The American Legal System

The American Legal System

Concepts and Principles

David Eliot Brody

University of Colorado at Denver

MEMBER OF THE COLORADO BAR

D. C. Heath and Company

Lexington, Massachusetts   Toronto

TO MY PARENTS

Preface

The American Legal System: Concepts and Principles is primarily intended for undergraduates in introductory law courses. This text presents a survey of the most significant facets of the entire American legal system. It gives students an overview of the many complex areas of that system and helps them to understand the relationships among those areas. This text was developed from material originally prepared for a course entitled "The Legal Process," which I have taught at the University of Colorado at Denver since 1974. It can also be used as an Introduction to Business Law text because the first eight chapters, particularly Chapters 7 and 8, discuss the more important principles and applications of American business law.

The chapters are organized to provide a cumulative analysis of the American legal system. The information is cumulative in both the chronological and the substantive senses. I have not made the assumption that the reader possesses advanced background knowledge of political science or constitutional law. The book carefully but briefly outlines the groundwork of our legal system, beginning in 1781 with the Articles of Confederation. It then describes the foundation of the legal process, the necessary preparation for and intricacies of a modern-day trial, and several selected areas of civil and criminal law.

The first five chapters describe the framework in which the American legal process functions and explain the reasons that framework is designed as it is. Chapter 1, the introductory chapter, gives a brief history of our legal system and some of the basic legal theories on which it is based and discusses the lawyers and judges who operate the system. Chapter 2 outlines the historical and constitutional background and the basic structure of the federal and state court systems. Chapter 3 discusses the judicial reasoning process and the importance of the system of precedents. Chapter 4 deals with the issues of the judicial power of federal and state courts and the relationships among and between them. Chapter 5 discusses three concepts that are useful in examining court decisions and the development of legal principles as they are presented in subsequent chapters. Chapter 6 then examines the actual preparation for, and conduct of, a typical personal injury case from the time of the injury through the trial.

Chapters 7 through 12 deal with several of the most basic and important substantive areas of the law. The discussion of these legal principles is by no means exhaustive, but it is extensive enough to give the reader a fundamental understanding of each area and to provide a basis on which to build and expand the discussion into topics not elaborated on herein. Chapter 7 discusses contracts, the requirements for their formation, and includes discussions of and defenses against claims of breach of contract. Chapter 8 examines business law and includes discussions of business organizations, the law of agency, the Uniform Commercial Code, and property.

Chapter 9 sets forth the principles of the law of torts and defenses against suits based on torts. Chapter 10 discusses three areas of the law that have particular contemporary importance—administrative law, consumer law, and environmental law. Chapters 11 and 12 consist of lengthy discussions of the principles of criminal law and criminal procedure, respectively. The Epilogue contains some closing thoughts on the study of law and the American legal system.

This text includes a number of edited cases, in which omitted substantive material is indicated by ellipsis points. A series of Appendixes, comprised of the United States Constitution, sample pleadings, and several model statutes, is also included.

A study of the law does not consist merely of memorizing the language of innumerable statutes. Throughout *The American Legal System* I have emphasized the social and historical basis for the development of the law. I have sought to eliminate many of the misconceptions surrounding our substantive legal principles by examining them using a common-sense approach. Such an approach is essential to a balanced view of our legal system. I hope this approach has served as a reminder to the reader that the law is largely a reflection of a society's needs and values and that the historical factors and requirements imposed by our society are the main reasons for most of the principles integral to our American system of law.

DAVID ELIOT BRODY

Acknowledgments

Bonnie L. Callen, who typed the manuscript drafts, did an excellent job throughout the many phases of this work ever since we began in the spring of 1976. Thanks also to Kathryn Price, who typed part of the first outline of the manuscript. Mike Maxwell's legal research, analysis, comments, and organization of the voluminous facts and statistics in the preparation of this book were invaluable. My colleague Jay Pansing was generous enough to spend hour after hour reading the manuscript drafts and discussing them with me. His comments concerning style and the substantive law contributed greatly to the final product. He provided such a detailed analysis of the manuscript that his incisive suggestions and analysis are reflected in every chapter of the book. Thanks, also, to my colleague, Allen G. Reeves, who spent many hours reading the manuscript and who provided a number of very useful suggestions. Also, I want to express my appreciation to the extremely helpful staff at D. C. Heath & Company.

I want to thank those writers and publishers who granted permission to use material from their works, including Harcourt Brace Jovanovich, Columbia University Press, Yale University Press, and the UCLA Law Review. Thanks, also, to those university presses that have adopted the resolution of the Association of American University Presses, allowing fair use without the need to obtain prior permission.

Summary of Contents

Contents

9 *The Law of Torts*   207

The American Legal System

1

Introduction

A. The American Legal System as an Embodiment of Common Sense and Morals

We sometimes hear complaints that the law does not make sense, that there is no rhyme or reason to the law, that there is no such thing as justice, and that the American legal system functions without regard to the real needs of society. There are many defects in the American legal system, and surely complaints such as these are often justified. However, such complaints can also result from a basic misunderstanding of the functioning of the legal system. The typical occasional contact that average citizens have with the legal system in the United States simply does not enable them to comprehend the theory and purpose behind the system as a whole and behind each individual area of the law. Although trial proceedings are often reported by the press, and local court and United States Supreme Court decisions receive television and newspaper coverage, the parties' extensive arguments and the theories behind the courts' decisions simply cannot be relayed to the reader or to the general public. Thus it is not surprising that the public often disagrees with the results of many cases and is unaware of the reasons underlying the courts' decisions.

Because of the way the American legal system functions, the development of our body of law has been a fairly orderly and logical one, and to a great extent all areas of the law embody common sense. Inherent in the development of the law is a continuous examination by the judges in the legal system, asking "What makes sense in this situation?" That is, what principle of law should be implemented by this court at this time that will serve as a general statement that this is the right and fair thing to do? Though not expressly made a part of court decisions, society requires that the law never cease to attempt to resolve the question of how persons must treat one another. In this respect it deals with the broader question of how the system should grow in the direction of the citizens' social and moral beliefs and their resultant demands, and how it can best reflect those standards, beliefs, and demands through its court decisions.

[handwritten margin note: common sense prevails]

Indeed, it has been said that all legal standards will have at least these three characteristics:[1]

1. They involve a certain moral judgment on conduct. They are to be fair, or conscientious, or reasonable, or prudent, or diligent.
2. They do not call for exact legal knowledge exactly applied, but for common sense about common things or trained intuition about things outside of everyone's experience.
3. They are not formulated absolutely and given an exact content, either by legislation or by judicial decision, but are relative to times and places and circumstances and are to be applied with reference to the facts of the case at hand. They recognize that, within certain fixed bounds, each case is to a certain extent unique.

Similarly, former Supreme Court Justice Benjamin Cardozo once stated that:[2]

> [T]he judge in shaping the rules of law must heed the mores of his day. . . . Law is, indeed, an historical growth, for it is an expression of customary morality which develops silently and unconsciously from one age to another. . . . But law is also the conscious or purposed growth, for the expression of customary morality will be false unless the mind of the judge is directed to the attainment of the moral end and its embodiment in legal forms. Nothing less than conscious effort will be adequate if the end in view is to prevail. The standards or patterns of utility and morals will be found by the judge in the life of the community.

Cardozo believed that custom and morality are vitally important to the judge's decision in all cases. He believed that the judge's duty to decide a case in accordance with reason and justice is part of his duty to decide it in accordance with custom.[3]

> [T]he judge is under a duty within the limits of his power of innovation, to maintain a relation between law and morals, between the precepts of jurisprudence and those of reason and good conscience. . . .
>
> You may say that there is no assurance that judges will interpret the mores of the day more wisely and truly than other men. I am not disposed to deny this, but in my view it is quite beside the point. The point is rather that this power of interpretation must be lodged somewhere, and the custom of the constitution has lodged it in the judges.

B. The Need for a Complex Judicial System in a Complex Society

Another often-heard criticism of our legal system is that it is overly complicated, and that both the court procedures and the substantive principles of law applied by the courts should be simplified. It is also said that legal documents are intentionally designed to confuse the layman. However, the only manner in which one can deal with complex legal problems in a highly sophisticated society is with a highly sophisticated legal system. The system must be complex not only with respect to the legal

---

[1] R. Pound, *An Introduction to the Philosophy of Law* (New Haven: Yale University Press, 1968), p. 58.
[2] B. Cardozo, *The Nature of the Judicial Process* (New Haven: Yale University Press, 1970), p. 104.
[3] Cardozo, pp. 133–35.

principles developed through court decisions but also with respect to the court procedures that govern the conduct of trials and the activities leading up to such trials. Great strides have been made over the last few decades in simplifying court procedure, but it has still been necessary to develop an extensive procedural framework to enable the parties and the courts to avoid wasting time on technical defects and formalities and to address the real issues of the case.

In addition, complex principles of American law have developed in response to complex questions that have been presented to the courts for resolution for two hundred years in the United States or for hundreds of years longer, in the case of American legal principles that originated in England's court system. There is no simple way to state principles of law that must apply to the myriad of relationships that exist in our society and at the same time establish principles that will endure and continue to logically apply to hundreds of millions of people.

An indication of the impossibility of providing principles or guidelines applicable to every particular fact and situation is the number of cases which are filed each year in the American legal system. In 1969 there were 112,606 cases filed in the United States District Courts alone; this figure had increased 27.2 percent by 1974, when 143,284 cases were filed in those courts. In the United States Circuit Courts of Appeals, there were 10,248 cases filed in 1969 and 16,436 cases filed in 1974, a 60.4 percent increase in the case load in those five years.[4]

As indicated in Table 1.1, these courts are experiencing a similar burden in the tremendous number of cases filed each year.[5] As indicated by this tremendous volume of cases, there are no "Ten Commandments" that could be responsive to the questions posed in the courts of the twentieth century. "As the relations with which the law must deal become more numerous and the situations calling for legal treatment become more complicated, it is no longer possible to have a simple, definite, detailed rule for every sort of case that can come before a tribunal, nor a fixed absolute for a legal transaction." [6] The breadth and the depth of legal principles, in this complex but highly organized American legal system, is the thread that maintains order in this society.

C. Background of American Legal Principles

1. Historical and Theoretical Basis

Defining the law and identifying the historical theory of the law is a necessary first step in determining what the law is or should be today. There are three views that are regarded as the main contending theories of law: (1) "that which is right"

---

[4] Administrative Office of the United States Courts, Management Statistics for U.S. Courts (1974), pp. 13, 120.

[5] The statistics shown in Table 1.1 were obtained from the following sources, respectively: *1975 Judicial Department of Arkansas Annotated Report; 1974 Colorado Annotated Statistical Report of the Colorado Judiciary; 1973 Florida Judicial System Statistical Report; 1974 Administrative Office of the Illinois Courts Annotated Report; 1973–74 Administrative Office of the Maryland Courts Annotated Report; 1974 Annual Report, Judicial Department of the State of New Mexico.*

[6] Pound, p. 77.

Table 1.1   State Court Case Loads

Arkansas

YEAR	CIRCUIT COURTS	CHANCERY COURTS
1969	21,158	18,921
1974	28,642	28,055
1975	32,795	28,791

Colorado   (New cases filed in fiscal year 1974–75)

Supreme Court and Court of Appeals	2,208
District Courts	74,921
County Courts	197,756

Florida   (New cases filed in 1973)

	CRIMINAL	CIVIL	JUVENILE	TOTAL
Circuit Courts	64,489	157,092	46,328	267,909
County Courts	222,475	146,310	—	368,785
				636,694

Illinois   (1974 cases)

Circuit Courts of Illinois	3,114,194

Maryland   (1973–74 fiscal year case load)

Circuit Courts	71,829
District Courts	915,959 (includes 506,650 motor vehicle cases)

New Mexico

	1969	1974
District Courts	26,159	40,118
Magistrates Courts	—	73,057

—the natural law concept; (2) "the will of the justices"—the positive law concept; and (3) "as others have done"—the sociological law concept. A basic statement of each of these, the problems each raises, and how they fit into the American legal system provides a brief background for the more specific discussion that is contained in succeeding chapters.

a. The Natural Law Tradition

The natural law tradition goes back as far as the Greek philosophers and is as modern as the Nuremberg trials of Nazi leaders for "crimes against mankind." The natural law theory assumes that there are fundamental and absolute concepts of law and justice that men have the ability to ascertain and to apply to their political and social affairs. The validity of a legal system, and of every decision taken under it, rests on the harmony of its rules and regulations with the principles of natural law. One main school of natural law is religious in character and rests on man's presumed ability to discover fundamental, rational principles of right and wrong by which to test man-made laws. In this way, man participates in God's divine reason. Another school, sometimes called *rationalistic natural law,* does not see natural law as flowing from divine origins but from a rational universe and man's self-developed moral codes. Whichever origin is assigned to the higher standard of law, the natural law advocate would say that a law that forbade anyone to practice anything but the national religion, or a national program that planned to systematically destroy a racial or ethnic group, would violate natural law standards. The essential point is that a higher morality limits all powers of government.

what is divinely right seems to rule. "the right thing to" from a divine source.

b. The Positivist Theory of Law

The second major theory of law, positivism, maintains that law is what the supreme political authority in the state commands and can enforce. Positivism sometimes cites a moral justification for its position—that it brings order out of the violent relations of men. The basic view of the positivist is that law must be separated from any standard of morality that is set by authorities other than the sovereign. This provides certainty about what must be accepted as binding law and ensures stability by rejecting any outside test of validity. The role of judges under positivist theory is to apply the law of the sovereign, not to substitute personal or religious notions of their own about what is wise.

positivist allows only the law does not allow any thing else to influence decision.

The positivist theory can be used by almost any political system. In a theocratic state, positive law would be the command of the church authority; in a monarchy, the will of a king; in a totalitarian system, the command of the leader; in a democracy, the act of the elected government. Positive law can thus be reactionary in one circumstance, reformist in another, or even revolutionary. Its essential point is that human political institutions are the sole source and measure of law.

c. The Sociological Theory of Law

A third basic theory defines law not as a set of rules measured against a higher moral standard or as the applied will of a particular sovereign but as a set of rules developed gradually by people over a period of time. Law is viewed as growing out of the family relationship in primitive societies, then out of tribal customs; it also developed in response to changes in technology and the organization of society. The moral aspirations of the society (natural law) as well as the particular policies of the sovereign (positivism) are embodied in the sociological theory of law.

Socialistic Laws that are developed over a period of time. Both natural & positivism are developed out of Socialistic. Basically— Evolutionary development

In addition to evolutionary development, sociological theory also stresses the realistic analysis of how lawmakers and law interpreters balance and adjust conflicting interests in society. For example, when legislation is proposed to create a federal loyalty program, sociological theory views legislators as weighing the need of the state to protect itself from internal subversion against the right of the individual to freedom of expression and social criticism. Judges weighing the constitutionality of such a measure are engaged in the balancing process, according to sociological theorists.

Thus, instead of discussing only the logic or the "right reason" of decisions, sociological theorists probe the economic, ideological, or psychological factors that influence judges. They then try to bring these into clear visibility so that society can see the factors afterward and decide whether they are the desired criteria to be applied by the judges. The essential point of sociological theory, therefore, is that it sees law as a product of society, by which conflicting interests of the day can be peaceably adjusted.

These legal theories have had a significant impact upon American constitutional and legal development. American law has been shaped by each of these three schools of thought as the country has moved from colonial times to the present. Natural law ideas in the writings of John Locke, Thomas Jefferson, and Thomas Paine, among many others, were important ingredients in America's revolutionary ideology. Statements that rulers could not abridge the "rights of mankind" and the laws of "Nature and Nature's God" permeated the documents of our independence era. Once the colonies were established as a nation, the United States Supreme Court began to interpret many of the broad provisions of the Constitution protecting individual rights, such as due process of law, equal protection of law, deprivation of liberty, and obligation of contract, as though these were shorthand terms for a body of natural law principles that the Founding Fathers had incorporated by reference into the Constitution. The idea that even the Constitution and the Supreme Court cannot justify violations of "higher law" has been another theme carried through American history.

An example of the positivist theory in the United States is the move, following the successful break with Great Britain, to limit the common law rules inherited from British law and applied by aristocratic judges. This limitation was accomplished through the adoption of codes by the state legislatures, a movement that was fairly widespread in the United States in the middle of the nineteenth century. The codes spelled out rules for major legal issues of property and procedure and represented an attempt to rationalize the American legal system. Other positivist themes in American law can be seen in the enduring assumption by many Americans that the legal system can legislate morality in matters ranging from drinking liquor and respecting religion to eliminating unpopular ideas about politics, economics, or society.

The contribution of the sociological theory to American law can be seen in the reaction against both natural concepts and positivist doctrines that political scientists and legal scholars associate with the ideas of Oliver Wendell Holmes, Jr., Roscoe Pound, Jerome Frank, and a number of other influential legal thinkers who changed the tone and outlook of American law from 1900 to the present. Their powerful analyses of the manner in which judges really decide cases, of how flexible the Constitution really is and must be in the face of new crises facing the nation, and of the basic role of legislation in adjusting conflicting group interests have become the common language of law taught in law schools.[7]

As regards contemporary usefulness or applicability, the sociological theory now far outweighs the other two concepts. Modern American legal theory and philosophy certainly do not regard the law as "a divinely ordained rule or set of rules for human action" or as "the recorded wisdom of the wise men of old who had learned the safe courses or the divinely approved course for human conduct" as maintained under the natural law concept. Traditional views of the American legal system do not regard the law as "a body of commands of the sovereign authority in a politically organized society as to how men should conduct themselves therein," resting ultimately on the authority of that sovereign, as the theory of positive law states. On the contrary, the present-day legal philosophy encompasses, to varying degrees, the three following concepts which are all aspects of the sociological theory of law:

a. The law is a system of precepts discovered by human experience, whereby the individual human will may realize the most complete freedom possible consistent with the like freedom of will of others.
b. The law is a system of principles, discovered philosophically and developed in detail by juristic writing and judicial decision, whereby the life of man is measured by reason, and whereby the will of the individual is harmonized with those of others.
c. The American legal system embodies the idea that the law is made up of dictates of economic and social laws with respect to the conduct of men in society; these are discovered by observation and expressed in precepts worked out through the human experience of what works and what does not work in the administration of justice.[8]

2. The Common Law

There are two chief sources of law: court decisions, or cases, and statutes.[9] The distinction between case law and statutory law is analogous to the distinction between the judicial branch and the legislative branch, the respective sources of each of those two types of law. This book deals almost entirely with the first of these, namely case law. The terms *court decisions, cases,* and *common law* will be

---

[7] Portions of the preceding discussion concerning the three theories of law and their impact are based on E. Redford, et al., *Politics and Government in the United States* (New York: Harcourt, Brace and World, Inc., 1965), pp. 471–75.

[8] Pound, pp. 28–29.

[9] There are administrative decisions, rules, and regulations that are also law but in a different sense, because those laws are made by administrative or regulatory bodies in the executive branch of state and federal government. These bodies derive their power to make such decisions, rules, and regulations only by virtue of statutes that must first be enacted by the legislature to give them this power. See Chapter 10, Part A, for a discussion of administrative agencies and administrative law.

used frequently throughout this discussion on the judicial branch. The difference in meaning between these terms should be kept in mind. A *case* is the general term for an action, cause, suit, or controversy between parties, that is, a question that is contested before a court of law. However, the term is not inclusive of or synonymous with all cases that are recognized at common law. Cases also include disputes over statutory law.[10] *Case law* is the aggregate of cases that form a body of jurisprudence for the law on a particular subject, but not including statutory law.[11] The term *common law,* on the other hand, is the body of law that was originated, developed, and formulated in England, and consists of judicial opinions that are only evidence of what the common law actually is. At the time of the separation of the colonies from England, the American legal system adopted the English common law and has continued to develop a large body of American common law.[12]

Before the Norman Conquest in 1066, feudal and other local courts administered a set of local customs that had been handed down for generations. After the Conquest these courts gave way to the King's Courts. Royal judges went from London to all parts of the realm, seeking to discover and apply the customs having the widest usage and attraction. Uniformity finally crystallized about the middle of the thirteenth century as a result of the enforcement of the doctrine of *stare decisis,* which declares that once a decision is reached by the superior court in a particular case it becomes a precedent, and all other cases of similar kind are to be decided according to the same rules. The royal judges, therefore, gradually forged a law that was "common" to all England.[13]

The term *common law* is also sometimes contrasted with what is designated as Roman, or *civil, law.* Civil law actually has two meanings, the more common of which is the law that is not criminal law. However, the term also refers to the system of jurisprudence that was administered in the Roman Empire, also called "civil" law. The laws that were compiled and promulgated in A.D. 529 by order of Emperor Justinian have supplied much of the foundation for the legal system in countries that adopted a civil law, rather than a common law, system. Roman influence is noticeable in the Napoleonic Code, and the French civil law has been used as a pattern for many continental European and Latin American countries. The two systems of jurisprudence, common law and civil law, are not entirely different. Many cases would reach the same result under both systems. However, the civil law is comprised solely of statutory law, rather than case law, and the judges decide each case on its

---

[10] *Black's Law Dictionary,* 4th ed. (St. Paul: West Publishing Company, 1968), p. 271; *Words and Phrases* (St. Paul: West Publishing Company, 1966), vol. 6, pp. 359–82; see Kelly v. Roetzel, 64 Okl. 36, 165 P. 1150 (1917); City of Akron v. Roth, 88 Ohio 456, 103 N.E. 465 (1913).

[11] *Black's Law Dictionary,* p. 272.

[12] *Black's Law Dictionary,* p. 346; *Words and Phrases,* vol. 8, pp. 107–18; see *In re Davis' Estate,* 131 N.J. 161, 35 A.2d 880 (1944).

[13] See generally A. Hogue, *Origins of the Common Law* (Bloomington: Indiana University Press, 1966); W. S. Holdsworth, *A History of English Law* (Boston: Little, Brown and Co., 1923), vol. 2, pp. 145–74. See Chapter 3, Part B, for a discussion of the doctrine of *stare decisis.*

independent merits by applying the law as it is enacted into the code and not in conformity with the system of *stare decisis,* that is, the system of precedents.

The English colonists brought the common law of England to the colonies. The original thirteen states adopted the common law, and other states followed their example as they were made part of the Union. Louisiana, however, retained the civil law which was in effect at the time that the Louisiana Territory was ceded to this country by France. With this exception, law in the United States had its origin in the English common law system of jurisprudence. Maryland's constitution, for example, provides "That the inhabitants of Maryland are entitled to the Common Law of England and the trial by jury, according to the course of that law." [14] That body of principles described as the common law does not consist of absolute, fixed, or inflexible rules, but rather broad and comprehensive principles based on justice, reason, and common sense. Its principles have been determined by the social needs of the community, and it reflects changes in such needs. Most importantly, the common law is able to adapt to new conditions, interests, relations, and usages as the progress of society may require.

Thus the term *common law* is a less limited term than the term *cases,* because case law, or a case, is only evidence of what the common law is; the two terms are rarely interchangeable. In the technical sense, cases are an application of common law to specific situations. From the common law "the judges make the actual law by a process of trying the principles and rules and standards in concrete cases, observing their practical operation and gradually discovering by experience of many causes how to apply them." [15]

Courts often decide cases in which they must interpret provisions of statutes or federal or state constitutions. Cases have almost the same relationship to constitutions as they do to statutes. Thus case law or court decisions can be, and often are, rendered on issues related to a statute or a constitution; other cases do not involve their interpretation. Whether they involve the interpretation of constitutions or not, cases must not be contrary to constitutional principles. The relationship between a constitution and any statute passed under it is that the constitution overrides a statute; but a statute, if consistent with the constitution, overrides the case-law determination of any judge. In this sense, judge-made law is secondary and subordinate to the law that is made by legislatures. However, statutes do not render the judge superfluous nor his work predetermined or mechancial. There are gaps to be filled, and there are often ambiguities to be cleared up by the courts.[16] The judicial function and the legislative function inevitably run into one another. It is the function of the legislative branch to make laws. That is, from the nature of our political system, the legislature cannot make laws so complete that the judicial branch will not be needed to exercise a law-making function also. The judicial function of supplementing, developing, and shaping from the legislative branch is a necessary part of judi-

---

[14] C. Post, *An Introduction to the Law* (Englewood Cliffs, N.J.: Prentice-Hall, Inc., 1963), p. 67.
[15] R. Pound, *The Spirit of the Common Law* (Boston: Jones Co., 1921), p. 176.
[16] See Cardozo, p. 14.

cial power, and most members of the profession view the function of and relationship between the two branches in that way. However, the famous legal philosopher Roscoe Pound suggested that "[o]ur political theory . . . has served merely to entrench in the professional mind . . . that legislative lawmaking is a subordinate function and exists only to supplement the traditional element of the legal system here and there and to set the judicial or juristic tradition now and then in the right path as to some particular item where it has gone astray." [17]

Except for extreme judicial activists, most judges and lawyers would disagree with Pound's observation and would maintain that, on the contrary, cases should supplement statutes.

In any event, however, the following chapters examine present-day legal principles that are embodied in court decisions. Many of these principles are found in cases that involved the interpretation of a statute, but most of the cases had no connection with any statute or any function of the legislative branch. These cases, modified and developed by American conditions and American needs, comprise the common law that is the basis for the settlement of controversies not governed by constitution or statute.

D. The Lawyers in the System

Who are the people who implement, help form, and use the legal system in the United States today? In 1977 the leading legal directory in the United States, Martindale-Hubbell, listed about 450,000 members of the legal profession. Although lawyers are found in cities and towns of all sizes in the United States, the profession has tended to be concentrated in major urban centers of commerce and government.

Statistics from the American Bar Association in 1977 indicated that 64.7 percent of all lawyers were in private practice; 12.9 percent were in governmental service; 10.6 percent were salaried employees in private industry; 2.4 percent were judges or court officers; and 9.4 percent were teachers in educational institutions or were active in law-related fields or politics.[18]

In an economic sense there is a general stratification within the profession. The most financially successful members are the partners of large law firms, counsel for major corporations, and some government lawyers at the level of the attorney general, solicitor general, and high-ranking assistants. Professors at the finest law schools in the country enjoy high esteem and a moderate to high income compared to other members of the profession. Partners in established and prosperous large urban law firms also have income in this range. Small-town lawyers and professors at lesser-quality law schools have an average income in relation to the rest of the profession. The lowest and most sporadic income, insofar as any classification or

---

[17] Pound, p. 51.
[18] American Bar Association, Information Service Center, Chicago, Illinois (1977).

generalization of the profession can be made, is among those attorneys who special-ize in divorce cases, traffic offenses, and other cases involving relatively small amounts of money. Most criminal lawyers also fall in this latter group. Although men like Clarence Darrow, Melvin Belli, and F. Lee Bailey are frequently in the spotlight and tend to raise the average income (and respect) of the criminal lawyer, the income of criminal lawyers is generally among the lowest in the profession. The fact that no criminal lawyers have ever become Supreme Court justices may also reflect the attitude of the bar toward this group, or the inability of less economically successful members of the profession to wield any significant influence.

E. The Judges in the System

In American society judges serve a very special function. They are regarded as custodians of society, a class apart from other governmental officers. They wear ceremonial robes. Awe-inspiring formalities of architecture, decoration, and proce-dure are part of the judicial surroundings. The people in the courtroom are in-structed to rise when a judge enters, and all must address the judge respectfully as "Your Honor." All this ritual and formality raises the question of whether the Amer-ican taxpayer's money should be spent in such a manner. However, it is argued that these symbols of power and importance lend respect, legitimacy, and stability to the judicial process and to the governmental structure as a whole. Thus the question becomes one of weighing the value of the respect, legitimacy, and stability gained through the use of these symbols and rituals against the high cost of perpetuating what may be a superficial image.

In any event, it has been the tradition of American government to call on its judges to restore integrity and to find the truth whenever public confidence in the political process has been shaken. Thus judges were used in the disputed presiden-tial election of 1876 to determine the victor, to investigate and clean up baseball after the Black Sox Scandal of 1919, to determine the cause of our devastating loss at Pearl Harbor in 1941, to prosecute on behalf of the nation in the Nuremberg War Crimes Trials in 1946, to chair the commission set up in 1963 to investigate the assassination of President Kennedy, and to preside over the numerous trials in the Watergate Affair during 1973 and 1974, as well as to consider various matters re-lated to Watergate, such as the Nixon tapes.

As reflected by these examples, society has historically regarded judges as being above politics. Although this ideal has not always been achieved in practice, society has felt that judges should be selected from among the best people available, with-out regard to political affiliation or prior party service; that political influences, whether of personal ideology, party, or interest groups, should not affect their deci-sions; and that they should be immune from political reprisals brought on by un-popular decisions or by controversial judicial philosophy. It is possible, at least in theory, for judges to make decisions without regard to their political beliefs. How-ever, as will be seen in later chapters, it is absolutely impossible to choose judges who will be able to divorce themselves from all the considerations and influences that normal human beings experience throughout their lives, and to have decisions made with perfect objectivity.[19]

QUESTIONS

1. In rendering their decisions, what moral and social factors should judges take into account?
2. Should judges be guided by their own moral beliefs or by those of the community in general? Why?
3. Describe the essential points of natural law, positive law, and sociological law. What examples of each of these theories can be seen in American government today?
4. What arguments can be made in support of the legislature's authority to enact statutes that override existing common law principles?

[19] See Redford, pp. 528–29.

2) Both; They should encampase there own moral Beliefs & also what the community in general will allow.

2

The Court System—
The Source of Cases

A. The Constitutional Basis for the Judicial System

1. The Federal Judiciary

A major factor contributing to the confusion and mystique in the public's understanding of the legal system is the number of courts and their varying responsibilities. There are traffic courts, probate courts, criminal courts, divorce courts; the list goes on and on. Also courts are divided into federal courts and state courts. The average citizen usually knows the physical location of these courts, and that federal courts are located in the federal buildings scattered throughout the country. Certainly it is well known that the most powerful and important court in the country is the United States Supreme Court.

Yet why do certain types of cases go to certain types of courts? Where does each type of court get its legal authority to hear certain types of cases? And how are the roles of the state courts and the federal courts divided? Without the answers to these questions, the legal system may seem like a great mass of courts arbitrarily established and costing the taxpayer too great a sum of money to maintain. However, once the basic origins and authority for the existence of each of our courts are examined, we will see that there are specific duties designed for each type of court, that the courts' functions are founded in a specific constitutional provision or statute, and that there is indeed a systematic and orderly distribution of cases throughout the court system.

Looking first at the federal judicial branch, we note that the Constitution of the United States was passed after the government had functioned unsuccessfully for several years under the Articles of Confederation. The Articles of Confederation was the first constitution of the United States; it was passed by the states and went into effect on March 1, 1781. In strong contrast to the present relationship between the federal government and the state governments, under the Articles of Confederation the states were independent and completely sovereign. They retained all powers over their citizenry. The powers of Congress over the states were merely advisory; there was no enforcement power.[1] Under the Articles, the legislative branch was considered a general congress and served the functions of all three branches of our present-day government. That is, the legislative branch under the Articles made policy and also was supposed to implement it, despite its lack of effective enforcement power. Each state sent a varying number of delegates to the central government, selected by any method the state desired to use in choosing such delegates.[2] The Congress was a unicameral legislature, and resolutions had to be passed by at least nine states in order to become law.

The legislative branch had broad authority reaching into both the executive and judicial areas, yet there was something vaguely resembling an executive branch under the Articles, although there was no executive-branch bureaucracy. When Congress was not in session, a committee of the states (consisting of one delegate per state) convened for the purpose of carrying out executive powers by managing the general affairs of the Confederation. On this committee, one delegate served as the president for no longer than one year and was elected by fellow delegates on the committee.[3]

Under the Articles the judicial branch actually did not exist because there was no independent judiciary. Instead Congress mediated all disputes between two or more states over any matters such as boundary, jurisdiction, or any other controversy concerning land title. Any other types of dispute were settled by the state judicial systems.[4]

The present Constitution was adopted primarily to remedy four weaknesses that existed in the structure of government under the Articles. The first was the revenue problem. The Articles of Confederation conferred no power of taxation on the Congress. The only source of revenue available to the central government was tax levied on each individual state; however, the Congress had no power to enforce the payment of such revenue. The power of the central government to contract debts with no accompanying power to raise revenue resulted in a war debt estimated at $42,000,000 in 1783.[5] In view of the weak financial status of the Confederation, foreign credit also evaporated.[6] In one address George Washington urged the people to reform the Articles, because in his opinion it was the only way to avert national bankruptcy.[7] The revenue problem was also vigorously addressed by Alexander Hamilton:[8]

---

[1] G. Curtis, *Constitutional History of the United States* (New York: Da Capo Press, 1974), vol. I, pp. 98–99, 116.

[2] The method of appointment by the governor was used in eleven states; in Connecticut and Rhode Island the delegates were elected by the people.

[3] Curtis, pp. 100, 136.

[4] Ibid., pp. 100, 173.

[5] Ibid., pp. 101–16.

[6] M. Birnbach, *American Political Life* (Homewood, Ill.: The Dorsey Press, 1971), pp. 142–43.

[7] Curtis, pp. 136, 141.

[8] *The Federalist Papers* (New York: The New American Library, Inc., 1961), Paper No. 30, p. 188. Hamilton also addressed the revenue problem in Papers No. 21, 31–36.

> A complete power . . . to procure a regular and adequate supply of revenue, as far as the resources of the community will permit, may be regarded as an indispensable ingredient in every constitution. From a deficiency in this particular, one of two evils must ensue: either the people must be subjected to continual plunder, as a substitute for a more eligible mode of supplying the public wants, or the government must sink into a fatal atrophy, and, in a short course of time, perish.

A second major problem under the Articles of Confederation was the lack of a centralized government. This led to chaos among the states, particularly in the field of commercial trade. Interstate rivalries were viewed as a bar to future development of the nation, as well as a bar to the ability to adopt any type of commercial law. The confusion resulting from individual states printing their own paper money and from import-export taxes between states are examples of the problems that faced the new nation.[9]

Under the Articles the lack of central power was a problem in all three branches of the government—executive, legislative, and judicial. An aspect of this lack was that there was no federal judiciary, as addressed in the Federalist Papers by Alexander Hamilton, in which he stated:[10]

> A circumstance which crowns the defects of the Confederation remains yet to be mentioned—the want of a judiciary power. Laws are a dead letter without courts to expound and define their true meaning and operation. The treaties of the United States, to have any force at all, must be considered as part of the law of the land. Their true import, as far as respects individuals, must, like all other laws, be ascertained by judicial determination.
>
> The treaties of the United States under the present constitution are liable to the infractions of thirteen different legislatures, and as many different courts of final jurisdiction, acting under the authority of those legislatures. The faith, the reputation, the peace of the whole Union are thus continually at the mercy of the prejudices, the passions, and the interests of every member of which it is composed. Is it possible that foreign nations can either respect or confide in such a government? Is it possible that the people of America will longer consent to trust their honor, their happiness, their safety, on so precarious a foundation?

In a separate Paper, Hamilton stated specifically that "the mere necessity of uniformity in the interpretation of the national laws decides the question. Thirteen independent courts of final jurisdiction over the same causes, arising upon the same laws, is a hydra in government from which nothing but contradiction and confusion can proceed." [11]

The third major problem facing the nation under the Articles of Confederation was that of a weak national defense.[12] The overriding purpose of the Confederation was cooperation among the states to win the War of Independence, and this incen-

---

9 Birnbach, pp. 142–44, 164.
10 *Federalist Papers*, No. 22, p. 150.
11 Ibid., No. 80, p. 476.
12 See *Federalist Papers* Nos. 8–15, 43.

tive was largely lost with the end of that war.[13] Coupled with the inability to raise money, the doubtful power of the Congress to create a peacetime army and navy thereby resulted in a weak national-defense posture.[14]

Fourth, the problem of the protection of property rights was a significant weakness under the Articles. It has been argued that the Founding Fathers wrote the Constitution in order to protect their own property interests. The fact that these rights had been adversely affected by the Articles of Confederation is regarded as having had a significant influence in the adoption of the Constitution. The lack of protection of property rights in money, public securities, manufacturing, trade, and shipping was a particular problem. Most or all of the initiators of the new union were personally interested in one or more of these areas of commerce.[15]

In addition to the four major weaknesses just discussed, another problem was that the Articles could be strengthened only by amendments proposed by Congress and ratified by the legislatures of every state. The defect in this procedure was revealed when the only two amendments proposed by Congress in 1789 failed as a result of less-than-unanimous ratification.[16]

As a result of these difficulties, Alexander Hamilton and George Washington began to advocate that the Confederation be replaced with "a solid coercive union." [17] To promote this idea, between July 12, 1781 and July 4, 1782 Hamilton wrote a series of anonymous articles entitled "The Continentalist." [18] The idea was furthered by the later writings of Jefferson, Madison, and Adams.[19] The sense of urgency of the need for an entirely new system of government was provided by Shays' Rebellion in the summer and fall of 1786 in Massachusetts, where dissatisfaction with the Articles of Confederation was strongest. The desire to amend and strengthen the Articles then led to the calling of the Constitutional Convention in Philadelphia beginning May 25, 1787. However, rather than merely amending the Articles, the Convention reconstructed the very constitutional foundations of the American government, even though none of the state legislatures authorized their delegates to make the basic changes that Hamilton, Madison, and Adams had long been advo-

---

13 Birnbach, p. 135.

14 Curtis, pp. 98–99.

15 C. Beard, *An Economic Interpretation of the Constitution of the United States* (New York: MacMillan Co., 1947), pp. 73–151; Birnbach, p. 165.

16 Ibid.

17 A. Mason, and R. Leach, *In Quest of Freedom* (Englewood Cliffs, N.J.: Prentice-Hall, Inc., 1959), p. 76.

18 Alexander Hamilton, "The Continentalist" (12 July 1781– 4 July 1782). Reprinted in Henry Cabot Lodge, ed., *The Works of Alexander Hamilton* (New York: G.P. Putnam's Sons, 1904), pp. 243–87.

19 Thomas Jefferson, *Notes on the State of Virginia* (Chapel Hill, N.C.: University of North Carolina Press, 1955), pp. 110–29; James Madison, *Vices of the Political System of the United States,* April 1787, reprinted in Gaillard Hunt, ed., *The Writings of James Madison* (New York: G.P. Putnam's Sons, 1901), vol. 2, pp. 361–69; John Adams, *A Defense of the Constitution of Government of the United States of America,* 1787–88, printed in Charles F. Adams, ed., *The Works of John Adams* (Boston: Little, Brown and Co., 1851), vol. 4, pp. 271–588.

cating. Out of the Convention, on September 17, 1787, came the present-day Constitution of the United States.[20]

In Article III of the new Constitution, the Founding Fathers formulated a judicial branch intended to operate completely independently of the legislature. Both the judicial and legislative branches continue to operate successfully almost two hundred years after their formation. The first sentence of Article III states: "The Judicial Power of the United States shall be vested in one supreme Court, and in such inferior Courts as the Congress may from time to time ordain and establish." This grant of authority to Congress, typical in its generality of many other provisions of the Constitution, gives Congress complete discretion in the establishment of lower, or "inferior," courts. The formation of most of the federal court system is based on this one short sentence. Article I, section 8, clause nine, of the Constitution contains a corresponding grant of power given to the Congress under its enumeration of powers. It states that the Congress shall have the power "To constitute Tribunals Inferior to the supreme Court."

In support of these provisions, when the Constitution was being presented to the states for ratification, Hamilton argued in Federalist Paper No. 81 in the following manner:[21]

> I proceed to consider the propriety of the power of constituting inferior courts, and the relations which will subsist between these and the [Supreme Court]. . . .
>
> [T]he evident design of the provisions is to enable the institution of local courts, subordinate to the Supreme, either in States or larger districts.
>
> The power of constituting inferior courts is evidently calculated to obviate the necessity of having recourse to the Supreme Court in every case of federal cognizance. It is intended to enable the national government to institute or *authorize*, in each State or district of the United States, a tribunal competent to the determination of matters of national jurisdiction within its limits. . . .
>
> I am not sure but that it will be found highly expedient and useful to divide the United States into four or five or half a dozen districts, and to institute a federal court in each district in lieu of one in every State. The judges of these courts, with the aid of the State judges, may hold circuits for the trial of causes in the several parts of the respective districts.

Thus the basic foundation for the federal court system was laid in Article III of the Constitution. Its development and present structure will be examined later in this chapter.

2. The State Judiciaries

A brief look at the historical background of the individual state governments in existence at the time of the enactment of the Constitution indicates the path of

---

[20] Mason and Leach, pp. 90, 98–130.
[21] *Federalist Papers*, No. 81, pp. 485–86.

development and the genesis of the various state judiciaries in this country. During the colonial period, prior to 1776, the Privy Council of England reversed any acts of the colonial legislatures if it believed such reversal was legally justified or could be justified on grounds of policy or expediency.[22] The colonies did have their own courts, but primarily the legislature, rather than the judiciary, reviewed the decisions of inferior courts, just as Congress did later under the Articles of Confederation.[23] In some states there were indications of the commencement of an independent judiciary as early as the mid-seventeenth century. However, the movement was extremely limited, both geographically and philosophically.[24]

The early state governments existing during the time of the Articles of Confederation and overlapping into the period under the new Constitution illustrate that early state constitutions did not recognize a separation of powers. This was primarily because of a general distrust of an independent judiciary.[25] As was common during the colonial period and characteristic under the Articles, the legislatures under the early state governments often revised judicial proceedings, authorized appeals, or interpreted the law existing in individual cases. The prevailing view was that the judiciary should have no power to invalidate legislation, even if such legislation was obviously unconstitutional.[26] The states of Pennsylvania, New York, and Vermont established a council of censors which was composed of delegates from the cities and counties in the state, and which censored the state legislatures by recommending the repeal of unconstitutional legislation and by ordering impeachments. The method was intended to control the actions of the legislature, but fell short of a judicial solution. However, eventually the conflicts between the legislative branch and the judiciary led to such great confusion that an autonomous judicial system was deemed necessary and began to evolve.[27]

After the Revolution the state constitutions began to recognize the concept of a separation of powers and an independent judiciary.[28] Each state began to develop its own supreme court, or court of errors in appeals. Thus a high court of last resort began to appear in the state governments. In addition, some states were beginning to establish lower courts. The states then began to model their judicial systems after the federal system established by the new Constitution, and the structure of the early state-court systems soon became very similar to the present structures of state judicial systems in most essential aspects. The constitutions of many states provided for the creation of a supreme court, while giving the state legislatures the power to

---

[22] C. Haines, *The American Doctrine of Judicial Supremacy* (New York: Da Capo Press, 1973), pp. 44–58.

[23] C. Callender, *American Courts: Organization and Procedure* (New York: McGraw-Hill Book Co., 1927), p. 18.

[24] Haines, p. 68.

[25] Ibid., p. 68; H. Glick, and K. Vines, *State Court Systems* (Englewood Cliffs, N.J.: Prentice-Hall, 1973), p. 21.

[26] Haines, p. 69.

[27] Ibid., p. 72; Glick and Vines, p. 21.

[28] Glick and Vines, p. 18.

establish inferior courts by statute.[29] For example, Figure 2.1 (p. 20) is the structure of the Virginia state court system at the time of the adoption of the United States Constitution.[30]

B. Constitutional and Statutory Requirements on Courts: Size, Composition, and Location

Not only was the number and geographical location of all federal courts left up to the discretion of the Congress, but the size, number of judges, and number of levels of courts inferior to the Supreme Court were also left to the discretion of Congress. As a result, a large number of statutes have been passed by Congress regarding these matters. Similarly, the individual states in the United States have adopted constitutions, each of which provides for the establishment of a court system, the number and hierarchy of which were left to the discretion of each individual state legislature.

1. Trial and Appellate Courts Distinguished

The major and most important separation in the levels of courts, both in the state judicial systems and in the federal system, is the distinction between *trial courts* and *appellate courts*. This distinction and the method of assigning roles to courts— the traditional distinction carried over from the English legal system—can be summarized as follows: *Trial courts* are those courts in which evidence is introduced, in the form of the testimony of witnesses or by documentary evidence, demonstrative evidence, or other means. The judge or jury listens to the testimony of the witnesses and weighs all other types of evidence in order to determine the true facts of a case. In trial courts a complete record of all the proceedings is made by a court reporter or by a tape recorder. *Appellate courts,* on the other hand, exist almost solely for the purpose of reviewing the proceedings which occurred in a lower, or inferior, trial court. No witnesses testify in an appellate proceeding, and no other type of evidence is introduced. Judges in appellate courts are limited to determining whether the trial judge ruled correctly on various legal questions during the course of the proceedings or at the conclusion of the trial, or whether the contending parties gave the jury sufficient evidence on which to base its decision. Appellate judges make their determinations on the basis of the record made during the trial, the legal briefs submitted, and the oral arguments made by the attorneys at the appellate hearing. Appellate courts are those to which an appeal may be made to review the proceedings that took place at the trial; they include the United States Supreme Court, state supreme courts, and state and federal intermediate courts of appeal.

---

[29] Callender, p. 19.
[30] M. Nelson, *Judicial Review in Virginia 1789–1928* (New York: AMS Press, Inc., 1967), p. 231.

The Virginia Court System, 1788–1829

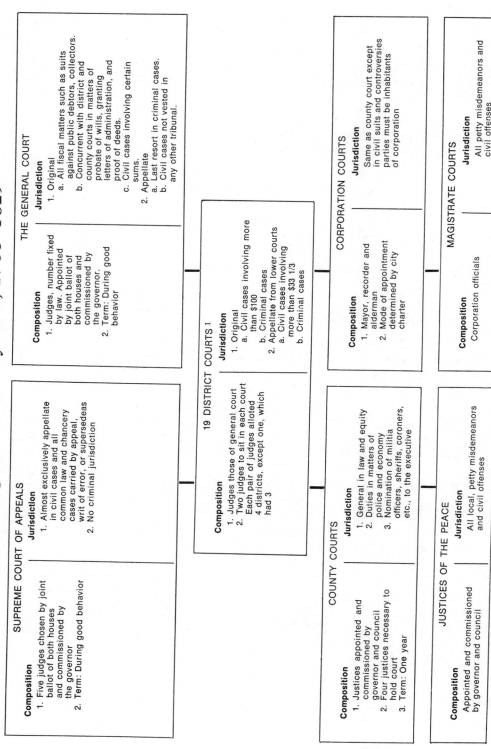

SUPREME COURT OF APPEALS

Composition
1. Five judges chosen by joint ballot of both houses and commissioned by the governor
2. Term: During good behavior

Jurisdiction
1. Almost exclusively appellate in civil cases and all common law and chancery cases carried by appeal, writ of error, or supersedeas
2. No criminal jurisdiction

THE GENERAL COURT

Composition
1. Judges, number fixed by law. Appointed by joint ballot of both houses and commissioned by the governor.
2. Term: During good behavior

Jurisdiction
1. Original
   a. All fiscal matters such as suits against public debtors, collectors.
   b. Concurrent with district and county courts in matters of probate of wills, granting letters of administration, and proof of deeds.
   c. Civil cases involving certain sums.
2. Appellate
   a. Last resort in criminal cases.
   b. Civil cases not vested in any other tribunal.

19 DISTRICT COURTS [1]

Composition
1. Judges those of general court
2. Two judges to sit in each court Each pair of judges alloted 4 districts, except one, which had 3

Jurisdiction
1. Original
   a. Civil cases involving more than $100
   b. Criminal cases
2. Appellate from lower courts
   a. Civil cases involving more than $33 1/3
   b. Criminal cases

CORPORATION COURTS

Composition
1. Mayor, recorder and alderman
2. Mode of appointment determined by city charter

Jurisdiction
Same as county court except in civil suits and controversies parties must be inhabitants of corporation

MAGISTRATE COURTS

Composition
Corporation officials

Jurisdiction
All petty misdemeanors and civil offenses

COUNTY COURTS

Composition
1. Justices appointed and commissioned by governor and council
2. Four justices necessary to hold court
3. Term: One year

Jurisdiction
1. General in law and equity
2. Duties in matters of police and economy
3. Nomination of militia officers, sheriffs, coroners, etc., to the executive

JUSTICES OF THE PEACE

Composition
Appointed and commissioned by governor and council

Jurisdiction
All local, petty misdemeanors and civil offenses

[1] In 1808–09 the district courts were abolished and 15 circuit or superior courts established in their places. The jurisdiction and composition remained about the same.

Figure 2.1

2. Historical Development of Federal District and Circuit Courts

The judicial branch of the federal government is founded in Article III of the Constitution. Under its provisions, Congress was authorized to form "such inferior Courts" as it "may from time to time ordain and establish." Pursuant to this authority, Congress enacted the Judiciary Act of 1789. The essential provisions of that Act not only gave the United States Supreme Court the basis for its functions but also created eleven inferior district courts, one for each state which at that time had ratified the Constitution. In addition, these eleven districts were divided into three circuits. Each circuit consisted of several districts from which appeals to the circuit could be made. Two justices of the United States Supreme Court and a district judge were assigned to each circuit. These three judges then sat to hear cases twice a year in each of the districts. When sitting in this capacity, these judges were designated as the "Circuit Court for the District of [name of state]." [31]

Since the Judiciary Act of 1789, Congress has from time to time added district courts to the judicial system, usually through individual pieces of legislation for each district added to the country or to an already existing state that was redistricted. As the nation expanded, it became necessary for Congress not only to increase the number of districts and district courts but also to enact legislation improving the structure and expanding the scope of activity of the judicial branch. By the year 1792 there were sixteen districts. In addition, under the Circuit Courts Act of 1801, Congress created six circuit courts, in a form much like that of the present-day circuit courts of appeal.[32] One of the main reasons for passage of the Act of 1801 was to relieve the Supreme Court justices of their duties outside of the Supreme Court. As early as 1792 Chief Justice John Jay and his associates had joined in a statement to President Washington in which they protested that the task of riding circuit was too burdensome. However, it was more than a century before the Supreme Court justices were entirely relieved of this burden.[33]

Although the Circuit Courts Act of 1801 was repealed in 1802, similar and more functional legislation was passed shortly thereafter, and by 1837 there were nine circuits set up under the framework originally established under the Judiciary Act of 1789.[34] As a practical matter, however, the pressure of the duties of the district judges was such that increasingly the circuit court was held by a single district judge. Then in 1869 Congress authorized the appointment of one circuit judge for each of the circuits and provided that a Supreme Court justice had to sit with the circuit court only once every two years in each district within his circuit. In 1891 the present system of the Circuit Courts of Appeals was established. However, additional circuits have been added since that time.[35]

---

[31] D. Billikopf, *The Exercise of Judicial Power 1789–1864* (New York: Vantage Press, 1973), pp. 21–27.
[32] See 28 United States Code §81–131.
[33] Billikopf, pp. 22–23; C. Wright, *Law of Federal Courts,* 2d ed. (St. Paul: West Publishing Co., 1970), p. 4.
[34] Billikopf, p. 23.
[35] See 26 Statutes at Large §826 (1891).

3. Federal District Courts

There are presently ninety-two trial-level, or district, courts in the federal judicial system. The territory, or district, covered by each of these courts generally coincides with state boundary lines or with county boundaries. Of the ninety-two federal district courts, approximately one-half cover a territory corresponding to the boundaries of one state. Within the remaining states, Congress has created additional district courts, usually as a result of the increased volume of federal cases in those states. Thus, for example, the state of New York is divided into four districts —eastern, western, northern, and southern. In addition, the states of California and Texas each have four districts. Alabama, Florida, Georgia, Illinois, Louisiana, North Carolina, Oklahoma, Pennsylvania, and Tennessee have three districts. Arkansas, Indiana, Iowa, Kentucky, Maine, Michigan, Mississippi, Missouri, Ohio, Virginia, Washington, West Virginia, and Wisconsin each have two districts. The remaining twenty-five states, as well as the District of Columbia and Puerto Rico, have one district each. There does not appear to be any correlation between the population of an area and the number of districts established therein. States with relatively low populations, such as Oklahoma, Arkansas, Maine, and West Virginia, have two or three districts, whereas several states with larger populations, such as Michigan, Ohio, Maryland, Massachusetts, and New Jersey, have only one or two districts established. There is no clear reason or rationale, for example, why Mississippi is divided into two districts, which are further divided into four and five divisions, while the whole state of Massachusetts constitutes a single district and single division.[36]

As an alternative to creating new districts, Congress has sometimes simply increased the number of judges within a particular district. The districts with the largest number of judges are shown in Table 2.1. In contrast, there are ten districts that have only 1 judge. (The average number of judges per district is 4.3.)[37]

Table 2.1   U.S. District Court Judges

DISTRICT	NUMBER OF JUDGES
Southern District of New York	27
Eastern District of Pennsylvania	19
Central District of California	16
District of Columbia	15
Northern District of Illinois	13
Northern District of California	11
Eastern District of Michigan	10
Western District of Pennsylvania	10

[36] Wright, p. 7.
[37] See 28 U.S.C. §§81–131, 133.

Table 2.2 State Judicial Districts

STATE	NUMBER OF JUDICIAL DISTRICTS
Alabama	37
Arkansas	16
California	58
Illinois	21
Maryland	8
Nebraska	18
New Mexico	13
New York	57

4. State Trial Courts

Just as Congress formed the trial (district) courts in the federal judicial branch under the power given to it by the Constitution, each of the state legislatures formed state trial courts pursuant to state constitutional provisions.[38] Each state system is comprised of several judicial districts. Just as federal court districts are comprised of a single state or of several counties within a state, state court districts usually have been established along county boundary lines, each district being comprised of one or more counties. As stated above, some states have more than one federal district contained therein, but *all* states have a much larger number of state districts and district courts than they do federal districts and district courts. For example, in the state of Colorado there are 22 state judicial districts and only 1 federal district; in Texas there are 216 state judicial districts and 4 federal districts. Other examples are seen in Table 2.2. The total number of state judicial districts in the United States is 1,569.[39]

5. Federal Appellate Courts

Under discretion granted to it in Article III of the Constitution, Congress has also established an intermediate group of appellate courts. That is, Congress has established a level between the district courts and the United States Supreme Court. These intermediate appellate courts, or United States Courts of Appeals, are spread throughout the country and serve as the first level to which a party may appeal from a decision rendered by a federal district court. There are eleven such federal appellate courts, and they are described in terms of numbered circuits, such as the "United States Court of Appeals for the Third Circuit." There is the U.S. Court of

---

[38] State trial courts are called by various names: Circuit Courts (Illinois, Indiana, Michigan); Superior Courts (California, Massachusetts); District Courts (Iowa, Minnesota, Oklahoma, Wyoming); Courts of Common Pleas (Ohio, Pennsylvania). For the purpose of clarity and consistency, state trial courts will be referred to as *district* courts throughout the book.

[39] United States Department of Justice, *Law Enforcement Assistance Administration National Survey of Court Organization* (Washington, D.C.: United States Government Printing Office, 1973), p. 3.

Appeals for the First Circuit (comprised of the states of Maine, New Hampshire, Massachusetts, and Rhode Island), the Court of Appeals for the Second Circuit (consisting of New York, Vermont, and Connecticut), and so forth, through ten circuits. The eleventh U.S. Court of Appeals is designated as the "United States Court of Appeals for the District of Columbia Circuit." (See Figure 2.2.)

Geographically, each circuit is comprised of several districts, each of which has a federal district court. One would file an appeal to a decision of a district court in the circuit court whose circuit encompasses the district in which that district court is located.

Cases in these appellate courts are normally heard by one of two or more divisions of judges set up within each court. Each division is comprised of three judges. The number of judges appointed to each court of appeals ranges from three to fifteen. Also the chief judge of the court of appeals may, and often does, designate and assign a district judge within the circuit to sit as a member of the court of appeals at any specific time.[40]

6. State Appellate Courts

The state court systems, on the other hand, vary in their structure. Some have no intermediate appellate courts, thus requiring a direct appeal to the state supreme court. Others have one or more courts of appeals. Since each state has been free to form its own judicial system, separate and distinct from all the other states and from the federal system, it is not surprising that the structure of the court systems in the states varies greatly. Twenty-eight states have no intermediate appellate court. These are primarily smaller, rural states, such as Arkansas, Iowa, Nebraska, and Wisconsin. Thirteen states have two or more intermediate appellate courts, which are divided into circuits or divisions. These are mostly larger states, such as California, Florida, Illinois, and New York. Some of these thirteen states have intermediate appellate courts for civil cases, and separate intermediate courts for criminal cases, such as in Alabama and Tennessee. In nine states there is one intermediate appellate court: Colorado, Georgia, Indiana, Maryland, Michigan, New Mexico, North Carolina, Oklahoma, and Oregon.[41]

7. The United States Supreme Court

a. *Constitutional and Historical Background*

The Supreme Court of the United States exists not by virtue of federal legislation, as in the case of the district courts and circuit courts of appeals, but by specific mention in Article III of the Constitution. However, most of the details pertaining to its justices and other matters were left up to Congress. In addition, Con-

---

[40] Wright, p. 8.
[41] *L.E.A.A. Survey,* p. 12.

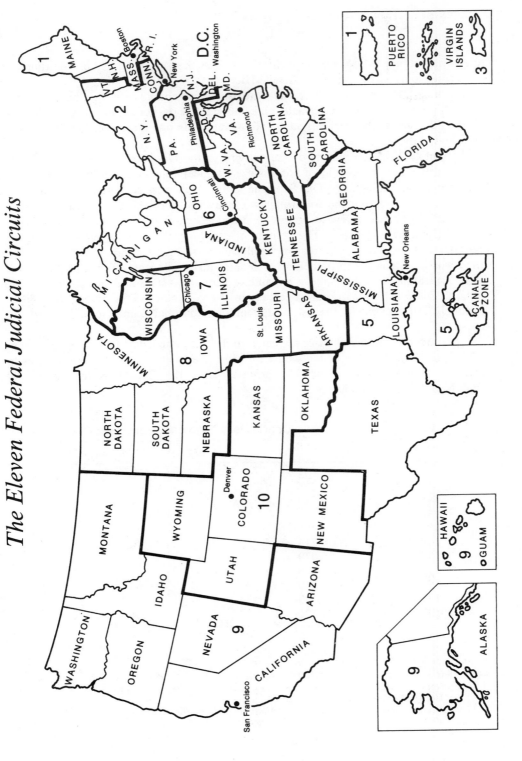

The Eleven Federal Judicial Circuits

Figure 2.2

gress has attempted to more specifically define the scope of the power that the Supreme Court was given under Article III.

Located in Washington, D.C., the Court sits in an annual term that begins on the first Monday in October and usually ends in the latter part of June. It reviews several thousand cases each year, although full written opinions are issued on only a few hundred of these.

A brief look at the history of the activity of the United States Supreme Court, and the increase in volume of cases since its inception, indicates the tremendous changes it has undergone. The Supreme Court's first session commenced on February 1, 1790. During the following two years the Supreme Court considered no cases. It did license a few attorneys to practice before it when appeals were submitted from lower courts.[42] The volume of cases remained extremely low until the post–Civil War period. The reason for the increase in the number of cases at that time was the significant broadening of federal jurisdiction as a result of post–Civil War legislation and the rapidly expanding economy, size, and population of the nation. There was a temporary decrease in the volume of cases during the 1890s, probably attributable to the establishment of additional federal circuit courts of appeals.[43]

Although the volume of cases appealed to the Supreme Court has increased three-fold since 1952, because of the Court's prerogative to choose the cases it desires to hear the number of cases actually argued before the Court has increased only slightly, as Table 2.3 indicates.[44]

Table 2.3   U.S. Supreme Court Cases Filed and Argued 1952–77

YEAR	CASES ON DOCKET	CASES GIVEN FULL ARGUMENT
1952	1,439	141
1955	1,856	123
1960	2,313	147
1965	3,284	131
1969	4,202	144
1970	4,213	151
1973	5,079	170
1974	4,620	173
1975	4,760	179
1976	4,747	179
1977	4,722	176

---

[42] L. Pfeffer, *This Honorable Court* (Boston: Beacon Press, 1965), pp. 42–43.

[43] C. Fairman, *History of the Supreme Court of the United States: Reconstruction and Reunion* (New York: MacMillan Co., 1971), p. 69.

[44] United States Department of Justice, *Annual Report of the Attorney General* (Washington, D.C.: U.S. Government Printing Office, 1963, 1973–75), pp. 49 (1963); 26 (1973); 28 (1974); 39 (1975); U.S. Supreme Court Public Information Office (1978).

Compare the figures in Table 2.3 with the early case load of the Supreme Court, as shown in Table 2.4.[45]

Since the early nineteenth century people have debated the function of the court system, particularly the Supreme Court, as a vehicle for social change in the United States. Many of Chief Justice Marshall's decisions reflected his attempts to influence the national conscience. Ever since that time people have raised questions concerning the proper scope of the Supreme Court's decisions. Should the Court serve as a force for social and economic reform? Stated more strongly, should courts in general substitute their social and economic beliefs for those of legislative bodies? These questions were asked more and more frequently beginning in the 1930s. The effects and the desirability of an activist Supreme Court reached a peak during the Warren Court in the 1950s and 1960s. It was during this era that the Court made substantial changes in its interpretation of the Constitution as it relates to free speech, the press, political liberty, the rights of criminal defendants, and race relations. It was during the 1950s, under Chief Justice Warren, that the Court acquired a self-conscious sense of judicial responsibility for minorities and for other groups that have historically been unable to influence the political process—and thus were unable to rely on the legislative branch to address their problems.

The Supreme Court's initial response to the growing pressures for racial equality was the decision in *Brown* v. *Board of Education*.[46] In this case the Court found that the Fourteenth Amendment's equal protection clause is violated by any state or local school district that creates a school system segregating children according to race or color. In rendering this decision the Court was not applying traditional constitutional principles. The Court reached the conclusion it did in order to fulfill the intent of the Fourteenth Amendment, namely to eliminate racial discrimination from official sources in the state.

Prompted by the Court's decisions on discrimination, state institutions have developed numerous mechanisms, guidelines, and quotas designed to assure minority opportunities in employment and education. Indeed, the Court's treatment of this social issue has given rise to a number of cases that allege "reverse discrimination," that is, discrimination against white applicants who claim that minority applicants

Table 2.4   U.S. Supreme Court Cases Filed and Argued 1790–1801

YEAR	CASES ON DOCKET	CASES GIVEN FULL ARGUMENT
1790	0	0
1796	28	27
1800	10	6
1790–1801	140	61

[45] J. Goebel, *History of the Supreme Court of the United States: Antecedents and Beginnings to 1801* (New York: MacMillan Co., 1971), p. 812.
[46] Brown v. Board of Education, 347 U.S. 483 (1954).

were selected for job or class openings in violation of the white applicants' right to equal protection.[47]

The Court has also entered traditional legislative spheres—reapportionment of voting districts, labor relations, school financing, and birth control and abortion—as well as its traditional provinces mentioned above—free speech, the press, and so on. This represents a clear move away from those decisions prior to the 1930s and 1940s wherein the Court dealt almost exclusively with matters of regulation of commerce, taxation, and antitrust.

It is clear that the Court has developed a philosophy that it has an obligation to make public policy under the guise of judicial review. As the most respected branch of government, perhaps it is best that the judicial branch, rather than the legislative branch, has adopted the role of social reformer. Its legitimacy and respect have allowed it to do so, although not without significant protest from segments of the public in many instances. Those protests have usually addressed the judiciary's philosophy of social change, rather than its power to render the decision in the first place.

The debate on the role of the Supreme Court and the judiciary as a whole in social reform continues vigorously. Conservatives argue that the Court should not assume the role of judicial legislator interfering with the decisions of elected officials. Liberals, on the other hand, generally defend the Supreme Court as a check upon unreasonably harsh legislation, as a protector of human rights, and as the only branch of government that is able to accurately perceive future trends in the public's views on social issues.[48]

b. The Supreme Court Justices

The United States Supreme Court consists of the Chief Justice of the United States and eight associate justices, appointed by the president for life or "during good Behaviour," with the advice and consent of the Senate. The Court has not always had a total membership of nine. The Judiciary Act of 1789 created a Supreme Court of six members, which was increased to seven in 1807, to nine in 1837, and to ten in 1864. An 1866 statute, enacted to prevent Andrew Johnson from making any appointments to the Court, provided that no vacancy should be filled until the number of associate justices was reduced to six. However, an 1869 statute was passed establishing the size of the Court at nine justices, where it has

---

[47] Bakke v. California, 438 U.S. — (decided June 28, 1978).

[48] See A. Cox, *The Role of the Supreme Court in American Government* (New York: Oxford University Press, 1976); A. Bickel, *The Supreme Court and the Idea of Progress* (New York: Harper and Row, 1970); C. Black, *The People and the Court: Judicial Review in a Democracy* (New York: MacMillan Co., 1960). Professor William Ray Forrester discusses the Supreme Court's role in "Are We Ready for Truth in Judging," *American Bar Association Journal* (September 1977), p. 212, where he urges that the legal system must first candidly recognize that the Supreme Court has evolved into what he terms a "Legiscourt." After recognizing this fact, the legal system may then be able to properly evaluate the merits of the Court's expanded function.

remained. President Roosevelt's proposed 1937 legislation would have authorized the appointment of an additional justice for each sitting justice over the age of seventy, up to a maximum of fifteen justices. A bitter fight followed this proposal, which came to be called the "court-packing" plan, and its defeat has resulted in a more firmly established and perhaps even permanently accepted concept of a nine-justice Court.[49]

The profile of the justices of the United States Supreme Court has remained constant from 1790 to the present. No person who is not a lawyer has yet to sit on the Supreme Court, although there is no constitutional or statutory bar to appointing a political scientist, a constitutional historian, or any other non-lawyer. Justices come from the same professions today as they did in the 1860s or 1920s: There are former cabinet members and executive officials; there are powerful party figures— men who must be rewarded for services done to the president's party; there are powerful members or immediately retired members of Congress, some of whom are placed on the Court for party reasons and some in order to clear the way for the president's policies; and there are prominent members of the bar and judges of the federal and state courts, again usually following broad party and sectional lines.

As these categories indicate, the Supreme Court, as a matter of occupational, career, and party lines, is an orthodox court. Former Chief Justice Earl Warren was a Republican governor of California and a Republican vice-presidental nominee in 1948; his appointment as Chief Justice in 1953 derived from President Eisenhower's desire to reward him for his services, although historians have suggested that the appointment derived from Eisenhower's desire to remove Warren from California politics. Hugo Black, Democratic senator from Alabama between 1928 and 1938, was appointed by President Franklin Roosevelt, partly because of Black's service in the United States Senate on behalf of Roosevelt's New Deal measures—including his support of the president's court reform proposal of 1937—and partly because Roosevelt knew that senatorial courtesy would prevent Black's nomination from encountering serious opposition in the Senate. William O. Douglas, though a law professor at Columbia and Yale in his early career, was a member and then chairman of the Securities and Exchange Commission during the New Deal; he was another instance of an executive official appointed to the Supreme Court.

The present Supreme Court continues this traditional profile: William J. Brennan, Jr., was a judge of the Supreme Court of New Jersey and, as an Irish Catholic and a registered Democrat, led an attempt by Dwight Eisenhower before the 1956 election to attract the votes of Catholics and "Eisenhower Democrats." Potter Stewart was a Federal Court of Appeals judge and former practicing lawyer. The only remaining Kennedy appointee on the present Supreme Court, Justice Byron White, was a member of the president's executive family, as Deputy Attorney General. The first (and only) Black appointed to the Supreme Court, Thurgood Marshall, was former counsel to the NAACP. Justice Marshall was appointed by President Johnson after a long career in the civil rights movement, including over twenty-seven

---

[49] Wright, p. 9.

years as counsel for the NAACP (where he argued, among other cases, *Brown* v. *Board of Education*[50]), three years as a U.S. Court of Appeals Circuit judge, and two years as Solicitor General of the United States under President Johnson. Chief Justice Warren Burger was Chief Judge of the United States Circuit Court of Appeals for the District of Columbia at the time he won favor with former President Nixon for his opinions attacking judicial activism and his speeches on law and order. Harry Blackmun, a lifelong Republican and a close friend of Chief Justice Burger, was appointed to the federal bench by Eisenhower in 1959 and then to the United States Supreme Court by Nixon in 1970. Supreme Court Justice Lewis Powell, a Richmond, Virginia, lawyer, had been chairman of the Richmond School Board and was president of the American Bar Association in 1965. Justice William Rehnquist was a top advisor to Senator Barry Goldwater during Goldwater's 1964 presidential campaign, prior to becoming an assistant attorney general in the Nixon Administration, presumably a reward for his support of Nixon on Vietnam and on Nixon's hard-line stance against protestors and liberal causes. Justice John Paul Stevens was a long-time member of the federal bench as judge on the United States Circuit Court of Appeals for the Seventh Circuit. When nominated by former President Ford, Stevens won more acclaim for his competence as a judge than had several previous nominees, particularly those of President Nixon.

A study of the 91 Supreme Court justices between 1789 and 1957 reveals that 87 of them were of English, Welsh, Scotch, Irish, or German origin. Of the 91 justices who served during that period of time, 82 were Protestants, 6 Roman Catholic, and 3 Jewish. Of those 91, 90 had held political positions of some kind before nomination (federal, state, or local elective, appointive, judicial, or party posts). As to their occupations before appointment, 49 were primarily politicians serving in elected office rather than devoting full time to law practice; 24 were primarily state or federal judges; 11 were primarily corporate lawyers; 4 were law professors; and 3 were general practitioners of law.[51]

8. State Supreme Courts

State supreme courts are provided for in the various state constitutions. Every state except New York has at least one supreme court that is the highest court in that state. New York's highest court is called its court of appeals rather than its supreme court, but it has the same function as the other states' supreme courts. New York does have a supreme court, but it is inferior to its court of appeals. The other state supreme courts (and New York's court of appeals) hear appeals from the judgments of the trial courts, either directly or in response to a second appeal from an intermediate state court of appeals to the state supreme court, in the same manner as the United States Supreme Court hears appeals from the rulings of lower

---

[50] Brown v. Board of Education, 347 U.S. 483 (1954).
[51] Redford, p. 508.

federal courts. Texas and Oklahoma have two supreme courts, one for criminal cases and one for civil cases.

The size of the state supreme courts varies from three justices in Delaware to nine justices in six other states: Alabama, Iowa, Mississippi, Oklahoma, Texas, and Washington. The District of Columbia, California, Colorado, Illinois, and New York each have seven justices. State supreme court justices are selected in various ways. For example, California justices are appointed by the governor, with the approval of the Commission on Judicial Appointments. Justices in California must then run in nonpartisan retention elections every twelve years. In Illinois, justices are elected on partisan ballots for ten-year terms. In Connecticut the process is analogous to the federal approach—the governor nominates a justice and the General Assembly confirms the nomination. Many states require that the justices be attorneys, a qualification the Constitution does not require of United States Supreme Court justices.

9. Special Federal Courts: Constitutional and Legislative Courts

In addition to the federal district courts, courts of appeals, and the Supreme Court, there are several other federal courts, originally called *legislative* courts because they were not formed under the authority given to Congress in Article III of the Constitution but were "created in virtue of the general rights of sovereignty which exists in the government . . . to make all needful rules and regulations." [52] Since their formation, there has been much controversy regarding whether they were in fact formed by Congress under its Article III powers or under some other congressional power conferred by the Constitution. Today, after much legislation and debate on the matter and numerous Supreme Court decisions, the only remaining legislative courts are the district courts for Guam, the Virgin Islands, and the Canal Zone. All of the special federal courts discussed below are now considered *constitutional* courts established under Article III, rather than legislative courts.[53]

Each of the constitutional courts has been established for a particular purpose. For example, the United States Court of Claims deals with claims against the United States, such as claims for compensation for property taken by the United States, for which the complainant does not believe he was adequately paid; claims relating to supply contracts; civilian and military personnel claims for back pay and retirement pay; and claims for the refund of federal income and excise tax. The United States Court of Customs and Patent Appeals deals with questions arising under the federal customs, patent, and trademark statutes. The United States Customs Court also deals with civil actions regarding the federal tariff laws. The United States Court of Military Appeals is associated with, although independent of, the United States Department of Defense and deals with certain military cases. Unlike the other special federal courts, the decisions of the United States Court of Military

---

[52] American Insurance Company v. Canter, 1 Pet. 511, 546, 7 L. Ed. 242, 257 (1828).
[53] Wright, pp. 10–13, 26–34.

Appeals are not reviewable by the United States Supreme Court. The United States Tax Court is a court which deals exclusively with claims made under the Internal Revenue Code. For example, cases heard in the United States Tax Court may deal with controversies regarding the deficiency or overpayment of income, estate, or gift taxes.

10. Other State Courts

In addition to the three-level state court system—district or trial-level courts at the lowest level, intermediate courts of appeal above that, and the state supreme court at the top of the judicial structure—all states also have a large number of other types of courts under the control of the state judicial system. These are the *county* and *municipal* government courts. These courts are very significant, and indeed most people have more contact with these municipal, county, and special state courts than with the trial-level district courts, state appellate courts, or state supreme court. These municipal, county, and special courts exist at the lowest level and do not include any types of appellate courts analogous to the state courts of appeals or supreme courts. Also the power of these lowest-level courts is more limited than the district courts and appellate courts in all of the state judicial systems.

For example, the state of Alabama has two juvenile courts in two of its counties. Special juvenile cases are heard in these courts, but there is no special juvenile court of appeals to which such a case may be appealed. Instead, such cases must be appealed to the Alabama Court of Appeals or Supreme Court, just like any other trial-level proceeding. In addition, Alabama has 1 probate court for each of its sixty-eight counties, 1 family court, which handles domestic matters, and 117 municipal courts (called reporters' courts) in cities with a population of at least 1,000 people.[54]

California has 77 municipal courts located in judicial districts with a population of over 40,000 people and 244 justice courts located in judicial districts with a population of less than 40,000.[55]

New York has a court of claims, with exclusive jurisdiction in claims to which the state of New York is a party with a citizen, any other state, or the federal government. The state also has 1 criminal court of the city of New York and 1 special civil court of the city of New York. Further, there are 2 special district courts, 61 city courts, 7 city justice courts, 7 city police courts, 7 recorders' courts, and 1,303 town and village justice courts.[56]

QUESTIONS

1. Under Article III, section 1, of the United States Constitution, was Congress *required* to establish inferior courts? Why or why not?

---

[54] *L.E.A.A. Survey,* pp. 82–88.
[55] Ibid., p. 103.
[56] Ibid., pp. 192–94.

2. What are the advantages and disadvantages to the public in having a tri-level state court system, as opposed to a bi-level system? Does the Constitution require that the *state* court systems provide for any appeal at all? Explain.

3. What moral or ethical obligation do the United States Supreme Court justices have to consider more cases than they do, or to consider all cases that may involve the violation of personal freedoms?

4. What, if any, arguments can be made that a political scientist or other lay person should be appointed to the United States Supreme Court? Should it be required that a person must have been a judge for a certain number of years in order to qualify for the United States Supreme Court?

3

The Case System and Appellate Decisions

A. Purpose and Importance of the Case System

1. Due Process

Although it is not expressly stated in the United States Constitution or any state constitution, a concept inherent in the judicial system in this country is that people must be given notice of the position that the courts of law have taken and most likely will take in the future on any given point of law. The idea of notice is a fundamental concept of fairness, and fairness is a major part of the concept of due process. It would be unfair for a court to be arbitrary and capricious in its decisions; courts must embody a system of predictability upon which individuals can rely. The courts must ensure that no matter who the parties are in each case, when those parties find themselves in a situation similar to that of parties in previous cases, they will be treated by the law in the same way.

Law must provide for social change through the statutes passed by elected organs of government and through the rulings of courts. Therefore, it must be an instrument of transition, adjusting older rules to the changing power relations and shifting ideals of society. However, law must also be the process that permits citizens to predict the probable legal consequences of their actions: "Obviously, a legal system in which judges could decide cases any which-way, manifesting prejudice, whimsy, ignorance and venality, each decision being an entity in itself unconnected with the theory, practices and precedents of the whole, would be a sorry system, or, one might say, no system at all, and a source of little comfort either to attorneys or litigants." [1] In the 1881 case of *Wilson* v. *Bumstead,* Judge Maxwell of the Supreme Court of Nebraska described the need for the system of precedents: "In the application of the principles of the common law, where the precedents are unanimous in the support of a proposition, there is no safety but in a strict adherence to such

---

[1] C. Post, *An Introduction to the Law* (Englewood Cliffs, N.J.: Prentice-Hall, Inc., 1963), p. 82.

precedents. If the court will not follow established rules, rights are sacrificed, and lawyers and litigants are left in doubt and uncertainty, while there is no certainty in regard to what, upon a given state of facts, the decision of the court will be." [2] The precedent system provides the needed certainty. The element of doubt concerning the court's anticipated actions is reduced greatly under the case system implemented by the courts. In this way the greatest affordable degree of notice is given to the public, thus satisfying the need for due process.

2. Stability and Legitimacy of Government

Equally important, and perhaps an overlapping concept, is that of stability in the constitutional system. For many reasons the governmental institutions of the United States command more respect than any other nation in the world. No other nation has existed under a written constitution for as long as the United States. The judicial system reflects and helps to perpetuate this stability, partly because of the exercise of the system of precedents—the case system. The greater the certainty of the judicial system, the greater its stability and credibility will be. This stable atmosphere and framework in turn foster economic and social progress. In *An Introduction to the Philosophy of Law* Roscoe Pound described the historical background and basis for institutionalizing the legal system: [3]

> A sure basis of authority resting upon something more stable than human will and power of those who govern to impose their will for the time being was required . . . for the problem of social control in the Greek city-state. In order to maintain the general security and the security of social institutions . . . in order to persuade or coerce both the aristocracy and the mass of the low born to maintain in orderly fashion the social status quo, it would not do to tell that law was a gift of God, nor that what offended the aristocrat, a radical bit of popular legislation enacted at the instance of a demagogue was yet to be obeyed because it had been so taught by wise men who knew the good old customs.

According to Pound, two needs have influenced philosophical thinking about the law: on the one hand, the paramount social interest in the general security, which "has led men to seek some fixed basis of a certain ordering of human action which should . . . assure a firm and stable social order"; on the other hand, the need to continually make compromises because of our constantly changing society. The need for change has called for frequent overhauling of legal precepts and for refitting them to unexpected situations. This has "led men to seek principles of legal development by which to escape from authoritative rules which they feared or did not know how to reject but could no longer apply to advantage." Pound warned, however, that these principles of change and growth might "easily prove inimical to the general

---

[2] Wilson v. Bumstead, 12 Nebr. 1 (1881).
[3] R. Pound, *An Introduction to the Philosophy of Law* (New Haven: Yale University Press, 1963), p. 82.

a process of search & comparison

security, [thus] it was important to reconcile or unify them with the idea of a fixed basis of the legal order." [4]

We now enjoy such a fixed legal basis, and one of its major purposes is not only to let the people that it serves know what treatment to expect should they become involved in the legal process but also to lend stability and legitimacy to our entire governmental process. "Adherence to precedent must . . . be the rule rather than the exception if litigants are to have faith in the even-handed administration of justice in the courts." [5]

B. Doctrine of *Stare Decisis*

stare decisis – let the decision stand.

1. General Meaning

The guiding principle in the system of judicial precedents is the doctrine of *stare decisis* (pronounced "stä′·rā dĕ·sĭ′·sĭs"), which requires that a principle established in prior cases must be followed by the court (and courts inferior to it) in the present case unless there is some overwhelming reason to change that principle or to distinguish the legal or factual issues of the present case from such precedent. Interpreted literally, the term *stare decisis* means "let the decision stand." When it is time to render a decision, this command should be ever-present in the mind of every judge. It should temper any tendency to act arbitrarily, and it should result in a decision and supporting rationale that will be sound and reasonable, so as to stand the test of time. The rendering of such a decision and rationale should be in accordance with earlier cases that are followed and cited by the court in its decision. The court attempts to build a case on those prior decisions, thereby showing that it is following the existing law on the subject and is acting in a predictable, fair, and reasonable manner. Judge Cardozo described the method of following precedent and adhering to the principle of *stare decisis* in this manner: [6]

> The first thing . . . [the judge] does is to compare the case before him with the precedents, whether stored in his mind or hidden in the books. . . . Back of precedents are the basic juridical conceptions which are the postulates of judicial reasoning, and farther back are the habits of life, the institutions of society, in which those conceptions have their origin, and which, by a process of interaction, have modified in turn. Nonetheless, in a system so highly developed as our own, precedents have so covered the ground that they fix the point of departure from which the labor of the judge begins. Almost invariably his first step is to examine and compare them. If they are plain and to the point, there may be need of nothing more. *Stare decisis* is at least the everyday working rules of our law. . . . It is a process of search, comparison, and little more. Some judges seldom get beyond that process in any case. Their notion of their duty is to match the colors of the

---

[4] Pound, pp. 2–3.
[5] B. Cardozo, *The Nature of the Judicial Process* (New Haven: Yale University Press, 1970), p. 34.
[6] Ibid., pp. 19–21.

case at hand against the colors of many sample cases spread out upon their desk. The sample nearest in shade supplies the applicable rule. But, of course, no system of living law can be evolved by such a process, and no judge of a high court, worthy of his office, views the function of his place so narrowly. If that were all there was to our calling, there would be little intellectual interest about it. The man who had the best card index of the cases would also be the wisest judge. It is when the colors do not match, when the references in the index fail, when there is no decisive precedent, that the serious business of the judge begins. He must then fashion law for the litigants before him. In fashioning it for them, he will be fashioning it for others.

Pound's analysis of the judge's duty consists of three necessary steps in the adjudication of a controversy:[7]

1. Finding the law and ascertaining which of the many rules in the legal system is to be applied, or, if none is applicable, establishing a new rule for the case (which may or may not stand as a rule for subsequent cases) by analogizing from existing cases;
2. Interpreting the rule so chosen or ascertained by determining its meaning and its intended scope; and
3. Applying to the present case the rule which has been so found and interpreted.

Pound further stated that finding the law "may consist merely in laying hold of a prescribed text of a code or statute. In that event the tribunal must proceed to determine the meaning of the rule and to apply it." [8] But both Pound and Cardozo repeatedly emphasized that many cases are not so simple. Also, of course, almost every case has unique facts. More than one source is at hand that might apply, and more than one rule may be applicable. "[T]he parties are contending which [rule] shall be made the basis of a decision." [9] In that event, the various rules must be interpreted in order for intelligent selection to be made. Pound pointed out that often the interpretation of the existing rules shows that none is adequate to cover the case and that a new one must be supplied:[10]

> Attempts to foreclose this process by minute-detailed legislation have failed signally, as, for example, in the overgrown code of civil procedure which long obtained in New York. Providing of a rule by which to decide the cause is a necessary element in the determination of a large proportion of the causes that come before our higher tribunals, and it is often because a rule must be provided that the parties are not content to abide by the decision of the court of first instance.

In criticizing and stating a somewhat cynical view of the manner in which the concept of *stare decisis* is sometimes implemented in our court system, Pound explained:[11]

---

[7] Pound, p. 48.
[8] Ibid., p. 50.
[9] Ibid., p. 50.
[10] Ibid., pp. 50–51.
[11] Ibid., pp. 59–60.

To a large and apparently growing extent the practice of our application of law has been that jurors or courts, as the case may be, take the rules of law as a general guide, determine what the equities of the cause demand, and contrive to find a verdict or render a judgment accordingly, wrenching the law no more than is necessary. Many courts have been suspected of ascertaining what the equities of a controversy require, and then raking up adjudicated cases to justify the result desired. . . . Occasionally a judge is found who acknowledges frankly that he looks chiefly at the ethical situation between the parties and does not allow the law to interfere therewith beyond what is inevitable.

. . . Necessary as it is, the method by which we attain a needed individualization is injurious to respect for law. If the courts do not respect the law, who will? There is no exclusive cause of the current [disrespectful] American attitude toward the law. But judicial evasion and warping of the law, in order to secure in practice a freedom of judicial action not conceded in theory, is certainly one cause.

Cardozo joined Pound in an indictment of the tendency of judges to apply existing principles either too loosely, incorrectly, or not at all, and to substitute their individual preferences for those embodied in the legal foundation theretofore established:[12]

The courts, then, are free in marking the limits of the individual's immunities to shape their judgments in accordance with reason and justice. That does not mean that in judging the validity of statutes they are free to substitute their own ideas of reason and justice for those of the men and women whom they serve. Their standard must be an objective one. In such matters, the thing that counts is not what I believe to be right. "While the courts must exercise a judgment of their own, it by no means is true that every law is void which may seem to the judges who pass upon it excessive, unsuited to its ostensible end, or based upon conceptions of morality with which they disagree. Considerable latitude must be allowed for difference of view as well as for possible peculiar conditions which this court can know but imperfectly, if at all." [Quoting *Otis* v. *Parker,* 187 U.S. 608 (1902)]

Throughout the examination of the precedent system, and despite the command of the doctrine of *stare decisis* and the warnings given by legal philosophers like Pound and Cardozo, we must remember that these legal principles are the judgment of mere men. There is no unanimous agreement on any legal principle or doctrine in the substantive areas of law discussed in the following chapters. These principles were established by judges looking at the facts through their own subjective eyes and through the myriad of experiences they have had throughout their lifetime and applying their own interpretations to them. This is a fundamental problem of the legal system; the administration of justice is carried out "by the more or less trained intuition of experienced magistrates." [13] As stated by Cardozo:[14]

There is in each of us a stream of tendency, whether you choose to call it philosophy or not, which gives coherence and direction to thought and action. Judges

---

[12] Cardozo, pp. 88–89.
[13] Pound, p. 54.
[14] Cardozo, pp. 12–13.

cannot escape that current any more than other mortals. All their lives, forces which they do not recognize and cannot name, have been tugging at them—inherited instincts, traditional beliefs, acquired convictions; and the resultant is an outlook on life, a conception of social needs. . . . We may try to see things as objectively as we please. Nonetheless, we can never see them without any eyes except our own.

2. The Need for Flexibility

Throughout the next several chapters many principles of law will be stated. In support, or as an example, of many of those principles, one or more cases will be cited in the footnotes. The cases illustrate only the legal principles for which they are cited. They are not intended to be either exhaustive of the jurisdictions that maintain a position or principle on a given point of law or representative of the greatest wisdom possible on such principles, because the minority position or a yet-unannounced or undiscovered position may possibly be more sound. In addition, the principles stated through these chapters are in no sense conclusive, inflexible, or final. Although the last judgment rendered on appeal carries with it a firmness not subject to challenge or further interpretation by the litigants in that case, the principles embodied in that decision serve only as legal guidelines for facts and situations in subsequent cases.

The legal principles set forth throughout this book reflect the principles in the various jurisdictions in this country. A majority position at one point in time may become the minority position a few years later as a result of courts changing their positions or by legislatures passing statutes applying to such principles. Thus the precedent system is an extremely flexible one, despite its stability and its capacity to prevent courts from handing down arbitrary and capricious decisions:[15]

> [T]he whole subject matter of jurisprudence is more plastic, more malleable, the molds less definitely cast, the bounds of right and wrong less preordained and constant, than most of us, without the aid of some such analysis, have been accustomed to believe. We like to picture to ourselves the field of the law as accurately mapped and plotted. We draw our little lines, and they are hardly down before we blur them.

Cardozo suggested that if we figure stability and progress as opposite poles, then at one pole we have the maxim of *stare decisis,* at the other the principles supporting the need for flexibility.[16] The former emphasizes uniformity and symmetry and follows fundamental conceptions to their ultimate conclusions, whereas the latter gives more consideration to equity and justice and to the value to society of the interests affected:[17]

> The one searches for the analogy that is nearest in point of similarity, and adheres to it inflexibly. The other, in its choice of the analogy that shall govern,

---

[15] Ibid., p. 161.
[16] B. Cardozo, *The Paradoxes of Legal Science* (New York: Columbia University Press, 1928), p. 8.
[17] Ibid., p. 8.

finds community of spirit more significant than resemblance in externals. . . . Each method has its value, and for each in the changes of litigation there will come the hour for use. A wise eclecticism employs them both.

The common law is not based upon "pre-established truths of universal and in-flexible validity" and "conclusions derived from them deductively." [18] Its method is inductive and draws its generalizations from particulars. Cardozo quoted with approval a statement by Monroe Smith:[19]

> In their effort to give to the social sense of justice articulate expression in rules and principles, the method of the law-finding experts has always been experimental. The rules and principles of case law have never been treated as final truths, but as working hypotheses, continually retested in those great laboratories of the law, the courts of justice. Every new case is an experiment; and if the accepted rule which seems applicable yields a result which is felt to be unjust, the rule is reconsidered. It may not be modified at once, for the attempt to do absolute justice in every single case would make the development and maintenance of general rules impossible; but if a rule continues to work injustice, it will eventually be reformulated. The principles themselves are continually retested; for if the rules derived from a principle do not work well, the principle itself must ultimately be re-examined.

This work of modification is gradual, and in the American legal system its effects cannot be measured from case to case or even from year to year. The results are seen only after decades and even centuries. "[T]hey are seen to have behind them the power and the pressure of the moving glacier." [20]

> Nothing is stable. Nothing absolute. All is fluid and changeable. There is an endless becoming. We are back with Heraclitus. That, I mean, is the average or aggregate impression which the picture leaves on the mind. Doubtless in the last three centuries, some lines, once wavering, have become rigid. We leave more to legislatures today, and less perhaps to judges. Yet even now there is change from decade to decade. The glacier still moves.
>
> In this perpetual flux, the problem which confronts the judge is in reality a twofold one: he must first extract from the precedents the underlying principles, the *ratio decidendi;* he must then determine the path or direction along which the principle is to move and develop, if it is not to wither and die.
>
> The first branch of the problem is one to which we are accustomed to address ourselves more consciously than to the other. Cases do not unfold their principles for the asking. They yield up their kernel slowly and painfully. The instance cannot lead to a generalization till we know it as it is.

---

18 Cardozo, *The Nature of the Judicial Process,* pp. 22–23.
19 M. Smith, *Jurisprudence* (New York: Columbia University Press, 1909), p. 21, as quoted in Cardozo, *The Nature of the Judicial Process,* p. 23.
20 Cardozo, p. 25, and pp. 28–29.

3. Mandatory and Persuasive Authority; Distinguishing Precedents

Class

The relationship between the court rendering a present decision and the court that rendered a decision now regarded as a precedent determines how binding the force of that precedent is on the present decision. A higher court decision, within either the state or federal judicial system, will bind the lower court in that same system, but the opposite is not true. Thus precedents from higher courts constitute *mandatory* authority over lower courts. One state court is not bound by the decisions of any other state's courts, despite the level of those other courts. However, it is not uncommon for a court to cite the decisions of other jurisdictions. These decisions, although not binding, are *persuasive* authority. Persuasive authority provides direction and support for a court on questions that suffer from a dearth of judicial guidance in a particular jurisdiction, or on questions that the court feels are in need of a change away from the existing trend or principles in that jurisdiction.

Despite the mandatory force of a state supreme court decision on a state district court in a later proceeding, for example, some judicial freedom is available to the lower court through the ability to distinguish unfavorable precedents. If such court can find sufficient distinction, in the facts or on a legal basis, between its present case and the precedent, so as to justify a decision not in line with the earlier case, it will not be bound by the prior decision. Prior decisions on a point of law are mandatory on a future case only if the same or substantially the same issue is involved. Also, the precedent must be considered in light of the facts.

The court's discretion and freedom to distinguish the present case from earlier ones is a basic component of the necessary flexibility just discussed. Thus the courts have available a justification or basis for avoiding what would otherwise constitute mandatory but often harsh and inappropriate precedents. Pound believed in the need for flexibility but maintained that judges have a tendency to abuse their right to exercise discretion.[21]

4. Overruling Precedents

Class

Besides their discretion and prerogative of distinguishing undesirable precedents, there is also the option of breaking with precedent altogether by acknowledging that such precedent should be expressly overruled, that is, a new principle of law should be established on the question presented to the court. Of course, an inferior court may not overrule a prior decision of a superior court. However, a court may overrule its own line of prior decisions or a line of prior decisions by a lower court. In the American judicial system, overruling a long-established principle on a particular point of law is a very rare step for a court to take and is justified by only the strongest of reasons. However, its significance as a method of avoiding stagnation and immobility should not be ignored. The doctrine of *stare decisis* represents

---

[21] Pound, p. 53.

the stability of the system, and the ability to overrule precedents represents the progressive element of the legal system:[22]

> [T]here is a good deal of discussion whether the rule of adherence to precedent ought to be abandoned altogether. I would not go so far myself. I think adherence to precedent should be the rule and not the exception.... [T]he labor of judges would be increased almost to the breaking point if every past decision could be reopened in every case, and one could not lay one's own course of bricks on the secure foundation of the courses laid by others who had gone before him.... But I am ready to concede that the rule of adherence to precedent, though it ought not to be abandoned, ought to be to some degree relaxed. I think that when a rule, after it has been duly tested by experience, has been found to be inconsistent with the social welfare, there should be less hesitation in frank avowal and full abandonment.... In such circumstances, the words of Wheeler, J., in Dwy v. Connecticut Co., 89 Conn. 74, 99, expressed the tone and temper in which problems should be met: "That court best serves the law which recognizes that the rules of law which grew up in a remote generation may, in the fullness of experience, be found to serve another generation badly, and which discards the old rule when it finds that another rule of law represents what should be according to the established and settled judgment of society, and no considerable property rights have become vested in reliance upon the old rule." If judges have woefully misinterpreted the mores of their day, or if the mores of their day are no longer those of ours, they ought not to tie, in helpless submission, the hands of their successors.

Indeed it has historically been the result of gradual but significant changes in the moral views or economic needs of society, rather than the court's earlier misinterpretation of such views or needs, which has brought about the repudiation and express overruling of long-standing precedents.

5. Precedents Established in Appellate Courts

Generally the cases relied on as precedents, either by the court in its opinion or by the attorneys arguing their respective positions on behalf of their clients, are decisions of appellate courts rather than trial courts. As explained in Chapter 2, the proceedings in trial courts consist of the presentation of evidence in the form of documentary evidence and testimony of witnesses. In trial courts there is a much greater concentration on the facts than on the legal points of the case. The proceedings in an appellate court, on the other hand, are strictly legal matters rather than factual matters. For example, if the losing party in a trial appeals the decision, the appeal would be based upon alleged errors made by the trial-court judge on matters of law such as admissibility of evidence or instructions that he gave to the jury. An appeal must be upon the failure of a trial court to follow the legal principles theretofore established in that jurisdiction. This fact alone indicates that precedents are more likely to be derived from appellate decisions that result from the review of a lower court's ruling. (However, a court or an attorney may sometimes cite a deci-

---

[22] Cardozo, pp. 149–52.

sion of a *trial* court from the same jurisdiction as a precedent of persuasive authority.)

In addition, a court or attorney is more likely to rely on appellate court decisions for the simple reason that they represent the position of a higher court and therefore carry with them much greater weight than the decision of a trial court. Another (and very practical) reason that the decisions cited as precedents are usually those of higher courts is that many jurisdictions simply do not publish the decisions of their trial courts, thereby making it impractical to locate, read, and base arguments upon such decisions.

QUESTIONS

1. What role does the system of precedents play in encouraging the settlement of lawsuits? When a close question of law is involved in a case, can either party be certain about what the judge's decision will be?

2. What is the relationship between the precedent system and the proceedings in a trial court, as opposed to an appellate court?

3. What factors should be considered most important in deciding whether to overrule a long-standing principle of law?

4. Give some examples of persuasive and mandatory authority. Are treatises by legal scholars persuasive authority?

4

The Concept of Jurisdiction

A. Definition

The word *jurisdiction* has several meanings; most commonly it is used to mean the power to hear and determine a case. However, jurisdiction has many facets. In order for a court's decision to have any effect, that court must have jurisdiction in all relevant respects. Several different tests may be used to determine each of the different types of jurisdiction. Yet the ultimate question to be answered is whether the court has the power to hear and determine the case.

One specific type of jurisdiction is jurisdiction over subject matter. Subject matter jurisdiction refers to the type or nature of the case. In the federal system, if a case is not the subject matter described in the United States Constitution as the type over which the federal courts may exercise jurisdiction, as described later in this chapter, then such a case must be filed in a state court. Any attempt by a federal district court to rule on a case improperly filed in that court may be rendered ineffective by a federal court of appeals or the United States Supreme Court, on the basis that the district court lacked subject matter jurisdiction. In terms of state court subject matter jurisdiction, different state courts are granted statutory authority over different types of cases. For example, a probate court does not have jurisdiction over a case involving a personal injury claim.

Another meaning of the word *jurisdiction* applies to a court's jurisdiction over the person. With certain exceptions, in order for a proceeding or a judgment of a federal or state court to have any effect on the defendant, such court must have personal, or *in personam,* jurisdiction. This is obtained by service of process in accordance with certain rules of procedure.[1] Usually state courts can exercise their power only over persons within the borders of the particular state, and who have been properly notified that an action has been commenced against them. While federal *in personam* jurisdiction extends throughout the country, a state's power out-

---

[1] See discussion in Chapter 5, Part A, concerning the Federal Rules of Civil Procedure.

side its own borders is quite limited. For purposes of obtaining jurisdiction over the person, a person or corporation must either be present in the state or have sufficient contacts there in order to be subject to suit therein. The case of *International Shoe Company* v. *Washington* illustrates the type of activities of a corporation that constitute its presence within a state, thus rendering the corporation subject to state taxation or litigation against it.

INTERNATIONAL SHOE COMPANY
v.
WASHINGTON

326 U.S. 310 (1945)

Supreme Court of the United States

Mr. Chief Justice STONE delivered the opinion of the Court:

The questions for decision are (1) whether, within the limitations of the due process clause of the Fourteenth Amendment, appellant, a Delaware corporation, has by its activities in the State of Washington rendered itself amenable to proceedings in the courts of that state to recover unpaid contributions to the state unemployment compensation fund exacted by state statutes, Washington Unemployment Compensation Act, and (2) whether the state can exact those contributions consistently with the due process clause of the Fourteenth Amendment.

The statutes in question set up a comprehensive scheme of unemployment compensation, the costs of which are defrayed by contributions required to be made by employers to a state unemployment compensation fund. The contributions are a specified percentage of the wages payable annually by each employer for his employees' services in the state. The assessment and collection of the contributions and the fund are administered by appellees. Section 14(c) of the Act authorizes appellee Commissioner to issue an order and notice of assessment of delinquent contributions upon prescribed personal service of the notice upon the employer if found within the state, or, if not so found, by mailing the notice to the employer by registered mail at his last known address.

That section also authorizes the Commissioner to collect the assessment by distraint if it is not paid within ten days after service of the notice. By §§14e and 6b the order of assessment may be administratively reviewed by an appeal tribunal within the office of unemployment upon petition of the employer, and this determination is by §6i made subject to judicial review on questions of law by the state Superior Court, with further right of appeal in the state Supreme Court as in other civil cases.

In this case notice of assessment for the years in question was personally served upon a sales solicitor employed by appellant in the State of Washington, and a copy of the notice was mailed by registered mail to appellant at its address in St. Louis, Missouri. Appellant appeared specially before the office of unemployment and moved to set aside the order and notice of assessment on the ground that the service upon appellant's salesman was not proper service upon appellant; that appellant was not a corporation of the State of Washington and was not doing business in the state; that it had no agent within the state upon whom service could be made; and that appellant is not an employer and does not furnish employment within the meaning of the statute.

The motion was heard on evidence and a stipulation of facts by the appeal tribunal which denied the motion and ruled that appellee Commissioner was entitled to recover the unpaid contributions. That action was affirmed by the Commissioner; both the Superior Court and the Supreme Court affirmed. 22 Wash.2d 146, 154 P.2d 801. Appellant in each of these courts assailed the statute as applied, as a violation of the due process clause of the Fourteenth Amendment, and as imposing a constitutionally prohibited burden on interstate commerce. The cause comes here on appeal, appellant assigning as error that the challenged statutes as applied infringe the due process clause of the Fourteenth Amendment and the commerce clause.

The facts as found by the appeal tribunal and accepted by the state Superior Court and Supreme Court, are not in dispute. Appellant is a Delaware corporation, having its principal place of business in St. Louis, Missouri, and is engaged in the manufacture and sale of shoes and other footwear. It maintains places of business in several states, other than Washington, at which its manufacturing is carried on and from which its merchandise is distributed interstate through several sales units or branches located outside the State of Washington.

Appellant has no office in Washington and makes no contracts either for sale or purchase of merchandise there. It maintains no stock of merchandise in that state and makes there no deliveries of goods in intrastate commerce. During the years from 1937 to 1940, now in question, appellant employed eleven to thirteen salesmen under direct supervision and control of sales managers located in St. Louis. These salesmen resided in Washington; their principal activities were confined to that state; and they were compensated by commissions based upon the amount of their sales. The commissions for each year totaled more than $31,000. Appellant supplies its salesmen with a line of samples, each consisting of one shoe of a pair, which they display to prospective purchasers. On occasion they rent permanent sample rooms, for exhibiting samples, in business buildings, or rent rooms in hotels or business buildings temporarily for that purpose. The cost of such rentals is reimbursed by appellant.

The authority of the salesmen is limited to exhibiting their samples and soliciting orders from prospective buyers, at prices and on terms fixed by appellant. The salesmen transmit the orders to appellant's office in St. Louis for acceptance or rejection, and when accepted the merchandise for filling the orders is shipped f.o.b. from points outside Washington to the purchasers within the state. All the merchandise shipped into Washington is invoiced at the place of shipment from which collections are made. No salesman has authority to enter into contracts or to make collections.

The Supreme Court of Washington was of opinion that the regular and systematic solicitation of orders in the state by appellant's salesmen, resulting in a continuous flow of appellant's product into the state, was sufficient to constitute doing business in the state so as to make appellant amenable to suit in its courts. But it was also of opinion that there were sufficient additional activities shown to bring the case within the rule frequently stated, that solicitation within a state by the agents of a foreign corporation plus some additional activities there are sufficient to render the corporation amenable to suit brought in the courts of the state to enforce an obligation arising out of its activities there. The court found such additional activities in the salesmen's display of samples sometimes in permanent display rooms, and the salesmen's residence within the state, continued over a period of years, all resulting in a substantial volume of merchandise regularly shipped by appellant to purchasers within the state. . . .*

Appellant . . . insists that its activities within the state were not sufficient to manifest its "presence" there and that in its absence the state courts were without jurisdiction, that consequently it was a denial of due process for the state to subject appellant to suit. It refers to those cases in which it was said that the mere solicitation of orders for the purchase of goods within a state, to be accepted without the state and filled by shipment of the purchased

---

* Author's Note: Ellipses in case text throughout this book indicate the omission of substantive material; omission of case citations is not indicated.

goods interstate, does not render the corporation seller amenable to suit within the state. And appellant further argues that since it was not present within the state, it is a denial of due process to subject it to taxation or other money exaction. It thus denies the power of the state to lay the tax or to subject appellant to a suit for its collection.

Historically the jurisdiction of courts to render judgment in personam is grounded on their de facto power over the defendant's person. Hence his presence within the territorial jurisdiction of a court was prerequisite to its rendition of a judgment personally binding him. Pennoyer v. Neff, 95 U.S. 714. But now . . . due process requires only that in order to subject a defendant to a judgment in personam, if he be not present within the territory of the forum, he have certain minimum contacts with it such that the maintenance of the suit does not offend "traditional notions of fair play and substantial justice." Milliken v. Meyer, 311 U.S. 457, 463.

Since the corporate personality is a fiction . . . it is clear that unlike an individual its "presence" without, as well as within, the state of its origin can be manifested only by activities carried on in its behalf by those who are authorized to act for it. To say that the corporation is so far "present" there as to satisfy due process requirements, for purposes of taxation or the maintenance of suits against it in the courts of the state, is to beg the question to be decided. For the terms "present" or "presence" are used merely to symbolize those activities of the corporation's agent within the state which courts will deem to be sufficient to satisfy the demands of due process. Those demands may be met by such contacts of the corporation with the state of the forum as make it reasonable, in the context of our federal system of government, to require the corporation to defend the particular suit which is brought there. An "estimate of the inconveniences" which would result to the corporation from a trial away from its "home" or principal place of business is relevant in this connection. "Presence" in the state in this sense has

never been doubted when the activities of the corporation there have not only been continuous and systematic, but also give rise to the liabilities sued on, even though no consent to be sued or authorization to an agent to accept service of process has been given. Conversely it has been generally recognized that the casual presence of the corporate agent or even his conduct of single or isolated items of activities in a state in the corporation's behalf are not enough to subject it to suit on causes of action unconnected with the activities there. To require the corporation in such circumstances to defend the suit away from its home or other jurisdiction where it carries on more substantial activities has been thought to lay too great and unreasonable a burden on the corporation to comport with due process.

While it has been held, in cases on which appellant relies, that continuous activity of some sorts within a state is not enough to support the demand that the corporation be amenable to suits unrelated to that activity, there have been instances in which the continuous corporate operations within a state were thought so substantial and of such a nature as to justify suit against it on causes of action arising from dealings entirely distinct from those activities. . . . It is evident that the criteria by which we mark the boundary line between those activities which justify the subjection of a corporation to suit, and those which do not, cannot be simply mechanical or quantitative. The test is not merely, as has sometimes been suggested, whether the activity, which the corporation has seen fit to procure through its agents in another state, is a little more or a little less. Whether due process is satisfied must depend rather upon the quality and nature of the activity in relation to the fair and orderly administration of the laws which it was the purpose of the due process clause to insure. That clause does not contemplate that a state may make binding a judgment in personam against an individual or corporate defendant with which the state has no contacts, ties, or relations.

But to the extent that a corporation exercises the privilege of conducting activities within a state, it enjoys the benefits and protection of the laws of that state. The exercise of that privilege may give rise to obligations, and, so far as those obligations arise out of or are connected with the activities within the state, a procedure which requires the corporation to respond to a suit brought to enforce them can, in most instances, hardly be said to be undue.

Applying these standards, the activities carried on in behalf of appellant in the State of Washington were neither irregular nor casual. They were systematic and continuous throughout the years in question. They resulted in a large volume of interstate business, in the course of which appellant received the benefits and protection of the laws of the state, including the right to resort to the courts for the enforcement of its rights. The obligation which is here sued upon arose out of those very activities. It is evident that these operations establish sufficient contacts or ties with the state of the forum to make it reasonable and just according to our traditional conception of fair

play and substantial justice to permit the state to enforce the obligations which appellant has incurred there. Hence we cannot say that the maintenance of the present suit in the State of Washington involves an unreasonable or undue procedure.

We are likewise unable to conclude that the service of the process within the state upon an agent whose activities establish appellant's "presence" there was not sufficient notice of the suit, or that the suit was so unrelated to those activities as to make the agent an inappropriate vehicle for communicating the notice. It is enough that appellant has established such contacts with the state that the particular form of substituted service adopted there gives reasonable assurance that the notice will be actual. Nor can we say that the mailing of the notice of suit to appellant by registered mail at its home office was not reasonably calculated to apprise appellant of the suit. . . .

Affirmed.

Thus, to bring a case against a corporation, the plaintiff must first show that that corporation is doing business in the state. For a corporation to be "doing business," the plaintiff must show that it availed itself of the privileges related to conducting business in the state, and that it therefore should be expected to incur corresponding obligations resulting from its activities in the state. As applied to both state and federal courts, personal jurisdiction requirements over individuals and corporations embody concepts of fair and adequate notice of the action to the defendant.

Jurisdiction can also mean a geographical area or a particular legal system. For example, it may be said that New York is the only jurisdiction where the highest court in the state is called the court of appeals rather than the supreme court.

B. Federal Jurisdiction as Established By the Constitution, Articles I and III

The meaning of the word *jurisdiction* throughout the remainder of this chapter and the book will be jurisdiction over subject matter, unless otherwise indicated. In examining subject matter jurisdiction, this chapter first addresses the following question: What is the scope of the power of the federal courts to hear cases? It has been stated previously that the power of the federal courts is limited, and that unlike the state courts, the federal courts can hear only certain types of cases. What are those limited areas of federal jurisdiction?

The post-Revolution events that established the structure of the federal judicial system—the enactment of the Constitution and the passage of the Judiciary Act of 1789—also established the scope of federal jurisdiction. Thus any discussion of the scope of federal jurisdiction must begin with these basic sources. This discussion will concentrate on the two most common types of cases over which the original thirteen states, through the pen of the Founding Fathers, granted the federal courts jurisdiction, namely *federal question* and *diversity of citizenship* cases.

The first sentence of Article III allows the Congress to establish the number and hierarchy of federal courts below the Supreme Court. However, the *authority* of the federal courts is limited by the theory upon which the entire federal government is based, namely a central government with limited power. The basic principle expressed throughout the *Federalist Papers* and the Constitutional Convention, and still repeated today, is that the federal government derives its power from the states. The federal government would not exist without the granting to it by the states of certain specific, yet limited, powers. This simple yet vitally important principle is the basic reason that federal courts can hear only certain types of cases, namely those cases that they have been given the authority to hear by the express provisions of the United States Constitution. In fact, all three branches of the federal government can act only in accordance with and within the scope of authority granted to them by the Constitution. Further, as the Tenth Amendment of the Constitution states, if powers have not been given to the federal government by the Constitution, those powers remain with the states or with the people. All of those limited areas carved out by the Constitution for the federal courts are contained in Article III of the Constitution.

1. Federal Question Cases

Section 2 of Article III in the Constitution states: "The judicial Power shall extend to all Cases in Law and Equity, arising under this Constitution, the Laws of the United States, and Treaties made, or which shall be made under their Authority . . ."

As used above, the term *judicial power* means the jurisdiction of the federal courts, that is, the constitutional authority giving those courts the power to hear cases arising under the Constitution, federal statutes, and treaties. The major problem with interpreting this clause is determining the meaning of "arising under." Does it mean that a case filed in the federal district court must (if only remotely) involve a federal law or the United States Constitution? Does it mean that there must be a specific federal statute that permits an individual to file the case in federal court?

The portion of Article III, section 2, of the Constitution quoted earlier is the basis for jurisdiction in the federal courts over what are commonly referred to as *federal question* cases. Cases wherein the plaintiff's claims are based on or "arise under" either the federal Constitution, federal statutes, or United States treaties naturally raise some type of federal issue, or question. Thus, under the Constitution, the federal courts are allowed to hear such cases.

However, although the meaning of the important phrase "arise under" has been the subject of voluminous writing by courts and scholars, no clear test has been developed yet to determine which cases "arise under" the Constitution, laws, or treaties of the United States. The first Supreme Court cases on the subject interpreted the phrase to mean that federal jurisdiction is present wherever some aspect of federal law is an "ingredient" of the cause of action. This test soon proved to be much too broad a guideline, one which could have potentially opened the door to excessive litigation in the federal courts.[2]

GULLY
v.
FIRST NATIONAL BANK IN MERIDIAN

299 U.S. 109 (1936)

Supreme Court of the United States

Mr. Justice CARDOZO delivered the opinion of the Court.

Whether a federal court has jurisdiction of this suit as one arising under the Constitution and laws of the United States is the single question here.

Petitioner, plaintiff in the court below, sued the respondent in a state court in Mississippi to recover a money judgment. The following facts appear on the face of the complaint: In June, 1931, the assets of the First National Bank *of* Meridian, a national banking association, were conveyed to the respondent, the First National Bank *in* Meridian, under a contract whereby the debts and liabilities of the grantor, insolvent at the time and in the hands of a receiver, were assumed by the grantee, which covenanted to pay them. Among the debts and liabilities so assumed were moneys owing to the petitioner, the state Collector of Taxes, or now claimed to be owing to him, for state, county, city, and school district taxes. In form the assessment was imposed upon the shares or capital stock of the bank, its surplus and undivided profits, exclusive of the value of the real estate. In law, so the pleader states, all taxes thus assessed were debts owing by the shareholders, which the bank was under a duty to pay as their agent out of moneys belonging to them, then in its possession. The new bank, in violation of its covenant, failed to pay the taxes of the old bank, which it had thus assumed and made its own. Judgment is demanded for the moneys due under the contract.

A petition was filed by the respondent for the removal of the cause to the federal court upon the ground that the suit was one arising "under the Constitution or laws of the United States." The state court made an order accordingly, and the federal District Court denied a motion to remand. Later, after a trial upon the merits, the complaint was dismissed. The Cir-

---

2 Osborn v. Bank of the United States, 9 Wheat. 738, 824, 6 L. Ed. 204, 224 (1824); Railroad Removal Cases, 115 U.S. 1 (1885).

cuit Court of Appeals for the Fifth Circuit affirmed the judgment of dismissal, overruling the objection that the cause was one triable in the courts of Mississippi. The decision was put upon the ground that the power to lay a tax upon the shares of national banks has its origin and measure in the provisions of a federal statute (Rev. Stat. §5219, 12 U.S.C.A. §548), and that by necessary implication a plaintiff counts upon the statute in suing for the tax. Because of the importance of the ruling, this Court granted certiorari, "limited to the question of the jurisdiction of the District Court."

How and when a case arises "under the Constitution or laws of the United States" has been much considered in the books. Some tests are well established. To bring a case within the statute, a right or immunity created by the Constitution or laws of the United States must be an element, and an essential one, of the plaintiff's cause of action . . . and the controversy must be disclosed upon the face of the complaint, unaided by the answer or by the petition for removal. . . . Indeed, the complaint itself will not avail as a basis of jurisdiction insofar as it goes beyond a statement of the plaintiff's cause of action and anticipates or replies to a probable defense. . . .

"A suit to enforce a right which takes its origin in the laws of the United States is not necessarily, or for that reason alone, one arising under those laws, for a suit does not so arise unless it really and substantially involves a dispute or controversy respecting the validity, construction or effect of such a law, upon the determination of which the result depends." . . .

Viewing the case at hand against this background of established principle, we do not find in it the elements of federal jurisdiction.

1. The suit is built upon a contract which in point of obligation has its genesis in the law of Mississippi. A covenant for a valuable consideration to pay another's debts is valid and enforceable without reference to a federal law. For all that the complaint informs us, the failure to make payment was owing to lack of funds or to a belief that a stranger to the con-

tract had no standing as a suitor or to other objections non-federal in their nature. There is no necessary connection between the enforcement of such a contract according to its terms and the existence of a controversy arising under federal law.

2. The obligation of the contract being a creation of the state, the question remains whether the plaintiff counts upon a federal right in support of his claim that the contract has been broken. The performance owing by the defendant was payment of the valid debts, and taxes are not valid debts unless lawfully imposed. From this defendant argues that a federal controversy exists, the tax being laid upon a national bank or upon the shareholders therein, and for that reason being void unless permitted by the federal law.

Not every question of federal law emerging in a suit is proof that a federal law is the basis of the suit. The tax here in controversy, if valid as a tax at all, was imposed under the authority of a statute of Mississippi. The federal law did not attempt to impose it or to confer upon the tax collector authority to sue for it. True, the tax, though assessed through the action of the state, must be consistent with the federal statute consenting, subject to restrictions, that such assessments may be made. It must also be consistent with the Constitution of the United States. M'Culloch v. Maryland, 4 Wheat. 316, 4 L. Ed. 579. If there were no federal law permitting the taxation of shares in national banks, a suit to recover such a tax would not be one arising under the Constitution of the United States, though the bank would have the aid of the Constitution when it came to its defense. That there *is* a federal law permitting such taxation does not change the basis of the suit, which is still the statute of the state, though the federal law is evidence to prove the statute valid.

The argument for the respondent proceeds on the assumption that because permission at times is preliminary to action the two are to be classed as one. But the assumption will not stand. A suit does not arise under a law renouncing a defense, though the result of the renunciation is an extension of the area of legislative power which will cause the suitor to prevail. Let us suppose an amendment of the Constitution by which the states are left at liberty to levy taxes on the income derived from federal securities, or to lay imposts and duties at their pleasure upon imports and exports. If such an amendment were adopted, a suit to recover taxes or duties imposed by the state law would not be one arising under the Constitution of the United States, though in the absence of the amendment the duty or the tax would fail. Here the right to be established is one created by the state. If that is so, it is unimportant that federal consent is the source of state authority. To reach the underlying law we do not travel back so far. By unimpeachable authority, a suit brought upon a state statute does not arise under an act of Congress or the Constitution of the United States because prohibited thereby. Louisville & N. R. Co. v. Mottley, 211 U.S. 149. With no greater reason can it be said to arise thereunder because permitted thereby.

Another line of reasoning will lead us to the same conclusion. The Mississippi law provides, in harmony with the act of Congress, that a tax upon the shares of national banks shall be assessed upon the shareholders, though the bank may be liable to pay it as their agent, charging their account with moneys thus expended. Miss. Code, §3138. Petitioner will have to prove that the state law has been obeyed before the question will be reached whether anything in its provisions or in administrative conduct under it is inconsistent with the federal rule. If what was done by the taxing officers in levying the tax in suit did not amount in substance under the law of Mississippi to an assessment of the shareholders, but in substance as well as in form was an assessment of the bank alone, the conclusion will be inescapable that there was neither tax nor debt, apart from any barriers that Congress may

have built. On the other hand, a finding upon evidence that the Mississippi law has been obeyed may compose the controversy altogether, leaving no room for a contention that the federal law has been infringed. The most one can say is that a question of federal law is lurking in the background, just as farther in the background there lurks a question of constitutional law, the question of state power in our federal form of government. A dispute so doubtful and conjectural, so far removed from plain necessity, is unavailing to extinguish the jurisdiction of the states.

This Court has had occasion to point out how futile is the attempt to define a "cause of action" without reference to the context. To define broadly and in the abstract "a case arising under the Constitution or laws of the United States" has hazards of a kindred order. What is needed is something of that common-sense accommodation of judgment to kaleidoscopic situations which characterizes the law in its treatment of problems of causation. One could carry the search for causes backward, almost without end. Instead, there has been a selective process which picks the substantial causes out of the web and lays the other ones aside. As in problems of causation, so here in the search for the underlying law. If we follow the ascent far enough, countless claims of right can be discovered to have their source or their operative limits in the provisions of a federal statute or in the Constitution itself with its circumambient restrictions upon legislative power. To set bounds to the pursuit, the courts have formulated the distinction between controversies that are basic and those that are collateral, between disputes that are necessary and those that are merely possible. We shall be lost in a maze if we put that compass by.

The judgment should be reversed and the cause remitted to the District Court with instructions to remand it to the court in Mississippi from which it was removed.

Reversed.

As the *Gully* case illustrates, later tests described in Supreme Court opinions have stated that a case arises under the Constitution, laws, or treaties of the United States if it substantially involves a dispute respecting the validity, construction, or effect of a federal law.[3] One commentator suggests that the test for federal question jurisdiction should be "a substantial claim founded 'directly' upon federal law."[4] A conclusive test has not yet been formulated, but an illustration may further clarify the concept of a federal question arising under the Constitution, laws, or treaties of the United States. For example, a private individual may file a case against the state in which he or she lives, complaining that the state unfairly confiscated some property. The case may arise under the Constitution on the basis that the state violated the Fourteenth Amendment of the United States Constitution, because that amendment requires that no state can deprive a person of his property without "due process of law." Depending on the manner by which the property is taken, the use for which it is intended, and the amount of money, if any, paid by the state for such property, taking an individual's property may indeed constitute taking it without due process of law. Therefore, such individual may file the case in a federal district court, and that court may properly determine the question presented to it, provided the individual expressly claims that the state has violated the Fourteenth Amendment.

Federal question cases have been said to justify a grant of exclusive jurisdiction in the federal courts because they touch on "the safety, peace, and sovereignty of the nation." They include, of course, not just the cases involving questions of due process, but all cases involving the citizens' First Amendment rights of freedom of speech, assembly, and religion, and the numerous issues involving the constitutional rights of criminal defendants.

2. Diversity of Citizenship Cases

Section 2 of Article III also states that "the judicial Power shall extend to all Cases, in Law and Equity . . . between Citizens of different states." This clause, together with authority given to the federal courts in the Judiciary Act of 1789, gives them jurisdiction in cases between citizens of different states. Such cases are commonly referred to as *diversity* or *diversity of citizenship* cases. Surprisingly, there is still no consensus on the historical justification or the current need for diversity jurisdiction, even though it was accepted without question at the Constitutional Convention. Neither the debates of the Convention nor the records of the First Congress shed any substantial light on the question of why the drafters of the Constitution granted the new government this type of jurisdiction.[5] However, the

[3] See Shulthis v. McDougal, 225 U.S. 561, 569 (1912); Gold-Washing and Water Company v. Keyes, 96 U.S. 199, 203 (1877).
[4] P. Mishkin. "The Federal 'Question' in the District Courts," 53 *Columbia Law Review* 157, 165, 168 (1953), as quoted in C. Wright, *Law of Federal Courts,* 2d ed. (St. Paul: West Publishing Co., 1970), p. 58. See also Wright, pp. 54–62.
[5] Wright, p. 73.

traditional explanation is that the designers of the Constitution recognized that local prejudice often puts out-of-state residents at a disadvantage when they commence actions in or are being sued in a state court in the other party's state. There is support for this explanation from other sources. For example, in arguing the need for a stronger federal judicial system, because "the laws of the whole are in danger of being contravened by the laws of the parts," Hamilton stated in Federalist Paper No. 22: [6]

> In this case, if the [State] Tribunals are invested with a right of ultimate jurisdiction, besides the contradictions to be expected from difference of opinion there will be much to fear from the bias of local views and prejudices and from the interference of local regulations.

Similarly, in discussing the scope of the judicial power as set forth in the proposed Constitution, Hamilton stated in Federalist Paper No. 80: [7]

> [T]he judiciary authority of the Union ought to extend . . . to all those [cases] in which the State tribunals cannot be supposed to be impartial and unbiased.

In a later portion of that same Paper Hamilton stated, with respect to diversity jurisdiction: [8]

> The reasonableness of the agency of the national court in cases in which the State Tribunals cannot be supposed to be impartial speaks for itself. No man ought certainly to be a judge in his own cause, or in any cause in respect to which he has the least interest or bias. This principle has not inconsiderable weight in designating the federal courts as the proper tribunals for the determination of controversies between different States and their citizens.

The Supreme Court believed this to be the rationale for diversity jurisdiction, as stated in the early case of *Martin* v. *Hunter's Lessee:* [9]

> The constitution has presumed . . . that state attachments, state prejudices, state jealousies, and state interest, might sometimes obstruct, or control . . . the regular administration of justice. Hence, in controversies . . . between citizens of different states . . . it enables the parties, under the authority of Congress, to have the controversies heard, tried, and determined before the national tribunals. No other reason than that which has been stated can be assigned, why some, at least, of those cases should not have been left to the cognizance of the state courts.

There were other, although significantly weaker, arguments supporting the establishment of diversity jurisdiction as a basis for federal jurisdiction. For example, it has been argued that there was a need to prevent federal judges from becoming "narrow technicians" in the field of federal questions, thus making it more difficult

---

[6] *The Federalist Papers* (New York: The New American Library, Inc. 1961), Paper No. 22, pp. 150–51.
[7] Ibid., No. 80, p. 475.
[8] Ibid., No. 80, p. 478.
[9] Martin v. Hunter's Lessee, 1 Wheat. 304, 347, 4 L. Ed. 97, 108 (1816).

to attract qualified personnel to "such a mundane position" as a federal judgeship. It has also been argued that there was a need for interplay between the federal and state courts, partly to educate lawyers in the superior procedures used in the federal court system, thus improving such procedures in the state courts. Finally, it has been argued, both at the time of the enactment of the Constitution and at the present time, that federal judges are better qualified to hear cases which deal with highly complex legal matters.[10]

During the years 1789–1801, 54 of the 140 cases (or 38.6 percent) filed in the federal courts were diversity cases.[11] More recent figures indicate that in the year 1962 there were 18,359 diversity cases out of a total number of civil cases in federal court of 61,836. Thus diversity cases comprised 29.7 percent of the total civil cases in that year. In 1972 the percentage of diversity cases decreased to 25.1 percent; there were 24,109 diversity cases out of a total number of civil cases of 96,173.[12] Over the last twenty years the percentage of federal cases based on diversity jurisdiction has gradually declined. This trend may be partly attributable to the passage of congressional legislation narrowing the definition of diversity cases, as explained below.

a. The Meaning and Determination of Citizenship

Diversity jurisdiction depends on the citizenship of the parties. Although the Fourteenth Amendment of the Constitution states that citizens of the United States are citizens of the state where they reside, physical presence or mere residence in a state has proven not to be sufficient for purposes of diversity jurisdiction. Citizenship is determined by *domicile,* which is that state in which a person has a fixed and permanent home and to which he or she intends to return. Thus in order for a person to change domicile or citizenship, that person must actually change his or her physical location and must intend to remain in the new state; neither alone is sufficient. However, the person need not intend to remain there permanently; the lack of an intent to go elsewhere is sufficient. The subjective intent element is generally determined by such factors as the exercise of political rights such as voter registration, payment of taxes, place of business, and statements made by the person.[13]

Citizenship for diversity purposes is determined as of the time of commencement of the action. If diversity exists between the parties at that date, it is not lost

10 H. Friendly, *Federal Jurisdiction: A General View* (New York: Columbia University Press, 1973) pp. 144–45, in which Judge Friendly criticizes the inclusion of diversity jurisdiction in the Constitution.
11 J. Goebel, *History of the Supreme Court of the United States, Antecedents and Beginnings to 1801* (New York: MacMillan Co., 1971), p. 807.
12 Friendly, p. 140.
13 See Wright, pp. 86–87.

as a result of one of the parties subsequently taking up domicile in the same juris-diction as the other party. Similarly, if no diversity existed when the action was commenced, it cannot be created by a change of domicile of one of the parties, al-though a new suit could be commenced.[14]

What if one of the parties is a corporation? Is a corporation considered a citizen within the meaning of the diversity clause of the Constitution? When first faced with this question, Chief Justice Marshall stated in 1809 that a corporation is "certainly not a citizen" because it is an "invisible, intangible, and artificial being." [15] In Jus-tice Marshall's view, the citizenship of the members of the corporation should deter-mine the corporation's citizenship for federal diversity purposes. However, the subsequent increase in the number of corporations led to the Supreme Court's state-ment in 1844 that a corporation given a charter for its operation in that state is "entitled, for the purpose of suing and being sued, to be deemed a citizen of that state." [16] Thus it is now well established that where the term *person* or *citizen* is used in any state or federal law or constitution, it is meant to include duly formed corporations as well as individual persons. Therefore for the purpose of diversity jurisdiction corporations may act as plaintiff or defendant just as individuals do.

As the above quotation indicates, a corporation used to be considered a citizen only of the state where it was formed, that is, where it was incorporated. However, as the federal courts became more and more crowded over the years with diversity of citizenship cases, Congress sought to reduce the number of cases eligible for fed-eral court consideration by reducing the number of cases that can qualify for diver-sity jurisdiction. In 1958 Congress enacted a statue which states that a corporation is now deemed to be a citizen of the state where it was incorporated *and* of the state where that corporation has its principal place of business.[17] Therefore, if a corpora-tion is either incorporated *or* has its principal place of business in the same state as any opposing or adverse party, there is not complete diversity and the action must be filed in a state court rather than in a federal district court. Prior to the 1958 law, the corporation could sue or be sued in federal court even if its principal place of business was in the same state as the place of citizenship of any of the adverse par-ties. The effect of this legislation has been to reduce the number of cases that other-wise would have qualified for diversity jurisdiction.

Despite the redefinition of corporate citizenship, the federal case load for diver-sity and federal question cases continues to increase. The reasons are not completely identifiable or subject to quantification; however, there are certain factors that ap-pear to be primarily responsible for this increase: the significant increase in the activism of the citizenry and the federal judiciary in the field of personal freedoms as contained in the Bill of Rights and the equal protection clause; another is the trend toward liberalizing the requirements enabling persons to obtain federal juris-

---

[14] See Wright, p. 93.
[15] Bank of the United States v. Deveaux, 5 Cranch 61, 86, 3 L. Ed. 38 (1809).
[16] Louisville, C. & C.R. Co. v. Letson, 2 How. 497, 555, 11 L. Ed. 353 (1844).
[17] 28 U.S.C. §1332(c), as amended by Act of July 25, 1958, section 2, 72 Statutes at Large 415.

diction; and the tremendous increase in congressional legislation in the fields of welfare, civil rights, social problems and regulation of industry.[18]

b. Exceptions to Diversity Jurisdiction

Congress has not only attempted to limit the number of cases qualifying for diversity jurisdiction but has also passed several statutory exceptions limiting the federal courts' jurisdiction over cases that initially appear to qualify. For instance, Congress has provided that there is no federal jurisdiction if a party, by assigning his or her claim, is made a party for the sole purpose of invoking federal jurisdiction. Also a federal court cannot entertain certain actions involving property, where the property is already in the custody of a state court of competent jurisdiction. These cases remain in the exclusive jurisdiction of the state courts. Related doctrines permit, and in some circumstances require, a federal court to decline jurisdiction or to postpone its exercise, even though the requirements of the diversity statute are satisfied. In addition, there are two areas where the federal courts will not act, even though diversity is present, namely domestic relations cases and probate matters. These two exceptions are regarded as areas of the law in which the states have an especially strong interest and a well-developed competence for dealing with them.[19]

3. Other Bases of Federal Jurisdiction

Article III, section 2, of the Constitution provides several other bases for federal jurisdiction, in addition to federal question and diversity cases. However, except for "controversies to which the United States shall be a party" the other types of cases are obscure and relatively insignificant. The most frequent litigant in the federal court is the United States itself. It is a party in approximately one-third of all civil cases filed in the federal district courts. In 1968, 71,449 civil cases were begun in the federal district courts; the United States was plaintiff in 10,221 of these cases and defendant in 9,445 cases.[20]

Since the Constitution clearly extends the federal judicial power to such controversies, there are no jurisdictional problems when the United States is a plaintiff. However, the issue of sovereign immunity becomes relevant to cases in which the United States is the defendant. It is now well established that the United States cannot be sued without consent. As a practical matter, however, this defense is rarely raised by the United States. Over the years, Congress has legislatively consented to numerous types of suits and has consistently broadened this consent. In addition,

---

[18] Friendly, pp. 15, 17–22.
[19] Wright, pp. 83–86.
[20] *Annual Report of the Director of the Administrative Office of the United States Courts* (Washington, D.C.: U.S. Government Printing Office, 1968), p. 194. In addition, there were 32,571 criminal prosecutions instituted by the federal government. *Annual Report,* p. 240.

the Supreme Court has not favored the defense of sovereign immunity and tends to liberally construe any waivers of such immunity.

Although there is no specific statutory jurisdiction over actions brought against *employees* of the federal government, when property rights of the government are challenged, the Supreme Court has firmly established the principle that such suits are actually against the United States and thus may be barred by sovereign immunity. On the other hand, a statute has been enacted which assures jurisdiction in certain specified situations in which the plaintiff seeks to compel an officer or employee in the United States to perform a duty owed to the plaintiff.[21]

4. Jurisdictional Amount

In order to qualify for federal jurisdiction, one must have not only either a federal question or diversity of citizenship case but also a case or controversy in which damages of at least $10,000 are claimed. The increase in the number of federal cases described earlier in this chapter might have been even greater today if Congress had not in 1958 raised the jurisdictional amount to $10,000.

Relative to other jurisdictional issues, cases are not often dismissed because of failure to meet the jurisdictional amount. However, as the case of *Giancana* v. *Johnson* illustrates, many federal judges are not inclined to ignore this requirement or to presume its existence.

GIANCANA v. JOHNSON

335 F.2d 366 (1964)

United States Court of Appeals, Seventh Circuit

KILEY, Circuit Judge.

The question is whether the district court had jurisdiction to entertain this "action to procure and protect the civil rights of plaintiff," growing out of alleged surveillance of plaintiff, his home and his recreation, by FBI agents under defendant's supervision and direction. We think the record shows the court did not have jurisdiction.

The Complaint, as amended, was based upon claim of a "federal question" arising under the Fourth and Fifth Amendments to the United States Constitution, and a civil rights violation. The district court denied defendant's motion to dismiss which challenged the complaint on jurisdictional grounds.

The district court, on the "sworn amended complaint, affidavits and evidence of the plaintiff," found that plaintiff's constitutional rights to privacy, personal liberty and freedom were violated by the surveillance; and that unless defendant was restrained plaintiff would suffer irreparable injury. The court granted a preliminary injunction. We stayed the effect of

---

[21] U.S.C. section 1361, 1391(e); see Wright, pp. 68–72. Governmental immunity, as distinguished from sovereign immunity, applies only to the taxing relationship between the federal and state governments and provides a limitation on the power of the federal and state governments to tax each other or each other's instrumentalities.

the injunction, pending appeal. Giancana v. Hoover, 322 F.2d 789 (7th Cir. 1963).

District courts are courts of limited jurisdiction, possessing only the jurisdiction that Congress has conferred upon them by statute. Klein v. Lee, 254 F.2d 188, 190 (7th Cir. 1958). And the jurisdiction conferred upon federal courts to entertain suits arising under the Constitution or laws of the United States has been "narrowly limited." Hague v. Committee for Industrial Organization, 307 U.S. 496, 507 (1939). Furthermore, this court has the duty to satisfy itself of the jurisdiction of the district court. Jackson v. Kuhn, 254 F.2d 555, 560 (8th Cir. 1958).

The vital question depends on whether the record shows that "the matter in controversy exceeds the sum or value of $10,000 . . ." so as to give the district court jurisdiction under 28 U.S.C. §1331.

Courts may not treat as a mere technicality the jurisdictional amount essential to the "federal question" jurisdiction, even in this case where there is an allegedly unwarranted invasion of plaintiff's privacy. The showing of that essential is not a mere matter of form, but is a necessary element. Congress in §1331 expressed the "federal question" jurisdiction in plain words. The district courts and suitors are bound by the words expressed. Congress . . . limited the jurisdiction by including the element of the sum or value of the matter in controversy, and the Congressional will is that unless that sum or value is shown there is no "federal question" presented and no jurisdiction.

Neither may a party invoke the district court's jurisdiction by treating that element as though not essential; nor choose not to amend his complaint or otherwise show, as plaintiff did here, that the jurisdictional sum or value is in controversy, thus opposing his will to the Congressional will.

. . . Here the complaint makes no express allegation of the essential jurisdictional sum or value. Plaintiff argues, however, that the jurisdictional sum or value should be inferred from the allegations, supported by unimpeached affidavits. But there are no facts from which that necessary element can be inferred. If, as plaintiff contends, the sum or value cannot be alleged because of the priceless rights involved, how can this court infer that essential element? And there is no finding of the essential sum or value and no evidence on which to base a finding.

Congress had a reason for setting the minimum jurisdictional sum or value in limiting the jurisdiction of the district court.[a] (It surely knew of the priceless nature of liberty and privacy when it required a showing of that element.) And placing the burden of estimating the value of one's claim upon him who sues is not unusual. If, for instance, plaintiff had chosen to sue for damages under §1331 for alleged violation of his Fourth and Fifth Amendment right of privacy—the basic claim here—he would have had to estimate the value of his claim. "Plaintiff is master of his claim," and it is no answer to failure to bring his claim within the jurisdictional prerequisite that the value is inestimable.

Finally plaintiff contends that the subject matter "in controversy"—the use of his home, his personal liberty and freedom, the tortious conduct of defendant and invasion of plaintiff's private rights—is admitted by defendant's motion to dismiss, and that the substantive issue of the amount of damage awaits ultimate resolution in the trial court upon hearing of the cause on the merits. We disagree. The validity of the court's ruling must be determined as of the time it was made.

To support his argument about deferring

---

a The purpose for setting the jurisdictional amount at $10,000 in 1958 was explained in the Senate Report accompanying the bill: "The recommendations of the Judicial Conference regarding the amount in controversy, which this committee approves, is based on the premise that the amount should be fixed at a sum of money that will make jurisidiction available in all substantial controversies where other elements of Federal jurisdiction are present. The jurisdictional amount should not be so high as to convert the Federal courts into courts of big business nor so low as to fritter away their time in the trial of petty controversies." S. Rep. No. 1830, 85th Cong., 2d Sess. (1958), 1958 U. S. Code Cong. & Ad. News, pp. 3099, 3101.

resolution of the jurisdictional question plaintiff relies upon McNutt v. General Motors Acceptance Corp., 298 U.S. 178 (1936). That case does not require, in the circumstances before us, that determination of the jurisdictional issue be deferred until plaintiff has an opportunity to furnish proof of his charges. We read McNutt, involving Indiana law regulating purchase of installment sales contracts, so far as pertinent here, to decide that if the requisite jurisdictional facts are alleged, and challenged, the plaintiff must support them by competent proof, and that in such a case an inquiry might be necessary to determine whether the facts support the allegations of jurisdiction; but that if the plaintiff fails to allege the facts

prerequisite to show jurisdiction he has no standing. 298 U.S. at 189, 56 S. Ct. 780.

The district court erred in entertaining the suit before us because, having only the jurisdiction conferred by Congress, its jurisdiction was limited, so far as it is based upon §1331, to controversies involving a sum or value in excess of $10,000, and plaintiff failed to allege, or otherwise show, his damage accordingly, or to allege, or otherwise show facts from which that essential jurisdictional element may be inferred. . . .

Judgment vacated and the cause remanded for proceeding not inconsistent with this opinion.

C. United States Supreme Court Jurisdiction

The Supreme Court's jurisdiction is divided into two parts—original and appellate jurisdiction. In cases involving foreign diplomats or in those cases described in Article III, section 2, of the Constitution in which a state is a party, the Supreme Court has *original jurisdiction.* This means that the justices hear the dispute as a *court of first instance,* that is, as a trial court, finding the facts as well as determining the legal issues involved in the matter. However, only a very small number of cases go directly to the Supreme Court as the court of original jurisdiction, and almost none of these have involved foreign diplomats. Between 1952 and 1974 only 182 original cases were filed, and 5 or fewer original cases were filed in seven of those years.[22] Despite the small number of such cases, those in which a state is a party are often legally important and politically volatile. Suits between states, involving land boundaries, water rights, and taxing authority, have been decided, with hundreds of millions of dollars resting on the Court's decisions. For example, in 1963 the Court decided a controversy between Arizona and California concerning water rights to the Colorado River.[23] Another important dispute in recent years was the fight between the federal and state governments for title to rich oil deposits under the tideland waters of several coastal states.[24]

In all other cases the Supreme Court has *appellate jurisdiction,* reviewing decisions which have already been made by trial courts and by lower, or inferior, appel-

---

[22] United States Department of Justice, *Annual Report of the Attorney General* (Washington, D.C.: U.S. Government Printing Office, 1963, 1973, 1975), pp. 52 (1963); 29 (1973); 42 (1975).

[23] Arizona v. California, 373 U.S. 546 (1963).

[24] United States v. Alaska, 422 U.S. 184 (1975); United States v. Texas, 339 U.S. 707 (1950); United States v. Louisiana, 339 U.S. 699 (1950); United States v. California, 332 U.S. 19 (1947).

late tribunals. There are two main groups of cases which come under the Supreme Court's appellate jurisdiction: those from the federal district courts and courts of appeal and those from the state supreme courts. Because the Supreme Court is the final tribunal in the federal judicial system, its review of lower federal court cases is a logical function. Review of state supreme court decisions, on the other hand, has been a controversial question since the Court's earliest days of operation under the Constitution. States' rights advocates contended, in a series of famous cases during the first decades after the adoption of the Constitution, that in a federal union with sovereign states and a limited national government, each state must have the final word on matters that lie within its territorial borders. The Supreme Court rejected this position and held that where a substantial federal question is determined by a state court, the need for protection of the citizen's federal constitutional rights and for uniformity of interpretation of the Constitution throughout the Union requires the United States Supreme Court to pass upon these questions, even though the question may have already been determined by the highest court in the state. The Court maintained that the nature of the case, not the court where it arises, governs federal review. The language of Article VI of the Constitution, the "supremacy clause," supports this view, because it states that the Constitution, federal statutes, and treaties "shall be the supreme law of the land," and "Judges in every State shall be bound thereby, any thing in the Constitution or laws of any State to the contrary notwithstanding."

In Federalist Paper No. 82 Hamilton argued in favor of a broad right of appellate jurisdiction in the United States Supreme Court over state courts, stating that such appellate jurisdiction should not be limited to appeals from the inferior federal courts but should also include appellate jurisdiction over appeals from state courts:[25]

> What relation would subsist between the national and State courts in these in-stances of concurrent jurisdiction? I answer that an appeal would certainly lie from the latter to the Supreme Court of the United States. The Constitution in direct terms gives an appellate jurisdiction to the Supreme Court in all the enumerated cases of federal cognizance in which it is not to have an original one, without a single expression to confine its operation to the inferior federal courts. The objects of appeal, not the tribunals from which it is to be made, are alone contemplated. From this circumstance, and from the reason of the thing, it ought to be construed to extend to the State tribunals. Either this must be the case or the local courts must be excluded from a concurrent jurisdiction in matters of national concern, else the judiciary authority of the Union may be eluded at the pleasure of every plaintiff or prosecutor. . . . [T]he national and State system are to be regarded as ONE WHOLE. The courts of the latter will of course be natural auxiliaries to the execution of the laws of the Union, and an appeal from them will as naturally lie to that tribunal which is destined to unite and assimilate the principle of national justice and the rules of national decision. . . . To confine, therefore, the general expression giving appellate jurisdiction to the Supreme Court to appeals from the subordinate federal courts, instead of allowing their extension to the State courts,

---

[25] *Federalist Papers*, No. 82, pp. 493–94.

would be to abridge the latitude of the terms, in subversion of the intent, contrary to every sound rule of interpretation.

Hamilton had made a similar argument in an earlier Paper in which he stated that one court, superior to all others in the nation, was necessary to "avoid the confusion which would unavoidably result from the contradictory decisions of a number of independent judicatories." [26] In the case of *Martin* v. *Hunter's Lessee* the Supreme Court clearly reflected Hamilton's philosophy and firmly established its jurdisdiction to review state court decisions that deal with federal questions.

MARTIN v. HUNTER'S LESSEE

1 Wheat. 304, 4 L. Ed. 97 (1816)

Supreme Court of the United States

The original suit was an action of ejectment, brought by the defendant in error, in one of the district courts of Virginia, holden at Winchester, for the recovery of a parcel of land, situate within that tract, called the northern neck of Virginia, and part and parcel thereof. A declaration in ejectment was served (April, 1791), on the tenants in possession; whereupon Denny Fairfax (late Denny Martin), a British subject, holding the land in question, under the devise of the late Thomas Lord Fairfax, was admitted to defend the suit. . . . The facts being settled in the form of a case agreed to be taken and considered as a special verdict, the court, on consideration thereof, gave judgment (24th of April, 1794), in favor of the defendant in ejectment. From that judgment the plaintiff in ejectment (now defendant in error) appealed to the Court of Appeals, being the highest court of law of Virginia. At April term, 1810, the Court of Appeals reversed the judgment of the District Court, and gave judgment for the then appellant, now defendant in error, and thereupon the case was removed into this court. . . .

STORY, J., delivered the opinion of the court:

This is a writ of error from the Court of Appeals of Virginia, founded upon the refusal of

that court to obey the mandate of this court, requiring the judgment rendered in this very cause, at February term, 1813, to be carried into due execution. The following is the judgment of the Court of Appeals rendered on the mandate: "The court is unanimously of opinion that the appellate power of the Supreme Court of the United States does not extend to this court, under a sound construction of the constitution of the United States; that so much of the 25th section of the act of Congress to establish the judicial courts of the United States, as extends the appellate jurisdiction of the Supreme Court to this court, is not in pursuance of the constitution of the United States; that the writ of error, in this cause, was improvidently allowed under the authority of that act; that the proceedings thereon in the Supreme Court were, coram non judice, in relation to this court, and that obedience to its mandate be declined by the court."

The questions involved in this judgment are of great importance and delicacy. Perhaps it is not too much to affirm that, upon their right decision, rest some of the most solid principles which have hitherto been supposed to sustain and protect the constitution itself. The great respectability, too, of the court whose decisions we are called upon to review, and the entire

---

[26] Ibid., No. 22, p. 150.

deference which we entertain for the learning and ability of that court, add much to the difficulty of the task which has so unwelcomely fallen upon us. . . .

Before proceeding to the principal questions, it may not be unfit to dispose of some preliminary considerations which have grown out of the arguments at the bar.

The constitution of the United States was ordained and established, not by the states in their sovereign capacities, but emphatically, as the preamble of the constitution declares, by "the people of the United States." There can be no doubt that it was competent to the people to invest the general government with all the powers which they might deem proper and necessary; to extend or restrain these powers according to their own good pleasure, and to give them a paramount and supreme authority. As little doubt can there be that the people had a right to prohibit to the states the exercise of any powers which were, in their judgment, incompatible with the objects of the general compact; to make the powers of the state governments, in given cases, subordinate to those of the nation, or to reserve to themselves those sovereign authorities which they might not choose to delegate to either. The constitution was not, therefore, necessarily carved out of existing state sovereignties, nor a surrender of powers already existing in state institutions, for the powers of the states depend upon their own constitutions; and the people of every state had the right to modify and restrain them, according to their own views of policy or principle. On the other hand, it is perfectly clear that the sovereign powers vested in the state governments, by their respective constitutions, remained unaltered and unimpaired, except so far as they were granted to the government of the United States.

These deductions do not rest upon general reasoning, plain and obvious as they seem to be. They have been positively recognized by one of the articles in amendment of the constitution, which declares, that "the powers not delegated to the United States by the constitution, nor prohibited by it to the states, are re-

served to the states respectively, or to the people."

The government, then, of the United States, can claim no powers which are not granted to it by the constitution, and the powers actually granted, must be such as are expressly given, or given by necessary implication. On the other hand, this instrument, like every other grant, is to have a reasonable construction, according to the import of its terms; and where a power is expressly given in general terms, it is not to be restrained to particular cases, unless that construction grow out of the context expressly, or by necessary implication. The words are to be taken in their natural and obvious sense, and not in a sense unreasonably restricted or enlarged.

The constitution unavoidably deals in general language. It did not suit the purposes of the people, in framing this great charter of our liberties, to provide for minute specifications of its powers, or to declare the means by which those powers should be carried into execution. It was foreseen that this would be a perilous and difficult, if not an impracticable, task. The instrument was not intended to provide merely for the exigencies of a few years, but was to endure through a long lapse of ages, the events of which were locked up in the inscrutable purposes of Providence. It could not be foreseen what new changes and modifications of power might be indispensable to effectuate the general objects of the charter; and restrictions and specifications which, at the present, might seem salutary, might, in the end, prove the overthrow of the system itself. Hence its powers are expressed in general terms, leaving to the legislature, from time to time, to adopt its own means to effectuate legitimate objects, and to mold and model the exercise of its powers, as its own wisdom and the public interests should require.

With these principles in view—principles in respect to which no difference of opinion ought to be indulged—let us now proceed to the interpretation of the constitution, so far as regards the great points in controversy.

The third article of the constitution is that

which must principally attract our attention. The first section declares, "the judicial power of the United States shall be vested in one Supreme Court, and in such other inferior courts as the Congress may, from time to time, ordain and establish." . . .

Such is the language of the article creating and defining the judicial power of the United States. It is the voice of the whole American people solemnly declared, in establishing one great department of that government which was, in many respects, national, and in all, supreme. It is a part of the very same instrument which was to act not merely upon individuals, but upon states; and to deprive them altogether of the exercise of some powers of sovereignty, and to restrain and regulate them in the exercise of others.

Let this article be carefully weighed and considered. The language of the article throughout is manifestly designed to be mandatory upon the legislature. Its obligatory force is so imperative that Congress could not, without a violation of its duty, have refused to carry it into operation. The judicial power of the United States shall be vested (not may be vested) in one supreme court, and in such inferior courts as Congress may, from time to time, ordain and establish. Could Congress have lawfully refused to create a supreme court, or to vest it in the constitutional jurisdiction? "The judges, both of the supreme and inferior courts, shall hold their offices during good behavior, and shall, at stated times, receive, for their services, a compensation which shall not be diminished during their continuance in office." Could Congress create or limit any other tenure of the judicial office? Could they refuse to pay, at stated times, the stipulated salary, or diminish it during the continuance in office? But one answer can be given to these questions: it must be in the negative. The object of the constitution was to establish three great departments of government: the legislative, the executive and the judicial departments. The first was to pass laws, the second to approve and execute them, and the third to expound and enforce them. Without the latter it would be impossible to carry into effect some of the express provisions of the constitution. How otherwise could crimes against the United States be tried and punished? How could causes between two states be heard and determined? The judicial power must, therefore, be vested in some court, by Congress; and to suppose that it was not an obligation binding on them, but might, at their pleasure, be omitted or declined, is to suppose that, under the sanction of the constitution, they might defeat the constitution itself; a construction which would lead to such a result cannot be sound. . . .

If, then, it is the duty of Congress to vest the judicial power of the United States, it is a duty to vest the whole judicial power. The language, if imperative as to one part, is imperative as to all. If it were otherwise, this anomaly would exist, that Congress might successively refuse to vest the jurisdiction in any one class of cases enumerated in the constitution, and thereby defeat the jurisdiction as to all; for the constitution has not singled out any class on which Congress are bound to act in preference to others.

The next consideration is as to the courts in which the judicial power shall be vested. It is manifest that a supreme court must be established; but whether it be equally obligatory to establish inferior courts is a question of some difficulty. If Congress may lawfully omit to establish inferior courts, it might follow that in some of the enumerated cases the judicial power could nowhere exist. The Supreme Court can have original jurisdiction in two classes of cases only, viz., in cases affecting ambassadors, other public ministers and consuls, and in cases in which a state is a party. Congress cannot vest any portion of the judicial power of the United States, except in courts ordained and established by itself; and if, in any of the cases enumerated in the constitution, the state courts did not then possess jurisdiction, the appellate jurisdiction of the Supreme Court (admitting that it could act on state courts) could not reach those cases, and, consequently, the injunction of the constitution, that the judicial power "shall be vested," would be disobeyed.

It would seem, therefore, to follow that Congress are bound to create some inferior courts, in which to vest all that jurisdiction which, under the constitution, is exclusively vested in the United States, and of which the Supreme Court cannot take original cognizance. They might establish one or more inferior courts; they might parcel out the jurisdiction among such courts, from time to time, at their own pleasure. But the whole judicial power of the United States should be, at all times, vested either in an original or appellate form, in some courts created under its authority.

This construction will be fortified by an attentive examination of the second section of the third article. The words are "the judicial power shall extend," etc. Much minute and elaborate criticism has been employed upon these words. It has been argued that they are equivalent to the words "may extend," and that "extend" means to widen to new cases not before within the scope of the power. For the reasons which have been already stated, we are of opinion that the words are used in an imperative sense. They import an absolute grant of judicial power. They cannot have a relative signification applicable to powers already granted; for the American people had not made any previous grant. The constitution was for a new government, organized with new substantive powers, and not a mere supplementary charter to a government already existing. The confederation was a compact between states; and its structure and powers were wholly unlike those of the national government. The constitution was an act of the people of the United States to supersede the confederation, and not to be ingrafted on it, as a stock through which it was to receive life and nourishment. . . .

It being, then, established that the language of this clause is imperative, the next question is as to the cases to which it shall apply. The answer is found in the constitution itself. The judicial power shall extend to all the cases enumerated in the constitution. As the mode is not limited, it may extend to all such cases, in any form in which judicial power may be exercised. It may, therefore, extend to them in the shape of original or appellate jurisdiction, or both; for there is nothing in the nature of the cases which binds to the exercise of the one in preference to the other. . . .

This leads us to the consideration of the great question as to the nature and extent of the appellate jurisdiction of the United States. We have already seen that appellate jurisdiction is given by the constitution to the Supreme Court in all cases, where it has not original jurisdiction; subject, however, to such exceptions and regulations as Congress may prescribe. It is, therefore, capable of embracing every case enumerated in the constitution, which is not exclusively to be decided by way of original jurisdiction. But the exercise of appellate jurisdiction is far from being limited by the terms of the constitution to the Supreme Court. There can be no doubt that Congress may create a succession of inferior tribunals, in each of which it may vest appellate as well as original jurisdiction. The judicial power is delegated by the constitution in the most general terms, and may, therefore, be exercised by Congress under every variety of form, of appellate or original jurisdiction. And as there is nothing in the constitution which restrains or limits this power, it must, therefore, in all other cases, subsist in the utmost latitude of which, in its own nature, it is susceptible.

As, then, by the terms of the constitution, the appellate jurisdiction is not limited as to the Supreme Court, and as to this court it may be exercised in all other cases than those of which it has original cognizance, what is there to restrain its exercise over state tribunals in the enumerated cases? The appellate power is not limited by the terms of the third article to any particular courts. The words are "the judicial power (which includes appellate power) shall extend to all cases," etc., and "in all other cases before mentioned the Supreme Court shall have appellate jurisdiction." It is the case, then, and not the court, that gives the jurisdiction. If the judicial power extends to the case, it will be in vain to search in the letter of the constitution for any qualification as to the tribunal where it depends. It is incumbent, then, upon those who assert such a qualification to show its existence by necessary implication. If the text be clear and distinct, no restriction upon its plain and obvious import ought to be admitted, unless the inference be irresistible.

If the constitution meant to limit the appellate jurisdiction to cases pending in the courts of the United States, it would necessarily follow that the jurisdiction of these courts would, in all the cases enumerated in the constitution, be exclusive of state tribunals. How otherwise could the jurisdiction extend to all cases arising under the constitution, laws and treaties of the United States, or to all cases of admiralty and maritime jurisdiction? If some of these cases might be entertained by state tribunals, and no appellate jurisdiction as to them should exist, then the appellate power would not extend to all, but to some, cases. If state tribunals might exercise concurrent jurisdiction over all or some of the other classes of cases in the constitution without control, then the appellate jurisdiction of the United States might, as to such cases, have no real existence, contrary to the manifest intent of the constitution. Under such circumstances, to give effect to the judicial power, it must be construed to be exclusive; and this not only when the casus fœderis should arise directly, but when it should arise, incidentally, in cases pending in state courts. This construction would abridge the jurisdiction of such courts far more than has been ever contemplated in any act of Congress.

On the other hand, if, as has been contended, a discretion be vested in Congress to establish, or not to establish, inferior courts at their own pleasure, and Congress should not establish such courts, the appellate jurisdiction of the Supreme Court would have nothing to act upon, unless it could act upon cases pending in the state courts. Under such circumstances it must be held that the appellate power would extend to state courts; for the constitution is peremptory that it shall extend to certain enumerated cases, which cases could exist in no other courts. Any other construction, upon this supposition, would involve this strange contradiction, that a discretionary power vested in Congress, and which they might rightfully omit to exercise, would defeat the absolute injunctions of the constitution in relation to the whole appellate power.

But it is plain that the framers of the constitution did contemplate that cases within the judicial cognizance of the United States not only might but would arise in the state courts, in the exercise of their ordinary jurisdiction. With this view the sixth article declares, that "this constitution, and the laws of the United States which shall be made in pursuance thereof, and all treaties made, or which shall be made, under the authority of the United States, shall be the supreme law of the land, and the judges in every state shall be bound thereby, anything in the constitution or laws of any state to the contrary notwithstanding." It is obvious that this obligation is imperative upon the state judges in their official, and not merely in their private, capacities. From the very nature of their judicial duties they would be called upon to pronounce the law applicable to the case in judgment. They were not to decide merely according to the laws or constitution of the state, but according to the constitution, laws and treaties of the United States— "the supreme law of the land."

A moment's consideration will show us the necessity and propriety of this provision in cases where the jurisdiction of the state courts is unquestionable. Suppose a contract for the payment of money is made between citizens of the same state, and performance thereof is sought in the courts of that state; no person can doubt that the jurisdiction completely and exclusively attaches, in the first instance, to such courts. Suppose at the trial the defendant sets up in his defense a tender under a state law, making paper money a good tender, or a state law, impairing the obligation of such contract, which law, if binding, would defeat the suit. The constitution of the United States has declared that no state shall make anything but gold or silver coin a tender in payment of debts, or pass a law impairing the obligation of contracts. If Congress shall not have passed a law providing for the removal of such a suit to the courts of the United States, must not the state court proceed to hear and determine it? Can a mere plea in defense be of itself a bar to further proceedings, so as to prohibit an inquiry into its truth or legal propriety, when no other tribunal exists to whom judicial cognizance of such cases is confided? Suppose an indictment for a crime in a state court, and the defendant should allege in his defense that the crime was created by an ex post facto act of the state, must not the state court, in the exercise of a jurisdiction which has already rightfully attached, have a right to pronounce on the validity and sufficiency of the defense? It would be extremely difficult, upon any legal principles, to give a negative answer to these inquiries. Innumerable instances of the same sort might be stated, in illustration of the position; and unless the state courts could sustain jurisdiction in such cases, this clause of the sixth article would be without meaning or effect, and public mischiefs, of a most enormous magnitude, would inevitably ensue.

It must, therefore, be conceded that the constitution not only contemplated, but meant to provide for cases within the scope of the judicial power of the United States, which might yet depend before state tribunals. It was foreseen that in the exercise of their ordinary jurisdiction, state courts would incidentally take cognizance of cases arising under the constitution, the laws and treaties of the United States. Yet to all these cases the judicial power, by the very terms of the constitution, is to extend. It cannot extend by original jurisdiction if that was already rightfully and exclusively attached in the state courts, which (as has been already shown) may occur; it must, therefore, extend by appellate jurisdiction, or not at all. It would seem to follow that the appellate power of the United States must, in such cases, extend to state tribunals; and if in such cases, there is no reason why it should not equally attach upon all others within the purview of the constitution. . . .

This is not all. A motive of another kind, perfectly compatible with the most sincere respect for state tribunals, might induce the grant of appellate power over their decisions. That motive is the importance, and even necessity, of uniformity of decisions throughout the whole United States, upon all subjects within the purview of the constitution. Judges of equal learning and integrity, in different states, might differently interpret a statute, or a treaty of the United States, or even the constitution itself. If there were no revising authority to control these jarring and discordant judgments, and harmonize them into uniformity, the laws, the treaties, and the constitution of the United States would be different in different states, and might, perhaps, never have precisely the same construction, obligation, or efficacy, in any two states. The public mischiefs that would attend such a state of things would be truly deplorable; and it cannot be believed that they could have escaped the enlightened convention which formed the constitution. What, indeed, might then have been only prophecy, has now become fact; and the appellate jurisdiction must continue to be the only adequate remedy for such evils. . . .

It will be recollected that the action was an ejectment for a parcel of land in the Northern Neck, formerly belonging to Lord Fairfax. The original plaintiff claimed the land under a patent granted to him by the state of Virginia, in 1789, under a title supposed to be vested in that state by escheat or forfeiture. The original defendant claimed the land as devisee under the will of Lord Fairfax. The parties agreed to a special statement of facts in the nature of a special verdict, upon which the District Court of Winchester, in 1793, gave a general judgment for the defendant, which judgment was afterwards reversed in 1810, by the Court of Appeals, and a general judgment was rendered for the plaintiff; and from this last judgment a writ of error was brought to the Supreme Court. The statement of facts contained a regular deduction of the title of Lord Fairfax until his death, in 1781, and also the title of his devisee. It also contained a regular deduction of the title of the plaintiff, under the state of Virginia, and further referred to the treaty of peace of 1783, and to the acts of Virginia respecting the lands of Lord Fairfax, and the supposed escheat or forfeiture thereof as component parts of the case. No facts disconnected with the titles thus set up by the parties were alleged on either side.

It is apparent, from this summary explanation, that the title thus set up by the plaintiff might be open to other objections; but the title of the defendant was perfect and complete, if it was protected by the treaty of 1783. If, therefore, this court had authority to examine into the whole record, and to decide upon the legal validity of the title of the defendant, as well as its application to the treaty of peace, it would be a case within the express purview of the 25th section of the [Judiciary] act; for there was nothing in the record upon which the court below could have decided but upon the title as connected with the treaty; and if the title was otherwise good, its sufficiency must have depended altogether upon its protection under the treaty. Under such circumstances it was strictly a suit where was drawn in question the construction of a treaty, and the decision was against the title specially set up or claimed by the defendant. It would fall, then, within the very terms of the act.

The objection urged at the bar is, that this court cannot inquire into the title, but simply into the correctness of the construction put upon the treaty by the Court of Appeals; and that their judgment is not re-examinable here, unless it appear on the face of the record that some construction was put upon the treaty. . . .

How, indeed, can it be possible to decide whether a title be within the protection of a treaty, until it is ascertained what that title is, and whether it have a legal validity? From the very necessity of the case, there must be a preliminary inquiry into the existence and structure of the title, before the court can construe the treaty in reference to that title. If the court below should decide that the title was bad, and, therefore, not protected by the treaty, must not this court have a power to decide the title to be good, and, therefore, protected by the treaty? Is not the treaty, in both instances, equally construed, and the title of the party, in reference to the treaty, equally ascertained and decided? Nor does the clause relied on in the objection impugn this construction. It requires, that the error upon which the appellate court is to decide shall appear on the face of the record, and immediately respect the questions before mentioned in the section. One of the questions is as to the construction of a treaty upon a title specially set up by a party, and every error that immediately respects that question must, of course, be within the cognizance of the court. The title set up in this case is apparent upon the face of the record, and immediately respects the decision of that question; any error, therefore, in respect to that title must be re-examinable, or the case could never be presented to the court. . . .

It is the opinion of the whole court that the judgment of the Court of Appeals of Virginia, rendered on the mandate in this cause, be reversed, and the judgment of the District Court, held at Winchester, be, and the same is hereby affirmed.

D. *Certiorari:* Discretion to Grant Judicial Review

The Supreme Court's appellate jurisdiction according to Article III was to be exercised "with such Exceptions, and under such Regulations as the Congress shall make." Under this power Congress has enacted several statutes, beginning with the Judiciary Act of 1789, defining the rules by which cases may be brought to the Supreme Court. The most important of these rules are those that allow the Supreme Court discretion to select those appeals that are truly important for developing a consistent and effective constitutional law for the nation, and to refuse to hear all others.[27] This discretion is called Supreme Court *certiorari* jurisdiction.[28] Discretionary cases are presented by "petitions for *certiorari,*" which ask the justices of the Supreme Court to call for the record of a state or federal court in a case and examine it for errors made in those courts. The Supreme Court can simply refuse to grant *certiorari* without having to give a reason if it believes the claim has no merit or does not want to consider a particular issue at the time.[29]

In addition to these discretionary cases, there are certain cases that come on appeal, rather than by petition for *certiorari,* from a state or federal court, and which the Supreme Court is theoretically obligated to hear. The federal statutes providing for such appeal generally deal with trial court decisions and allow a direct appeal to the Supreme Court. However, as a practical matter the Supreme Court can also dismiss these types of cases if it finds that such cases suffer from procedural defects in taking the appeal or do not present a substantial federal question.[30] Thus even the cases that the Supreme Court is theoretically bound to hear may be disposed of as it pleases.

However, this method must be available to the Court if it is not to be so inundated that it cannot give careful attention to the matters of crucial importance. It would simply be impossible for the Court to consider all cases that it is asked to consider. Thousands of cases are petitioned or appealed to the Supreme Court each year; thus the device of *certiorari* has been accepted in order to lighten this intolerable burden of cases. It is only through its discretionary power to hear or deny these petitions for "cert" that the Court is able to devote the time and care necessary to the important issues. Therefore, in contrast to the process in the federal and state *trial* courts, before the parties (or anyone else) can even find out whether the Supreme Court will hear the case, a petition for a writ of *certiorari* must be filed with the Supreme Court, which the Court will then either grant or deny.

There are several situations in which the Supreme Court is more likely to grant the petition and issue the writ. For example, if several of the federal circuit courts of appeal are in disagreement on a certain principle of law, the Supreme Court is likely to grant the writ in a case that presents that principle of law; thus it will clear up the disputed principle, with the result that circuit courts will thereafter render consistent decisions. Also, if the matter has substantial national importance or concerns an urgent national issue, the Court is more likely to grant *certiorari.*[31]

---

[27] 28 U.S.C. 1254; Revised Rules of the Supreme Court of the United States, Rule 19 (as amended, 1973).

[28] Pronounced "sur-shē-ǝ-rår'-ē."

[29] Rule 19 of the Revised Rules of the Supreme Court provides that "a review on writ on certiorari is not a matter of right, but of sound judicial discretion, and will be granted only where there are special and important reasons therefor." In any particular year, the Supreme Court grants *certiorari* in 10–15 percent of the cases on its appellate docket. *Annual Report of the Director* (1977) pp. 170–72.

[30] Although the Court renders decisions on the majority of cases appealed to it, most of those cases are ruled on summarily without an opinion or without hearing oral argument on the matter, as where the Court states that it lacks jurisdiction or that there is no substantial federal question. See Wright, pp. 471–98.

[31] Rule 19 of the Revised Rules of the Supreme Court lists seven factors that indicate reasons which may induce the Supreme Court to grant *certiorari.*

A denial of *certiorari* is not generally considered an indication of the Supreme Court's position in any respect. That is, one should not regard a denial of *certiorari* as implying that the Supreme Court approves of the lower court's decision on the matter, and that the Supreme Court would therefore want the decision to stand. Although lawyers often read between the lines, there are simply too many variables and considerations involved, thus precluding any inferences to be drawn from a denial of *certiorari*. The late Supreme Court Justice Felix Frankfurter stated that a variety of considerations underlie a denial of the writ, such as: a review may be sought too late; the judgment of the lower court may not be final; it may not be the judgment of the State court of last resort; or the decision may be supportable as a matter of state law.[32]

E. State Jurisdiction as All Judicial Power That Is Not Exclusively Federal

At the time this nation was formed, the colonists almost considered each state to be a nation in itself; the central government was given only those limited powers thought necessary for the common survival, protection, and economic well-being of all the states. All powers that were not exclusively granted to the central government were reserved by the individual states.[33] This principle need not have been stated in the Constitution, but as an assurance that it would be followed under the new union, it was stated in Amendment IX: "The enumeration in the Constitution, of certain rights, shall not be construed to deny or disparage others retained by the people." It was further stated in Amendment X: "The powers not delegated to the United States by the Constitution, nor prohibited by it to the States, are reserved to the States respectively, or to the people."

These principles of state sovereignty apply to the judiciary with the same strength as they do to the other two branches of government. Each state, therefore, has always been free to develop its own legal system, and more importantly, has retained jurisdiction over all cases that have not been exclusively given to the federal courts or expressly taken away from the States by the Constitution. Thus state courts hear not only exclusively state matters and cases involving citizens of the same state but also hear federal question cases and diversity of citizenship cases. Although the federal courts also have the power to hear federal question and diversity cases, there is no reason why the state courts cannot exercise concurrent jurisdiction over those types of cases. In his discussion of the question of the relationship between the respective jurisdictions of the state and federal courts in Federalist Paper No. 82, Hamilton attempted to reassure those fearing an overly powerful central government by pointing out:[34]

---

[32] Maryland v. Baltimore Radio Show, Inc., 338 U.S. 912, 917–18 (1950).

[33] *Federalist Papers,* Nos. 45–46. Congress has made federal jurisdiction exclusive in bankruptcy proceedings; patent and copyright cases; cases involving fines, penalties, forfeitures, or seizures under laws of the United States; crimes against the United States; and in less significant areas. See Wright, p. 24n.19.

[34] *Federalist Papers,* No. 82, p. 492.

[T]he States will retain all *pre-existing* authorities which may not be exclusively delegated to the federal head; and ... this exclusive delegation can only exist in one of three cases: where an exclusive authority is, in expressed terms, granted to the Union; or where a particular authority is granted to the Union and the exercise of a like authority is prohibited to the States; or where an authority is granted to the Union with which a similar authority in the States would be utterly incompatible.... [T]he State court will retain the jurisdiction that we now have, unless it appears to be taken away in one of the enumerated modes. ...

When ... we consider the State governments and the national governments, as they truly are ... as parts of ONE WHOLE, the inference seems to be conclusive that the State courts would have a concurrent jurisdiction in all cases arising under the laws of the Union where it was not expressly prohibited.

F. Other Aspects of the Relationship Between the Federal and State Court Systems

1. Removal

As mentioned previously, the federal court system and the state court systems are two separate systems, one formed by the Congress of the United States and the other formed by each of the individual state legislatures. Each state judicial system is free to operate in its own separate and distinct manner, apart from the other states' systems and apart from the federal judicial system, consistent with the federal Constitution and subject to Supreme Court review. The types of cases handled by the federal court system are limited to those special types described in the Constitution, but the state courts are free to hear almost all types of cases. If the Constitution does not specifically grant the federal judicial system the power to hear a particular type of case, that case must be filed in and heard by a state court. In many cases the state and federal courts both have jurisdiction. Of course, the plaintiff must make a choice between one or the other.

After having been filed but before being tried in a state court, a case over which the federal district court could have had jurisdiction may, upon request of the defendant, be transferred, or "removed," from the state court to such federal court. This is another aspect of the relationship between state and federal courts. Not only may cases that have been decided in state supreme courts be appealed to the United States Supreme Court but also certain cases, before being decided, may be transferred to a federal district court, provided the case is of the type described in Article III of the Constitution, and in the case of a diversity action, provided none of the defendants is a citizen of the state in which the action was originally brought by the plaintiff.[35] Although the Constitution does not specifically authorize removal of cases from state court to federal court, ever since the Judiciary Act of 1789 this procedure has been authorized by statute. As stated by the Supreme Court: "This power of removal is not to be found in express terms in any part of the constitution;

---

[35] 28 U.S.C. section 1441(b).

if it be given, it is only given by implication, as a power necessary and proper to carry into effect some express power." [36]

2. State Court Decisions in Federal Diversity Cases

Another aspect of the relationship between state and federal courts is the requirement that in diversity cases all federal district courts must follow the principles of the cases of the state court where that federal court is located. In federal question cases, the federal courts are bound to follow federal decisions, because the issues in these cases primarily involve federal matters. The requirement that federal courts apply state principles in diversity cases developed from two important Supreme Court decisions that were rendered almost one hundred years apart. The Judiciary Act of 1789, passed by the newly formed Congress, included a portion called the Rules of Decision Act. The Rules of Decision Act stated that "the law of the several states" shall be applied in the federal courts unless the federal Constitution, statutes, or treaties provide otherwise. Then in 1842, in the case of *Swift* v. *Tyson,* the Supreme Court was asked to decide the question of whether "law of the several states" meant state statutory law only, or whether it also included state court decisions.[37] The Supreme Court decided in that case that such "law" was in fact limited to state statutes, thus allowing the federal district courts to develop their own court decisions, or substantive *federal common law,* in all fields not covered by state statutes.

This simultaneous development of state case law and federal case law by the federal courts sitting within those states brought about the untenable situation, in diversity cases, of giving the plaintiff a choice of filing a case in the forum that had the more favorable case law. The fact that there was a choice is not necessarily objectionable; there is presently and always has been a choice in diversity cases between filing in state court or in federal court. The point is that the choice was motivated by the difference in legal principles applicable to the plaintiff's claim. This allowed a plaintiff to examine the state common law and the federal common law and then decide to which "side of the street" he would go, depending upon which court's common law was more favorable.

Principles of fairness and justice in the eyes of the law should be based upon ground more solid than the difference in tribunals, but it took many years before the Supreme Court remedied the problem in the 1938 decision of *Erie R.R.* v. *Tompkins.*[38] In *Erie,* the Court held that the principle set forth in *Swift* v. *Tyson* was not only unfair but also flew in the face of consistency of the judicial system and a logical relationship between the state and federal court systems. Therefore, in overruling *Swift* v. *Tyson,* the Supreme Court held in the *Erie* case that it had misconstrued the Rules of Decision Act in its 1842 decision of *Swift* v. *Tyson,* and that "law of the several states" includes not only state statutes but also the judicial decisions of the states. This marked the end of federal common law in diversity cases.

---

[36] Martin v. Hunter's Lessee, 1 Wheat. 304, 349, 4 L. Ed. 97 (1816).
[37] Swift v. Tyson, 16 Pet. 1, 10 L. Ed. 865 (1842).
[38] Erie Railroad Company v. Tompkins, 304 U.S. 64 (1938).

G. Other Types of Jurisdiction

In addition to the definitions of the term *jurisdiction* discussed at the beginning of this chapter, there are a few other types of jurisdiction that should be discussed.

1. Original Jurisdiction

A court with original jurisdiction has the power to hear the case at its inception, rather than being limited to considering the case on appeal after it has been tried by a lower court. All trial courts have original jurisdiction. Also it has been explained previously that the United States Supreme Court is a court that considers appeals from state supreme courts or from the federal circuit courts. This is true; however, Article III, section 2, of the Constitution also gives the Supreme Court *original* jurisdiction in certain specified cases. The Constitution further specifies that it shall have appellate jurisdiction in all other cases, including appellate jurisdiction over the subject matter that has already been discussed, namely federal question and diversity of citizenship cases. In those cases in which the Supreme Court has original jurisdiction it acts as a *trial* court, not as an appellate court. Many state supreme courts have original jurisdiction for the issuance of special writs. However, they do not have the type of original jurisdiction that the United States Supreme Court has.[39]

2. Concurrent Jurisdiction

Concurrent jurisdiction exists when more than one court has the power to hear and determine a case. This means that the parties have a choice as to the court in which the case may be filed. For example, there is concurrent jurisdiction in a federal district court and a state district court for nearly all diversity of citizenship and federal question cases.

3. Appellate Jurisdiction

Appellate jurisdiction is the power vested in the courts above the trial courts to review the decisions and correct legal errors of the lower courts and to revise the judgment of the lower courts in accordance with such corrections. Such errors are corrected either by remanding the case to the trial court for a new trial to be conducted in accordance with the appellate court's instructions, or by reversing the lower court's decision. State supreme courts spend approximately 90 percent of their time on matters involving their appellate jurisdiction.[40]

4. Ancillary Jurisdiction

Ancillary jurisdiction is jurisdiction assumed by federal courts that extends beyond the judicial power conferred upon them expressly by the Constitution or by

---

[39] See Wright, pp. 499–506.
[40] United States Department of Justice, *Law Enforcement Assistance Administration National Survey of Court Organization* (Washington, D.C.: United States Government Printing Office, 1973), p. 3.

federal statutes. Under the concept of ancillary jurisdiction, a federal district court acquires jurisdiction over issues that otherwise would be determinable only in a state court as an incident of disposition of a closely related federal matter that is *properly* before such federal court. This type of jurisdiction generally involves either proceedings that are concerned with pleadings, records, or judgments of court, or proceedings that affect property that is already in the federal court's jurisdiction. The concept has been established largely as a convenience to the parties, because it allows the court to hear ancillary claims when the court properly has jurisdiction of the principal claim, even though the ancillary claims otherwise would be improper in the federal court because of the citizenship of the parties, the amount in controversy, or any other factor determinative of jurisdiction.

5. Pendent Jurisdiction

Pendent jurisdiction is the jurisdiction of federal courts in cases in which the plaintiff joins a federal claim (or the defendant does so with a counterclaim) with a state-law claim and both are based on a single event or series of events that are said to constitute a single cause of action. The test to determine whether the federal court has pendent jurisdiction to hear the state claim (as well as the federal claim) is whether the same evidence will serve to prove both claims.

QUESTIONS

1. If the International Shoe Company had conducted business in the state of Washington through the mail, rather than by the use of salesmen, would the state have had *in personam* jurisdiction? Why or why not?

2. Give some examples of cases "arising under" the Constitution.

3. In order for a federal court to have subject matter jurisdiction in a diversity case, does the case have to involve a federal question? Explain.

4. Was the court being unreasonably restrictive in its interpretation of the jurisdictional amount requirement in the *Giancana* case? Why or why not?

5. What alternatives could be implemented or used by the Supreme Court or Congress to enable the Court to review a greater number of cases than it presently reviews?

6. Explain whether there is a contradiction between the principles contained in the Preamble of the Constitution, as discussed in *Martin* v. *Hunter's Lessee,* and the concept (discussed elsewhere in this chapter) of the states retaining the ultimate power in forming the central government.

7. What was the Supreme Court's interpretation of "law of the states" in the case of *Erie R.R.* v. *Tompkins?* Should the doctrine stated in the *Erie* case have any effect on federal question cases? Why or why not?

5

Other Foundational Considerations

A. Procedure and Substance

1. Definition

The legal system defines *procedure* as those rules or legal decisions that do not bear directly on the outcome of the court's decision. Procedure is the machinery for carrying on the suit, or the mechanics of the legal process. Rules of procedure exist so that substantive law can be implemented. Accordingly, one main objective of procedural law is to give each party to a dispute an equal opportunity to present his or her case. Substantive principles of law, or *substance,* on the other hand, are those principles that directly affect the court's decision and determine the respective rights and duties at issue in the case—in other words, all issues in the case that might materially affect the outcome. Most procedural rules govern the commencement and conduct of a case. Examples include rules stating that "a civil action is commenced by filing a complaint with the court" and that "the defendant shall serve his answer within twenty days after the service of the summons and complaint upon him. . . ." Note that these procedural rules are quite distinct from substantive principles of law, one example of which is: a landowner is not liable for injuries suffered by trespassers on his or her land, despite the negligence of that landowner. Substantive law is comprised of both statutes and court decisions, but most substantive law has been developed by the latter. Procedural rules, on the other hand, are formulated almost exclusively by Congress and the state legislatures. However, just as any statute can be *interpreted* by the judicial branch, the courts are continuously developing common law or case law interpretation of the rules of procedure.

In the case of *Hanna* v. *Plumer*[1] Chief Justice Earl Warren stated that the procedure-substance distinction cannot be determined "by application of any automatic 'litmus paper' criterion, but rather by reference to the policies underlying the

---

[1] Hanna v. Plumer, 380 U.S. 460 (1965).

. . . rule" stated in the case of *Erie R.R.* v. *Tompkins*.[2] He summarized these policies as: (1) discouragement of forum shopping and (2) avoidance of inequitable administration of the laws.[3] An earlier case distinguished procedure and substance on the theory that the latter was "outcome-determinative" and that "in all cases where a federal court is exercising jurisdiction solely because of the diversity of citizenship of the parties, the outcome of the litigation in the federal court should be substantially the same, . . . as it would be if tried in a State court." [4] This, of course, was the policy embodied in the *Erie* case.[5] But although *Erie* clearly established that the federal courts must apply the state's substantive legal principles in diversity cases, the exact definition of what constitutes substantive—as opposed to procedural—legal principles still needed clarification after *Erie*. Thus cases such as *Hanna* v. *Plumer* and *Guaranty Trust* have provided guidelines to aid federal courts in deciding whether they must apply the law of the state in which they sit—if substantive law, in accordance with the *Erie* doctrine—or whether they are free to apply federal procedural rules, on which *Erie* has no effect.

2. Rules of Civil Procedure

Because the "laws of the several states" as interpreted in the *Erie* case refers to substantive law only, in the areas in which procedure and substance can be distinguished under the *Hanna* case, the federal courts have remained free to establish their own procedural rules and principles for the conduct of federal trials and appeals. In these trials the federal courts apply procedural rules called the Federal Rules of Civil Procedure. This is true even in diversity cases, despite the *Erie R.R.* case. At approximately the same time as *Erie* was decided, the Supreme Court, by the authority delegated to it by Congress in the Act of June 19, 1934, established the Federal Rules of Civil Procedure.[6] These rules prescribe detailed procedures governing all federal proceedings in all federal district courts, and they continue (with amendments) to govern all procedural matters within those courts. The only limitation on the authorization contained in the 1934 Act was that the new rules of procedure could not alter any substantive rights. The Act provided that the rules were to take effect six months after their promulgation. In response to this grant of authority, the Supreme Court appointed an Advisory Committee of practitioners, professors, the president of the American Law Institute, and several other experts and assigned them the duty of preparing and submitting a draft of these rules. In December 1937 the Advisory Committee to the Supreme Court submitted the proposed rules to the Supreme Court and then to the United States Attorney General. They were then submitted to Congress in January 1938 and approved later that year.

---

[2] Erie R.R. Company v. Tompkins, 304 U.S. 64 (1938).
[3] Hanna v. Plumer, 380 U.S. at 468.
[4] Guaranty Trust Company of New York v. York, 326 U.S. 99, 109 (1945).
[5] See discussion concerning *Erie* case in Chapter 4, Part F.
[6] 28 U.S.C. Section 2072.

There have been several changes, mostly minor ones, since that time. On April 4, 1960 the Chief Justice of the United States Earl Warren, acting pursuant to the Act of Congress of July 11, 1958, appointed six standing committees to maintain continuous study of the Rules, in order to recommend any improvements and to keep the Rules up to date. Under this law any recommendations of these committees go to the Supreme Court, which then disapproves of such recommendations or presents them to Congress. If Congress does not expressly reject such recommendations, they then become effective ninety days after presentation to Congress for adoption.[7]

The Federal Rules of Civil Procedure generally have worked effectively since the time of their adoption in 1938. Wright states that: "The success of the Federal Rules of Civil Procedure has been quite phenomenal. They provide for the federal courts a uniform procedure in civil actions . . . that is flexible, simple, clear and efficient." [8]

The positive impact of the Rules has been so great that since the time of their enactment in 1938 thirty-four states have adopted rules of procedure modeled after the Federal Rules. The few states that have not yet adopted rules modeled after the Federal Rules continue to use outdated and somewhat more cumbersome procedural rules.

B. Conflict of Laws

Since different states have different substantive laws, courts sometimes have to reconcile conflicts between them in cases that involve parties from different states or events that occurred in more than one state. The study of conflict of laws deals, among other concepts, with this relationship between the laws of the various states. This discussion of conflict of laws will be limited to one area, namely choice of law. Choice of law deals primarily with the question of which state's law is to be applied by the forum to a case that involves factors, or contacts, with different states.

A typical example of a choice of law problem is the following: One plaintiff (the driver of an automobile) is a citizen of state A, a second plaintiff (a passenger in the automobile) is a citizen of state B, the defendant (the driver of a second vehicle) is a citizen of state C, and an automobile accident occurred between the two vehicles on the highways of state D, causing physical injury and property damage to the plaintiffs. The law of most states would permit the filing of the complaint in this hypothetical case to take place in any one of those four states. Assuming the case is filed in the state district court of state A, under conflicts of law—choice of law—rules, it is then the duty of the state A trial court to carefully analyze the facts involved in the case and determine whether it is fair and logical to apply the substantive legal principles of state A, or whether it makes greater sense to invoke the substantive legal principles of any of the other three states. The applicable legal principles in each state may differ so much that the plaintiffs would win if the court

---

[7] See C. Wright, *Law of Federal Courts* (St. Paul: West Publishing Co., 1970), pp. 257–60.
[8] Ibid., p. 260.

applied the law of state A or B, but lose under the law of state C or D. Thus this initial choice of law question may become crucial in such multijurisdiction cases. The judge hearing the case in the state in which it is filed is free to examine the other states' legal principles and apply them if he or she determines that one of the other states has a more significant interest in the application of its policies and principles to the incident.

One may ask why the law of the local forum shouldn't be applied in every case. First, each state simply applying its own legal principles in all cases would encourage plaintiffs to "forum shop"—looking to the various jurisdictions in which the action could be commenced in search of the state whose applicable legal principles were most favorable to their cases and then suing in those courts. However, if the courts in each state invoke the same principles, then uniformity of results are assured, despite the location of the forum chosen. Second, in many cases application of the forum's own principles may not be consistent with fairness and justice to the litigants. If the forum has no material interest in the litigation other than the fact that it is the location of the court chosen by the plaintiff, and all of the important factors relate to another state, then it is more logical and usually more just to apply the laws of the other state.

Once the forum has determined that it should apply the substantive legal principles of another jurisdiction, the question becomes *what* other jurisdiction. There are five main approaches in determining which state's law should be applied to the controversy:

1. Center of gravity approach: The forum applies the law of the state having the greatest weight of contacts. If there is no clear weight outside the forum, it would apply its own law.
2. Governmental interests approach: A few jurisdictions base the choice of law decision on the relative importance of the interests and policies underlying each state's legal principles. Thus the forum must first determine what such policies or purposes are and then determine to what extent application of one law, as opposed to another, would tend to further the interests of the states involved.
3. *Lex fori* approach: Some courts regard the law of the forum as being applicable unless another state has an overriding interest in the application of its laws.
4. Better law approach: A few authorities in the field of conflict of laws believe that the sole purpose of choice of law rules should be to effectuate justice between the parties, and that the forum therefore should select the law best designed to achieve that end. That is, it should be a choice of law, not a choice between jurisdictions.[9]

---

[9] R. Leflar, *American Conflicts Law* (New York: Bobbs-Merrill Co., 1968), p. 216; see generally, D. Cavers, *The Choice of Law Process* (Ann Arbor: University of Michigan Press, 1965) for an in-depth discussion of the problems with this approach. See also F. Harper, "Policy Basis of the Conflict of Laws: Reflection on Rereading Professor Lorenzen's Essays," 56 *Yale Law Journal* 1155 (1947); Siegalman v. Cunard White Star, Ltd., 221 F.2d 189 (2d Cir. 1955) (Frank, J., dissenting).

5. Most significant contacts approach: The trend, and the soundest approach, is to determine which state has the most significant relationship to the particular issue. The states that follow this approach generally derive their analysis from the Restatement of Conflict of Laws 2d,[10] which requires consideration of the following factors:

a. the needs of the interrelationship between the states, such as discouraging forum shopping;
b. the relative importance of the forum's policies compared with the policies of other interested states;
c. the parties' expectations of what law would be applied to their dealings or relationship with each other;
d. the basic policies underlying the particular field of law involved;
e. the need for certainty, predictability, and uniformity of results;
f. the ease in determination and application of the law to be applied.

The Restatement provides that certain factors are more significant in some types of cases than in others. Thus the most significant contacts factor in a contracts case may indicate one state's law for the issue of performance and another state's law for the issue of damages.

In the example involving states A, B, C, and D mentioned earlier facts constituting significant contacts might include the residence of the parties, the state in which the vehicles are registered, the place of work of the parties, and the state where the injuries were suffered. The case of *First National Bank in Fort Collins* v. *Rostek* illustrates the application of the significant contacts approach as contained in the Restatement of Conflicts.

FIRST NATIONAL BANK IN FORT COLLINS
v.
ROSTEK

514 P.2d 314 (1973)

Supreme Court of Colorado

PRINGLE, Chief Justice.

This case arises out of events surrounding a tragic airplane accident which took the lives of Carol Hardin Rostek and her husband, John E. Rostek. The First National Bank in Fort Collins, plaintiff below (petitioner herein), is the guardian of the natural children of Carol Hardin Rostek. The respondent is the administratrix of the estate of John E. Rostek.

... [P]etitioner filed a wrongful death action in Colorado district court alleging that negligent operation of the aircraft on the part of

---

[10] *Restatement of Conflict of Laws 2d,* section 6 (St. Paul: American Law Institute Publishers, 1971).

John E. Rostek caused the accident and the ensuing death of his guest-passenger, Carol Hardin Rostek.

The respondent filed a motion for summary judgment alleging the rights of the parties are governed by the South Dakota Aircraft Guest Statute, S.D.C.L.1967, 50-13-15. This South Dakota statute requires proof by the guest-passenger of *willful* or *wanton* misconduct on the part of an operator of an aircraft.

For purposes of the summary judgment motion the parties stipulated that *at most* the petitioner's evidence would show simple negligence on the part of John Rostek. The parties also stipulated that John and Carol Rostek were both citizens and residents of the state of Colorado, and that Carol Rostek's natural children, who are her sole heirs at law, resided with her in Colorado. With respect to the events in question, the stipulation stated:

"That on or about December 29, 1969, John E. Rostek, deceased, accompanied by his wife, Carol Hardin Rostek, deceased, took off from Colorado enroute to Iowa and Vermillion, South Dakota. That the Rosteks intended to remain in Vermillion, South Dakota, overnight, but after ascertaining that a board of directors meeting could not be held that evening, decided to return to Fort Collins the same night.

"That the Rosteks took off in their twin engine plane that evening from Harold Davidson Airport, Vermillion, South Dakota. That two days later, the plane was found approximately 500 feet from the end of the runway."

The trial court granted the respondent's motion for summary judgment and held:

". . . The parties have agreed that if the trial court is to adopt the law of the place of the wrong, *lex loci,* the case must be dismissed. If the Court is to adopt the law in which the trial is held, *lex fori,* the motion must be denied.

"The law in Colorado is that the claim is governed by *lex loci delicti,* rather than *lex fori.*"

The petitioner then petitioned this court . . . for a writ of certiorari to review the summary judgment of the trial court. We granted certio-rari for the sole purpose of determining if Colorado courts are compelled to apply the doctrine of *lex loci delicti* (the law of the place of the wrong), under the facts and circumstances of this case.

I.

A brief review of Colorado case law convinces us that the issue presented in this case has in reality never been previously decided by this court, and that the doctrine of *lex loci delicti* appears in Colorado law more by default than by design.

In both Atchison T.&S.F.R. Co. v. Betts, 10 Colo. 431, 15 P. 821 (New Mexico law applied where a suit was brought for the killing of plaintiff's mule by defendant railroad in New Mexico) and Denver & R.G.R. Co. v. Warring, 37 Colo. 122, 86 P. 305 (New Mexico law applied to determine if legal action by a personal representative of deceased was proper when accident occurred in New Mexico), the question of whether any rule other than *lex loci delicti* should be applied was never raised. In both cases the court applied the law of the place of the wrong without recognition of the choice of law issue and without a discussion of any choice of law doctrine. This is, of course, typical of cases from all jurisdictions in the days when *A.T.&S.F.* and *D.&R.G.R.* were decided. *Lex loci delicti* was accepted doctrine then and none challenged it or gave any thought to its jurisdiction or its fairness.

The only Colorado case which expressly mentions the doctrine of *lex loci delicti* is Pando v. Jasper, 133 Colo. 321, 295 P.2d 229. . . . This reference to *lex loci delicti* is unquestionably *dicta,* and the court reached this conclusion without citing any previous Colorado cases as precedent. Further, in *Pando,* as in previous cases where the court applied the law of the place of the wrong, no issue was raised concerning the applicability or scope of the doctrine of *lex loci delicti* or any other choice of law rule.

. . . We conclude, therefore, that *stare decisis* does not compel this court to apply the rule of *lex loci delicti* without regard to the facts and circumstances in the particular case. Instead, this court must decide, as a matter of first impression, whether the broad rule of *lex loci delicti* should be adopted and applied to this case, or whether a more flexible choice of law rule should control.

II.

When the doctrine of *lex loci delicti* was first established in the mid-nineteenth century, conditions were such that people only occasionally crossed state boundaries. Under those circumstances, there was legitimacy in a rule which presumed that persons changing jurisdictions would be aware of the different duties and obligations they were incurring when they made the interstate journey. Further, even if persons making these occasional journeys into neighboring states were not actually aware of the changing duties and responsibilities, enforcing the laws of the jurisdiction in which they were wronged was justified because of the "vested rights" doctrine that was prevalent and widely accepted at that time. Thus, the rule of *lex loci delicti* was originally viewed as a practical formula by which individuals could govern their actions in accordance with prevailing attitudes and customs, providing both uniformity of application and predictability of results.

However, with the industrial revolution and the passage of time, the interstate mobility of the citizenry increased in speed and availability to such an extent that persons no longer regarded an interstate journey as a rare occurrence entailing a significant change of surroundings. As these attitudes and conditions changed, it became clear that the mechanical application of *lex loci delicti* to every multistate tort controversy often yielded harsh, unjust results, unrelated to the contemporary interests of the states involved or the realistic expectations of the parties.

To avoid the growing number of undesirable results which strict adherence to *lex loci delicti* produced, courts devised various methods of characterizing the issues in the controversy to allow them to deviate from the application of *lex loci delicti* without offending *stare decisis*.

By labeling a matter as "procedural" rather than "substantive," or "contractual" rather than "tortious," courts were able to apply law other than the law of the place of the wrong. See, e.g., Kilberg v. Northeast Airlines, Inc., 9 N.Y.2d 34, 211 N.Y.S.2d 133, 172 N.E.2d 526; Grant v. McAuliffe, 41 Cal.2d 859, 264 P.2d 944. In the process the courts were, in effect, making a choice of law decision without exposing the real choice influencing factors for objective classification and criticism. This constant search for a result which would comport with reason and justice made it evident by the mid-twentieth century that the doctrine of *lex loci delicti* no longer provided the high degree of predictability and uniformity which were considered its primary virtues.

The questionable viability of the *lex loci delicti* rule in today's society has been recognized by courts and commentators alike. In the last ten years, while several states have retained adherence to the broad *lex loci delicti* rule, a greater number of jurisdictions have abandoned or rejected *lex loci delicti* in favor of a more flexible and rational choice of law approach in multistate tort cases. The majority of those cases rejecting the *lex loci delicti* rule have involved the application of host-guest statutes or the question of interspousal liability for injuries received in automobile or airplane accidents. Additionally, the overwhelming majority of commentators are opposed to the mechanical application of the place of wrong rule, largely for the reasons previously discussed.

The rationale of the cases rejecting *lex loci delicti,* the views of eminent authorities in the field of tort law, and our own observations and experience convince us a more flexible and rational approach than *lex loci delicti* affords is necessary. We fully appreciate the arguments made by the defendant that *lex loci delicti* retains some predictabiilty of result and ease of application by courts. Yet, the facts in the case at bar classically demonstrate the injustice and irrationality of the automatic application of the *lex loci delicti* rule. Both Carol and John Rostek were citizens of Colorado. The airplane in question was registered in Colorado and was returning to Colorado when the accident occurred. The lawsuit was brought in a Colorado forum with a Colorado resident as defendant. It becomes evident, therefore, that South Dakota's only interest in this controversy is the fortuitous occurrence of the accident within its borders. Thus the trial court's decision to apply South Dakota law to this case can be affirmed only if we are to adhere to a mechanical and unfailing application of the place of wrong rule, regardless of the interests of the states involved or the expectations of the parties. This we refuse to do.

III.

Although most courts and commentators are united in their opposition to the use of the general *lex loci delicti* rule, there is disagreement as to which approach should be adopted. Some would emphasize the law of the place of the forum, while others would place more emphasis on the expectations of the parties. Still others stress the need to consider the interests of the various governmental entities involved. All of the generally accepted approaches, however, suffer from a similar defect; namely, they are all "approaches," to be applied in a more or less *ad hoc* fashion, and containing indeterminate language with no concrete guidelines. Thus, quite naturally, these approaches have exhibited a certain lack of both predictability of result and uniformity of application. This situation cannot be completely disregarded. While we recognize that a rational and equitable approach to choice of law is desirable, we now harmonize that approach with the genius of the common law which always sought to provide to its consumers some degree of predictability and consistency in application. As we have said, accidents occurring in states not the domicile of all of the parties are commonplace in today's society. The law should not deal with them as if they were rare and exotic hypotheticals, to be solved by exercises in intellectual gamesmanship. The events in this case, and the probable reoccurrence, are real world concerns, and the law in this area should provide a concrete and viable system for the equal application of just laws.

Because of the lack of consistency and predictability exhibited by various proposed choice of law "approaches," the principal question in choice of law today is whether or not to adopt rational choice of law "rules," or to deal with each case as it comes to us on an *ad hoc* basis. Rules are employed in most areas of the law because they provide the benefits of certainty and predictability. . . .

Thus, in order to provide some predictability of result and uniformity of application, this court turns to the adoption of some rules dealing with choice of law. In so doing, we begin with the particular issue presented in this case, namely, the application of a guest statute to a host-guest controversy. We consider this issue a narrow one, occurring with enough frequency and repetitiveness to enable us to extract specific guidelines that will satisfactorily regulate this issue.

Our search for a workable choice of law rule in the guest-host area leads to the majority opinion in Neumeier v. Kuehner, 31 N.Y.2d 121, 335 N.Y.S.2d 64, 286 N.E.2d 454 (1972), written by Chief Judge Fuld. In *Neumeier* the court was faced with a guest-host accident situation involving a citizen of Canada and a resident of New York. Judge Fuld admitted that the recent choice of law "approach" in guest-host controversies, initiated in Babcock v. Jackson, had, until *Neumeier,* lacked consistency. The New York court then proceeded to formulate a specific rule governing the application of guest statutes in multistate tort controversies. This rule generally embodies the rational underpinnings of the newer approaches to choice of law problems, emphasizing the expectations of the parties and the interests of the different jurisdictions involved. We are persuaded that it is just and equitable and ought to be accepted in Colorado with respect to the first two sections thereof and we now do so. As stated by the New York court, those sections provide:

"1. When the guest-passenger and the host-driver are domiciled in the same state, and the [vehicle] is there registered, the law of that state should control and determine the standard of care which the host owes to his guest.

"2. When the driver's conduct occurred in the state of his domicile and that state does not cast him in liability for that conduct, he should not be held liable by reason of the fact that liability would be imposed upon him under the tort law of the state of the victim's domicile. Conversely, when the guest was injured in the state of his own domicile and its law permits recovery, the driver who has come into that state should not—in the absence of special circumstances—be permitted to interpose the law of his state as a defense."

IV.

We must now apply the aforementioned choice of law rule to determine if the South Dakota guest statute should be applied to the case at bar. Both the guest-passenger and the host-pilot were domiciled and residing in Colorado, and the airplane was registered in Colorado. Thus, the facts in this case are governed by the first statement of the rule. Under this statement, the rights and liabilities of the parties are governed by the law of the place of domicile which in this case is Colorado. Accordingly, South Dakota law, including its Airplane Guest Statute, is not the appropriate law to apply under this new rule. . . .

V.

Since the scope of our decision to reject the mechanical application of the rule of *lex loci delicti* extends to all multistate tort controversies, we must now address ourselves to the question of what rules govern choice of law in

Colorado outside the rules laid down with respect to host-guest controversies which fit those rules. We announce that Colorado will adopt the general rule of applying the law of the state with the most "significant relationship" with the occurrence and the parties, as presented and defined in the Restatement, (Second) Conflict of Laws, Vol. 1, Sec. 145 (1969). Generally, the Restatement requires the application of separate rules to various kinds of torts, and defines "significant contacts" in terms of the issues, the nature of the tort, and the purposes of the tort rules involved. While this Restatement rule is somewhat broad, it is no less precise than the concepts of "reasonableness" or "due process" which courts have applied for many years. Hopefully, at some time in the future, as the body of case law develops, we can lay down more specific choice of law rules governing other areas, as we have done today in the area of guest statutes. However, at present, in all areas of multistate tort controversies other than those involving the situations we have dealt with in the specific rules laid down today, we will use and apply the rule articulated in Sec. 145 of the Second Restatement on Conflict of Laws.

VI.

Since Colorado law was the appropriate law to be applied to the issues in this case, it was error for the trial court to grant respondent's summary judgment motion on the grounds that South Dakota law barred the suit.

The judgment is reversed and the cause remanded to the trial court for further proceeding not inconsistent with the views herein expressed.

C. Comparison of Civil and Criminal Law

The next several chapters closely examine several substantive areas of the law. Before those discussions, we must make a distinction between the two major areas of the law—civil and criminal. First, these are mutually exclusive and exhaustive classifications; if a matter does not fall within the realm of criminal law, then it must necessarily be a civil case, and vice versa. Although some statutes deal with both criminal and civil penalties, the actual nature of a case heard in the courts must be either civil or criminal. That is, a court cannot in the same proceeding hear both civil and criminal issues.

An example of a statute that contains criminal sanctions and civil remedies is the Sherman Antitrust Act, under which an injured party may recover treble damages (civil damages) for injuries due to a violation of the Act.[11] This law also provides that the federal government can prosecute the violator for criminal conduct for which, if convicted, the defendant could be imprisoned.[12]

The Sherman Antitrust Act is a federal law. Many states also have statutes containing civil penalties. For example, the state of Colorado provides that under certain conditions a tenant can recover treble damages from a landlord for the latter's wrongful failure to refund a security deposit.[13] Despite its punitive nature, this law is a *civil* one because it protects a private right rather than the public interest.

1. Difference in Adversaries

As the preceding examples show, the most obvious distinction between criminal law and civil law is the difference in adversaries. In a civil action a plaintiff is seeking compensation from one or more defendants in the form of monetary damages or is requesting the court to order the defendant to do or cease doing some act. In a criminal action, a representative of the state or the people, namely the prosecuting or district attorney (or city attorney in a case involving violation of a municipal ordinance) is asking the court to impose a fine upon or order the imprisonment of the defendant; no pecuniary compensation to the injured party is involved in a criminal proceeding.[14] Thus, although both types of actions involve defendants, only private persons or private entities can bring a complaint in a civil action, whereas in a criminal action only a representative of the public may prosecute the defendant. This of course does not include civil cases brought by or against a state, the federal government, or any political subdivision or agency. The government can sue or be sued in a civil action just as an individual can, and the fact that the government is a party does not change the nature of the case from civil to criminal. On the other hand, if it is a criminal case the government, of course, will be a party.

2. Difference in Theoretical Basis

Another distinction between civil and criminal law lies in their respective theoretical bases. Under civil law, as mentioned earlier, the plaintiff seeks compen-

---

[11] 15 U.S.C. Section 15, *et seq.*
[12] 15 U.S.C. Section 1.
[13] Colorado Revised Statutes 38–12–103 (1973).
[14] However, a few states have enacted statutes that establish a victim-compensation fund funded by state revenues and intended to aid victims of crimes. Florida, Pennsylvania, and North Carolina have very recently instituted state experimental programs to provide aid directly from the defendant to the victim.

sation in the form of money, property, or conduct from the defendant. Criminal law, on the other hand, is based on the concepts of punishment, protection, retribution, deterrence, and rehabilitation. The relative importance assigned each of these factors by the prosecution or the jury will differ among cases. One or more of these concepts is the basis for all criminal trials. This theoretical basis differs from that of the civil theory of compensation, by which the law attempts to resolve the case so that the plaintiff is justly compensated or returned as near as possible to the state he or she enjoyed before the injury inflicted by the defendant.

3. Similarities

Civil and criminal law are, however, similar in several respects: One similarity is that the concept of fault or blame pervades both. Although the emphasis is on compensation in civil cases the law assumes that the defendant should suffer in the course of compensating the plaintiff, just as it assumes in criminal cases that the defendant should be punished for wrongdoing. Another common denominator is that the same court has jurisdiction in both civil and criminal cases, although, as stated earlier, these issues cannot be heard in the same proceeding. Although unlikely, it is possible that the cases could be heard consecutively by the same judge in the same courtroom in two separate actions. For example, an individual who is struck by an automobile while attempting to cross the street could be the plaintiff in a civil action suing the driver of the automobile and seeking to recover damages for his or her injury. The same person could also be the complaining witness in a criminal action arising from the same accident brought on behalf of the state and prosecuted by the district attorney; in such a case the driver of the automobile, if convicted, could lose his or her license and be fined and possibly imprisoned for reckless driving resulting in the injury to that witness. If the injured party were killed by the driver of the automobile, his or her estate could sue the defendant for wrongful death. Based on the same facts, the state could try the defendant in a separate proceeding for vehicular homicide or involuntary manslaughter. These civil and criminal actions would be completely distinct from one another. They could be filed in the same court and heard in the same courtroom by the same judge on succeeding days or weeks, and they could involve nearly identical testimony. The critical distinction is that the civil case would be brought by the plaintiff for the purpose of compensating him or her, while the criminal case would be brought by the state for the purpose of punishing the defendant, protecting society, deterring future similar activities, or to satisfy any of the other concepts on which our criminal justice system is based.

QUESTIONS

1. How can a distinction be made between procedure and substance if the outcome of a case is materially affected as a result of one party's failure to follow a procedural rule? How would you describe the difference between substance and procedure?

2. What would the result have been in the *First National Bank in Fort Collins* v. *Rostek* case if the court had applied one of the other choice of law approaches? Apply each approach to the facts of the case.

3. In what order of importance should the five bases for the criminal law be listed? why? Does the importance of each basis change in each situation and with the unique personality of each criminal defendant?

6

Civil Litigation

Having discussed the constitutional basis of the law, the structure of the court system, the meaning of jurisdiction, and other concepts, we next examine the steps by which a case reaches the court system and proceeds to its conclusion. This chapter discusses the litigation process (primarily civil litigation) from preparation and commencement through the trial of a case.

A. Establishing the Facts

The first event leading to an adversary proceeding in a civil action is the injury of the potential plaintiff, either financial or physical (known as *personal* injury) and that person's belief that he or she has suffered a type of damage for which the legal system provides relief. Assuming that such a person is unable to represent himself or herself in court, and assuming that the damage suffered is significant enough to require hiring an attorney, the client will seek out the help of an attorney to determine whether he or she has a legitimate basis for legal action. If such a basis exists, the client will retain the attorney and instruct him or her to proceed with the action. Suppose that Mr. Pope comes to his attorney and discloses the following:

> At 4:00 a.m. on the morning of January 1, 1978, Mr. Pope was proceeding down a steep hill in his 1975 automobile on California Street in downtown San Francisco. As he approached an intersection the traffic light turned yellow, at which time he attempted to stop, but was unable to. An approaching vehicle, driven by Mr. Drake, attempted to make a left-hand turn by crossing in front of Mr. Pope, whereupon Mr. Pope slammed his brakes and veered to the left, avoiding the collision with Drake's automobile but colliding with a light pole on one corner of the intersection.
>
> As a result of the crash, Pope suffered a broken arm, minor head injuries, and two severe facial cuts from the windshield glass. Drake suffered no injuries or damage to his vehicle.
>
> In addition, Pope stated that he was traveling at approximately 40 mph before applying his brakes, and that Drake's left headlight was not functioning at the time

of the incident. The roads were fairly wet, and there was one street light at the intersection.

The attorney must now determine whether the client has any legally enforceable rights and to so advise Mr. Pope. As part of this obligation the attorney must fully inform the client whether the extent of the damages, and therefore the potential recovery, is large enough to justify litigation.

The attorney should also inform Mr. Pope of the three typical methods of paying attorneys' fees. Most legal work is compensated at an hourly rate. For example, a client may request an attorney to draft a contract governing a business venture into which the client is about to enter with a third person. During the course of the following week the attorney might spend an hour on the telephone with the client obtaining all the pertinent facts about the proposed business venture; five hours drafting the contract; an hour meeting with the client; a half hour driving to the third party's attorney's office to negotiate the matter; and three hours in conference with the client, the third party, and the third party's attorney. Therefore, the attorney would bill the client for a total of 10½ hours at a previously agreed-upon hourly rate. The rate may range from $35 an hour for an attorney recently out of law school to $100 an hour for a more experienced attorney.

The second method of compensation is by a predetermined set amount, or flat rate. For example, an attorney may charge $150 for all noncontested divorces and $250 for all simple wills he or she drafts, even though the amount of time required often varies significantly among cases. The third method of compensation, and the one most frequently used in personal injury cases such as Pope's, is the contingent fee. Under this arrangement the plaintiff-client agrees to pay the attorney a specified portion (usually one-third or one-fourth) of the recovery, if any, obtained at the conclusion of the litigation. If the plaintiff does not recover, he or she pays only the actual costs of the suit, such as filing fees, court reporter fees, and other relatively minor expenses; if the plaintiff loses, the attorney receives no compensation, regardless of the time spent on the case.

If the potential recovery is large enough to justify the expenditure of attorney's fees, the attorney should further inform the client of the likelihood of the court or jury ruling in the client's favor. If the legal issues involved are not too complex, or if the attorney happens to be very well informed on them, there may be little or no need for research. If the questions are more complex, the answers may require several days of legal research of the precedents of that particular jurisdiction before the attorney can determine whether an action should even be commenced.

Based on the facts in Mr. Pope's case, his attorney would probably inform him that he has a relatively strong civil case, based on negligence, against Mr. Drake for recovery of damages for the injuries suffered as a result of the accident. However, Pope's attorney would further inform him that, although he had the right-of-way in the intersection, he may have contributed to the cause of the accident because of his excessive speed down an incline on a wet road. Further, the fact that Pope attempted to stop for the light would be raised by Drake to point out that

Drake had reason to believe Pope *would* stop for the light, thereby allowing Drake to make his turn. Other factors important to Pope's case are the questions of Drake's location at the time the light turned yellow, Drake's speed, and how far Drake had pulled into the intersection before Pope attempted to avoid colliding with him. Pope's attorney will inform his client of the importance of these facts, because the controlling legal principles in the state of California applied to these facts are: (1) An automobile approaching an intersection constitutes an immediate hazard to a motorist intending to make a left turn, under the California statute providing that the motorist intending to make such a left turn shall yield the right-of-way to an approaching vehicle within the intersection or close enough to it to constitute such a hazard. (2) If a motorist turns in front of an approaching automobile, the motorist is liable for negligence and conduct that could not reasonably have been anticipated.[1] (3) The degree of care required of a person for his or her own safety is ordinary care, although in some circumstances the amount of care required to reach the degree of ordinary care is greater than other circumstances.[2] (4) If the motorists are driving along the same street in opposite directions, and the second motorist to reach the intersection gives a signal for a left-hand turn, the first motorist's action imposes a duty on the second motorist to keep his or her automobile under control. (5) If an automobile has actually entered an intersection before another automobile approaches it, the driver of the first automobile has the right to assume that he or she will be permitted to pass through without danger of collision and that the driver of the other automobile will obey the law, slow down, and yield the right-of-way if slowing down is necessary to prevent a collision. (6) A motorist is not required to yield the right-of-way to a second motorist a considerable distance away, whose duty is to slow down while crossing an intersection.[3] (7) A motorist must maintain a proper lookout and keep his or her automobile under control.[4] (8) If the driver of an automobile is traveling at a lawful speed on a through highway protected by traffic lights, and if that driver assumes that other drivers will obey traffic lights and yield the right-of-way, and if the other driver does not do so, the first driver can be charged with negligence only if he or she fails to use the care of an ordinary prudent person from the time he or she knew, or in the exercise of due care should have known, what the other driver would do.[5]

B. The Lawyer as Negotiator

If the attorney determines that the client has suffered damages that could form the basis of a successful civil action, the next question he or she must answer is what approach should be taken vis-à-vis the potential defendant, Mr. Drake. The attorney will contact the potential defendant either by telephone or by letter and set forth

---

[1] Carr v. Holtslander, 246 P.2d 678 (Calif. 1952).
[2] Cucinella v. Weston Biscuit Co., 265 P.2d 513 (Calif. 1954).
[3] Osgood v. City of San Diego, 62 P.2d 195 (Calif. 1936).
[4] Grasso v. Cunial, 235 P.2d 32 (Calif. 1951).
[5] Shivers v. Van Lobensels, 240 P.2d 635 (Calif. 1952).

his or her client's position and version of the facts. The attorney will probably make a request or demand for a certain sum of money as compensation for the client's injury. However, in some situations a suit should be commenced without even contacting or discussing the matter with the other party; if it is determined that contacting the party will be a futile act—that the party will flatly refuse or ignore any possibility of resolving the matter prior to the commencement of an action—then this course should be taken. Sometimes the potential defendant wants to avoid substantial attorney's fees, is well aware of the likelihood of losing the case, and therefore will be quite agreeable to negotiating an out-of-court settlement. It is likely that the attorneys would meet, with or without their clients, to discuss settlement.

However, in many cases a potential defendant will seek the advice of an attorney to determine whether the potential plaintiff has cause for an action and the chances of the action's success. In this situation both attorneys perform a very significant function—preventing, rather than encouraging, the commencement of litigation. This role is not recognized as much as the more dramatic role of trial attorney. Most lawyers spend the vast majority of their time in their offices negotiating contracts or settlements of cases rather than trying cases in court. Either in the process of avoiding a potential suit or in simply drafting a legal document, such as a contract or articles of incorporation for a business, the lawyer has one object foremost in mind—*preventing* any future litigation. This object is accomplished by carefully drafting documents in order to have a clear solution to all potential problems that might arise from an agreement between parties under a contract or during the course of a business relationship governed by a document drafted by an attorney. It would be impossible to estimate the number of cases that would have been commenced except for the foresight of attorneys in drafting agreements or other documents. However, of those cases that have been commenced, attorneys' efforts in halting such litigation and in promoting early settlement are illustrated by the following figures: In 1973, 91.6 percent of the cases commenced in federal district courts were settled out of court prior to trial. Approximately 80 percent of all state cases filed are settled prior to trial.[6] Much of the credit can be attributed to the attorneys who controlled the situation from the time of the commencement of such actions, and who for various reasons encouraged their amicable or practical settlement. These figures do not include controversies that arise between people and are referred to their attorneys but are resolved before an action is begun.

Case law has an important impact upon the documents prepared by lawyers, in that many cases deal with the interpretation and meaning of words or phrases contained in such documents. Once a principle of law is established on the interpretation of a word or phrase, lawyers drafting documents will be sure to clearly include or exclude that word or phrase or to include language in the document elaborating

---

[6] H. Edwards and J. White, *The Lawyer as a Negotiator* (St. Paul: West Publishing Co., 1977), p. 8, citing G. Williams, et al. "Effective, Average and Ineffective Legal Negotiators," in *Psychology and the Law: Research Frontiers*, ed. G. Berment, et al. (Lexington, Mass.: Lexington Books, 1976).

upon it, so as to expressly carry out the meaning given it by the court's recent decision.

In the *Pope* case the attorney for Pope might wait for all of Pope's medical expenses to be added up and for an opportunity to determine the long-term effect of his injuries. Information helpful in making this determination would include medical reports, the results of any operations for the facial injuries resulting from the accident, and so on. After all of this information is gathered, probably several months after the accident, Pope's attorney would probably write a letter to Drake, indicating the amount of damages suffered by Pope as a result of Drake's alleged negligence and demanding immediate payment of that amount. As stated earlier, a potential defendant in such a situation would probably seek the advice of an attorney, just as the plaintiff did. Drake's attorney would analyze the facts and the law, just as Pope's attorney did, and would probably respond to Pope's attorney's letter, indicating that the matter has been turned over to him or her for reply. Drake's attorney would probably state that Drake denies all liability for any injuries suffered by Pope on the basis that Pope was the cause of his own injuries, that he was speeding at the time of the accident, and that Drake yielded the right-of-way to Pope.

What role would the insurance companies in this hypothetical case play? For the purposes of this case, we will not consider the role of either party's insurance company. The fact of insurance is inadmissible in any court proceeding, and the injured party normally has the right to recover the amount of damages he or she is able to prove and to which he or she is entitled, regardless of additional coverage by an insuror. Another fact that we will omit in this hypothetical case is that in this type of situation Drake would also contact his insuror, in which case the attorneys for the insurance company, rather than the attorney for Drake, would probably handle the matter. However, other than the fact that the insurance company attorneys would be representing Drake and that Pope may be entitled to damages not only from Drake's insurance company but also from Drake, this hypothetical case is representative of many similar negligence cases that have occurred and do occur very frequently.

C. Commencement of Court Involvement

Assuming that the parties' attorneys are unable to arrive at an out-of-court settlement, Mr. Pope must now commence suit. If there is a basis for federal jurisdiction, as described in Chapter 4, Pope's attorney must determine whether it would be more advantageous to file the action in federal court or in state court. The attorney might consider a great variety of factors in making this choice: crowding of the trial docket, comparative costs, quality and attitudes of the judges, advantages or disadvantages of different rules of evidence, convenience to the party and witnesses, differences in the procedural rules, past decisions of each court, and amount of damages awarded in previous cases. Whether the case is filed in state or federal court, the first step is the preparation and filing of a complaint by the plaintiff. (A form of complaint that Pope's attorney might draft and file in this hypothetical case is shown in Appendix B.) As described in Chapter 5, the rules of civil procedure govern the conduct of all procedural matters in federal court and in most state courts. Rule 3 of these uniform state and federal rules typically states: "A civil action is commenced by filing a complaint with the court." Some state rules of civil procedure provide that the transmittal, or service, of a summons upon the defendant, or the filing of the complaint, whichever occurs first, constitutes the commencement of a civil action. The summons is simply an instruction by the court to the defendant ordering the defendant to file an answer to the plaintiff's complaint by a specified date. Regardless of whether it is the filing or service that commences the action, a complaint must be filed with the court and given to the defendant to apprise the defendant of the nature of the allegations being made by the plaintiff.

The word *process* is defined as "a formal writing, or writ, issued by authority of law," [7] such as a summons (and a complaint by virtue of being incorporated in a summons). Therefore, transmittal of these documents by the plaintiff's agent, either a private person, the sheriff, or in the case of a federal complaint, a United States marshal, is described as service of process. The method by which service of process must be made is described in detail in Rule 4 of the rules of civil procedure. For example, Rule 4(d)(1) of the Federal Rules of Civil Procedure states in part:

> Service shall be made . . . upon an individual . . . by delivering a copy of the summons and of the complaint to him personally or by leaving copies at his dwelling house or usual place of abode with some person of suitable age and discretion then residing therein or by delivering a copy of the summons and of the complaint to an agent authorized by appointment or by law to receive service of process.

The last portion of this quotation, referring to "an agent authorized by appointment or by law to receive service," is relevant with respect to corporations, which in most jurisdictions are required to file with the secretary of state the name and address of a registered agent designated to receive service of process in the event such corporation is sued. If no agent is designated, then service must usually be made upon the secretary of state. Rule 4(d)(3) of the Federal Rules of Civil Procedure provides that service on a corporation may also be "to any other agent authorized by appointment or law to receive such process," and if a statute so requires, a copy should also be mailed directly to the defendant corporation. In addition, Rule 4(d)(7) permits service in "the manner prescribed by any statute of the United States or . . . by the law of the state." For example, a Texas statute allows service on the secretary of state, the assistant secretary of state, or on any clerk having charge of the corporation department of the secretary of state's office. Other provisions in this statute have been construed to allow service on a traveling

---

[7] United States v. Fore, 38 F. Supp. 142, 143 (S. D. Cal. 1941), as quoted in S. Gifis, *Law Dictionary* (Westbury, N.Y.: Barron's Educational Series, Inc., 1975), p. 164.

sales representative of a corporation while he or she is in the state, or on any other officer or local agent of that corporation.[8]

In cases in which jurisdiction over the person is required and the party cannot be located, Rule 4(d)(7) incorporates various methods of service other than *personal* service, such as by mail to a last known address, by publication in a newspaper, or by service upon a representative of the defendant. These methods are called *substitute* service. For example, substitute service is available if a statute allows service by mailing the summons to the defendant at his or her last known address or affixing the summons to the door of his or her place of business, dwelling house, or usual place of abode.[9] Some state statutes allow the court to prescribe a manner of substitute service if expressly authorized modes are impracticable. Such methods are able to withstand due process attacks, provided they are "reasonably calculated to give [the defendant] actual notice of the proceedings and an opportunity to be heard."[10]

Substitute service is commonly used if the defendant is not present in the jurisdiction and thus not subject to personal service, and if the subject of the litigation is property belonging to the defendant and located within the state. The court may make binding decisions regarding such property but may not hold the defendant personally liable in such cases. This is called *in rem* jurisdiction. In cases of *in rem* actions, service on the defendant may be had by personal service or the substitute methods of mailing or publication.

After having been properly served with a summons and complaint by Pope, and after having had an opportunity to ascertain the allegations Pope is making against him, Drake must now respond to the complaint in accordance with the rules of civil procedure. The first sentence of Rule 12 of the Federal Rules of Civil Procedure provides that "a defendant shall serve his answer within 20 days after the service of the summons and complaint upon him." (See Appendix C for a typical answer to a complaint such as Pope's.)

Rule 12 also lists a number of responses, other than an answer, that a defendant can make to a complaint. That is, a defendant isn't necessarily required to file an answer to the complaint; he or she may file other pleadings within the prescribed time period of twenty days. Such other pleadings must contain the reasons for the defendant's failure to file an answer. For example, if the defendant believes that the action should have been filed in the state court, and that the federal court does not have the jurisdiction to hear the particular type of action, the defendant can file a motion to dismiss based on lack of jurisdiction over the subject matter. This response can be made in a diversity of citizenship case in which the plaintiff believes that the defendant is a citizen of a jurisdiction other than that of the plaintiff, while in actuality both parties are citizens of the same jurisdiction, thereby precluding

---

[8] Vernon's Annotated Texas Statutes, Business Corporation Act, Article 8.10; See Harbich v. Hamilton-Brown Shoe Company, 1 F. Supp. 63 (S.D. Tex. 1932).

[9] See 2 *Moore's Federal Practice*, Paragraph 4.19.

[10] Milliken v. Meyer, 311 U.S. 457 (1940).

federal jurisdiction based on diversity of citizenship. If there is in fact a lack of diversity, then the federal district court will be forced to dismiss the case, and the plaintiff will have to refile the same action in a state district court if he or she wants to continue the suit.

Another motion often filed in response to a complaint is a motion to dismiss based on the plaintiff's failure to state a claim upon which relief can be granted. The theory of this motion is that, even if all the allegations in the plaintiff's complaint were admitted and deemed to be true, such allegations do not constitute a violation of the plaintiff's rights and therefore do not allow the plaintiff to recover anything from the defendant. The defendant contends, therefore, that the plaintiff has failed to state a claim upon which relief can be granted. This type of motion is listed in Rule 12(b)(6) of the Federal (and most state) Rules of Civil Procedure and is sometimes referred to simply as a 12(b)(6) motion. Appendix D contains Drake's motion to dismiss Pope's complaint under Rule 12(b)(6).

If any of these Rule 12 motions are filed instead of an answer, or if any other motions are filed prior to the defendant's answer, a hearing is scheduled at which the parties' attorneys can argue the legal principles behind and against such pleadings. The court must then determine whether it has jurisdiction in the case, or whether it should dismiss the complaint. If the court dismisses the complaint, it has the discretion to allow and almost always does allow the plaintiff to amend the complaint to cure the defect.

Assuming that in the present case Pope's complaint is not dismissed and Drake is required to file an answer to the complaint, Drake will state his version of the facts in his answer (as indicated in Appendix C), generally disputing the facts set forth in Pope's complaint and denying any liability on Drake's part. At this point, the parties having disagreed with each other's statement of the facts or the law or both, the allegations of the complaint are "put at issue," thereby setting the stage for the resolution of the dispute in the trial court.

D. Discovery

1. Theory and Purpose of Discovery

The term *discovery* means the procedure of obtaining facts by both parties prior to the actual trial. Before the adoption of the modern rules of civil procedure in 1938, the theory behind litigation was that many facts could remain concealed until the time of the trial; at trial such facts would be disclosed for the first time. Trials, therefore, were often filled with surprises, and the "sporting theory of justice" was the rule of the day.[11]

The theory of modern-day civil trials is that all significant facts should be brought out before the trial, and that both parties should be fully apprised of all aspects of the opponent's case. Indeed rules of civil procedure (state and federal) 26 through

---

[11] C. Wright, *Law of Federal Courts,* 2d ed. (St. Paul: West Publishing Co., 1970), p. 354n.5.

37 provide the mechanism by which the parties are entitled to discover these facts, and to ascertain the overall legal and factual bases for the claims and defenses made in the pleadings. These rules rest[12]

> on a basic philosophy that prior to trial every party to a civil action is entitled to the disclosure of all relevant information in the possession of any person, unless the information is privileged. No longer are civil trials to be "carried on in the dark." . . . Victory is intended to go to the party entitled to it, on all the facts, rather than to the side that best uses its wits.

Rule 26(b)(1) states:

> Parties may obtain discovery regarding any matter, not privileged, which is relevant to the subject matter involved in the pending action, whether it relates to the claim or defense of the party seeking discovery or to the claim or defense of any party, including the existence, description, nature, custody, condition and location of any books, documents or other tangible things and the identity and location of persons having knowledge of any discoverable matter.

Both parties use this right of discovery, commencing shortly after the filing of the complaint and usually continuing intermittently for several months until at least thirty days prior to trial, or as otherwise ordered by the court.

2. Methods of Discovery

There are five general methods of discovery available to all parties: depositions upon oral examination or written question, interrogatories, production of documents, physical and mental examination, and requests for admission. These methods complement each other and constitute an integrated mechanism for obtaining the facts of a controversy. They also promote the settlement of controversies prior to trial because discovery enables the parties to readily assess their chances of winning in the light of their respective legal theories and versions of the facts. Unless the action is of such a limited nature or involves such a small amount of damages that it doesn't warrant the expenditure of substantial attorney's fees resulting from extensive discovery, at least one of the five methods normally will be used by the parties in their trial preparation. Depositions upon oral examination and interrogatories are the two most frequently used methods of discovery. Because depositions upon written questions are used infrequently, they will not be discussed.

In the case of *Pope* v. *Drake,* the plaintiff would attempt to discover such things as the condition of Drake's vehicle at the time of the accident, Drake's speed, his physical condition at the time of the incident, including his eyesight, hearing, and so forth, his estimates of such matters as distances and speeds, and other relevant matters. Drake would want to discover similar information. Both Pope and Drake could use all five methods of discovery to obtain this information.

---

[12] Ibid., p. 354.

a. Depositions Upon Oral Examination

Rule 30 of the rules of civil procedure states in part that "after commencement of the action, any party may take the testimony of any person, including a party, by deposition upon oral examination." This most frequently used method of discovery simply involves one party, Drake for example, giving notice to Pope that the latter party's testimony is requested by the first party. Note, however, that under Rule 30 either Pope or Drake could request the deposition not only of each other but also of any person who is not a party to the action. The notice provides a date and location for the taking of the deposition. A subpoena must be served on a person whose deposition is to be taken if that person is not a party. If a corporation is involved, the discovery is obtained from persons who are authorized to speak on behalf of the corporate entity. During the actual taking of the deposition, the attorneys for both parties are present, as well as the party being deposed. Also present is a reporter who will record everything stated during the deposition by means of a special typewriter known as a stenographic recorder. (A reporter also records court proceedings to preserve all statements made at hearings and trials.)

After Pope has sworn to tell the truth, Drake's attorney will ask him a series of questions about the claims he made. For example, Drake's attorney would probably ask Pope very detailed and extensive questions about the matters mentioned previously, which may have a bearing on the legal or factual issues in the case. Depositions usually last for at least several hours. It is the only discovery method that allows examination and cross-examination of a witness by counsel prior to trial and is thus the most valuable of the five methods. Often the deponent's attorney, who is present at the deposition, will consult with the deponent before he gives an answer. The deponent's attorney may also state objections for the record but nevertheless will normally allow the deponent to answer the questions.

If the deponent refuses to answer a question and the deposing party believes that under the rules of procedure it must be answered, the latter can file a motion with the court requesting that the refusing party be required to answer. The court must then determine whether the party is required to answer the question. However, such determination by the court will occur after the conclusion of the deposition and will require a separate pretrial hearing and argument by the parties. It is unusual for a deponent to completely refuse to answer questions, because Rule 26(b)(1) states:

> It is not ground for objection that the information sought will be inadmissible at the trial if the information sought appears reasonably calculated to lead to the discovery of admissible evidence.

This indicates that information given during a deposition will not necessarily be admissible at the trial. Different standards of admissibility govern the evidence allowed at trial than those regulating the information obtainable during the discovery process. At trial the party providing the information is free to object to its admissibility for the first time on any basis that may exclude it. Another reason that all questions are usually answered is that the court generally requires the losing party to pay court costs in connection with all motions, including a motion requesting the court to order the deponent to answer questions posed during a deposition.

b. Interrogatories

Interrogatories, prescribed and authorized by Rule 33 of the Rules of Civil Procedure, are another commonly used method of discovery. The rule states in part:

> Any party may serve upon any other party written interrogatories to be answered by the party served . . . who shall furnish such information as is available to the party . . . .
> The party upon whom the interrogatories have been served shall serve a copy of the answers, and objections if any, within 30 days after service of the interrogatories . . .

Rule 33 is thus somewhat less flexible than Rule 30, since the former is restricted to parties to the action; interrogatories cannot be served on potential witnesses or any other persons not parties to the litigation. Under Rule 33, either before or after the taking of a deposition, any party may serve upon any other party written questions about various aspects of the case, the answers to which could be helpful at trial. Like depositions, the questions usually seek information about the plaintiff's allegations in the complaint or about any defenses to the plaintiff's claims. There may be a few interrogatories or there may be hundreds, depending upon the complexity of the litigation. Further, it is not unusual for a party to serve a second set of interrogatories to answer questions raised by the answers to the first set of interrogatories. A party may use the various discovery methods in any order or combination he wishes. (See Appendix E for Pope's interrogatories to Drake.)

c. Production of Documents

Most cases, particularly business related ones, involve a number of documents prepared by both parties. For example, documents may relate to the performance of a contract that one party believes the other party has breached. Consider a hypothetical situation: A subcontractor in a housing development claims that the general contractor has not paid all the money to which the subcontractor believes he or she is entitled under the terms of the contract. The subcontractor therefore sues the contractor. As a critical part of his or her discovery prior to trial, the defendant general contractor seeks to examine all the invoices that the subcontractor alleges were submitted to the contractor under the terms of the contract. The contractor could, of course, serve interrogatories upon the subcontractor and ask him or her to list the number and amounts of all invoices, or the contractor could depose the subcontractor and obtain a record of the subcontractor's invoices in that way. However, it would be much less expensive and more accurate, and would result in more information from the subcontractor, if the general contractor were shown all the allegedly unpaid invoices.

The method by which the contractor would obtain the invoices would be by requesting the production of documents pursuant to Rule 34 of the Rules of Civil Procedure. The Rule states in part:

> Any party may serve on any other party a request to produce and permit the party making the request . . . to inspect and copy any designated documents . . . or to inspect and copy, test, or sample any tangible things which constitute or contain matters within the scope of Rule 26(b) and which are in the possession, custody or control of the party upon which the request is served . . . .
>
> The party upon whom the request is served shall serve a written response within 30 days after the service of the request.

Like interrogatories, the use of Rule 34 is limited to discoverable material in the possession of parties only. In the example given earlier, the general contractor would have an opportunity to examine all invoices submitted by the subcontractor and to view the subcontractor's books and records, bank deposits, and any other relevant documents that may have a bearing on the question of the general contractor's liability.

Conversely, under Rule 34 the subcontractor would have an opportunity to obtain the canceled checks that the general contractor stated, in answer to the complaint, were sent to the subcontractor, cashed, and deposited by him as full payment for the subcontractor's services.

Thus each party would have an opportunity to learn all the facts prior to the trial. As stated earlier, in many cases during the discovery process the parties decide that a trial would be a waste of time and expense; they can thus reach a settlement much more easily under these completely open and straightforward rules of discovery. During discovery the parties can ascertain the strengths and weaknesses of their respective cases and are thus much better able to anticipate what a judge or jury would decide if the case were to go to trial.

In the *Pope* case Drake may use Rule 34 to obtain medical reports, copies of bills for medical supplies, and any other documents representing expenses that the plaintiff claims were caused by the defendant's alleged negligence.

d. Physical and Mental Examination

In personal injury cases it is very common for the parties to dispute the true condition of the plaintiff. To resolve such a dispute and provide evidence to the court and the jury about that physical condition, the defendant may obtain a physical examination of the plaintiff by a physician other than the plaintiff's physician. Prior to the adoption of the Federal Rules of Civil Procedure, a federal court could not order such an examination unless express authorization was granted by the laws of the state in which the federal district court was located. Now, however, the court may order such an examination through the provisions of Rule 35, which states in part:

> When the mental or physical condition (including the blood group) of a party, or of a person in the custody or under the legal control of a party, is in controversy,

the court in which the action is pending may order the party to submit to a physical or mental examination by a physician. . . .

Usually, after both parties' physicians have examined the plaintiff, the extent of the plaintiff's injuries is still in dispute. The respective parties' physicians usually present conflicting testimony on this subject, and the court or the jury must determine which party's expert witnesses are more accurate in their evaluation of the seriousness and extent of the injuries. For example, Pope's physician may believe that the plaintiff is permanently disabled and will never be able to resume a normal life, while Drake's physician may testify that it will take only six months before Pope is able to resume his normal physical functions. The jury's decision on this question will directly affect the amount of damages the plaintiff is awarded. If he is permanently disabled, he may be entitled to damages equal to his potential earnings for the rest of his life; but if he is only temporarily incapacitated, his recoverable damages will be significantly less.

e. Requests for Admission

The last method of discovery, contained in Rule 36, is used by the parties to establish the authenticity of documents that may be significant during the course of the trial and to force a party to admit the truth of certain statements that may also be important during the course of the trial. The effect of admitting the authenticity of any document or the truth of any matter is that it is conclusively established for the purposes of the trial.

In certain respects, Requests for Admission are similar to interrogatories in that the requesting party is asking a question, namely whether the other party admits that a statement is true or that a document is authentic. The responding party either admits or denies the truth or authenticity. However, unlike interrogatories, under Requests for Admission the matters inquired into are deemed admitted automatically unless, within thirty days after service of the request, the party to whom the Requests are directed serves upon the party requesting the admission a written answer or objection. The court, however, may void the admission if the response is untimely, or it may permit the admission to be amended or withdrawn.

In one sense, Rule 36 is not actually a discovery procedure, because it presupposes that the party requesting the admissions already knows the facts or has the document and is only seeking to obtain confirmation of the truth or authenticity from his opponent. Thus the purpose of the rule is to expedite the trial and to relieve the parties of the cost of proving facts that will not be disputed at trial, the truth of which can be ascertained by reasonable inquiry.[13]

3. Sanctions

The success of any of the rules of discovery depends on their enforceability and on the answering party responding specifically enough and within the time

---

[13] Ibid., p. 393.

prescribed. The court is not directly involved in the course of discovery. Depositions are generally taken in lawyers' offices out of the presence of the court; interrogatories are sent directly from one party to another; and the other discovery methods are also accomplished outside of any formal court proceeding presided over by a judge. However, because the case has begun and all of the parties' conduct that occurs after commencement of the case is within the jurisdiction of the court, if any disputes arise during the course of discovery, the court has the authority to determine which party should prevail.

Disputes arising from the discovery process are governed by Rule 37 of the rules of civil procedure, entitled "Failure to Make Discovery: Sanctions." For example, assume that a number of interrogatories were served upon Drake, most of which he answered. He refused, however, to answer those requesting information about his past driving record, and he gave no reason for this refusal. In such a case Pope would look to Rule 37, part of which provides:

> If a party fails to answer an interrogatory submitted under Rule 33, the discovering party may move for an order compelling an answer. . .
>
> If the motion is granted, the court shall, after opportunity for hearing, require the party or deponent whose conduct necessitated the motion or both of them to pay to the moving party the reasonable expenses incurred in obtaining the order . . .

In the example given, if a hearing were held on Pope's motion for sanctions under Rule 37, Drake would be ordered to answer the interrogatories about his past driving record. In addition Drake may be forced to pay the expenses that Pope incurred in connection with preparing the written motion under Rule 37 and all directly related expenses.

Rule 37 further provides sanctions in the event that the party fails to comply with an order that has already been obtained under Rule 37. These sanctions include: contempt of court, allowing the court to refuse to allow the disobedient party to support or oppose designated claims or defenses, and prohibiting him or her from introducing designated matters in evidence. If the disobedient party continues to ignore court orders and fails to comply with valid requests for discovery by the other party, the court may even order final judgment in favor of the requesting party and against the disobedient party.

4. Protective Orders

The rules not only provide ways to enforce discovery sought but also provide ample protection against a party using discovery to oppress his or her opponent. Rule 26(c) provides that:

> Upon motion by a party or by the person from whom discovery is sought, and for good cause shown, the court in which the action is pending . . . may make any order which justice requires to protect the party or person from annoyance, embarrassment, oppression or undue burden or expense . . .

In addition to this general statement, the rule also specifies eight particular types of protective orders that a court may make: (1) that the discovery not be answered at all, although in view of the philosophy of complete and open discovery embodied in the rules of civil procedure, this type of motion for relief is usually denied;[14] (2) that discovery be answered only on specified terms and conditions and at a designated time and place; (3) that the discovery be answered by a different method; (4) that certain matters not be inquired into, or that the scope of the discovery be limited to certain matters; (5) that discovery be conducted with no one present except persons designated by the court; (6) that a deposition, after being sealed, shall be opened only by order of the court; (7) that a trade secret or other confidential research, development, or commercial information not be disclosed or disclosed only in a designated way; or (8) that the parties simultaneously file specified documents or information enclosed in sealed envelopes, to be opened as directed by the court.

These eight specific provisions illustrate the general power of the court to protect the party responding to discovery. Because it is impossible to set out in a rule all circumstances that could arise, the rule only provides limited suggestions that are not meant to preclude any other orders that the court may deem appropriate under the circumstances.[15]

E. Motion for Summary Judgment

As mentioned earlier, it is not unusual for motions to be made to the court prior to the actual commencement of the trial. For example, the defendant may file a motion to dismiss the plaintiff's complaint soon after that complaint is filed, or either party may file a motion for sanctions under Rule 37 as a result of the other party's failure to respond to interrogatories, requests for admission, or other methods of discovery. In response, the court will set a date for a hearing on the motion, and the respective attorneys will present legal arguments on behalf of their clients' position. The court will then rule on the motion in favor of one party or the other. (Juries are never empaneled for such pretrial motions.)

Another pretrial motion common in civil actions is the motion for summary judgment, as provided for in Rule 56 of the Rules of Civil Procedure (state and federal). The theory of the motion is that there is no need to proceed to trial when the parties are not in disagreement over the facts. Because the purpose of all trials is to introduce evidence and to allow the jury or the judge to view and examine the evidence, listen to the testimony of the witnesses, and decide which party's assertions are more accurate and truthful, this evidence consists solely of facts and doesn't include legal issues. If the parties agree on the *facts* of the dispute, and simply disagree on the applicable *legal* principles there is no need for testimony or any other type of evidence.

---

[14] See W. Barron and A. Holtzoff (Wright, ed.) 2A *Civil Practice and Procedure* (St. Paul: West Publishing Co., 1960) Section 715.1, notes 87–94; Wright, p. 370.

[15] See Wright, p. 372.

Rule 56 has been interpreted by literally thousands of cases over the years. Its purpose has been stated so many times that there is a consensus about the intent and function of the rule. Because a motion for summary judgment is an extraordinary type of proceeding, the courts have been particularly reluctant to grant it. Rule 56 and the cases decided under it clearly establish the principle that the motion should be granted only when the party making the motion has established the absence of any genuine disagreement between the parties over the facts.[16] In accord with the statements in the rule itself and their purpose and intent, the courts have been careful to limit the granting of the motion to special situations in which they have reviewed all factual inferences introduced by the parties in the light most favorable to the party opposing the motion.[17] Thus the purpose of Rule 56 is expeditious disposal of cases in which the pleadings do not present any material factual issues. However, the rule must be cautiously applied and never used to deprive a litigant of a determination of whether such issues exist.[18]

In many instances one party will move for summary judgment under Rule 56 because the party believes that there is no dispute over the facts and therefore no need for a trial. However, the other party may want a trial, either because he or she believes that the facts are in dispute or because he or she believes that a jury would be more likely to rule in the party's favor than a judge would be. Thus the second party will oppose the motion for summary judgment filed by the first party. At that time there will be a hearing on whether one or more material facts are in dispute; the court, not the parties, will resolve that question.

If the parties disagree merely on the insignificant facts of the case, the court may still grant a motion for summary judgment. Also, if the parties agree that the defendant is liable, but disagree on the amount of damage caused by the defendant's wrongful or negligent activities, the court may grant a motion for *partial* summary judgment on the issue of liability alone and order a separate trial dealing solely with the question of the amount of damages. Rule 56(c) states:

> The judgment sought shall be rendered forthwith if the pleadings, depositions, answers to interrogatories, and admissions on file, together with the affidavits, if any, show that there is no genuine issue as to any material fact and that the moving party is entitled to a judgment as a matter of law. A summary judgment . . . may be rendered on the issue of liability alone although there is a genuine issue as to the amount of damages.

If one party seeks summary judgment and the other party opposes it, the court examines the file containing the complaint and the answer, the results of discovery efforts by both parties, and any supporting affidavits that have been filed in favor of

---

[16] See, e.g., Dzenits v. Merrill Lynch, Pierce, Fenner & Smith, Inc., 494 F.2d 168 (10th Cir. 1974); James v. Atchison, Topeka and Santa Fe Railway Co., 464 F.2d 173 (10th Cir. 1972); Bowlds v. Smith, 144 Ohio App. 21, 180 N.E.2d 184 (1961).

[17] See, e.g., Mustang Fuel Corp. v. Youngstown Sheet and Tube Co., 516 F.2d 33 (10th Cir. 1935); Harman v. Diversified Medical Investments Corporation, 488 F.2d 111 (10th Cir. 1973); Bowlds v. Smith, 114 Ohio App. 21, 180 N.E.2d 184 (1961).

[18] See Avrick v. Rockmont Envelope Co., 155 F.2d 568 (10th Cir. 1946).

or in opposition to the motion for summary judgment. The court may also allow or require oral argument on the motion. The court must then determine whether there really is a dispute over the facts, but it cannot try any facts at the hearing on the motion. The court can consider only whether there are any factual issues to be tried. If there is no dispute over the facts the court *must* apply the applicable legal principles and determine whether "the moving party is entitled to a judgment as a *matter of law*." If depositions or other results of discovery indicate no dispute, contradictions of material facts in the defendant's answer to the complaint will not be sufficient to defeat the plaintiff's motion for summary judgment.

F. Trial

1. The Jury System[19]

a. Constitutional and Statutory Requirements

The Sixth Amendment of the United States Constitution provides that "in all *criminal* prosecutions, the accused shall enjoy the right to a speedy and public trial, by an impartial jury." With respect to *civil* cases in federal court, the Seventh Amendment states: "In suits at common law, where the value in controversy shall exceed twenty dollars, the right of trial by jury shall be preserved. . . ." Rule 38(a) of the Federal Rules of Civil Procedure incorporates this guarantee where it states that "the right of trial by jury as declared by the Seventh Amendment to the Constitution or as given by a statute of the United States shall be preserved to the parties inviolate."

In all *criminal* cases, all states except Louisiana provide a right to trial by jury in their constitution.[20] The Colorado Constitution provides that the right to jury "shall remain inviolate in criminal cases." [21] The Kentucky Constitution provides that "the ancient mode of trial by jury shall be held sacred and the right thereof remain inviolate subject to such modification as may be authorized by this Constitution." The state constitutions of Georgia and West Virginia contain similar provisions.[22] Minnesota provides that the right shall remain inviolate, shall extend to all cases at law without regard to the amount in controversy, and may be waived by agreement of both parties.[23] The Ohio Constitution similarly provides that the right to jury in

---

[19] The jury in this discussion is called a *petit* jury as opposed to a grand jury, as in criminal investigation procedures and indictments. See Chapter 12, Part F.

[20] The reason for the Louisiana exception is not that it is less conscious of its criminal defendants than other states, but because of its unique judicial heritage of French civil law legal principles, rather than English common law as in all other states. (See Chapter 1, pp. 7–9.) Under the French system the jury was not as important an institution as it was in England. M. Bloomstein, *Verdict: The Jury System* (New York: Dodd, Mead & Co., 1969), p. 28.

[21] Constitution of Colorado, Article II, section 23.

[22] Constitution of Kentucky, Section 7; see *Constitutions of the United States, National and State*, 5 vols. (Dobbs Ferry, N.Y.: Oceana Publishing Co., 1974).

[23] Constitution of Minnesota, Article I, section 4.

criminal cases "shall be inviolate." (Ohio, however, specifically states that this right shall not be guaranteed in civil cases.) Ohio is also unusual in allowing a verdict of three-fourths of the jurors rather than requiring a unanimous agreement. Oregon guarantees the right to jury not only in criminal cases but also in civil cases. In Utah the guarantee of a jury remains inviolate only in capital cases, and the constitution of Utah provides that such guarantee may "be made available" in other types of cases. In Utah civil cases don't require a jury unless one of the parties demands it.[24]

There are several constitutions that deal specifically with a right to jury in *civil* cases also. For example, Alaska provides for a jury in civil cases in which the amount of damages asked exceeds $250; in Hawaii the amount in dispute must exceed $100; in Oregon and West Virginia, $20. New Hampshire has the same limit as Hawaii as to the minimum amount of the claim, but grants no right to a jury where the title to real estate is involved in the controversy. In Georgia one of the parties in civil cases must demand a jury. Unlike New Hampshire, the states of Maine, Virginia, and North Carolina guarantee the right to jury in civil cases where property is concerned. In Indiana the right to a jury in civil cases "shall remain inviolate." [25]

These statements about juries in civil cases pertain only to guarantees in the state constitutions, not to state statutes. With some exceptions, states generally do not have statutes specifically providing for the right to jury trial in civil cases; most of them rely on their constitutional provisions. In Louisiana the right to a jury trial in civil cases, according to the state statute, depends on the nature and amount of the principal demand, and no such right exists if the claim is for less than $1,000. Louisiana also provides that there is no right to a jury trial in suits on unconditional obligations to pay a specific sum of money, unless the defendant's argument is based on forgery, fraud, error, or lack of consideration.[26]

As a general rule, the right to a jury trial in civil cases is not available in divorce, paternity, custody and related domestic matters, probate, admiralty, court-martial, and special summary proceedings.[27] The constitutional guarantees of the rights to jury and due process do not require a jury in these types of cases because of the belief that the individual's right to a fair trial does not rest on the availability of a jury of peers. Also speed of trial is an important consideration in such cases and generally outweighs the benefits of a jury.

It is interesting that the main body of the Constitution as passed (without the Bill of Rights) contained no mention of a guaranteed right to trial by jury in civil or

---

[24] Constitution of Oregon, Article I, section 1, 17; Constitution of Utah, Article I, section 10.

[25] Constitution of Alaska, Article I, section 16; Constitution of Georgia, Article VI, section 4, subsections 7, 8; Constitution of Hawaii, Article I, section 10; Constitution of New Hampshire, Article I, section 20; Constitution of Indiana, Article I, section 20; Constitution of Maine, Article I, section 20; Constitution of Virginia, Article I, section 11; Constitution of North Carolina, Article I, section 19; Constitution of Oregon, Article I, section 17; Constitution of West Virginia, Article III, section 13.

[26] Louisiana, CCP section 1731, et seq. See also South Dakota Statutes Annotated, Section 15–6–38(a), Section 15–6–39(a).

[27] 47 *AmJur* 2d, "Jury," section 41.

criminal cases. In Federalist Paper No. 83, Hamilton suggested one reason for this:[28]

> [T]here is a material diversity . . . in the extent of the institution of trial by jury in civil cases, in the several states. . . . [N]o general rule could have been fixed upon by the convention which would have corresponded with the circumstances of all the States; and . . . more or at least as much might have been hazarded by taking the system of any one State for a standard, as by omitting a provision altogether and leaving the matter as it has been left, to legislative regulations.

Although the state and federal constitutions address the right to trial by jury, they do not detail the respective functions of the judge and jury. This description was not necessary, because the traditional roles of the judge and the jury in the Anglo-American legal system at the time of the adoption of the United States Constitution were presumed to apply to both the state judicial systems and the newly formed federal government. Traditionally, the judge is responsible for ruling on the applicable *legal* principles on such questions as admissibility of evidence and which party has the burden of proof. The jury, on the other hand, is strictly responsible for determining which side presented the more sound interpretation of the *facts* and which side is telling the truth concerning disputed facts.

b. History of the Jury System

The jury system is literally thousands of years old. The jury existed at least as early as ancient Greece, in the seventh century B.C.[29] At that time juries were called "decuries," and were chosen by lot; they rendered decisions on both the facts and the law without an appeal available to either party. Quite different from the juries that now usually consist of twelve people, the decuries had 200 to 500 members, with up to 2,000 persons acting as jurors in the more important trials. In ancient Rome the government established a trial system that used *judices* (judges); the system used no real judges, but rather lawyers who acted somewhat as judges do in establishing the guidelines for the trial procedure. The judices were abolished in A.D. 352.

In early Germany groups of landholders were formed to help the courts make decisions. These groups usually consisted of seven people, or twelve for the more important cases. Germany was the first nation to seclude juries during their deliberations.[30] In the year A.D. 788, during the reign of Charlemagne, the Franks established the *inquisitio*. This system, under which the parties were interrogated during the "trial," became widespread in the Norman provinces during that period.[31]

The Saxons had used the *oath of compurgation* as a substitute for the jury in the

---

[28] *The Federalist Papers* (New York: The New American Library, Inc., 1961), p. 503.
[29] L. Moore, *The Jury* (Cincinnati: W. H. Anderson Co., 1973), p. 2.
[30] M. Bloomstein, *Verdict: The Jury System* (New York: Dodd, Mead & Co., 1968), pp. 3–7.
[31] Moore, pp. 13–17.

ninth and tenth centuries.[32] Under this method of oath taking, the plaintiff swore his innocence in response to interrogation. Both parties were then supported by *compurgators,* who swore not to the facts but to the principal's truthfulness.[33] The English jury system began to take on some of its contemporary aspects after the invasion in 1066 of William the Conqueror, who came from France's Norman provinces.

By the twelfth century the oath of compurgation had been discarded and juries had begun to come into use. The early jury was a body of neighbors called the *assize,* who decided facts disputed by the parties. They were expected to be familiar with the facts; thus in effect they were not only regarded as the persons to decide disputed facts but also as witnesses in a sense. However, by 1350 the functions of the juror and the witness were becoming distinct from each other. During this period the Crown had a significant influence on juries, unlike the more independent juries of modern times. The main form of control over juries at that time was the action of *attaint* under which jurors were held subject to fine and imprisonment for a wrongful verdict. The process of attaint continued until about 1670.[34]

During early American colonial times it was often difficult to find twelve persons who were fit to serve on a jury; thus a smaller number of people was sometimes used. In 1765 Blackstone's *Commentaries on the Common Law* appeared in England, and his comments on the jury system led to enthusiasm for the institution of the jury system in the American colonies.[35] However, at the time of the American Revolution, jurors in most of the colonies were still deciding law rather than confining themselves to determining facts. Soon afterwards the modern jury system was incorporated into various state constitutions and the federal Constitution, guaranteeing the right to trial by jury in criminal cases and in most civil cases, as described earlier.[36]

c. Number of Jurors

Juries have historically consisted of twelve persons. We can only speculate on the reason for this number. It may have been the traditional number used in the Saxon compurgation process, even though that process also used other numbers, such as 6, 9, 36, 40, and 66. An English publication dated 1682 suggested that the number was based on the Biblical twelve prophets and twelve apostles.[37] But the most accurate answer may be, as United States Supreme Court Justice Byron White stated in the case of *Williams* v. *Florida,* that the number twelve was a "historical accident." [38]

---

[32] Bloomstein, p. 9; W. Holdsworth, *A History of English Law,* vol. I (London: Methuen Co., 1903), p. 312.
[33] Moore, p. 29.
[34] Holdsworth, pp. 317, 323, 325–26; Bloomstein, p. 16; Moore, p. 43.
[35] Bloomstein, pp. 21, 24.
[36] Moore, pp. 107, 143.
[37] Ibid., pp. 91, 107.
[38] Williams v. Florida, 399 U.S. 78, 102 (1970).

The trend in recent years among the states has been to permit the establishment of juries of fewer than twelve people. As of 1976, twenty-six states allowed juries of fewer than twelve.[39] Most states provide the required number of jurors in their state constitutions rather than by statute. If the state constitution permits the legislature to establish juries of fewer than twelve, or if the constitution does not specify the number, smaller juries are commonly authorized in cases that involve small amounts of money, or in hearings in less important courts (such as courts in which no record of the trial proceeding is kept, or courts that are inferior to the general trial courts in each jurisdiction).

California's constitution provides that both in civil and criminal matters there must be twelve jurors, although the parties may stipulate a lesser number. In Colorado, the constitution states that there will be twelve jurors or "as prescribed by law," thus permitting the state legislature to allow for fewer than twelve. The Alaska constitution provides for twelve people but also states that six to twelve may be authorized by statute in courts that are not "of record" (that is, courts that do not preserve a record of the proceedings). The Georgia constitution provides for a minimum of five jurors in courts other than general trial courts and municipal courts. Idaho specifies that there must be twelve jurors, unless the parties agree to a lesser number, but further specifies that there may be only six if the amount in controversy is less than $500.[40]

There is a significant variation in the number of jurors among the states whose constitutions allow for the state statutes to prescribe the number of jurors. For example, Oregon statutes now provide for a jury of six in the circuit courts. In Georgia and Louisiana the state statutes merely provide that the parties may stipulate a number of jurors fewer than twelve.[41]

There is no federal statute prescribing the number of jurors. The only federal provision is in Rule 48 of the Federal Rules of Civil Procedure, which states that the parties may stipulate that the jury will consist of fewer than twelve. Neither the federal statutes nor the federal Constitution provides for smaller juries in any specific situation. Early United States Supreme Court cases, though not dealing specifically with the number of jurors required in federal cases, addressed related questions. These cases defined *trial by jury* as a trial by jury as understood and applied by common law at the time the United States Constitution was adopted, including the stipulation that the jury consist of twelve persons, and no more or fewer. These common law features of the jury system were regarded as embedded in the

---

[39] Alaska, Arizona, Colorado, Georgia, Iowa, Michigan, Missouri, Nebraska, New Jersey, New Mexico, North Dakota, Oklahoma, South Carolina, South Dakota, Utah, Washington, Wyoming, California, Florida, Idaho, Illinois, Kentucky, Montana, Texas, Virginia, West Virginia. Bloomstein, p. 32.

[40] Constitution of California, Article I, section 7; Constitution of Colorado, Article II, section 23; Constitution of Alaska, Article I, section 16; Constitution of Georgia, Article VI, section 16, subsection 1; Constitution of Idaho, Article 1, section 7.

[41] Oregon Statutes, sections 46.175, 46.180, 5.110, 17.105; Georgia Statutes, section 81A147; Louisiana CCP section 1761.

Constitution and thus beyond the authority of Congress to change.[42] However, the more recent case of *Williams* v. *Florida* contains language indicating that the Supreme Court may be relaxing its position on the number of jurors required in federal cases.[43] The case deals with the number of jurors considered constitutional under the *state* constitutions, but its language indicates what the court might say if the specific question of the number of jurors required under the *federal* Constitution were presented to the Supreme Court. For example, Justice White stated that:[44]

> The performance of [the jury's] role is not a function of the particular number of the body which makes up the jury. . . . [W]e find little reason to think that these goals are in any meaningful sense less likely to be achieved when the jury number is six, than when it numbers twelve—particularly if the requirement of unanimity is retained. And, certainly the reliability of the jury as a fact-finder hardly seems likely to be a function of its size.
>
> . . . [N]either currently available evidence nor theory suggests that the twelve-man jury is necessarily more advantageous to the defendant than a jury composed of fewer members.

d. Value of the Jury System

The jury system in the American legal process has sometimes been the subject of controversy, but it has stood firm against being eliminated. The system has acquired strength through tradition, and it withstands criticism because of the widespread belief that it submits the administration of the law to community scrutiny and also provides a mechanism for the mitigation of legal doctrines that are often too harsh if implemented by a judge alone. Because it submits the legal system to community scrutiny, the jury system enables the community to keep in much closer contact with the entire legal system. On the other hand, some argue that judges are equally or more capable of evaluating facts than are juries, that juries are inconsistent in their application and understanding of legal principles, and that trial by jury is cumbersome, overly time-consuming, and extremely expensive.

In weighing the arguments for and against a constitutional guarantee of trial by jury, Hamilton stated:[45]

> The strongest argument in its favor is that it is a security against corruption. As there is always more time and better opportunity to tamper with a standing body of magistrates than with a jury summoned for the occasion, there is room to suppose a corrupt influence would more easily find its way to the former than to the latter. . . . As matters now stand, it would be necessary to corrupt both the court and jury; for where the jury have gone evidently wrong, the court would generally grant a new trial, and it would be in most cases of little use to practice upon the jury unless the court could be likewise gained. Here then is a double security; and

---

[42] Patton v. United States, 281 U.S. 276, 288, 290 (1930).
[43] Williams v. Florida, 399 U.S. 78 (1970).
[44] 399 U.S. at 102.
[45] *The Federalist Papers,* No. 83, p. 500.

it will readily be perceived that this complicated agency tends to preserve the purity of both institutions. By increasing the obstacles to success, it discourages attempts to seduce the integrity of either.

2. Role of the Judge

As stated above, in jury trials in the American legal system the judge's role is to rule on the law, while the jury's role is to find the facts. But more often than not there is no jury in a trial, and the judge must not only rule on the legal questions but also find the facts. Of all cases that go to trial, the majority are tried to a judge rather than to a jury, either because no right to jury trial exists or because the parties have waived such a right. Non-jury cases generally have fewer procedural and evidentiary problems than do cases in which a jury is present. For example, many of the rules of evidence are the product of the jury system and have been devised in an effort to prevent juries from misinterpreting or giving overdue weight to certain types of evidence. In the *Pope* v. *Drake* case, for example, Pope might try to produce testimony that Drake had been at a New Year's Eve party shortly before the accident. Based on that evidence, a jury might assume that Drake had been drinking and perhaps was drunk. A judge would give no weight to such testimony, unless evidence of actual intoxication were introduced. Further, rules designed to protect certain confidentialities or privileges, though applied equally in nonjury cases, as a practical matter simply need not be as rigidly applied in nonjury cases as in jury cases. Indeed certain rules of civil procedure tend to reduce the number of situations in nonjury cases in which the judge rules to exclude evidence that has been challenged under one of the exclusionary rules. This difference in attitude is largely a result of the trial judge's appreciation of the view that the appellate court takes of the lower court proceedings:[46]

> In the trial of a non-jury case, it is virtually impossible for a trial court to commit reversible error by receiving incompetent evidence, whether objected to or not. . . . On the other hand, a trial judge, who, in the trial of a non-jury case, attempts to make strict rulings on the admissibility of evidence, can easily get his decision reversed by excluding evidence which is objected to but which, on review, the appellate court believes should have been admitted.

In all trials, with or without a jury, the judge has a substantial amount of control over the proceedings. The control is even greater in the federal courts, particularly because federal judges have the power to comment on the evidence, a power not present in most state judicial systems. Among the powers that judges possess, either under the rules of civil procedure or at common law, are the powers to order separate trials of issues, to order a joint trial of two separate actions or consolidation thereof, to take a voluntary dismissal, or nonsuit by the plaintiff, and to dismiss the case involuntarily for want of prosecution by the plaintiff, or for failure of the plaintiff to comply with the rules of civil procedure or with an order of the court.

---

[46] Builders Steel Co. v. Commissioner, 179 F.2d 377, 379 (8th Cir. 1950).

3. Rules of Evidence

The law of evidence is the study of the legal regulation of proof and persuasion at trial, the means by which alleged matters of fact are established or disproved. In a trial the evidence presented to the court and the jury is the sole means by which each party presents his or her case. Therefore, the ability to introduce such evidence is critical to both parties. Often the parties cannot introduce all the evidence that they want to because of prejudice, irrelevance of the information, unreliability, or other reasons. In 1974 the Congress and Supreme Court made effective a body of rules of evidence now used in all federal district court trials. The majority of state courts still follow the common law or case law decisions regarding the admissibility of evidence and other evidentiary matters.

In either case there are specific guidelines that a judge is required to follow in determining whether evidence is admissible (that is, allowed to be presented to and considered by the trier of fact) and what may be done or stated by the attorneys or judge concerning that evidence. The first requisite for evidence to be admissible is that it must be relevant to something at issue under the applicable substantive law. Evidence is relevant if a reasonable fact finder would feel that it renders a fact at issue more probable than it appeared before the introduction of that evidence.

Although relevancy is a requisite to admissibility, there are counterbalancing considerations that may outweigh such evidence and make it inadmissible. The question of admissibility is controlled by exclusionary rules that have been devised to prevent juries from giving evidence more weight or effect than it deserves. That is, it has been felt that juries could not be trusted to give certain evidence its logical, rational weight or to perceive that it had none. The test applied under exclusionary rules is whether the jury is likely to overinflate such evidence to the extent that a fair decision in the trial would be more likely without the evidence. One type of evidence to which juries are likely to give too much weight is *prejudicial* evidence. The amount of prejudice is one of the factors that must be balanced against the relevancy or probative nature of the evidence. One example of evidence that is prejudicial because of the tremendous emotional impact that it may have is introduction of a mutilated body in a murder case (though such evidence is conclusive proof of death). Another example is the introduction of the previous convictions of a criminal defendant, though this type of evidence may tend to prove that he or she is the type of person who breaks the law. In civil cases a court will not permit the introduction of horribly gruesome and bloody pictures of the plaintiff, if the relevant facts to be proved can be supported by alternative proof that is equally available and not prejudicial.

Considerations in addition to prejudice that must be balanced against relevancy include surprise, consumption of time, and confusion of the judge or jury. However, even if a judge is very careful in excluding any evidence, the probative value of which is outweighed by any of these factors, certain evidence that should have been excluded does sometimes erroneously come before the jury. In such cases the judge will either order a mistrial or will instruct the jurors to disregard that evidence. But even when jurors are ordered to disregard a piece of evidence, it is only human nature to be influenced by it, anyway, probably to a greater extent than if it had not come before them in the first place. For example, suppose a jury in a criminal case is instructed to disregard a confession because it was involuntary. Suppose further that the jury knows that the gun was found where the confession states that the defendant buried it. In such a case the effect of the instruction to disregard such evidence will be minimal. Therefore, the only proper course of action for the judge to take would be to order a mistrial.[47]

A term commonly heard in the context of evidence is *hearsay*. The basic evidentiary principle relating to hearsay is called *the hearsay rule*. It provides that evidence of a statement offered to prove the *truth* of the matter stated, but which was made by someone other than a witness testifying at the hearing, is hearsay evidence and inadmissible. The typical situation to which the hearsay rule applies involves the testimony of a witness who attempts to report what he or she heard another person state out of court, if such other person's statement is offered as evidence to establish the truth of that statement. In this case such witness's testimony would be inadmissible in the absence of an applicable exception to the rule. The basic theory and rationale of the rule is that if a statement is made out of court, without the benefit of cross-examination and without the declarant's demeanor being exposed to the judge or jury, the statement should not be admitted as evidence. The adversary system of justice relies on courtroom confrontation, cross-examination, the open display of the witness on the stand, the oath, and the possibility of penalty for perjury and contempt to establish the truth in a case.

There are numerous exceptions to the hearsay rule. They are divided into two types—apparent exceptions and real exceptions. Apparent exceptions allow the introduction of an out-of-court statement, not to show the truth of that statement but for some other purpose, such as to show what the *state of mind* of the declarant was at the time he or she made the statement. For example, a witness may be permitted to testify that he or she heard the store manager instruct an employee to mop up a wet spot in the store an hour before the plaintiff in the case slipped and injured himself or herself on the wet spot, thus indicating that the defendant store knew of a dangerous condition and failed to correct it within a reasonable time. The credibility of the out-of-court statement is *not* the issue in this example. Whether the floor was actually wet or not may be proved by other means, such as the testimony of the plaintiff.

The preceding example was an apparent exception to the hearsay rule, because the statement was introduced for a purpose other than to show the truth of the statement. There are many *real* exceptions to the hearsay rule in which the out-of-court declaration is admitted, even though its purpose *is* to prove the truth of the statement. For example, official written statements, such as police reports, are admissible under the *business records exception* to the rule. Such exceptions are based

---

[47] See P. Rothstein, *Evidence in a Nutshell* (St. Paul: West Publishing Company, 1970).

upon the special necessity for and the special truthworthiness of the particular hear-say evidence embraced by the exception.

As the case of *Dallas County* v. *Commercial Union Assurance Co., Ltd.* illus-trates, admission of an out-of-court statement for the purpose of proving the truth of such statement may be justified by the rationale behind the exceptions to the rule while not expressly relying on such exceptions. In this case the court found, in effect, that the hearsay rule was not applicable.

DALLAS COUNTY
v.
COMMERCIAL UNION ASSURANCE COMPANY, LTD.

286 F.2d 388 (1961)

United States Court of Appeals, Fifth Circuit

WISDOM, Circuit Judge.

This appeal presents a single question—the admissibility in evidence of a newspaper to show that the Dallas County Courthouse in Selma, Alabama, was damaged by fire in 1901. We hold that the newspaper was admissible, and affirm the judgment below.

On a bright, sunny morning, July 7, 1957, the clock tower of the Dallas County Courthouse at Selma, Alabama, commenced to lean, made loud cracking and popping noises, then fell, and telescoped into the courtroom. Fortunately, the collapse of the tower took place on a Sunday morning; no one was injured, but damage to the courthouse exceeded $100,000. An examination of the tower debris showed the presence of charcoal and charred timbers. The State Toxicologist, called in by Dallas County, reported the char was evidence that lightning struck the courthouse. Later, several residents of Selma reported that a bolt of lightning struck the courthouse July 2, 1957. On this information, Dallas County concluded that a lightning bolt had hit the building causing the collapse of the clock tower five days later. Dallas County carried insurance for loss to its courthouse caused by fire or lightning. The in-surers' engineers and investigators found that the courthouse collapsed of its own weight. They reported that the courthouse had not been struck by lightning; that lightning could not

have caused the collapse of the tower; that the collapse of the tower was caused by structural weaknesses attributable to a faulty design, poor construction, gradual deterioration of the struc-ture, and overloading brought about by re-modeling and the recent installation of an air-conditioning system, part of which was con-structed over the courtroom trusses. In their opinion, the char was the result of a fire in the courthouse tower and roof that must have oc-curred many, many years before July 2, 1957. The insurers denied liability.

. . . The case went to the jury on one issue: did lightning cause the collapse of the clock tower?

The record contains ample evidence to sup-port a jury verdict either way. The County pro-duced witnesses who testified they saw lightning strike the clock tower; the insurers produced witnesses who testified an examination of the debris showed that lightning did not strike the clock tower. Some witnesses said the char was fresh and smelled smoky; other witnesses said it was obviously old and had no fresh smoky smell at all. Both sides presented a great mass of engineering testimony bearing on the design, construction, overload or lack of overload. All of this was for the jury to evaluate. The jury chose to believe the insurers' witnesses and brought in a verdict for the defendants.

During the trial the defendants introduced a

copy of the Morning Times of Selma for June 9, 1901. This issue carried an unsigned article describing a fire that occurred at two in the morning of June 9, 1901, while the courhouse was still under construction. The article stated, in part: "The unfinished dome of the County's new courthouse was in flames at the top, and ... soon fell in. The fire was soon under control and the main building was saved. ..." The insurers do not contend that the collapse of the tower resulted from unsound charred timbers used in the repair of the building after the fire; they offered the newspaper account to show there had been a fire long before 1957 that would account for charred timber in the clock tower.

As a predicate for introducing the newspaper in evidence, the defendants called to the stand the editor of the Selma Times-Journal who testified that his publishing company maintains archives of the published issues of the Times-Journal and of the Morning Times, its predecessor, and that the archives contain the issue of the Morning Times of Selma for June 9, 1901, offered in evidence. The plaintiff objected that the newspaper article was hearsay; that it was not a business record nor an ancient document, nor was it admissible under any recognized exception to the hearsay doctrine. The trial judge admitted the newspaper as part of the records of the Selma Times-Journal. The sole error Dallas County specifies on appeal is the admission of the newspaper in evidence.

In the Anglo-American adversary system of law, courts usually will not admit evidence unless its accuracy and trustworthiness may be tested by cross-examination. Here, therefore, the plaintiff argues that the newspaper should not be admitted: "You cannot cross-examine a newspaper." [a] Of course, a newspaper article *is*

---

[a] This argument, a familiar one, rests on a misunderstanding of the origin and the nature of the hearsay rule. The rule is not an ancient principle of English law recognized at Runnymede. And, gone is its odor of sanctity.

Wigmore is often quoted for the statement that "cross-examination is beyond any doubt the greatest legal engine ever invented for the discovery of the truth." 5 Wigmore §1367 (3rd ed.). In over 1200 pages devoted to the hearsay rule, however, he makes it very clear that: "[T]he rule aims to insist on testing all statements by cross-examination, *if they can be*.... No one could defend a rule which pronounced that all statements thus untested are worthless; for all historical truth is based on uncross-examined assertions; and every day's experience of life gives denial to such an exaggeration. What the Hearsay Rule implies—and with profound verity—is that all testimonial assertions *ought to be* tested by cross-examination, as the best attainable measure; and it should not be burdened with the pedantic implication that they must be rejected as worthless if the test is unavailable." 1 Wigmore §8c. In this connection see Falknor, The Hearsay Rule and Its Exceptions, 2 UCLA L. Rev. 43 (1954).

In The Introductory Note to Chapter VI, Hearsay Evidence, American Law Institute, Model Code of Evidence (1942), Edmund M. Morgan, Reporter, it is pointed out that "the hearsay rule is the child of the adversary system." The Note continues: "During the first centuries of the jury system, the jury based its decision upon what the jurors themselves knew of the matter in dispute and what they learned through the words of their fathers and through such words of these persons whom they are bound to trust as worthy.... Until the end of the sixteenth century hearsay was received without question.... The opportunity for cross-examination is not a necessary element of a jury system, while it is the very heart of the adversary system.... As the judges began their attempts to rationalize the results of the decisions dealing with evidence, they first relied upon the general notion that a party was obliged to produce the best evidence available, but no more. Had they applied this generally, hearsay would have been received whenever better evidence could not be obtained. Therefore the judges discovered a special sort of necessity in ... exceptional cases ... [making] the admissible hearsay less unreliable than hearsay in general.... [By 1840] it became the fashion to attribute the exclusion of hearsay to the incapacity of the jury to evaluate, and in the development of exceptions to the rule, courts have doubtless been influenced by this notion.... Modern textwriters and judges have purported to find for each exception some sort of necessity for resort to hearsay and some condition attending the making of the excepted statement which will enable the jury to put a fair value upon it and will thus serve as a substitute for cross-examination. A careful examination of the eighteen or nineteen classes of utterances, each of which is now recognized as an exception to the hearsay rule by some respectable authority, will reveal that in many of them the necessity resolves itself into mere convenience and the substitute for cross-examination is imperceptible.... In most of the exceptions, however, the adversary theory is disregarded. There is nothing in any of the situations to warrant depriving the adversary of an opportunity to cross-examine; but those rationalizing the results purport to find some substitute for cross-examination. In most instances one will look in vain for anything more than a situation in which an ordinary man making such a statement would positively desire to tell the truth; and in some the most that can be claimed is the absence of a motive to falsify." For the history of the rule see 5 Wigmore, Evidence, §1364 (3rd ed.); 9 Holdsworth's History of English Law, 214 (1926).

hearsay, and in almost all circumstances is inadmissible. However, the law governing hearsay is somewhat less than pellucid.[b] And, as with most rules, the hearsay rule is not absolute; it is replete with exceptions. Witnesses die, documents are lost, deeds are destroyed, memories fade. All too often, primary evidence is not available and courts and lawyers must rely on secondary evidence. . . .

There are no cases clearly in point—at least none that we have found—in Alabama decisions, in the decisions of other states, or in the federal decisions. We decide this case, therefore, on general principles of relevancy and materiality, guided, as in [Monarch Insurance Company of Ohio v. Spach, 281 F.2d 401 (5th Cir. 1960)], by the liberal language of Rule 43(a), F.R. Civ. P. 28 U.S.C.A. Rule 43(a) provides:

"All evidence shall be admitted which is admissible under the statutes of the United States, or under the rules of evidence heretofore applied in the courts of the United States on the hearing of suits in equity, or under the rules of evidence applied in the courts of general jurisdiction of the state in which the United States court is held. In any case, the statute or rule which favors the reception of the evidence governs and the evidence shall be presented according to the most convenient method prescribed in any of the statutes or rules to which reference is herein made."

---

b "The fact is, then, that the law governing hearsay today is a conglomeration of inconsistencies, developed as a result of conflicting theories. Refinements and qualifications within the exceptions only add to its irrationality. The courts by multiplying exceptions reveal their conviction that relevant hearsay evidence normally has real probative value, and is capable of valuation by a jury as well as by other triers of fact. This is further demonstrated by the majority view that inadmissibe hearsay received without objection may be sufficient to sustain a verdict. Most statutes regulating procedure before administrative tribunals make hearsay admissible. And it is by no means clear that the administrative official ordinarily presiding at a hearing has more competence to value testimony than has a jury acting under the supervision of a judge. The number of cases tried before juries as compared with the number tried before judges without juries and before administrative tribunals, is small indeed." ALI Model Code of Evidence, p. 223 (1942).

Thus, "in a federal court, the rule, whether federal or state, which favors the reception of the evidence governs." New York Life Ins. Co. v. Schlatter et al., 5 Cir., 1953, 203 F.2d 184, 188.

Rule 43(a) affirmatively expands the scope of admissibility. It is a rule of admissibility, not exclusion. Although the rule specifies three categories of evidence that shall be admitted, it does not prohibit the receipt of probative evidence outside the three categories. So, this Court said in Monarch: "[The rule] defines the three standards of admissibility. But it does not purport to prohibit the admission of other relevant material probative evidence which, in the considered exercise of judicial wisdom, is trustworthy. . . . [I]n today's litigation with its endless complexities many of which are an outgrowth of our scientific age we would hardly think that a court instituted with all of the power the organic constitution could invest in it would have to stand helpless in the face of a new situation." Even if Rule 43(a) should be interpreted as carrying the necessary implication that evidence to be admissible must fit into one of the three categories specified in the rule, the cryptic reference to "rules of evidence heretofore applied in the courts of the United States on the hearing of suits in equity" is so uncertain in its meaning as to give broad latitude to a trial judge in his rulings on admissibility. The trial judge may exercise his discretion, if he keeps the hearing within reasonable bounds. In finding and applying rules of evidence applicable to hearings of suits in equity, his chief censor is the conscience of a Chancellor.

If they are worth their salt, evidentiary rules are to aid the search for truth. Rule 43(a), notwithstanding its shortcomings, carries out that purpose by enabling federal courts to apply a liberal, flexible rule for the admissibility of evidence, unencumbered by common law archaisms. . . .

Wigmore on Evidence [states] . . . that "the requisites of an exception to the hearsay rule are necessity and circumstantial guaranty of trustworthiness."

. . . As to necessity, Wigmore points out this requisite means that unless the hearsay statement is admitted, the facts it brings out may otherwise be lost, either because the person whose assertion is offered may be dead or unavailable, or because the assertion is of such a nature that one could not expect to obtain evidence of the same value from the same person or from other sources. Wigmore, §1421 (3rd ed.). "In effect, Wigmore says that, as the word necessity is here used, it is not to be interpreted as uniformly demanding a showing of total inaccessibility of firsthand evidence as a condition precedent to the acceptance of a particular piece of hearsay, but that necessity exists where otherwise great practical inconvenience would be experienced in making the desired proof. . . . If it were otherwise, the result would be that the exception created to the hearsay rule would thereby be mostly, if not completely, destroyed." United States v. Aluminum Co. of America, D.C. 1940, 35 F. Supp. 820, 823.

The fire referred to in the newspaper account occurred fifty-eight years before the trial of this case. Any witness who saw that fire with sufficient understanding to observe it and describe it accurately, would have been older than a young child at the time of the fire. We may reasonably assume that at the time of the trial he was either dead or his faculties were dimmed by the passage of fifty-eight years. It would have been burdensome, but not impossible, for the defendant to have discovered the name of the author of the article (although it had no by-line) and, perhaps, to have found an eyewitness to the fire. But it is improbable—so it seems to us—that any witness could have been found whose recollection would have been accurate at the time of the trial of this case. And it seems impossible that the testimony of any witness would have been as accurate and as reliable as the statement of facts in the contemporary newspaper article.

The rationale behind the "ancient documents" exception is applicable here: after a long lapse of time, ordinary evidence regarding signatures or handwriting is virtually unavailable, and it is therefore permissible to resort to circumstantial evidence. Thus, in Trustees of German Township, Montgomery County v. Farmers & Citizens Savings Bank Co., Ohio Com. Pl. 1953, 113 N.E.2d 409, 412, affirmed Ohio App., 115 N.E.2d 690, the court admitted as ancient documents newspapers eighty years old containing notices of advertisements for bids relating to the town hall: "Such exhibits, by reason of age, alone, and unquestioned authenticity, qualify as ancient documents." The ancient documents rule applies to documents a generation or more in age. Here, the Selma Times-Journal article is almost two generations old. The principle of necessity, not requiring absolute impossibility or total inaccessibility of first-hand knowledge, is satisfied by the practicalities of the situation before us.

The second requisite for admission of hearsay evidence is trustworthiness. According to Wigmore, there are three sets of circumstances when hearsay is trustworthy enough to serve as a practicable substitute for the ordinary test of cross-examination: "Where the circumstances are such that a sincere and accurate statement would naturally be uttered, and no plan of falsification be formed; where, even though a desire to falsify might present itself, other considerations, such as the danger of easy detection or the fear of punishment, would probably counteract its force; where the statement was made under such conditions of publicity that an error, if it had occurred, would probably have been detected and corrected." These circumstances fit the instant case.

There is no procedural canon against the exercise of common sense in deciding the admissibility of hearsay evidence. In 1901 Selma, Alabama, was a small town. Taking a common sense view of this case, it is inconceivable to us that a newspaper reporter in a small town would report there was a fire in the dome of the new courthouse—if there had been no fire. He is without motive to falsify, and a false report would have subjected the newspaper and him to embarrassment in the community. The usual dangers inherent in hearsay evidence, such as lack of memory, faulty narration, intent to influence the court proceedings, and plain lack of truthfulness are not present here. To our minds, the article published in the Selma Morning-Times on the day of the fire is more reliable, more trustworthy, more competent evidence than the testimony of a witness called to the stand fifty-eight years later.

We hold, that in matters of local interest, when the fact in question is of such a public nature it would be generally known throughout the community, and when the questioned fact occurred so long ago that the testimony of an eye-witness would probably be less trustworthy than a contemporary newspaper account, a federal court, under Rule 43(a), may relax the exclusionary rules to the extent of admitting the newspaper article in evidence. We do not characterize this newspaper as a "business record," nor as an "ancient document," nor as any other readily identifiable and happily tagged species of hearsay exception. It is admissible because it is necessary and trustworthy, relevant and material, and its admission is within the trial judge's exercise of discretion in holding the hearing within reasonable bounds.

Judgment is affirmed.

---

4. Burden of Proof

Because it is the plaintiff or the state who makes the complaint containing the allegations against the defendant, it is the duty of the plaintiff or the state to substantiate those allegations. This duty is the "burden of proof." Thus the plaintiff or the state must be the first party to introduce evidence and establish the facts, in order to convince the judge or the jury (whichever is the trier of facts) of the truth of the claims made against the defendant.

In civil cases the plaintiff must prove a case by a *preponderance of the evidence,* while in criminal cases the state must prove its case by the more stringent standard of *beyond a reasonable doubt.* Preponderance of the evidence in civil cases requires that the plaintiff's evidence must merely tip the scale in his or her favor, when compared with the defendant's evidence.[48]

5. Establishing a *Prima Facie* Case

To fulfill the burden of proof, the plaintiff's first step is to establish a *prima facie* case. For example, to prove negligence against the defendant, the plaintiff must prove that there was a duty not to injure the plaintiff, that the defendant did not fulfill that duty, and that damages to the plaintiff resulted. Once the plaintiff has introduced facts that prove these elements, he or she has established a *prima facie* case of negligence. At this point the plaintiff has met the burden of proof on the allegations made in the complaint. Assuming that the court agrees that the plaintiff has met the burden of proof and established a *prima facie* case of negligence, it is incumbent upon the defendant to rebut the plaintiff's case by introducing his or her

---

[48] However, some types of civil actions require "clear and convincing" proof, such as proof of illegitimacy and proof of dependency to make a child a ward of the court in domestic relations proceedings, proof in commitment proceedings for alcoholics and the mentally ill and in certain aspects of probate matters.

version of the facts and to attempt to convince the trier of facts that the defendant's evidence is more persuasive than that of the plaintiff.

6. Motions During and After Trial

Parties to a case may file motions and have hearings not only prior to commencement of the trial, but also during, and after the trial. For example, if Drake does not believe that Pope has established a *prima facie* case at the trial, before Drake attempts to rebut Pope's evidence he will make a *motion for a directed verdict*. This means that Drake will request the court to direct the verdict away from the jury (that is, not allow the jury to render a verdict) and simply dismiss the case at that point because Pope has not presented enough evidence to prove any liability on Drake's part. If the motion for a directed verdict is granted, the trial will end at that point, because without any valid claims at issue, there is no point in proceeding any further with the trial.

Conversely, after Pope has established a *prima facie* case, and Drake has either failed to make a motion for a directed verdict or has made one that has been denied, and after he has attempted to rebut Pope's evidence, Pope may also make a motion for a directed verdict. Pope's theory here would be that his *prima facie* case has been established and that Drake has failed to rebut it, thereby entitling Pope to a verdict without the case going to the jury. The theory of the directed verdict, whether requested by plaintiff or defendant, is that the facts are so clearly in one party's favor that there is no point in wasting time by giving the case to the jury for determination. If "reasonable men could not differ" about the facts being in one party's favor, what would otherwise be a factual matter becomes a *legal* matter; thus the judge is allowed to direct the verdict.

Preventing the jury from considering a case at all is a radical ruling by a judge. The motion for a directed verdict is rarely granted, particularly because of the possibility that the judge's action in taking the case away from the jury might be interpreted as unfair to one party or the other, and because, as stated previously, the appellate court may reverse the judge's decision, in which case the entire trial may have to be conducted over again from beginning to end.

In most circumstances the court will reserve decision on either party's motion for a directed verdict, submit the case to the jury, and then rule on the legal sufficiency of the evidence on a motion made after the verdict has been rendered, namely a motion for *judgment notwithstanding the verdict*. Because the motion is granted or denied after the trial has taken place and the jury has made a decision, the need for a second trial is avoided if an appellate court later reverses the trial court's granting of the motion, because the jury's decision can then be reinstated. The theory of this motion is that even after the *prima facie* case has been established, the defendant has attempted to rebut it, and the jury has made its decision, it is conceivable that there simply was not enough evidence to support the jury's decision. As with the motion for a directed verdict, the moving party asserts that the opponent's evidence failed to create an issue on which reasonable men could differ, and that as a *matter of law* the losing party should be awarded judgment notwithstanding the verdict. It is on this basis that one party or the other may make the motion (referred to as *judgment n.o.v.,* which stands for the Latin *non obstante verdicto*). This motion is also rarely granted and is generally made by the parties simply as a formality and to maintain consistency with any subsequent appeal the moving party may make.

A very common motion made subsequent to the verdict is a motion for a new trial. It has long been understood that "if the trial judge is not satisfied with the verdict of a jury, he has the right—and indeed the duty—to set the verdict aside and order a new trial." [49] A motion for a new trial may be granted on the basis of insufficient evidence. Other bases for granting a motion for a new trial are improper admission or exclusion of evidence; verdict contrary to the evidence; erroneous instruction; excessive or inadequate damages; coercion of the jury; misconduct of the court, jury, or counsel; disqualification of the judge or a juror; or newly discovered evidence. Thus, contrary to a motion for a directed verdict or for judgment n.o.v., the credibility of witnesses and the weight and sufficiency of the evidence are proper considerations on a motion for a new trial. This motion is also rarely granted but is usually made to preserve the moving party's right to a subsequent appeal.

G. Judgment

The court's judgment is the final decisive act defining the rights of the parties. If the court has rendered judgment in the plaintiff's favor and the defendant has exhausted all rights of appeal, the plaintiff is entitled to whatever relief is provided for by the judgment, either the right to collect the money the court or jury has awarded, the transfer of certain property, the performance of a contract, or any other possible type of relief. (In criminal cases, the judgment is in the form of a suspended sentence, a fine or imprisonment, or a combination of these.) However, the right to such relief in civil cases is of no value whatsoever unless the plaintiff has the power to enforce such right, or the defendant voluntarily agrees to comply with the order rendered by the court.

For example, if the judgment in the *Pope* case was for money damages against Drake, what would Pope do if Drake refused to pay, or if Drake alleged that he did not have the money to pay? Just as there are methods of enforcing the rules of discovery, there are methods of enforcing a court order for payment of a judgment. If Pope was unaware of the whereabouts or value of any of Drake's property, Pope would be entitled to force Drake to come into court under a proceeding provided in Rule 69 of the Rules of Civil Procedure and disclose to Pope and the court the whereabouts and value of all such property. Assuming that Drake still refused to pay the amount ordered, Pope's next step would probably be to obtain a court order called a *writ of execution* from the court that rendered the judgment. This writ would authorize and instruct the sheriff to "execute" upon and "levy" (that is,

---

[49] Wright, p. 420.

seize) any of Drake's real or personal property. A writ of execution would also entitle Pope to the wages or funds in any of Drake's bank accounts. If Drake's real or personal property is executed upon, Pope would be entitled to have that property sold by the sheriff of the county in which the property is located and to recover the amount of the judgment, plus costs, out of the proceeds of such sale. The sheriff would have to remit the remaining amount, if any, to Drake. If Pope were to garnish Drake's wages, bank accounts, or other funds that were in the custody of a disinterested third party, the garnishment issued by the court would order the third party to transfer the funds directly to Pope.

QUESTIONS

1. Basing your reasoning on the facts in the *Pope* case and on the California principles Pope's attorney described to him, who should prevail? Explain.

2. Should Drake respond to the complaint with a motion? If so, what motion?

3. What is the theory behind the discovery rules? What additional rules of procedure or discovery should be adopted to improve civil litigation?

4. What additional interrogatories, other than those in Appendix E, should Pope ask Drake? Prepare Drake's answers to Pope's Interrogatories.

5. Should the right to a jury in civil cases be as broad as it is in criminal cases? Why or why not?

6. What arguments can be made for or against requiring a unanimous verdict? for a jury of twelve persons as opposed to any other number?

7. Under what circumstances is hearsay evidence sufficiently trustworthy to serve as a substitute for cross-examination?

7

The Law of Contracts

A. Its Importance for a Stable Society

In all areas of the law, the court seeks to establish principles of fairness in dealings between individuals. This is equally true in the law of contracts. The guiding principle here is that both parties must be able to rely on the legal system if one party to an agreement does not fulfill his or her part of the bargain. Stated another way, the basic principle in the law of contracts is that certain standards should govern the dealings between parties, so that those parties can rely on each other's word with the knowledge that if that word is broken there will be recourse in the courts to enforce those promises. As stated by Pound, in *An Introduction to the Philosophy of Law*:[1]

> Wealth, in a commercial age, is made up largely of promises. An important part of everyone's substance consists of advantages which others have promised to provide or to render to him; of demands to have the advantages promised, which he may assert not against the world at large but against particular individuals. Thus the individual claims to have performance of advantageous promises secured to him. He claims the satisfaction of expectations created by promises and agreements. If this claim is not secured friction and waste obviously result.... [I]n such a society men must be able to assume that those with whom they deal in the general intercourse of the society will act in good faith, and as a corollary must be able to assume that those with whom they so deal will carry out their undertakings according to the expectations which the moral sentiment of the community attaches thereto. Hence in a commercial and industrial society, a claim or want or demand of society that promises be kept and that undertakings be carried out in good faith, a social interest in the stability of promises as a social and economic institution, becomes of the first importance.

---

[1] R. Pound, *An Introduction to the Philosophy of Law* (New Haven: Yale University Press, 1968), pp. 133–34.

In the web of our complex social and economic structure the concepts of the law of contracts are simple threads that seek to maintain order in society and to provide stability in the relationship between its members. Traditionally the courts have been the watchdog and ensurer of such stability.

In recent years both the judicial and legislative branches of the government have come under attack for interfering with relations between private individuals relating to private contracts. In addition, administrative regulations promulgated under the executive branch significantly affect the law of private contracts. This interference with private contracts sometimes manifests itself in the judiciary by the tendency of some courts to relieve the contracting parties from the obligations originally undertaken:[2]

> While it is true that defendant ... failed to read the entire contract, this Court believes that a contract which locks an individual into a contract for any physical disability not reported within four business days, is against public policy. ... The limiting language of the paragraph in question, flies in the face of the all-out efforts being made to protect the consumer who frequently deals on an unequal basis with a sophisticated corporation such as plaintiff.

Pound recognized and criticized this trend many years ago:[3]

> If letting people of full age and sound mind contract freely and holding them rigidly to the contracts they made was carried to an extreme in the last century, a system of restricting free contract and relaxing the obligation of contract may be carried as far in reaction, and the spirit of the times seems to be pushing everywhere to that other extreme. ...
>
> ... The one-time general proposition that courts cannot make contracts over for the parties, that freedom of contracts implies the possibility of contracting foolishly, is giving way to a power of the ... state to act as guardian of persons of age, sound mind, and discretion, and relieve them of judicial action from their contracts, or make their promises easier for them. ... Often the words finally written in a contract after a long negotiation are the result of hard-fought compromises. They are not ideal provisions from the standpoint of either side, but are what each is willing to concede in order to reach agreement. After some frustrating event has happened and a party who has suffered a damage from nonperformance is suing for it, to say he intended and would have consented to insert a condition which the court conjures up to relieve the promisor is to make a new contract under a fiction of interpretation.

Cardozo reached the same conclusion as Pound did, namely that the courts should not relieve the promisor of the obligation imposed by the express words of the contract. But Cardozo arrived at that conclusion by a different approach:[4] "If we were

---

[2] Holiday of Plainview, Ltd. v. Bernstein, 350 N.Y.S.2d 510, 512 (1973); see also GTI Corp. v. Calhoon, 309 F. Supp. 762 (1969).

[3] Pound, pp. 166–67.

[4] B. Cardozo, *The Nature of the Judicial Process* (New Haven: Yale University Press, 1970), pp. 139–40.

to consider only the individual instance, we might be ready to release the promisor. We look beyond the particular to the universal, and shape our judgment in obedience to the fundamental interest of society that contracts shall be fulfilled." Thus Cardozo was prepared to release the promisor, despite the fact that the contract indicated otherwise. This temptation was outweighed in Cardozo's view by a fundamental need in society "that contracts shall be fulfilled." Pound, on the other hand, believed that adherence to the express terms of the contract should be based not only upon the long-range needs of society but also upon the particular individual's right to rely on the promise as originally made. In either case an apparent trend in the direction of more liberal construction and interpretation of contracts remains in disfavor among commentators:[5]

> [I]n the future there will be greater restrictions imposed by courts in the exercise of their function of developing the common law. There has been increasing recognition in legal literature that the bargaining process has become more limited in modern society. In purchasing a new automobile, for example, the individual may be able to dicker over price, model, color and certain other factors, but, if he wishes to consummate the contract to purchase, he usually must sign the standard form prepared by the manufacturer (although he is contracting with an independent dealer). He has no real choice. He must take that form or leave it. Such contracts, called contracts of "adhesion," have frequently been denied their intended effects by a process of strained interpretation.

Such disfavor may be well founded, in the interests of maintaining a stable society and of preventing too broad an application of the theory of unconscionability of contracts.[6] This theory is an attempt by some judges and the Uniform Commercial Code to nullify the express agreements of "people of full age and sound mind" in an effort to provide relief from an undefinable category of business sales practices that occasionally result in financial hardship for an undefinable category of buyers. This attitude of some courts and the social context in which the doctrine of unconscionable contracts is invoked are not the same as some judges' *justified* refusal to "interpret contracts with meticulous adherence to the letter when in conflict with the spirit." [7]

B. Definition of and Requirements for Contracts

A *contract* is a promise or a set of promises for the breach of which the law provides a remedy, or the performance of which the law recognizes as a duty.[8] The

---

[5] J. Calamari and J. Perillo, *The Law of Contracts* (St. Paul: West Publishing Co., 1970), section 3, p. 5, citing Boll v. Sharp & Dohme, Inc. 281 App. Div. 568, 121 N.Y.S.2d 20 (1st Dept. 1953), aff'd 307 N.Y. 646 (agreement to relieve drug company of liability rendered ineffective by narrow construction), and Tunkl v. Regents of Univ. of Cal., 60 Cal.2d 92, 32 Cal. Rptr. 33, 383 P.2d 441 (1963) (agreement by patient to relieve hospital of liability held void).

[6] See Chapter 8, p. 190.

[7] Cardozo, p. 100.

[8] *Restatement of Contracts 2d* (1973), section 1.

requirements for the formation of a contract may be summarized as follows: (1) there must be at least two parties; (2) both parties must have the legal capacity to incur contractual duties; (3) there must be a manifestation of assent by all parties to the contract; and (4) there must be consideration supporting a contractually enforceable promise.[9]

1. Two Parties

This requirement simply means what it says: a person cannot contract with himself or herself; there must be at least two parties, though not necessarily two individual people. There may be two corporations, or a corporation and a person, or some other combination. Of course there may be more than two parties, and it is very common for a larger number of parties to sign one document, which constitutes one contract among them.

2. Capacity

Legal incapacity can arise from minority or infancy (being under a specified age), or from artificial creation, as in the case of corporations. The term capacity is also used to include those situations in which one party may not be mentally capable of comprehending the concept of entering into a contract, as well as those situations in which one of the parties was so intoxicated that he or she did not have the capacity to enter into contractual obligations at that time.[10]

At common law an infant is a person under the age of twenty-one. Many states have enacted statutes providing that persons under a certain age have the legal capacity to enter into binding contracts but may withdraw from the obligations imposed under such contracts. These minors have the ability to void their contractual duties at their option, and therefore they have the ability or the capacity to incur *voidable* contractual duties. Emancipation of infants from their parents, such as by marriage, gives them the right to their earnings and releases them from their parents' control. However, it does not remove their disability of incapacity or make contracts binding upon them. The case of *Kiefer* v. *Fred Howe Motors, Inc.* discusses the issue of capacity and the policy behind an infant's ability to void his or her contracts.

---

[9] United States v. Alaska S.S. Company, 491 F.2d 1147 (9th Cir. 1974); Hosler v. Beard, 54 Ohio 398, 43 N.E. 1040 (1896); Trujillo v. Glen Falls Insurance Company, 88 N.M. 279, 540 P.2d 209 (1975); Fries v. United Mine Workers of America, 30 Ill. App.3d 575, 333 N.E.2d 600 (1975).

[10] Smalley v. Baker, 262 Cal. App.2d 824, 69 Cal. Rptr. 521 (1968) (mental incapacity); 41 *AmJur* 2d, "Incompetent Persons," sections 75–77 (intoxication).

KIEFER v. FRED HOWE MOTORS, INC.

39 Wis.2d 20, 158 N.W.2d 288 (1968)

Supreme Court of Wisconsin

WILKIE, Justice.

Three issues are presented on this appeal. They are:

1. Should an emancipated minor over the age of eighteen be legally responsible for his contracts?

2. Was the contract effectively disaffirmed?

3. Is the plaintiff liable in tort for misrepresentation?

LEGAL RESPONSIBILITY OF EMANCIPATED MINOR

The law governing agreements made during infancy reaches back over many centuries. The general rule is that "... the contract of a minor, other than for necessaries, is either void or voidable at his option." The only other exceptions to the rule permitting disaffirmance are statutory or involve contracts which deal with duties imposed by law such as a contract of marriage or an agreement to support an illegitimate child. The general rule is not affected by the minor's status as emancipated or unemancipated.

Appellant does not advance any argument that would put this case within one of the exceptions to the general rule, but rather urges that this court, as a matter of public policy, adopt a rule that an emancipated minor over eighteen years of age be made legally responsible for his contracts.

The underpinnings of the general rule allowing the minor to disaffirm his contracts were undoubtedly the protection of the minor. It was thought that the minor was immature in both mind and experience and that, therefore, he should be protected from his own bad judgments as well as from adults who would take advantage of him. The doctrine of the voidability of minors' contracts often seems commendable and just. If the beans that the young naive Jack purchased from the crafty old man in the fairy tale "Jack and the Bean Stalk" had been worthless rather than magical, it would have been only fair to allow Jack to disaffirm the bargain and reclaim his cow. However, in today's modern and sophisticated society the "infancy doctrine" seems to lose some of its gloss.

Paradoxically, we declare the infant mature enough to shoulder arms in the military, but not mature enough to vote; mature enough to marry and be responsible for his torts and crimes, but not mature enough to assume the burden of his own contractual indiscretions. In Wisconsin, the infant is deemed mature enough to use a dangerous instrumentality—a motor vehicle—at sixteen, but not mature enough to purchase it without protection until he is twenty-one.

No one really questions that a line as to age must be drawn somewhere below which a legally defined minor must be able to disaffirm his contracts for nonnecessities. The law over the centuries has considered this age to be twenty-one. Legislatures in other states have lowered the age. We suggest that the appellant might better seek the change it proposes in the legislative halls rather than this court. . . .

Undoubtedly, the infancy doctrine is an obstacle when a major purchase is involved. However, we believe that the reasons for allowing that obstacle to remain viable at this point outweigh those for casting it aside. Minors require some protection from the pitfalls of the market place. Reasonable minds will always differ on the extent of the protection that should be afforded. For this court to adopt a rule that the appellant suggests and remove the contractual disabilities from a minor simply because he becomes emancipated, which in most cases would be the result of marriage, would be to suggest that the married minor is somehow vested with more wisdom and maturity than his single counterpart. However, logic would not seem to dictate this result especially when today a youthful marriage is oftentimes indicative of a lack of wisdom and maturity.

DISAFFIRMANCE

The appellant questions whether there has been an effective disaffirmance of the contract in this case.

Williston, while discussing how a minor may disaffirm a contract, states:

"Any act which clearly shows an intent to disaffirm a contract or sale is sufficient for the purpose. Thus a notice by the infant of his purpose to disaffirm . . . a tender or even an offer to return the consideration or its proceeds to the vendor . . . is sufficient."

The testimony of Steven Kiefer and the letter from his attorney to the dealer clearly establish that there was an effective disaffirmance of the contract.

MISREPRESENTATION

Appellant's last argument is that the respondent should be held liable in tort for damages because he misrepresented his age. Appellant would use these damages as a set-off against the contract price sought to be reclaimed by respondent.

The 19th-century view was that a minor's lying about his age was inconsequential because a fraudulent representation of capacity was not the equivalent of actual capacity. This rule has been altered by time. There appear to be two possible methods that now can be employed to bind the defrauding minor: He may be estopped from denying his alleged majority, in which case the contract will be enforced or contract damages will be allowed; or he may be allowed to disaffirm his contract but be liable in tort for damages. Wisconsin follows the latter approach.

Having established that there is a remedy against the defrauding minor, the question becomes whether the requisites for a tort action in misrepresentation are present in this case.

The trial produced conflicting testimony regarding whether Steven Kiefer had been asked his age or had replied that he was "twenty-one." Steven and his wife, Jacqueline, said "No," and Frank McHalsky, appellant's salesman, said "Yes." Confronted with this conflict, the question of credibility was for the trial court to decide, which it did by holding that Steven did not orally represent that he was "twenty-one." This finding is not contrary to the great weight and clear preponderance of the evidence and must be affirmed.

Even accepting the trial court's conclusion that Steven Kiefer had not orally represented his age to be over twenty-one, the appellant argues that there was still a misrepresentation. The "motor vehicle purchase contract" signed by Steven Kiefer contained the following language just above the purchaser's signature:

"I represent that I am 21 years of age or over and recognize that the dealer sells the above vehicle upon this representation."

Whether the inclusion of this sentence constitutes a misrepresentation depends on whether elements of the tort have been satisfied. They were not. In First Nat. Bank in Oshkosh v. Scieszinski it is said:

"A party alleging fraud has the burden of proving it by clear and convincing evidence. The elements of fraud are well established:

" ' "To be actionable the false representation must consist, first, of a statement of fact which is untrue; second, that it was made with intent to defraud and for the purpose of inducing the other party to act upon it; third, that he did in fact rely on it and was induced thereby to act, to his injury or damage." ' "

No evidence was adduced to show that the plaintiff had an intent to defraud the dealer. To the contrary, it is at least arguable that the majority of minors are, as the plaintiff here might well have been, unaware of the legal consequences of their acts.

Without the element of scienter being satisfied, the plaintiff is not susceptible to an action in misrepresentation. Furthermore, the reliance mentioned in *Scieszinski* must be, as Prosser points out, "justifiable reliance." We fail to see how the dealer could be justified in the mere reliance on the fact that the plaintiff signed a contract containing a sentence that said he was twenty-one or over. The trial court observed that the plaintiff was sufficiently immature looking to arouse suspicion. The appellant never took any affirmative steps to determine whether the plaintiff was in fact over twenty-one. It never asked to see a draft card, identification card, or the most logical indicium of age under the circumstances, a driver's license. Therefore, because there was no intent to deceive, and no justifiable reliance, the appellant's action for misrepresentation must fail.

Judgment affirmed.

HALLOWS, Chief Justice (dissenting).

The majority opinion on the issue of whether an emancipated minor legally should be responsible for his contracts "doth protest too much." After giving very cogent reasons why the common-law rule should be abandoned, the opinion refrains from reshaping the rule to meet reality. Minors are emancipated by a valid marriage and also by entering military service. If they are mature enough to become parents and as-

sume the responsibility of raising other minors and if they are mature enough to be drafted or volunteer to bear arms and sacrifice their life for their country, then they are mature enough to make binding contracts in the market place. The magical age limit of 21 years as an indication of contractual maturity no longer has a basis in fact or in public policy.

My second ground of the dissent is that an automobile to this respondent was a necessity and therefore the contract could not be disaffirmed. Here, we have a minor, aged 20 years and 7 months, the father of a child, and working. While the record shows there is some public transportation to his present place of work, it also shows he borrowed his mother's car to go to and from work. Automobiles for parents under 21 years of age to go to and from work in our current society may well be a necessity and I think in this case the record shows it is. An automobile as a means of transportation to earn a living should not be considered a nonnecessity because the owner is 5 months too young. I would reverse.

3. Mutual Assent

In determining whether a contract exists, cases rarely involve the question of whether there were two parties to the agreement or whether the parties had the legal capacity to incur contractual duties. Cases on formation usually deal with the question of whether the parties actually had a meeting of the minds and mutually assented, or agreed, to create legally binding obligations with one another.

Mutual assent normally takes the form of an offer and an acceptance. Most jurisdictions will determine whether an offer and acceptance have been made by the objective theory of mutual assent. Under this approach a contracting party is bound by the outward or apparent intention manifested to the other contracting party, irrespective of what the actual or secret intention may have been. The phrase *meeting of the minds* means that the parties must reach an agreement on the same bargain on the same terms and at the same time. This usually involves negotiations until one of the parties makes a definite proposition or promise (such as to pay money or render goods or services), which is conditioned on the other party promising to render goods or services or pay money in return. This proposition or promise is called an offer. The offeree's agreement to render goods or services or pay money in return is called the acceptance. The acceptance may come in the form of the actual performance, rather than the promise to perform, but it generally takes the form of a promise to perform.

a. Intent to Create Legal Obligation

There must be a manifestation of intent on the part of both parties in order to create legal obligations.[11] What constitutes a manifestation of intent? It is an outwardly communicated desire to enter into legally binding obligations. Mutual assent must not only be outwardly manifested; it must also be communicated. Subjective considerations are relevant only where there has been no objective manifestation. One test used in determining whether such intent is present is whether the offeree reasonably believes that the offeror seriously extended the offer. In the case of *Barnes* v. *Treece,* the court noted that: "When expressions are intended as a joke and are understood or would be understood by a reasonable person as being so intended, they cannot be construed as an offer and accepted to form a contract." [12] As the case of *Yeager* v. *Dobbins* indicates, the court will also examine whether such offer was ready to be accepted and whether the offeror extended an offer to contract, not merely an offer to enter into further negotiations with only a vague intention that a contract might someday be consummated as a result of such negotiation.[13]

YEAGER v. DOBBINS

252 N.C. 824, 114 S.E.2d 820 (1960)

Supreme Court of North Carolina

Plaintiff's complaint is summarized as follows: Defendant is the widow of C. N. Dobbins who died 15 June 1958. She is sole devisee and legatee and executrix under the will of deceased. She is sued in her representative capacity. On and prior to 21 October 1948 plaintiff was a resident of Lansdowne, Pennsylvania, where he owned his home and was employed in the insurance business. At this time C. N. Dobbins owned a 210-acre farm in Yadkin County, North Carolina and, "in writing, contracted with and promised" plaintiff if he would give up his residence and employment in Pennsylvania, bring his family to North Carolina and take over, operate and work the farm, Dobbins would convey or devise it to plaintiff. The contract was subject to the condition that if Dobbins' sons, Charles and James, or either of them, should join plaintiff in operating and working the farm, it would be conveyed or devised to plaintiff and such son or sons in equal shares, otherwise to plaintiff solely. In reliance upon the contract, plaintiff sold his home, gave up his employment, moved his family to the farm, lived thereon and operated and worked it until the death of C. N. Dobbins. Neither of the sons joined with plaintiff in operating and working the farm. The land was not conveyed

---

[11] Three-Seventy Leasing Corporation v. Ampex Corp., 528 F.2d 993 (5th Cir. 1976); Morgan v. Board of State Lands, 549 P.2d 695 (Utah 1976).

[12] Barnes v. Treece, 549 P.2d 1152, 1155 (Wash. App. 1976); see also Meyer v. Benko, 55 Cal. App.2d 937, 127 Cal. 846 (1976).

[13] Hill v. McGregor Manufacturing Corp., 23 Mich. App. 342, 178 N.W.2d 553 (1970) (cursory memorandum insufficient to evidence intent to make offer without further actions); Lefkowitz v. Great Minneapolis Surplus Store, 251 Minn. 188, 86 N.W.2d 689 (1957) (advertisement adequate to constitute offer ready to be accepted); Willowood Condominium Assn. v. HNC Realty Co., 531 F.2d 1249 (5th Cir. 1976); Transamerica Equipment Leasing Corp. v. Union Bank, 426 F.2d 273 (9th Cir. 1970).

to plaintiff, and in breach of the contract Dobbins willed it to his wife, the defendant. The farm, at the death of Dobbins, was worth $105,000, including $50,000 in improvements placed thereon by plaintiff at his own expense. Plaintiff filed claim with defendant for the sum of $105,000 but payment was refused.

In consequence of a motion by defendant that the complaint be made more definite and certain and that the writing relied on by plaintiff be fully set out, plaintiff filed an amendment and alleged that the writing is a letter from C. N. Dobbins to plaintiff. It was made a part of the complaint and attached thereto as an exhibit.

The letter is dated 21 October 1948, addressed to "Dear Frank" and signed, "Your dad, C. N. Dobbins." Omitting nonessentials, it is as follows:

"I wanted that you should make the decision yourself so that . . . I wouldn't feel that I had over persuaded you. . . . I've been getting the corn out of the field and sowing grain, which is mighty close akin to work . . . the payoff comes next summer with the harvest.

"Now to answer more specifically your questions. I had hoped that you, Charles and James could and would take the farm over and operate it as a jointly owned piece of property. There is sufficient land and sufficient work for all of you to have a full time job. However I realize that partnerships are rather hard to make operate and it would probably be just as well or better to divide the place 3 ways even though it should be operated as an entity. Who knows for sure what James or Charles will want to do when older? They may not want to farm. You might not like it after a trial. I would like for any of you boys to have the farm only if you would keep it and work it.

"I would like to turn the whole thing over to you to make as much as you can until Charles gets through school and comes home; then the two of you to do likewise until James can join you and then the three of you carry on from there. It appears that I am about through except in an advisory capacity and possibly that too. I naturally would like to have

you and Grace nearby and even more especially Kathy and Christine.

"The decision is yours to make, Frank. I'd love to have you come on down as soon as possible. . . .

"As for a house for you to live in, we might at odd times build one. I selected one out of the October Country Gentleman as being about what would be needed for you boys to live in. You have better ideas probably. . . .

"One thing is certain you would never be out of a job. . . .

"For my part will try to make it interesting from every angle.

"I am not sure this covers everything you wanted to know. If not I would be glad to explain further on request."

Defendant demurred to the complaint as amended on the ground that it does not state facts sufficient to constitute a cause of action, in that the action, sounding in contract, is based solely and entirely upon the above letter, which upon its face is wholly insufficient in law to constitute an offer to contract, a contract, "or any other thing upon which plaintiff can as a matter of law maintain the action."

The court sustained the demurrer. Plaintiff appealed and assigned error. . . .

MOORE, Justice.

The complaint alleges that the agreement or contract on the part of C. N. Dobbins is in writing. Plaintiff amended the complaint and alleged that the writing relied on is the letter of C. N. Dobbins dated 21 October 1948. It is not alleged that Dobbins agreed or offered to do anything more than appears in the letter.

The question for decision is whether the letter constitutes a contract or offer to contract sufficient to support an action for damages for breach of its terms.

Where the alleged contract is made a part of the complaint and is relied on as the sole basis of recovery, the court will look to its particular provisions rather than the more broadly stated allegations in the complaint or the conclusions of the pleader as to its character and meaning.

Williamson v. Miller, 231 N.C. 722, 726, 58 S.E.2d 743. . . .

Upon proper construction of the letter in question depends the propriety of the judgment sustaining the demurrer. The letter is not a complete contract within itself. This is obvious and requires no discussion. The real question is whether it contains a valid offer in express terms or by necessary implication, the acceptance of which and the performance of conditions therein contained give rise to a binding contract, the breach of which will support an action for damages.

The writer comes to the main purpose of the letter in this wise: "Now to answer more specifically your questions." Here he discusses some ideas he has concerning the farm. He *had hoped* that plaintiff, Charles and James could and would take the farm over and operate it as a *jointly owned* piece of property. There is work enough for all. However he realizes that partnerships are "hard to make operate." It would probably be as well or better to divide the place three ways but it should be operated as a unit. He doesn't know whether James or Charles will want to farm when they are older. Plaintiff might not like it if he tried it. Writer would like for any of the three boys to have the farm *"only"* if they *"would keep it and work it."*

It is our opinion that the foregoing portion of the letter does not comprise an offer to convey or devise the farm or any part thereof. The writer is merely discussing ideas and possibilities. He is giving background information for possible future disposition of the farm. He has reached no definite decision. He wants plaintiff and writer's sons to have the farm *only* if they should like farming, that is, "would keep it and work it." It would appear that the writer does not wish to convey the land to plaintiff, Charles or James until he is convinced they like farming and want to farm. There is no positive offer of the land on any definite conditions. The writer is reserving his decision as to the disposition of the farm until future developments disclose the attitudes of plaintiff and the sons

toward farming. This is borne out by his summary or conclusion of the matter.

The writer concludes by making the following proposal: "I would like to turn the whole thing over to you to make as much as you can until Charles gets through school and comes home; then the two of you do likewise until James can join you and then the three of you carry on from there." It is clear that writer offers an interim arrangement. Plaintiff may come to North Carolina, take over the farm and *make as much as he can* until Charles and James finish school. Then the three are to "carry on from there." There is still no offer to convey or devise. Again final decision and disposition must await developments.

"When an offer and acceptance are relied on to make a contract, 'The offer must be one which is intended of itself to create legal relations on acceptance. It must not be an offer intended merely to open negotiations, which will ultimately result in a contract, or intended to call forth an offer in legal form from the party to whom it is addressed.' " "If a proposal is one merely to open negotiations which may or may not ultimately result in a contract, it is not binding though accepted. . . . Care should be taken not to construe as offers letters which are intended merely as preliminary negotiations."

"In the formation of a contract an offer and an acceptance are essential elements; they constitute the agreement of the parties. The offer must be communicated, must be complete, and must be accepted in its exact terms. Mutuality of agreement is indispensable; the parties must assent to the same thing in the same sense, *idem re et sensu,* and their minds must meet as to all the terms."

We are of the opinion, and we so hold, that C. N. Dobbins did not make an offer to convey or devise the farm that will support plaintiff's contention and theory of the case. The court below properly sustained the demurrer. . . .

The judgment below is

Affirmed.

In addition to the requirements discussed in *Yeager,* the offeree must reasonably believe that the offeror contemplates contractual relations rather than some other type of relation that is noncontractual, such as the receipt of a gift.[14] The significance of this distinction is that if a gift is offered by the offeror and accepted by the offeree, and if the offeror subsequently changes his or her mind, then the offeree cannot resort to the courts for enforcement of that offer. However, if the offeror contemplated contractual relations at the time the offer was made, and if the offeree reasonably believed that the offeror contemplated contractual relations and subsequently accepted the offer, thus forming a contract that was then not performed by the offeror, such action on the part of the offeror would constitute a breach. Therefore the contract would be enforceable in a court of law.

The case of *Meyer* v. *Benko* illustrates that the court will base its determination of whether assent existed more on the parties' objective and outward manifestations than on any subsequent statements concerning their lack of knowledge about the contents of the document they sign.

MEYER v. BENKO

55 Cal. App. 2d 937, 127 Cal. 846 (1976)

California Court of Appeals, Second District

STEPHENS, Associate Justice.

This is an action for specific performance of a contract of sale of real property, or in the alternative, damages. Plaintiffs William and Deborah Meyer, purchasers, appeal from a judgment that no contract existed or was created between them and the defendants, Howard and Irene Benko, sellers.

FACTS

On December 28, 1972, plaintiffs and defendants executed a document entitled "DEPOSIT RECEIPT and AGREEMENT OF SALE" (hereinafter, Deposit Receipt). Under its terms, the Deposit Receipt required plaintiffs to deposit $250 of a total of $23,500 purchase price for a residence owned by defendants and, in pertinent part, further specified:

"Buyer to obtain and qualify for a new (_____ VA 20½ yr. _____ FHA _X_ FHA Vet 30 yr.) loan in the amount of $22,650

at the prevailing (_____ VA _X_ FHA) interest rate at close of escrow (plus ½ % to FHA Mutual mortgage insurance). Buyer to pay 1 pt. loan origination fee and ½ % VA funding fee, if applicable, and those costs required by (_____ VA _X_ FHA) lender including an impound account for taxes and hazard insurance. Payments to be approximately $214.00 per month including principle [*sic*] interest and impounds for taxes and hazard insurance. Seller to pay no more than _4.5_ loan discount points for new loan. (_X_ Seller _____ Buyer) to pay for (_____ VA _X_ FHA) appraisal and *seller to do any necessary work at his expense. . . .*" (Emphasis added.)

The defendants signed this document on the lines prefaced by the word "Seller," immediately below a statement acknowledging that the sellers "have read, understood, approved and received [a] copy of this agreement. . . ." Plaintiffs' signatures appear on the lines labeled

---

[14] In re Baer's Estate, 92 N.Y.S.2d 359 (1949).

"Buyer," immediately below the following statement:

"We, the undersigned, agree to purchase the above described property for the price and terms outlined above. We have read and understood this agreement and acknowledge receipt of a copy of this *contract*. . . ." (Emphasis added.)

Following the execution of these documents, the plaintiffs procured a loan commitment from Colonial Associates Incorporated in the amount of $22,650, guaranteed by the Federal Housing Authority, payable over a thirty-year period at an interest rate of 7½ percent per annum. However, as a condition to guaranteeing the loan, the FHA required that a new roof be installed on the residence. Both the plaintiffs and the defendants refused to pay the $515 cost of a new roof. As a result, the loan commitment lapsed and the defendants never conveyed possession or title to the residence.

Plaintiffs instituted this action, alleging that the aforementioned Deposit Receipt constituted an enforceable contract, and that despite the fact that the plaintiffs had performed all conditions precedent to conveyance, the defendants refused to convey the subject property. After a trial without a jury, the court concluded that no contract existed between the parties. This conclusion was based upon findings that the Deposit Receipt merely constituted an offer subject to various unsatisfied contingencies.

DISCUSSION

In considering the merits of this appeal, we heed certain guidelines:

"The interpretation of a written instrument . . . is essentially a judicial function to be exercised according to the general accepted canons of interpretation so that the purpose of the instrument may be given effect. Extrinsic evidence is 'admissible to interpret the instrument, but not to give it a meaning to which it is not reasonably susceptible' and it is the instrument itself that must be given effect." (Parsons v. Bristol Dev. Co., 62 Cal. 2d 861, 865, 44 Cal. Rptr. 767, 770, 402 P.2d 839, 842.) In addition, it is "solely a judicial function to interpret

a written instrument unless the interpretation turns upon the credibility of extrinsic evidence. Accordingly, 'An appellate court is not bound by a construction of the contract based solely upon the terms of the written instrument without the aid of evidence [citations], where there is no conflict in the evidence.' (Estate of Platt, 21 Cal. 2d 343, 352, 131 P.2d 825, 830.)" (Parsons v. Bristol Dev. Co., 62 Cal. 2d 861, 865, 44 Cal. Rptr. 767, 770, 402 P.2d 839, 842.) In the case at bar, we have determined that there is no conflict in the relevant evidence. Therefore, we are not bound by the trial court's construction of the Deposit Receipt.

Every contract requires the mutual assent or consent of the parties. The existence of mutual consent is determined by objective rather than subjective criteria, the test being what the outward manifestations of consent would lead a reasonable person to believe. Accordingly, the primary focus in determining the existence of mutual consent is upon the acts of the parties involved. In the case at bar, this focus is directed toward the Deposit Receipt and related documents, and the actions of the parties during the period of time encompassing the execution of these documents.

The utilization of the objective test of mutual consent demonstrates that the Deposit Receipt is in fact a contract. The fact that this document was signed by *both* parties indicates that the parties entered into an enforceable agreement. "Ordinarily, one who accepts or signs an instrument, which on its face is a contract, is deemed to assent to all its terms. . . ." Although the parties introduced conflicting testimony as to whether or not the terms of the Deposit Receipt were explained to the defendants before they signed that document, this evidence was not sufficient to establish a lack of mutual consent. "The general rule is that when a person with the capacity of reading and understanding an instrument signs it, he is, in the absence of fraud and imposition, bound by its contents, and is estopped from saying that its explicit provisions are contrary to his intentions or understanding." (Larsen v. Johannes, 7 Cal. App. 3d 491, 501, 86 Cal. Rptr. 744,

749.) In addition the material factors common to a contract for the sale of real property are contained within the terms of the Deposit Receipt. The Deposit Receipt named the sellers, named the buyers, identified the property being sold, and specified the price for which that property was being sold. Further, it detailed the method of financing the transaction, as well as providing an allocation of various incidental costs and duties. The presence of these material factors upon the face of the document raises two inferences, both of which indicate the existence of mutual consent. First, these factors indicate that the parties had proceeded beyond the stage of mere preliminary negotiations and into the stage of actual contract formation. Moreover, the presence of this material in the document gave notice to the subscribing parties, notably the defendants, that they were entering into a binding contract by subscribing their signatures upon that document. The evidence introduced by the defendants relating to their lack of knowledge about the implications of the terms contained in the Deposit Receipt fails to rebut these inferences. . . .

In toto, the various facts discussed above lead to the inescapable conclusion that, based upon an objective test of contract formation, the parties mutually assented to the formation of a contract on the terms and conditions set forth in the Deposit Receipt. Accordingly, pursuant to the term obligating the seller "to pay for . . . FHA appraisal and . . . to do any necessary work at his expense," the defendants were bound to pay for the new roof. . . .

The judgment is reversed.

KAUS, P. J., and HASTINGS, J., concur.

---

b. Definity of the Offer

Part of the problem in determining whether there has been an offer and acceptance involves the question of the definity of the offer and acceptance. The nature of the contractual relationship must be reasonably certain, or there is no mutual assent. That is, the offer must contain sufficient definity, or require such definity in the acceptance, as to apprise both parties of the true nature of their obligations. Absolute certainty, however, is not required.[15]

Courts have developed various rules of construction to aid them in their effort to provide terms in the contract that would otherwise not be definite enough to constitute the requisite meeting of the minds. The following are examples of such rules: (1) indefinite provisions or unexpressed conditions may be cured or provided by reference to accepted standards;[16] (2) whenever reasonable, terms of a contract will be interpreted as consistent rather than conflicting; (3) the law will favor an interpretation that gives a lawful and effective meaning to all terms over an interpretation that will leave a part of the contract unlawful or without effect; (4) specific terms are given greater weight than general terms; (5) the intent of the parties controls if ascertainable; (6) language will be given its generally prevailing meaning in the absence of a different intention;[17] (7) custom in the business community will explain what would otherwise be indefinite provisions in an offer or acceptance; (8) words that appear to be incapable of adequate definition may become contrac-

---

[15] Barnes v. Huck, 540 P.2d 1352 (Idaho 1975); Forest, Inc. v. Guarantee Mortgage Company, 534 S.W.2d 853 (Tenn. App. 1975).

[16] See 17 *AmJur* 2d, "Contracts," section 240 et seq.

[17] See *Restatement of Contracts 2d* (1973), sections 228, 229, 232, 233.

tually acceptable as a result of numerous past interpretations by courts. In these cases the intent of the parties with respect to specific matters is presumed, and the contract is enforced in accordance with those presumptions.[18]

c. Termination of the Offer; Method of Acceptance

An offeree is often precluded from mutually assenting to an offer because the offer terminates before it is accepted. By making an offer, the offeror creates a continuing power in the offeree to create a contract by acceptance. However, such power continues only for the duration of the offer, which can be limited or terminated. There are three primary ways by which an offer may terminate:

i. REJECTION

The offer terminates by rejection when the offeree communicates to the offeror an intent to decline the offer.[19] If the offeree responds with another offer that differs in any significant respect from the original offer, the offeree's return offer is a counteroffer. It also acts as a rejection and terminates the original offer that was made.[20] However, in this latter situation there remains a second offer made by the original offeree, which the original offeror now can either accept or reject.

For the rejection to be effective, it must be communicated directly to the offeror. A rejection is not effective or functional until the offeror receives it. Thus a rejection that an offeree sends through the mail is ineffective if it becomes lost. An acceptance, on the other hand, is effective when it is mailed.[21] Therefore, in a situation in which A makes an offer to B and B mails a rejection by regular delivery mail but thereafter sends an acceptance by special delivery so that the acceptance is received first, there is a binding contract formulated at the point in time when B's acceptance was placed in the mail. This is referred to as the mailbox rule, which originated in *Adams* v. *Lindsell*.[22] The leading American case with respect to the rule is *Morrison* v. *Thoelke*.[23] The rationale for the rule originated in a fiction that was indulged by the

---

[18] National Car Rental System, Inc. v. Council Wholesale Distributors, Inc., 393 F. Supp. 1128 (M.D. Ga. 1974); Zappanti v. Berge Service Center, 549 P.2d 178 (Ariz. App. 1976); Wells Fargo Bank, National Assn. v. Huse, 57 Cal. App.3d 927, 129 Cal. 522 (1976) (words in private instruments should be accorded the effect given them by statutory or case law in absence of showing of contrary intent).

[19] Peretz v. Watson, 324 N.E.2d 908 (Mass. App. 1975); Nodland v. Chirpich, 240 N.W.2d 513 (Minn. 1976).

[20] Coffman Industries, Inc. v. Gorman-Taber Co., 521 S.W.2d 763 (Mo. App. 1975); Greenberg v. Stewart, 236 N.W.2d 862 (N.D. 1975); Anderson v. Shain, 1 Wash. App. 469, 462 P.2d 566 (1970). But see the discussion on pp. 183–87 in Chapter 8 concerning the Uniform Commercial Code, Section 2–207, which provides that an acceptance with added or different terms operates as an acceptance unless it is expressly made conditional on assent to the added or different term.

[21] McClure Insurance Agency v. Hudson, 238 Ark. 5, 377 S.W.2d 814 (1964); Palo Alto Town & Country Village, Inc. v. BBTC Corp., 521 P.2d 1097, 113 Cal. 705 (1974). See also *Restatement of Contracts 2d* (1973), section 39.

[22] Adams v. Lindsell, 1 Barn. & Ald. 681, 106 Eng. Rep. 250 (K.B. 1818).

[23] Morrison v. Thoelke, 155 So.2d 889 (Fla. App. 1963).

courts at the time of the *Adams* v. *Lindsell* case, namely that since the offeror's offer is mentally continuous after it is mailed, a contract is formed by the offeree's overt act of posting the letter of acceptance. This theory satisfied the requirement that the minds of the parties meet on the same proposal at the same time and also satisfied the court's unwillingness to extend the offer beyond the point in time when the offeree manifested assent by an overt act.[24]

The *method* by which the acceptance is communicated to the offeror is also important in determining whether an operative acceptance has occurred, and thus whether there has been mutual assent as is required for the formation of the contract. The offeror may prescribe or require an exact method of acceptance, in the absence of which no contract will be formed, except as described below.[25] However, if the offeror merely suggests a method of acceptance, the offeree may use any method he or she desires to accept the offer.[26] When the offeree uses his or her own method of accepting the offer, then the following rules govern the question of formation:

1. Where the offeror does not indicate a particular method of acceptance, the acceptance is binding on the offeror at the time it leaves the offeree's possession, provided the offeree uses the same method of transmission as the offeror used, or if he or she uses any other customary method of transmission.
2. Even if the offeree uses an unauthorized method of transmitting his or her acceptance, it is binding on the offeror when it is received, provided it arrives within the time that an authorized acceptance would have been received.[27]

Therefore, if A makes an offer to B that states "send your answer by return mail," and B telegrams his or her acceptance, which telegram arrives before return mail would have arrived, the acceptance is binding upon its receipt.

In the event the offeror seeks an *act* by the offeree in response to his or her offer, rather than a verbal acceptance by offeree, performance of such act by the offeree constitutes acceptance. The offeror is bound at the time that performance is rendered by the offeree in accordance with the offer. This is true even if the offeror is not immediately aware of the offeree's performance.[28] However, the offeree must give notice of his or her performance within a reasonable time if it appears unlikely that the offeror will soon discover such performance. For example: A states to B, "If you paint my winter home in Arizona by September 1, then I will pay you $1,000." B then paints the house on August 28. A, who is outside the state of Arizona, is not aware of B's performance. Then B notifies A of his performance on September

[24] See L. Simpson, *Law of Contracts* (St. Paul: West Publishing Co., 1965), section 37.
[25] Nelson, Inc. v. Sewerage Commission of Milwaukee, 72 Wis.2d 400, 241 N.W.2d 390 (1976); Crockett v. Lowther, 549 P.2d 303 (Wyo. 1976).
[26] United States Ore Corp. v. Commercial Transport Corp., 369 F. Supp. 792 (E.D. La. 1974); In re Klauenberg's Estate, 108 Cal. 669 (Cal. App. 1973).
[27] Bruegger v. National Old Line Insurance Co., 387 F. Supp. 1177 (D.C. Wyo. 1975); Hayne v. Cook, 525 Iowa 1012, 109 N.W.2d 188 (1961); Farmers' Produce Co. v. McAlester Storage & Commission Co., 48 Okla. 488, 150 P. 483 (1915).
[28] Garrett v. American Family Mutual Insurance Co., 520 S.W.2d 102 (Mo. App. 1974).

2. Even though A was unaware of B's performance prior to the September 1 dead-line, A would be obligated to pay B the $1,000 offered.

ii. LAPSE OF TIME

Once an offer has been made, how much time does the offeree have to make up his or her mind whether to accept or reject that offer? An offer remains open for the length of time expressly stated by the terms of the contract. Where it is not stated, the court must rely on a rule of construction. The majority of jurisdictions hold that an offer that does not specify the length of its continuance remains open for a reasonable time.[29] The judge or jury in each case must determine what constitutes a reasonable time. Generally, the nature of the subject matter of the offer or the proposed contract influences the determination of how long the offer was intended to remain open. For example, an offer to sell publicly traded shares of stock is presumed to remain operable for only a very short time, since it would not be fair to the offeror to allow the offeree to wait until the market value of those stocks increased tremendously before accepting the offer at the original price, which is now substantially below the price the offeree can obtain for the stock in the open market. On the other hand, an offer to purchase or sell real estate may reasonably be expected to remain open for a week or more. Thus a "reasonable time" will vary significantly depending upon the subject matter of the offer.

iii. REVOCATION

The third method by which an offer may be terminated is by the offeror retracting his or her offer prior to acceptance by the offeree.[30] Contrary to the requirement in the case of rejection, a revocation may be communicated to the offeree by either direct or indirect means. That is, if any act of the offeror that is inconsistent with the offer is communicated to the offeree, even by third persons, the offer is considered revoked.[31] For example, if the offeror makes an offer to the offeree, and prior to its acceptance the offeror sells the item previously offered to the offeree to a third person, then, although not directly communicated to the of-feree, such an action on the part of the offeror will be considered a revocation of the original offer, resulting in the original offeree's inability to form a contract by acceptance.

---

[29] Stewart v. Cunningham, 219 Kan. 374, 548 P.2d 740 (1976); Martin v. Basham, 223 S.E.2d 899 (Va. 1976).

[30] *Restatement of Contracts 2d* (1973) Section 35. See also Richards v. Simpson, 111 Ariz. 415, 531 P.2d 538 (1975); Coffman Industries, Inc. v. Gorman-Taber Co., 521 S.W.2d 763 (Mo. App. 1975). The general rule does not apply to bid offers, such as contractor-subcontractor situations, Claitor v. Delta Corp., 279 So.2d 731 (La. App. 1973), and does not apply to option contracts, Kidd v. Early, 222 S.E.2d 392 (N.C. 1976).

[31] Hoover Motor Express Co. v. Clements Paper Co., 193 Tenn. 6, 241 S.W.2d 851 (1951) (any inconsistent act is sufficient); Frank v. Stratford-Handcock, 13 Wyo. 37, 77 P. 134 (1904) (prior sale of goods). The leading case is Dickinson v. Dodds, 2 Ch. D. 463 (C.A. 1876). See also 77 *AmJur* 2d., "Vendors and Purchasers," section 20.

4. Consideration

The fourth and final requirement for the formation of a contract is that of consideration. Both parties to a contract must convey consideration to and receive consideration from one another.[32] This occurs if the parties incur a legal detriment by promising to do what they are not otherwise legally bound to do, or by promising not to do what they are legally privileged to do.[33] That is, the parties must in some respect suffer a detriment induced by the promise of the other party. If one party's promise induces a promise from the other party, they are said to be engaging in bargaining.[34] Thus there must be actual bargaining between the parties in order for consideration to be present.

Consideration is not present in a situation in which a father wants to make a gift of real estate to his son and promises to "sell" a $100,000 piece of property to him for only 50¢. There is no contract in this situation because there was no real bargaining intent, (a) even though an actual exchange was made, namely the property for 50¢, (b) even though there were two parties, both having the legal capacity to incur contractual obligations, and (c) even though there was mutual assent. Since the parties did not intend an actual bargain, the court would rule that the consideration was inadequate.[35]

In addition, the consideration must be a present consideration.[36] Thus, if individual A saved B's life two years ago, and B now promises to convey a certain tract of real estate to A as a result of A's past heroics, no contract will exist because there is no present consideration, no present bargaining, and no benefit flowing from A to B. Instead such a promise by B would be regarded as a gift promise rather than a contract to sell property, and if a gift promise is not kept, the promisee cannot enforce fulfillment of such promise. "He gave nothing for it, loses nothing by it, and upon its breach he suffers no recoverable damage." [37]

C. Other Contractual Situations

Having examined the four basic requirements for the formation of a contract, we next discuss situations involving the existence of an already formed valid and binding contract. These situations involve the legal interpretation of existing contracts and the requirements of performance upon the parties involved.

---

[32] Bearden v. Ebcap Supply Co., 108 Ga. App. 375, 133 S.E.2d 62 (1963); Manwill v. Oyler, 11 Utah 2d 733, 361 P.2d 177 (1961).

[33] Reed, Roberts Associates, Inc. v. Bailenson, 537 S.W.2d 238 (Mo. App. 1976).

[34] Richman v. Brookhaven Servicing Corp., 363 N.Y.S.2d 731 (1975); Tigrett v. Heritage Building Co., 533 S.W.2d 65 (Tex. Civ. App. 1976).

[35] The leading case on this point is Fisher v. Union Trust Co., 138 Mich. 612, 101 N.W. 852 (1904).

[36] Bogley's Estate v. United States, 514 F.2d 1027 (Ct. Claims 1975).

[37] Stonestreet v. Southern Oil Co., 226 N.C. 261, 31 S.E.2d 676 (1946).

1. Third-party Beneficiaries

A third-party beneficiary is one who is entitled to enforce a promise made for his or her benefit, even though he or she is a complete stranger to both the contract and the consideration that was conveyed by both parties to each other.[38] The law of third-party beneficiaries relates to situations in which an offeror is obligated to perform for the benefit of a third person who is not a party to the contract but who has the right to seek such performance. It is not necessary that any consideration move from the third-party beneficiary in order for that person to have enforceable rights. Of course, in order for the third-party beneficiary to enforce the contract, the contract itself must be valid. Also, the fact that a third-party beneficiary may enforce the contract does not limit or otherwise affect the promisee's right to enforce it. The third-party beneficiary's rights under the contract will not be greater than the rights of the promisee—that is, the party entering into the contract for the benefit of the third party.[39]

The primary factors determining whether the third party is entitled to enforceable rights are: the intentions of the parties to the contract; and the requirement that the benefit to the third party must be the direct result of the promisor's performance of the contract.[40] "Before an injured party may recover as a third party beneficiary . . . it must clearly appear from the provisions of the contract that the parties thereto intend to confer a *direct benefit* on the alleged third party beneficiary." [41]

The law recognizes the concept of third-party beneficiaries and permits the enforcement of their rights in order to effectuate the intent of the parties to the contract, and to avoid circuitous and unnecessary litigation. The concept is illustrated in Figure 7.1 (p. 138).

There are two classifications of third-party beneficiaries: creditor beneficiaries and donee beneficiaries. A creditor to whom a party (promisee) owes or believes he or she owes a legal obligation becomes a third-party creditor beneficiary when two parties enter into a contract in which one party (promisor) agrees to pay or agrees to perform the other party's legal obligation to that creditor.[42] For example, if A buys a house and B is the mortgagee, and A then sells the house to C, who assumes the mortgage, then C is personally liable to B, the creditor beneficiary, on the mortgage note. This situation is illustrated in Figure 7.2 (p. 138).

---

[38] The leading case in this area is Lawrence v. Fox, 20 N.Y. 268 (1859). See also United States v. Ogden Technology Laboratories, Inc., 406 F. Supp. 1090 (E.D.N.Y. 1973); Martin v. Edwards, 219 Kan. 466, 548 P.2d 779 (1976).

[39] Zahn v. Canadian Indemnity Co., 57 Cal. App.3d 509, 129 Cal. 276 (1976); Rumsey Electric Co. v. University of Delaware, 358 A.2d 712 (Del. 1976).

[40] Backus v. Chilivis, 236 Ga. 500, 224 S.E.2d 370 (1976) ("in order for a third party to have standing to enforce a contract . . . it must clearly appear from the contract that it was intended for his benefit"); Martin v. Edwards, 219 Kan. 466, 548 P.2d 779 (1976) (the intent of the contracting parties as to the rights of a third-party beneficiary is a question of construction for the court, subject to the usual rules of construction).

[41] Bernal v. Pinkerton's, Inc., 382 N.Y.S.2d 769 (1976).

[42] Horne v. Radiological Health Services, P.C., 371 N.Y.S.2d 948 (N.Y. Sup. 1975); *Restatement of Contracts 2d* (1973), section 133(1)(a) and comment B.

Third-Party Beneficiary

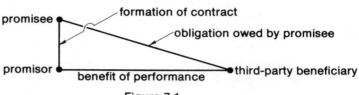

Figure 7.1

The creditor beneficiary has enforceable rights under the contract, on the theory that the parties intend to benefit him or her even though the actual intent of the promisee is not so much to benefit the creditor as it is to relieve himself or herself of the debt.

A situation in which there is a donee beneficiary arises when two parties enter into a contract whereby the promisee intends to make a direct *gift* to the third party through the medium of the promisor's performance, as shown in Figure 7.3. Here A intends that C's payment of $500 to B (in exchange for services performed by A for C) constitutes a gift to B. As third-party beneficiary, B is entitled to enforce the contract if C fails to make the $500 payment.

Even though the third party may in fact also be a creditor of the donor-promisee, the donor-promisee will not discharge his or her obligation to the beneficiary unless he or she *intends* the promisor's performance to function as a discharge.[43] For example, A owes B $500 and A does a painting for C. A then instructs C to pay the portrait price of $1,000 to B rather than to A. In this situation, A *intends* the $1,000 to be a gift. Thus B is a donee beneficiary, and A still owes B $500. This is diagrammed in Figure 7.4.

Creditor Beneficiary

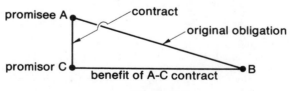

Figure 7.2

---

[43] King v. National Industries, Inc., 512 F.2d 29 (6th Cir. 1975); Wolfe v. Morgan, 11 Wash. App. 738, 524 P.2d 927 (1974); *Restatement of Contracts 2d* (1973), section 133(1)(b) and comment C.

Donee Beneficiary

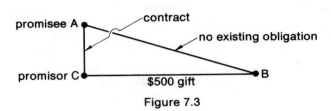

Figure 7.3

There is still another type of third-party beneficiary, namely the incidental beneficiary. A third party to whom a merely incidental, indirect, or consequential benefit accrues as a result of a contract between two parties has no enforceable rights against either the promisor or promisee; this person is described as an incidental beneficiary. "Where the contract is primarily for the benefit of the parties thereto, the mere fact that a third person would be incidentally benefited does not give him a right to sue for its breach." [44] For example, A, in return for services, promises to finance B's tuition through college. The college is then an incidental beneficiary.

Beneficiaries with enforceable rights need not know of the contract when it is entered into, nor need they rely upon the contract in order to have enforceable rights.[45] In addition, the third-party beneficiary need not be designated nor identified by name in the contract; however, the beneficiary must be ascertainable at the time the promisor is to perform his or her obligation.[46]

Donee Beneficiary (as creditor)

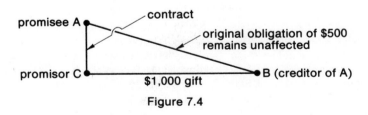

Figure 7.4

---

[44] 17 *AmJur* 2d, "Contracts," section 307, as cited in Martin v. Edwards, 219 Kan. 466, 548 P.2d 779, 785 (1976).

[45] Martin v. Edwards, 219 Kan. 466, 548 P.2d 779 (1976); Peters Grazing Association v. Legerski, 544 P.2d 449 (Wyo. 1975).

[46] Bond v. Home Furniture Co., 516 S.W.2d 224 (Tex. Civ. App. 1974) (plaintiff-beneficiary sufficiently designated even though no specific mention of plaintiff).

2. Assignments

An assignment is a manifestation by the owner (the assignor) to presently transfer an interest in a contractual right or other property to another (the assignee). An assignment does not have to be in writing, but if it is not in writing, it is revoked by the death of the assignor, by a subsequent assignment by the assignor to a second assignee, or by notice of revocation given by the assignor to the assignee or given to the assignor's debtor.[47] If the assignor chooses to put the assignment in writing, thus making it irrevocable, that writing must make it sufficiently clear that the assignor intends to surrender his or her right to the assignee.

As illustrated in the case of *Macke Co.* v. *Pizza of Gaithersburg, Inc.,* an assignor may assign any right he or she desires or delegate any duty, even without the permission of the original promisee of the contract, unless the substitution of the assignee for the original promisee materially varies the duty of the promisee or increases the promisee's contractual risk. Often in assigning these rights under a contract, the assignor may also delegate performance of the duty that conditions his or her right. However, where the duty is a personal duty, it is not delegable. Therefore, under an employment contract, the duties of an employee, such as a school teacher or sales representative, are not delegable without the employer's assent, since the personal trust or confidence has been placed in the employee.

MACKE COMPANY
v.
PIZZA OF GAITHERSBURG, INC.

259 Md. 479, 270 A.2d 645 (1970)

Court of Appeals of Maryland

SINGLEY, Judge.

The appellees and defendants below, Pizza of Gaithersburg, Inc.; Pizzeria, Inc.; The Pizza Pie Corp., Inc. and Pizza Oven, Inc., four corporations under the common ownership of Sidney Ansell, Thomas S. Sherwood and Eugene Early and the same individuals as partners or proprietors (the Pizza Shops) operated at six locations in Montgomery and Prince George's Counties. The appellees had arranged to have installed in each of their locations cold drink vending machines owned by Virginia Coffee Service, Inc., and on 30 December 1966, this arrangement was formalized at five of the locations, by contracts for terms of one year, automatically renewable for a like term in the absence of 30 days' written notice. A similar contract for the sixth location, operated by Pizza of Gaithersburg, Inc., was entered into on 25 July 1967.

On 30 December 1967, Virginia's assets were purchased by The Macke Company (Macke) and the six contracts were assigned to Macke by Virginia. In January, 1968, the Pizza Shops

---

[47] Miller v. Wells Fargo Bank International Corp., 406 F. Supp. 452 (S.D.N.Y. 1975); Mitchell v. Shoreridge Oil Co., 24 Cal. App.2d 382, 75 P.2d 110, rehearing denied, 77 P.2d 221 (1938).

attempted to terminate the five contracts having the December anniversary date, and in February, the contract which had the July anniversary date.

Macke brought suit in the Circuit Court for Montgomery County against each of the Pizza Shops for damages for breach of contract. From judgments for the defendants, Macke has appealed.

The lower court based the result which it reached on two grounds: first, that the Pizza Shops, when they contracted with Virginia, relied on its skill, judgment and reputation, which made impossible a delegation of Virginia's duties to Macke; and second, that the damages claimed could not be shown with reasonable certainty. These conclusions are challenged by Macke.

In the absence of a contrary provision—and there was none here—rights and duties under an executory bilateral contract may be assigned and delegated, subject to the exception that duties under a contract to provide personal services may never be delegated. . . . Crane Ice Cream Co. v. Terminal Freezing & Heating Co., 147 Md. 588, 128 A. 280 (1925) held that the right of an individual to purchase ice under a contract which by its terms reflected a knowledge of the individual's needs and reliance on his credit and responsibility could not be assigned to the corporation which purchased his business. In Eastern Advertising Co. v. McGaw & Co., 89 Md. 72, 42 A. 923 (1899), our predecessors held that an advertising agency could not delegate its duties under a contract which had been entered into by an advertiser who had relied on the agency's skill, judgment and taste. . . .

We cannot regard the agreements as contracts for personal services. They were either a license or concession granted Virginia by the appellees, or a lease of a portion of the appellees' premises, with Virginia agreeing to pay a percentage of gross sales as a license or concession fee or as rent, . . . and were assignable by Virginia unless they imposed on Virginia duties of a personal or unique character which could not be delegated.

The appellees earnestly argue that they had dealt with Macke before and had chosen Virginia because they preferred the way it conducted its business. Specifically, they say that service was more personalized, since the president of Virginia kept the machines in working order, that commissions were paid in cash, and that Virginia permitted them to keep keys to the machines so that minor adjustments could be made when needed. Even if we assume all this to be true, the agreements with Virginia were silent as to the details of the working arrangements and contained only a provision requiring Virginia to "install . . . the above listed equipment and . . . maintain the equipment in good operating order and stocked with merchandise." We think the Supreme Court of California put the problem of personal service in proper focus a century ago when it upheld the assignment of a contract to grade a San Francisco street:

"All painters do not paint portraits like Sir Joshua Reynolds, nor landscapes like Claude Lorraine, nor do all writers write dramas like Shakespeare or fiction like Dickens. Rare genius and extraordinary skill are not transferable, and contracts for their employment are therefore personal, and cannot be assigned. But rare genius and extraordinary skill are not indispensable to the workmanlike digging down of a sand hill or the filling up of a depression to a given level, or the construction of brick sewers with manholes and covers, and contracts for such work are not personal, and may be assigned." Taylor v. Palmer, 31 Cal. 240 at 247–248 (1866).

Moreover, the difference between the service the Pizza Shops happened to be getting from Virginia and what they expected to get from Macke did not mount up to such a material change in the performance of obligations under the agreements as would justify the appellees' refusal to recognize the assignment. . . .

As we see it, the delegation of duty by Virginia to Macke was entirely permissible under the terms of the agreements. In so holding, we do not put ourselves at odds with Eastern Advertising Co. c. McGaw, 89 Md. 72, 42 A. 923, for in that case, the agreement with the agency contained a provision that "the advertising cards were to be 'subject to the approval of Eastern Advertising Company as to style and contents,' " at 82, 42 A. at 923, which the court found to import that reliance was being placed on the agency's skill, judgment and taste, at 88, 42 A. 923. . . .

Judgment reversed as to liability; judgment entered for appellant for costs, on appeal and below.

In *Macke Co.,* despite the fact that the defendant had chosen the assignor service company (not a party to the litigation) specifically because the defendant liked the way the company did business, the court held that the assignment did not affect the defendant's rights materially, and the defendant therefore was bound to the contract with the assignee service company. On the other hand, a person with an insurance policy on a *brick* house cannot assign the rights owed him or her by the insurance company to an assignee for coverage on the assignee's *straw* house, because such assignment would materially alter and increase the duty of the insurance company. Of course, the promisee may expressly prohibit such assignment of rights in the original contract.

D. Conditions in Contracts

A condition is any fact or event other than a lapse of time that qualifies a promisor's duty of performance or nullifies liability for a prior breach by the promisor. There are three types of conditions: conditions precedent, concurrent conditions, and conditions subsequent. If the condition or event must exist or occur before the promisor is bound to perform, it is a condition precedent. If conditions precedent are to be rendered or required to occur simultaneously, they are called concurrent conditions. If the condition nullifies liability for an already existing breach or discharges the promisor's duty of performance that has already arisen, it is a condition subsequent.

An example of a condition precedent would be the following: A commissions B, an artist, to paint a landscape of A's estate. B is to receive $5,000 for painting the picture on the express condition that it wins first or second prize in an art contest in which it is to be entered. The picture does not win first or second prize. Because the condition was not met by B, B has no claim against A for payment of the $5,000. (Of course, A will not be entitled to keep the work.) The point here is that even though the parties had formed a valid contract prior to its performance, A is not obligated to pay B the $5,000 because the express condition was not met. This is an example of a condition precedent, because the condition of winning first or second prize qualified A's duty to pay the $5,000.

If an event occurs *subsequent* to the time that the promisor became obligated to perform, and if the parties have agreed that such an event would discharge the promisor's liability for damages already accrued, the event is a condition subsequent. Thus, where goods are sold under a contract that requires the buyer to pay for them on delivery but also gives the buyer the right to return the goods after a specified inspection period, the buyer can discharge the liability (for failing to pay on delivery) by returning the goods.

The distinction between conditions precedent and conditions subsequent is not important substantively but is very important procedurally. The burden of proving conditions precedent is on the plaintiff promisee, while the burden of proof for conditions subsequent is on the defendant promisor. The rationale is that the promisor cannot be in breach of contract until all conditions to his or her duty exist or have occurred. Thus the plaintiff must allege and affirmatively prove the existence or occurrence of such conditions. On the other hand, the defendant promisor must raise the affirmative defense that a condition subsequent has occurred in order to prove that he or she was relieved of the duty to compensate the plaintiff for the breach alleged in the complaint.

E. Defenses to Breach of Contract

1. Mistake as to a Material Fact

The requirement of mutual assent in the formation of a contract means that the parties must have a meeting of the minds and must agree reasonably well on the meaning of the terms in order to form a contract. Similarly, if the parties are mistaken as to a material fact of the contract, there is no mutual assent, thus no contract. No contract is formed if the parties, each without the knowledge of the other, attach different meanings to the particular words in question.[48] The same result occurs if each party knows that the other party is defining ambiguous words differently, because they are equally at fault for allowing the misunderstanding to develop. Thus there is no reason to hold either contractually liable. If there is a mutual mistake of fact, and that mutual mistake induces the formation of the contract, then the contract is voidable. The court in the case of *Interstate Industrial Uniform Rental Service, Inc.* v. *Couri Pontiac, Inc.* stated as follows: "A mistake of fact occurs if the parties entertain a conception of the facts which differs from the facts as they really exist. The mistake must be mutual, that is, the minds of the parties must fall prey to the same misconception with respect to the bargain . . ."[49] This case also points out that the mistake must relate to the subject matter of the contract and cannot be a merely collateral matter, that is, it must be a material mistake of fact.[50] For example, suppose A agrees to sell B a ring for $1,000. Both of the parties

48 Walther & Cie v. United States Fidelity & Guaranty Co., 397 F. Supp. 937 (M.D. Pa. 1975); Frigaliment Importing Co. v. B.N.S. International Sales Corp., 190 F. Supp. 116 (S.D.N.Y. 1960).

49 Interstate Industrial Uniform Rental Service, Inc. v. Couri Pontiac, Inc., 355 A.2d 913, 918 (Me. 1976).

50 See Bellwood Discount Corp. v. Empire Steel Building Co., 175 Cal. App.2d 432, 346 P.2d 467 (1959); First Regional Securities, Inc. v. Villella, 377 N.Y.S.2d 424 (N.Y. City Civ. Ct. 1975).

believe the ring to be an emerald. Actually it is glass. In this situation the contract would be voidable by B.

However, if the words are uncertain or ambiguous to one party and not the other, then the party who is aware of the ambiguity is bound to the meaning that he or she knows the other party intends.[51] For example: A contracts to buy B's car for $500. However, B has two cars, a 1961 Ford and a 1975 Ford. A is only aware of the 1975 Ford, and B is aware that A only knows about that car. Therefore the 1975 Ford is the subject matter of the contract, and the contract is enforceable by A, despite the fact that B had intended to demand the $500 from A upon presentation of the 1961 Ford to A.

2. Statute of Frauds

There is much misunderstanding about the significance or validity of a written contract as opposed to an oral one. However, except for specific contracts that must be in writing, as described later in this section, there is absolutely no difference in the validity of oral and written contracts. They are equally enforceable, equally valid, and identical in the eyes of the law. The issue of *provability* is incorrectly confused with the question of validity. Just as it is more difficult to prove any unwritten fact than a written one, it is often difficult to *prove* the necessary elements of a contract when all evidence of such elements is oral and, most importantly, is in dispute. There are, however, certain types of contracts that must be placed in writing in order to be enforceable by either party. In general these contracts are likely to involve large amounts of money. Every state in the United States has enacted some form of a statute that is commonly referred to as the Statute of Frauds. The statute is intended to produce certainty in the parties' obligations and to eliminate the possibility of a plaintiff proving a nonexistent contract by the use of perjured evidence. There are a number of areas covered by most statutes of fraud; however, three of these are most important.

a. Contracts for Interest in Land

Most statutes of fraud provide that every contract for the sale of land or any interest in land is unenforceable unless that contract or some note or memorandum expressing the consideration is in writing and is signed by the party against whom the contract is to be enforced.

b. Contracts that Cannot Be Performed within One Year

A second provision common in the statutes of fraud is the requirement that a contract must be in writing if it cannot be fulfilled within one year from the

---

[51] Meyer v. Benko, 55 Cal. App. 2d 937, 127 Cal. 846 (1976); Trujillo v. Glen Falls Insurance Co., 88 N.M. 279, 540 P.2d 209 (1975).

date that it is made. However, courts tend to interpret this provision as not requiring a written contract if there is *any* possibility that the contract can be performed within that one-year period.[52] A common dispute that arises on this matter is whether employment contracts are regulated by the statute of frauds. Typically they are not. For example: A orally contracts to support B for the rest of his or her life. B is twenty-two years old and in good health. Because it is *possible* for B to die within a year, in which case the contract would be completely performed, this contract, though oral, is enforceable, and the provisions and requirements of the statute are avoided.

c. Sales for $500 or More

The third common provision under statutes of fraud deals with the sale of goods in the amount of $500 or more. In order for such contracts to be enforceable, they must be in writing.[53] However, there are certain exceptions to this requirement in most jurisdictions, including the following: (a) an oral contract for specially manufactured goods in excess of $500 is enforceable; (b) goods received and accepted or paid for may render an oral contract enforceable; and (c) written confirmation by one merchant under an oral contract (for goods in excess of $500), if the written confirmation requires a written rejection, allows for the enforcement of that oral contract.

3. Statute of Limitations

All jurisdictions have enacted statutes that place a specific time limit on an injured party's right to commence an action based on breach of contract, as well as other statutes relating to the time limit for commencing all other types of actions. These are referred to as statutes of limitations. The period of time usually begins when the injury occurred, or when the plaintiff should have reasonably discovered the occurrence of such injury. The effect of such statutes is to permanently bar any claim from being made after the specified period of time, which may be anywhere from one year for breach of contract in some jurisdictions to six or eight years in others.

However, if the statute of limitations bars a claim, such claim may be revived by a new promise to pay any amount owed under the contract, or by an acknowledgment of debt and of the duty to pay it, or by part payment by the breaching party. In such a case, the act or promise of the debtor does not require new consideration

---

[52] See e.g., Kiyose v. Trustees of Indiana University, 333 N.E.2d 886 (Ind. App. 1975); Koman v. Morrissey, 517 S.W.2d 929 (Mo. 1975); Kramer v. Kramer, 26 Md. App. 620, 339 A.2d 328 (1975) (child support agreement not within statute because it would be performed in less than a year if the child were to die); Chandler v. Rosewin Coats, Inc., 515 S.W.2d 184 (Mo. App. 1974).

[53] Uniform Commercial Code, section 2–201.

running from the debtor to the creditor in order to continue the obligation beyond the period of time stated in the statute of limitations.

QUESTIONS

refers to Personal [illegible handwritten note]

1. In what respects might society suffer if judges are allowed to rewrite contracts on the basis of moral rather than legal considerations? Can the two considerations be separated?

2. In the case of *Kiefer* v. *Fred Howe Motors, Inc.,* discuss the significance of the following issues: capacity; emancipation; disaffirmance of contract; contract liability, as opposed to liability in tort for fraud and misrepresentation; and the automobile as a necessity.

3. If the principles in the case of *Meyer* v. *Benko* had been applied to the *Kiefer* case, would the court have reached a different decision in *Kiefer?* Why or why not?

Example of conditions precedent & subsequent

4. On Thursday at 9:00 A.M., Smith called Anderson Supply Store and ordered 1,000 pounds of barley seed at $1.03 per pound for the spring planting on the Smith farm. During the conversation Smith informed Anderson that he needed the seed delivered by the following Wednesday morning, because Smith intended to begin the three days of planting work that day, and because he had hired some hands for Wednesday.

    mid term type item — ques

    On the following Wednesday at 10:00 A.M. the seed had not been delivered yet. Smith called Anderson twice, but was not able to get through either time because the line was busy. So Smith called Lincoln Farm Supply and ordered 1,000 pounds of barley seed (at $1.26 per pound) for immediate delivery. At 12:15 the Anderson and Lincoln trucks both drove into the Smith driveway.

    What are the issues? Should Smith refuse the Anderson delivery? the Lincoln delivery? why? Who is entitled to damages? how much?

5. What, if any, conditions are present in the situation described in paragraph 4 above?

Statute of Fraud — 500.⁰⁰ or more.

8

Business Law

A. Nature and Source of Business Law

Unlike the law of contracts, business law is not a well-defined area of the law. Rather it is a conglomeration of several narrow substantive areas of the law that are often loosely combined under the general heading of business law. One of these substantive areas is contracts, which has already been discussed in Chapter 7. This chapter covers four other such areas—business organizations, agency, the Uniform Commercial Code, and property. Each of these five substantive areas comprises a separate course in law school.

The source of modern business law is the same as the source of the civil law discussed in Chapter 1—the common law of England. However, business law has been codified to a greater extent than other areas of the civil law. Throughout this chapter, statutes such as the Uniform Partnership Act, the Uniform Limited Partnership Act, the Uniform Commercial Code, and other uniform acts will be mentioned. These statutes cover areas of the law that were previously controlled by court decisions or case law. The codification of commercial law is similar to the adoption of uniform criminal codes in many jurisdictions. Also, as seen in Chapters 5 and 6, great changes occurred in both state and federal civil procedure with the adoption of uniform rules of civil procedure for the federal judicial system and for almost all state judicial systems.

The National Conference of Commissioners on Uniform State Laws, appointed by the governors of the states, worked with the American Law Institute, a private foundation, to draft these uniform laws. The Conference has encouraged the states to adopt the laws in the form recommended or in similar form. The desire for modernization, uniformity, and consistency among the states' treatment of the many aspects of commercial law resulted in formation of the Uniform Commercial Code (UCC). We will examine some of the principles of this voluminous law in Part D of this chapter. The UCC deals with all aspects of commercial transactions, including the contract of sale, the security device that may be used to ensure payment to the seller, the instrument of payment given to the seller by the buyer, such as a check or promissory note, and the document of title to goods being sold. The UCC also deals with commercial matters such as bulk sales, investment securities, and the bank collection process. Forty-nine states have now enacted some form of the Uniform Commercial Code. Similarly, most states have adopted some form of the Uniform Partnership Act, the Uniform Limited Partnership Act, and the Model Business Corporation Act. These acts, discussed in this chapter, are contained in Appendices F through I.

B. Business Organizations

Businesses operate under a variety of forms, the most common of which are the sole proprietorship, the partnership, the limited partnership, and the corporation. Some less common business organizations are professional service corporations, joint stock companies, business trusts, and joint ventures. Only the first four will be discussed in this chapter. The particular form a business takes has a significant influence on its ability to function, its taxation, and other factors. Thus people forming, planning, or intending to expand or restructure a business should examine the factors that could affect that business and determine which form of organization would be the best framework for the conduct of the business. There are advantages and disadvantages with each form. The most important factors to be considered are taxation, control, liability, continuity, and legal capacity. The method of creating each of the four types of business organizations and the characteristics of each will be examined in connection with these five factors.

1. Sole Proprietorship

A business in the form of a sole proprietorship is simply a business owned by one person. Such a business may employ any number of persons, but the actual ownership rests in one person. Income earned by the owner of a sole proprietorship is taxed as ordinary income, just as if that person were being paid a salary. Sole proprietors are entitled to deduct all business expenses as well as all personal non-business deductions in arriving at net taxable income. Control is also a very simple matter and is usually an advantage in a sole proprietorship, because all decisions ultimately rest with the owner, despite the fact that authority is often delegated to managers or other employees for certain tasks or for specified periods of time.

Personal liability is usually considered a disadvantage when compared to the limited partnership or corporate form of business organization. The sole proprietor is the sole owner of the business, and remains solely and personally responsible for all debts incurred by the business. Thus *all* of the sole proprietor's assets are available for satisfying business-incurred debts, including the owner's property that is not connected with the business, such as his or her house and family car. The sole proprietor takes all the profits but also assumes all the risks.

The lack of continuity of a sole proprietorship is another disadvantage of this form of business entity. If the owner dies, or becomes too ill to continue the operation of the business, there is no separate legal entity in existence with which the public, creditors, or suppliers can deal to ensure the continuity of the business. Of course, if the sole proprietor has a number of employees to whom various duties had been delegated, those employees could make management decisions. However, the legal essence of the business is absent if the sole proprietor is absent. By contrast with a corporation, when one of the shareholders of a corporation dies, the shares representing the business organization itself would pass on to the heirs of that shareholder, and the business entity itself would survive. In the sole proprietorship the assets of the business would pass to the heirs upon his or her death. The business itself would terminate at that point, unless one of the heirs wanted to continue it, in which case the ownership of the business would be vested in a new sole proprietor.

Legal capacity refers both to the capability of the business to sue and be sued in its own name and to the capacity of the business to own and dispose of property and to enter into contracts. A sole proprietor has the sole legal capacity to sue and be sued for damages resulting from the operation of the business. Damages to the business are damages to the individual sole proprietor; damages to other persons caused by the business are damages caused by the individual sole proprietor. Thus the business is not considered a separate entity having its own legal capacity. The same principle applies to entering into contracts and disposing of property owned by the sole proprietor.

2. General Partnership

a. General Description

The law of partnership originated in the common law of England, and much of the present law on the subject is the result of hundreds of years of development. As mentioned earlier, the law of partnership has been significantly affected by statutory developments. The efforts to codify partnership law culminated in England with the Partnership Act of 1890 and in the United States with the Uniform Partnership Act, completed by the Commissioners on Uniform State Laws in 1914.[1] Forty-three states have now adopted the act. Like all uniform laws, the Uniform Partnership Act is primarily a restatement and reorganization of the case law that existed at the time of its original enactment. Through subsequent amendments, the statute continues to reflect the soundest legal principles.

Partnerships are classified as either *general* or *limited*. The main distinctions between the two classifications are that: (a) one or more partners in the limited partnership have limited liability—that is, their liability is limited to the extent of their investment in the partnership—whereas all partners in a general partnership have unlimited liability; and (b) limited partners have no control over the everyday

---

[1] See L. Smith and G. Roberson, *Business Law* (St. Paul: West Publishing Co., 1971), pp. 730 *et seq.*

management of the partnership, whereas general partners have a voice in the every-day management. The limited partnership will be discussed later.

A *general partnership* is an association of two or more persons to carry on, as co-owners, a business for profit. This generally accepted definition is the one given by § [Section] 6 of the Uniform Partnership Act. Other definitions are less popular but more comprehensive.[2] Although as a practical matter in the course of day-to-day business activities this association is regarded as an entity in itself, the common law does not recognize a partnership as a legal entity.[3] Rather it is regarded as an aggre-gation of individuals. Thus, unlike a corporation, a partnership is not a fictional person with a distinct legal existence apart from its members. This was not only the theory at common law, but also the view written into §§ (Sections) 6 and 7 of the Uniform Partnership Act. This characterization of a partnership as an associa-tion of individuals is reflected in the legal considerations of taxation, liability, con-trol, continuity, and legal capacity discussed below.

b. Formation

We will first examine the requirements for the formation of a general partnership. The question of whether a partnership exists should be the first one addressed when examining a situation in which the form of the business is not clear. A partnership is created by an agreement of the parties who are to be the owners and managers of the business. Sometimes the parties enter into a written agreement called the "Articles of Partnership" or "Partnership Agreement." In other situa-tions, the partners may orally agree to form a partnership. A partnership not only may be formed by such an express written or oral agreement but also may arise among parties doing business with each other, as a result of their conduct.[4] It is in the latter situation that the basic question of whether a partnership exists is likely to arise.

Thus the question of whether a partnership exists may be complex, but it must be conclusively determined in many situations, because liability will ultimately de-pend upon whether the parties are deemed to be in business by themselves or in a partnership. The question must also be determined in situations in which one alleged partner may have a cause of action against his or her alleged copartners. Difficult facts and situations often arise because of the partners' failure to become associated in more than an informal way or by an incomplete arrangement, thereby

---

[2] For example, "partnership . . . is usually defined to be a voluntary contract between two or more competent persons to place their money, effects, labor and skills, or some or all in lawful commerce or business, with the understanding that there shall be a communion of the profits thereof between them." J. Story, *Commentaries On The Law of Partnership,* W. Wharton, ed. (Boston: Little, Brown, and Co., 1881), p. 1; similar to definition in 59 *AmJur* 2d, Partner-ship, section 5.

[3] Pinellas County v. Lake Padgett Pines, 333 So.2d 472 (Fla. App. 1976); see also 59 *AmJur* 2d, Partnership, section 6.

[4] Garner v. Garner, 31 Md. App. 641, 358 A.2d 583 (1976) (advertising under firm name in phone directory, on letterheads, and in insurance policies was evidence that parties conducted themselves as if they were a partnership).

leaving unspecified their rights, their duties, and the nature of their relationship. Problems arise if the parties claim to have a relationship other than a partnership, such as a loan, a lease, or a contract of employment, and if their relationship actually possesses the elements of a partnership. They may not know that they have formed a partnership, nor desire one. But if the relationship they desire constitutes a partnership under the law, it will be considered as such both between them and in relation to third persons.[5]

CREST CONSTRUCTION COMPANY
v.
INSURANCE COMPANY
OF NORTH AMERICA

417 F. Supp. 564 (1976)

United States District Court, Western District Oklahoma

DAUGHERTY, District Judge.

In this diversity action Plaintiff Crest Construction Company (Crest) seeks recovery on a "Comprehensive Crime Policy" of insurance issued to it by Defendant Insurance Company of North America (I.N.A.). . . .

The Petition alleged that Defendant issued to Plaintiff a "Comprehensive Crime Policy" No. TDD 12 73 which was effective from January 3, 1973 to January 6, 1976; that this policy insured Plaintiff against the fraudulent or dishonest acts of its employees; that between January 15, 1973 and August 2, 1973 Plaintiff was a contractor on an apartment project; that during this same period Roy Cribbs (Cribbs) was an employee of Plaintiff working on this project; that during this time Cribbs took from Plaintiff tools and materials worth more than $20,000; and that Plaintiff has demanded that Defendant pay its losses but Defendant has refused to pay. Defendant denies both liability and the amount of Plaintiff's claim. At the Pretrial Conference the issues of liability (or coverage) and loss were separated. The first issue has been submitted to the Court on a Stipulation of Facts of the parties.

The question before the Court on the liability issue is whether, at the time of the alleged thefts, Cribbs was an employee of Crest as claimed by Plaintiff or a joint adventurer or partner with Crest's President and 100% owner, Dale Smith (Smith), and Crest's Controller, David C. Gallion (Gallion) as claimed by Defendant. The parties agree that if at the time of the alleged thefts Cribbs was an employee of Crest any losses occasioned by his defalcations would be covered by the policy but that if Cribbs was a partner or joint adventurer with Smith and Gallion such losses would not be covered by the policy. . . .

The depositions of Smith and Gallion show that at some time before January 15, 1973 Crest entered into a series of sub-contracts for the performance of construction work on the Buena Vista Apartments in Alva, Oklahoma. Two or three weeks after January 15, 1973 Smith, Cribbs, and Gallion executed an agreement relating to various functions to be performed by the parties with respect to the construction of the apartments. This agreement was prepared by Gallion on January 15, 1973 and bears that date. This agreement is as follows:

---

[5] Howard Gault & Son v. First National Bank of Hereford, 541 S.W.2d 235 (Tex. Civ. App. 1976).

MEMORANDUM

To: Dale Smith
　　Roy Cribbs
From: David Gallion
Re: General Agreement
Date: January 15, 1973

This memo is to reduce to writing some of the areas covered in prior conversations that are applicable to the association of Smith, Cribbs, and Gallion.

RESPONSIBILITY:

Smith (Crest): To provide financial stability in the initial stages of operations, until such time as undertakings can.

To provide a vehicle that will give an (illegible) for purchasability and transacting business that is established and going.

To provide overall control in all areas.

To advise and counsel in the making of decisions, and to have the responsibility to make a final decision, if necessary.

Cribbs: Responsible for on-site supervision, which would include all areas in the running of a job.

To estimate prospective work, and/or to assist in the estimating of jobs.

To devote full time of his expertise in any area that will inhance (sic) the progress of the association of Smith, Cribbs and Gallion. (sic)

To follow any and all procedures that are (illegible) may be established for effective control association.

Gallion: Responsible for the installation and the administration of any and all procedures that are and that may be established.

To devote such time as is necessary in all areas to insure that all necessary documentation is being accumulated for effective control.

To follow any and all procedures that are and that may be established.

REMUNERATION:

Smith (Crest): To participate in any net profit at rate of 52.50%.

To be reimbursed for any and all expenses that are applicable to any work of this association.

Cribbs: Salary to be $300.00 per week until such time that monies due Cribbs for prior work done on Haujntolla Nursing Home are received, then salary will be $275.00 per week.

To be advanced a 'petty cash' in the amount of $50.00 for expenses that are directly applicable to job cost. This amount to be maintained by a weekly reimbursement of expenses, as reported (illegible) report.

A place of lodging will be provided at the expense of the particular job in situations (illegible) is a second place of lodging.

To be furnished a pickup for use in the carring-on of and the pursueing of work that involves this association. (sic)

To participate in any net profit at the rate of 23.75%.

Gallion: Salary to be $1,250.00 per month, payment to be made from Crest Construction 'Special' account which has been opened primarily for the (illegible) of the above mentioned associations' business. (sic) Whenever possible an allocation, for reimbursement to the 'Special' account, will be made in any time applicable to work that is not a part of this particular association.

To be reimbursed for all out of pocket expenses on the date of each pay period.

Expenses of operating and maintaining an automobile, that is primarily used for company business, to be paid by the association.

To participate in any net profit at the rate of 23.75%.

We understand that the areas here-to-fore mentioned in this memorandum, are not all inclusive but are the basic agreements as this association starts operation, and that additions and/or decisions can be made as need be.

We the undersigned agree in general (illegible) all items included in this memorandum, and furthermore we agree that at the completion of the two jobs, these being Buena Vista and Huajntolla Nursing Home, or by January 15, 1974, that this memorandum will be revised and adjustments made as agreed by Smith, Cribbs and Gallion. (sic)

The parties entered into performance under this agreement. Thereafter dissension arose among the parties in that Cribbs was excessively absent from the job. Smith considered terminating Cribbs but did not. After a conversation with Smith, Cribbs' job performance improved. Smith then was informed that Cribbs was taking materials from the job to build a personal home. At this point Smith either fired Cribbs or terminated their agreement.

The crux of this case is the January 15, 1973 agreement. It is Defendant's position that this agreement creates a partnership or joint adventure between Smith, Cribbs, and Gallion, and, therefore, its policy provides no coverage for Cribbs' defalcations. It is Plaintiff's position that this agreement does not create a partnership or joint adventure; that Cribbs was a Crest employee, and, therefore, it is entitled to recover under the policy.

A partnership is an association of two or more persons to carry on as co-owners a business for profit. A joint adventure is a special combination of two or more persons, whether corporate, individual, or otherwise which seeks a joint profit in a specific venture. Partnerships and joint adventures are separate legal relationships although they are generally governed by the same rules of law. The principal difference between the two relationships is that a joint adventure is usually limited to a single transaction while a partnership encompasses a continuing course of business. The essential elements of a partnership are: (1) an intent by the parties to form a partnership, (2) participation by all parties in both profits and losses, and (3) such a community of interest as far as third persons are concerned as enables each partner to make contracts, manage the business and dispose of partnership property. The essential elements of a joint adventure are: (1) a joint interest in the property by the parties sought to be held as partners; (2) agreement, express or implied, among the parties to share in the profits and losses of the venture; and (3) ac-

tions or conduct showing cooperation in the project.

With regard to the first element of partnership, intent of the parties to form a partnership, the issue is whether the January 15, 1973 agreement shows an intent by Smith, Cribbs and Gallion to carry on a business as co-owners for profit. It is clear that the parties intended to carry on a business for profit because the agreement provides for the division of profit after the completion of the subject job(s). However, the agreement is not clear on the question of ownership. Smith was to provide all necessary funds. Cribbs and Gallion were to provide the labor. The contract which was the subject matter of the agreement was held by Crest. As a general rule, in order to constitute a partnership, the parties must have a community of interest as common owners of the business which constitutes their joint undertaking. However, in view of the fact that the contribution of a partner need not be money or property, but may consist of services or skill, a partnership may exist where the members have an interest in the profits only and no interest in the property from which the profits are to be derived. Thus, where persons who are associated in a common business share both profits and losses, it is not necessary to the existence of a partnership that there be joint ownership of the property or capital used to carry on the business.

In this case, the property used to carry on the business was Crest's contract(s) with the owners of the subject apartment(s). There is no indication that Cribbs and Gallion had any ownership interest in this contract(s). However, in view of the above rule it is not absolutely necessary to the existence of a partnership that all partners own a portion of the business capital. If Cribbs and Gallion contributed skill and labor to the enterprise and were to share in the profits and losses thereof, a partnership could exist even though they did not own the capital. Thus, the second element of partnership, sharing in the profits and losses, must be considered in order to determine the first. However, as the second element of both joint adventure and partnership are the same, the first element of joint adventure will be considered next.

The first element of a joint adventure has been stated by the Oklahoma Supreme Court to be "a joint interest in the property by the parties sought to be held as partners." This statement is far from being self-explanatory, and the decisions have not been overly explicit as to what constitutes a joint interest in the property. However, it is clear that joint interest is not joint ownership. Joint ownership of the property used in carrying on the business is not necessary to the existence of a joint adventure. Nor does joint interest necessarily equate with joint control. While the right of mutual control of subject matter of the enterprise is essential to the creation of a joint adventure, the rights of the parties with respect to management and control of the adventure may be fixed by agreement. Thus, it appears that "joint interest in the property" as used by the Oklahoma Supreme Court means only that the parties need be engaged in an enterprise in which they have a community of interest and a common purpose in its performance.

In this case Smith (Crest) was to provide all necessary funds. Cribbs and Gallion were to provide their services. Profits were to be divided after expenses were returned to Smith (Crest). Thus, it appears that the parties had a community of interest and a common purpose. The community of interest was the pooling of capital and labor. The common purpose was the maximization of profits. Therefore, the first element of a joint adventure is found to exist in the subject agreement.

The second element of both a partnership and a joint adventure is the same, participation in both profits and losses by all members. In order for an association to constitute a joint adventure it is necessary that the parties agree to share both in the profits and losses of the enterprise. The absence of an express agreement to share in the losses is, however, not fatal. An agreement to share in losses may be implied from an agreement to share in profits. 48 C.J.S. Joint Adventure §2. Cf. Tulsa County

Truck & Fruit G. Ass'n v. McMurphey, 185 Okl. 132, 90 P.2d 927 (1939); Albina Engine and Machine Works, Inc. v. Abel, 305 F.2d 77 (Tenth Cir. 1962). The rule respecting partnerships is similar. It is essential to the partnership relationship that the parties share both in the profits and losses of the enterprise. Whitney v. Harris, 169 Okl. 288, 36 P.2d 872 (1934). However, it is not necessary to the partnership relationship that there be an express agreement to share in the losses. Such an agreement may be implied if the intent of the parties to form a partnership is otherwise made clear. Cf. Municipal Paving Co. v. Herring, 50 Okl. 470, 150 P. 1067 (1915); Chowning v. Graham, 74 Okl. 232, 178 P. 676 (1918).

In this case there is no express agreement to share losses. Smith (Crest) undertook to provide financing for the enterprise. Smith (Crest) was to participate in profits at the rate of 52.50% and was to be reimbursed for its financing. Cribbs was to be paid a salary from a special Crest account, participate in the profits at the rate of 23.75%, provided with expense money and a place of lodging. Gallion was to be paid a monthly salary out of the special Crest account, but the account was to be reimbursed for work done by Gallion which was not attributable to the association. Gallion was also to participate in profits at the rate of 23.75% and be reimbursed for expenses.

Thus, Cribbs stood to lose nothing by a failure of the enterprise except a share of the net profits. Cribbs did not furnish his skill in the sole expectation of receiving a share of the profits as he was compensated for his time and expenses. If Cribbs had provided his services solely in return for a share of expected profits, it could be seen that he stood to share in the losses of the enterprise as well as its profits. Lost labor could be valued as highly as lost capital. However, Cribbs was being compensated for both his labor and expenses. Cribbs stood only to lose a share of the profits. This is not sufficient to constitute a sharing of the losses of the enterprise. In order to constitute a partnership or joint enterprise members must stand to sustain an actual loss by the failure of the enterprise. Of course, a member of a partnership or joint adventure might provide his services in return for a minimal compensation in the hopes of sharing in the profits of the enterprise and thereby stand to sustain a loss by the failure of the enterprise. However, such is not the case here. Cribbs was to be compensated at a rate of $275–300 per week. This is not a minimal amount. Nor has it been shown that this is less than Cribbs would normally take to do such work, or that he took a reduced salary in the hopes of a share of the profits. Therefore it must be concluded that Cribbs did not stand to share in the losses of the enterprise and a joint adventure or partnership did not exist between Smith, Cribbs and Gallion for that reason.

Moreover, this is not a case in which an agreement to share in losses can be implied.

In order to imply such an agreement the intent of the parties to form a partnership or joint adventure would have to be clear. There is no such clear intent expressed in the instant agreement. In view of the facts that the project was to be financed entirely by Smith (Crest), that Cribbs and Gallion were to be paid salaries by Smith (Crest) and there is no express or implied agreement for Cribbs or Gallion to share in the losses of the enterprise, it must be concluded that the relationship created by the subject agreement is essentially that of employer/employee.

Accordingly, as to the first separated issue the Court finds and concludes that Cribbs was an employee of Plaintiff, and Defendant's policy of insurance would cover any defalcations attributable to him.

Shares in profits and losses.

As seen in the *Crest* case, co-ownership of an asset does not necessarily establish a partnership. If such co-ownership relates to a business and includes the incidents of partnership, such as the sharing of profits and losses and the right to manage and control the business, such a relationship is likely to constitute a partnership. However, if persons are associated for mutual financial gain on only a limited or temporary basis involving a single transaction or a few isolated transactions, there is no partnership. The parties must be engaged in a continuous series of commercial activities for the relationship to be considered a partnership.[6]

As mentioned earlier, partnership liability may be imposed upon a person by a third person because of words or conduct that preclude the alleged partner denying that he or she was a member of a partnership. This principle is called *partnership by estoppel*. It does not cause the partner by estoppel to actually become a member of the partnership; it relates only to the duties and liabilities of such a person who, though not a partner, has a relationship with third persons who assume that he or she *is* a partner. As provided in §16 of the Uniform Partnership Act, a person not actually a partner is liable *as a partner* if that person has represented or allowed others to represent himself or herself by words, conduct, or acquiescence as a partner to one or more third persons who were not partners of that person.[7]

In order to create partnership liability by estoppel, the parties involved must accept the representation of a partnership.[8] For example, A and B are members of a

---

[6] Koesling v. Basamakis, 539 P.2d 1043 (Utah 1975).

[7] Time Financial Services, Inc. v. Hewitt, 139 Ga. App. 270, 228 S.E.2d 176 (1976); Carlton v. Grissom Co., 98 Ga. 118, 26 S.E. 77 (1896).

[8] See 59 *AmJur* 2d, Partnership, Section 71, citing numerous cases, including Thompson v. First National Bank, 11 U.S. 529 (1884).

partnership. However, C states to T that he is a member of the partnership with A and B; relying upon C's statement, T enters into a contract with A and B to sell goods to A and B. T believes he is selling to A, B, *and C* as copartners. If A and B fail to pay for the goods, T has the right to hold A, B, *and C* liable as partners. By his statement to T, C is estopped from denying that he is a member of the partnership. The same result would occur if A introduced C as a member of the firm to T, and C did not object to that introduction. C's failure to deny A's statement of C's membership in the partnership is sufficient basis for T's belief that C is a partner. Thus, in an action by T against A, B, and C as partners, C could not successfully defend himself by claiming that A's statement was false and that he was not in fact a partner. In the first situation, in which C states to T that he is a member of the partnership and T sues A, B, and C as partners, T may successfully sue A and B (as well as C) because A and B agreed to purchase the goods from T.

c. Taxation

Because a partnership is not a legal entity, it is not required to pay federal income tax. However, it must file an informational return each year, stating the income or profits realized by each of the partners, who are required in turn to report and pay an individual tax on such income or profits. The partnership informational return allocates each of the individual partners' proportionate share of profits or losses derived from operation, dividend income, capital gains or losses, and other income of the partnership. In many situations the income is not actually received by the individual partner, since it may be left in the partnership in accordance with the agreement among the individuals. Nevertheless, each partner must report his or her proportionate share of such income and pay the tax on it, whether it was received or not.

d. Liability

Because each partner is an agent of the partnership as well as an agent of each of the other partners, each partner is also the principal of every partner. Therefore an act by one partner binds the entire partnership and results in the partnership and each partner being liable for the obligations undertaken by that partner.[9] The Uniform Partnership Act specifies that the liability assumed by the partners and the partnership is confined to the parties' acts performed in conducting the business of the partnership. Therefore each partner is individually liable for his or her conduct outside of the partnership, and such conduct does not bind the other partners. Section 9 of the Act further provides that unless authorized by all of the partners, the

---

[9] Battista v. Lebanon Trotting Assn., 538 F.2d 111 (6th Cir. 1976); Matter of Fowler, 407 F.Supp. (W.D. Okla. 1975). See also Cook v. Brundidge, et al., 533 S.W.2d 751 (Tex. 1976), finding that the extent of the partner's authority to bind the partnership is determined by essentially the same principles measuring the scope of authority of an agent. See Part C in this Chapter.

following conduct by fewer than all of the partners does not bind the entire partnership: (1) assignment of partnership property for the benefit of its creditors; (2) disposal of the good will of the business; (3) any act that would make it impossible to carry on the ordinary business of the partnership; (4) confession of a judgment; (5) submission of a partnership claim or liability to arbitration or to a referee.

But many acts by individual partners do bind the partnership. An admission or representation by any partner concerning partnership affairs within the scope of his or her authority may be introduced into evidence in a court action involving the partnership.[10] Similarly, a partnership is bound by notice any partner receives about any matter relating to partnership affairs.[11] Section 12 of the Uniform Partnership Act provides that the partnership is also bound by the knowledge that a partner acted in a particular matter, if that knowledge was acquired while he or she was a partner. Section 15 of the Act states that partners are jointly liable on all debts and contract obligations of the partnership. This statement means that each partner must be joined as a defendant to any legal action brought by the creditor. If partners are jointly liable, a release of one joint obligor releases all the other joint obligors. By contrast, in a situation in which the partners may be severally liable, either the partner-obligors may be joined as defendants in one suit or they may each be sued in separate actions, and release of one does not release the others.

Once a judgment against the partnership is obtained, the question of whether that judgment may be satisfied out of partnership assets or out of the individual assets of the partners or both, depends on the persons named as defendants in the suit and the scope of the judgment rendered by the court. If the suit is against a partnership in its partnership name, only partnership assets are subject to the judgment. If a suit is against individually named partners who do business under the partnership name, the judgment is enforceable against partnership property *and* against the individually owned property of each partner-defendant.[12]

Although §15 of the Uniform Partnership Act requires joint liability on all debts in the contract obligations of the partnership, the liability of partners for a *tort* committed by one of the partners or by an employee of the partnership in the course of partnership business is joint *and* several.[13] Thus all of the partners may be sued jointly in an action based on tort liability or they may be sued in separate actions resulting in separate judgments obtained against each of the partners.

e. Control

Under the principles of common law and under the Uniform Partnership Act, each partner has the right to take part in the management of the business, to

---

[10] See 73 A.L.R. 447, Annotation.

[11] North Peachtree I-285 Properties, Ltd. v. Hicks, 136 Ga. App. 426, 221 S.E.2d 607 (1975).

[12] However, as indicated in Matter of Fowler, 407 F. Supp. 799 (W.D. Okla. 1975), a creditor may be required to first apply partnership assets on the judgment.

[13] Battista v. Lebanon Trotting Assn., 538 F.2d 111 (6th Cir. 1976); Cooley v. Slocum, 326 So.2d 491 (La. 1976).

handle partnership assets for partnership purposes, and to act as an agent of the partnership. Thus, unless the partnership agreement provides otherwise, each partner has a voice in the control of the business. Each of the partners has a number of rights, both at common law and under the Act. Because the purpose of a partnership is to carry on a business for profit, each partner may share in the profits and must bear a proportionate share of any losses. In the absence of an agreement stating otherwise, the partners share profits and losses equally, regardless of the ratio of their financial contributions to the business. Other rights of partners, relating to control of the business, include: upon termination of the partnership, the right to be repaid his or her contribution of capital; the right to full information on all partnership matters upon demand at any time; the right to reject or accept as a partner any person whom he or she chooses; the right to an accounting whenever a partner is wrongfully excluded from the partnership business or possession of its property by his or her copartners or whenever other circumstances render it just and reasonable. Most importantly, each of the partners has an absolute right to know how the business operates, and each of them has an equal voice in its management.[14] As a practical matter, of course, partners generally pool their individual resources in an effort to use each of their special talents to the best advantage. Thus, for purposes of operating efficiency, one partner may supervise the accounting activities of the business, while another will be in charge of marketing and retail sales activities. When a disagreement arises, the majority prevails under both the Uniform Partnership Act and common law principles of partnership.[15] If an equal division of opinion results in a tie vote, some jurisdictions allow a partner to proceed with his or her desired course of action without suffering liability to the partnership, while other jurisdictions hold to the contrary.[16]

f. Continuity and Legal Capacity

A partnership may be dissolved at any time, either by act of the parties or by operation of law. Dissolution by act of the parties may occur by (1) agreement; (2) withdrawal or addition of a partner; (3) violation of the partnership agreement by one of the parties; or (4) accomplishment of the purpose for which the partnership was formed. Dissolution by operation of law may be by (1) the death of a partner; (2) the bankruptcy of a partner or the partnership; (3) the illegality of the partnership; or (4) by order of a court.

Dissolution is not the complete end of partnership activity; even though the partnership is dissolved, it does not actually terminate until the partnership affairs are

---

[14] See 60 *AmJur* 2d, Partnership, section 108, citing Uniform Partnership Act, §§18–22.

[15] Thompson Door Co. v. Haven Fund, 351 A.2d 864 (Del. 1976). The general rule does not apply to acts contrary to the partnership agreement nor to certain other acts specified in section 9 of the Uniform Partnership Act.

[16] There is some authority that if a partnership agreement does not provide for a solution in the event of an equal division among the partners, the power of the firm to act is suspended indefinitely. 60 *AmJur* 2d, Partnership, section 110.

completed. This completion, or winding up of its affairs, is called termination. Between dissolution and termination the liquidation of the partnership occurs; in this process business affairs are put in order, receivables are collected, accountings are made, payments to creditors are made, and the remaining assets distributed to the partners as provided in the Uniform Partnership Act.

3. Limited Partnership

Unlike the general partnership, the limited partnership was not recognized under common law but has been developed by state statutes to accomplish certain purposes. Its formation and activities are strictly controlled by the limited partnership acts of forty-seven states. These acts were modeled after the Uniform Limited Partnership Act drafted by the Commissioners on Uniform State Laws. A limited partnership is made up of general partners with unlimited liability and limited partners with limited liability. Another major difference between a limited partnership and a general partnership is that the limited partners have no control over the everyday management of the partnership business. Thus it has the characteristics of both a general partnership and a corporation.

Under the Uniform Limited Partnership Act, in order to form a limited partnership, two or more persons must sign and swear to a certificate of limited partnership, which must set forth a number of facts relating to the partners and the nature of their business, including the name of the partnership; the character of the business; the location of the principal place of business; the name and place of residence of each member, general and limited partners being indicated; the term for which the partnership is to exist; the amount of cash and description of any other property contributed by each limited partner; and various rights of the limited partners, such as the right of the partners to admit additional limited partners. This certificate is then filed or recorded in the office of a designated public official, such as the clerk and recorder of the county in which the principal office of the limited partnership is to be located. This allows any person desiring to do business with the firm to learn the nature of the association, who its members are, and the ones whose personal credit may be relied on.

Limited partners are in a position similar to that of shareholders in a corporation, in that they are primarily investors and can take no part in the management or operation of the business. In addition, they are not agents of the partnership as general partners are. However, by definition a limited partnership also includes general partners who in most respects have the same amount of control and liability as members of a general partnership.

4. The Corporation

a. *Its Role in Society*

The mention of the word *corporation* frequently stirred controversy on college campuses over the past decade. During the Vietnam War the word seemed to symbolize to much of the nation, and to college students in particular, the undesirable ramifications of our capitalist society. The fact is, however, that without the corporate form of business in this society, the social and technological progress of the past one hundred years could not have been accomplished. Every aspect of our lives is directly affected by the ability of corporations to accumulate tremendous amounts of capital and thereby accomplish goals in business and technology. Without corporations, this task would have required the joint activity of literally thousands of individuals working independently but toward the same goal. The efficiency and large concentrations of wealth in the larger, publicly owned corporations have transformed this nation into the most productive industrial economy in the world.

Because this artificial, invisible, and intangible person has such a tremendous role in the nation's economy, it is inevitable that it will also have a role in private and governmental social policy, both domestic and international. Through the collective decisions of its policymakers, the corporation may possess and reflect, at least by implication, a moral position on those social policies. Thus, by their tacit or overt participation in the activities of the U.S. and foreign governments, corporations have sometimes felt the wrath of those opposed to such activities. The social well-being of this society has depended largely upon the right of private citizens to express such opposition to any public or private cause. However, in defense of the corporate *form* of business, one must remember that the corporation possesses no inherent or innate tendency to disregard moral and ethical considerations. A corporation is merely the medium through which human beings—its shareholders, officers, and directors—carry on a particular business enterprise. Those individuals should not suffer opposition to and criticism of their activities simply because of the vehicle they use to carry on the business. If criticism is justified, it should be based on the lack of merit or moral acceptability of the decisions made and implemented through the corporation. Therefore it should be directed at the individuals responsible for such decisions, not at the medium or form they are using.

b. Formation

Although formation of a corporation is a relatively easy matter today, prior to the middle of the nineteenth century it took an act of the legislature to create a corporation. The first railroads were founded under special acts of the legislatures of their respective states. However, as it became evident that this form of business fostered progress, and that it would be an intolerable burden on the government if each corporation could be formed only by a special statute, the state legislatures enacted general laws under which a designated state official, such as the secretary of state, could issue a charter or certificate of incorporation to people who complied with the statute's provisions. Thus a corporation today remains a creature of the legislature, but it is formed by the provisions of a general statute rather than by a special act designed for each particular corporation.

Like the uniform acts regarding partnerships, the Model Business Corporation Act (the Model Act, or the Act) was drafted in 1959 and has been amended several times since then. The Model Act is designed to provide for the organization of business corporations to the extent consistent with special statutory provisions in each of the states governing corporations. As of the end of 1977, thirty-six states had adopted the Act with minor variations. In the states that have not yet adopted the Model Act, corporations are governed by a large body of common law and by various other statutes of limited applicability, such as those relating to utilities, reservoir companies, and nonprofit organizations. Because the Model Act is largely a reflection of the case law prevailing at the time of its original enactment, and because most jurisdictions have adopted the Model Act, this discussion will focus on corporate law as embodied in the Model Act, unless otherwise stated.

The Model Act, as revised in 1969, is reproduced in Appendix H. Under it, a corporation's name must contain the word *corporation, company, incorporated,* or *limited,* or an abbreviation thereof. No name may indicate that the corporation is formed for a purpose other than that specified in its articles of incorporation. Further, no name may be the same as or deceptively similar to the names of other corporations on file in the jurisdiction [Section 8 of the Model Act]. In order to form a corporation, one or more people must sign and deliver the articles of incorporation to the secretary of state, together with the appropriate filing fees [§53]. The Act outlines in detail the provisions that must be stated in the articles, such as name, period of duration, purpose, shares, incorporators, directors, and address of the registered agent of the corporation [§54]. Any other provisions that are not inconsistent with law, or that may be stated in the corporation's bylaws, may be inserted in the articles of incorporation for the regulation of the corporation's internal affairs.

If a registered agent is not maintained at the registered office as provided in the articles, or cannot be found there, the secretary of state becomes the agent for the purpose of receiving the service of all legal papers [§§12–14]. The articles of incorporation may be amended, provided the amended articles contain only provisions that are lawful at the time of such amendment [§§58–65]. The Act expressly provides for certain matters that may be the subject of amendment, such as widening the corporate goals or increasing the number of authorized shares of stock [§58]. Proposing such an amendment, as provided in the Act, requires a resolution of the board of directors. The adoption of the amendment requires the affirmative vote of a majority of the shares of stock entitled to vote [§59]. Although these are the provisions of the Act, a higher or lower percentage of votes from shareholders may be and has been required by various states' versions of the Model Act. Also, whatever the statutory requirement, the articles of incorporation may require a higher percentage.

Under the Act, the corporation is officially born upon issuance of the certificate of incorporation by the secretary of state. The certificate is conclusive evidence of compliance with the conditions precedent to incorporation, and it is also conclusive evidence of proper incorporation [§56]. However, upon subsequent discovery of the corporation's failure to comply with the provisions of the Act or other law, the state may institute proceedings to cancel or revoke the certificate [§56].

If the founders have substantially complied with the statutory requirements and the state has issued a certificate of incorporation, a *de jure* (by law or by right) corporation exists.[17] If the founders have failed to comply with the statutory conditions and the state has *not* issued a certificate but the founders have in good faith attempted to comply with the statute and have in general complied with the law and have exercised or used the corporate powers, then a *de facto* corporation exists.[18]

If the defect in incorporation is too serious to justify a finding of a *de facto* corporation, the corporation may sometimes invoke the doctrine of *corporation by estoppel* (sometimes called the doctrine of *corporation by admission*). The founders may claim estoppel if the association has held itself out as a corporation and a third person has done business with it as such. In an action brought by such a third person, the third person is estopped from claiming (that is, prevented from asserting) that the existence or capacity of the corporation to act or own property may be questionable.[19] Estoppel does not *create* a corporation, but it prevents the third person from holding the individuals in the corporation personally liable, provided such persons were innocent of the defect in the corporation.

The principles of *de jure* and *de facto* corporations and estoppel affect not only who will be liable but also the validity of the contractual and other business relationships of the corporation and its agents. Persons who claim to act as a corporation are jointly and severally liable under the Model Act for the debts and liabilities resulting from their actions [§146].

c. Corporate Characteristics

Once properly formed, the corporation possesses a number of characteristics that are unique to the corporate form and that make the form very desirable. First, because a corporation is a separate legal entity, it can sue, be sued, own property, make contracts, and engage in any other types of activity that a person can engage in [§4]. The corporate characteristic with the greatest significance is that shareholders are liable only for the par or fixed value of the shares, unless they have contracted with the corporation to the contrary, or unless some special statutory provision makes the shares of stock assessable. Thus the owners of the corporation enjoy limited liability, unless they have not paid the par or fixed value of the shares [§25]. Another important characteristic of the corporate entity is that corporate life is perpetual if so provided in the articles of incorporation [§4]. Other generally favorable characteristics include the following: shares of stock may be freely sold or exchanged without affecting the operation of the corporation; there does not necessarily have to be public disclosure of beneficial ownership of the shares (although this is more often true with small, closely held corporations);

---

[17] Western Machine Works v. Edward Machine and Tool Corp., 223 Ind. 655, 63 N.E.2d 535 (1945).

[18] Robertson v. Levy, 197 A.2d 444 (D.C. Ct. App. 1964).

[19] Cargill, Inc. v. American Pork Producers, Inc., 415 F. Supp. 876 (D.S.D. 1976); Cranson v. International Business Machines Corp., 234 Md. 477, 200 A.2d 33 (1964).

clearly established lines of authority and highly centralized management are possible; and comprehensive and liberal corporation laws permit a great degree of flexibility of action [§§15–21].

d. Powers and Liability

The Act provides a number of corporate powers that all corporations have, and that need not be expressly set forth in the articles of incorporation. A corporation has the power to sue and be sued; to enter into contracts; to acquire, deal with, sell, mortgage, and dispose of real and personal property; to borrow money [§4].

If a corporation acts beyond the scope of its corporate authority, such an action may subject the corporation, or in some circumstances the officers and directors, to liability for that action [§7]. Acts that are beyond the scope of the corporate authority are termed *ultra vires,* which means "without right, without authority, or in excess of powers." *Ultra vires* activities include acts that are not permitted by statute or are not within the purposes set forth in the articles of incorporation. Because of the broad authority given corporations today, actions based on *ultra vires* are not common. Under the Model Business Corporation Act, the scope of corporate acts deemed invalid because of *ultra vires* activities is limited to specific situations in which proceedings are brought by a shareholder, by the corporate entity itself, or by the attorney general in dissolution or injunctive proceedings [§7]. An individual cannot bring an action based on *ultra vires* under the Model Act.

At common law an *ultra vires* contract cannot be enforced by either party, if it has been formed, but not performed by either party, until all shareholders have approved it.[20] If both parties have performed in part, it is effective, despite the *ultra vires* conduct of the corporate party.[21] If only the corporation performed it, the other party cannot claim *ultra vires* in an effort to escape liability for failure to perform it.[22] This principle is similar to the principle of corporation by estoppel, by which a third person cannot deny the existence of a corporation if he or she has dealt with it as a corporation.[23]

The doctrine of *ultra vires* does not apply to tort liability and may not be used by the corporation to limit its tort liability. Liability for torts allegedly committed by the corporation is imposed on it under the common law doctrine of *respondeat*

---

[20] See *AmJur* 2d, Corporations, section 965. According to Haynie v. Milan Exchange, Inc., 458 S.W.2d 23 (Tenn. App. 1970), *ultra vires* is no defense if shareholders have ratified the act and if there is no question of public policy or involvement of a state or public right. There is some authority that *ultra vires* acts cannot be ratified by the shareholders, Komanetsky v. Missouri State Medical Assn., 516 S.W.2d 545 (Mo. App. 1974).

[21] See 19 *AmJur,* Corporations, section 974.

[22] Total Automation, Inc. v. Illinois National Bank and Trust Co., 40 Ill. App. 3d 266, 351 N.E.2d 879 (1976). Similarly, a corporation may not claim *ultra vires* if the other party has performed. Witter v. Triumph Smokes, Inc., 464 F.2d 1078 (5th Cir. 1972); Stephan v. Equitable Savings & Loan Assn., 522 P.2d 478 (Ore. 1974).

[23] See text accompanying note 19.

superior, which covers wrongful acts and omissions committed by corporate agents within the scope of their authority.[24] An action against a corporation may sometimes result in an uncollectable judgment, because of insufficient corporate assets. If this is so, and if the corporate entity was used to fraudulently shield its principals (who are less judgment-proof than the corporation) from liability, the plaintiff can seek to "pierce the corporate veil" and obtain a judgment directly against the individual for whom the corporation is the alter ego.

ZUBIK v. ZUBIK

384 F.2d 267 (1967)

United States Court of Appeals, Third Circuit

VAN DUSEN, District Judge.

This consolidated appeal is from multiple judgments in admiralty entered in the District Court against Charles Zubik (Charles, Sr.), individually, and Charles Zubik & Sons, Inc. (Zubik Corporation). The claimed damages to personal property and equipment occurred early on the morning of March 6, 1964, when an unusually large ice flow coming down the Allegheny River broke several of the appellants' sand and gravel barges from their moorings at the 16th Street landing in the City of Pittsburgh. The drifting vessels caused damage to the several appellees having a total value of $207,540.

Appellants make [the] argument . . . that, even if the Zubik Corporation was liable, the court erred in disregarding the corporate entity and treating Charles, Sr. and Zubik Corporation as one and the same. . . .

The issue of Charles Zubik, Sr.'s personal liability occupied a large part of the trial below. The trial judge's several findings of fact concerning the interrelation of Charles, Sr.'s personal affairs and the affairs of Zubik Corporation led him to the conclusion that:

"The corporate defendant is nothing more than the alter ego of the individual defendant. . . . All of the defendant's finances, activities, operation of the corporation business were intertwined with that of the corporation. The overwhelming weight of the evidence indicates that there is no demarcation between the individual and corporate defendants."

This conclusion of "lack of demarcation" or conclusion that the corporation was the "alter ego" of Charles, Sr. rested upon Findings of Fact concerning the Zubik business operation. In these Findings the trial judge stressed that Zubik Corporation was "purely an operating company" with records inadequate even to designate what property owned by Charles, Sr. was leased to the corporation and at what rent. The intertwining of Charles, Sr.'s personal affairs with the corporation was inferred, particularly from the fact that all of his personal expenses were paid directly by the corporation with merely a bookkeeping entry against Charles, Sr.'s credit account. Emphasis was placed upon the fact that Charles, Sr. was the only one authorized to sign corporate checks, although, via a personal power of attorney, his daughter often signed for him. A disregard of the corporate formalities of meetings for some years, the use of oral leases of equipment from Charles, Sr. at fluctuating rentals, and the general "intertwining" of personal and corporate finances, relating to the sale of barges and the borrowing of money, provided additional "facts" from which the trial judge concluded

---

[24] See Part C in this chapter for discussion of *respondeat superior.*

that the corporate "fiction" of Zubik Corporation could not be relied upon by Charles, Sr.

Consideration of the record as a whole, however, requires the conclusion that libellants did not sustain their burden of proving that the corporate entity should be disregarded. An examination of the record has established that the additional facts summarized below are supported by uncontradicted evidence. Zubik Corporation was formed in 1948 on the advice of counsel when Charles, Sr. became too ill to continue physically in his business and when he wanted to let his children run the business he had created. Engaged primarily in the sand and gravel business, after 1957 the corporation expanded into the related field of producing concrete. In both businesses, the corporation paid its own expenses of operation, hired its own employees, paid their wages and made the various tax, social security, and unemployment payments. Although the corporation borrowed from Charles, Sr. on several occasions it borrowed from other stockholders as well. The corporation kept records reflecting such loans.

Considerable testimony was heard concerning the leasing of barges and other assets owned by Charles, Sr. Although the bulk of the equipment used by Zubik Corporation was leased from Charles, Sr., some barges were leased from others and the corporation owned some assets of its own (over $67,000, one witness testified) such as cement, gravel, sand, gasoline, tools and rope. The great bulk of the "assets," however, were owned by Charles, Sr., including those used in the cement business, and leased in their entirety to Zubik Corporation. Charles, Sr. owned very little he did not lease. Some controversy existed over the financial arrangement of such leases from Charles, Sr.; however, all sides seem to agree that payments to Charles, Sr., including his salary, took the form of credits to his account with the company. Whether these payments and leases are characterized as "purported" or not, Charles, Sr.'s credit account was carefully debited to reflect payment of all of Charles, Sr.'s personal expenses. In this fashion, Charles, Sr. was "paid" his salary, rental and loans, by having the corporation

"pay" for his personal expenses. All of the evidence concerning the written and oral leases, as well as the bookkeeping and activities concerning sale, purchase, sub-letting, repairs, and maintenance of equipment, tended to show a possible lack of arm's-length dealing between Charles, Sr. and the corporation or a lack of some of the formal elements of a lessor-lessee relationship found outside a closely held corporation. This informality extended to the observance of corporate procedure as to meetings [no records for 1961 through 1963] and as to expenses, oral renewals of leases, and alteration of rentals and salaries to reflect the success of operations. But there is no evidence that funds oscillated at will between Charles, Sr. and Zubik Corporation, and the Internal Revenue Service apparently forced some uniformity, at least as to fair and consistent rentals.

Since the trial judge did not disbelieve or reject the testimony concerning oral leases of marine equipment, it is difficult to understand his Conclusion of Law 8 that the barges which broke away "were not under lease" to Zubik Corporation "at the time of the breakaway."

The Zubik family paid attention to the separate corporate entity of the closely held Zubik family corporation in many respects. It was particularly required for tax purposes. Members of the family were given shares of stock by their father which he paid for in cash. The children served as officers of the corporation and also as its "active heads." In addition to the uncontradicted evidence of regular meetings of Zubik Corporation in years prior to 1961 and in 1964, there is testimony of corporate meetings during the years 1961–1963, even though no minutes were produced. Moreover, the separate corporate existence cannot be denied merely because Charles, Sr. and the corporation had the same attorney or the same accountant. The fact that Charles, Sr.'s records and the corporate records were both kept by his daughter, the fact that the corporation kept his notes and deeds, or the fact that his daughter signed corporate checks pursuant to a personal power of attorney from Charles, Sr. seems irrelevant to the issue of separate corporate existence, particularly since Charles, Sr. could neither read nor write. Even if Charles, Sr. remained the "last word" within the corporation, his sons ran the business, asking their father only for his experienced advice. As to daily operations, Charles, Sr. was really a spectator, whether from the upper deck of their office boat or from his car on the river road. The fact that Charles, Sr. kept all his personal money in the corporation, Finding of Fact 4, seems adequately explained by the testimony that he sought to avoid government attachment, and that the corporation made money in only one year and, therefore, not only declared no dividends but was forced to "juggle the best way we know how to try to get along."

Since business on the river was apparently filled with the constant threat of litigation, over collisions for instance or even over real estate, it was natural in 1948 for a sick man, no longer able to play an active role in the business, to seek to limit his personal liability.

As all parties to this appeal agree, the appropriate occasion for disregarding the corporate existence occurs when the court must prevent fraud, illegality, or injustice, or when recognition of the corporate entity would defeat public policy or shield someone from liability for a crime. . . .

In applying the test, however, any court must start from the general rule that the corporate entity should be recognized and upheld, unless specific, unusual circumstances call for an exception. E.g., Erie Drug Company Case, 416 Pa. 41, 43, 204 A.2d 256 (1964). Care should be taken on all occasions to avoid making "'the entire theory of the corporate entity . . . useless." Cases in bankruptcy or in taxation call for an entirely different evaluation of "fraud" or "injustice" than cases of controlled corporate subsidiaries, or as in this instance, a case of corporate tort. The defrauded creditor or "victim" of a business transaction with an undercapitalized corporation, for instance, often has a strong case for piercing the veil of a "sham" corporation. The controversy in such cases in-variably involves some degree of reliance by the plaintiff, contributing to the fraud, or undue advantage or trick accenting the injustice. But the injured tort claimant stands on a different footing. It is not contended that the claimants here relied upon Zubik Corporation's being more than a "mere operating company."

Limiting one's personal liability is a traditional reason for a corporation. Unless done deliberately, with specific intent to escape liability for a specific tort or class of torts, the cause of justice does not require disregarding the corporate entity. The corporate form itself works no fraud on a person harmed in an accident who has never elected to deal with the corporation.

Once fraud or injustice demand piercing the corporate veil, then the intertwining of personal affairs with a family corporation can provide additional grounds for arguing that the defendant cannot be heard to complain. In such cases, the failure of various corporate formalities either contributes to the fraud involved or strengthens the argument for injustice by holding the individual in effect estopped. But in the case of an old (71 at the time of trial), illiterate, ill man, the conduct of personal affairs through a family corporation not only has its separate justification unrelated to fraud or injustice but it fails as a "make weight" argument for ignoring the corporate entity. Nothing in the record indicates that an "operating company" such as Zubik Corporation was unique, or that it perpetrated a fraud on the Pittsburgh river community. Neither does it justify a finding that the libellants in this case were defrauded in any respect by lack of corporate formalities of Zubik Corporation or the fact that it paid Charles, Sr. by debiting his account, rather than drawing a regular salary check to his order. Nowhere does it appear that anyone failed to insure or felt protected in reliance upon Zubik Corporation's assets.

This record does not justify holding Charles Zubik, Sr. individually liable by disregarding the corporate existence of Zubik Corporation.

Directors may be liable for *ultra vires* activities of the corporation, despite the concept of limited liability inherent in the corporate form. As a general proposition the concept of limited liability applies only to the owners (the shareholders) of the corporation. Directors, on the other hand, may sometimes be personally liable for damages suffered by third parties as a result of the corporation's actions, although the general rule tends to protect directors from such liability.[25] If directors act honestly but mistakenly and enter into a contract beyond the corporate authority, they will not be held personally liable for any resulting loss.[26] In addition there is a growing trend toward imposing criminal fines upon a corporation and criminal liability upon its officers and directors for criminal violations.[27]

e. Ownership and Capital

Under the Model Act a corporation may create and issue any number of shares, provided that number is stated in its articles of incorporation. These shares of stock may be divided into classes. Each class may be granted the right specified in the articles [§5]. Usually common stock is the basic stock and has voting rights but no particular preferences (claims) to corporate income and no fixed dividend. Preferred stock usually has particular preferences to income over the common stock, as stated in the articles of incorporation. Although termed preferred, this type of stock is not superior to the common stock; it is merely different from it.

Issuing stock in exchange for money is the most common method of attracting capital to the business. The corporation may also obtain capital by borrowing money, usually by issuing debt instruments such as notes, debentures, or bonds [§4]. Such debt securities may be secured or unsecured. Although the shares of stock represent shares in the business enterprise, the payment of debt instruments takes precedence over the payment of stock or equity securities.

f. Control and Management

The general management of a corporation is vested in its board of directors. The number of directors may be set by the bylaws [§36]. If there are nine or more directors, the articles of incorporation may provide for classes of directors whose terms of office may be staggered [§37]. The first board of directors is designated in the articles of incorporation, but thereafter the shareholders elect the directors at the next annual meeting, unless classes of directors have been established. Upon a vote of the majority of the shareholders, one or more directors may be removed with or without cause [§39].

Directors have a fiduciary responsibility toward management of the corporation.

---

[25] See 19 *AmJur* 2d, Corporations, section 1341.
[26] Simon v. Soconoy-Vacuum Oil Co., 38 N.Y.S.2d 270 (Sup. Ct. 1942); Gilbert v. Burnside, 183 N.E.2d 325 (N.Y. 1962).
[27] See Z. Cavitch, *Business Organizations with Tax Planning,* vol. 5 (New York: Matthew Bender, 1977), Section 103.04.

a relationship founded on trust.

That is, they have a duty, as directors, to act primarily for the benefit of the corporation in matters connected with their roles as directors. Although a director can delegate a certain amount of authority to other individuals, he or she cannot delegate his or her entire authority. An example of normal delegation of authority is electing officers and employing other agents to act on behalf of the corporation.

The fiduciary responsibilities of directors also extend to their duties of care and loyalty toward the corporate entity and its shareholders. Thus a director may be subject to liability for unfair contracts entered into between himself or herself and the corporation for the benefit of that director and to the detriment of the corporation.[28] Also a director cannot divert a business opportunity to himself or herself if the corporation expected that opportunity.[29] If a director receives benefits in violation of a fiduciary duty owed to the corporation, the director must account to the corporation for profits or other benefits.[30] There is also a growing trend among the courts to hold the directors liable for profits made from the purchase of shares of stock from shareholders who do not have the benefit of special information possessed by the director or another insider, if such information makes the shares worth more than the selling shareholder believed them to be worth.[31]

Under the Model Act a director may be held personally liable if he or she votes for or assents to the distribution of an improper dividend; a distribution of assets to shareholders during liquidation without providing for all known debts, obligations, and liabilities of the corporation; a loan to an officer or director (unless approved in accordance with the provisions of the Act); or any other corporate action contrary to law [§48].

Like the relationship of a partner to the partnership entity, the authority of a corporate officer is governed by general agency principles and is founded upon bylaw provisions, resolutions by the board of directors, and the generally accepted authority of such officers.[32]

Although the management of a corporation is vested in its board of directors and

---

28 Wieberg v. Gulf Coast Land & Development Co., 360 S.W.2d 563 (Tex. Civ. App. 1962) (if the contract is fair and just the shareholders may ratify the contract after full disclosure by the director).

29 Burg v. Horn, 380 F.2d 897 (2d Cir. 1967) ("property acquired by a corporate director will be impressed with the constructive trust as a corporate opportunity only if the corporation had an interest or a 'tangible expectancy' in the property when it was acquired."). See also Litwin (Rosemarin) v. Allen, 25 N.Y.S.2d 667 (Sup. Ct. 1940); Irving Trust Co. v. Deutsch, 73 F.2d 121 (2d Cir. 1934).

30 Byrne v. Barrett, 268 N.Y. 199, 197 N.E. 217 (1935); Diamond v. Oreamuno, 24 N.Y.2d 494, 301 N.Y.S.2d 78, 248 N.E.2d 910 (1969) ("the primary concern . . . is not to determine whether the corporation has been damaged but to decide, as between the corporation and the defendants, who has a higher claim to the proceeds. . . . In our opinion there can be no justification for permitting officers and directors . . . to retain for themselves profits . . . which they derived solely . . . by virtue of their inside position as corporate officials").

31 Diamond v. Oreamuno. See also Feder v. Martin Marietta Corp., 406 F.2d 260 (2d Cir. 1969), cert. denied, 396 U.S. 1036 (1970), construing section 16(b) of the Securities Exchange Act of 1934, which is designed to prevent "short-swing" profits by corporate insiders.

32 See F. Kempin, "The Corporate Officer and the Law of Agency," 44 *Virginia Law Review* 1273 (1958).

implemented through its officers and other agents, *ultimate* control remains with the shareholders, who elect the board of directors. Under the Model Act and under common law, shareholders possess a number of additional rights. For example, shareholders have the right to examine corporate books for any proper purpose and to attend and vote at shareholders' meetings [§§29, 52]. A quorum of shareholders consists of a majority of the outstanding shares entitled to vote, unless the articles provide otherwise. However, a quorum can be no less than one-third of such shares [§32]. Under the Act each voting share may vote on each matter submitted for a vote, except for classes of stock not allowed to vote. Shareholders have the right to vote their shares cumulatively for the election of directors, unless the articles expressly state otherwise [§33]. This provision means that a shareholder can multiply his or her shares by the number of positions to be filled and then distribute the total as he or she chooses. In effect, cumulative voting opens the way for proportional representation of minority shareholders on the board of directors. In noncumulative elections shareholders vote their full number of shares for as many persons as are to be elected. Shareholders may execute proxies to other persons. A proxy is simply a power of attorney allowing that other person to vote the shares of the shareholder. Under the Act a proxy must be in writing and is effective for eleven months [§33].

As a general rule, shareholders may vote their shares any way they desire, regardless of their own personal interest or motives. However, the courts have tended to recognize a limited fiduciary obligation owed by majority shareholders toward the minority shareholders.[33] Thus major shareholders may sell their shares for more than the minority shareholders receive for theirs, provided there is no deception or inducement by the majority to cause the minority to sell for the lower price. Similarly, the majority shareholders may not sell their control to third persons if they know that such third persons intend to drain the corporation of its assets by voting bonuses and other compensation to themselves as officers or directors or by benefiting themselves by contractual relationships with the corporation, to the detriment of the minority shareholders.[34]

In situations in which a minority shareholder seeks to hold directors or majority shareholders accountable for actions considered injurious to the minority shareholders, the latter may bring a shareholders' *derivative action* against such directors or majority shareholders [§49]. The theory of the derivative action is that defendants have failed to do their duty, not to the individual shareholder, but to the corporation. Therefore a minority shareholder "derives" the right to sue on behalf of the corporation by virtue of his or her position as a part owner. In such case the defendants have injured the corporation directly and the shareholder indirectly, through depletion or mismanagement of the corporate assets. (In some situations both an individual action and a derivative action may be proper.) If a derivative action is sought, the plaintiff-shareholder must first show that the directors have

---

[33] Jones v. H. F. Ahmanson & Co., 81 Cal. 592, 460 P.2d 464 (1964) (majority shareholders must act in a "fair, just, and equitable manner"); Perlman v. Feldman, 219 F.2d 173 (2d Cir.) cert. denied, 349 U.S. 952 (1955).
[34] Gerdes v. Reynolds, 28 N.Y.S.2d 622 (1941); Brown v. Halbert, 76 Cal. 781 (1969).

refused to bring a proper action on behalf of the damaged corporation.[35] Unlike the usual role of a shareholder, in a derivative suit the plaintiff-shareholder fully controls the action.

g. *Corporate Securities Laws*

One usually thinks of the major publicly held corporations, such as those whose stock is traded on the New York and American Stock Exchanges, as the typical corporations. However, the vast majority of corporations are smaller and closely held, with very few shareholders and infrequently traded stock. Both state and federal law regulate the offering or sale of securities to the public. Under most state securities laws (generally called "blue sky laws") and the Federal Securities Act of 1933, an offering is not public if the seller reasonably believes the securities purchased are taken for investment and if each offeree, by reason of his or her knowledge about the affairs of the issuing corporation, does not require the information that would be set forth in a registration statement. A registration statement is a comprehensive description of the activities of the corporation required to be filed with the Securities and Exchange Commission or state securities commission, in order to allow investors to make a reasonably informed judgment about the investment.[36] Prompted by the crash of 1929, the federal government enacted the Securities Act of 1933 and the Securities Exchange Act of 1934 in an effort to require the complete disclosure of all material facts relating to the issuance of stock by any corporations, in order to prevent the widespread fraudulent activity and the use of "shell" corporations that contributed greatly to that economic disaster. Over the last several decades, the states have followed suit by enacting their own securities laws (the "blue sky laws"), which require disclosure of all facts, thereby giving the potential investor information on which to base a decision. The acts do not mean that the federal or state governments make a value judgment on the stock being issued to the public. However, they can make registration so difficult that it becomes tantamount to a value judgment. If it is subsequently determined that the issuing corporation has misstated or omitted any material facts, the corporation and those involved in the issuance of its stock may be found liable under the Securities Acts.

Often the issuer will attempt to sell the stock as a private rather than public offering, maintaining that it meets the tests of a private offering as described below. However, even in these situations the issuer must obtain from the state or federal agency permission to make such a private offering. In determining whether or not an offering is public or private, an agency uses such criteria as the sophistication of the offerees and their access to information. The number of offerees is another factor, but it is usually not as significant as the sophistication and access criteria.

Stock is generally transferred by means of negotiable certificates, except if re-

---

[35] See Federal Rules of Civil Procedure, 23.1.
[36] See, e.g., Securities and Exchange Commission v. Ralston Purina, 346 U.S. 119 (1953), describing the purposes of the Securities Act of 1933.

strictions on transfer are stated on the certificate. Under Article 8 of the Uniform Commercial Code, there is authority for imposing restrictions upon the transferability of stock. Such a restriction must be stated conspicuously on the certificate itself, so as to apprise the transferee of any limitation to which he or she may be subject as the new owner.

h. Dissolution, Liquidation, and Winding Up

The terms *dissolution, liquidation,* and *winding up* apply to corporations much as they do to partnerships. That is, dissolution is the formal conclusion of corporate existence. Liquidation of the corporate assets and winding up of the corporate business must be completed after dissolution but prior to the actual termination, which occurs upon issuance of a certificate of dissolution. Under the Act dissolution may occur by action of the incorporators of the corporation, by unanimous consent of the shareholders, or by action of the board of directors and approval by a majority of all shares entitled to vote [§§82–93].

In addition the attorney general may involuntarily dissolve the corporation, on the basis that it procured articles of incorporation by fraud, exceeded or abused its authority, failed to maintain a registered agent in the jurisdiction, or failed to file a statement of change of its registered agent or office [§§94–96]. Further, under the Act any shareholder may seek liquidation, winding up, and dissolution through court action in order to prevent irreparable injury to the corporation [§97]. Similarly, a creditor may seek liquidation, winding up, and dissolution through court action if such creditor's claim has been reduced to judgment and the corporation shown to be insolvent, or if the corporation admits in writing that the creditor's claim is due and the corporation is shown to be insolvent [§97].

C. Law of Agency

As shown earlier, an officer's, director's, or partner's authority to act affects the liability of other partners or the liability of the entity itself. The law of agency is most important for analyzing the authority of officers or partners and thus determining the extent of the liability of the parties involved. Although this area of the law has its own particular principles, questions of the law of agency generally arise in the context of larger business issues dealing with broader legal questions, such as those related to the law of partnerships, corporations, or contracts.

Agency is a consensual, fiduciary relationship between at least two parties, concerning contractual and tort rights, liabilities, and duties between the two parties and to third parties. There does not have to be a contract between the parties in order for a principal-agent relationship to be present. In its broadest sense the law of agency encompasses not only the principal-agent relationship but also the employer-employee (otherwise known as master-servant) and employer–independent contractor relationships. Strictly speaking, the law of agency encompasses only the principal-agent relationship. All three relationships will be discussed in this part.

1. Principal and Agent

a. *Contractual Rights and Liabilities of the Principal Resulting from the Acts of the Agent*

A principal is a person who has permitted or directed another person to act for his or her benefit and to be subject to the principal's direction and control while so acting. An agent is one who, by mutual agreement with the principal, is authorized to act for the principal's benefit. There are two main characteristics of a principal-agent relationship distinguishing it from the other types named in the preceding section: First, agents are distinguished from servants and independent contractors in that they act on behalf of their principals and have the power or consent, either express or implied, to bind their principals contractually with a third party; that is, agents are fiduciaries of their principals. Second, agents generally do not perform physical work for their principals and have discretion in the accomplishment of their principals' mission. The primary characteristic of the principal-agent relationship is that it deals with situations in which acts or statements of the agent bind the principal to a contract. Thus the most common principal-agent issue is whether the principal has acted through another person. In order to answer this question, it must be determined whether the principal has granted the agent authority to act on his or her behalf. A third party dealing with an agent has the right to assume that the agent has the usual authority that the societal-business relationship requires, in order for that agent to adequately deal with the third party and complete the transaction. For example, someone dealing with a business over the telephone has the right to assume that the person answering the phone has the authority to transact normal business.[37] Sometimes, however, the third party may be obligated to inquire into the actual extent of the agent's authority.[38]

The authority that the principal has granted the agent is called the *actual* authority. This is the authority by which the agent has the power to accomplish whatever his or her principal has explicitly or implicitly assigned him or her to do. There are four types of actual authority: express (clearly stated by the principal); implied (indicated by the principal by conduct or general circumstances); incidental (authority to handle matters usually incidental to accomplishing the object of the agency); and necessary (authority to act as the agent reasonably believes necessary to prevent loss to the principal).

The authority the third party, on the other hand, *believes* the agent possesses is regarded as *apparent* authority. Thus, despite the actual limited extent of the authority given by the principal to the agent, the principal may be bound to a transaction with a third party who reasonably believed the agent had the authority to

---

[37] Crawford Savings & Loan Assn. v. Dvorak, 40 Ill. App. 3d 288, 352 N.E.2d 261 (1976); Three-Seventy Leasing Corp. v. Ampex Corp., 528 F.2d 993 (5th Cir. 1976) (agent has authority to act in the usual and proper way for the business in which he is employed).

[38] DeBoer Construction, Inc. v. Reliance Insurance Co., 540 F.2d 486 (1976); Bunge Corp. v. Biglane, 418 F. Supp. 1159 (S.D. Miss. 1976).

act as he or she did.[39] The third party has the right to reasonably believe the agent had such authority as a result of some indication by the *principal,* but not one by the *agent,* to the third party. In such a case, in order to hold the principal liable, the third party must prove that the principal actually was responsible for the manifestation or appearance of authority given to the agent. Thus the third party must prove that because the principal allowed the agent to appear to have authority, the third party's belief was a reasonable one.

b. Effect of Agent's Contracts

If the agent acted with authority, either actual or apparent, and the third party knew that the agent was acting on behalf of a principal, the principal is liable for the contract the agent, on the principal's behalf, entered into with the third party. If, however, the agent acted without authority, only the agent is bound to the transaction with the third party, because he or she breached an implied promise to that third party that he or she in fact had the authority to bind the principal.[40] Thus, if no actual authority existed, the third party cannot sue the principal unless he or she can prove that the principal, either accidentally or intentionally, led the third party to believe that the agent had the necessary authority to deal with the third party.

c. Rights and Liabilities Between Principal and Agent

Because an agent is a fiduciary, he or she owes a number of duties to the principal, the breach of which may result in the agent's liability to the principal. For example, the agent cannot engage in self-dealing, acquire secret profits, or conceal facts essential to the principal in the conduct of the business.[41] The agent's obligation to act solely for the principal in all matters connected with the agency prohibits the agent's competing in business against the principal or acting as agent for another principal without consent of each or in concert with others in competition with the principal. Also the agent must exercise reasonable care, skill, and diligence in his or her work.[42] The agent must carry out the principal's instructions.

---

[39] Cordaro v. Singleton, 229 S.E.2d 707 (N.C. App. 1976); Lewis v. Citizens & Southern National Bank, 139 Ga. App. 855, 229 S.E.2d 765 (1976) (existence of apparent authority is a question of fact); Feltman v. Sarbov, 366 A.2d 137 (D.C. App. 1976).

[40] Burg v. Action Enterprises, Inc., 197 Neb. 38, 246 N.W.2d 724 (1976); Talmadge Tinsley Co. v. Kerr, 541 S.W.2d 207 (Tex. Civ. App. 1976).

[41] County of Cook v. Barrett, 36 Ill. App. 3d 623, 344 N.E.2d 540 (1975) (good faith no defense in self-dealing); Conklin v. Joseph C. Hofgesang Sand Co., 407 F. Supp. 1090 (W.D. Ky. 1975) (profits of an agent realized through the agency belong to the principal in the absence of an agreement to the contrary); Grundmeyer v. McFadin, 537 S.W.2d 764 (Tex. Civ. App. 1976) (duty of full disclosure of material facts).

[42] Regarding competition, see 3 *AmJur* 2d, Agency, section 220–22; regarding standard of care, see Roland A. Wilson and Associates v. Forty-O-Four Grand Corp., 246 N.W.2d 922 (Iowa, 1976). Although an agent has an obligation to act solely for the principal, the principal is allowed to compete against the agent. Allied Financial Services, Inc. v. Foremost Insurance Co., 418 F. Supp. 157 (D. Neb. 1976).

Failure to fulfill any of these obligations may result in liability in contract or in tort for any loss of profits or other damages the principal suffers as a result of the agent's neglect.

The principal also owes duties to the agent: First, the principal must indemnify the agent for any losses or damages the agent incurs in the course of discharging his or her agency duties.[43] Also the principal owes the agent the agreed-upon or reasonable fee for the agent's services and must maintain an accurate account of such money owed.[44] The most frequent litigation between a principal and an agent is in situations in which the agent is a sales representative for the principal, and the latter contends that the advances paid to the salesperson were to be deducted from commissions earned, while the salesperson or agent contends such advances were paid as salary. In the absence of an explicit contractual provision, most courts will regard such draw or advance by the principal to be salary rather than a loan that must be repaid or deducted from the salesman's commissions.[45]

In addition, unless the agreement between the principal and agent provides otherwise, the following rules apply to the principal's duties to the agent: (1) depending on the circumstances under which the agreement was made, the principal by implication owes the agent an opportunity for work; (2) if the principal has a duty to provide work for the agent, he or she must refrain from unreasonably interfering with the agent's work; and (3) a principal has a duty to inform the agent of risks of physical or financial harm that the principal has reason to know exist.

d. Termination of Agency Powers

There are five methods by which agency power may be terminated:

1. Expiration of term—the agency relationship terminates upon the expiration of a specified term; if no term is specified, the agency terminates after a reasonable time. If the employment contract is for an indefinite time, it is presumed that the relationship may be terminated at any time, without cause or liability, by either the principal or the agent.
2. Consummation of event—the agency may terminate upon the accomplishment of the object for which the relationship was created.
3. Death—the agency terminates upon the death of either the principal or the agent.
4. Operation of law—the agency may also terminate as a result of a legal requirement, such as the bankruptcy of the principal or the agent, the insanity of either party, or the loss, destruction, or sale of the subject matter of the agency relationship.

---

[43] Contractors Equipment Co. v. Gottfried, 139 Ga. App. 784, 229 S.E.2d 558 (1976); 3 *AmJur* 2d, Agency, section 247–48.
[44] Scott v. Allstate Insurance Co., 20 Ariz. App. 236, 553 P.2d 1221 (1976); Castille v. Folck, 338 So.2d 328 (La. App. 1976).
[45] Kleinfeld v. Roburn Agency, Inc., 60 N.Y.S.2d 485 (1946).

5. Renunciation or revocation—if the agent has the power to terminate the relationship and does so, this act is termed a *renunciation* of the agency. Similarly, a principal may terminate the agency by *revocation*. Termination by either party may occur for cause, that is, a breach of a duty owed by one party to the other. If termination is for cause and the principal is able to prove such a breach, no liability will attach to the principal for terminating the agency. However, if termination is without cause by either party, that is, in violation of the agency agreement, the relationship terminates nevertheless, but may give the aggrieved party grounds for an action for damages against the party who caused the termination.

2. Tort Liability of Master for Acts of Servant

The master-servant relationship involves a servant performing physical services for a master, with no power to bind the master contractually with a third party. A master has control of, or the right to control, the servant's physical activities during the course of the employment. A master-servant relationship is the same as an employer-employee relationship, and the terms are used interchangeably. The performance of physical services sometimes involving the commission of a tort by the employee usually characterizes the employer-employee relationship.

This relationship is relevant in situations in which a third party seeks to hold the employer liable for negligent or otherwise tortious acts of the employee if committed while acting within the scope of the employment. The rationale for holding an innocent master or employer vicariously liable for a tort committed by a servant within the scope of the employment relationship is founded primarily upon social and economic policy. Referred to as the doctrine of _respondeat superior,_ this principle is necessary to allow the free flow of commerce and the assurance to persons dealing with employees that any wrongful actions by those employees will be compensable to the injured party by the employer. This practical principle, referred to as the "deep pocket" doctrine, requires that the generally more affluent or insured employer respond to the third party for damages caused by the employee. On a strictly moral basis, and under normal concepts of culpability and justice, it is unfair for the innocent employer to be held liable for the employee's negligence. However, social policy and economic consideration for the injured party necessitate judicial recognition of the doctrine of *respondeat superior,* which means "let the master answer." Social policy further requires that the employer assume responsibility for the employee's torts because it is the employer who puts the employee in contact with the plaintiff.

Another indication of the social considerations lying behind the doctrine of *respondeat superior* is the "family car doctrine." This doctrine, recognized by many jurisdictions, requires that the operator of a family vehicle be considered the servant of the economic master of the family unit. Thus vicarious liability is imposed upon the family head if he or she explicitly or implicitly consented to the general use of the vehicle and the operator, or servant, was driving it in the course of conducting the "family business."

In order to determine whether the injured party may hold the master liable for the acts of the servant, the first question to answer is whether a master-servant relationship exists. The relationship may be created by oral or written consent or by express or implied consent. Consideration is not necessary in order to form the relationship; the master will be liable if he or she accepts the free services of a servant.[46] If the master has the right to control and direct the activities of the employee, vicarious liability may be imposed upon the master. If, however, the person causing the damage is found to be an independent contractor under the guidelines discussed further on, the master will not be liable for the acts of the contractor or for the acts of a servant of the contractor.[47]

Once the master-servant relationship is proved, the injured plaintiff must further prove that the servant was acting within the scope of employment at the time of the injury. The plaintiff must prove that the servant who caused the injury was engaged in work for the master of the type that the employee was hired to perform.[48] If the servant's conduct was motivated by a desire to further the master's interests during the scope of the employment, and his or her activities were generally the same as or incidental to the conduct authorized by the employment relationship, the injured party may hold the master liable.[49] The facts about the servant's intent, the method by which he or she attempted to accomplish the service, and the servant's actual working hours become critical in determining the scope of the employment relationship.

The fact that the master may be liable to the injured party does not preclude that party from also bringing an action against the servant for his or her own negligent activity. The servant is always personally liable for his or her own tort. In addition, the master has the right to sue the servant for damages for which the master became liable to a third party as a result of the servant's torts.

In addition to the imposition of vicarious liability under the doctrine of *respondeat superior,* a master may be held liable on the basis of conventional tort prin-

---

[46] Roring v. Hoggard, 326 P.2d 812 (Okla. 1958). See also Hulahan v. Sheehan, 522 S.W.2d 134 (Mo. App. 1975). The master must nevertheless have control over the gratuitous servant if *respondeat superior* is to apply, Usrey v. Dr. Pepper Bottling Co., 385 S.W.2d 335 (Mo. App. 1964).

[47] The question of the master-servant or independent-contractor relationship is a question for the trier of the facts. Rademaker v. Archer Daniels Midland Co., 247 N.W.2d 28 (1976); Truck Insurance Exchange v. Yardley, 556 P.2d 494 (Utah 1976); Martin Marietta Corp. v. Evening Star Newspaper Co., 417 F. Supp. 947 (D.C. 1976); Burkett v. Crulo Trucking Co., 355 N.E.2d 253 (Ind. App. 1976). See also Ostrander v. Billie Holm's Village Travel, Inc., 386 N.Y.S.2d 597 (1976) (an employer is not liable for damages caused by an independent contractor unless the subject of the contract is unlawful, the subject creates a public nuisance, a duty is imposed by statute or ordinance, the employer has a nondelegable duty to perform, the work is inherently dangerous, or the employer assumes the duty pursuant to contract).

[48] Dell v. Heard, 532 F.2d 1330 (10th Cir. 1976); Pesqueira v. Talbot, 7 Ariz. App. 476, 441 P.2d 73 (1968); Williams v. Wachovia Bank & Trust Co., 30 N.C. App. 18, 226 S.E.2d 210 (1976).

[49] Massey v. Henderson, 138 Ga. App. 565, 226 S.E.2d 750 (1976). See also Mays v. Pico Finance Co., 339 So.2d 382 (La. App. 1976) (it is also essential to consider whether an employee's act was closely connected in time, place, and causation to employment duties).

ciples, such as if he or she directed or authorized the servant to perform a tortious act, or if the master was negligent in employing an incompetent servant in the first place. If the master knew or should have known that the servant was likely to perform negligently, the master may be liable for the negligent hiring.[50] Further, if the master negligently delegated the duty to the servant, the master will be held liable for the servant's negligent activities.

A master may be liable to his or her servant, either for the master's negligence or for the negligence of a fellow servant employed by the master. In almost all jurisdictions, however, workmen's compensation statutes cover these situations; they provide maximum amounts of recovery and preclude the employee from bringing a normal tort action. In cases not covered by workmen's compensation, or if the parties have waived the benefits of such statute, common law liability for injuries to servants is available. Even if the plaintiff is suing under common law principles, all jurisdictions impose by statute a limit on monetary damages for injuries incurred during the course of employment.[51]

3. Employer–Independent Contractor Relationship

The third type of agency relationship is that of employer–independent contractor. This type of relationship has characteristics of both the principal-agent relationship and the master-servant relationship, as well as its own distinctive features. As with the master-servant relationship, there is an expressed or implied contract between the employer and independent contractor. However, this contract has a specialized objective that the independent contractor is supposed to accomplish; there is no general employment. Unlike the master-servant relationship, but similar to the principal-agent relationship, the employer in an independent-contractor situation has no right to control the means by which the independent contractor accomplishes the particular objective that the parties have in mind. Other characteristics of the employer–independent contractor relationship are: an independent contractor does not bind the employer contractually with third parties as an agent would; it is less personal than the principal-agent relationship; the independent contractor is usually engaged in an independent business; the independent contractor usually furnishes his or her own equipment; and he or she receives full payment without deductions for income taxes or social security.

Often the same person may act both as an agent and as a servant, depending upon the powers and duties that have been given to him or her. Or the person may be both servant and independent contractor to the same master-employer. The relationship depends upon the particular activity in which the person was engaged during the occasion in question. For example, a storekeeper may be an *agent* of

---

[50] Becker v. Manpower, Inc., 532 F.2d 56 (7th Cir. 1976); Thahill Realty Co. v. Martin, 388 N.Y.S.2d 823 (1976).

[51] See 53 *AmJur* 2d, Master & Servant, section 341 et seq.; 81 *AmJur* 2d, Workmen's Compensation, section 1.

the store owner because of the duty to hire and fire personnel and purchase goods. However, he or she may also be a *servant* of the store owner with respect to the duty to keep records, to maintain the premises, and to unload shipments of goods. Similarly, a master may employ a person as a distributor of the master's goods, in which case that person would be an *independent contractor*.

McLEAN v. ST. REGIS PAPER COMPANY

6 Wash. App. 727, 496 P.2d 571 (1972)

Court of Appeals of Washington

PEARSON, Judge.

This is an action for personal injuries and damages in which the plaintiffs, Fulton and Dorothy McLean, sought to establish the vicarious liability of defendant, St. Regis Paper Company, for the negligent actions of defendant, Alan Roland. A jury rejected plaintiff's theories that Roland was either an employee or agent of St. Regis at the time the car he was driving rolled backward down a hill, crushing Mrs. McLean against the wall of a building. Plaintiff's principal contention is that an agency was established as a matter of law, creating vicarious liability by application of the doctrine of "respondeat superior." We affirm the judgment of dismissal.

At the time of the accident, on Monday, August 21, 1967, Roland was en route to Western Clinic in Tacoma to undergo a physical examination to determine his fitness for employment with St. Regis. Roland had interviewed a Mr. Harold Snow at the St. Regis personnel center on Friday, August 18, 1967. Snow advised Roland that there were job openings in the sawmill. Shift times, wages and benefits were discussed. Although Snow never said, "You're hired," Roland testified that he thought he had a job. By the time Roland had talked with another man and filled out some forms, it was too late to go to Western Clinic for a required physical examination. He was told to come back on Monday, pick up a form, proceed to Western Clinic, wait for the form to be completed, and then return it to St. Regis. The physical examination was paid for by St. Regis,

and was an absolute prerequisite to employment.

Upon return from the physical examination, Roland understood that he was to take a dexterity test and thought he would then begin work on the Monday afternoon shift. On the morning of Monday, August 21, the receptionist at St. Regis told Roland where Western Clinic was located, but not how to get there. Roland began his drive to the clinic in a car he had borrowed from a friend, taking a longer route to avoid some steep hills. The accident occurred on his way to the clinic.

The trial itself was limited in nature. Roland did not appear, and both attorneys agreed he was negligent. The only real issues submitted to the jury were damages and the question of the vicarious liability of St. Regis. The jury returned a verdict in favor of McLean, against Roland, in the sum of $377,000, but found also that St. Regis was not liable to plaintiffs.

Plaintiffs concede on appeal that the issue of whether or not Roland was an employee of St. Regis at the time of the accident was a question of fact for the jury. They contend, however, that whether or not Roland was an employee of St. Regis, he was an agent for the latter *as a matter of law* for the express purpose of obtaining an employment physical and returning to St. Regis with the results. If this were true, it is contended St. Regis would *necessarily* be liable for the damage amount under the doctrine of respondeat superior. These contentions raise the central issue of this appeal. What is the vicarious tort liability of a principal for the negligent physical acts of a non-servant agent?

Assuming that Roland was not employed by St. Regis at the time of the accident, and assuming arguendo that he was an agent of St. Regis for the purpose of obtaining a pre-employment physical, we do not agree that vicarious liability would otherwise attach as a matter of law under agency principles. The general rule of vicarious tort liability applicable to non-servant agents is set forth in Restatement (Second) of Agency §250 (1958), as follows:

"A principal is not liable for physical harm caused by the negligent physical conduct of a non-servant agent during the performance of the principal's business, if he neither intended nor authorized the result nor the manner of performance, *unless he was under a duty to have the act performed with due care.* (Italics ours.)"

The comments following this and subsequent sections of the Restatement of Agency make it clear that vicarious liability of a principal for the negligent acts of any agent or servant is dependent upon whether the principal controls or has the right to control *the details of the physical movements* of the agent while such person is conducting the authorized transaction. *See* Restatement (Second) of Agency §250, comment a (1958).

In accord with this general principle are two eminent legal scholars, namely, Warren A. Seavey, and William L. Prosser. In W. Prosser, Law of Torts, ch. 13 §69 at 479 (3d ed. 1964) the rule is stated and rationalized as follows:

"Since an agent who is not a servant is not subject to any right of control by his employer over the details of his physical conduct, the responsibility ordinarily rests upon the agent alone, and the principal is not liable for the torts which he may commit." (Footnotes omitted.)

If the rule were otherwise, then in many true agency situations unwarranted vicarious tort liability would attach; for example, the client would be responsible for the negligent physical conduct of his attorney; or the factor, the broker, the independent contractor salesman, or the architect—all who are agents in the broad, generic sense could impose liability on their respective clients for negligent physical acts wholly beyond the client's ability to control.

The Washington courts have not previously considered the vicarious tort liability of the principal of a non-servant agent. Both parties in their briefs have approached the question as though vicarious tort liability were dependent upon the *creation* of an agency relationship. Consequently, St. Regis urges, on the one hand, that agency requires proof of (1) mutual consent, and (2) control by the principal, and that in this instance the requirement of control was lacking.

Plaintiff, on the other hand, urges that Washington recognizes gratuitous agents (Coombs v. R. D. Bodle Co., 33 Wash. 2d 280, 205 P.2d 883 (1949)) and that mutual consent for the undertaking which would benefit both parties was factually established. This mutual manifestation of consent, it is contended, gives rise to the existence of agency as a matter of law. Restatement (Second) of Agency §15 (1958).

For the most part, the sections of the Restatement and other authorities cited by both parties do not deal with tort liability, but address the question of the ability of one to bind another in contractual dealings with third parties. In our view, the question of vicarious tort liability involves different policy considerations than the question of an agent's ability to bind his principal in business dealings with third persons.

For instance, we have no hesitation in accepting the premise that St. Regis authorized Roland to do an act which was of mutual benefit to both. He was authorized to act for St. Regis in obtaining a physical examination at Western Clinic. In this sense, he was an agent within the broad definition of Restatement (Second) of Agency §15 at 82 (1958), which provides:

"An agency relation exists only if there has been a manifestation by the principal to the agent that the agent may act on his account, and consent by the agent so to act.". . .

Both Section 1 and Section 15 of the Restatement (Second) of Agency deal with contractual conceptions of agency and not with tort liability. "Subject to his control" referred to in *Moss* as an element for the creation of agency refers not to control of the physical conduct of agent, but control of the business dealings to which the relationship refers. Consequently, these general statements are of little value in analyzing the question of vicarious tort liability.

The doctrine of respondeat superior, which is the basis of vicarious tort liability in this jurisdiction whether an agent or an employee is involved, requires that the one charged with imputed liability have control of or the right to control the physical actions of the negligent actor....

We thus conclude that the label "employee," or "agent" does not per se create vicarious tort liability. Vicarious tort liability arises only where one engaging another to achieve a result controls or has the right to control the details of the latter's physical movements. *See* Restatement (Second) of Agency §250 (1958).

Conceding then, arguendo, that Roland was

an "agent" for St. Regis for the limited purpose of obtaining a pre-employment physical examination, we are not persuaded that St. Regis, as a matter of law, controlled or had a right to control his physical movements while he was carrying out the authorized transaction.

Roland was told only where Western Clinic was, not how to get there. He provided his own transportation and was in every sense on his own. He was under no obligation to actually take the physical examination, nor to return to St. Regis afterward. The trial court, by instruction 14, quite properly required the jury to find that St. Regis had "the right to exercise control over the conduct of" Roland in order to find vicarious tort liability. Such instruction and the others given pertaining to this issue were wholly consonant with the rule announced above. We conclude that no error occurred in submitting to the jury the issue of vicarious liability based upon agency....

Judgment affirmed.

PETRIE, C. J., and ARMSTRONG, J. J. concur.

As the *McLean* case indicates, the particular activity in which the employee was engaged will determine the liability of the parties in a particular situation. Sometimes an employer or a principal may be held liable for the wrongful action or for the binding statements of the employee or the agent, while the same activity or statements of an independent contractor will *not* bind the employer. Thus the facts in each situation must be examined in order to determine the exact nature of the relationship, which in turn will determine the liability of the parties involved.

D. The Uniform Commercial Code

As stated earlier, the field of commercial law has been the subject of extensive legislation as well as government regulation. The legislation has taken the form of numerous uniform acts, such as the Uniform Partnership Act, the Uniform Limited Partnership Act, and the Model Business Corporation Act. Another uniform act sponsored by the National Conference of Commissioners on Uniform State Laws is the Uniform Commercial Code, here referred to as the UCC or the Code. The UCC has been adopted in all states except Louisiana and is also law in the District of Columbia and the Virgin Islands. As is the case with any uniform state law, the UCC is enacted by each individual state legislature and is not subject to control for conformity by the National Conference, the federal government, or any other state. However, in the interest of national uniformity and uniformity among judicial decisions affecting commercial law, the states have enacted the UCC largely unchanged from its recommended form. Those who conceived of, designed, and sponsored this great achievement have made a permanent contribution to commercial law.

The Uniform Commercial Code is divided into the following ten articles:

Article 1. General Provisions
Article 2. Sales
Article 3. Commercial Paper
Article 4. Bank Deposits and Collections
Article 5. Letters of Credit
Article 6. Bulk Transfers
Article 7. Warehouse Receipts, Bills of Lading and Other Documents of Title
Article 8. Investment Securities
Article 9. Secured Transactions; Sales of Accounts, Contract Rights and Chattel Paper
Article 10. Effective Date and Repealer

This discussion will consider only Articles 2 and 3, the most important articles in the UCC because of the extent to which they affect and are relied upon in everyday business activities. In courses on the UCC most law schools concentrate largely, if not exclusively, on these two articles. As seen in Appendix I, the Articles are subdivided into parts, each of which in turn is subdivided into sections. These sections are numbered in the UCC text in a manner indicating both the article and the part. Thus reference to §2-201 indicates that it is in Article 2, Part Two. As with most other uniform statutes enacted by states, the jurisdictions enacting the Code followed the arrangement, sequence, and the numbering system of the uniform text recommended by the National Conference of Commissioners.

Because of the wide acceptance of the UCC, as indicated by its almost unanimous adoption among the states, it receives much well-deserved attention in business law courses and in law schools. However, this attention tends to mislead students into thinking that the UCC not only is a panacea for all commercial law problems but that it also has replaced common law contract and most other common law principles applicable to the business field. This misconception must be clarified at the outset. The Uniform Commercial Code does not apply to the sale of realty, nor to security interests in realty (except fixtures), even though these are commercial matters. Nor does the Code apply to the formation, performance, and enforcement of insurance contracts. It does not control the bankruptcy laws. Article 2, dealing with the sale of goods, is not a comprehensive codification of all sales. That is, it has absolutely no bearing on the issue of contracts that do not deal with goods. Common law principles continue to govern the law of real estate and service contracts.

As with all statutes there is a rapidly growing body of case law interpreting the UCC statutory provisions that are brought into question in the course of litigation. Enactment of uniform laws can never eliminate the need for their interpretation by the judicial branch. They can and do clarify the state of the law on numerous issues in the commercial field, but continuing judicial activity in the application of uniform laws is still necessary even with such codification. Despite the attempt at uniformity in commercial transactions throughout the nation, each jurisdiction has made changes as it adopts the UCC, and the courts of the various jurisdictions have given and will inevitably continue to give certain phrases different meanings and constructions. This process will continue because it is a function of the courts to apply the common law principles of their jurisdiction to questions arising under all statutes within the jurisdiction. Cases cannot be decided solely upon the text of the Code. Judicial integrity, maintained through well-reasoned decisions and decisions that are consistent with prior case law in that particular jurisdiction, far outweighs any possibility that the UCC will be interpreted identically in every jurisdiction.

Because of the length and complexity of Articles 2 and 3 of the UCC, it would be impossible to analyze in detail all sections of the Code and the case law developed in connection with it. The following discussion will indicate the basic content and purpose of Articles 2 and 3 and identify their major areas of concern. Article 2 is dealt with in some detail, and Article 3 is treated more briefly. In studying these Articles, there is no substitute for carefully reading each of them. Also it is more important to acquire the essential concepts of each Article than to remember section numbers or specific definitions.

1. Article 2: Sales

a. Formation of the Contract

The first step in analyzing Article 2 of the UCC is to determine how to recognize a situation to which this Article applies. In order for this Article to apply to a contract situation between a buyer and seller, the contract must contemplate a sale constituting the passing of title from the seller to the buyer for a price [§2-106(1)]. Title cannot actually pass until there has been identification of the items being sold under the contract [§§2-401(1) and 2-501(1)]. Other types of transfers must be distinguished from the sale type of transfer, because they are not covered by Article 2. For example, a lease does not include the passing of title. Also the transfer of a gift does not include the necessary element of price.

The sale must also be a sale of goods, or it will not fall under Article 2 [§2-102]. Goods are defined in §2-105(1) as all things that are movable at the time of identification to the contract. Even if the goods are not both existing and identified in the contract, such a contract for sale relating to future goods is valid as a contract to sell [§§2-105(2), 2-106(1)]. Any contract covering the sale of real property or a contract for services does not fall under this Article, because realty and services are not goods. However, if a contract for the sale of goods and services is combined, the goods portion of such a contract may fall under Article 2. In addition, if the essence of the contract relates more to the goods aspect than the services aspect, Article 2 may govern the entire contract.

Once it is determined that a particular situation involves the sale of goods as defined by Article 2, the next question is whether an actual contract for the sale of goods has been formed in accordance with the article, and if so, whether that contract is enforceable by either party pursuant to the terms of the article. This article contains a number of common law principles or principles codified in previous uniform acts that relate to these issues of formation and enforceability.[52]

i. FIRM OFFER

Section 2-205 of the Code deals with the *formation* of the contract. Under common law contract principles, an offer to buy or sell may be revoked prior to the time that the offer is accepted. However, under §2-205, if an offer to buy or sell is stated to be firm, is from a merchant, is in writing and signed, states that it will remain open for a particular time, and is separately signed if the offeree has supplied the contract form, then such offer cannot be revoked by the offeror for the specified time period. If no time is stated, the offer cannot be revoked for a reasonable time not exceeding three months.

ii. OFFER AND ACCEPTANCE

Section 2-206 also relates to formation of the contract. Contrary to common law contract principles, the offeree may accept an offer in any reasonable manner and by any reasonable medium regardless of the manner in which the offer was communicated [§2-206(1)(a)].[53] Even when the goods do not conform to the order or offer to buy, they may be accepted, resulting in the formation of a contract.

iii. BATTLE OF THE FORMS

Perhaps the most significant change in the common law principles of contract formation is in §2-207 of the Code, which contains principles of offer and acceptance referred to as the "battle of the forms." We saw in Chapter 7 that if an acceptance differs in any material respect from the offer, such acceptance constitutes a rejection of the offer and may itself constitute a counter offer, thereby eliminating the possibility of any meeting of the minds and formation of a contract.[54] However, the object of §2-207 of the UCC is to stretch the common law concept of "meeting of the minds" and to find that a contract was formed if it is at all possible to do so, despite the fact that there is not a meeting of the minds in the common law contract sense. Assuming that the offer does not contain conditions expressly limiting acceptance to the terms of such an offer, and that both parties are merchants, an offer

---

[52] See, e.g., 67 *AmJur* 2d, Sales, sections 1–3, discussing the predecessor of Article 2, the Uniform Sales Act; regarding formation and enforceability, see 67 *AmJur* 2d, Sales, sections 57–63, 65–128.
[53] See Chapter 7, pp. 133–34.
[54] See Chapter 7, p. 133.

from A to buy or sell goods, followed by a definite and timely expression of acceptance by B or a written confirmation from B sent within a reasonable time, operates as an acceptance by B, despite the fact that B's acceptance contains *new terms* [§§2-207(2)(a), 2-207(1)]. A contract may also be found to exist in a series of transmittals of orders and responses or acceptances. Among merchants dealing in goods, this correspondence often occurs on preprinted forms; thus the outcome of the battle of the forms determines whether a contract has been formed under §2-207.

Even though this situation would result in the existence of a valid contract, A is not necessarily bound by the new terms proposed by B. Those new terms are subject to A's acceptance or rejection. If A does not expressly accept the new terms proposed by B, they will become part of the contract [§2-207(2)]. However, if A informs B that the new terms are rejected, a contract will be formed under the terms of A's original offer. This result is contrary to the result under common law, under which B's response to A's offer would be a counter offer and rejection. The case of *Application of Doughboy Industries, Inc.* illustrates a typical battle of the forms.

APPLICATION OF DOUGHBOY INDUSTRIES, INC.

17 A.D.2d 216, 233 N.Y.S.2d 488 (1962)

Supreme Court of New York, Appellate Division

BREITEL, Justice.

This case involves a conflict between a buyer's order form and a seller's acknowledgment form, each memorializing a purchase and sale of goods. The issue arises on whether the parties agreed to arbitrate future disputes. The seller's form had a general arbitration provision. The buyer's form did not. The buyer's form contained a provision that only a signed consent would bind the buyer to any terms thereafter transmitted in any commercial form of the seller. The seller's form, however, provided that silence or a failure to object in writing would be an acceptance of the terms and conditions of its acknowledgment form. The buyer never objected to the seller's acknowledgment, orally or in writing. In short, the buyer and seller accomplished a legal equivalent to the irresistible force colliding with the immovable object.

Special Term denied the buyer's motion to stay arbitration on the ground that there was no substantial issue whether the parties had

agreed to arbitrate. For the reasons to be stated, the order should be reversed and the buyer's motion to stay arbitration should be granted. As a matter of law, the parties did not agree in writing to submit future disputes to arbitration (Civil Practice Act, §§1448, 1449).

Of interest in the case is that both the seller and buyer are substantial businesses—a "strong" buyer and a "strong" seller. This is not a case of one of the parties being at the bargaining mercy of the other.

The facts are:

During the three months before the sale in question the parties had done business on two occasions. On these prior occasions the buyer used its purchase order form with its insulating conditions, and the seller used its acknowledgment form with its self-actuating conditions. Each ignored the other's printed forms, but proceeded with the commercial business at hand.

The instant transaction began with the buyer, on May 6, 1960, mailing from its office in

Wisconsin to the seller in New York City two purchase orders for plastic film. Each purchase order provided that some 20,000 pounds of film were to be delivered in the future on specified dates. In addition, further quantities were ordered on a "hold basis," that is, subject to "increase, decrease, or cancellation" by the buyer. On May 13, 1960 the seller orally accepted both purchase orders without change except to suggest immediate shipment of the first part of the order. The buyer agreed to the request, and that day the seller shipped some 10,000 pounds of film in partial fulfillment of one purchase order. On May 16, 1960, the buyer received the seller's first acknowledgment dated May 13, 1960, and on May 19, 1960 the seller's second acknowledgment dated May 16, 1960. Although the purchase orders called for written acceptances and return of attached acknowledgments by the seller no one paid any attention to these requirements. Neither party, orally or in writing, objected to the conditions printed on the other's commercial form. Later, the buyer sent change orders with respect to so much of the orders as had been, according to the buyer, on a "hold basis."

The dispute, which has arisen and which the parties wish determined, the seller by arbitration, and the buyer by court litigation, is whether the buyer is bound to accept all the goods ordered on a "hold basis." The arbitration would take place in New York City. The litigation might have to be brought in Wisconsin, the buyer's home state.

The buyer's purchase order form had on its face the usual legends and blanks for the ordering of goods. On the reverse was printed a pageful of terms and conditions. The grand defensive clause reads as follows:

"ALTERATION OF TERMS—None of the terms and conditions contained in this Purchase Order may be added to, modified, superseded or otherwise altered except by a written instrument signed by an authorized representative of Buyer and delivered by Buyer to Seller, and each shipment received by Buyer from Seller shall be deemed to be only upon the terms and conditions contained in this Purchase Order

except as they may be added to, modified, superseded or otherwise altered, notwithstanding any terms and conditions that may be contained in any acknowledgment, invoice or other form of Seller and notwithstanding Buyer's act of accepting or paying for any shipment or similar act of Buyer."

The buyer's language is direct; it makes clear that no variant seller's acknowledgment is to be binding. But the seller's acknowledgment form is drafted equally carefully. On its front in red typography one's attention is directed to the terms and conditions on the reverse side; and it advises the buyer that he, the buyer, has full knowledge of the conditions and agrees to them unless within 10 days he objects in writing. The seller's clause reads:

"IMPORTANT—Buyer agrees he has full knowledge of conditions printed on the reverse side hereof; and that the same are part of the agreement between buyer and seller and shall be binding if either the goods referred to herein are delivered to and accepted by buyer, or if buyer does not within ten days from date hereof deliver to seller written objection to said conditions or any part thereof."

On the reverse side the obligations of the buyer set forth above are carefully repeated. Among the conditions on the reverse side is the general arbitration clause.

This case involves only the application of the arbitration clause. Arguably, a different principle from that applied here might, under present law, govern other of the terms and conditions in either of the commercial forms. . . .

It should be evident, as the buyer argues, that a contract for the sale of goods came into existence on May 13, 1960 when the seller made a partial shipment, especially when following upon its oral acceptance of the buyer's purchase order. The contract, at such time, was documented only by the buyer's purchase order form. However, that is not dispositive. It is equally evident from the prior transactions between these parties, and general practices in trade, that more documents were to follow. Such documents may help make the contract, or modify it. Whether the subsequent documents were necessary to complete the making of the contract (as would be true if there had been no effective or valid acceptance by partial shipment), or whether they served only to modify or validate the terms of an existing contract (as would be true if there had been a less formal written acceptance, merely an oral acceptance, or an acceptance by partial shipment of goods) is not really too important once the commercial dealings have advanced as far as they had here. By that time, there is no question whether there was a contract, but only what was the contract.

Recognizing, as one should, that the business men in this case acted with complete disdain for the "lawyer's content" of the very commercial forms they were sending and receiving, the question is what obligation ought the law to attach to the arbitration clause. And in determining that question the traditional theory is applicable, namely, that of constructive knowledge and acceptance of contractual terms, based on prior transactions and the duty to read contractual instruments to which one is a party. . . .

But, and this is critical, it is not only the seller's form which should be given effect, but also the buyer's form, for it too was used in the prior transactions, and as to it too, there was a duty to read. Of course, if the two commercial forms are given effect, they cancel one another. (Certainly, the test is not which is the later form, because here the prior form said the buyer would not be bound by the later form unless it consented in writing. It needs little discussion that silence, a weak enough form of acceptance, effective only when misleading and there is a duty to speak, can be negatived as a misleading factor by announcing in advance that it shall have no effect as acceptance.)

[T]he problem of conflicting commercial forms is one with which there has been much concern before this, and a new effort at rational solution has been made. The new solution would yield a similar result. The Uniform Commercial Code takes effect in this State September 27, 1964 (§10–105). It reflects the latest legislative conclusions as to what the law ought to be. It provides:

"§2–207 Additional Terms in Acceptance or Confirmation

"(1) A definite and seasonable expression of acceptance or a written confirmation which is sent within a reasonable time operates as an acceptance even though it states terms additional to or different from those offered or agreed upon, unless acceptance is expressly made conditional on assent to the additional or different terms.

"(2) The additional terms are to be construed as proposals for addition to the contract. Between merchants such terms become part of the contract unless:

"(a) the offer expressly limits acceptance to the terms of the offer;

"(b) they materially alter it; or

"(c) notification of objection to them has already been given or is given within a reasonable time after notice of them is received.

"(3) Conduct by both parties which recognizes the existence of a contract is sufficient to establish a contract for sale although the writings of the parties do not otherwise establish a contract. In such case the terms of the particular contract consist of those terms on which the writings of the parties agree, together with any supplementary terms incorporated under any other provisions of this Act."

While this new section is not in its entirety in accordance with New York law in effect when the events in suit occurred, in its particular application to the problem at hand it is quite useful. . . .

On this exposition, the arbitration clause, whether viewed as a material alteration under subsection (2), or as a term nullified by a conflicting provision in the buyer's form, would fail to survive as a contract term. In the light of the New York cases, at least, there can be little question that an agreement to arbitrate is a material term, one not to be injected by implication, subtlety or inveiglement. And the conclusion is also the same if the limitation contained in the offer (the buyer's purchase order) is given effect, as required by subsection 2(a) of the new section.

Accordingly, the order denying petitioner-appellant buyer's motion to stay arbitration should be reversed, on the law, with costs to petitioner-appellant and the motion should be granted.

Order, entered on April 13, 1962, denying

petitioner-appellant buyer's motion to stay arbitration, unanimously reversed, on the law, with $20 costs and disbursements to appellant, and the motion granted. All concur.

---

b. Enforceability of the Contract

i. STATUTE OF FRAUDS

Article 2 contains its own statute of frauds with respect to the sale of goods. The statute of frauds section of Article 2 [§2-201] does not indicate whether a contract has been formed; it only determines whether or not a contract, once formed, is enforceable. As discussed later, §2-204 must be examined in order to determine whether the contract has first been formed. The question of enforceability rests primarily on the requirement that there be "some writing" if the price of the goods is $500 or more [§2-201(1)]. In addition, such writing must be signed by the party sought to be held to the contract [§1-201(39)]. Assuming there is sufficient written evidence to conclude that the contract has been formed under §2-204, it is not necessary that *all* terms be in writing. The quantity term is the only term that must be in writing. Terms other than quantity, such as price and delivery, may be omitted from the written memoranda or evidence, because the court presumes them. Section 2-201(3) provides for situations in which the statute may be satisfied; that is, the statute may provide for enforceability of the contract under §2-201(3) despite the absence of a writing signed by the party sought to be held if, for example, the buyer has received and accepted the goods for which the seller is seeking payment.

ii. PAROL EVIDENCE

Parol evidence likewise does not relate to formation but to the evidence that can be admitted to prove the contract terms. The UCC codifies the common law principle of parol evidence, which states that a written contract without ambiguities that is intended by the parties as a final expression of the agreement may not be contradicted by evidence of a prior agreement (either written or oral) or evidence of a contemporaneous oral agreement [§2-202]. However, as is typical of most otherwise absolute principles, the parol evidence rule allows exceptions, namely that even a final expression may be explained or supplemented by "consistent additional terms" or by "course of performance," "course of dealing," or "usage of trade" [§§2-202(a), 2-208(1), 1-205].

c. Warranties: Performance and Breach

Once it has been determined that a contract has been formed, that such contract falls within the purview of Article 2 of the UCC, and that enforcement by the injured party is not precluded by the statute of frauds, the next question is what aspect, if any, of the contractual relationship the defendant has breached.

In dealing with the sale of goods, this issue often involves the question of breach of warranty. A warranty is an assurance by one party to a contract of the existence of a fact upon which the other party may rely. Such an assurance is intended to relieve the other party of any duty to personally ascertain the fact. The net result is a promise to compensate the other party, usually the buyer, for any loss in the event such warranted fact is later proven untrue. The UCC establishes several principles concerning various types of warranties.

i. Warranty of title

Under §2-312 of the Code, a contract of sale automatically includes a warranty of title. Any seller, whether a merchant or not, warrants that the title conveyed to the buyer is good and that the seller claims title in himself or herself, thereby making the transfer of the goods proper [§2-312(1)(a)]. A contract of sale also includes a warranty by the seller that the goods are being delivered free of any interest or lien held by a third party of which the buyer does not have knowledge [§§2-312(1)(b), 1-201(25), (26) and (27)].

ii. Express warranties

Section 2-313 of the Code describes the three methods by which the seller may create an express warranty. The first method is by an affirmation of fact or a promise made by the seller that becomes part of the basis of the bargain. Examples include statements that an automobile tire will not wear out for a specified number of miles, that a pump has a certain pumping capacity, or that a refrigerator will maintain a particular temperature.

The second and third methods by which express warranties may arise are from any "description of goods" and from any "sample or model" that is made part of the basis of the bargain. The former category includes technical specifications and blueprints or contract provisions; the latter category may include a sample that is taken from the goods on hand, or a model that represents the goods that are not actually on hand. The characteristics of such sample or model become express warranties regarding the goods to be purchased.

The key phrase in this section is "basis of the bargain." This is another example of a somewhat general guideline to be applied to specific situations. The common-sense interpretation of the phrase would indicate that any promise or warranty that has become a basic assumption on which the contract was made constitutes part of the basis of the bargain. Some sense of reliance on the warranty by the buyer also seems to be an inherent element of this phrase.[55]

---

[55] Land v. Roper Corp., 513 F.2d 445 (10th Cir. 1976); Hrosik v. J. Keim Builders, 37 Ill. App. 3d 352, 345 N.E.2d 514 (1976). But see Comment 3 of UCC §2–313, that no particular reliance need be shown. See Alan Wood Steel Co. v. Capital Equipment Enterprises, 39 Ill. App. 3d 48, 349 N.E.2d 627 (1976); Interco, Inc. v. Randustrial Corp., 533 S.W.2d 257 (Mo. App. 1976).

In order for an express warranty to be included in a contract, there does not have to be any particular word used, such as *warranty* or *guarantee*. Representations by the seller as to the value of the goods, or his or her opinion or recommendation concerning the value, are generally regarded as "puffing," and do not create an express warranty [§2-313(2)]. However, if there is an explicit oral or written representation that is an "affirmation of fact or promise . . . which relates to the goods," then an express warranty has been made.[56]

iii. IMPLIED WARRANTY OF MERCHANTABILITY

An implied warranty of merchantability can only be created when the seller is a merchant with respect to the particular goods he or she is selling. Section 2-314(2) outlines the requirements for goods to be merchantable. Because this warranty is very closely related to strict tort liability, and because product liability cases are often tried under the claim of breach of implied warranty of merchantability, this section of the Code is an extremely important one. The plaintiff need not prove negligence on the part of the defendant under this section but must prove that the goods deviated from the standard of merchantability outlined in §2-314 and that this deviation caused the plaintiff's injury. Under this section the plaintiff must prove (1) that a merchant sold goods, (2) that were not merchantable at the time of sale, and (3) injury and damages to the plaintiff or his or her property (4) were caused proximately and actually by the defective nature of the goods, and that (5) notice of the injury was given to the seller.[57]

iv. IMPLIED WARRANTY OF FITNESS

An implied warranty of fitness for a particular purpose arises, whether the seller is a merchant or not, if the seller, at the time of entering into the contract for the sale of goods, has reason to know any particular purpose for which the goods are required and that the buyer is relying on the seller's skill or judgment in selecting or furnishing suitable goods [§2-315]. It may be said that the implied warranty of merchantability is a warranty regarding the fitness for the *ordinary* purpose for which goods are used, while the warranty of fitness is for a *particular* purpose. The implied warranty of fitness under §2-315 is a narrower and more precise type of warranty than the warranty of merchantability under §2-314.

The particular purpose that the buyer has in mind is generally communicated to the seller during the course of negotiations and is sometimes expressly stated in the contract itself. In proving the buyer's reliance on the seller's skill and judgment, as required under the section, the relative knowledge of the two parties is extremely

---

[56] Leveridge v. Notaras, 433 P.2d 935 (Okla. 1967). Compare Shore Line Properties, Inc. v. Deer-O-Paints and Chemicals, Ltd., 24 Ariz. App. 331, 538 P.2d 760 (1975) (if a final written agreement has been executed, evidence of express oral warranty is inadmissible). See also Rogers v. Crest Motors Co., Inc., 516 P.2d 445 (Colo. App. 1973) (express warranty implied from turned-back odometer).

[57] See 67 *AmJur* 2d, Sales, sections 63–67, 728–738.

relevant.[58] That is, it can generally be assumed that the seller is more knowledgeable than the buyer, thereby indicating the latter's reliance on the former's skill and judgment.

v. THE UNCONSCIONABLE CONTRACT

Under §2-302, contract terms held by a court to be unconscionable cannot be enforced. Although the UCC does not define the term *unconscionable,* the courts have applied it to delete terms in contracts in situations in which the seller has taken unfair advantage of the buyer. The concept of the fair bargaining process is absent in those situations in which unconscionability is found to be present. Examples of clauses deemed by judicial decision to be unconscionable include the following: (a) clauses limiting the time for the communication of complaints about latent defects in goods that could be discovered only by microscopic analysis; (b) clauses permitting the seller to allow the delivery date to be indefinitely postponed upon the buyer's failure to supply shipping instructions; (c) blanket clauses prohibiting rejection of the goods by the buyer; (d) clauses disclaiming all warranties in cases in which the court believes there should be an implied warranty of fitness; (e) contracts containing exorbitant prices in cases in which consumer goods are involved.[59]

Unconscionable provisions under §2-302 would not necessarily constitute fraud, although many of the elements are the same in both situations. One might argue that a contract validly entered into should be enforceable. Just because the buyer exercised poor judgment in entering into a one-sided bargain, he or she should not be protected by any legal doctrine. Further, the codification of the concept of unconscionability may provide some liberal courts with a basis for exercising an unlimited discretion sometimes unjustifiably sympathetic to the unsuspecting and careless consumer. But the rationale in support of the doctrine of unconscionability is that public policy requires that a buyer who is not on an equal bargaining basis with the seller deserves greater protection by the court.

Most of the people who rely on the §2-302 unconscionability theory are consumers, and those cases where courts have decided in the consumers' favor involve the poor or otherwise disadvantaged consumer. If a merchant is suing another merchant, and the latter attempts to raise the unconscionability defense, the courts have not been nearly as receptive as they have in cases in which a consumer was involved.

vi. REMEDIES

Sections 2-701 through 2-710 of the UCC set forth the alternative remedies available to the *seller* against a breach by an insolvent buyer. Summarized, these remedies are that the seller may refuse delivery of the goods except for cash

---

[58] Cagney v. Cohn, 13 UCC Rep. 998 (D.C. Sup. Ct. 1973); Lewis v. Mobil Oil Corp., 438 F.2d 500 (8th Cir. 1971).

[59] See, e.g., Luick v. Graybar Electric Co., 473 F.2d 1360 (8th Cir. 1973); Majors v. Kalo Laboratories, Inc., 407 F. Supp. 20 (N.D. Ala. 1975); McCarty v. E. J. Korvett, Inc., 28 Md. App. 421, 347 A.2d 253 (1975); Chrysler Corp. v. Wilson Plumbing Co., 132 Ga. App. 435, 208 S.E.2d 321 (1974); Toker v. Perl, 103 N.J. Super. 500, 247 A.2d 701 (1968); Zabriskie Chevrolet v. Smith, 99 N.J. Super. 441, 248 A.2d 195 (1968).

[§2-702(1)], stop delivery [§2-705], or reclaim the goods from the buyer upon demand within ten days after receipt [§2-702(2)]. If the buyer is solvent but breaches the contract, the seller may withhold delivery [§2-703], stop delivery [§2-705], or "identify" the goods under the contract [§2-501(1)], hold the goods for the buyer [§2-704], and sue for the price of such goods [§2-709]. The seller may resell the goods [§2-706], recover damages [§2-708], recover the price [§2-709], and cancel the contract, as defined in §2-106(4).

The method of measuring the seller's damages is usually determined by the difference between the market price at the time of performance and the unpaid contract price, plus the incidental damages under §2-710, less any expenses saved as a result of the buyer's breach [§2-708(1)]. This is referred to as the contract-market formula.

The Code also states remedies available to the *buyer* in the case of a breaching seller. The buyer's *rights* are stated in §§2-601 through 2-616. The buyer's *remedies* that are available after exercising such rights are described in §§2-711 through 2-717. First, the buyer has the right to reject the goods if they do not conform to the contract [§2-601]. If the buyer chooses to reject the goods, the rejection must comply with §2-602, that is, the buyer must make it within a reasonable time and with a seasonable notice of rejection. Further, if the buyer is a merchant and the seller has no agent or place of business at the location of the rejection, the merchant-buyer must follow the reasonable instructions from the seller, or, if no instructions were given and the goods are perishable, the buyer must sell the goods on behalf of the seller, and the seller must bear the expenses of the sale. The buyer is not obligated to incur an excessive amount of expense in order to protect nonconforming goods [§2-603]. If the buyer rightfully rejects the goods and the seller gives no instructions about them, the buyer may store, reship, or resell them [§2-604]. Even if the buyer accepts the goods under §2-602(1) or 2-606, he or she may still revoke acceptance of them within a reasonable time after acceptance if he or she has been misled about the seller's intention to eliminate any nonconformity [§2-608].

If the buyer accepts and retains the nonconforming goods, his or her damages are measured in any reasonable manner [§2-714]. The measure of damages in such cases is the difference between the value of the goods as accepted and the value of the goods if they had been as promised under the terms of the contract [§2-714(2)].

2. Article 3: Commercial Paper

Commercial paper is a specialized branch of contract law, which often involves concepts of property law and the law of agency. The three basic types of commercial paper dealt with under Article 3 of the Uniform Commercial Code are the promissory note, the draft, and the check. Although governed primarily by Article 3, Articles 2, 4, and 9 may also become involved in the analysis of a commercial-paper problem. For example, a seller may receive a check in connection with a sale of goods. Article 2 would govern the sale, Article 4 would govern the rules of the bank collection process in connection with the check, while Article 9 would cover the security interest that the seller may want in the goods sold.

The main concept embodied in and governed by Article 3 of the UCC is that of negotiability. Not all commercial paper is negotiable. Although a person may hold commercial paper, he or she does not necessarily hold a negotiable instrument. It is desirable that such an instrument be negotiable; later we will discuss the requirements of negotiability.

There are differences among the three types of commercial paper covered by Article 3. The *check,* the most widely used type of commercial paper, is an order issued by the drawer to the drawee (the bank) to pay money to a third party (a payee). The check is distinguished from the note and the draft in that it is always drawn on a bank and is payable on demand [§3-104(2)(b)]. The *draft* is usually used in large commercial sales transactions rather than in consumer transactions. Rather than take a check from the buyer in such a situation, the seller draws a draft himself or herself and is therefore the drawer. By doing so, the drawer-seller orders the buyer (drawee) to pay the price to the seller's (payee's) order. Often the draft involves only two parties, who are appearing in three distinct capacities; one party is both drawer and payee. The *promissory note* is an instrument generally used in credit sales, in which the buyer signs such a note as part of his or her agreement with the seller to defer payment for the goods purchased. Thus transactions involving promissory notes usually involve the payment of interest. Unlike the check and the draft, which contains three parties, the note contains only two parties, the maker (buyer) and the payee (seller). A further distinction from the check and the draft is that the note is a promise by the maker to pay the payee, rather than an order directed to the maker's bank [§§3-102(1)(b),(c) and 3-104(2)(d)].

The reason that the concept of negotiability is so significant to commercial paper as governed by Article 3 is that a "holder in due course" of a negotiable instrument takes it free from all personal defenses of the maker (in the case of a promissory note) or the drawer (in the case of a check or draft). Thus if the buyer signs a negotiable promissory note and gives it to the seller as the payee, and the seller negotiates that note to a third party, and if the third party qualifies as a holder in due course, the original buyer (maker of the note) is forced to pay the note to the third-party holder even if the goods sold to the buyer turn out to be defective or if any other defense would otherwise normally be available. However, before this rule applies: (1) the note must be negotiable; (2) the third party must have taken the note through negotiation; (3) the third party must qualify as a holder in due course; and (4) the buyer must not have available any defenses other than personal defenses. The extensive and complex provisions contained in Article 3 cannot be dealt with in detail here, but the following discussion analyzes those four requisites.

a. Formal Requisites of Negotiability

In order to be negotiable, the note, check, or draft must be:

1. a writing [§§1-201(46), 3-118],
2. signed by the maker (in the case of a note) or drawer (in the case of a check or draft) [§§3-401, 1-201(39)],

3. containing an unconditional promise or order to pay [§3-105],
4. a sum certain [§3-106],
5. in money [§§1-201(24), 3-107],
6. on demand or at a definite time [§§3-108, 3-109, 1-208],
7. to the order of the payee or to the bearer [§§3-110, 3-111].

Each one of these elements possesses a special meaning defined by the sections cited, and each has been further refined by court decisions interpreting the provisions of Article 3.

b. Transfer and Negotiation

Transfer and negotiation are dealt with in Part 2 of Article 3 (§§3-201 through 3-208). As stated previously, the advantage of negotiable instruments is primarily based upon the rights of a holder in due course. However, before a person can claim to be a holder in due course, he or she must qualify simply as a holder of the instrument. In order to do this, he or she must take the instrument by negotiation rather than by mere transfer. The difference between taking by negotiation and taking by transfer is that in the latter situation the transferee obtains only such rights as the transferor had. This would be the same as the assignee of a contract as explained in Chapter 7.[60] Negotiation, on the other hand, transfers the instrument in such a way that the transferee becomes a holder and may further qualify as a holder in due course.

The sections of Article 3 dealing with transfer and negotiation describe in detail the different types of indorsements by which an instrument may be transferred or negotiated and the effect of each type of indorsement. These rules become critical in determining whether an instrument has been negotiated or transferred. For example, an instrument payable to order and indorsed "in blank" becomes payable to bearer and thus may be negotiated by delivery alone, rather than by delivery and a *further* indorsement [§3-204].

c. Holder in Due Course

Section 3-302 requires that in order to be a holder in due course, a holder must take the instrument (1) for value, (2) in good faith, and (3) without notice that it is overdue or has been dishonored or has any defense against or claim to it by any person. [Also see §§3-303, 3-304, and 1-201(19), (25).] Some of the basic rights of any holder, including a holder in due course, include the right to enforce it in his or her own name [§3-301], the right to transfer or negotiate it [§3-301], and the right to obtain judgment on it unless the payor proves that the signature is not his or hers or otherwise establishes a defense [§3-307]. This latter right is in contrast to a suit on a contract, which requires that the plaintiff prove consideration,

---

[60] See Chapter 7, pp. 140–42.

mutual assent, and the other requirements for a *prima facie* case of breach of contract.

d. Defenses

i. PERSONAL DEFENSES

The holder in due course of a negotiable instrument takes such an instrument free from the following *personal* defenses of the drawer, maker, or indorser [§3-306]: (a) failure of consideration or breach of warranty with respect to the goods sold and exchanged for the instrument; and (b) fraud in the inducement to enter into the transaction. However, a holder in due course must take the instrument without notice of any such defenses against it or any claims to it on the part of any person [§§1-201(25), 3-304(1)].

ii. REAL DEFENSES

Although the holder in due course takes free of all personal defenses of the defendant, he or she does not take the instrument free from what are termed real defenses, as set forth in §3-305(2). In addition, a person claiming the rights of a holder in due course has the burden of establishing that he or she is such a holder in all respects [§3-307].

iii. INTERPRETIVE AND STATUTORY DEFENSES

Judicial decisions interpreting the phrase "holder in due course" have made inroads in the defenses that can be raised against a holder in due course. For example, many cases have held that if the purchaser of the note is closely related to the seller of the goods, he or she cannot occupy the favored position of a holder in due course. This is sometimes referred to as the *close connectedness doctrine.* One early and well-known case establishing this principle is *Henningsen* v. *Bloomfield Motors, Inc.,* in which the court found that the payee (seller of goods) of a note and his transferee (lender to the maker-buyer) were so closely connected that the transferee could not be a holder in due course.[61] Factors that the courts have emphasized in determining whether the doctrine applies in each particular case include whether the transferee and payee conduct independent checks on the credit of the debtor and whether there is a common or connected ownership or management between the seller and the lender.[62]

Legislation in several jurisdictions has also narrowed the rights of the holder in due course. For example, many states simply prohibit the use of negotiable notes in

---

[61] Henningsen v. Bloomfield Motors, Inc., 32 N.J. 358, 161 A.2d 69 (1960).
[62] Slaughter v. Jefferson Federal Savings & Loan Assn., 361 F. Supp. 590 (D.C.D.C. 1973); Vasquez v. Superior Court of San Joaquin County, 94 Cal. 796, 484 P.2d 964 (1971); Jones v. Approved Bancredit Corp., 256 A.2d 739 (Del. 1969).

consumer transactions. This limitation is contained in the Uniform Consumer Credit Code, as adopted in each of those states.[63]

E. Property

1. Definition

In a strictly legal sense, the word *property* signifies the *relationship* between persons and things, not the things themselves. Although the thing itself is commonly understood to be property and is referred to in that manner even by courts, the word actually means the lawful right to use, control, or dispose of that thing. (It will be used in the normal rather than technical or legal manner throughout this discussion.) Complete control over the thing, or the property, for the rights of use, control, and disposition can be divided into the following categories: present, concurrent, future, conditional, and special. Therefore many persons can have property or an interest in property as it relates to *one* thing.

Property can be classified according to its physical characteristics as *tangible* property or *intangible* property. Tangible property includes land and all other items that can be possessed. Intangible property includes items such as stock certificates, bonds, promissory notes, or other representations of the actual property, which are only evidence of the tangible property right.

Property can also be classified as *real* property or *personal* property. Real property or realty is not only land and whatever is growing on the land but also includes improvements such as structures or other items that are securely affixed to or built on the land, and various rights connected with that land. Real estate also includes items that were formerly not attached and part of real estate, that is, items that were previously personal property, but that have lost their personal-property nature and have now become part of the realty. These are referred to as fixtures. An item is a fixture if the intention of the person who attached the item to the realty was to make it part of the realty. Personal property, on the other hand, sometimes referred to as *chattels* or *personalty,* is moveable items that are not attached to the realty or that can be severed without injury to the realty. Both real and personal property can be either tangible or intangible.

2. Freehold Estates

Because interests in property can represent fractional interests and different interests in time, ownership in real estate may be for the duration of a particular person's life or for a period of time of some other uncertain duration. If the interest in real estate is for an uncertain duration that lasts at least as long as the life of the present holder, then it is a freehold estate. If it is for a period of time less than the life of the present holder, it is a nonfreehold estate (discussed later).

---

[63] Uniform Consumer Credit Code, §3–307.

Historically there are three types of freehold estates: the *fee simple,* the *fee tail,* and the *life estate.* The fee simple estate (also called fee simple absolute) represents the greatest interest that a person can have in real estate, because it signifies an estate of infinite duration free of any conditions, limitations, or restrictions. The fee tail, on the other hand, establishes a fixed line of inheritance in the eldest son. Therefore it creates succession of the property in a manner that cuts off what would otherwise be the normal heirs at law. The life estate is an estate whose duration is limited to or measured by the life of a particular person, either the person holding the land or some other person. Thus if A conveys an estate to B for life, the estate of B will terminate by its own express limitation upon the death of B. In the meantime A has retained the vested fee simple estate, which is called the *reversion,* subject to the life estate of B. Upon B's death the property reverts to A in fee simple. If B conveys his or her life estate to C, C is said to have a life estate *per autre vie,* that is, a life estate for the life of another. Thus when B dies, C's estate terminates. If C dies before B, the life estate will descend to the heirs of C and will similarly terminate when B dies.

In the preceding examples, A retains a reversionary interest. However, if A had conveyed his or her estate to B for life, with a *remainder* to D, A would have parted with his or her entire fee simple estate, because instead of retaining the reversionary interest that would come back to A or to his or her heirs after the end of the life estate, A would have allowed the remaining interest to go to another person, namely to D or to his or her heirs. Thus a remainder rather than a reversion is created if the balance of the fee simple estate is conveyed simultaneously with the creation of the life estate. Reversions and remainders are types of future interests.

3. Landlord-Tenant Relationship

The landlord-tenant relationship is a nonfreehold estate. It is characterized by the tenant's ownership of a leasehold estate in property. The leasehold estate is the most important type of nonfreehold or less-than-freehold estate. In effect, a lease or leasehold is the creation of an estate by *agreement.* The freehold estate is created by an express grant by only *one* person.

The common law substantially favored the landlord in this relationship and accordingly developed certain rules of law in his favor, even if such rules or requirements were not expressly contained in any written or oral agreement between the landlord and the tenant. They are referred to as covenants and establish the general rights and duties of the parties in a landlord-tenant relationship: (a) a tenant has a covenant to repair any damages caused by floods, fires, or acts of third parties;[64] (b) a tenant is liable to the landlord for waste, such as deterioration or other material

---

[64] Borders v. Roseberry, 216 Kan. 486, 532 P.2d 1366 (1975). See also Euco Corp. v. Ross, 528 S.W.2d 20 (Tenn. 1975) (any obligation of the landlord must rest on the contract); Flame v. Oak Lane Shopping Center, Inc., 369 A.2d 1220 (Pa. 1977) (lease provided for the obligation of the landlord to repair the property).

change in the nature and character of the leased property, even if the value of the property increases during the tenancy;[65] and (c) the tenant must support the landlord's title to the property,[66] thus requiring that: (i) a tenant cannot assist an adverse claimant; (ii) a tenant cannot claim that the landlord does not have a valid title to the property; (iii) if the tenant acquires superior title, it automatically inures to the benefit of the landlord; and (iv) if a tenant indicates that he or she believes that the title of the property is valid in someone other than the landlord, he or she thereby forfeits the lease. The landlord is not obligated under an implied warranty of fitness regarding the leased premises.[67] This means that the tenant takes the premises in their condition at the time the lease is entered into, regardless of any defects discovered later. Also the landlord does not have a duty to repair the property, except in common areas.[68] Of course, any rights or duties under common law may be expressly modified or invalidated in the lease. These harsh common law covenants have been substantially eroded by modern court decisions and statutes.

In contrast, only three rules at common law favor the tenant: (a) the landlord owes an implied covenant of "quiet enjoyment;"[69] (b) a tenant is no longer obligated under the lease if he or she is evicted or "constructively evicted" (such as by the landlord's causing or failing to repair uninhabitable conditions);[70] and (c) the tenant has no duty to pay rent if it is not specified in the lease.[71] As a practical matter, the duty to pay rent is always stated.

If a landlord conveys his freehold estate to a third person, the grantee of the freehold becomes the landlord of the tenant under the same terms that existed between the parties prior to the conveyance.[72] Similarly, if the lessee-tenant assigns his or her leasehold interest to a third person, the assignee of the leasehold steps into the shoes of the original tenant.[73]

However, there is a distinction between an assignment of the tenant's entire interest in the lease and a conveyance of only part of the leasehold interest. For

---

[65] Cluff v. Culmer, 556 P.2d 498 (Utah 1976); Olson v. Bedke, 97 Idaho 825, 555 P.2d 156 (1976).

[66] McKownville Fire Dist. v. Bryn Mawr Bookshop, 388 N.Y.S.2d 699 (1976); Freed v. Young, 21 Ill. App.3d 64, 315 N.E.2d 72 (1973); Kirby Lumber Corp. v. Laird, 231 F.2d 812 (5th Cir. 1956); Stewart v. Joiner, 105 So.2d 448 (Ala. 1958).

[67] Blackwell v. Del Bosco, 558 P.2d 563 (Colo. 1976); Gade v. National Creamery Co., 324 Mass. 515, 87 N.E.2d 180 (1949). But compare Ingalls v. Hobbs, 156 Mass. 348, 31 N.E. 286 (1892) (recognizing an exception for short-term leases of furnished premises); Javins v. First National Realty Corp., 428 F.2d 1071 (D.C. Cir. 1970) (a landmark case recognizing a general implied warranty of fitness of the premises).

[68] Freygang v. Borough of Verona, 146 N.J. Super. 310, 369 A.2d 959 (1977). Compare Brown v. Robyn Realty Co., 367 A.2d 183 (Del. Sup. 1976) (based on modern landlord-tenant codes changing the common law rule and expanding duties of landlord).

[69] Dyatt v. Pendleton, 8 Cow. 727 (N.Y. 1826).

[70] East Haven Associates v. Gurian, 313 N.Y.S.2d 927 (1970); Dyatt v. Pendleton, above.

[71] Industrial Funding Corp. v. Megna, 384 N.Y.S.2d 955 (1976).

[72] Prados v. So. Central Bell Telephone Co., 309 So.2d 386 (La. App. 1975) (noting that this rule applies even if the sale contained no assignment of the lease and no special reference to the lease was made in the deed); National Forge Co. v. Carlson, 452 Pa. 516, 307 A.2d 902 (1973); Bank of New York v. Hirschfeld, 374 N.Y.S.2d 100, 366 N.E.2d 710 (1975).

[73] Nybor Corp. v. Ray's Restaurants, Inc. 225 S.E.2d 609 (N.C. App. 1976).

example, if a landlord leases a building to a tenant for six years and the tenant transfers all his or her interest in the premises to a third party after three years, this is an assignment because it conveys all of the tenant's remaining interest in the lease. In this case the landlord obtains the right to collect directly from the assignee all rent incurred after the assignment.[74] In addition the landlord retains the right to collect from the original tenant based upon the original contractual arrangement in the lease.[75]

However, if a landlord leases a building to a tenant for six years, and after three years the tenant transfers all his or her interest in the premises to a third party for only two of the remaining three years, the tenant is a *sublessor* (not an assignor) and the third party is a *sublessee,* because the transfer is of less than all of the tenant's remaining interest in the lease. In this situation the landlord's right to collect rent after the sublease continues to relate only to the original tenant, and the sublessee has no duty to pay rent to the landlord. The sublessee's rental obligation runs only to the sublessor.[76] In the event the original tenant fails to pay the rental, the landlord has the right to terminate the lease, in which case the sublease would automatically be terminated also.[77]

These examples regarding assignments and subleases assume that the lease agreement does not prohibit such transfers. Nothing prevents such prohibition from being expressly provided in the lease agreements, and in fact most modern-day leases do include a provision that the tenant shall not assign or sublease the premises without the prior written consent of the landlord. Such prohibitions in leases are strictly construed by courts, and a prohibition against an assignment does not prohibit subleasing, and vice versa.[78]

There are three types of leasehold estates: a *lease for a definite term,* a *tenancy at will,* and a *periodic tenancy.* A grant of an estate for a definite period of time or until a specific date is a leasehold, even though that time may be longer than any possible life span. This is a lease for a definite term, and it expires by its own limitation without the need for any notice from either the landlord or the tenant. A tenant who remains in possession after the end of a lease for a definite term is called a *tenant at sufferance* and may be ejected at any time without notice unless the landlord recognizes the tenancy as a continuing one. If the landlord still recognizes the ten-

---

[74] National Ins. Trust v. First Nat'l Bank of Alburquerque, 88 N.M. 514, 543 P.2d 482 (1975). The assignee is also liable on the other obligations under the lease. Paul v. Kanter, 172 So.2d 26 (Fla. App. 1965).

[75] Thomas v. United States, 505 F.2d 1282 (Ct. Cl. 1974) (unless landlord releases the assignor—the original lessee—from liability); Viera v. Soto, 240 F. Supp. 541 (D. Vir. Is. 1965).

[76] First American National Bank v. Chicken System of America, Inc., 510 S.W.2d 906 (Tenn. 1974); Board v. B & B Vending Co., 512 S.W.2d 702 (Tex. Civ. App. 1974); Haynes v. Eagle-Picher Co., 295 F.2d 761 (10th Cir. 1961).

[77] Glenn v. State Roads Commission, 365 A.2d 297 (Md. App. 1976); Xerox Corp. v. Listmark Computer Systems, 142 N.J. Super. 232, 361 A.2d 81 (1976).

[78] Smith v. Hegg, 214 N.W.2d 789 (S.D. 1974). See also Kroger Co. v. Chemical Securities Co., 526 S.W.2d 468 (Tenn. 1975); P. Rohan, ed., *Powell on Real Property* (New York: Matthew Bender and Co., 1977), section 246.

ancy, such as by acceptance of tendered rent, the tenancy will either be automatically renewed under the original arrangement of the definite term or it will become a tenancy at will or a periodic tenancy, depending upon the circumstances. The majority of courts favor the finding of a periodic tenancy in this situation, that is, if a lease for a definite term has terminated, the tenant has held over, and the landlord has recognized the continuance of some type of landlord-tenant relationship.[79]

A tenancy at will is the least common type of leasehold. It is a leasehold for an indefinite period of time. In this case the tenancy is terminable by either the landlord or the tenant at any time, without a period of notice. Because a tenancy at will is terminable at any time, the tenant cannot assign or grant the estate to a third person.[80] The tenancy at will and the tenancy at sufferance are similar in that they are both for an indefinite period. However, in a tenancy at will the tenant originally entered into the tenancy for an indefinite term and is not a holdover, as in the case of a tenant at sufferance. Also a tenancy at sufferance cannot arise from an agreement, as can a tenancy at will.

The third type of tenancy is the periodic tenancy, which is the most common. This type of tenancy is a leasehold relationship during successive periods of time, such as from year to year, from month to month, or for any other repetitive period of time. It renews automatically and indefinitely until it is terminated in the manner described later. If the nature of the tenancy is unclear, courts tend to find a periodic tenancy based upon the equivalent of the rental payment period.[81] For example, if rent is stated at so much per month, it will be deemed a monthly tenancy, that is, a periodic tenancy from month to month. Most states have enacted statutes that govern the manner by which a periodic tenancy may be terminated. For example, many jurisdictions provide that if a tenancy is for a period of one year or longer, either party may terminate the tenancy by giving written notice to the other party no later than three months prior to the end of such period of one year or longer. (Common law requires six months' notice in tenancies renewable yearly.) If the tenancy is for a period of six months to one year, the written notice must be given no later than one month prior to the end of the period. If the tenancy is for one to six months, ten days' notice must be given. If it is a one-week to one-month tenancy, three days' notice is required, and if it is less than one week, one day's notice is required. However, if the lease provides for notice other than as stated in the statute, the provisions in the lease will govern the respective rights and duties of the parties.

If a tenant abandons the leased property prior to the termination of the lease, he or she still remains liable for all of the rent due under the terms of the lease. In most jurisdictions this is true even if the landlord makes no effort to re-lease the premises. In other jurisdictions, however, the landlord is obligated to mitigate the damages by taking affirmative action to lease the premises after the original tenant has

---

[79] See, e.g., American Oil Co. v. Colonial Oil Co., 130 F.2d 72 (4th Cir. 1942); *C.J.S.,* Landlord & Tenant, section 137(b).

[80] Bellis v. Morgan Trucking, Inc. 375 F. Supp. 862 (D. Del. 1974) (no assignment); Mossler Acceptance Co. v. Martin, 322 F.2d 183 (5th Cir. 1963) (no assignment or grant).

[81] Camp v. Matich, 197 P.2d 345 (Cal. App. 1948).

abandoned them.[82] If he does not do so, he cannot seek recovery against the original tenant for the unpaid balance due. In the majority of jurisdictions, if mitigation is not required, abandonment sometimes creates a dilemma for the landlord as to whether he should retake possession of the premises and attempt to relet them, or allow the property to remain vacant and attempt to collect rent from the departed tenant as it comes due. If the landlord relets the premises (even at a lower rental rate or for a shorter term), he may be said to have released the previous tenant from his obligation under the lease. However, if the landlord does not relet the premises, he faces the very real possibility that he will be unable to collect from the departed tenant.

4. Cotenancies

a. Joint tenancy

Property is owned in joint tenancy if it is a single estate of land owned by two or more persons, created under one instrument and at one time, with all such persons having an equal right to share in the use and enjoyment of the property during their respective lives. On the death of a joint tenant, the rights of the property pass to the surviving tenants, not to the heirs who would normally take the estate of the deceased.

A joint tenancy exists only if the required four *unities* are present: (a) *unity of time*—each joint tenant's interest arose at the same time; (b) *unity of possession*—each joint tenant has an undivided interest in the whole property, rather than an in-interest in a particular physical segment of the property; (c) *unity of title*—the joint tenants derived their interests by the same document, such as a deed or a will; and (d) *unity of interest*—the joint tenants have estates of the same type.[83]

A joint tenancy may be terminated by a physical partition of the property at the request of any of the joint tenants, or by any transaction that involves the property and is inconsistent with the continuation of the joint tenancy.[84] For example, transfer by one joint tenant of his or her interest destroys the four unities just enumerated, and therefore the joint tenancy is terminated and the tenants hold as tenants in common.

b. Tenancy in Common

A tenancy in common is an interest held by two or more persons, each having a possessory right deriving from a title in the same piece of land. A tenancy

---

[82] Camelback Land & Investment Co. v. Phoenix Entertainment Corp., 2 Ariz. App. 250, 407 P.2d 791 (1965).

[83] Tenhet v. Boswell, 133 Cal. Rptr. 10, 554 P.2d 330 (1976); Hass v. Hass, 248 Wisc. 212, 21 N.W.2d 398 (1945). See also A. J. Casner, ed., *American Law of Property* (Boston: Little, Brown and Co., 1952), section 6.1.

[84] See, e.g., West's Anno. Cal. Code, Civ. Proc. Code, Section 872 et seq. (as amended, 1976); McKinney's Consolidated Laws of New York, Real Property Actions Law, Section 901, et seq. (1967); Yannopoulos v. Sophos, 365 A.2d 1312 (Pa. Super. 1976); Manta v. Manta, 391 N.Y.S.2d 680 (1977); Shepherd v. Shepherd, 336 So.2d 497 (Miss. 1976).

in common is characterized by unity of possession. Although cotenants may have unequal shares in the property, they are each entitled to equal use and possession of it.[85] Thus, like joint tenants, tenants in common have unity of possession but do not need the other three unities. Tenants in common may acquire their interests at different times, under different instruments, and from different persons. Also the interests do not have to be of the same duration. One significant difference between joint tenancy and tenancy in common is that upon the death of a tenant in common, his or her interest in the property will descend to the heirs or pass under the will. In contrast with joint tenancy, there is no survivorship passing the interest of a tenant in common to other tenants in common.

c. Tenancy by the Entirety

Tenancy by the entirety is a type of ownership of property by a husband and wife together. As with joint tenancy, the survivor of the marriage is entitled to the whole estate. However, in addition to the four unities of time, title, interest, and possession, in order for a tenancy by the entirety to exist there must be *unity of person*. At common law the husband and wife were said to be seized as one person.[86] Thus, as part of this fiction, neither was allowed to convey any part of the property without the consent of the other.

The survivorship feature of this type of tenancy can be terminated by mutual agreement between the husband and wife, a conveyance of the property joined in by both parties, the death of either party, or by divorce or the dissolution of the marriage.[87]

Modern statutes in some states have effectively eliminated this type of interest in property by treating all tenancies by the entirety as tenancies in common, and by eliminating the parties' inability to destroy the survivorship feature without mutual agreement.[88]

5. Subsurface and Above-Surface Ownership Rights

According to ancient statements of the legal extent of a person's ownership in land, a person owned the land below his surface to the center of the earth and above his surface *ad infinitum*.[89] However, it has long been recognized that separate estates in real property may be created embracing the content of the land below the

---

[85] Thompson v. Flynn, 102 Mont. 446, 58 P.2d 769 (1936).
[86] Bechtel v. Bechtel's Estate, 330 So.2d 217 (Fla. App. 1976); Boehringer v. Schmid, 254 N.Y. 355, 173 N.E. 220 (1930); W. Burby, *Hornbook on Real Property* (St. Paul: West Publishing Co., 1943), pp. 293–94.
[87] Walker v. Walker, 336 So.2d 649 (Fla. App. 1976) (conveyance by both husband and wife); Newman v. Chase, 70 N.J. 254, 359 A.2d 474 (1976) (death of either); Kinney v. Mosher, 100 So.2d 644 (Fla. App. 1958) (agreement by husband and wife); Millar v. Millar, 200 Md. 14, 87 A.2d 838 (1952) (divorce). And see generally P. Rohan, ed., *Powell on Real Property* (Matthew Bender & Co., New York, N.Y. 1977), section 624.
[88] *Powell*, section 621.
[89] 63 *AmJur* 2d, Property, section 12.

surface; and since human beings began to fly above the surface, court decisions have made it clear that property rights do not extend upward infinitely.[90]

The typical subsurface estate is in some mineral, such as oil, gas, or coal. However, the fee ownership below the surface does not have to be in a mineral; it may be merely applied to a designated space beneath the surface. Fee ownership of minerals is usually created in one of two ways. It is either granted to another person by the person who owns the entire estate (surface and subsurface) and the mineral estate is thereby severed from the surface ownership, or it is reserved in the surface owner at the time he or she transfers the surface to another person, which also creates a severance of the mineral and surface estates. From that point onward, the "chains of title" of ownership remain separate and distinct, unless of course the mineral owner and the surface owner subsequently transfer their interests to the same person. If the surface and mineral estates are severed, the mineral owner is entitled to reasonable use of the surface in order to realize the benefits from the minerals that he or she owns below the surface. In fact, in the majority of jurisdictions the mineral estate is the dominant estate, which means that if there is a conflict in the use of the two estates, the surface estate must give way to the mineral estate in order to allow reasonable use and development of the minerals therein. The mineral owner is not required to pay damages to the surface owner in making such reasonable use of the surface.[91]

This principle is applicable to a situation in which the surface owner has a 320-acre farm with a farmhouse, related buildings, and irrigated crops such as corn, and another person owns the oil and gas lying several thousand feet below the surface and wishes to drill an oil well. In the absence of any municipal or state regulations precluding the development of the oil, the surface owner could not prohibit the mineral owner from proceeding with the development of the oil well, even though the surface owner would receive no benefit from the discovery of oil and may suffer damages to his or her growing crops.

Another element is typically present in the development of minerals such as oil and gas. Because it is so expensive and speculative to drill for oil and gas, the average mineral owner is unable to bear the risk and cost of such an endeavor. Therefore, the mineral estate is usually leased to an oil company, with the owner retaining a royalty interest in any minerals discovered, produced, and sold. The lessee–oil company has the right to proceed with development of the resource without interference from the surface owner. That is, under the typical oil and gas lease the lessee is expressly assigned and granted all the rights connected with the ownership of the mineral estate, except for the royalty interest (usually one-eighth) retained by the mineral owner.

The majority of courts now consider an estate in land to extend upward as far as may be necessary to protect any actual use of the air space.[92] Several states have

---

[90] 8 *AmJur* 2d, Aviation, section 3; 54 *AmJur* 2d, Mines & Minerals, section 108; 63 *AmJur* 2d, Property, section 12.
[91] Cole v. Ross Coal Co., 150 F. Supp. 808 (S.D.W.Va. 1957); Wall v. Shell Oil Co., 25 Cal. Rptr. 908 (Cal. App. 1963); See also, Gulf Oil Corp. v. Walton, 317 S.W.2d 260 (Tex. Civ. App. 1958).

statutes that specify that the air space is owned by the surface owner, but that air-craft have the right to fly through it.[93] However, even in these states, aircraft are not permitted to interfere with the surface owner's *actual* use of his or her own airspace.

A relatively new concept in above-surface ownership has evolved in recent years with the advent of the condominium and townhouse. This method of ownership has generally been authorized by statutes that allow for the ownership of an estate that is above the surface of the ground, even though it is not contiguous thereto. Thus certain condominium statutes provide that condominium ownership consists of a fee simple estate in an individual air-space unit that is part of a multiunit property and is combined with an undivided fee simple interest in common elements such as walls, floors, halls, corridors, parking areas, and garden areas.

6. Incorporeal Interests in Property

Incorporeal interests are rights or interests that grow out of or are connected to land but that are not interests in the real estate itself. The following discussion briefly examines several of the most common incorporeal interests in property.

a. Easements

An easement is the right to use some or all of the land of another person. The land over which the easement runs is called the *servient tenement*. The land that the easement serves is called the *dominant tenement*. The most common types of easements are for the right to maintain or install utilities such as power lines or gas pipelines. However, there are also easements for right-of-way or passages over another person's land, and easements for light, air, and the flow of water. This right can be distinguished from the right to actually use the water that goes across one's *own* land, which is a corporeal interest. The right to simply have the water flow across another person's land to a designated place is an incorporeal interest.

In general the scope of an easement granted orally or in writing is based on the intent of the parties and on reasonable use. If the easement was granted in writing, its scope is controlled by the express provisions in such written easement in light of the circumstances existing at the time of the grant of the easement. However, the law also recognizes the creation of an easement through *continued use* of a particular area across another person's surface for a specified period of years (usually twenty years). This is called an *easement by prescription.* Easements obtained by prescription are limited in their scope to the type of use actually made during the period when the easement was being established, and to the use of the dominant tenement during that period.[94]

---

[92] 8 *AmJur* 2d, Aviation, section 3.

[93] West's Anno. Calif. Code, Public Utility Code, Section 21402 (1965); Purdon's Pa. Stat. Anno. 1 P.S. 1467 (1963).

[94] Sylva v. Kuck, 49 Cal. Rptr. 512 (Cal. App. 1966); Merriam v. 352 West 42nd St. Corp., 183 N.Y.S.2d 950 (1959); Kerr Land & Timber Co. v. Emmerson, 233 Cal. App.2d 200, 43 Cal. Rptr. 333 (1965).

An easement can also be implied by the circumstances surrounding the physical characteristics of land. For example, if the conveyance of a piece of property leaves it without a right of access, an easement of necessity will be implied, because any other result would be contrary to the obvious intentions of the parties. With the rapidly growing use of solar-energy facilities in private homes, a new body of court decisions can be expected that will establish the right of a solar easement implied by necessity. This is necessary to assure the user that a neighbor's trees or buildings will not block the solar panels' access to the sun.

b. Rents, Profits, and Licenses

If a person owns a *rent,* he or she is entitled to receive from the tenant the portion of the product of the land stated in the grant or reservation of the rent. The rent may be in the form of a portion of the product of the land, such as a crop, or it may be a specified amount of money.

A *profit* is the right to remove from the land of another some substance, such as the right to cut timber, the right to mine minerals, or the right to remove gravel. Like rents, profits may be conveyed along with the dominant estate or apart from it. Also rents and profits must be distinguished from the ownership of the substance in place, as with the actual fee ownership of minerals by the mineral owner. Of course, the mineral owner may convey a profit in such minerals to another person, but the right consists of the right to remove the minerals and not the actual ownership of them while they exist below the surface.

A *license* is a consent by the landowner to perform an act that would otherwise constitute a trespass to the landowner. (This type of license is not the same as a license granted by governmental authority, such as a driver's license or liquor license). If a landowner grants a license related to property, it is revocable at the will of that landowner. Also licenses are regarded as personal to the licensee and are therefore not assignable to another person. Thus the license is terminated upon the death of either the licensor or the licensee. An exception to the principle that a license is revocable is if such a license is coupled with an interest. For example, if a landowner sells the timber on his or her land and grants a license to the purchaser to enter and remove the timber, the purchaser has a license coupled with an interest permitting him or her to enter. This license cannot be revoked by the landowner.

The difference between a profit and a license is that the latter does not give the licensee an interest in the premises itself. It is simply a right of *use* for a given length of time.

c. Restrictive covenants

The term *restrictive covenants* is heard most commonly in connection with housing developments. The owner of a housing development and his or her grantees often seek to maintain a certain set of standards in the neighborhood by imposing specific requirements on all future owners of the houses as to architecture, streets, utilities, and various uses of the land in the neighborhood. They want their neighbors' grantees to maintain those standards if such standards are not expressly provided in the deeds to such grantees. The most effective way to accomplish this goal is to restrict the ability of successive owners of land to alter their own homes by imposing private restrictive covenants that are described as running with the land. These covenants thus ensure that architectural or other types of requirements survive the change of ownership in the land. This is accomplished by recording the housing development plat in the appropriate records of the county in which the land is located. This automatically makes the plat, including the covenants and restrictions, part of all subsequent purchasers' title. Recording it provides constructive notice to any successive owners, even if they purchased the house and property several years after the development occurred and the covenants were recorded. Because conformity with the covenants is in the interest of all the homeowners in the development, any of them may enforce the covenants by court action against any owner not complying with them.

QUESTIONS

1. A general partnership is an association of two or more persons to carry on, as co-owners, a business for profit. Does this mean that the partnership must retain all profits, or can all profits be passed through to the partners?

2. Which of the essential elements of a general partnership were lacking in the *Crest* case?

3. What are the differences between a general partnership and a limited partnership?

4. What are the differences between a limited partnership and a corporation?

5. Give some examples indicating the scope of responsibility of corporate directors compared to that of corporate officers. Does the Model Business Corporation Act require that a corporation have both directors *and* officers? If so, how many?

6. What are some of the fiduciary responsibilities that directors and officers have toward the shareholders?

7. In the following situation, who is liable? An employer is awarded a contract by the city to construct a public building and hires an independent contractor to perform the work. A third-party pedestrian is then injured as a result of the independent contractor's negligence during construction of the building.

    As a general rule, is an employer liable for the independent contractor's negligence? for the negligence of an employee of the independent contractor? Is the situation described here an exception to the rule? why?

8. Applying the Uniform Commercial Code to the hypothetical case in paragraph 4 of the Chapter 7 Questions, what result do you reach? Discuss. Does the case

involve a sale of goods or services? Is the UCC statute of frauds (§2-201) relevant to this case? Explain. What rights are available to Smith under §§2-601 through 2-616? What remedies are available to the parties under §§2-701 through 2-717?

9. What is the difference between an implied warranty of merchantability and an implied warranty of fitness? Give some examples of such warranties from newspaper or television advertisements.

10. In promissory note cases involving the close-connectedness doctrine, what other factors should the court consider in deciding whether to allow the purchaser of the note to qualify as a holder in due course?

11. What do you assume were the prevailing economic conditions and social considerations at the time when the common law landlord-tenant covenants were established? Based on contemporary social and moral factors, what arguments can be made in favor of eliminating those covenants that favor the landlord?

12. What is the difference between an assignment and a sublease?

13. Why should a buyer of real estate carefully check the ownership of the minerals under the land before purchasing?

9

The Law of Torts

[handwritten note: a tort is any unlawful act against another not covered by a contract.]

A. Definition and Introduction

A *tort* is an unprivileged act or failure to act, independent of a contract, that causes injury to a legally protected interest of another and subjects the person committing the act to liability for damages in a civil suit.[1] The essential elements of a tort are the existence of a legal duty owed by the defendant to the plaintiff, breach of that duty, and a causal relationship between the defendant's conduct and the resulting damages incurred by plaintiff. If the defendant's conduct is tortious, then it will subject him or her to tort liability. The term *tort* comes from the Latin *tortus,* meaning "twisted." In England, through common usage, the word came to mean "wrong." Later the word lost its common usefulness and disappeared from the English language; however, it has remained a legal term, gradually acquiring the technical meaning given here.[2]

The law of torts contains three broad areas: negligence, intentional torts, and torts based on strict liability. Certain other torts do not fall into these categories and will be considered separately. Most people are familiar with the first type of tort, negligence, which is generally the cause of the typical automobile accident and of other common personal injuries. In most tort cases the basis for liability is negligence.

1. Duty

As stated in the definition, one may sue in tort because the defendant has breached a legal duty owed to the plaintiff. The first question is how that legal duty arises. What is its origin, and why is such a duty recognized by the court system and by the public in general? With a few exceptions, such as imputed negligence and

---

[1] W. Prosser, *The Law of Torts* (St. Paul: West Publishing Co., 1971), pp. 1–3.
[2] C. Post, *An Introduction to the Law* (Englewood Cliffs, N.J.: Prentice-Hall, Inc., 1963), p. 68.

strict liability statutes, legal duty as applied to the law of torts does not arise out of any statutes passed by the legislature. It is a duty brought into existence by the courts because of a need for guidelines in people's dealings with one another. In order to function in an orderly and efficient manner, society should deter people from causing injury to one another, and when such injury occurs, people must have a means to be compensated for it by the person who caused it:[3]

> In the state of nature, where everything is common, I owe nothing to him whom I have promised nothing; I recognize as belonging to others only what is of no use to me. In the state of society all rights are fixed by law, and the case becomes different.

According to Pound, the original theory of liability consisted in a duty to buy off the vengeance of the person to whom the injury had been done.[4] As the social interests of peace and order came to be secured more effectively by regulation, compensation came to be regarded as a duty to repair the injury, rather than to prevent vengeance by the injured party:[5]

> [T]he crude beginnings of liability in a duty to compound for insult or affront to man or gods or people, lest they be moved to vengeance . . . [later] developed into liability to answer for injuries caused by oneself or done by those persons or those things in one's power, and liability for certain promises made. . . . Thus, the basis for liability has become twofold. It rests on the one hand upon duty to repair injury. It rests on the other hand upon duty to carry out formal undertakings.

2. Standard of Conduct

In a sense, the torts guidelines represent what the average person in society regards as normal behavior, and they attempt to establish parameters within which society allows its members to function. Once one steps outside those parameters, one is vulnerable to a person who wishes to seek legal relief for damages he or she suffered as a result of the "abnormal" conduct:[6]

> Is it not . . . [a] postulate that in civilized society men must be able to assume that their fellow man, when they are in a course of conduct will act with due care, that is, with the care which the ordinary understanding and moral sense of the community exacts, so as not to impose an unreasonable risk of injury upon them?

The impermissible conduct, that is, the activity outside the parameters that comprise the law of torts, may be either intentional or accidental conduct. Whether intentional or accidental, the question of whether the action has in fact breached

---

[3] Jean Jacques Rousseau, *The Social Contract,* trans. G.D.H. Cole, in C. Morris, ed., *The Great Legal Philosophers* (Philadelphia: University of Pennsylvania Press, 1971), p. 223. See also Jean Dabin, *General Theory of Law,* trans. K. Wilk, in C. Morris, ed., *The Great Legal Philosophers,* pp. 466–494.

[4] R. Pound, *An Introduction to the Philosophy of Law* (New Haven: Yale University Press, 1968), p. 74.

[5] Ibid., p. 76.

[6] Ibid., p. 86.

society's guidelines for acceptable conduct becomes a value judgment. The French Civil Code stated in the nineteenth century that "every act of man which causes damage to another obliges him through whose fault it happened to make reparation." [7] In discussing this provision, Pound observed: [8]

> Liability is to be based on an act, and it must be a culpable act. Act, culpability, causation, damages were the elements. This simple theory of liability for culpable causation of damage was . . . taken up by text writers on torts in the last half of . . . [the nineteenth] century . . . [and] had much influence on Anglo-American law.

The legal system judges what constitutes a culpable act over the long term through a continuous body of decisions made by judges and juries. The question of whether the conduct is acceptable or "normal" is answered by the judge or jury in each individual case. But the standard is a changing and sometimes elusive one. The standard of what is normal in the field of torts is analogous to the changing concept of liberty. Indeed, imposing restrictions on a person's freedom of action in some sense restricts his or her liberty. [9]

> Liberty is not defined. Its limits are not mapped and charted. How shall they be known? Does liberty mean the same thing for successive generations? May restraints that were arbitrary yesterday be useful and rational and therefore lawful today? May restraints that are arbitrary today become useful and rational and therefore lawful tomorrow? I have no doubt that the answer to these questions must be "yes."

The public's conception of standards of acceptable conduct is as dependent on present customs, economic beliefs, and other changing social currents as is its concept of liberty at any given time. Judges as well as the public are subject to these changes. According to Cardozo, however, judicial freedom to redesign legal guidelines was not always available. In response to the questions he posed in the preceding quotation, Cardozo stated that: [10]

> There were times in our judicial history when the answer might have been "no." Liberty was conceived of at first as something static and absolute. The Declaration of Independence had enshrined it. The blood of Revolution had sanctified it. The political philosophy of Rousseau and of Locke and later of Herbert Spencer and of the Manchester School of economists had dignified and rationalized it. *Laissez faire* was not only a counsel of caution which statesmen would do well to heed. It was a categorical imperative which statesmen, as well as judges, must obey. The "19th century theory" was "one of eternal legal conceptions involved in the very idea of justice and containing potentially an exact rule for every case to be reached by an absolute process of logical deduction."

Though a particular act or mode of conduct may in one century be considered to fall outside the parameter of normal activity and in another century fall within it,

---

[7] As quoted in Pound, p. 81.
[8] Ibid., pp. 81–82.
[9] B. Cardozo, *The Nature of the Judicial Process* (New Haven: Yale University Press, 1970), pp. 76–77.
[10] Ibid., pp. 77–78.

the general principle of the law of torts is unaffected and continuously applicable. The principle is that everyone has a legal duty not to interfere with, invade, or breach any legally protected interest of any other person. Most importantly, the law of torts establishes and makes visible those duties and interests; it organizes and gives concreteness to what is otherwise a set of abstract concepts. This organization is accomplished, of course, through the court system. This area of the law, perhaps more than any other, conforms to standards established through case law, and legislative control has little effect on it:[11]

> Inheritance and succession, definition of interests in property and the conveyance thereof, matters of commercial law . . . have proved a fruitful field for legislation. In these cases the social interest in the general security is the controlling element. But where the questions are . . . of the weighing of human conduct and passing upon its moral aspects, legislation has accomplished little. No codification of the law of torts has done more than provide a few significantly broad generalizations.

However, the state courts did attempt to eliminate the flexibility of some tort principles and turn the English principles of tort law into hard and fast rules:[12]

> If one crossed a railroad he must stop, look, and listen. It was negligence, *per se,* to get on or off a moving car . . . and the like.

All attempts to eliminate the exercise of discretion in applying legal standards eventually collapsed. The result was a reaction in the courts; many states turned over all questions of negligence to juries, without very much advice from the bench. Jurisdictions have also delegated many subjects to administrative boards and commissions. In any event, whether a jury applies the standard of due care in an action for negligence, or a public service commission applies the standard of reasonable facilities for transportation, the process is one of judging the quality of conduct under its special circumstances and with reference to ideas of fairness as understood by the layman, or ideas of what is reasonable as understood by the (more or less) expert commissioner. "Common sense, experience, and intuition are relied upon, not technical rules and scrupulously mechanical application." [13]

B. Negligence

Negligence is an act or failure to act which constitutes: (1) a failure to exercise the due care of a reasonably prudent person under the circumstances; or (2) a failure to exercise the degree of care that a prudent person would exercise under the same circumstances, by which the person or property of another is exposed to an unreasonable risk of injury and does in fact sustain injury. Thus the term refers to conduct that falls below the standard established by the law for the protection of

---

[11] Pound, p. 69.
[12] Ibid., p. 58.
[13] Ibid., pp. 58–59.

others against unreasonable risk of harm.[14] By this definition other types of torts are implicitly excluded. That is, negligence does not include any type of conduct that either intentionally disregards the interest of others or that constitutes the intentional infliction of injury on a person. In addition, negligence can result not only from an affirmative act but also from an omission or failure to act.

1. *Prima Facie* Case

As a first step in proving that the defendant has invaded the plaintiff's legally protected interest, the plaintiff must establish the basic elements constituting a case of negligence. The basic elements of any cause of action are termed the *prima facie* case. In the law of torts, a *prima facie* case of negligence consists of the facts that on their face establish a sufficient case of negligence, not requiring any further support to establish its existence, validity, or credibility. Understandably, the plaintiff should have the burden of establishing the *prima facie* case, because it is the plaintiff who brought the case to court in the first place, and it is the plaintiff who is making allegations about the defendant's supposedly negligent activities. In the plaintiff's complaint he or she stated one or more acts that allegedly constitute negligence, and the plaintiff should thus be required to show the court and the jury that not only did the activities occur but, as prescribed in the law of torts, those activities constitute negligence on the part of the defendant. Thus the initial step for the plaintiff in any trial is to establish the four basic elements of a *prima facie* case of negligence: duty, breach of duty, causation, and damages.

a. Duty

i. DUE CARE

Negligence, as defined earlier, includes a "failure to exercise the due care of a reasonably prudent person under the circumstances." Thus one owes a duty of due care. The phrase "due care" means that amount of care proportionate to the amount of threatened or apparent danger to which the plaintiff is foreseeably exposed.[15] The more dangerous the situation, the more care is required. For example, irrespective of any speed limits imposed by statute, the driver of an automobile going through a crowded city street owes more due care than the driver of an automobile on a deserted road. The first driver may be driving at the rate of 20 mph while the latter may be driving at 50 mph, yet both may be exercising due care, that is, care proportioned to the amount of apparent danger.

---

[14] DeMichaeli & Associates v. Sanders, 340 N.E.2d 796 (Ind. App. 1976); Pence v. Ketchum, 326 So. 2d 831 (La. 1976).

[15] Silvers v. TTC Industries, Inc., 395 F. Supp. 1312 (E.D. Tenn. 1970); Shuler v. Clabough, 38 Tenn. App. 333, 274 S.W.2d 17 (1954).

ii. REASONABLY PRUDENT PERSON

The phrase "reasonably prudent person" (traditionally known as a "reasonably prudent man") must be understood in the context of the law of torts as an embodiment of guidelines of conduct acceptable to the majority of the members of society. The reasonably prudent person is a hypothetical person whose conduct represents the community's ideal of reasonable behavior.[16] That is, the conduct of such a person always falls within those guidelines. In determining whether the defendant has acted negligently, then, his or her conduct is compared with that of the reasonably prudent person. With tongue in cheek, A. P. Herbert[17] defines the reasonable man as one who

> invariably looks where he is going, and is careful to examine the immediate foreground before he executes a leap or a bound; who neither star-gazes nor is lost in meditation when approaching the trap-doors or the margin of a dock; who records in every case upon the counterfoils of cheques such ample details as are desirable . . . who never mounts a moving omnibus and does not alight from any car while the train is in motion; . . . who never from one year's end to the other makes an excessive demand on his wife, his neighbors, his servants, his ox, or his ass; who in the way of business looks only for that narrow margin of profit which twelve men such as himself would reckon to be "fair," and contemplate his fellow merchants, their agents, and their goods, with that degree of suspicion and distrust which the law deems admirable; who never swears, gambles, or loses his temper, who uses nothing except in moderation, and even while he flogs his child is meditating only on the golden mean. Devoid, insured, of any common weakness, with not one single saving vice . . . this excellent but odious creature stands like a monument in our Courts of Justice, vainly appealing to his fellow-citizens to order their lives after his own example.

As interpreted by the courts, the attributes of the reasonably prudent person are at least minimum intelligence, the mental capacity of the normal person of the community, a normal memory, and normal perception.[18] However, the law in most jurisdictions requires that the defendant be compared with a reasonably prudent person who also has such *superior* qualities as that particular defendant possesses or pretended to the injured party to possess.[19] The theory here is that people who represent themselves as having certain special attributes that they do not actually have should be held to account for their actions in light of these additional qualities, provided the injury allegedly suffered by the plaintiff resulted from or had some connection with those superior qualities or the lack of them. For example, if someone represents himself or herself as a doctor, whether he or she is a doctor or not, and the plaintiff submits to that person's care for some professional service, and injuries subsequently result from the rendering of that service, it would be totally

---

16 See 57 *AmJur* 2d, "Negligence," section 68.
17 A. Herbert, *Uncommon Law* (London: Methuen & Co., Ltd., 1935), pp. 3–4.
18 See Prosser, pp. 149–54.
19 See, e.g., Johnson v. County Arena, Inc., 29 Md. App. 674, 349 A.2d 643 (1976).

unfair to the plaintiff to measure the defendant merely against the reasonably prudent person of the community who is not a doctor. Surely the reasonable person of the community cannot be expected to provide the same degree of care in the actions that resulted in the plaintiff's injury as the reasonably prudent *doctor* is expected to provide.

iii. DUTY OWED BY WHOM

Who owes the duty? That is, to whom do these standards concerning the average, reasonable person and the degree of due care apply? The answer is that they apply to all persons. Every case is governed by the rule of general application that *all persons* are required to use ordinary care to prevent others from being injured as a result of their conduct.[20] Simply as a member of society, each person has responsibility to act within society's guidelines and parameters.

Even children are held to the standard of the reasonable person, although the age, intelligence, and experience of the individual child are considered part of the circumstances of each particular case.[21] Thus, if a ten-year-old child is the defendant, the question becomes, "How would the average, reasonable person have acted if that person were ten years old, and of the same intelligence and experience as the child who is the defendant in this particular case?" [22]

Persons with physical disabilities are also held to the standard of the reasonable person, in which case their disability is one of the circumstances taken into account.[23] However, such defendants would also be charged with knowledge that they have such a disability; so they may be found negligent simply because they engaged in an activity that a reasonable person with such a disability would not have attempted.[24] For example, when measured against the reasonable person, a defendant with poor vision is held only to the standard of care that a reasonable person with poor vision would exercise. If it was unreasonable for such a defendant to drive a car, that is, if a reasonable person with poor vision would have realized that it was unsafe to drive the car, then the defendant's driving would constitute negligence and his or her liability would not be lessened by virtue of having poor vision.

---

20 Weirum v. RKO General, Inc., 123 Cal. Rptr. 468, 539 P.2d 36 (1975); M & T Chemicals, Inc. v. Westrick, 525 S.W.2d 740 (Ky. 1974) (every person owes a duty to every other person to exercise ordinary care in his or her activities to prevent any foreseeable injury from occurring to those other persons).

21 Starr v. United States, 393 F. Supp. 1359 (N.D. Tex. 1975) (standard of care for minor child under fourteen years of age is that care that a child of the same age, intelligence, and experience would use); Sramek v. Logan, 36 Ill. App. 3d 471, 344 N.E.2d 47 (1976).

22 However, where a minor assumes to act as an adult, he or she may be judged by an adult standard of care. Starr v. United States, footnote 21.

23 Prosser, pp. 151–52, citing cases concerning blindness, age, sex, epilepsy, sleepiness, drunkenness, weight, etc. But see Carter v. Tatum, 212 S.E.2d 439 (Ga. App. 1975) (a defendant is normally held to the same standard of care regardless of infirmities).

24 Sterling v. New England Fish Co., 410 F. Supp. 164 (W.D. Wash. 1976) (physically disabled person is required to act with reasonable prudence for person under such disability); Karmazin v. Penn R.R., 82 N.J. Super. 123, 196 A.2d 803 (1964) (persons aware of impaired faculties must conduct themselves reasonably in light of such disability).

iv. DUTY OWED TO WHOM

It is clear that everyone must submit to the parameters embodied in the law of negligence, and that *all* persons have a duty to act with the due care of a reasonably prudent person. However, is it equally clear that the duty of due care is owed *to all* members of society? That is, given the fact that the duty of due care is one that is owed *by* every person, is that duty owed *to* all other persons? If not, then to whom is the duty of due care owed? Who may complain when such a duty is breached? After much debate and disagreement on this question, there now seem to be two main positions: the majority of jurisdictions hold that the defendant's duty of due care is owed to anyone who suffers injuries as a proximate or direct result of the defendant's actions. The minority view is that the defendant owes a duty of due care only to those persons to whom the average reasonable person would have foreseen a risk of harm under the particular circumstances of the case. The distinguishing feature between these two positions is that the majority position does not include the element of foreseeability as a prerequisite to the defendant's liability. The minority view, however, requires that in order for the defendant to have been under any duty of care to any other person, the average, reasonable person must have foreseen that a risk of harm to the plaintiff (or to a class of persons to which the plaintiff belongs) was present.

The most widely cited statement of these two positions is contained in the case of *Palsgraf* v. *Long Island R.R. Co.,* in which the majority opinion was written by Judge Benjamin Cardozo, and a dissenting opinion was written by Judge Andrews.[25] The facts of the *Palsgraf* case were as follows: A passenger (not a party in the action) was running to catch one of the defendant railroad's trains. In the process of assisting the passenger to board the train, one of the defendant's employees accidentally knocked a package from the possession of the passenger. The package happened to contain fireworks and other explosives, which exploded violently, causing the loosening of a set of scales on the railroad platform several feet from the explosion. These scales fell upon and injured the plaintiff, Mrs. Palsgraf. Judge Andrews, addressing the question of whether the railroad owed a duty to Mrs. Palsgraf, stated that the defendant's duty was owed not merely to the passenger being assisted on the train by an agent of the railroad, but to anyone in the world who might be injured by that agent's activities. On this theory the plaintiff was entitled to recover, in the opinion of Judge Andrews, whether or not the manner of injury was foreseeable. On the other hand, Cardozo's view (the majority opinion in this case) stated that while a risk of harm to the passenger or to the passenger's package was foreseeable, the reasonable, prudent person could not have foreseen any risk to Mrs. Palsgraf, because she was a considerable distance away. Therefore, by Judge Cardozo's reasoning, the plaintiff was not within what he termed the "zone of danger," and no duty was owed to the plaintiff; thus the court awarded no recovery.

---

[25] Palsgraf v. Long Island R.R. Co., 248 N.Y.339, 162 N.E. 99 (1928).

The "zone of danger" test may not be as narrow as it seems at first glance. Under Cardozo's view the zone of danger not only includes those persons foreseeably imperiled by the defendant's conduct but also those who reasonably go to the rescue of those foreseeably imperiled. Therefore, the defendant may be liable for injuries sustained by someone rescuing an already imperiled or injured person, provided it is a reasonable attempt to assist the person endangered by the defendant's conduct. The rationale behind this extension of the zone of danger lies in the phrase "danger invites rescue." That is, if a reasonable person would foresee a risk of harm to an injured person, then the defendant owes a duty of care not only to the injured party, but to all those persons who might foreseeably go to the rescue of that person.

The most famous statement of the "danger invites rescue" doctrine was rendered by Judge Cardozo in the case of *Wagner* v. *International Railway Co.*[26] Arthur Wagner and his cousin, Herbert, boarded an electric car operated by the International Railway Co. connecting the cities of Buffalo and Niagara Falls, New York. At one point the railroad crossed the New York Central and Erie tracks over a long trestle. Upon approaching the trestle there was a gradual incline of about twenty-five feet, a curve, and then a bridge over the tracks below, followed by another turn, and concluding upon a descent back to grade level. At the time the Wagners boarded the train the car was crowded and they had to hang onto nearby open doors. Moving slowly up the incline, the car reached the curve, then lurched violently, throwing Herbert Wagner out. The car proceeded down the incline on the far side and finally stopped. Arthur Wagner then walked back up the incline and crossed the trestle, hoping to find the body of his cousin. Other people walked under the trestle and found Herbert Wagner's body. Then, as the other people stood by Herbert's body, Arthur's body struck the ground beside them. In the darkness Arthur had apparently missed his step and fallen, sustaining serious injuries.

In determining the applicable legal principles in this situation, the trial court held that the negligence toward Herbert Wagner on the part of the defendant railway company would not impose liability on the company for injuries suffered by the plaintiff, Arthur Wagner, "unless two other facts were found: First, that the plaintiff had been invited by the conductor to go upon the bridge; and second, that the conductor had followed with a light." Under such tests the trial court found no liability. Upon appeal to the New York Court of Appeals, Cardozo eliminated such limitations and reversed the trial court. He established a principle that in effect excuses and justifies any negligence on the part of the plaintiff if the act that was performed negligently has first been made necessary by the defendant, and if such negligence of the *plaintiff* can only be regarded as a normal reaction to the situation caused by the defendant's negligence and thus within the zone of danger. Under the Andrews view the same result would follow, provided the rescuer's acts were reasonable and thus deemed to be the normal response to the defendant's negligence.

Under either the Cardozo or Andrews approach it is also possible that the defendant could be liable for causing third persons to cause an injury. That is, the

---

[26] Wagner v. International Railway Co., 232 N.Y. 176 (1921).

reasonable person standard not only requires the defendant to exercise due care to avoid injuring the plaintiff through his or her own conduct but also requires the defendant to avoid exposing the plaintiff to the foreseeable risks of harm caused by the acts of third parties.[27] For example, if a defendant blocked a public sidewalk and thus forced pedestrians into the street, he or she would have created a foreseeable risk of harm caused by third parties driving in the street. Under the Cardozo approach, the zone of danger includes persons exposed by the defendant to the foreseeable injuries from the third person, as well as from the defendant's own conduct. Similarly, under the Andrews position, the acts of third persons would be within the scope of the original duty owed by the defendant.

b. Breach of Duty

This element of the *prima facie* case is fairly self-explanatory. It simply requires proof that the defendant's conduct has fallen short of the duty of due care which the defendant owed to the plaintiff. This proof must show that the defendant's conduct fell outside of the parameters and guidelines of the conduct of the hypothetical reasonably prudent person.

c. Causation

Two types of causation are required to establish the *prima facie* case of negligence: actual cause and proximate cause.

i. ACTUAL CAUSE

In order to establish actual cause ("cause in fact") the defendant's act must have been physically responsible for the injury to the plaintiff.[28] Two tests are recognized in determining whether the defendant's acts were the actual cause of the plaintiff's injury. First, the *but for* rule requires that the plaintiff would not have been injured "but for" the defendant's act.[29] If the plaintiff would have sustained the same injury despite the conduct of the defendant, then the act is not the cause of the injury.

Also recognized as a test for determining whether the defendant's conduct was the actual cause of the plaintiff's injury is the *substantial factor* test, which states that a defendant is liable if his or her conduct was a substantial factor in causing the injury, even if the plaintiff sustained injury as a result of conduct from the de-

---

[27] Prosser, pp. 170–76.
[28] Shelton v. Aetna Casualty & Surety Co., 334 S.2d 406 (La. 1976).
[29] Salk v. Alpine Ski Shop, 342 A.2d 622 (R.I. 1975), citing F. Harper and F. James, *The Law of Torts,* vol. 2 (Boston: Little, Brown and Co., 1956), section 20.2, p. 1110.

fendant *and* a third party. If damage would have occurred in the absence of a party's negligence, the negligent conduct must be shown to have been a substantial factor in causing the harm, in order for the party to be responsible.[30] For example, if two automobiles hit the automobile of the plaintiff one immediately after the other and cause the plaintiff injury, then *either* of the first vehicles would be deemed the cause of the plaintiff's injury, because each of the defendant's conduct was a substantial factor in causing such injury. The question is not whether either alone would have caused injury. If the defendant's negligence contributes substantially to the injury, it need not be the sole physical cause of it.[31] Whether the defendant's acts were substantial factors is ordinarily a question of fact if evidence conflicts or if different inferences can be drawn from it.[32]

Another test applied in certain situations is the rule of concurrent liability, in which the separate, negligent acts of the defendant and a third party concur. If the evidence indicates that the plaintiff would *not* have been injured but for the concurrence of the conduct of *both* the defendant and the third party, the defendant and the third party are both liable, that is, concurrently liable.[33]

Actual causation may be proven by either the but for test or the substantial factor test. However, the majority of jurisdictions in the United States presently follow the substantial factor rule, which is the sounder of the two tests.[34] The weakness of the but for test is evident in a situation such as the example given under the substantial factor rule. In that example, if the but for test were applied, the defendant and a third party potential defendant would both escape liability, because the answer would be that the injuries to the plaintiff *would have* occurred in the absence of or "but for" the acts of the defendant. Thus the test fails to prove actual causation on the part of the defendant. The but for test is useful, however, in determining whether specific conduct actually caused a particular aspect of the harmful result in question.

ii. PROXIMATE CAUSE

Liability for negligence is predicated upon a causal connection between the allegedly negligent conduct and the plaintiff's injury. The existence of merely some causal connection between them is insufficient to satisfy the legal causation requirement of the *prima facie* case. Thus, in proving the *prima facie* case, the plaintiff must prove that the defendant's conduct was that cause, which in a natural and continued sequence, "unbroken by an efficient independent intervening cause,"

---

[30] State Department of Environmental Protection v. Jersey Central Power and Light Co., 69 N.J. 102, 351 A.2d 337 (1976), citing *Restatement (2d) Torts,* section 432(1) (1965).

[31] Schultz v. Brogan, 251 Wisc. 390, 29 N.W.2d 719 (1947).

[32] Recognized as a leading case in this area is Anderson v. Minneapolis, S.P. and S.S.M. R.R., 146 Minn. 430, 179 N.W. 45 (1920).

[33] Burton v. Douglas Co., 14 Wash. App. 151, 539 P.2d 97 (1975); Burdette v. Maust Coal and Coke Corp., 222 S.E.2d 293 (W. Va. 1976).

[34] Prosser, pp. 238–240.

produced the result of which the plaintiff complains.[35] That is, not only must the conduct of the defendant be the actual physical cause, but it must be the direct and efficient cause of the injuries of the plaintiff. This has traditionally been referred to as proximate cause.

By definition, the question of proximate cause necessarily raises problems of liability for unforeseeable consequences and the further problems of the effect of intervening forces. If an independent force intervenes between the allegedly negligent conduct of the defendant and the injury to the plaintiff, then such an intervening force may relieve the defendant of liability for his or her acts. A defendant is not liable for unforeseen damages caused by third persons subsequent to or simultaneously with the defendant's conduct, or forces of nature whose consequences could not have been foreseen.[36]

On the other hand, a defendant who places another person in peril must anticipate that the latter will attempt to avoid the peril, and in doing so may injure himself or herself or other persons. The plaintiff's act of attempting to escape is deemed to be an "instinctive reaction," thus an automatic act and therefore foreseeable.[37] The defendant is not relieved of liability in the case of an instinctive reaction. Even if the plaintiff's acts are not instinctive, the defendant may be liable for such acts or the acts of third parties if they are reasonably foreseeable.[38]

If one refers back to the theory of substantial factor in the discussion of actual cause, then the theory of intervening forces becomes more clear. If an intervening force is so great that the defendant's conduct can no longer be considered a substantial factor, then the defendant must necessarily be relieved of liability for his or her acts. Something unforeseeable and extraordinary reduces the defendant's acts to something *less than* a substantial factor; such intervening forces make the defendant's conduct remote.[39] The question of whether such an intervening force was extraordinary or unforeseeable must be answered on a case-by-case basis by the fact finder, that is, the jury or the judge.[40] However, the general principles and the tests to be applied in each case make such a determination easier and provide the necessary guidelines in establishing the *prima facie* case. The case of *Spurlin* v. *General Motors Corporation* involves the issues of breach of duty and proximate cause, including the question of intervening forces.

---

[35] Long v. City of Weirton, 214 S.E.2d 832 (W. Va. 1975).

[36] Exner Sand & Gravel Corp. v. Petterson Lighterage & Towing Corp., 258 F.2d 1 (2d Cir. 1958); Prosser, pp. 281–88; 57 *AmJur* 2d, "Negligence," sections 192–98. But see Leib v. City of Tampa, 326 So.2d 52 (Fla. App. 1976).

[37] Hill v. Associated Transport, Inc., 345 Mass. 55, 185 N.E.2d 642 (1962) (person's leaping from bed was instinctive reaction to truck crashing through front door of home, and slipping on rug was sufficient evidence to allow jury determination of defendant's liability).

[38] See, e.g., Landeros v. Flood, 123 Cal. Rptr. 713 (Cal. App. 1975).

[39] Gerber v. McCall, 175 Kan. 433, 264 P.2d 490 (1953) (unpredictable flood); McLaughlin v. Mine Safety Appliances Co., 111 N.Y.2d 62, 181 N.E.2d 430 (1962) (gross negligence of third party); Batts v. Faggart, 260 N.C. 641, 133 S.E.2d 504 (1963).

[40] Landeros v. Flood, 123 Cal. Rptr. 713 (Cal. App. 1975); Milwaukee & St. Paul R.R. v. Kellogg, 94 U.S. 469 (1876).

SPURLIN
v.
GENERAL MOTORS CORPORATION

528 F.2d 612 (1976)

United States Court of Appeals, Fifth Circuit

TUTTLE, Circuit Judge:

This diversity suit arises out of a school bus crash which occurred in Morgan County, Alabama, on April 23, 1968, when the bus's brakes failed. Two wrongful death suits and twenty-two personal injury actions were filed, on behalf of the children who were in the bus at the time, against the manufacturer of the school bus chassis, General Motors Corporation. Following consolidation of the cases for trial by the district court, a six-person jury heard evidence for approximately two weeks. The court then submitted the cases on the theory of alleged negligent design of the braking system, and the jury returned a verdict for the plaintiffs, awarding damages in the amount of $70,000 each in the wrongful death cases. The district court, however, granted defendant's post-trial motions for judgment notwithstanding the verdict and, in the alternative, a new trial, on the ground that the verdict was not supported by the evidence. This appeal followed. We consider the district court's two post-trial rulings in turn, beginning with its grant of General Motors' motion for judgment notwithstanding the verdict.

I. CORRECTNESS OF THE DISTRICT COURT'S GRANT OF JUDGMENT NOTWITHSTANDING THE VERDICT

A. The Standard of Review

The applicable standard of review for judging the correctness of a district court's grant or denial of a motion for judgment notwithstanding the verdict was carefully delineated by this Court in Boeing Co. v. Shipman, 411 F.2d 365 (5th Cir. 1969) (*en banc*):

"On motions for directed verdict and for judgment notwithstanding the verdict the Court should consider all of the evidence—not just that evidence which supports the non-mover's case—but in the light and with all reasonable inferences most favorable to the party opposed to the motion.... [I]f there is substantial evidence opposed to the motions, that is, evidence of such quality and weight that reasonable and fair-minded men in the exercise of impartial judgment might reach different conclusions, the motions shall be denied, and the case submitted to the jury.... There must be a conflict on substantial evidence to create a jury question. However, it is the function of the jury as the traditional finder of the facts, and not the Court, to weigh conflicting evidence and inferences, and determine the credibility of witnesses." 411 F.2d at 374–375 (footnotes omitted).

This test requires us to scrutinize the record carefully, considering all the evidence which was submitted to the jury for its consideration, but viewing it in the manner most favorable to the plaintiffs, as the parties opposed to the motion for judgment n. o. v. It is important to note at the outset, therefore, that defendant General Motors has not assigned, as separate grounds for cross-appeal, the commission of any errors by the district court in admitting into evidence any particular items or testimony given by any of the witnesses. This Court, therefore, is not required to consider the issue of the scope of the evidence which was properly before the jury in reaching its verdict, but is free to examine and rely upon all the evidence which the district court charged the jury it could consider in deciding the case.

B. Plaintiffs' Theory of Recovery

Briefly stated, the theory upon which the cases were submitted to the jury was one of alleged negligent design of the bus's braking system by General Motors, coupled with a failure to warn of the unique problems and need for frequent servicing and maintenance associated with operating school buses. Specifically, the plaintiffs contended that the braking system with which the 1965 66-passenger school bus at issue was equipped was not reasonably safe for the use for which it was intended in that: (1) the single hydraulic braking system on the bus was a dangerous system because of the inevitability of total failure of braking power in the event of a loss of brake fluid through undetected leakage; (2) there was no effective emergency brake on the bus, only a parking brake which was not intended to stop a loaded, moving vehicle such as this one; and (3) there was no warning device of any sort, such as a gauge or warning light to indicate when the brake fluid in the reservoir was running low. Furthermore, the plaintiffs alleged, the owner's manual which came with the bus suggested brake fluid level checks only every 6,000 miles, which on a school bus would be only once a year, whereas safe maintenance practices would actually require checking the brake fluid in such a vehicle every two weeks to a month.

C. Sufficiency of the Evidence Under the Boeing Co. Test

In charging the jury, the district court clearly and correctly outlined the four elements necessary for recovery in a negligence action: (1) the existence of a duty on the part of the defendant; (2) a breach of that duty; (3) the existence of a causal relationship between the defendant's conduct and the plaintiff's injury, and (4) resulting injury to the plaintiff. *Ward v. Hobart Manufacturing Co.,* 450 F.2d 1176 (5th Cir. 1971). Since the existence of the final element was in effect uncontested in any of the consolidated cases, and since the existence and nature of the scope of the duty owed by a particular defendant is a question of law for the court . . . and neither side has asserted that the district court erred in defining GM's duty in this case, we find it necessary to examine the sufficiency of the evidence introduced at trial

only with respect to the second and third elements of the plaintiffs' cause of action.

1. The Breach of Duty Issue

The district court instructed the jury that General Motors, as an automotive manufacturer, had a duty to design and build a bus chassis reasonably fit for the purpose for which it was made, without hidden or latent defects which would make it "imminently and inherently dangerous" to persons using it. The defendant was required to exercise reasonable care in the adoption of a safe plan or design, the court charged the jury, and the standard by which its conduct was to be judged was that of a "reasonably prudent manufacturer of school bus chassis in 1965."

Given this definition of the defendant's duty, the jury was then in effect required to decide whether the braking system used on the bus at issue was "imminently" or "inherently" dangerous so as to render the vehicle unsafe for its intended use, keeping in mind the state of the art in the automotive industry in 1965 and the extent to which alternative braking systems which were reasonably safe were available. While it is unnecessary to catalogue in detail the evidence presented on these issues at trial, a brief summary of the mechanics involved in the braking system in use on this particular bus, and the testimony offered by witnesses on both sides regarding its safety will serve to support our holding that there was sufficient "substantial evidence," as required by *Boeing Co. v. Shipman,* for the jury to have found that the braking system on the bus was not reasonably safe and consequently that GM had breached its duty as a manufacturer.

The bus which crashed was a 1965 66-passenger school bus, the chassis portion of which was designed and built by General Motors. It was equipped with a single hydraulic braking system, containing a single reservoir in the master cylinder supplying all of the brake fluid which transmits pressure to the brake cylinders on each wheel. In such a system, a leak which exhausts the brake fluid in the reservoir causes a sudden and total failure of braking ability, as happened in this case. A dual hydraulic braking system, on the other hand, is equipped with two brake fluid reservoirs, each of which services the brake cylinders on two separate wheels, so that in the event of loss of fluid from one of the reservoirs, whether from leakage or some other cause, the vehicle continues to have braking power on the wheels serviced by the other reservoir. The only other braking mechanism with which the bus in this case was equipped was a parking brake, which by the admission of all those who testified at the trial was never intended to function as an emergency brake.

We find that the evidence offered at trial on the safety of the braking system as described above was more than sufficient to withstand a motion for judgment n. o. v. under the test set out in *Boeing.* Although a GM Senior Design Engineer, Paul Fisher, testified that he considered a dual hydraulic braking system to be less reliable than a single system (because of the existence of more parts and consequently a greater possibility that one of them could malfunction), the plaintiffs put on expert testimony that the single hydraulic braking system in use on the bus at issue was not reasonably safe for the purpose for which it was intended.... Certainly the jury could have found, from this expert testimony admitted by the district court, that the braking system on the bus was not a sufficiently safe one.

Furthermore, on the issue of the emergency brake, the testimony on both sides was virtually unanimous that a safe system must include an emergency brake and that the parking brake with which the bus was equipped was never intended to function as an emergency brake, in the sense of stopping a large loaded moving vehicle. It was designed to hold the vehicle stationary when parked. There was, however, conflicting evidence on the actual stopping ability of the parking brake; GM personnel testified that simulated tests were made under "substantially similar" circumstances at GM testing grounds in Detroit which proved that the park-

ing brake on the bus could have stopped the bus in about 230 feet if it had been in working order and if the driver had applied it. The state trooper who investigated the accident, however, admitted on the witness stand that it might have been dangerous to attempt to stop the bus with the parking brake; since the brake operated by making contact with the drive shaft, there was a possibility of the drive shaft breaking if the parking brake were to be applied while the bus was travelling at 25 or 30 miles per hour, as was the case here. Given the existence of substantial conflicting evidence from which reasonable persons might draw differing conclusions, it is clear that the jury could have concluded that the absence of an effective emergency brake on the bus also constituted negligent design on the part of the defendant.

Having concluded that there was sufficient evidence presented from which the jury could find that the braking system on the bus rendered it not reasonably safe for the use for which it was intended, we now turn to the issue of the evidence concerning the state of the art with respect to braking systems in the automotive industry in 1964, when the bus involved here was manufactured. The judge instructed the jury that it could consider the following evidence which had been admitted at trial, all of which, in the opinion of this Court, constitutes substantial evidence of the kind required by Boeing Co. v. Shipman before a grant of judgment notwithstanding the verdict can be reversed. First, it was established without contradiction at trial that both Cadillac and American Motors passenger cars had been equipped with dual hydraulic braking systems for several years prior to 1964. Second, plaintiffs' expert witnesses testified that dual hydraulic systems were not only in use on large buses in England and Europe prior to 1964 but were actually required by law in some countries. Finally, it was established that both interstate buses and many public transit buses in the United States in 1964 were equipped with air brakes, a system which is "failsafe" in that in the event of a malfunction, the brakes automatically take effect; additionally, GM Engineer Fisher testified that air brakes were optional equipment on the type of bus chassis which the Morgan County School Board ordered in this case, thus showing that at least one "failsafe" braking system was developed and available for use on school bus chassis in 1964. General Motors offered counterevidence seeking to show that the dual hydraulic braking system contended for by plaintiffs was not sufficiently developed so as to be available on large vehicles in 1964; however, a GM engineer gave testimony at trial from which it could have reasonably been inferred that work on the dual system was delayed as a result of an economic policy decision at GM in order to give precedence to further development work on passenger car engines. It thus appears clear that considering the record as a whole there was substantial evidence "of such quality and weight" that reasonable persons might draw differing conclusions as to the state of the art with respect to the automotive braking system for school buses which were reasonably safe in comparison to the single hydraulic braking system.

Since we have concluded that there was sufficient evidence under Boeing Co. v. Shipman to go to the jury on both the issue of the reasonable safety of the braking system in use on the bus, and on the issue of the state of the art of braking systems in 1964, it follows that there was enough evidence from which the jury could find that General Motors had breached its duty as a manufacturer. Thus the only remaining question to be considered in determining whether the court below erred in granting GM's motion for judgment n. o. v. is whether there was sufficient evidence to create a jury question on the issue of proximate cause.

2. Proximate Cause

As stated previously, in order for the plaintiffs to recover in this case, they had to prove to the jury's satisfaction that the defendant's negligence in designing the braking system on the bus caused the accident resulting in the injuries and deaths underlying the instant law-

suits. As the district court instructed the jury, the law requires that the defendant's negligence act as the proximate, as opposed to a remote, cause of the plaintiff's injury. See, e.g., City of Mobile v. Havard, 29 Ala. 532, 268 So. 2d 805 (1972). General Motors' primary defense in this case was that the leakage of brake fluid which ultimately resulted in the brake failure at issue was due to negligence on the part of school board officials who failed to have the bus properly serviced and maintained at the necessary intervals. The district court therefore properly instructed the jury that if they found that there was an intervening act of negligence, either on the part of the school board or on the part of the driver (in failing to notice that the brake pedal was "giving" more than normal, indicating some loss of fluid), which acted as the sole cause of the accident, GM could not be held liable. The court further instructed the jury, however, that even if they found independent negligence by the Board or the driver, GM could nevertheless be held liable if: (1) the other negligent act was concurrent with that of the defendant, so that both acts jointly caused the injury, see, e.g., Greyhound Corp. v. Brown, 269 Ala. 520, 113 So. 2d 916 (1959); or (2) the intervening act of negligence, i.e., failure to maintain and service the bus frequently and properly, was one which was foreseeable by the defendant. Clendenon v. Yarbrough, 233 Ala. 269, 171 So. 277, 278 (1936); Union Pacific v. Jarrett, 381 F.2d 597 (9th Cir. 1967). Although defense counsel objected to these last two instructions at the time the court charged the jury, no specific grounds were assigned and General Motors has not urged the giving of these instructions as constituting grounds for a cross-appeal here. This Court will therefore examine the evidence on the issue of proximate cause in order to determine whether a jury question existed on any of the three theories outlined by the district court under which GM's negligence could be found to be sufficiently causally linked to the injury for the jury to find liability. If sufficient evidence existed to support a finding of liability on behalf of GM under any one of the above three approaches, the district court erred in granting the motion for judgment notwithstanding the verdict.

The evidence offered by the defense on the condition of the bus at the time it crashed was extensive and damaging to the plaintiff's case. Testimony by the state trooper investigating the accident and by General Motors personnel who inspected the braking system afterwards established that most of the wheel cylinders were completely or partially frozen, and that most of the cylinder pistons on the rear brakes were leaking. The trooper testified that improper realignment of an anchor pin and brake shoe (presumably resulting from summer maintenance work on the bus) was probably the cause of increased friction and heat within the affected brake drum and likely caused excessive leakage of fluid from the transmission lines. He stated that in his opinion lack of sufficiently frequent maintenance had been the cause of the failure to detect the loss of brake fluid and the resulting accident.

To counter this evidence, plaintiffs elicited testimony from their expert witnesses tending to establish that had the braking system on the bus been a dual rather than a single hydraulic system, the chances of leakage developing in both reservoirs simultaneously would have been quite significantly lower, and hence the presence of the additional fluid reservoir servicing two of the brake cylinders independently of the other two would probably have prevented this accident. More importantly, however, the plaintiffs put on evidence relating to the brake servicing instructions in the 1969 GM Owner's Manual and Shop Maintenance Manual from which this Court finds the jury could have concluded either that the Morgan County officials were not negligent in servicing the vehicle's braking system, or that if they were, such negligence was foreseeable by GM and hence the defendant could still be held liable.

Plaintiffs introduced into evidence copies of the 1965 GM owner's and shop maintenance manuals, both of which stated the fluid in the brake fluid reservoir should be checked every 6,000 miles. In addition, the owner's manual stated that "[t]he Chevrolet braking system re-quires very little care. The braking system should be checked occasionally for indications of fluid leaks. If leaks are found necessary repairs should be made at once. Keep the brakes properly adjusted, check all vacuum hose connections for leaks." The 1965 truck shop manual contained only the following additional warning: "Sustained heavy duty and high speed operation, or operation under adverse conditions may require more frequent servicing."

Plaintiffs alleged, and sought to prove, that statements in the manuals were inadequate and grossly misleading in that checking the brake fluid level on a school bus every 6,000 miles would mean inspecting it only once a year, whereas GM engineers who testified at trial admitted that it would be necessary to check the fluid level on a school bus several times a month in order to conform with good maintenance practices. . . .

Given the existence of all this conflicting evidence bearing on the issue of the adequacy of the warnings in the two GM manuals that came with the bus chassis purchased by Morgan County in 1964, this Court is of the opinion that sufficient evidence was adduced at trial to create a jury issue on the negligence *vel non* of the Morgan County officials and whether such negligence, if it occurred, was foreseeable by GM. With respect to the possibility of intervening negligence in the form of the bus driver's failure to notice operational signs indicating possible loss of brake fluid, we note that the driver denied noticing either any signs of leakage or the gradual development of any significant "give" in his brake pedal prior to the accident, thus creating a jury question on this issue also.

From the above analysis, then, it appears that there was ample evidence introduced at trial under the Boeing Co. v. Shipman test to warrant submitting the issue of proximate cause to the jury. Since we have already determined that there was sufficient evidence to go to the jury on the breach of duty issue, it follows that the plaintiffs put on the kind and quantity of evidence which this Court had held is required to withstand a defense motion for judgment

n. o. v., and the district court's grant of that motion by GM must therefore be reversed. . . .

As stated before, we have studied the record carefully and have concluded that the jury verdict here was not against the "*great* weight of the evidence," as required in this Circuit in order to justify a grant of a new trial. The judgment of the district court granting appellee General Motors judgment notwithstanding the verdict is therefore reversed, the alternative grant of a new trial is also reversed, and the district court is hereby directed to enter judgment on the verdict for plaintiffs-appellants.

---

d. Damages

The last essential element of the *prima facie* case is that of damages.[41] It requires that the plaintiff prove actual damage to his or her person or property in order to establish the liability of the defendant based on negligence. The purpose of requiring the defendant to pay damages is to restore the plaintiff to the same condition, insofar as possible, as prior to the injury. As discussed in Chapter 5, the emphasis is on compensating the plaintiff rather than punishing the defendant. In explaining the concept of a person's duty to compensate the injured party, Pound stated that:[42]

> A final step is to put [liability] in terms of reparation. These steps are taken haltingly and merge into one another so that we may hear of a "penalty of reparation." But the result is to turn composition for vengeance into reparation for injury.

There are two types of compensatory (sometimes called actual) damages which may be recoverable if proven by the plaintiff: *general* damages and *special* damages. They apply to all loss recoverable as a matter of right. General damages are those that the law implies or presumes to have accrued from the wrong complained of by the plaintiff.[43] The reason that general damages are implied is that they are the immediate, direct, or proximate result of the defendant's conduct; they are deemed to be inherent in the injury itself. An example of general damages is pain and suffering. It is quite difficult to prove the monetary value of pain and suffering, or to place a price tag upon loss of limb or other physical impairment or disability. Putting a value upon such damages becomes a subjective determination by the judge or jury. However, methods of valuing pain and suffering or specific physical injuries have been developed over the years in personal injury trials, and some guidelines are generally recognized. Throughout the course of a trial, the plaintiff's attorney attempts to educate the jury on such guidelines and to convince it to adopt these accepted valuations of types of injuries in deciding the amount to be awarded to the plaintiff.

The second type of compensatory damages is special damages, those to which the plaintiff is entitled as a result of the injury, but which are a result of special circumstances or conditions. Special damages are those actually suffered, but which are not the *necessary* result of the injury as are general damages. For example, in

---

[41] See Prosser, pp. 143–144.
[42] Pound, pp. 74–75.
[43] 22 *AmJur* 2d, "Damages," section 15.

the case of an automobile accident, general damages would include expenses for any actual physical injury, including pain and suffering, physical damage to the vehicle, and reduced earnings that resulted from the physical disability caused by the accident. Items such as financial losses resulting from the plaintiff's inability to use the vehicle in his or her business, lost profits, or the reduction of one's services to one's own business are all special damages.

In addition to compensatory damages, the plaintiff is sometimes awarded exemplary or punitive damages. These are damages given as a punishment to the defendant and as a deterrent to others, because of the wanton, reckless, or malicious character of the defendant's conduct. They are not granted as compensatory damages but are in addition to such damages. Exemplary damages are not considered to be criminal punishment—they are enlarged damages for a civil wrong.

Finally the court may award nominal damages but no compensatory or exemplary damages. Nominal damages (usually one dollar) are awarded where there has been an invasion of a right but no actual monetary or physical injury, or where some compensable injury has been shown, but the *amount* of that injury has not been proven.

2. *Res Ipsa Loquitur*

In establishing the *prima facie* case, the necessary facts may be proven by circumstantial evidence. Circumstantial evidence is evidence of one fact, or a set of facts, from which the existence of the fact to be determined may reasonably be inferred. For example, it may be reasonable to infer from automobile skid marks that an automobile was driven at an excessive speed.

Thus the *prima facie* case may be submitted to the jury although evidence of specific allegedly negligent acts of the defendant has not been introduced. The doctrine allowing the case to be submitted to the jury in this situation is called the doctrine of *res ipsa loquitur,* which means "the thing speaks for itself."

The typical situation in which the doctrine has been applied is one in which the item that has caused the injury to the plaintiff is shown to have been under the sole control of the defendant or his or her servants, and the accident is of the type that would not ordinarily occur if those persons had used proper care. The following elements must be present in order for the doctrine to be applicable: (1) in the normal course of events the plaintiff would not have suffered injury unless there was negligence; (2) the instrument, agency, or source of harm was under the sole and exclusive control of the defendant at the time of the alleged wrongful or negligent activity; (3) the plaintiff could not reasonably be expected to know the specific negligent acts of the defendant, and the defendant can be assumed to know such information; (4) the instrument was capable of causing the harm received; (5) there is no contributory negligence on the part of the plaintiff. The case of *Escola* v. *Coca Cola Bottling Co. of Fresno,* while not expressly dividing the requirements into the same five categories, discusses all of the conditions that are necessary for the application of the doctrine.

ESCOLA
v.
COCA COLA BOTTLING CO. OF FRESNO

150 P.2d 436 (1944)

Supreme Court of California

GIBSON, Chief Justice.

Plaintiff, a waitress in a restaurant, was injured when a bottle of Coca Cola broke in her hand. She alleged that defendant company, which had bottled and delivered the alleged defective bottle to her employer, was negligent in selling "bottles containing said beverage which on account of excessive pressure of gas or by reason of some defect in the bottle was dangerous . . . and likely to explode." This appeal is from a judgment upon a jury verdict in favor of plaintiff.

Defendant's driver delivered several cases of Coca Cola to the restaurant, placing them on the floor, one on top of the other, under and behind the counter, where they remained at least thirty-six hours. Immediately before the accident, plaintiff picked up the top case and set it upon a near-by ice cream cabinet in front of and about three feet from the refrigerator. She then proceeded to take the bottles from the case with her right hand, one at a time, and put them into the refrigerator. Plaintiff testified that after she had placed three bottles in the refrigerator and had moved the fourth bottle about 18 inches from the case "it exploded in my hand." The bottle broke into two jagged pieces and inflicted a deep five-inch cut, severing blood vessels, nerves and muscles of the thumb and palm of the hand. Plaintiff further testified that when the bottle exploded, "It made a sound similar to an electric light bulb that would have dropped. It made a loud pop." Plaintiff's employer testified, "I was about twenty feet from where it actually happened and I heard the explosion." A fellow employee, on the opposite side of the counter, testified that plaintiff "had the bottle, I should judge, waist high, and I know that it didn't bang either the case or the door or another bottle . . . when

it popped. It sounded just like a fruit jar would blow up. . . ." The witness further testified that the contents of the bottle "flew all over herself and myself and the walls and one thing and another."

The top portion of the bottle, with the cap, remained in plaintiff's hand, and the lower portion fell to the floor but did not break. The broken bottle was not produced at the trial, the pieces having been thrown away by an employee of the restaurant shortly after the accident. Plaintiff, however, described the broken pieces, and a diagram of the bottle was made showing the location of the "fracture line" where the bottle broke in two.

One of defendant's drivers, called as a witness by plaintiff, testified that he had seen other bottles of Coca Cola in the past explode and had found broken bottles in the warehouse when he took the cases out, but that he did not know what made them blow up.

Plaintiff then rested her case, having announced to the court that being unable to show any specific acts of negligence she relied completely on the doctrine of res ipsa loquitur.

Defendant contends that the doctrine of res ipsa loquitur does not apply in this case, and that the evidence is insufficient to support the judgment.

Many jurisdictions have applied the doctrine in cases involving exploding bottles of carbonated beverages. . . . It would serve no useful purpose to discuss the reasoning of the foregoing cases in detail, since the problem is whether under the facts shown in the instant case the conditions warranting application of the doctrine have been satisfied.

Res ipsa loquitur does not apply unless (1) defendant had exclusive control of the thing causing the injury and (2) the accident is of such a nature that it ordinarily would not occur in the absence of negligence by the defendant. . . .

Many authorities state that the happening of the accident does not speak for itself where it took place some time after defendant had relinquished control of the instrumentality causing the injury. Under the more logical view, however, the doctrine may be applied upon the theory that defendant had control at the time of the alleged negligent act, although not at the time of the accident, *provided* plaintiff first proves that the condition of the instrumentality had not been changed after it left the defendant's possession. . . . Plaintiff must also prove that she handled the bottle carefully. The reason for this prerequisite is set forth in Prosser on Torts at page 300, where the author states: "Allied to the condition of exclusive control in the defendant is that of absence of any action on the part of the plaintiff contributing to the accident. Its purpose, of course, is to eliminate the possibility that it was the plaintiff who was responsible. If the boiler of a locomotive explodes while the plaintiff engineer is operating it, the inference of his own negligence is at least as great as that of the defendant, and res ipsa loquitur will not apply until he has accounted for his own conduct." It is not necessary, of course, that plaintiff eliminate every remote possibility of injury to the bottle after defendant lost control, and the requirement is satisfied if there is evidence permitting a reasonable inference that it was not accessible to extraneous harmful forces and that it was carefully handled by plaintiff or any third person who may have moved or touched it. Cf. Prosser, p. 300. If such evidence is presented, the question becomes one for the trier of fact, . . . and, accordingly, the issue should be submitted to the jury under proper instructions.

In the present case no instructions were requested or given on this phase of the case, although general instructions upon res ipsa loquitur were given. Defendant, however, has made no claim of error with reference thereto on this appeal.

Upon an examination of the record, the evidence appears sufficient to support a reasonable inference that the bottle here involved was not damaged by any extraneous force after delivery to the restaurant by defendant. It follows, therefore, that the bottle was in some manner defective at the time defendant relinquished control, because sound and properly prepared bottles of carbonated liquids do not ordinarily explode when carefully handled.

The next question, then, is whether plaintiff may rely upon the doctrine of res ipsa loquitur to supply an inference that defendant's negligence was responsible for the defective condition of the bottle at the time it was delivered to the restaurant. Under the general rules pertaining to the doctrine, as set forth above, it must appear that bottles of carbonated liquid are not ordinarily defective without negligence by the bottling company. In 1 Shearman and Redfield on Negligence (Rev. Ed. 1941), page 153, it is stated that: "The doctrine . . . requires evidence which shows at least the probability that a particular accident could not have occurred without legal wrong by the defendant."

An explosion such as took place here might have been caused by an excessive internal pressure in a sound bottle, by a defect in the glass of a bottle containing a safe pressure, or by a combination of these two possible causes. The question is whether under the evidence there was a probability that defendant was negligent in any of these respects. If so, the doctrine of res ipsa loquitur applies.

The bottle was admittedly charged with gas under pressure, and the charging of the bottle was within the exclusive control of defendant. As it is a matter of common knowledge that an overcharge would not ordinarily result without negligence, it follows under the doctrine of res ipsa loquitur that if the bottle was in fact excessively charged an inference of defendant's negligence would arise. If the explosion resulted from a defective bottle containing a safe pressure, the defendant would be liable if it negligently failed to discover such flaw. If the defect were visible, an inference of negligence would arise from the failure of defendant to discover it. Where defects are discoverable, it may be assumed that they will not ordinarily escape detection if a reasonable inspection is made, and if such a defect is overlooked an inference arises that a proper inspection was not made. A difficult problem is presented where the defect is unknown and consequently might have been one not discoverable by a reasonable, practicable inspection. In the *Honea* case we refused to take judicial notice of the technical practices and information available to the bottling industry for finding defects which cannot be seen. In the present case, however, we are supplied with evidence of the standard methods used for testing bottles.

... [T]here is available to the industry a commonly used method of testing bottles for defects not apparent to the eye, which is almost infallible. Since Coca Cola bottles are subjected to these tests by the manufacturer, it is not likely that they contain defects when delivered to the bottler which are not discoverable by visual inspection. Both new and used bottles are filled and distributed by defendant. The used bottles are not again subjected to the tests referred to above, and it may be inferred that defects not discoverable by visual inspection do not develop in bottles after they are manufactured. Obviously, if such defects do occur in used bottles there is a duty upon the bottler to make appropriate tests before they are refilled, and if such tests are not commercially practicable the bottles should not be re-used. This would seem to be particularly true where a charged liquid is placed in the bottle. It follows that a defect which would make the bottle unsound could be discovered by reasonable and practicable tests.

Although it is not clear in this case whether the explosion was caused by an excessive charge or a defect in the glass there is a sufficient showing that neither cause would ordinarily have been present if due care had been used. Further, defendant had exclusive control over both the charging and inspection of the bottles. Accordingly, all the requirements necessary to entitle plaintiff to rely on the doctrine of res ipsa loquitur to supply an inference of negligence are present.

It is true that defendant presented evidence tending to show that it exercised considerable precaution by carefully regulating and checking the pressure in the bottles and by making visual inspections for defects in the glass at several stages during the bottling process. It is well settled, however, that when a defendant produces evidence to rebut the inference of negligence which arises upon application of the doctrine of res ipsa loquitur, it is ordinarily a question of fact for the jury to determine whether the inference has been dispelled.

The judgment is affirmed.

SHENK, CURTIS, CARTER, and SCHAUER, J. J., concurred.

C. Defenses to Negligence

Once the plaintiff has succeeded in establishing the *prima facie* case, that is, once he or she has introduced evidence sufficient to show that each of the four elements necessary for a *prima facie* case is present, then the burden shifts to the defendant. At this point, if the defendant does not introduce any evidence to rebut the evidence already introduced by the plaintiff, the judge must find in favor of the plaintiff. If the facts are undisputed and a reasonable conclusion can be drawn from the evidence, the question of negligence becomes a matter of law (rather than a factual matter) to be decided by the court rather than the jury.[44] However, as a practical matter no defendant would allow this to take place. Instead the defendant

---

[44] McDrummand v. Montgomery Elevator Co., 97 Idaho 679, 551 P.2d 966 (1976).

would usually approach the presentation of his or her case from two distinct angles. The first would be to attempt to directly rebut the evidence of the four elements of the *prima facie* case that the plaintiff has introduced. For example, the defendant would try to show that the defendant owed no duty to the plaintiff in the first place. Perhaps, in a jurisdiction where the Cardozo theory of duty is used by the courts, he or she would be able to show that the plaintiff was outside the zone of danger. The defendant might also try to prove that even if a duty did exist between the parties, the defendant did not breach it. Even if there was a duty, and the defendant breached that duty, perhaps there were intervening causes that made the defendant's conduct less than a substantial factor in the resulting injuries to the plaintiff. The defendant might seek to prove that even if there was a duty and a breach, and even if the defendant's conduct did proximately cause the injuries to plaintiff, still the injuries were so slight and insignificant that no damages should be awarded, and the fourth element necessary for the establishment of the *prima facie* case, namely damages, is not present. The defendant's attempt to disprove the existence of proximate cause and damages may include such evidence as expert testimony concerning the actual cause of any physical injuries allegedly incurred by the plaintiff. Other evidence might be the testimony of witnesses who have knowledge that the plaintiff's present physical condition is much better than he or she alleges, thereby indicating that the damages allegedly suffered by the plaintiff are not as extensive as claimed.

Another part of the defendant's attempt to rebut the plaintiff's *prima facie* case would be to show that there was a justification for the defendant's actions, in which case even if a duty existed there may not have been a breach. The method of determining whether such conduct was justified generally involves weighing the utility of the defendant's conduct against the magnitude of the risk created by it.[45] As to the utility of the conduct, the court must consider the social value that the law attaches to the defendant's conduct, the likelihood that the conduct will achieve some desirable end, and the possibility of danger. In determining the magnitude of the risk, the court considers the social value that the law attaches to the interests imperiled by the defendant's conduct, the likelihood of an actual injury by such conduct, the extent or degree of injury threatened, and the number of individual interests imperiled.

The second major approach a defendant might take would be to raise defenses to negligence. That is, the defendant would admit that negligence has in fact been established but claim that he or she should be relieved of liability because of the plaintiff's own actions. The purpose of the first approach is to disprove or negate the very existence of the *prima facie* case, and thereby eliminate the necessity for proceeding any further with the trial. But if the defendant is unable to rebut the plaintiff's *prima facie* case, the only chance of avoiding liability would be to prove that the plaintiff contributed to his or her own injury, or was willing to take a chance and voluntarily place himself or herself in a dangerous situation. Under these circumstances it would make sense to prevent the plaintiff from being compensated for any injuries.

---

[45] Prosser, p. 148.

The defendant proves this by asserting affirmative defenses to the negligence that the plaintiff's proof has established in the *prima facie* case. There are two basic defenses to negligence: contributory negligence and assumption of risk.

1. Contributory Negligence

Contributory negligence is conduct on the part of the *plaintiff* that contributes to his or her own injuries or that falls below the standard of conduct to which the plaintiff should conform in order to protect himself or herself against the foreseeable risks to which he or she is exposed.[46] By definition, the actions of the plaintiff may be a substantial factor in his or her own injury. If the plaintiff's conduct is determined to be a substantial factor, then the defendant's conduct no longer is the proximate cause of the plaintiff's injury. Once the necessary element of proximate cause is eliminated by proof of contributory negligence, then the plaintiff's case must necessarily fail, and he or she is precluded from recovering *anything* for the injury, even if the plaintiff's degree of negligence was very slight in comparison with the defendant's negligence.

The doctrine of contributory negligence was first pronounced in 1809 in the English case of *Butterfield* v. *Forrester,* in which the plaintiff was denied recovery for injuries sustained in a horse-riding accident because he was found to be partially responsible for the mishap.[47] From that case evolved a legal precept that denied recovery to one who was even slightly negligent. This idea found acceptance in England and the United States.[48]

The defendant proves contributory negligence in the same way that the plaintiff proves negligence. The defendant must establish the same necessary elements of a *prima facie* case. However, there is a distinction in the establishment of the *prima facie* case for contributory negligence, in that the duty element is not owed to any particular person; instead it is a duty to exercise due care under the circumstances in order to avoid exposing *oneself* to injury at the hands of another.[49] It is not a duty to exercise due care to avoid exposing *another* person to injury. Yet it is still a duty to exercise due care as would the reasonable, prudent person in the community.

Although the result is the same under the defense of contributory negligence as in the first approach in which the defendant rebuts the plaintiff's *prima facie* case, no reference was made in the first approach to the *plaintiff's* contribution to his or her own injury as is done in raising the contributory negligence defense.

---

[46] Simpson v. Davis, 219 Kan. 584, 549 P.2d 950 (1976); Scott v. I. L. Lyons & Co., 329 So. 2d 795 (La. App. 1976); Carreras v. Honeggers and Co., 68 Mich. App. 716, 244 N.W.2d 10 (1976).

[47] Butterfield v. Forrester, 11 East, 60, 103 Eng. Rep. 926 (1809).

[48] The first American case was Smith v. Smith, 2 Pick., Mass., 621 (1824). See R. Laugesen, "Colorado Comparative Negligence," 48 *Denver Law Journal* 469 (1972).

[49] Menish v. Polinger Co., 277 Md. 553, 356 A.2d 233 (1976).

2. Assumption of Risk

The second defense to negligence is assumption of risk. This defense is based on the plaintiff's consent, either implied or expressed, to the defendant's acts. If the plaintiff consents to take the chance of harm from a particular risk created by the defendant, then he or she is held under the principles of law governing this defense to have assumed that risk. His or her consent thus relieves the defendant of any duty to the plaintiff. In order for the defendant to successfully prove assumption of risk, the plaintiff must normally (1) be aware of the risk; (2) appreciate the danger involved; and (3) armed with such knowledge, voluntarily choose to encounter the danger.[50]

Often, in contrast with contributory negligence, the plaintiff's conduct may be quite reasonable under assumption of risk circumstances. For example, it is perfectly reasonable for a person to attend a baseball game and sit in a front-row box seat. However, by doing so, a plaintiff may have impliedly consented to the threat of being hit by a foul ball.[51] Similarly, if one voluntarily participates in a raft trip or a safari in the jungles of Africa, then one has impliedly consented to a number of normal risks that accompany such activities.

3. Comparative Negligence

The two defenses to negligence just discussed have been established through court decisions over hundreds of years, as have the elements of the plaintiff's case of negligence. Following their early development, there seemed to be justification in refusing to allow recovery to one who himself or herself is at fault. However, where the level of culpability was disproportionate, the harshness of the contributory negligence doctrine soon became apparent. As a consequence increasing dissatisfaction developed among twentieth-century American legal scholars regarding the absolute defense of contributory negligence.[52] This dissatisfaction led to attempts within various states to find a substitute method of dealing with cases in which negligence existed on the part of both parties. For example, the doctrine of "last clear chance," which evolved in England, was adopted by a majority of jurisdictions in the United States in an attempt to soften the effect of the strict rule of contributory negligence. However, none of these developments satisfactorily alleviated the harshness of the contributory negligence defense and fairly allocated culpability when both parties were at fault.

In an effort to alleviate the harshness of the common law defense of contributory negligence, a number of jurisdictions across the country have adopted legislation

---

[50] See 57 *AmJur* 2d "Negligence," section 274, et seq.

[51] See Brown v. San Francisco Ball Club, Inc., 99 Cal. App. 2d 484, 222 P.2d 19 (1950). Compare Thurman v. Ice Palace, 36 Cal. App. 2d 364, 97 P.2d 999 (1939) (plaintiff hit with ice hockey puck; court distinguished between baseball and hockey on basis that risks inherent in baseball game are deemed common knowledge, while risks of attending hockey games are not).

[52] See Prosser, section 67, pp. 433–34nn., 52–59.

known as comparative negligence statutes. These statutes typically provide that even if the plaintiff was contributorily negligent, he or she may still be able to recover a certain amount of damages from the defendant rather than being completely barred from recovery, as provided under the doctrine of contributory negligence.

In 1861 Georgia became the first state to adopt a statutory remedy for the inequities of the contributory negligence bar by enacting a number of regulations that permitted the application of comparative principles in tort claims. In 1910 Mississippi enacted a "pure" comparative negligence statute. This was followed in 1913 by the enactment of the Nebraska Act, which classifies the parties' negligence as "slight" or "gross." In 1931 Wisconsin passed a statute that permitted comparison of the plaintiff's and the defendant's respective liabilities, but that barred recovery when both parties were equally at fault. South Dakota followed in 1941 with an act similar to that of Nebraska; Arkansas in 1955 enacted a "pure" comparative negligence act much like Mississippi's, but repealed it in 1957 in favor of a statute which more closely resembles the present Wisconsin law. As of the end of 1977, fifteen states had adopted some form of comparative negligence statute and have thus eliminated contributory negligence as a defense to tort recovery. These states are Arkansas, Colorado, Georgia, Hawaii, Idaho, Maine, Massachusetts, Minnesota, Mississippi, Nebraska, New Hampshire, Rhode Island, South Dakota, Vermont, and Wisconsin.

Comparative negligence legislation presently takes three forms. Statutes in Nebraska and South Dakota typify the first variety: the plaintiff's recovery is limited to situations in which his or her negligence has been slight while that of the defendant has been gross, when comparing one party's negligence to the other's. The determination of degrees is of course left to the jury. The second form of statutory enactment is the "pure" comparative negligence. Under this approach a plaintiff may recover his or her damages *less* the percentage of negligence attributable to him or her. Thus a plaintiff who is determined to have been 90 percent responsible for his or her own injuries may still recover 10 percent of his or her damages from the party who is found to have been 10 percent at fault. Only Mississippi presently employs this apportionment scheme. The third variation is the "modified" or "equal to or greater than" rule, which reduces the plaintiff's recovery by the percentage of his or her own negligence and denies recovery if the plaintiff's negligence exceeds that of the defendant. This was the form taken by the Wisconsin Act and has been the most popular among states more recently enacting comparative negligence statutes.

This third type of comparative negligence statute—the modified rule—requires that the fact finder, either the judge or the jury, assign a percentage of negligence to each party. For example, if the plaintiff is 40 percent negligent and the defendant is 60 percent negligent, then under both of these types of statutes the plaintiff's recovery will be 60 percent of the actual damages suffered by the plaintiff. However, under the modified comparative negligence statute, if the plaintiff's negligence is *greater* than that of the defendant, then not only would the plaintiff be precluded from recovering anything; but if the defendant made a counterclaim for damages against the plaintiff, then the defendant may be able to recover from the plaintiff a certain percentage of damages that he or she may have suffered as a result of the plaintiff's contributory negligence.

The modified negligence statutes have four basic features:

1. the percentage of negligence assigned to each party determines whether the defendant is liable; a plaintiff cannot recover unless his or her negligence is of a lesser degree than the negligence of that person against whom he or she seeks recovery;
2. this comparison of negligence also serves the purpose of reducing damages in proportion to the causal negligence of the person seeking recovery;
3. the jury theoretically does not know the results of its findings, because the plaintiff is not permitted to inform the jury either as to the result and operation of the statute or that the jury's percentage findings are applied to the amount of damages proven; and
4. the court applies the doctrine upon facts found by the jury in terms of percentages of negligence attributed to each person contributing to the injury for which recovery is sought.[53]

The comparative negligence statutes have a relation only to the contributory principle and do not affect the assumption of risk doctrine. This is so primarily because the theory behind the assumption of risk doctrine had its origin in contract and was simply a form of consent. It can thus be applied without any form of fault. Therefore a jurisdiction that has adopted a comparative negligence statute will also have the assumption of risk doctrine established by cases. In jurisdictions that have not adopted the comparative negligence statute, the contributory negligence and assumption of risk doctrines will continue to be available as defenses. A jurisdiction cannot recognize both comparative negligence and contributory negligence, because it would not make sense to simultaneously implement two methods of relieving the defendant, at least partially, of liability because of the plaintiff's negligence.

4. Last Clear Chance

The most commonly accepted common law modification of the strict rule of contributory negligence is the doctrine of the last clear chance. Last clear chance is not a defense to negligence. On the contrary, it is a judge-made effort to aid *plaintiffs* against the harshness of the contributory negligence defense. This doctrine had its origin in 1842 in the English case of *Davies* v. *Mann,* in which the plaintiff left his mule fettered in the highway, and the defendant drove into it.[54] It was held that the plaintiff should recover, notwithstanding any negligence of his own, if the defendant might have by proper care avoided injuring the animal. The rationale suggested for this principle is that if the defendant has the last clear opportunity to

---

[53] Laugesen, "Colorado Comparative Negligence," p. 469; Prosser, section 67.
[54] Davies v. Mann, 10 M. & W. 546, 152 Eng. Rep. 588 (1842).

avoid the harm, the plaintiff's negligence is not a proximate cause of the injury.[55]

Since the doctrine of last clear chance developed as a rule designed to soften the harsh effect of contributory negligence, it would seem that the necessity for such a rule is eliminated when comparative negligence becomes applicable. However, Nebraska has retained the doctrine of last clear chance and has virtually eliminated the slight/gross negligence standards of comparison, so as to apply the last clear chance doctrine in all cases, unless the plaintiff's negligence was active and continuing until the very moment of the injury. South Dakota has also retained the doctrine of last clear chance and has determined it to be compatible with comparative negligence. Arkansas, Mississippi, Maine, and Wisconsin have apparently abrogated the last clear chance rule and used the apportionment, comparison, and reduction features of their comparative negligence statutes instead.[56]

The case of *Rachal* v. *Brookshire Grocery Stores, Inc.* deals with defenses to negligence and with the doctrine of last clear chance. Although the court discussed the plaintiff's contributory negligence, it appears that the plaintiff assumed the risk of a known danger, and the court simply failed to distinguish between the two defenses (contributory negligence and assumption of risk).

RACHAL

v.

BROOKSHIRE GROCERY STORES, INC.

336 So. 2d 1014 (1976)

Court of Appeal of Louisiana, Third Circuit

DOMENGEAUX, Judge.

This is a tort suit wherein damages are sought for injuries sustained by plaintiff, Mrs. Lillian Rachal when she slipped and fell on the floor while shopping in defendant's supermarket. After trial on the merits the District Judge, rendering written reasons, concluded that the plaintiff had failed to prove actionable negligence on the part of the defendant, but assuming arguendo that there was such negligence, the plaintiff herself was guilty of contributory negligence which barred her recovery. From a judgment dismissing her demands, plaintiff had appealed. We affirm.

The accident occurred on June 6, 1975. The plaintiff was a regular customer at defendant's

supermarket. Accompanied by her 6 year old daughter, she entered the establishment shortly before 9:00 A.M., cashed a check at the office situated in the front portion of the building, picked up a push cart and commenced to do her grocery shopping. She eventually reached an area in the supermarket designated as Aisle 6. Donald Harris, the janitor for the defendant was in the process of mopping up the remains of a broken bottle of pine oil which had fallen from the shelf previously inside the aisle. Leaving the push cart and her 6 year old daughter near the entrance of the aisle, plaintiff proceeded past Mr. Harris to secure a bottle of Purex, which was on sale. After obtaining the Purex she turned around, started forward, and

---

[55] Prosser, section 66.
[56] See Laugesen, "Colorado Comparative Negligence," p. 485.

slipped, but did not fall. She nevertheless continued walking and slipped again, this time falling to the floor and causing the injuries of which she complains. Her accident occurred in the area where the pine oil had spread, and where Harris had been mopping.

NEGLIGENCE OF THE PARTIES

The evidence shows that the janitor, Donald Harris, came to work at 6 A.M. He completed his general cleanup work by approximately 8:30 A.M. which consisted of sweeping the store, buffing the floor, mopping up the places which needed mopping, and then buffing again. Harris then returned to the back of the store in furtherance of his job duties. At approximately 8:35 A.M. a bottle of pine oil which was on a shelf in Aisle 6 fell to the floor and broke. The record does not indicate who or what caused the pine oil to fall, but Mr. Claude Adcock, the Assistant Manager for the defendant, who was in his office, heard the break and saw the broken bottle and its contents on the floor. He immediately summoned Mr. Harris over the loudspeaker to clean up. The janitor promptly got a bucket and mop and then a box and dust pan and proceeded to Aisle 6. When he arrived at the scene he saw a broken 32 oz. bottle of pine oil on the floor. He picked up the broken glass and placed same in the box, pushed the box aside, and began to wet and then dry mop the pine oil substance. While he was so engaged the plaintiff arrived at the scene as aforesaid.

Mrs. Rachal admitted that she saw Harris mopping the area, utilizing the bucket and the mop, and that the mop looked wet to her. She said that she spoke to Harris and told him "you cleaning up and I'm going to come mess up." She admitted that the area was damp, but that she nevertheless proceeded down the aisle past Harris. She also admitted that she did not take her daughter down the aisle but rather left her, together with the grocery cart, near the spot where Harris was mopping. She testified that there was no one else in the aisle and that she did not see anything on the floor before she fell and neither did she smell the pine oil. She denied that she was warned of any substance on

the floor and specifically denied that Harris warned her not to go there because it was slippery. She stated that when she first slipped she caught herself and prevented a fall, at which time she looked on the floor and saw nothing but a "plain damp floor". She admitted, after that episode, that she started out again, at which time she slipped a second time, resulting in the fall. . . .

While Harris was cleaning up as aforesaid, it is conceded that there was no sign, barricade, or rope blocking off the area. However, the mop bucket was lettered with the words "Wet Floor."

Generally, a storekeeper has the responsibility of providing a safe place for his customers. He is not the insurer of their safety, however, and he need only keep floors and passageways in a reasonably safe condition for use in a manner consistent with the purpose of the premises, that is, free from defects or conditions in the nature of hidden dangers, traps or pitfalls which are not known to the invitee and would not be observed by him in the exercise of reasonable care. The invitee assumes the obvious, normal or ordinary risks attendant on the use of the premises, and the storekeeper is not liable for injuries to an invitee whose injuries result from a danger which should have been observed by the latter in the exercise of reasonable care. See Jones v. W. T. Grant Company, 187 So. 2d 470 (La. App. 3rd Cir. 1966), and cases cited therein.

Under the facts of this case we find no manifest error in the trial court's conclusion that plaintiff failed to prove actionable negligence on the part of the defendant, and we will not elaborate further on that aspect of the case in view of the obvious negligence on the part of the plaintiff herself. Such being the case, she cannot recover even if there was some violation of any duty owed plaintiff as an invitee.

Owners of business establishments are not liable for injuries to an invitee when those injuries result from a danger which should have been observed by the latter in the exercise of reasonable care; the invitee assumes the obvious, normal or ordinary risks attendant on the use of the business premises. Nurdin v. Connecticut Fire Insurance Company, 211 So. 2d 688 (La. App. 4th Cir. 1968).

In the instant case Mrs. Rachal knew or should have known of the possible danger of traversing the area in Aisle 6 under the circumstances described hereinabove. She should have realized the possibility of slipping but apparently thought that she could traverse the area safely. She took her chances. . . .

LAST CLEAR CHANCE

Alternatively in her petition, plaintiff pleaded the doctrine of the Last Clear Chance and argues likewise on appeal.

The doctrine of the Last Clear Chance, stated broadly, is that the negligence of the plaintiff does not preclude a recovery for the negligence of the defendant where it appears that the defendant, by exercising reasonable care and prudence might have avoided injurious consequences to the plaintiff notwithstanding the plaintiff's negligence. In order for the doctrine to be applied the plaintiff herein was obligated to prove three essential facts: (1)

That she was in a position of peril of which she was unaware or from which she could not extricate herself; (2) That the defendant actually discovered or should have discovered her peril; and, (3) That after the defendant actually discovered or should have discovered plaintiff's peril, said defendant had a reasonable opportunity to avoid the accident. . . . In order to apply the doctrine there must be negligence on the part of both parties.

We conclude, based on the factual context of this case, that the Last Clear Chance doctrine is not applicable herein for either of two reasons: (a) The trial judge concluded that the plaintiff failed to prove any actionable negligence on the part of the defendant and we find no manifest error in that conclusion; (b) Plaintiff failed to prove one of the essential facts required to apply the doctrine, i.e., that she was in a position of peril of which she was unaware. . . .

For the above and foregoing reasons, the judgment of the district court which dismissed plaintiff's suit is hereby affirmed at her costs.

Affirmed.

intented conduct + intended results.

D. Intentional Torts

As stated previously, the law imposes certain standards or guidelines upon the members of society relating to their accidental, or unintentional, conduct that causes injury to others. The same is true for intentional conduct. The guidelines imposed on those intentionally causing injury contain a more clearly defined standard of conduct than that embodied in the legal principles relating to negligence. The reasonable person standards imposed by the principles of negligence represent a statement by society, through the courts, that the defendant should compensate the plaintiff for injuries caused by the defendant's unintentional negligent conduct. The guidelines in the field of intentional torts, on the other hand, deal with defendants who *knowingly* perform an act that is outside of those guidelines. Unlike a case of negligence, the defendant in an intentional torts case knew beforehand that he or she was performing the act causing the injury. The defendant does not necessarily realize at the time he or she performs such an act that it constitutes a tort. However, in the vast majority of intentional torts cases, the defendant at least knows that his or her intentional conduct constitutes an unprivileged act. Under negligence principles, no conscious decision is made by the defendant intending the consequences of his or her act.

Because intentional torts are more culpable, defendants found liable for them are sometimes required to pay greater damages than those found liable for negligence. Courts have addressed this issue and have held that in actions brought for intentional or malicious torts, the wrongdoer will be responsible for direct injuries, even if such injuries lie outside the limit of natural and apprehended results applied to unintentional torts. That is, the range of injuries for which a plaintiff can claim damages resulting from an intentional tort is wider than in a case of negligence. The effect of this is to subject the intentional wrongdoer to a greater potential liability for damages.[57]

Intential torts have no bearing on any criminal actions that may also be brought. Terms such as *assault* and *battery* are common to both the criminal field and the field of intentional torts. However, although similar terminology is used and similar elements of proof are required in both areas of the law, this discussion concerns civil law and is restricted solely to actions between private individuals for compensation to the injured party.

1. Battery

A battery is an act that directly or indirectly is the legal cause of "harmful or offensive conduct" with another's person, when that act is done: (1) with the intention of causing the contact or apprehension of it to the other's person or to a third person; (2) when the contact is not consented to, or when it is procured by fraud or duress; and (3) when the contact is not otherwise allowed.[58] The type of intent necessary on the part of the defendant in order to find him or her liable for the intentional tort of battery may consist of either the intention of causing the *contact* or the intention of causing the *apprehension* of the contact.

Harmful or offensive contact requires the touching of the plaintiff or an object so closely associated with the plaintiff as to make the touching tantamont to a physical invasion of the plaintiff's person against his or her will. The contact may be indirect, provided the defendant caused it or set it in motion. Examples of such indirect batteries include sending poison candy to the plaintiff or stretching a rope across a walkway.[59] Even if the defendant intended to confer a benefit upon the plaintiff or to play a joke, he or she may nevertheless be liable.[60] The defendant's motives are usually immaterial. The principles concern only whether or not the physical act itself was willfully done.

---

[57] See 22 *AmJur* 2d, "Damages," section 82; Sandler v. Lawn-A-Mat Chemical & Equipment Corp., 141 N.J.Super. 437, 358 A.2d 805 (1976).

[58] Bakker v. Baza'r, Inc., 551 P.2d 1269 (Ore. 1976); Whitley v. Andersen, 551 P.2d 1083 (Colo. App. 1976) (intent to cause physical injury is not a prerequisite); 6 *AmJur* 2d, "Assault and Battery," section 111.

[59] Smith v. Smith, 194 S.C. 247, 9 S.E.2d 584 (1940); 6 *AmJur* 2d, "Assault and Battery," section 113.

[60] Newman v. Christensen, 149 Neb. 471, 31 N.W.2d 417 (1948); Moore v. El Paso Chamber of Commerce, 220 S.W.2d 327 (Tex. Civ. App. 1929) (rodeo horse play); Markley v. Whitman, 95 Mich. 236, 54 N.W. 763 (1893).

The plaintiff does not have to be aware of the contact at the time that it occurs. Therefore, if the defendant makes offensive physical contact with the plaintiff while the latter is asleep (that is, it would have been offensive had he or she known about it at the time it occurred), but does not awaken or harm him or her, the contact may be sufficient to establish liability, even though the plaintiff learns of the contact later. Another classic case of this type arose when the plaintiff was under an anesthetic at the time of the alleged battery.[61]

The *transferred intent* doctrine, discussed in the case of *Alteiri* v. *Colasso,* is often involved in battery cases. This doctrine states that a mistake as to the identity of the victim does not negate the defendant's intent, and further states that if the defendant intends to commit a battery upon A, but A manages to avoid the injury and the defendant causes injury to B instead, the courts will "transfer" the defendant's wrongful intent from A to B in order to hold the defendant liable, even though the defendant did not intend to cause any injury to B.[62]

ALTEIRI v. COLASSO

168 Conn. 329, 362 A.2d 798 (1975)

Supreme Court of Connecticut

LOISELLE, Associate Justice.

This action is one for battery brought by a minor, the plaintiff Richard Alteiri, to recover for injuries he suffered, and by his mother, the named plaintiff, to recover for expenses incurred. The complaint alleges that while the minor plaintiff was playing in the back yard of a home at which he was visiting, the defendant threw a rock, stone or other missile into the yard and struck the minor plaintiff in the eye and "[a]s a result of said battery by the defendant, the plaintiff Richard Alteiri suffered severe, painful and permanent injuries.". . .

Six interrogatories were submitted to the jury. Two interrogatories were answered in the affirmative as follows: "On April 2, 1966, did the defendant, John Colasso, throw a stone which struck the plaintiff, Richard Alteiri, in the right eye?" Answer: "Yes." "[W]as that stone thrown by John Colasso with the intent to scare any person other than Richard Alteiri?"

Answer: "Yes." The jury answered "No" to four other questions concerning whether the defendant had intended to strike either the minor plaintiff or any other person and whether he had thrown the stone either negligently or wantonly and recklessly. A plaintiffs' verdict was returned. The defendant has appealed from the judgment rendered. . . .

Error is assigned in the court's denial of the defendant's motions to set aside the verdict and for judgment notwithstanding the verdict. The defendant claims that the jury could not have reasonably and logically rendered a verdict under our law when in their answers to the interrogatories they expressly found that the defendant did not throw the stone with intent to strike either the minor plaintiff or any other person and did not throw the stone either negligently or wantonly and recklessly. In this state an actionable assault and battery may be one committed wilfully or voluntarily, and there-

---

[61] Mohr v. Williams, 95 Minn. 261, 104 N.W. 12 (1905); Hively v. Higgs, 120 Ore. 588, 253 P. 363 (1927).

[62] See 6 *AmJur* 2d, "Assault and Battery," section 114; Prosser, pp. 32–34.

fore intentionally; one done under circumstances showing a reckless disregard of consequences; or one committed negligently. By their answers to the interrogatories it is clear that the jury found that the battery to the minor plaintiff was one committed wilfully. The issue to be determined on this appeal is whether a jury upon finding that the defendant threw the stone with the intent to scare someone other than the one who was struck by the stone can legally and logically return a verdict for the plaintiffs for a wilful battery.

In Rogers v. Doody, 119 Conn. 532, 534, 178 A. 51, in discussing the distinction between reckless disregard and wilfulness the court stated that a "wilful and malicious injury is one inflicted intentionally without just cause or excuse. It does not necessarily involve the ill will or malevolence shown in express malice. Nor is it sufficient to constitute such an injury that the act resulting in the injury was intentional in the sense that it was the voluntary action of the person involved. Not only the action producing the injury but the resulting injury must be intentional." The defendant claims, in reliance upon this principle, that as there was no intention either to injure the minor plaintiff or to put him in apprehension of bodily harm there could be no recovery for a wilful battery. The intention of the defendant was not only to throw the stone—the act resulting in the injury

was intentional—but his intention was also to cause a resulting injury, that is, an apprehension of bodily harm. If the stone had struck the one whom the defendant had intended to frighten, the defendant would have been liable for a battery. The statement in *Rogers* that the "resulting injury must be intentional" would be satisfied as the injury intended was the apprehension of bodily harm and the resulting bodily harm was the direct and natural consequence of the intended act.

It is not essential that the precise injury which was done be the one intended. An act designed to cause bodily injury to a particular person is actionable as a battery not only by the person intended by the actor to be injured but also by another who is in fact so injured. . . . This principle of "transferred intent" applies as well to the action of assault. And where one intends merely an assault, if bodily injury results to one other than the person whom the actor intended to put in apprehension of bodily harm, it is battery actionable by the injured person. . . .

It follows that the jury could logically and legally return a plaintiffs' verdict for wilful battery, and that the court in accepting that verdict and denying the defendant's motions was not in error.

There is no error.

In this opinion the other judges concurred.

---

2. Assault

The elements of assault are: (1) an intention to inflict a harmful or offensive contact or to make a person apprehensive that one will be inflicted; and (2) the performance of an act, other than the mere speaking of words, when the act does cause apprehension.[63] As in the case of battery, in order for the defendant to be found liable for civil assault, he or she must have the intent either to cause contact or to cause apprehension of contact. The distinguishing feature between the two torts is that in the case of assault the existence of apprehension replaces the existence of actual contact required in battery. Thus, unlike battery, assault requires an analysis of the state of mind of *both* the actor (defendant) and the victim (plaintiff). In

---

[63] Crouter v. Rogers, 193 Neb. 497, 227 N.W.2d 845 (1975).

the case of battery only the defendant's state of mind needs to be analyzed, since no actual apprehension need be present in the plaintiff.

Because the *defendant's* intention remains a requirement in finding liability for assault, the question arises as to whether the defendant intended to put the plaintiff in apprehension of harmful or offensive contact. Certainly, in a case in which the defendant points a water gun at the plaintiff, the defendant does not intend to inflict a harmful or offensive contact, but he or she may intend to make the plaintiff *believe* that such contact is imminent. Thus an assault would have occurred.

The apprehension must be of an immediate nature; the threat causing the apprehension in the plaintiff cannot exist far in the future. Therefore the plaintiff must prove that the defendant had either the actual or the apparent ability to inflict an immediate, harmful, or offensive touching of the plaintiff's person.[64]

Conditional threats do not constitute an assault.[65] Consistent with the requirement of apprehension of an *immediate* harmful or offensive contact, if the defendant points a gun at the plaintiff and says "I would kill you if I had a silencer on this gun," the plaintiff may be frightened, but he or she is not in apprehension of an immediate offensive contact. Therefore there is no assault. This is an example of a conditional threat, or a limitation contained in the statement, which negates the reasonable belief that the plaintiff is in immediate danger.

The majority of jurisdictions require that such a state of apprehension in the plaintiff's mind be a reasonable belief; it is not a completely subjective analysis of the plaintiff's state of mind.[66] For example, if the defendant points an unloaded gun at the plaintiff, it will depend on all of the surrounding circumstances as to whether or not it is a reasonable apprehension or belief that the gun is loaded.

The plaintiff must be in apprehension of a touching to his or her own person. Threats to property, or to the person or property of another, are not sufficient to establish assault.

3. Infliction of Mental Distress

One who intentionally and willfully causes severe emotional distress to another person may be liable in tort for that emotional distress. The majority of jurisdictions require that physical harm or illness resulting directly from the emotional distress accompany it.[67] The main reason for this requirement is to prevent frivolous lawsuits and suits based on perjured evidence. However, several more liberal jurisdictions do not require the accompanying physical harm or illness, and the trend of

---

[64] Gelhaus v. Eastern Air Lines, 194 F.2d 774 (5th Cir. 1952); Cucinotti v. Ortmann, 399 Penn. 26, 159 A.2d 216 (1960); Castiglione v. Galpin, 325 So.2d 725 (La. App. 1976) ("present ability"); Durivage v. Tufts, 94 N.H. 265, 51 A.2d 847 (1947) ("present apparent ability").

[65] Holcombe v. Whittaker, 318 So.2d 289 (Ala. 1975).

[66] Prosser, p. 39, pointing out that courts are reluctant to protect timid individuals from exaggerated fears.

[67] Johnson v. Board of Jr. College District No. 508, 334 N.E.2d 442 (Ill. App. 1975); Gibson v. Greyhound Bus Lines, Inc., 409 F. Supp. 321 (M.D. Fla. 1976).

the courts is to recognize the tort of intentional mental disturbance without physical harm attached.[68]

The concept of the tort of *negligent* infliction of emotional harm is similar to intentional infliction of mental distress. The majority of jurisdictions also require that in order to obtain recovery under this tort, it must be accompanied by physical harm.[69] However, the trend with negligent infliction of emotional harm is to recognize the tort without any accompanying physical harm.

4. Trespass

a. Trespass to Land

The three types of intentional torts just discussed all require a specific intent on the part of the defendant. However, the intentional tort of trespass does not require such conscious intent in order for the defendant to be found liable. Trespass to land is an intentional and unprivileged act whereby another's right of exclusive possession in land is invaded. Trespass to land does not require a conscious intent to trespass, only to do the physical act which constitutes the trespass.[70] Thus the defendant need not realize that the land belongs to another person. The defendant may enter the land in good faith, believing that he or she is the owner, and still be liable for the trespass. The trespass may also consist of the defendant's failure to leave the land, once having entered it lawfully or with the plaintiff's permission.[71]

The trespass must be physical.[72] This can be contrasted with the nontrespassory tort of nuisance, as in concussion damage from an adjacent explosion or blasting work, or a defendant's factory emitting smoke, dust, vibrations, or noise. When the invasion is nonphysical in nature, then the courts usually treat the action as a nuisance action rather than a trespass.[73]

The law holds that landowners own the land beneath the surface to the center of the earth (subject to mineral ownership, as discussed in Chapter 8) and all space above the surface. Therefore an airplane flying above a person's property may be trespassing on that property. There are four views about this type of trespass generally accepted by various jurisdictions across the country: (1) there is a trespass only when the flying takes place in the owner's *effective* zone of use; (2) there is a trespass only when the flying takes place in the owner's *actual* zone of use; (3)

---

[68] Meyer v. Nottger, 241 N.W.2d 911 (Iowa 1976); Grimsby v. Samson, 85 Wash. 2d 52, 530 P.2d 291 (1975); 38 *AmJur* 2d "Fright, Shock, etc.", section 13.

[69] 38 *AmJur* 2d, "Fright, Shock, etc.," sections 13, 15, 29, and 36.

[70] Chartrand v. State, 46 A.D.2d 942, 362 N.Y.S.2d 237 (1974).

[71] Harrison v. Rapach, 132 Ill. App.2d 915, 271 N.E.2d 399 (1971); Southwestern Electric Power Co. v. Hammock, 283 So.2d 817 (La. App. 1973); Busada v. Ransom Motors, Inc., 358 A.2d 258 (Md. App. 1976); Ucci v. Mancini, 344 A.2d 367 (R.I. 1975).

[72] Fairlawn Cemetery Assn. v. First Presbyterian Church of Oklahoma City, 496 P.2d 1185 (Okla. 1972).

[73] See Celebrity Studios, Inc. v. Civetta Excavating Inc., 340 N.Y.S.2d 694 (N.Y. Super. 1973) (denial of recovery of damages for trespass resulting from noise and vibration caused by blasting and pile-driving operations on adjoining land).

flight cannot be regarded as a trespass, but only (possibly) as a nuisance or negligence; (4) (the majority position) any amount of "reasonable" flight is a privileged trespass, and therefore not actionable.[74]

b. Trespass to Chattels

A *chattel* is any tangible or movable item; it is an item of personal property, as opposed to real property or real estate. The term is interchangeable with the word *personalty*. Thus the intentional tort of trespass to chattels is an act intentionally invading another's right of possession in chattels. The necessary elements for a *prima facie* case of trespass to chattels are (1) the performance of the trespassory act by defendant; (2) an intent on the part of defendant to perform such an act, although not necessarily an intent to commit a trespass; (3) an invasion of the chattel interest; (4) the plaintiff's possession of the chattel or his or her right to immediate possession; and (5) damages.

The act of a trespasser to chattels is similar to the act of a trespasser to land. That is, there must be some volitional movement by the defendant or some part of his or her body, resulting in an intrusion into the plaintiff's rightful possession to the chattel.[75] The element of intent is also quite similar to that required for trespass to land. The defendant must have done the act that causes the intrusion with the intent to deal with the chattel as he or she did.[76] Mistake or claim of right to the chattel are not defenses, even though the defendant may have been acting under a reasonable misapprehension.[77]

In order for the plaintiff to show that there has been an invasion of his or her chattel interest, he or she must prove that the defendant's volitional act, or some force set in motion by it, resulted in either a dispossession or an intermeddling with the plaintiff's chattel.[78] A *dispossession* is conduct which amounts to an assertion by the defendant of a possessory interest in the chattel. This type of invasion extends to thefts of the chattel, destruction of it, or even the barring of the righful owner's access to it. An *intermeddling* is conduct by the defendant that is just short of challenging the rightful owner's interest in the chattel, although the defendant may have gone so far as to carry the chattel away. For example, intermeddling may be throwing a stone at another's automobile, stampeding another's herd of cattle, or "joy

---

[74] See Smith v. New England Air Craft Co., 270 Mass. 511, 170 N.E. 385 (1930) for the first view. Prosser, p. 71, indicates that the third view is "finding increasing support." The fourth view has been adopted by twenty-two states.

[75] Socony-Vacuum Oil Co. v. Bailey, 109 N.Y.S.2d 799 (Supp. Ct. 1952); Shell Petroleum Corp. v. Liberty Gravel & Sand Co., 128 S.W.2d 471 (Tex. Civ. App. 1939).

[76] Texas-New Mexico Pipeline Co. v. Allstate Construction Co., 70 N.M. 15, 369 P.2d 401 (1962); Socony-Vacuum Oil Co. v. Bailey, 109 N.Y.S.2d 799 (Sup. Ct. 1952) ("The actor may be innocent of moral fault, but there must be an intent to do the very act which results in the immediate damage").

[77] Byrne v. Frank Cunningham Stores, Inc., 89 F. Supp. 489 (D.C.D.C. 1950); Jaquith v. Stanger, 310 P.2d 805 (Idaho 1957).

[78] Mountain States Telephone & Telegraph Co. v. Horn Tower Construction Co., 363 P.2d 175 (Colo. 1961); Glidden v. Szybiak, 95 N.H. 318, 63 A.2d 233 (1949).

riding" in another's car, but without intent to assert ownership rights in those chattels.

The next necessary element—possession or right to possession—is fairly self-explanatory. Anyone in possession of a chattel, under at least a "colorable" claim of right to it, at the time of defendant's interference, can maintain an action for trespass to chattels.[79] The original common law rule required that the plaintiff be in possession of the chattel at the time of the trespass, or the action could not be maintained. This rule was relaxed slightly at a later date, in order to allow trespass to be maintained by one who is entitled to immediate possession, or upon demand.

The final element for the *prima facie* case is that of damages. If the defendant's act accomplishes only an intermeddling, as just described, damages to the chattel must be shown, or the plaintiff must have been deprived of the use of the chattel for a substantial period. However, there is no such requirement for proof of actual damages when the defendant's conduct amounts to a dispossession.[80]

E. Defenses to Intentional Torts

As in the case of negligence, several defenses are available to the defendant against the plaintiff's claim of intentional tort. Along with the attempt to rebut the *prima facie* case of intentional tort established by the plaintiff, the defendant will raise one or more defenses to negate the liability for an alleged invasion of the plaintiff's person or an alleged invasion of the plaintiff's real or personal property. It should be kept in mind that it is the defendant raising the points discussed next, even though it appears at times that the actions of the plaintiff could have been the basis for an action commenced by the defendant against the plaintiff.

1. Defenses Against Torts to the Person

If the plaintiff alleges an intentional tort to his or her person, such as an assault or battery, the defendant has a number of defenses against the claim.

a. Consent

The defense of consent negates the wrongful element of the defendant's acts and prevents the existence of the tort. There are three types of consent. The first is *actual* or *express* consent. The second is *apparent* consent—consent implied by the plaintiff's conduct. For example, if the plaintiff does not object to a vaccination given to him or her by the defendant, this may be deemed an implied consent to what the plaintiff is now alleging to be a tortious invasion of his or her person. Similarly, one who enters into a contact sport consents to the normal contacts char-

---

[79] Pentagon Enterprises v. Southwestern Bell Telephone Co., 540 S.W.2d 477 (Tex. Civ. App. 1976). Constructive possession or an equitable right to possession may also be sufficient.

[80] Zaslow v. Kroenert, 29 Cal.2d 541, 176 P.2d 1, reversed on other grounds, 29 Cal.2d 878, 176 P.2d 8 (1946).

acteristic of that activity. The third type of consent is *consent implied by law:* the plaintiff's consent may be implied by law if an interference is necessary to save the plaintiff's life or to protect some other important interest in his or her person or property. An example of consent implied by law is the performance of an operation, provided the plaintiff is unable to consider the matter and grant or withhold consent, an immediate decision is necessary, there is no reason to believe that the plaintiff would not give consent if he or she were able to do so, and a reasonable person in the plaintiff's position would consent.[81]

Consent is not available as a defense if the interference goes beyond the limits of the consent actually given.[82] For example, even though the plaintiff consents to an operation to remove his or her appendix, for the surgeon to also remove the plaintiff's kidney is an unprivileged battery, because the surgeon went beyond the limits of the consent.

A physician has a duty to inform the patient of the dangers inherent in any proposed treatment or surgery. If he or she does not, the patient's "consent" to the treatment will not be effective to bar an action against the doctor for battery.[83] The rationale for this requirement, of course, is that had the plaintiff been informed, he or she may have declined the proposed treatment. Consent is also ineffective when it has been granted while the plaintiff is under duress.[84] Finally, consent is not available as a defense if it is given by a person legally incapable of consenting, such as an incompetent person, a minor, or one who is intoxicated or unconscious.[85]

b. Self-defense

The defendant may be relieved of liability because of his or her right to use the force reasonably appearing to be necessary in order to avoid an invasion of his or her person.[86] Thus the defendant may be entitled to neutralize the plaintiff's attack; however, the law does not condone retaliation and retribution as part of this defense. The defense must be suitable and appropriate.[87] Further, the danger against which the defendant allegedly was protecting himself or herself must be a present

---

[81] Pedesky v. Bleiberg, 59 Cal. Rptr. 294 (Cal. App. 1967). For the classic case regarding implied consent without an emergency situation, see O'Brien v. Cunard S.S. Co., Ltd., 28 N.E. 266 (Mass. 1891).

[82] For example, consent to operate on the right ear does not apply to the left ear; consent to examination does not apply to extraction of all one's teeth. Prosser, 104. Also, consent to a boxing match is not consent to the use of brass knuckles. On the other hand, if A permits B to punch him in the chest as hard as he can, and due to a defective heart A drops dead, the consent is effective. Prosser, p. 103n.54.

[83] Belcher v. Carter, 13 Ohio App.2d 113, 234 N.E.2d 311 (1967). But compare Prosser, p. 106: Most decisions now regard failure to disclose as involving negligence.

[84] According to Prosser, p. 106, there are few cases regarding duress in tort law. One example is Millsap v. National Funding Corp., 56 Cal. App.2d 772, 135 P.2d 407 (1943).

[85] Hollerud v. Malamis, 20 Mich. App. 748, 174 N.W.2d 626 (1969) (intoxication); Bolton v. Stewart, 191 S.W.2d 798 (Tex. Civ. App. 1945) (mental incompetence); Robalina v. Armstrong, 15 Barb., N.Y. 247 (1852) (infant). See also Watts v. Aetna Casualty & Surety Co., 309 So.2d 402 (La. App. 1976); Eisentraut v. Madden, 97 Nebr. 466, 150 N.W. 627 (1915).

[86] See Prosser, pp. 108–112.

[87] Jahner v. Jacob, 233 N.W.2d 791 (N.Dak. 1975).

danger and not a future one.[88] The defendant cannot claim that the plaintiff provoked him or her by mere words; the provocation must include some type of act in order for the defendant to rely on self-defense.[89]

Although the courts have been divided in their opinions, if it reasonably appears unsafe for the defendant to retreat from the imminent danger caused by the plaintiff, the majority of jurisdictions hold that the defendant does not have to "retreat to the wall" before defending himself or herself. The minority of jurisdictions hold that the defendant must retreat if it appears safe to do so.[90]

If one is attacked within one's present dwelling place, if one is being dispossessed from one's dwelling place, or if one is being forced to abandon a lawful arrest, nearly all jurisdictions state that one may use all reasonable force necessary to protect oneself from such attacks, even force likely to cause serious bodily harm or death to the plaintiff.[91] But the defendant is never allowed to use the degree of force likely to cause serious bodily harm or death in retaliation against the plaintiff *after* the plaintiff has been disarmed or has ceased to threaten the defendant, and the defendant is aware of that disarming or cessation of threat.[92]

c. Defense of Third Persons

The defendant is entitled to use reasonable force to defend a third person, just as one may defend himself or herself under the principles just described.[93] The majority position is that the defense of a third person is not permitted if the defendant was reasonably mistaken as to the necessity of such a defense. It is not enough that it reasonably *appeared* that the third person would have been permitted, under the principles discussed earlier, to defend himself or herself. If the defendant interferes, causing an assault or battery to the plaintiff, the defendant must stand in the shoes of the party he or she is defending. Thus, in jurisdictions holding this position in the absence of the third party's *actual* right to defend himself or herself in the circumstances, the defendant will be liable for assault or battery.[94]

---

[88] Clark v. Ziedonis, 513 F.2d 79 (7th Cir. 1975) (must be "imminent" danger); Maichle v. Jonovic, 230 N.W.2d 789 (Wis. 1975) (belief that he is likely to suffer bodily harm *at the time*).

[89] Daigle v. Goodwin, 311 So.2d 921 (La. App. 1975). One is also barred from self-defense if he or she causes the incident by provocation on his or her part. Bernstine v. Natchitoches, 335 So.2d 51 (La. App. 1976).

[90] This majority view is based on a high regard for the individual's dignity and sense of honor and prevails in the American South and West. Prosser, p. 111. See e.g., Brown v. United States, 256 U.S. 335 (1921); Burton v. Waller, 502 F.2d 1261 (5th Cir. 1974). An example of the minority view is State v. Cox, 23 A.2d 634 (Me. 1941).

[91] See, e.g., Price v. Gray's Guard Service, Inc., 248 So.2d 461 (Fla. App. 1974); Prosser, pp. 111–12.

[92] Germolus v. Sausser, 83 Minn. 141, 85 N.W. 946 (1901); McCombs v. Hegarty, 205 Misc. 937, 130 N.Y.S.2d 547 (1954) (kicking man when he is down).

[93] Sandman v. Hagan, 154 N.W.2d 113 (Iowa 1967); Rhoden v. Booth, 344 S.W.2d 481 (Tex. Civ. App. 1961).

[94] For majority view see People v. Young, 11 N.Y.2d 274, 229 N.Y.S.2d 1, 183 N.E.2d 319 (1962). For minority view, see Patterson v. Kuntz, 28 So.2d 278 (La. App. 1946). See also Commonwealth v. Martin, 341 N.E.2d 885 (Mass. 1976) (minority position may now be majority—at least twenty-one states have adopted sounder minority view by statute, namely that honest and reasonable mistake will relieve defendant of liability).

d. Defense of Land or Chattels

The defendant may use reasonable force necessary to defend his or her property. In fact, the majority of jurisdictions hold that the defendant is privileged to use *deadly* force in defense of his or her person[95] or home.[96] If the person or home are not threatened, only the amount of force necessary to counter the intrusion is permitted. Some courts insist that in order to use deadly force both the person and the home must reasonably appear to be in serious danger.[97] Thus this right to defend land or chattels is closely related to the privilege of self-defense, as described earlier.

In all jurisdictions a condition of the defendant's privilege to defend his or her land or chattels through the use of force is that the defendant, prior to the use of such force, demand that the plaintiff desist or leave. If the demand is ignored, or if it is reasonable to assume that such a demand would be useless, futile, or would have further endangered the defendant's property, then that condition has been met.

e. Recovery of Possession of Land Wrongfully Withheld

Although the common law rule allowed it, the majority position is that there is no privilege to use force to recover possession of land that is being wrongfully withheld. If the defendant owner uses force to regain possession, he or she is liable for injury to the plaintiff or the plaintiff's property in so doing, even though the plaintiff was not entitled to possession.[98] The defendant's title or right to possession is not a defense. The rationale for this position is that the forceable entry and unlawful detainer statutes that have been passed in most jurisdictions provide a quick and effective judicial remedy for the recovery of possession of land wrongfully withheld. These statutes express the public policy of encouraging resort to the courts for the purpose of settling land disputes and discouraging the use of force by private persons.

f. Recovery of Possession of Chattels Wrongfully Withheld

One may use force not likely to cause death or serious bodily harm when the plaintiff has wrongfully taken a chattel from the defendant's rightful possession, provided that the defendant uses such force during an immediate pursuit. A timely or reasonably fast recovery of the chattel by the defendant and a demand for and a refusal to return the chattel are also required.[99] If it would be futile or would

---

[95] Eldred v. Burns, 182 P.2d 397 (Ore. 1947).

[96] See State v. Bonano, 59 N.J. 515, 284 A.2d 345 (1971); 40 *AmJur* 2d, "Homicide," section 167.

[97] State v. Cessna, 153 N.W.2d 194 (Iowa 1915); 6 *AmJur* 2d, "Assault & Battery," section 176.

[98] Daluiso v. Boone, 78 Cal. Rptr. 707, 455 P.2d 811 (1969).

[99] Bobb v. Bosworth, 16 Ky. 81 (1808); *Restatement of Torts 2d*, Section 103. See Prosser, pp. 117–19.

further endanger the chattel, the demand is unnecessary. If the plaintiff received rightful possession of the chattel in the first place, the defendant must resort to legal remedies. On the other hand, the defendant *may* resort to force to recover his or her chattel even though the plaintiff claims a right, provided no right actually exists.[100]

g. Privilege of Arrest

The often-used phrase "citizen's arrest" is generally misunderstood. Under what circumstances can a private person attempt to arrest or detain another person without being subjected to a civil action for assault, battery, or false imprisonment? A private citizen is privileged to arrest another person without a warrant for a felony only if the felony has in fact been committed, and if the defendant has reasonable grounds for believing that the person he or she arrests committed the felony.[101]

According to the majority view, both officers and private citizens may arrest a person for a misdemeanor without a warrant, if such a misdemeanor was a breach of the peace and was committed in the presence and knowledge of the arresting party, and if the arresting party makes the arrest immediately after the commission of the misdemeanor.[102]

When the arrest is for a misdemeanor, either a police officer or a private person is privileged to use that degree of force necessary to effect the arrest; however, deadly force is never permitted in an arrest for a misdemeanor. When the arrest is for a felony, deadly force may be used by police officers or private persons, although many states limit such extreme force to arrests for serious felonies, such as murder, rape, and robbery.[103]

Police officers and private citizens can use only the amount of force that reasonably appears necessary to effect the arrest. Police officers will not be held liable for using deadly force to arrest for a felony, even though they may be reasonably mistaken as to the identity of the felon. However, when a private person uses deadly force, the majority position is that no mistaken belief is permitted, reasonable or unreasonable, as to the identity of the felon or the occurrence of the felony.[104]

The privilege of arrest carries with it the privilege of entering onto the plaintiff's land for the purpose of effecting that arrest. The minority of jurisdictions deny such a right to forcefully enter dwellings when only a misdemeanor is involved.[105]

---

[100] 6 *AmJur* 2d, "Assault & Battery," section 169.

[101] Montiero v. Howard, 334 F. Supp. 411 (D.R.I. 1971).

[102] Moll v. United States, 413 F.2d 1233 (1969); People v. Dixon, 392 Mich. 691, 222 N.W.2d 749 (1974).

[103] State v. Clarke, 61 Wash.2d 138, 377 P.2d 449 (1962) (private citizens); People v. Lawrence, 308 P.2d 821 (Cal. App. 1957) (police officers).

[104] Commonwealth v. Cheimansky, 430 Pa. 170, 242 A.2d 237 (1968).

[105] Hart v. State, 145 N.E. 492 (1924).

2. Defense of Land and Chattels

The defenses just described are raised by the defendant in cases in which the plaintiff has claimed the occurrence of an intentional tort (assault or battery) upon his or her person or body. The following defenses are raised when the plaintiff claims that the defendant has committed either trespass to land or trespass to chattels.

a. Consent and Recovery of Possession of Chattels Wrongfully Withheld

The defense of consent has been discussed in 1(a) and the defense of recovery of possession of chattels in 1(f). These two defenses contain the same principles in response to claims of invasion of the plaintiff's personal property as in defenses to the claim of invasion of his or her person. Therefore sections 1(a) and 1(f) explain these two defenses.

b. Privilege to Exclude or Evict Trespassing Chattels of Another

The defendant may use reasonable force to evict or exclude chattels possessed by the plaintiff if such force is necessary or is reasonably believed to be necessary in order to protect the defendant's interest in the exclusive possession of his or her own land or chattels.[106] The reasonableness of force used by the defendant is determined by: (1) the necessity for immediate action to prevent the injury or destruction that is threatened by plaintiff's invading chattels; (2) whether the force used by the defendant was excessive or was necessary to terminate or prevent the intrusion by plaintiff's chattels; and (3) the comparative value of the defendant's threatened property and the value of plaintiff's chattels to which the defendant's force is applied.

c. Privileged Invasion of Another's Land or Chattels as a Public Necessity

The defendant may enter the plaintiff's land or destroy his or her property without liability for damage if the defendant acts to prevent or mitigate the effect of a disaster, if such a disaster endangers the welfare of a community or part of it.[107] Such a privilege extends as far as the defendant's breaking and entering fences and buildings, including dwellings. Further, if the plaintiff-owner resists the defendant's attempt to enter the land or deal with the plaintiff's chattels, the defendant may use whatever force is reasonably necessary, including deadly force.[108] The rationale for the broad extent of this privilege is that if a public disaster is imminent, a single

---

[106] Maryland Telephone & Telegraph Co. v. Ruth, 68 A. 358 (Md. App. 1907).
[107] Bowditch v. Boston, 101 U.S. 16 (1879); State v. Hoyt, 21 Wis.2d 254, 128 N.W.2d 645 (1964).
[108] State v. Waggoner, 49 N.M. 399 (1946).

life should not endanger the lives of the multitude. A common law outgrowth of the necessity of protecting oneself in the face of natural hazards, this principle provides that a traveler on an impassable public road is privileged to continue a journey by entering another's neighboring lands, as a matter of public right.[109]

d. Privileged Invasion of Another's Land or Chattels as a Private Necessity

The defendant may also enter the plaintiff's land or interfere with his or her chattels if such conduct appears reasonably necessary to avoid serious harm to oneself, chattels, or land.[110] Contrary to the defense of *public* necessity, the defendant using the defense of *private* necessity is liable for actual damages done to the plaintiff's person or property.[111] Otherwise the private necessity defense is the same as the public necessity defense. However, because greater public policy factors are present in the latter situation, it is unlikely that the use of deadly force would ever be privileged in the case of a private necessity.

e. Privileged Invasion of Land or Chattels to Abate a Nuisance

The defendant is privileged to invade the land or chattels of another for the purpose of abating a private nuisance created or maintained on the land or chattels of the plaintiff, provided that: (1) the defendant is the owner of land or chattels injuriously affected by the plaintiff's nuisance; (2) the defendant has first made a demand that the nuisance be abated, unless it reasonably appears that such a demand is impractical or would be futile; and (3) the defendant uses only reasonable force to effect the abatement.[112] If the nuisance is a public one, a private individual is not privileged to abate it unless the nuisance is causing the defendant some injury "peculiar" in kind, so that to him or her it is a private nuisance as well as a public one.[113]

F. Strict Liability

In certain circumstances the law of torts imposes liability upon the defendant despite the exercise of all reasonable care. Under the concept of strict liability there is no moral wrongdoing, yet a person is at fault. This is not a new concept under

---

[109] Gulf Production Co. v. Gibson, 234 S.W. 906 (Tex. Civ. App. 1921); Shriver v. Marion Ct., 66 S.E. 1062 (W.Va. App. 1910).

[110] See 75 *AmJur* 2d, "Trespass," section 42.

[111] See Prosser, pp. 66–67.

[112] See 58 *AmJur* 2d, "Nuisance," section 209, noting that demand is not necessary if danger to health, life, or property is imminent and the necessity of prompt removal of the nuisance is urgent. See, e.g., Childers v. New York Power & Light Corp., 275 A.D. 133, 89 N.Y.S.2d 11 (1949). See discussion of nuisance in Part G of this chapter.

[113] See 58 *AmJur* 2d, "Nuisance," section 210; 75 *AmJur* 2d, "Trespass," section 38; Restatement of Torts 2d, section 203(2).

the law of torts; the concept of fault has never been exactly synonymous with moral blame. Often the law imposes liability for conduct that is actually morally proper, such as if a trespasser enters another person's land with the reasonable belief that the land is his or her own. The fault of a person's conduct sometimes lies in ignorance or an honest mistake.

The feature that distinguishes strict liability from other areas of the law of torts is that the defendant not only cannot be charged with any *moral* wrongdoing, but he or she has not departed in any way from a reasonable standard of care. In fact the defendant's conduct or activity may even be desirable. However, requirements of social policy necessitate the imposition of liability.

In its early stages, strict liability was imposed upon the keepers of animals which caused injury to others, if the owner knew or should have known about some vicious propensity of the animals.[114] Under modern principles, strict liability is imposed upon the defendant for damages arising out of activities in which a high degree of risk to others was foreseeable. Examples are blasting, drilling oil wells, storing explosives, and impounding waters, all considered ultrahazardous activities.[115] Most jurisdictions have statutes that specify activities deemed to be ultrahazardous, thus imposing strict liability in the case of any injuries resulting from them.[116]

The law does not propose to prevent the activity from being carried out, but social policy requires that, despite the absence of blame, the damages should be borne by the party who intentionally exposed those in the vicinity to such a tremendous risk. In addition, that party is usually the one most financially able to pay for the damages.

The doctrine of strict liability for ultrahazardous or abnormally dangerous activities developed from the leading case of *Rylands* v. *Fletcher,* decided in England in 1868.[117] The *Rylands* case established the principle that a force that is brought on to the defendant's land and is a "nonnatural" use of such land, and that is likely to cause substantial harm to adjacent land if it escapes, in spite of reasonable care by the defendant, is an ultrahazardous activity for which the defendant is responsible. The case involved the construction of a reservoir upon the defendant's land. The water broke into an underground shaft of an abandoned coal mine and flooded along underground connecting passages into the adjoining mine of the plaintiff. The defendants did not even know of the old coal mine, and no basis existed for a finding of negligence or trespass. However, the court held that a person should

---

[114] See Prosser, pp. 496 et seq. See e.g., Crunk v. Glover, 167 Nebr. 816, N.W.2d 135 (1959); Page v. Hollingsworth, 7 Ind. 317 (1855).

[115] See, e.g., Smith v. Lockheed, 56 Cal. Rptr. 128 (Cal. App. 1967); Pumphrey v. J.A. Jones Construction Co., 94 N.W.2d 737 (Iowa 1959); Luthringer v. Moore, 190 P.2d 1 (Cal. 1948); Greene v. General Petroleum Co., 270 P. 952 (Cal. 1928).

[116] See, e.g., West Anno. Calif. Code, Health & Safety Code, Section 13115 (Supp. 1977); Mass. Gen. Laws Anno., ch. 148, section 20C (Supp. 1976).

[117] Rylands v. Fletcher, House of Lords 1868, L.R. 3, H.L. 330. Compare Fletcher v. Rylands, Exchequer Chamber 1866, L.R. 1, Ex. 265.

[handwritten marginal note: "a series of Brooks wrote on a series of subjects"]

be held absolutely liable for all damage that is the natural consequence of the likely escape of anything he or she brings onto his or her land.

The Restatement of Torts defines an ultrahazardous activity as one that (1) involves a risk of serious harm to the persons or property of others; (2) creates a risk that cannot be eliminated by due care; and (3) is not a matter of common usage (thereby excluding dangerous conditions such as automobiles, fires, firearms, and airplanes). Under Section 402A of the Restatement of Torts a form of strict liability is imposed upon sellers of goods. This rule most frequently arises in connection with commonly used household appliances. Based on statutes that have adopted the Restatement position and on the recent trend in the courts, strict liability in tort is now being extended to the manufacturers and suppliers of such products.

The concurring opinion in the *Escola* case is a widely cited discussion of the policy considerations behind the doctrine of strict liability. Through this case and others Judge Traynor made a significant contribution to the present-day principles of the doctrine.

ESCOLA

v.

COCA COLA BOTTLING CO.
OF FRESNO

[See opinion on page 226]

TRAYNOR, J., concurring.

I concur in the judgment, but I believe the manufacturer's negligence should no longer be singled out as the basis of a plaintiff's right to recover in cases like the present one. In my opinion it should now be recognized that a manufacturer incurs an absolute liability when an article that he has placed on the market, knowing that it is to be used without inspection, proves to have a defect that causes injury to human beings. MacPherson v. Buick Motor Co., 217 N.Y. 382, 111 N.E. 1050, established the principle, recognized by this court, that irrespective of privity of contract, the manufacturer is responsible for an injury caused by such an article to any person who comes in lawful contact with it. . . . In these cases the source of the manufacturer's liability was his negligence in the manufacturing process or in the inspection of component parts supplied by others. Even if there is no negligence, however,

public policy demands that responsibility be fixed wherever it will most effectively reduce the hazards to life and health inherent in defective products that reach the market. It is evident that the manufacturer can anticipate some hazards and guard against the recurrence of others, as the public cannot. Those who suffer injury from defective products are unprepared to meet its consequences. The cost of an injury and the loss of time or health may be an overwhelming misfortune to the person injured, and a needless one, for the risk of injury can be insured by the manufacturer and distributed among the public as a cost of doing business. It is to the public interest to discourage the marketing of products having defects that are a menace to the public. If such products nevertheless find their way into the market it is to the public interest to place the responsibility for whatever injury they may cause upon the manufacturer, who, even if he is not negligent in the manufacture of the product, is responsible for its reaching the market. However intermittently such injuries may occur and however haphazardly they may strike, the risk of their occurrence is a constant risk and a general one. Against such a risk there should be general and constant protection and the manufacturer is best situated to afford such protection.

The injury from a defective product does not become a matter of indifference because the defect arises from causes other than the negligence of the manufacturer, such as negligence of a submanufacturer of a component part whose defects could not be revealed by inspection, or unknown causes that even by the device of res ipsa loquitur cannot be classified as negligence of the manufacturer. The inference of negligence may be dispelled by an affirmative showing of proper care. If the evidence against the fact inferred is "clear, positive, uncontradicted, and of such a nature that it can not rationally be disbelieved, the court must instruct the jury that the nonexistence of the fact has been established as a matter of law." Blank v. Coffin, 20 Cal. 2d 457, 461, 126 P.2d 868, 870. An injured person, however, is not ordinarily in a position to refute such evidence or identify the cause of the defect, for he can hardly be familiar with the manufacturing process as the manufacturer himself is. In leaving it to the jury to decide whether the inference has been dispelled, regardless of the evidence against it, the negligence rule approaches the rule of strict liability. It is needlessly circuitous to make negligence the basis of recovery and impose what is in reality liability without negligence. If public policy demands that a manufacturer of goods be responsible for their quality regardless of negligence there is no reason not to fix that responsibility openly. . . .

The liability of the manufacturer to an immediate buyer injured by a defective product follows without proof of negligence from the implied warranty of safety attending the sale. Ordinarily, however, the immediate buyer is a dealer who does not intend to use the product himself, and if the warranty of safety is to serve the purpose of protecting health and safety it must give rights to others than the dealer. In the words of Judge Cardozo in the MacPherson case: "The dealer was indeed the one person of whom it might be said with some approach to certainty that by him the car would not be used. Yet the defendant would have us say that he was the one person whom it was under a legal duty to protect. The law does not lead us to so inconsequent a conclusion." While the defendant's negligence in the MacPherson case made it unnecessary for the court to base liability on warranty, Judge Cardozo's reasoning recognized the injured person as the real party in interest and effectively disposed of the theory that the liability of the manufacturer incurred by his warranty should apply only to the immediate purchaser. It thus paves the way for a standard of liability that would make the manufacturer guarantee the safety of his product even when there is no negligence.

This court and many others have extended protection according to such a standard to consumers of food products, taking the view that the right of a consumer injured by unwholesome food does not depend "upon the intricacies of the law of sales" and that the warranty of the manufacturer to the consumer in absence of privity of contract rests on public policy. . . . Dangers to life and health inhere in other consumers' goods that are defective and there is no reason to differentiate them from the dangers of defective food products. . . .

In the food products cases the courts have resorted to various fictions to rationalize the extension of the manufacturer's warranty to the consumer: that a warranty runs with the chattel; that the cause of action of the dealer is assigned to the consumer; that the consumer is a third party beneficiary of the manufacturer's contract with the dealer. They have also held the manufacturer liable on a mere fiction of negligence: "Practically he must know it [the product] is fit, or take the consequences, if it proves destructive." Such fictions are not necessary to fix the manufacturer's liability under a warranty if the warranty is severed from the contract of sale between the dealer and the consumer and based on the law of torts. . . . Warranties are not necessarily rights arising under a contract. An action on a warranty "was, in its origin, a pure action of tort," and only late in the historical development of warranties was an action in assumpsit allowed. "And it is still generally possible where a distinction of procedure is observed between actions of tort and of contract to frame the declaration for breach of warranty in tort." 4 Williston, §970. . . . The consumer no longer has means or skill enough to investigate for himself the soundness of a product, even when it is not contained in a sealed package, and his erstwhile vigilance has been lulled by the steady efforts of manufacturers to build up confidence by advertising and marketing devices such as trade-

marks. Consumers no longer approach products warily but accept them on faith, relying on the reputation of the manufacturer or the trade mark. . . . The manufacturer's obligation to the consumer must keep pace with the changing relationship between them; it cannot be escaped because the marketing of a product has become so complicated as to require one or more intermediaries. Certainly there is greater reason to impose liability on the manufacturer than on the retailer who is but a conduit of a product that he is not himself able to test. . . .

The manufacturer's liability should, of course, be defined in terms of the safety of the product in normal and proper use, and should not extend to injuries that cannot be traced to the product as it reached the market.

Rehearing denied; EDMONDS, J., dissenting.

Although the scope of the duty under the doctrine of strict liability extends to any injuries to persons or property resulting from the ultrahazardous activity, the concept of foreseeability is retained to some degree, in that the duty the defendant owes is only toward "foreseeable plaintiffs." Thus, in order for the defendant to be held liable, the injury must have occurred to persons to whom a reasonable person would have foreseen the risk of harm under the circumstances, and the injury must be within the scope of the risk that could have been anticipated.[118]

The plaintiff's contributory negligence is not a defense, unless it was the actual and direct cause of the injury, such as when the plaintiff negligently collides with the dangerous instrumentality, such as explosives, thereby directly causing his or her own injury.[119] Even if a plaintiff's activity is not the sole cause of his or her own injury, his or her negligence may be deemed such a substantial factor that the defendant's liability is cut off by its remoteness, as it would be eliminated as the result of an unforeseeable intervening force. Assumption of risk, on the other hand, is ordinarily a good defense to strict liability.[120] Thus plaintiffs who voluntarily bring

---

[118] Polk v. Ford Motor Co., 529 F.2d 259 (8th Cir. 1976); Deem v. Woodbine Manufacturing Co., 89 N.M. 50, 546 P.2d 1207 (1976).

[119] Kassouf v. Lee Brothers, Inc., 209 Cal. App.2d 568, 26 Cal. Rptr. 276 (1962); Jasper v. Skyhook Corp., 89 N.M. 98, 547 P.2d 1140 (1976); General Motors Corp. v. Hopkins, 535 S.W.2d 880 (Tex. Civ. App. 1976).

[120] Hiigel v. General Motors Corp., 544 P.2d 983 (Colo. 1975); Heil Co. v. Grant, 534 S.W.2d 916 (Tex. Civ. App. 1976). See also Johnson v. Clark Equipment Co., 274 Ore. 403, 547 P.2d 132 (1976) (assumption of risk has different test in strict liability case—defendant must show that plaintiff actually knew and appreciated the particular risk, that plaintiff voluntarily encountered the risk while realizing the danger, and plaintiff's decision was unreasonable).

themselves in reach of an animal that they know to be dangerous, or who intentionally irritate or provoke it, have no cause of action if the animal attacks. The plaintiff's appreciation or realization of the risk, and his or her voluntary consent to encounter it, will generally be a question for the jury.

G. Other Torts

A number of other torts do not readily fall under the heading of intentional tort, negligence, or strict liability. Such torts can be caused by either intentional or negligent conduct on the part of the defendant. Although usually intentional, they differ significantly in their nature from the other intentional torts discussed earlier. A suit based on any of these other torts must be predicated on at least one of the three previously considered bases for liability. Thus it is important to ascertain which basis of liability is relied upon, because this will determine the defenses that may be asserted and the scope of liability imposed on the defendant.

1. Nuisance

There are two types of nuisance: *private* and *public*. The term private nuisance generally applies to interferences with the use and enjoyment of land. In these cases an actual physical invasion of the plaintiff's land is not necessary, as it is with trespass to land. Rather the nuisance consists of a use of the *defendant's* land that is inconsistent with the free enjoyment by the plaintiff of his or her land.[121] Thus the defendant's actions actually deprive the plaintiff of the free use of his or her property, as opposed to any interference with his or her person. The nuisance can arise through the intentional, negligent, or ultrahazardous activities of the defendant. An action based upon nuisance is appropriate if, for example, the plaintiff is complaining of obnoxious odor, damaging vibrations, or excessive noise from the defendant's adjacent property.

In order for liability to be based upon private nuisance, substantial harm must be proven.[122] Here the claim for relief largely depends upon the recurring and continuous nature of the irritation. Adding to the difficulty of obtaining recovery based upon private nuisance is the fact that most courts will weigh the harm caused to the plaintiff's enjoyment and use of his or her land against the social utility of the defendant's activity. This balancing of the equities takes into consideration such factors as the public's interest in the defendant's activity, whether the plaintiff was present in the locality before the defendant, the economic ability of the defendant to cease the activity, the plaintiff's ability to avoid the interference, and the defendant's motive.[123]

---

[121] Hein v. Lee, 549 P.2d 286 (Wyo. 1976).

[122] Smejkal v. Empire Lite-Rock, Inc., 547 P.2d 1363 (Ore. 1976).

[123] Vern. J. Oja and Associates v. Washington Park Towers, 15 Wash. App. 356, 549 P.2d 63 (1976) (degree of risk, gravity of harm, whether risk can be eliminated by reasonable care, whether the activity is of common usage, appropriateness of the location, and value of the activity to the community).

A public nuisance, on the other hand, is an act or omission that causes inconvenience or damage to the public in general, such as endangering its health, safety, or morals. In order for a public nuisance to be present it does not have to affect the entire community simultaneously; the activity or condition may successively interfere with those who come in contact with it in exercising their public right, such as an obstruction on a public highway.[124] In addition to the common law basis for public nuisance, many jurisdictions have enacted statutes that declare specific activities to be public nuisances, such as noise in excess of certain decibel levels.

A person is privileged to use reasonable force or take other steps in order to abate a private or public nuisance that threatens to damage the person; however, the right to inflict personal injury is never allowed.[125] The wiser course is to seek an injunction against the nuisance prior to the time actual harm occurs. A court will grant such an injunction if it appears that the defendant's contemplated activity will probably cause irreparable harm.[126]

2. Defamation

Defamation is the general term given to the torts of libel and slander. These are actions which involve the unprivileged publication to a third person of defamatory matter that concerns and injures the plaintiff. The term *publication* as used in this context has a much more general meaning than in normal use. Publication is the communication of defamatory matter intentionally or by a negligent act to a person other than the person defamed. Publication need not be in writing; any communication fulfills this requirement.[127]

Persons other than the original publishers can be found liable for the publication and repeated republication of the defamation.[128] One who repeats or republishes the defamatory matter is liable even if the republisher claims that he or she doesn't believe the defamation. In addition, the original defamer is liable for the repetition caused by third persons, when those repetitions were or should have been anticipated by the original defamer.[129] The liability of the original publisher is limited somewhat, however, under what is referred to as the single publication rule, which holds

---

[124] Board of Supervisors v. United States, 408 F. Supp. 556 (E.D. Va. 1976); Smejkal v. Empire Lite-Rock, Inc., 547 P.2d 1363 (Ore. 1976); Busche v. Projection Room Theater, 118 Cal. Rptr. 428 (Cal. App. 1974); General Corp. v. State ex rel. Sweeton, 320 So. 2d 668 (Ala. 1975).

[125] Maddran v. Mullendore, 111 A.2d 608 (Md. 1955); Childes v. N.Y. Power & Light Corp., 275 App. Div. 133, 89 N.Y.S.2d 11 (1949); State ex rel. Herman v. Cardon, 112 Ariz. 548, 544 P.2d 657 (1976).

[126] Harrison v. Indiana Auto Shredders Co., 528 F.2d 1107 (7th Cir. 1975). Compare McQuade v. Tucson Tiller Apartments, Ltd., 25 Ariz. App. 312, 543 P.2d 150 (1975) (injunction may issue against an anticipated nuisance if it is "highly probable").

[127] Southland Corp. v. Garren, 138 Ga. App. 246, 225 S.E.2d 920 (1976); General Motors Corp. v. Piskor, 352 A.2d 810 (Md. 1976) (may be spoken words, gestures, or actions).

[128] Lyle v. Waddle, 144 Tex. 90, 188 S.W.2d 770 (1945) (generally not liable for publication by plaintiff); Davis v. Askin's Retail Stores, 211 N.C. 551, 191 S.E. 33 (1937) (liable under certain circumstances).

[129] Barres v. Holt, Rinehart & Winston, Inc., 141 N.J. Super. 563, 359 A.2d 501 (1976).

that the entire edition of a newspaper or book is considered one publication, instead of treating each copy or reprint as a publication.[130]

If the alleged defamation is not apparent on the face of the publication, then in order to prove the case the plaintiff must establish through pleading and proof those additional facts (called *inducements*), together with the defamatory meaning of the publication in light of those inducements (the meaning is called *innuendo*), and must finally prove that the inducements and innuendo specifically lead to a reference to the plaintiff (the reference is called *colloquium*).[131] In order for the plaintiff to recover, he or she does not have to prove that the person to whom the defamation was published actually believed it; it is only necessary that the person seeing, hearing, or reading the defamation understood the statement and further understood that it referred to the plaintiff.[132] If the defamatory statement appears to refer to a group, an individual member of the defamed group may successfully bring an action if he or she is able to prove that a personal reference was actually intended, or if the group is so small that the remark must have been intended to defame each individual member.[133]

a. Libel

Libel is a form of defamation that is communicated by sight and embodied in a more or less permanent physical form. It has been argued that the better test in distinguishing libel from slander is one of scope rather than permanence. Therefore there are commentators who would construe any defamatory radio broadcast as libelous because of the audience reached.[134] Case law in many jurisdictions provides that if the libel is clear on its face, it is *libel per se,* thereby eliminating the requirement that the plaintiff prove actual damages. If the libel is not evident on its face, then damages must be alleged and proven as part of the *prima facie* case, as with any other tort. In the majority of jurisdictions, this damage must be of a pecuniary nature; damage such as social ostracism is not sufficient.[135]

---

[130] Neyrey v. Lebrun, 309 So.2d 722 (La. App. 1975).

[131] General Motors Corp. v. Piskor, 340 A.2d 767 (Md. App. 1975). See also Bordoni v. N.Y. Times, Inc., 400 F. Supp. 1223 (S.D.N.Y. 1975).

[132] Smith v. Huntington Publishing Co., 410 F. Supp. 1270 (S.D. Ohio 1975) (test whether a reasonable person could believe that the article referred to plaintiff); Gregory v. McDonnell Douglas Corp., 127 Cal. Rptr. 825 (Cal. App. 1976) (person to whom matter is communicated must be likely to understand it).

[133] Cahill v. Hawaiian Paradise Park Corp., 543 P.2d 1356 (Hawaii 1975) (recovery allowed for individual's family); Webb v. Sessions, 531 S.W.2d 211 (Tex. Civ. App. 1975) (no recovery—group too large and term used too general).

[134] L. Vold, "The Basis for Liability for Defamation by Radio," 19 *Minnesota Law Review* 611 (1935); A. Haley, "The Law on Radio Programs," 5 *George Washington Law Review* 1157 (1937). See also Prosser, pp. 753–54.

[135] Rosanova v. Playboy Enterprises, 411 F. Supp. 440 (S.D.Ga. 1967); Allard v. Church of Scientology, 129 Cal. Rptr. 797 (Cal. App. 1976). The general trend today seems to be away from the earlier position: Fuqua Television Inc. v. Fleming, 134 Ga. App. 731, 215 S.E.2d 694 (1975) (may recover for hurt feelings; recovery not limited to pecuniary loss); Wilson v. Capital City Press, 315 So.2d 393 (La. App. 1975) (may recover for harm to reputation even if proof of pecuniary loss is impossible). See also, Time, Inc. v. Firestone, 424 U.S. 448 (1976); Buckley v. Littell, 394 F. Supp. 918 (S.D.N.Y. 1975).

b. Slander

Slander is a form of defamation communicated by the spoken word or by a transitory gesture. The principal characteristic of slander is that it is defamation in less permanent and less physical form than libel. Contrary to libel, and primarily because slander is not considered as serious as libel, it requires proof of damages, even where the slander is clear on its face.[136] However, exceptions to this rule are that compensatory damages need not be proven where the slander concerns (1) a criminal offense involving moral turpitude; (2) a presently existing offensive and communicable disease; (3) the improper conduct or characteristic of a lawful business, occupation, or profession; or (4) a woman's lack of chastity.[137] These are considered *slander per se*. This indicates a further distinction between libel and slander, in that libel per se depends upon the clarity of the defamation, while slander per se is determined by the nature or subject of the defamatory statement.

c. Defenses to Defamation

Defenses to defamation may be categorized as (1) absolute privilege, (2) qualified (sometimes called conditional) privilege, (3) consent, and (4) truth. If a person has an absolute privilege, any malice he or she may have had toward the plaintiff is immaterial in applying such a defense; the purpose and motive cannot be considered. Under an absolute privilege, what would otherwise be defamatory may be stated with impunity by judges, attorneys, witnesses, or jurors in the course of performing a judicial function, and provided the statement relates to the matter at hand. Federal legislators are privileged to say anything they please while performing their legislative function. The president, governors, and cabinet members are absolutely privileged during the exercise of their governmental functions.

If the defamation was published in good faith and for proper motives, and if the publication was not excessive, the defendant may raise the defense of qualified privilege.[138] A speaker has a qualified privilege if he or she has a social, moral, or legal obligation to speak about the plaintiff. Statements are qualifiedly privileged if their subject is of a common interest, for example, relevant to private groups or labor unions. Similarly, a person may comment on matters of public interest provided the comment is made in good faith, and further provided that the underlying facts on which the comment is based are true. In this case the allegedly defamatory comment and its factual basis are qualifiedly privileged. Statements made by or to public officials related to the discharge of their duties may be successfully defended on the basis of qualified privilege. Finally, *consent,* given by the invitation or at the

---

[136] Big O Tire Dealers, Inc. v. Goodyear Tire & Rubber Co., 408 F. Supp. 1219 (D. Colo. 1976); Picone v. Talbott, 29 Md. App. 536, 349 A.2d 615 (1975).

[137] Atkinson v. Equitable Life Assurance Society, 519 F.2d 1112 (5th Cir. 1975); Kirk v. Village of Hillcrest, 335 N.E.2d 535 (Ill. App. 1975).

[138] Weening v. Wood, 349 N.E.2d 235 (Ind. App. 1976); Krumholz v. TRW, Inc., 142 N.J. Super. 80, 360 A.2d 413 (1976).

instigation of the plaintiff, and the *truth* of the defendant's statement are complete defenses.[139]

Another defense to defamation may be based on constitutional grounds. In *New York Times Co.* v. *Sullivan,*[140] the Supreme Court had held that the First Amendment right of free speech and press requires that *public officials* may not recover damages for defamatory statements relating to their official conduct without proof of knowledge of the falsity of the statement or reckless disregard of whether the statement was false on the part of the defendant. *Curtis Publishing Co.* v. *Butts* expanded the *New York Times* test to include *public figures* other than public officials.[141]

The question remaining after those cases was whether there was a constitutional privilege when the defamer made statements about *private* individuals. In *Rosenbloom* v. *Metromedia, Inc.,* the Court could manage only a plurality opinion indicating there *might* be such a privilege in this situation, at least if it was a matter of public concern.[142] *Gertz* v. *Robert Welch, Inc.* purported to answer the question.[143] Elmer Gertz, an attorney who represented the family of a youth killed by a Chicago policeman in a civil action against the officer, was falsely accused by a right-wing publication of involvement with communist organizations and of having a criminal record. The jury awarded Gertz $50,000, but the District Court granted judgment to the defendant, notwithstanding the verdict, based on the *New York Times* case.[144] The Court of Appeals affirmed. The Supreme Court pointed out that the real problem was to balance the interest in a free and uninhibited press against the interest of private individuals to be free from injury by false statements about them. Public officials and public figures enjoy easy access to the media to refute false statements, and they voluntarily assume a position subject to public scrutiny. In addition, the public right to know is involved. However, the private individual does not enjoy these advantages or voluntarily expose himself or herself to public scrutiny and is thus entitled to greater protection.

In order to protect private individuals, the Court held that in cases of defamatory falsehood that harms *private* individuals, each state must define the appropriate standard of publisher or broadcaster liability, with the important limit that states may not impose liability without fault. In other words, some degree of intent or negligence must still be shown, but the test need not be as strict as the *New York Times* test. The Court further held that the interest in protecting individuals extended only so far as to allow recovery of actual damages and not presumed or punitive damages.

---

[139] Barticula v. Paculdo, 411 F. Supp. 392 (W.D.Mo. 1976); DeLay First National Bank & Trust Co. v. Jacobsen Appliance Co., 243 N.W.2d 745 (Nebr. 1976) (truth). Prosser, p. 784 (consent).

[140] New York Times Co. v. Sullivan, 376 U.S. 254 (1964).

[141] Curtis Publishing Co. v. Butts, 388 U.S. 130 (1967).

[142] Rosenbloom v. Metromedia, Inc., 403 U.S. 29 (1971).

[143] Gertz v. Robert Welch, Inc., 418 U.S. 323 (1974).

[144] For a discussion of judgment notwithstanding the verdict (judgment n.o.v.), see Chapter 6, pages 117–18.

In the *Gertz* case the Court further defined "public figures." Gertz had been active in the community and his profession and was quite well-known. However, because he had no "general fame or notoriety in the community" and was not pervasively involved in the affairs of society, he was not a "public figure." Thus the Supreme Court held that the *New York Times* standard of liability was inapplicable and thus incorrectly applied by the trial court. The case was reversed and remanded for a new trial.

There were four dissents in *Gertz,* but the most incisive was that of Justice White. White argued that *Gertz* "federalized" the law of defamation by changing the common law rules regarding damages. Since actual damages are so difficult to prove in this type of case, the law of defamation is greatly limited. Furthermore, the view that there can never be strict liability shifts the "risk of falsehood" to the innocent victim rather than the publisher, with whom the risk had previously rested.

Another problem with *Gertz* is the great diversity that may well develop from state to state. National publishers or broadcasters now may have to consider the varying laws of defamation in fifty states in determining whether something is safe to print.

Another relatively recent case, *Time, Inc.* v. *Firestone*, was not the groundbreaking case that *Gertz* was, but its treatment of the public figure concept is important.[145] While the plaintiff was a well-known socialite, the fact that she was not involved in public affairs and that she was involuntarily cast into the public eye made her a private individual. (However, Justice Marshall, dissenting, could not not see how Mrs. Firestone could be anything but a public figure under the old tests.) The *Firestone* case also represents a further grant of discretion to the states. The damages-fault impacts assailed by Justice White in the *Gertz* case were lessened. The Court went out of its way to find the "fault" necessary to avoid the *Gertz* bar on strict liability. It also expanded the view of "actual" damages, thus reopening the door to larger recovery. Thus the overall effect of *Firestone* is to place a greater burden on publishers to ascertain the truth of what they print.

3. Fraud

In order to establish a *prima facie* case of the tort of fraud, the plaintiff must show that the defendant (1) intentionally (2) made a misrepresentation of a fact (3) that presently exists (4) to the plaintiff (5) with the intent that the plaintiff should act in reliance upon such a fact and that (6) in fact the plaintiff did substantially reply upon it reasonably under the circumstances, resulting in his or her pecuniary injury.[146]

Matters of opinion and circumstances in which a person is "puffing," such as in attempting to make a sale, are not actionable as fraud. However, in many jurisdic-

---

[145] Time, Inc. v. Firestone, 424 U.S. 448 (1976).
[146] In re Romero, 535 F.2d 618 (10th Cir. 1976); Keck v. Wocker, 413 F. Supp. 1377 (D.Ky. 1976); Banks v. Merritt, 537 S.W.2d 494 (Tex. Civ. App. 1976).

tions, if a speaker had a duty to speak only with reasonable care, and the plaintiff is a person or a member of a class for whom the misrepresentation was intended, then liability will be imposed for verbal negligence.[147] In this case, even though intentional fraud is absent, the courts will substitute for it the lack of reasonable care and will find fraud when such conduct is combined with the other requirements of the *prima facie* case.

4. Invasion of privacy

The majority of jurisdictions now recognize the tort called invasion of the right of privacy. A few states have established this right through the enactment of statutes. The gist of this cause of action is not injury to a person's character or reputation, as in defamation, but a direct wrong of a more personal type arising out of interference with an individual's right to be let alone. The damages lie in an injury to the plaintiff's feelings, without regard to the effect of the defendant's actions on the plaintiff's property, business, or standing in the community.

The law's recognition of this tort arises directly out of a now-famous law review article written by Samuel D. Warren and Louis D. Brandeis in 1890.[148] The article discussed several cases in which courts had granted relief based upon defamation, invasion of property rights, or breach of contract. The authors concluded that the awarding of damages in these cases was actually based upon a broader yet unexpressed principle that these courts should have independently recognized, primarily because of the press's growing abuses of private individuals' lives. After the article was published, several courts began to accept the existence of the right of privacy proposed by Warren and Brandeis. Although the New York Court of Appeals rejected the concept, the New York legislature enacted a statute making it a misdemeanor and a tort to use the name, portrait, or picture of any person for "advertising purposes or for the purposes of trade" without his or her written consent.[149] Thereafter Georgia and several other states began to recognize this tort by case law.[150] Other jurisdictions have now enacted statutes recognizing the right.[151]

A *prima facie* case of invasion of privacy is established by proving the defendant intended to do an act that invades the right of privacy of the plaintiff.[152] Since the time of the Warren and Brandeis article, several hundred cases have been decided concerning invasion of the right of privacy. Prosser and other leading commentators in the field of torts divided the development of this area of law into four distinct types of invasion of privacy.[153] Thus, regarding the invasion element of the *prima*

---

[147] Griffin v. Wheeler-Leonard & Co., 290 N.C. 185, 225 S.E.2d 557 (1976).

[148] S. Warren and L. Brandeis, "The Right to Privacy," 4 *Harvard Law Review* 193 (1890).

[149] Roberson v. Rochester Folding Box Co., 171 N.Y. 538, 64 N.E. 442 (1902).

[150] Pavesich v. New England Life Insurance Co., 122 Ga. 190, 50 S.E. 68 (1905), is the leading case.

[151] According to Prosser, p. 804, New York, Oklahoma, Utah, and Virginia have such statutes.

[152] Froelich v. Werbin, 548 P.2d 482 (Kan. 1976).

[153] See McNally v. Pulitzer Publishing Co., 532 F.2d 69 (8th Cir. 1976); Marks v. Bell Telephone Co., 331 A.2d 424 (Pa. 1975).

facie case, the defendant's act must result in a serious and unreasonable invasion in any one of the following respects.

a. Intrusion

Any type of intrusion of solitude constitutes invasion of the right of privacy. Common examples are phone tapping, uninvited bursting into homes, and any other sort of intrusion into a person's private life or affairs. The intrusion must be of the type that would be offensive or objectionable to a reasonable person.[154]

b. Disclosure

This form of invasion of privacy involves the public disclosure of private facts. As this branch of the law of privacy has developed, the courts have required that the suit must be based on publicity of private facts that are highly objectionable or embarrassing to the plaintiff, despite their truth.[155] It has been held an invasion of privacy, for example, to publish in the newspaper that the plaintiff has not paid his or her debts, or to disclose the present identity of a reformed prostitute.[156]

c. Appropriation

This invasion of the right of privacy consists of the appropriation of the plaintiff's name or picture for the defendant's benefit. The first case that carved out this area of the law of privacy involved the defendant's use of the plaintiff's picture, without his consent, to advertise the defendant's product.[157] Other cases have involved the plaintiff's pictures on packages containing articles of the defendant company, or pictures used for other business purposes.[158]

When a name is appropriated and used in a book or in the name of a corporation, in order for the plaintiff to recover it must be apparent from the context of the book, or circumstances surrounding the appropriation, that the name is actually that of

---

[154] Nader v. General Motors Corp., 307 N.Y.S.2d 647, 255 N.E.2d 765 (1970).

[155] Atchison, Topeka and Santa Fe R.R. v. Lopez, 216 Kan. 108, 531 P.2d 455 (Kan. 1975); Beaumont v. Brown, 65 Mich. App. 455, 237 N.W.2d 501 (1975).

[156] Midwest Glass Co. v. Stanford Development Co., 34 Ill. App.3d 130, 339 N.E.2d 274 (1975) (plaintiff who hadn't paid debts); Melvin v. Reid, 112 Cap. App. 285, 297 P. 91 (1931) (reformed prostitute).

[157] See, e.g., Flake v. Greensboro News Co., 212 N.C. 780, 195 S.E. 55 (1938); Edison v. Edison Polyform Manufacturing Co., 73 N.J. Eq. 136, 67 A. 392 (1907). See also Roberson v. Rochester Folding Box Co., footnote 149.

[158] Selsman v. Universal Photo Books, Inc., 238 N.Y.S.2d 686 (1963) (plaintiff's picture on packages); Bureau of Credit Control v. Scott, 345 N.E.2d 37 (Ill. App. 1976) (other commercial uses). Compare Reilly v. Rupperswill Corp., 377 N.Y.S.2d 488 (1975) (not every commercial use is protected against); Zacchini v. Scripps-Howard Broadcasting Co., 47 Ohio St. 2d 224, 351 N.E.2d 545 (1976) (minority rule—even some noncommercial uses are protected against).

the plaintiff. That is, the appropriation must clearly identify the plaintiff, rather than being a mere coincidence.[159]

d. False Light

This type of invasion of privacy consists of either: (1) publicly attributing to the plaintiff some opinion or statement without authorization; or (2) using the plaintiff's picture to illustrate a book or an article with which he or she has no connection, thereby implying that such a connection exists. The false light does not have to be defamatory, although an action will often be for both defamation and invasion of privacy.

e. Defenses to Invasion of Privacy

Because the essence of this tort is the right to solitude and the right to privacy in personal affairs, the fact that the matter is true does not constitute a defense. However, there are defenses which may be raised under any of the four types of invasion of privacy. First, if the plaintiff has consented to the alleged invasion, then no cause of action exists.[160] Second, if the matter that has been publicized is deemed to be newsworthy, then the defendant is privileged to publicize it.[161] This principle is based upon the rationale that freedom of speech and press require a free flow of information that is of interest to the public at large.

The public interest defense of newsworthiness has even been recognized as a constitutional privilege. The Supreme Court has held that any publication that is of legitimate public interest is privileged, unless the plaintiff proves that the defendant published the report with knowledge of its falsity or offensiveness, or in substantial disregard of such falsity or offensiveness.[162] This explains why celebrities have found it particularly difficult to successfully bring cases involving invasion of their right of privacy. The courts have stated that a celebrity has abandoned his or her entire right to privacy and cannot object to offensive publicity, unless of course such publicity falls under some other tort, such as libel or slander.

The leading case regarding the effect of the United States Constitution on actions for invasion of privacy is *Time, Inc.* v. *Hill*.[163] *Hill* held that the constitutional protections of speech and press preclude recovery for false light invasions of privacy without proof that the defendant acted with knowledge of the falsity of its reports or in reckless disregard of the truth.

---

[159] Hendrickson v. California Newspapers, Inc., 121 Cal. Rptr. 429 (Cal. App. 1975); Maggio v. Charles Scribner's Sons, 130 N.Y.S.2d 514 (1954).

[160] Dennis v. Adcock, 226 S.E.2d 292 (Ga. App. 1976).

[161] Friedan v. Friedan, 414 F. Supp. 77 (S.D.N.Y. 1976); Kapellas v. Kofman, 81 Cal. Rptr. 360, 459 P.2d 912 (1969).

[162] Time Inc. v. Hill, 385 U.S. 374 (1967).

[163] Time, Inc. v. Hill, footnote 162. See also Cantrell v. Forest City Publishing Co., 419 U.S. 245 (1974), where the Supreme Court again applied the *Hill* test in a false light situation.

In *Cox Broadcasting Corp.* v. *Cohn,* the Court invoked the constitutional privilege concept in a public disclosure invasion of privacy case.[164] The issue was whether a state may provide a cause of action for damages for invasion of privacy caused by publishing the name of a deceased rape victim whose identity was previously publicly known from judicial records that were open to public inspection. After noting that even though there was a zone of privacy surrounding each individual, the Court held that in this case the public's right to know was paramount, and therefore a state cannot provide such a cause of action. However, a careful reading of *Cox* shows that it does not go as far as some commentators have indicated. It does not address the question of what is required for a successful defense to an action against a publication for disclosing *private* facts. Justice White, who wrote the Court's majority opinion, very carefully limited the decision to holding that the Constitution protects the publication of facts already part of a *public* court record.

Cantrell v. *Forest City Publishing Co.* and *Cox* leave little doubt that there are constitutionally imposed limits on causes of action for invasion of privacy, at least those involving publicity and the media. However, they do not go significantly beyond the holding in *Time, Inc.* v. *Hill* in defining the limits of the constitutional privilege; *Cox,* however, does indicate that the privilege may be quite extensive in public disclosure situations.

QUESTIONS

1. What are some examples of other legal and social concepts that, like the concept of liberty and the standard of care in torts, change along with changes in customs, economic beliefs, and other social currents?

2. Analyze the *Pope* v. *Drake* case in Chapter 6 in light of the four elements of a *prima facie* case.

3. What are the two main opposing positions concerning the extent or scope of a person's legal duty toward other persons?

4. Is foreseeability as important in determining proximate cause as it is in determining duty? That is, if an injury is only remotely connected with the defendant's conduct, then was the injury foreseeable, and if not, then how could there have been a duty owing by the defendant? Stated otherwise, if the defendant's conduct was the proximate cause of the plaintiff's injury, then didn't the defendant necessarily owe a duty of due care to protect the plaintiff against such a foreseeable injury? Are all direct and proximate causes foreseeable?

5. Describe the general and special damages that may be recoverable by the plaintiff in the *Pope* case.

---

[164] Cox Broadcasting Corp. v. Cohn, 420 U.S. 469 (1975).

6. What is the primary difference between the defenses of contributory negligence and assumption of risk?

7. What is the primary difference between the torts of assault and battery?

8. What arguments can be made for and against Judge Traynor's suggestion that strict liability should be extended to all consumer products?

9. Give an example of a private nuisance and a public nuisance.

10. How does an action based on defamation differ from one based on invasion of privacy?

10

Other Areas of Civil Law

All three areas of the law discussed in this chapter (administrative law, consumer law, and environmental law) have their origins in legislation and continue to be based primarily upon numerous state and federal statutes. The judicial interpretation and application of the statutes contributes to the ever-increasing body of law in these areas. The law governing the administrative agencies (administrative law) is an essential element in the operation of our state and federal governments. Consumer and environmental law deal with many issues having great contemporary significance. All three of these areas of the law now have a tremendous impact on our lives.

A. Administrative Law

1. Definition

Administrative law is that body of law governing the legal authority of administrators in agencies and departments of the government's executive branch to promulgate and enforce regulations affecting private persons. Administrative law not only limits the scope of authority of these administrators but also prescribes the the manner in which that authority may be exercised.

Administrative law should not be confused with the actual rules and regulations made by the administrators of such agencies and departments. Nor is administrative law the same as decisions made in adjudicatory hearings in administrative agencies and executive branch departments. For example, when the Federal Trade Commission promulgates a rule prohibiting cigarette advertisements on television, the rule itself is not administrative law. However, principles of administrative law established in the judicial branch of government determine whether the FTC has the authority to make the rule in the first place, and whether the procedure followed by the agency in publicizing, implementing, and enforcing the rule was legally proper.

2. Delegation of Powers

The United States Constitution specifies that all legislative powers of the United States Government "shall be vested in a congress of the United States." It also states that "the judicial Power of the United States, shall be vested in one supreme Court, and in such inferior Courts as the Congress may from time to time ordain or establish." Is it not unconstitutional, then, for Congress to delegate legislative and judicial functions to administrative agencies? The answer is that the only possible modern-day interpretation of the Constitution allows Congress to delegate a number of legislative functions and delegate certain judicial functions to the administrative agencies. When the Constitution was adopted in 1789, there was no need to delegate authority to administrative agencies. Indeed the "agency" is not mentioned anywhere in the Constitution. The Constitution emphasizes the role of Congress, as opposed to the judiciary or the executive. The Founding Fathers viewed the presidency as an office to be given only that amount of authority that was absolutely necessary and that would be sufficient to correct the deficiencies of the Articles of Confederation, as explained in Chapter 1. At the time of the adoption of the Constitution, there were only three million people in the United States, and the largest city had a population of only 25,000. There was no need for the administrative process then; the agency is largely an outgrowth of modern business conditions and technology.

The complexity of our society now requires that such agencies perform legislative and judicial functions, even though they are actually a component of the executive branch. Congress has given agencies a number of functions, usually of economic importance, such as the power to grant subsidies, approve corporate mergers, raise and lower tariffs, and regulate banks, advertising, and the prices of goods of major industries. Not all administrative agencies perform the same functions. Some act as investigative or advisory bodies, while others possess those powers as well as rule-making power. The scope of a particular agency's power can be ascertained only by an examination of the statute that created it. Because administrative agencies are solely created by statute, they have no general common law powers.

The specific legal basis upon which courts have upheld the delegation of legislative and judicial powers is that such delegation is proper, provided "adequate standards" are furnished in order to guide the agency in its administrative action.[1] The reason for requiring the standards is to allow the administrator, and any court subsequently reviewing the agency's action, to ascertain the legislature's intent. If the administrator and the court are able to determine the legislative intent, this ensures that the administrative action is within the scope of authority granted by the legislature to the agency and its head.

There have been only two Supreme Court cases invalidating delegation of legislative or judicial authority by the Congress to an administrative agency. Those cases

---

[1] The development of the rule began in Buttfield v. Stranahan, 192 U.S. 470 (1904) and United States v. Grimaud, 220 U.S. 506 (1911). The leading case for the concept itself is Hampton v. United States, 276 U.S. 394 (1928). See also cases cited in note following.

are *Panama Refining Company* v. *Ryan* and *Schechter Poultry Company* v. *United States,* in which the Court held that the lack of adequate standards was tantamount to an unfettered and thus unconstitutional discretion given to the administrator of the agency.[2]

3. Right to Hearing in Agency Proceedings

Most agencies perform both legislative and judicial functions. The general rule is that when an agency is performing legislative or rule-making functions, constitutional due process does not require that the affected persons be given the type of hearing to which they would be entitled in an actual judicial proceeding in court.[3] In general there are far fewer constitutional and statutory requirements on agencies during their legislative or rule-making activities than during their adjudicatory functions. Although the federal Administrative Procedure Act and state administrative procedure acts contain provisions relating to the procedure to be followed during the rule-making process, these provisions are much less detailed than those relating to administrative adjudication.[4] For example, the federal Administrative Procedure Act devotes only one-tenth of its space to rule-making matters. The nature of rule-making requires brevity, simplicity, and flexibility.

The basic reason for the difference in treatment between these two administrative functions—legislative and judicial—is that the agencies simply cannot provide a hearing for each of the millions of individuals who are directly affected by the passage of such agencies' rules. On the other hand, adjudicatory matters usually involve the rights of very few individuals, the same as a case in court. If the agency is adjudicating, constitutional due process requires a trial-type hearing. There are numerous principles that determine how closely the administrative hearing must resemble a judicial trial. For example, when an agency relies on secret investigations to secure facts, there is a right of confrontation and cross-examination of the agency's witnesses.[5] On the other hand, strict rules of evidence need not be adhered to in administrative hearings. Incompetent evidence is usually admissible. Evidence which would constitute hearsay in a court, and therefore would be inadmissible, may form the basis for the agency's order arising out of an administrative proceeding.[6]

---

[2] Panama Refining Co. v. Ryan, 293 U.S. 388 (1935); Schecter Poultry Co. v. United States, 295 U.S. 495 (1935).

[3] P.A.M. News Corp. v. Butz, 514 F.2d 272 (D.C. Cir. 1975); United States v. Florida East Coast Railway Co., 410 U.S. 224 (1973); Automotive Parts & Accessories Association v. Boyd, 407 F.2d 330 (D.C. Cir. 1968).

[4] Administrative Procedure Act, 5 U.S.C., sections 551 et seq.

[5] Greene v. McElroy, 360 U.S. 474 (1958). But see Hannah v. Larche, 363 U.S. 420 (1959) (no right to confrontation where such a procedure is authorized by Congress and there is no power to adjudicate; this case involved the Civil Rights Commission).

[6] Martin-Mendoza v. Immigration and Naturalization Service, 499 F.2d 918 (9th Cir. 1974) cert. denied, 419 U.S. 1113 (test for admissibility is fundamental fairness and probativeness). See also Richardson v. Perales, 402 U.S. 389 (1971).

Due process does not require an internal separation of functions in the adjudicating agency. Thus investigation and prosecution may be performed by members of the same agency that holds the adjudicatory hearing in which the results of that investigation are to be presented.[7]

4. Judicial Review of Administrative Action

In establishing administrative agencies, legislatures could grant such agencies authority to render *final* decisions in their respective areas of action. However, legislatures do not do so; agencies are never granted the authority to render nonreviewable decisions. The judicial branch retains the power to review any final decision of an administrative agency. Judicial review allows a court to determine not only the constitutionality of administrative action but the legality of the actions of any government official, agency, or legislative body. The purpose of judicial review as it applies to administrative agencies is to redress or prevent abuses of administrative power.

Even where the act establishing the agency is silent as to judicial review, there remain constitutional and general common law theories upon which to base the right of the judicial branch to review the administrative action. Any other result would not make sense, because agencies could otherwise be granted unlimited authority by the legislature, and the scope or limits of the authority of such agencies could be clarified or interpreted only by further legislation.

Numerous principles govern a person's right to judicial review of administrative action. For example, the person seeking review must have *standing,* and the court will not review orders of agencies unless the order is a *final* order of that agency. Other principles of administrative law deal with the method of obtaining judicial review and its permissible scope.

In the case of *Fein* v. *Selective Service System,* the United States Supreme Court examined the question of whether the statutes and case law involved in this case allow for judicial review of the agency's actions.

FEIN v. SELECTIVE SERVICE SYSTEM

405 U.S. 365 (1972)

Supreme Court of the United States

BLACKMAN, J., delivered the opinion of the Court.

Petitioner Oliver T. Fein is a doctor of medicine. In February 1969 he filed this pre-induction suit in the United States District Court for the Southern District of New York. . . . Fein challenged, on due process grounds, the constitutionality of his Selective Service appeal procedures and sought declaratory and injunctive relief that would prevent his induction into

---

[7] Withrow v. Larkin, 421 U.S. 35 (1975).

military service. The defendants are Fein's local board at Yonkers, New York, the Appeal Board for the Southern District, the State Selective Service Director, and the National Appeal Board.

. . . Certiorari was granted, so that this Court might consider the important question whether §10(b)(3) of the Military Selective Service Act of 1967, 50 U.S.C. App. §460(b)(3), permits this pre-induction challenge to Selective Service appeal procedures.

I.

Fein, born May 5, 1940, registered with his Yonkers local board at age 18. He was assigned a II–S student deferment during his undergraduate years at Swarthmore College and, subsequently, during the period of his attendance at Case-Western Reserve University School of Medicine. Upon graduation from medical school, Fein was assigned a II–A occupational deferment because of his internship at Cleveland Metropolitan General Hospital.

In September 1967, while still an intern, Fein wrote his local board "to declare myself a conscientious objector to war and the institution which propagates war, the military." He requested and received SSS Form 150 for conscientious objectors. He promptly completed and returned the form to the local board. . . .

Upon receiving Fein's Form 150 and letters supportive of his claim, the local board invited him to appear personally before it. He did so on November 15, 1967. After the interview the board denied him a I–O classification "at this time." Inasmuch as Fein then held his II–A classification, this action by the board was consistent with Selective Service Regulation 32 C.F.R. §1623.2 providing that a registrant be placed in the lowest class for which he is eligible.

In February 1968, however, Fein was reclassified I–A. He immediately asked for another personal appearance before the board. The request was granted and he appeared on May 27. The board then classified him as I–O and thus gave him his desired conscientious objector classification.

On June 4 the State Director, pursuant to 32 C.F.R. §1626.1, wrote the appeal board requesting an appeal and stating, "It is our opinion that the registrant would not qualify for a I–O classification as a conscientious objector." Notice of this was given Dr. Fein by mail. Fein then wrote seeking "a statement indicating the basis for the State Director's appeal" and an opportunity to reply. No explanation was forthcoming.

The local board forwarded the file to the appeal board. Accompanying the file was a so-called "brief." This, as petitioner has conceded, was merely a summary of the file prepared by a lay employee of the board. The appeal board, by a unanimous 4–0 vote on June 20, classified Dr. Fein I–A and thus rejected his claim to conscientious objector status. The board stated no reason for its decision. Fein was notified of his reclassification.

Under 32 C.F.R. §1627.3 a registrant was not entitled to take an appeal to the presidential, or national, appeal board from an adverse classification by the state appeal board made by a unanimous vote. Fein was in this position. Accordingly, he wrote the National Director of Selective Service in July and asked that the Director appeal on his behalf under 32 C.F.R. §1627.1(a). Fein's letter to the Director was detailed. It emphasized his above-stated beliefs and the way of life to which those beliefs had guided him. "It should be clear, that I am willing to serve my country, but only in activities consistent with my conscience." Fein outlined the administrative proceedings and listed five claimed inequities: (1) the appeal board's rejection, upon the appeal by the State Director, of the local board's classification; (2) the failure of the Director to state the basis for his challenge; (3) the absence of an opportunity to submit supplemental information before the file was forwarded; (4) the absence of an opportunity to rebut the State Director's decision to take an appeal; and (5) the absence of an opportunity for a personal appearance before the appeal board.

On July 31 Fein was ordered to report for induction September 6.

The National Director, however, complied with Fein's request and noted an appeal. Fein's outstanding induction order was canceled. He again asked the State Director for a statement of reasons. He was now advised that in the State Director's opinion he did not qualify for a Class I–O deferment and that the decision to appeal "was based upon the information contained in [his] selective service file."

On November 26, 1968, the national board, by a vote of 3–0, classified Dr. Fein I–A. No reason for this action was stated.

No new order that Fein report for induction has been issued.

Fein then instituted this suit. The complaint alleged that the statute and regulations governing Fein's classification and appeal violated the Due Process Clause of the Fifth Amendment in that they did not provide for a statement of reasons to the registrant for the State Director's decision to appeal, or for the appeal board's subsequent decision denying Fein a I–O classification. It also alleged that the defendants acted unconstitutionally by failing to provide Fein with the statements of reasons, by failing to permit him to submit additional material for consideration by the appeal boards, and by refusing him an opportunity to rebut the State Director's decision to appeal.

The District Court did not reach the merits of the constitutional claims. While expressing concern about Fein's ability to establish jurisdiction, the court assumed, arguendo, that he had done so, but then concluded that the suit was barred by §10(b)(3).

The Second Circuit affirmed. . . .

II.

The case pivots, of course, upon the meaning and reach of §10(b)(3), and this Court's decisions in [Oestereich v. Selective Service Board, 399 U.S. 233 (1968); Clark v. Gabriel, 393 U.S. 256 (1968); Boyd v. Clark, 287 F. Supp. 561 (S.D.N.Y. 1968), affd. 393 U.S. 316 (1969)] . . . and in Breen v. Selective Service Board, 396 U.S. 460 (1970).

Section 10(b)(3) states flatly that a classification decision of the local board "shall be final, except where an appeal is authorized . . ." and that the classification decision on appeal also "shall be final. . . ." It further provides, "No judicial review shall be made of the classification or processing of any registrant . . . except as a defense to a criminal prosecution . . . after the registrant has responded either affirmatively or negatively to an order to report for induction. . . ." Even then, the review "shall go to the question of the jurisdiction . . . only when there is no basis in fact for the classification. . . ."

The "except" clause and the "no basis in fact" language came into §10(b)(3) with the 1967 statute by way of prompt congressional reaction provoked by the Second Circuit's decision in Wolff v. Selective Service Local Bd., 372 F.2d 817 (1967).

Section 10(b)(3), as so amended, was promptly challenged. In *Oestereich* the Court refrained from striking down the statute on constitutional grounds. It held, however, that pre-induction judicial review was available to that petitioner who, as a divinity student, claimed his local board had wrongfully denied him a statutory exemption from military service. To rule otherwise "is to construe the Act with unnecessary harshness." And, "No one, we believe, suggests that §10(b)(3) can sustain a literal reading." This construction, it was said, leaves the section "unimpaired in the normal operations of the Act." . . .

In the companion *Gabriel* case, on the other hand, the registrant was asserting a conscientious objector claim. The Court said: "Oestereich, as a divinity student, was by statute unconditionally entitled to exemption. Here, by contrast, there is no doubt of the Board's statutory authority to take action which appellee challenges, and that action inescapably involves a determination of fact and an exercise of judgment. . . . To allow pre-induction judicial review of such determinations would be to permit precisely the kind of 'litigious interruptions of procedures to provide necessary military manpower' which Congress sought to prevent when it enacted §10(b)(3)." The constitutionality of the statute again was upheld. . . . *Oestereich* was complemented by *Breen* a year later with respect to a registrant statutorily entitled to a deferment rather than to an exemption.

Finally, pre-induction review was denied under §10(b)(3) in Boyd v. Clark, 287 F. Supp. 561 (SDNY 1968), a decision affirmed here, 393 U.S. 316 (1969), with only a single reference to *Gabriel,* decided just four weeks before. In *Boyd,* four registrants, each classified I–A, challenged student deferment on the ground that it discriminated against those financially unable to attend college. They did not otherwise contest their own I–A classifications.

Thus *Oestereich, Gabriel, Breen,* and *Boyd* together establish the principles (a) that §10(b)(3) does not foreclose pre-induction judicial review in that rather rare instance where administrative action, based on reasons unrelated to the merits of the claim to exemption or deferment, deprives the registrant of the classification to which, otherwise and concededly, he is entitled by statute, and (b) that §10(b)(3) does foreclose pre-induction judicial review in the more common situation where the board, authoritatively, has used its discretion and judgment in determining facts and in arriving at a classification for the registrant. In the latter case the registrant's judicial review is confined —and constitutionally so—to the situations where he asserts his defense in a criminal prosecution or where, after induction, he seeks a writ of habeas corpus. By these cases the Court accommodated constitutional commands with the several provisions of the Military Selective Service Act and the expressed congressional intent to prevent litigious interruption of the Selective Service process.

III.

These principles do not automatically decide Fein's case. The doctor, unlike Oestereich and unlike Breen, cannot and does not claim a statutory exemption or a statutory deferment on the basis of objectively established and conceded status. On the other hand, while *Gabriel* focuses on the administrative and discretionary process, it does not necessarily foreclose Fein's claim. This is so because Fein challenges the constitutionality of the very administrative procedures by which, he claims, the presentation of his case was adversely affected. . . .

We again conclude that the line drawn by the Court between *Oestereich* and *Breen,* on the one hand, and *Gabriel* and, inferentially, *Boyd,* on the other, is the appropriate place at which, in the face of the bar of §10(b)(3), to distinguish between availability and unavailability of pre-induction review. We therefore adhere to the principles established by those cases. . . .

The case strikes us, as did *Gabriel,* as representative of a category that, if allowed pre-induction review, would tend to promote the "litigious interruptions of procedures to provide necessary military manpower" that Congress intended to prevent. The conscientious objector claim is one ideally fit for administrative determination. . . .

The judgment of the Court of Appeals is therefore to be affirmed. We express no view upon the merits of Dr. Fein's conscientious objector claim other than to observe the obvious, namely, that his claim is not frivolous.

Affirmed.

B. Consumer Law

1. Description

Consumer law is comprised of several narrow areas of the law, much like business law and environmental law. For example, Articles 2 (Sales) and 3 (Commercial Paper) of the Uniform Commercial Code, discussed in Part D of Chapter 8, are integral parts of consumer law. Many states have enacted consumer protection statutes, such as the Uniform Consumer Credit Code, that are designed to protect the buyer from certain deceptive trade practices.[8] These statutes, as well as such federal statutes as the Federal Consumer Credit Protection Act (commonly called the Truth-in-Lending Act), constitute the major part of consumer law.[9]

Most of these consumer law statutes are of relatively recent origin. However, many statutes have been a part of the American legal system for years, such as the federal and state statutes related to usury and bankruptcy.[10] Under the usury laws the states attempt to protect debtors by limiting the amount of interest that may be charged upon borrowed money. Contracts by which the lender may receive more than the maximum legal interest rate are said to be usurious. Bankruptcy laws have long provided methods for relieving debtors of their obligation to creditors or for postponing the time in which they may make payment to such creditors. According to the United States Constitution, all bankruptcy proceedings are within the exclusive jurisdiction of federal courts.[11] The main purpose of the bankruptcy laws is to relieve honest debtors of the indebtedness, thus allowing them to get back on their feet financially and avoid being indebted for the rest of their lives. The bankruptcy laws also provide a method of dividing the debtor's remaining assets equitably among his or her creditors.

Case law developed in the context of contract and tort law also protects the consumer in sales transactions. Such case law consists primarily of defenses that the consumer can raise in a suit commenced by the seller. In Chapter 8 the doctrine of unconscionability was discussed, illustrating that courts may sometimes relieve a buyer from oppressive obligations.[12] In Chapter 9 it was seen that there is a cause of action in tort based upon fraud and deceit perpetrated by the buyer.[13] In addition, courts will not enforce illegal contracts.[14] An illegal contract is one that is prohibited by statute, is contrary to the common law, or is contrary to public policy—meaning that it tends to injure an important interest of society or interferes with the public health, safety, morals, or general welfare. Other case law defenses that are sometimes used by consumers include the contractual defenses of mutual mistake of fact, breach of warranty, and incapacity (for example, allowing a minor to disaffirm a sales contract).

2. The Federal Truth-in-Lending Act

The purpose of the Truth-in-Lending Act is "to assure a meaningful disclosure of credit terms so that the consumer will be able to compare more readily

---

[8] E.g., West's Annotated California Code, Business and Professional Code, section 17000 et seq. (1969); Colorado Revised Statutes Annotated 6-2-101 et seq. (1973); Vernon's Texas Statutes Annotated, Civil Statutes section 7426 et seq. (1958).

[9] The Federal Consumer Credit Protection Act and the Uniform Consumer Credit Code (not related to, or to be confused with, the Uniform Commercial Code) are discussed in Sections 2 and 3 of Part B of this chapter.

[10] *E.g., West's Annotated California Code,* Civil Code, sections 1916-1 et seq. (1969).

[11] See 11 U.S.C., section 1 et seq.

[12] See Chapter 8, pp. 190.

[13] See Chapter 9, pp. 259–60.

[14] International Dairy Queen, Inc. v. Bank of Wadley, 407 F. Supp. 1270 (D. Ala. 1976); First National Bank of Barron v. Strimling, 241 N.W.2d 478 (Minn. 1976).

the various credit terms available to him and avoid the uninformed use of credit." [15]
The Act does not regulate the interest rates themselves; the rate remains within the
jurisdiction of the states. The thrust of the Act is to *disclose* what the consumer is
paying for the credit. The Act applies only to those transactions in which: (1) the
lender is in the business of extending credit in connection with a loan, a sale, or the
furnishing of services; (2) the debtor is a person (as opposed to a corporation or
other business entity); (3) a finance charge may be imposed; and (4) the credit is
obtained by the consumer primarily for the purpose of personal, family, household,
or agricultural purposes.

The Act accomplishes its objective by requiring disclosure to the customer of all
finance charges, figured annually and expressed as the annual percentage rate
(APR). This is in addition to disclosure of all dollar amounts that the consumer is
required to pay. Included in the finance charge are interest, service charges, loan
fees, points, finders' fees, fees for appraisals, credit reports for investigations, and
any life and health insurance required as a condition of the loan.

The finance charge and APR are made known to consumers through a financing
statement. The statement must be communicated to the consumer before the creditor extends credit, and it must also contain information about charges that may result from a default or late payment and about any property used as security.

The Act also provides for both civil and criminal penalties that may be imposed
when a creditor violates the Truth-in-Lending Act. The Act gives the borrower an
opportunity to rescind or cancel the transaction within a period of seventy-two
hours from the date of the loan or from the date that the borrower is given notice of
such rights, whichever is later.

3. Uniform Consumer Credit Code

As of the end of 1977, the Uniform Consumer Credit Code (UCCC) had
been adopted in eleven states.[16] The purpose of the UCCC is to permit competition
in pricing of borrowed money and obtaining credit in much the same way as the
Truth-in-Lending Act. However, the UCCC goes beyond the Truth-in-Lending Act
in certain respects, such as abolishing usury (thus actually regulating rates of interest) and providing limitations on creditors' remedies. The UCCC also prohibits
the unsolicited distribution of credit cards, regulates the advertising of consumer
credit, and governs home-solicitation sales. The UCCC does not affect the existing
methods of obtaining, perfecting, extending, and terminating security interests in
personal property as governed by Article 9 of the Uniform Commercial Code.

The following excerpt discusses home solicitation (door-to-door sales)—one of
the practices against which the UCCC is designed to protect the consumer:[17]

---

[15] 15 U.S.C., section 1601.

[16] The UCCC was drafted by the National Conference of Commissioners on Uniform State
Laws starting in 1964, with an initial publication date in 1968.

[17] Reprinted from Project, "The Direct Selling Industry: An Empirical Study," 16 *U.C.L.A.
Law Review* 883, 895–903 (1969).

DOOR-TO-DOOR SALES

1. THE PROBLEM

The high-pressure sale can result in the purchase of an item which a consumer neither needs nor desires. Although badgering and physical coercion are sometimes used in door-to-door sales, more subtle and sophisticated techniques are generally employed to achieve this result. The use of psychologically coercive tactics can create pressures equivalent to those associated with the more overt forms of coercion, and can cause with equal effectiveness a breakdown in the traditional contractual concept of equal parties bargaining freely. Thus, the high-pressure sale should be distinguished from both the purely fraudulent sale and the low-income consumer's purchase of poor quality merchandise at an inflated price because of his inability to purchase elsewhere.

2. INCIDENCE OF PRESSURE

High-pressure selling is not unique to door-to-door sales. However, psychological "high-pressure" . . . is particularly common in direct selling. The prevalence of this kind of pressure in door-to-door sales can be traced to the following factors:

a. *The Commission System.* Individual salesmen usually work on a commission rather than a salary basis of compensation. Commissions generally vary between 20 and 50 percent of the retail selling price, depending upon the company and the type of product sold. None of the now common employee benefits such as social security, workman's compensation or retirement plans are available to him because he is designated by virtually all companies as an independent dealer. Under these circumstances, the salesman's entire livelihood depends upon the number of sales he makes. For this reason, even salesmen representing reputable companies may resort to high-pressure techniques.

b. *The Context of the Sale.* Unlike the normal retail sales context where a consumer who feels pressured can leave the store, the context of the door-to-door sale is right in the consumer's own home. Once the salesman gains entrance, the consumer is trapped and, unless he abandons his home, can find relief only by taking affirmative action to remove the salesman. In this constricted atmosphere, pressure may build to the point where the consumer will agree to make a purchase merely to get rid of the salesman. Indeed, this "high-pressure" context is one of the door-to-door salesman's chief advantages; it explains why "getting inside the door" is so important to his success.

c. *The Customer-Salesman Relationship.* Most door-to-door sales are "one shot" affairs. After giving the salesman his order, the customer deals solely with the company. The order is company processed and the goods are delivered by a company representative. Likewise, the company administers the payment plan and handles any subsequent complaints. Under these circumstances, the salesman has little reason to concern himself with the impression he leaves with his customer. Hence, the customer-salesman relationship normally present in retail sales is absent as a bar to "high-pressure" in the direct sale.

d. *Ineffective Company Control.* Even though the use of high-pressure sales techniques is contra to the announced policy of most direct selling companies, their systems of control makes it almost impossible for them to implement this policy. There is a vast distance between the Home Office of most direct selling companies and their field sales personnel. The national hierarchical structure, the most prevalent among those companies studied, typically consists of a large company engaged in multistate operations, with a chain of command established through regional, district, and branch offices located throughout the country. The Branch Office is the closest link that the Home Office has with individual salesmen.

The Branch Manager is the critical factor in this link. He is responsible for recruiting and training sales personnel, assigning territories and establishing sales quotas. Frequently his own salary is based partially upon a percentage of the sales of the people working under him. Moreover, his personal advancement in the company may be tied to the performance of his salesmen. Therefore, it is necessary for the Branch Manager to maintain sufficient pressure upon his sales personnel to keep the sales totals for his office rising at an appropriate rate. As a consequence, the manager may ignore the techniques used by his salesmen and focus only upon their results. In the process he may actually or tacitly encourage his personnel to use any available method to make a sale. Hence, the salesman's only link to the Home Office is likely to prove ineffective as a check upon high-pressure selling.

e. *Industry Beliefs.* Throughout this Project, references are continually made to "reputable" and "disreputable" companies in the direct selling industry. The line between them is usually drawn on the basis of quality prices and sales techniques. However, even the "reputable" companies are objected to for the high-pressure and "gimmickry" which accompany almost all sales pitches. Although some companies have earned a reputation for selling quality products, it nevertheless remains an article of faith within the direct sales industry that gimmickry plus pressure is necessary to sell. The widespread acceptance of this myth has perpetuated the highly-developed and often misleading "high-pressure" sales pitches for which the industry is so well known.

3. LOCATING THE CUSTOMER

Because potential door-to-door consumers do not actively seek out their products, direct sales companies face a unique merchandising problem in attempting to establish customer contact. Some companies believe that the systematic coverage of every residence in a selected neighborhood is the most effective means of maximizing customer contact. Because this type of selling is usually done without any previous customer contact, it is usually called "cold canvassing." Whether or not a company employs "cold canvassing" is generally dependent upon the extent of its product's appeal to the consuming public. Thus, for example, a needed item such as the vacuum cleaner is frequently sold cold door-to-door, while the Fotron Camera, which has a more limited appeal, is never sold in this manner.

Most companies no longer rely on the "cold canvass" to isolate potential customers. More sophisticated marketing methods have been developed to accomplish this objective. One approach, for example, is to first blanket a given geographical area by mail. A return slip is enclosed for interested residents to notify the company. Another approach is to exhibit the company's products at local fairs and other comparable events. Information sign-up cards are used to compile a list of prospective customers. Still another method is to advertise the company's product in the media at an incredibly low price. Come-on statements such as "first time in this area" or "limited time only" are used to whet the consumer's interest. At the same time, the company prominently offers a "free home demonstration" or "free estimate" and indicates a phone number that can be called day or night to arrange an appointment. Callers are generally promised a "free gift" and are assured that "there is absolutely no obligation." Numerous home decorating services such as carpeting and upholstering are marketed in this manner.

One of the most commonly used techniques relies upon information obtained from sources which specialize in locating prospective customers. Large numbers of telephone calls are made by these people and information is solicited under the guise of taking a "survey" or compiling a "neighborhood listing." All of the questions asked relate directly to the subject's desirability as a potential customer. For example, one person who responded to a "survey" gave her age, salary, make and year of her car, age of television and if color or not, and her preference for cash or credit as a means of payment. With these few questions the caller is able to construct a consumer profile which is revealing enough to establish the subject as a target for a variety of sales attempts. Lists of such "prime prospects" are prepared and sold to direct sales companies. Salesmen then contact only preselected consumers and are able to tailor their openings to the individual "needs" of the people to whom they are selling.

In a variant of this approach, company representatives telephone every resident in a specially selected geographical area. The residents are told that they have been chosen to compete in a contest and that if they answer some questions correctly they will win a prize. The questions are generally quite simple. For example, the subject may be asked to identify the last three Presidents of the United States. If the questions are answered successfully, the subject is informed that he has become eligible to purchase the company's product at a "drastically reduced" price. If the subject fails to respond correctly, he may nevertheless be offered the same option as a "consolation" prize. If he expresses interest, a follow-up salesman is dispatched to the customer's home to close the transaction.

In theory, it would seem to be more likely that high-pressure sales techniques will be used on a consumer solicited during a "cold canvass" than on one chosen by one of the more specific solicitation methods. In the latter instances, the consumer has already indicated some interest in the product and presumably it conforms to his individual needs. For this reason, the salesman should not have to resort to high pressure to make a sale. The problem with this analysis is that there is frequently a gross disparity between the deal that is advertised and the actual transaction into which the consumer enters. The terms of the transaction are almost never clearly stated and the product sold may not even be the one that was advertised. Thus, the more selective marketing methods often amount to no more than the most effective means of isolating those consumers who are most susceptible to high-pressure sales techniques.

4. Getting Inside the Door

If the salesman has obtained a fixed interview time beforehand, he does not have the problem of gaining entry. More often, however, he must face another of the unique problems encountered in direct selling—getting inside the door. To maximize his effectiveness and thereby increase the probability of making a sale, the salesman must gain entry into the consumer's home before any part of the sales talk, or "pitch," is attempted. Without entry, the consumer retains the power to easily foreclose the salesman's presentation at any time by making a convenient excuse and closing the door. This power makes it difficult, if not impossible, to create the necessary sales environment. Once physical entry into the home is obtained, however, a good salesman will persevere until his pitch is completed unless the disinterested consumer is somehow able to convince him that there is no chance to make a sale. In that event, it is to the salesman's advantage to leave quickly so that he can find a better prospect.

The most direct method of gaining entry is for the salesman to simply outline briefly some vague purpose and then ask, "May I come in for a minute?" Often he will not even wait for a reply before entering. More frequently, however, he must resort to some form of deception or gimmickry to gain entry. Thus, it is common for salesmen to open with the disclaimer "I'm not selling anything." This is highly recommended within the industry as a standard part of any successful approach. The salesman will then represent that he is taking a survey, introducing a new product, wants only an endorsement, is doing a special promotion in connection with a national program, merely wants to place the goods in the consumer's home for the neighbors to see, or even that he knows the consumer's absent spouse. In any event, the door-to-door salesman rarely begins by stating his actual purpose.

The "free gift" is another generally recognized gimmick used throughout the direct selling industry to obtain entry. Gifts may actually be free, or their cost may be included in the sale price of the product that is being merchandised. They tend to be very inexpensive items, ranging from a small cosmetic aid given by the Fuller Brush man to a bottle of perfume given by a pots and pans salesman. The value depends upon the nature of the product being sold. The gift flatters the consumer while arousing interest sufficient to enable the salesman to get into the door. This is because it usually is offered upon the contingency that the consumer will allow the salesman to demonstrate his product. The gift may also be used to obtain a "referral sale." The salesman offers a discount or gift in return for which the buyer must give the name of a friend or relative that is a likely sales prospect. By using the buyer as a reference and opening with "Mrs. Buyer just purchased one of my products and *she* thought that you might be interested," the salesman may frequently gain an advantage in obtaining entrance.

The contest is similar to the gift as a means of achieving entry. A real prize is awarded to preserve the legitimacy of the contest, but the main objective is to obtain the names and addresses of prospective customers. One pots and pans salesman interviewed stated that he usually wore a large button advertising a radio contest for assorted items including his product. He walked the sidewalks of downtown Los Angeles during working hours and gave out entry blanks to young women while casually asking if they were married, whether they lived with their family, and if they possessed a good set of pots and pans. Those who gave a negative reply to all three questions were solicited on the spot for an appointment later. A variant of the contest technique is to visit the "lucky" participant at her home to inform her that she has won the second prize, a discount on the salesman's pots and pans. These approaches are effective and the price may be adjusted upward to cover the discount.

5. THE SALESMAN'S PITCH

A thoroughly trained salesman can, and sometimes to make a sale must, overwhelm the unwary consumer. His "pitch," or sales talk, must be designed to make the sale quickly and with as much certainty as possible. The well-organized pitch must proceed from point to point without giving the consumer an opportunity to reflect upon his economic position. The pitch must either create a need in the consumer's mind or sufficiently demonstrate actual need so that the consumer will agree to make a purchase.

a. *A Sample Pitch.* The approaches to creating a successful pitch vary. Many direct selling organizations recommend to their salesmen a standardized, highly refined talk. Others set no guidelines whatsoever and let their salesmen use any method they wish. Many sales organizations, however, thoroughly drill their salesmen to overcome the most popular objections to their products with memorized answers. Being properly prepared to meet any contingency is a highly developed professional skill and in some firms training never ends. . . .

U.C.C.C. SECTIONS 2.501–2.505

§2.501. Definition: "Home Solicitation Sale"

"Home solicitation sale" means a consumer credit sale of goods, other than farm equipment, or services in which the seller or a person acting for him engages in a personal solicitation of the sale at a residence of the buyer and the buyer's agreement or offer to purchase is there given to the seller or a person acting for him. It does not include a sale made pursuant to a preexisting revolving charge account, or a sale made pursuant to prior negotiations between the parties at a business establishment at a fixed location where goods or services are offered or exhibited for sale.

§2.502. Buyer's Right to Cancel

(1) Except as provided in subsection (5), in addition to any right otherwise to revoke an offer, the buyer has the right to cancel a home solicitation sale until midnight of the third busi-

ness day after the day on which the buyer signs an agreement or offer to purchase which complies with this Part.

(2) Cancellation occurs when the buyer gives written notice of cancellation to the seller at the address stated in the agreement or offer to purchase.

(3) Notice of cancellation, if given by mail, is given when it is deposited in a mailbox properly addressed and postage prepaid.

(4) Notice of cancellation given by the buyer need not take a particular form and is sufficient if it indicates by any form of written expression the intention of the buyer not to be bound by the home solicitation sale.

(5) The buyer may not cancel a home solicitation sale if the buyer requests the seller to provide goods or services without delay because of an emergency, and

   (a) the seller in good faith makes a substantial beginning of performance of the contract before the buyer gives notice of cancellation, and
   (b) in the case of goods, the goods cannot be returned to the seller in substantially as good condition as when received by the buyer.

(6) If a home solicitation sale is also subject to the provisions on debtor's right to rescind certain transactions (Section 5.204), the buyer may proceed either under those provisions or under this Part.

§2.503. Form of Agreement or Offer; Statement of Buyer's Rights

(1) In a home solicitation sale, unless the buyer requests the seller to provide goods or services without delay in an emergency, the seller must present to the buyer and obtain his signature to a written agreement or offer to purchase which designates as the date of transaction the date on which the buyer actually signs and contains a statement of the buyer's rights which complies with subsection (2).

(2) The statement must
   (a) appear under the conspicuous caption: "Buyer's Right to Cancel," and
   (b) read as follows: "If this agreement was solicited at your residence and you do not want the goods or services, you may cancel this agreement by mailing a notice to the seller. The notice must say that you do not want the goods or services and must be mailed before midnight on the third business day after you sign this agreement. The notice must be mailed to: _____

_____
(insert name and mailing address of seller)

If you cancel, the seller may keep all or part of your cash down payment."

(3) Until the seller has complied with this section the buyer may cancel the home solicitation sale by notifying the seller in any manner and by any means of his intention to cancel.

§2.504. Restoration of Down Payment; Retention of Cancellation Fee

(1) Except as provided in this section, within 10 days after a home solicitation sale has been cancelled or an offer to purchase revoked the seller must tender to the buyer any payments made by the buyer and any note or other evidence of indebtedness.

(2) If the down payment includes goods traded in, the goods must be tendered in substantially as good condition as when received by the seller. If the seller fails to tender the goods as provided by this section, the buyer may elect to recover an amount equal to the trade-in allowance stated in the agreement.

(3) The seller may retain as a cancellation fee 5 per cent of the cash price but not exceeding the amount of the cash down payment. If the seller fails to comply with an obligation imposed by this section, or if the buyer avoids the sale on any ground independent of his right to cancel provided by the provisions on the buyer's right to cancel (subsection (1) of Section 2.502) or revokes his offer to purchase, the

seller is not entitled to retain a cancellation fee.

(4) Until the seller has complied with the obligations imposed by this section the buyer may retain possession of goods delivered to him by the seller and has a lien on the goods in his possession or control for any recovery to which he is entitled.

§2.505. Duty of Buyer; No Compensation for Services Prior to Cancellation

(1) Except as provided by the provisions on retention of goods by the buyer (subsection (4) of Section 2.504), within a reasonable time after a home solicitation sale has been cancelled or an offer to purchase revoked, the buyer upon demand must tender to the seller any goods delivered by the seller pursuant to the sale but he is not obligated to tender at any place other than his residence. If the seller fails to demand possession of goods within a reasonable time after cancellation or revocation, the goods become the property of the buyer without obligation to pay for them. For the purpose of this section, 40 days is presumed to be a reasonable time.

(2) The buyer has a duty to take reasonable care of the goods in his possession both before cancellation or revocation and for a reasonable time thereafter, during which time the goods are otherwise at the seller's risk.

(3) If the seller has performed any services pursuant to a home solicitation sale prior to its cancellation, the seller is entitled to no compensation except the cancellation fee provided in this Part.

---

4. Creditors' Remedies

The basic remedies available to creditors have already been outlined in the discussion of judgments in Part G, Chapter 6.[18] Most jurisdictions still permit what is called the cognovit note, in which the purchaser agrees in advance of a default that if he or she defaults in the future, the seller may automatically obtain a judgment and take immediate possession of the items sold and secured on credit, rather than having to file a legal action and obtain a judgment prior to levy and execution upon any assets. In the absence of such "confessions" of judgment, creditors in consumer transactions must follow the same procedures in foreclosure and execution as required of any other judgment creditor. In consumer transactions it is more common that a creditor is secured by the items sold to the consumer. This is in contrast to a situation in which the judgment is obtained by a person who is entirely unsecured, as in the case of *Pope* v. *Drake*. If the creditor is secured, he or she is entitled to delivery of the secured piece of property after obtaining a judgment against the debtor consumer.

In the event a creditor obtains a judgment against a debtor consumer, certain statutory exemptions available to the debtor protect certain property against persons who do not have a security interest in it. These exemptions vary from state to state, but generally include a homestead exemption, which secures a certain amount of equity in a person's home against attachment, levy, and sale by general creditors. These statutes also exempt such items of personal property as an automobile, furni-

---

[18] See Chapter 5, pp. 118–19.

ture and household goods, tools of trade, and various clothing and jewelry. In addition, they exempt a certain percentage of a person's wages from garnishment by an unsecured creditor.

C. Environmental Law

1. Historical Development

Since the late 1960s environmental law has developed more rapidly and widely than any other area of the law. This development created a need for lawyers with expertise in the environmental field, which is only beginning to be filled. Until very recently there was no such thing as a well-trained environmental lawyer. Now, almost solely as a result of the outpouring of federal environmental regulations, the field has become a specialty requiring lawyers in varying capacities. Environmental law is practiced by government lawyers in the federal and state regulatory agencies, such as the Environmental Protection Agency; by industry lawyers whose responsibilities are to keep abreast of requirements imposed on their companies and to protect the companies from unreasonable regulation; and by lawyers representing the public environmental groups, such as the Natural Resources Defense Council, Environmental Defense Fund, Sierra Club, and Friends of the Earth.

Over the last ten years, events such as the 1968 Santa Barbara oil spill, the construction of the Alaska pipeline, and the oil and gas shortages of the summer of 1973 and winter of 1977, respectively, have focused the public's attention on environmental and energy issues. American society has developed an economic superstructure and a standard of living that both allows and requires serious federal and state attention to these matters.

In terms of long-range national goals, economic progress and environmental protection do not necessarily conflict or compete with each other. However, the immediate result of the environmental regulation imposed on industry and the economy in general has been a tremendous increase in government regulation and in the cost of doing business. Yet society has demanded that a clean environment be given a priority equal to a strong economy. The fact that both concerns now occupy equal stature in national policy, and that our economy and overall governmental structure continue to flourish, is a tribute to leaders in industry, government, and environmental groups. Environmental lawyers in all three areas deal with an increasingly complex set of laws and regulations, some of which are discussed next.

2. National Environmental Policy Act of 1969

The first major event in environmental regulation was the passage of the National Environmental Policy Act of 1969 (NEPA).[19] The impact of NEPA has been much greater than anticipated, and surprising in view of its brevity and

---

[19] National Environmental Policy Act, 42 U.S.C., sections 4321, 4331–35, 4341–47.

the ease with which it became law. It is only a few pages long, and at first it was uncontroversial, becoming law by unanimous consent in the Senate, with only fifteen nays in the House, after just two days of hearings in both houses.

The most significant provision contained in NEPA is §102(2)(C), which provides that "all agencies of the Federal Government shall include in every major Federal action significantly affecting the quality of the human environment, a detailed statement by the responsible official on the environmental impact of the proposed action." This is the basis for all the federal environmental impact statements that are so often publicized and so often controversial. Environmental impact statements have been the subject of several hundred lawsuits since 1970, when NEPA actually became law. NEPA established a new decision-making procedure for all agencies of the federal government. Federal environmental impact statements are required when a federal agency or department or other federal entity takes some action considered a "major federal action" that "significantly affects the quality of the human environment." Predictably, there has been much litigation on the threshold question of whether a particular action falls within the meaning of these phrases in §102(2)(C). In one case in which the Law Enforcement Assistance Administration issued a grant to build a state correctional facility, the court deemed the grant to be a "major federal action" requiring the preparation of an impact statement, despite the routine nature of the grant program.[20] Yet in another case a training exercise involving 900 marines in Reid State Park, Maine, was held by the court not to be a major federal action.[21] There remains a great inconsistency among federal courts as to what constitutes a "major federal action."

Other controversies under §102(2)(C) have questioned the adequacy of impact statements. For example, does the statement adequately examine "alternatives to the proposed action" as required by §102(2)(C)(iii)? The Act does not *appear* to mandate any particular substantive environmental standards. Thus it would seem that even if unfortunate environmental impacts result from a particular project, as long as there is proper consideration of the impacts and of possible alternatives in the course of the review process, and as long as the decision reached by the federal agency as to whether to take the action is not arbitrary, then the decision will pass judicial scrutiny. NEPA establishes a decision-making procedure and requires "rigorous exploration and objective evaluation of alternative actions that might avoid some or all of the adverse environmental effects." [22]

Even though neither the Act nor its legislative history mention judicial review, the courts have vigorously reviewed federal agency compliance with NEPA. As mentioned, the Act appears to refer only to procedural, not substantive, compliance. Yet in the courts' efforts to require informed agency decision making and to require the discussion and consideration of alternatives and greater public accessibility, many decisions have become so involved in NEPA's implementation that they are

---

[20] Ely v. Velde, 451 F.2d 1130 (4th Cir. 1971).
[21] Citizens for Reid State Park v. Laird, 336 F.Supp. 783 (D. Me. 1972).
[22] Council on Environmental Quality Guidelines, 36 Fed. Reg. 7725 (1971).

tantamount to substantive opinions on the agency action. Indeed NEPA has been interpreted by some courts to contain substantive provisions in §101, which reads in part as follows:

> *§101.* (a) The Congress, recognizing the profound impact of man's activity on the interrelations of all components of the natural environment, particularly the profound influences of population growth, high-density urbanization, industrial expansion, resource exploitation, and new and expanding technological advances and recognizing further the critical importance of restoring and maintaining environmental quality to the overall welfare and development of man, declares that it is the continuing policy of the Federal Government, in cooperation with State and local governments, and other concerned public and private organizations, to use all practicable means and measures, including financial and technical assistance, in a manner calculated to foster and promote the general welfare, to create and maintain conditions under which man and nature can exist in productive harmony, and fulfill the social, economic, and other requirements of present and future generations of Americans.
>
> (b) In order to carry out the policy set forth in this Act, it is the continuing responsibility of the Federal Government to use all practicable means, consistent with other essential considerations of national policy, to improve and coordinate Federal plans, functions, programs, and resources to the end that the Nation may—
>
> 1. Fulfill the responsibilities of each generation as trustee of the environment for succeeding generations;
> 2. Assure for all Americans safe, healthful, productive, and esthetically and culturally pleasing surroundings;
> 3. Attain the widest range of beneficial uses of the environment without degradation, risk to health or safety, or other undesirable and unintended consequences;
> 4. Preserve important historic, cultural, and natural aspects of our national heritage, and maintain, wherever possible, an environment which supports diversity, and variety of individual choice;
> 5. Achieve a balance between population and resource use which will permit high standards of living and a wide sharing of life's amenities; and
> 6. Enhance the quality of renewable resources and approach the maximum attainable recycling of depletable resources.

Courts, in reviewing the agencies' decisions under this section, have found in some cases that the proposed actions are not permitted under NEPA.[23] The first opinion stating the view that NEPA imposes judicially reviewable substantive requirements was the case of *Environmental Defense Fund* v. *Corps of Engineers,* in which the court stated:[24]

> Given an agency obligation to carry out the substantive requirements of the Act, we believe that courts have an obligation to review substantive agency decisions on

---

[23] See, e.g., Citizens to Preserve Overton Park v. Volpe, 401 U.S. 402 (1971); Akers v. Resor, 339 F.Supp. 1375 (W.D. Tenn. 1972); Environmental Defense Fund v. Froehlke, 473 F.2d 346 (8th Cir. 1972); Conservation Council of North Carolina v. Froehlke, 473 F.2d 664 (4th Cir. 1973); Sierra Club v. Froehlke, 486 F.2d 946 (7th Cir. 1973).
[24] Environmental Defense Fund v. Corps of Engineers, 470 F.2d 289 (8th Cir. 1972).

the merits. Whether we look to common law or the Administrative Procedure Act, absent "legislative guidance as to reviewability, an administrative determination affecting legal rights is reviewable unless some special reason appears for not reviewing. . . ." Here, important legal rights are affected. NEPA is silent as to judicial review, and no special reasons appear for not reviewing the decision of the agency. To the contrary, the prospect of substantive review should improve the quality of agency decisions and should make it more likely that the broad purposes of NEPA will be realized.

More recent cases continue to follow the interpretations set forth in the *Environmental Defense Fund* case. The trend is clearly away from reviews that are limited to procedural compliance and in the direction of reviews that more precisely define the allowable scope of agency discretion under NEPA.[25]

NATURAL RESOURCES DEFENSE COUNCIL, INC.
v.
MORTON

458 F.2d 827 (1972)

United States Court of Appeals, District of Columbia Circuit

LEVENTHAL, Circuit Judge:

This appeal raises a question as to the scope of the requirement of the National Environmental Policy Act (NEPA) that environmental impact statements contain a discussion of alternatives. Before us is the Environmental Impact Statement filed October 28, 1971, by the Department of Interior with respect to its proposal, under §8 of the Outer Continental Shelf Lands Act, for the oil and gas general lease sale, of leases to some 80 tracts of submerged lands, primarily off eastern Louisiana. . . . Opening of bids for the leases was scheduled for December 21, 1971, and three conservation groups brought this action on November 1, to enjoin the proposed sale. On December 16, the District Court held a hearing and granted a preliminary injunction enjoining the sale of these leases pending compliance with NEPA.

The Government appealed, and filed a motion in this court for summary reversal and immediate hearing. We granted the immediate hearing, and on December 20, heard the presentations and issued an order permitting the bids to be received on condition they remain unopened pending further order of the court. As to the motion for summary reversal, we conclude that this must be denied. . . .

What NEPA infused into the decision-making process in 1969 was a directive as to environmental impact statements that was meant to implement the Congressional objectives of Government coordination, a comprehensive approach to environmental management, and a determination to face problems of pollution "while they are still of manageable proportions and while alternative solutions are still available" rather than persist in environmental deci-

---

[25] Several circuits now adhere to the position that NEPA requires substantive judicial review of agency decisions. See Sierra Club v. Morton, 514 F.2d 856 (D.C. Cir. 1975), stating at note 25 that six circuits follow this interpretation, and citing numerous cases. For a more detailed treatment of this issue, see also articles cited in E. Dolgin and T. Guilbert, eds., *Federal Environmental Law* (St. Paul. West Publishing Co., 1974), p. 303n.230.

sion-making wherein "policy is established by default and inaction" and environmental decisions "continue to be made in small but steady increments" that perpetuate the mistakes of the past without being dealt with until "they reach crisis proportions." S. Rep. No. 91–296, 91st Cong., 1st Sess. (1969) p. 5.

. . . In this as in other areas, the functions of courts and agencies, rightly understood, are not in opposition but in collaboration, toward achievement of the end prescribed by Congress. So long as the officials and agencies have taken the "hard look" at environmental consequences mandated by Congress, the court does not seek to impose unreasonable extremes or to interject itself within the area of discretion of the executive as to the choice of the action to be taken.

Informed by our judgment that discussion of alternatives may be required even though the action required lies outside the Interior Department, the Secretary will, we have no doubt, be able without undue delay to provide the kind of reasonable discussion of alternatives and their environmental consequences that Congress contemplated.

Motion denied.

Environmental impact statements are not required under NEPA where a state, an individual, a corporation, or other private entity takes an action that significantly affects the human environment—these are not *Federal* actions." In such cases protection of the environment is regulated through compliance with *state* environmental impact statement requirements and with federal and state laws that deal with specific activities, such as the discharge of materials into waterways and the emission of pollutants into the air.

3. The Environmental Protection Agency and Other Federal Statutes

NEPA did not establish the Environmental Protection Agency (EPA). EPA came into existence by Executive Order shortly after the passage of NEPA, in 1970, and it has assumed the role of environmental policeman through its regulatory and enforcement functions as granted in that order. As a matter of course, almost all environmentally related legislation that Congress passes delegates to EPA the authority to implement such legislation. Thus the Agency has grown rapidly and now has over 10,000 federal employees and ten large regional offices throughout the United States.

Prior to 1970 federal responsibility for pollution control regulation was scattered among several agencies. For example, water pollution was the responsibility of the Interior Department, and air pollution was regulated by the National Air Pollution Control Administration, located in the Department of Health, Education and Welfare. Now, according to Reorganization Plan Number 3 of 1970, which created the Environmental Protection Agency, EPA controls the major programs regulating air and water pollution, environmental radiation, pesticides, solid waste, and other matters that affect the environment. The head of the agency reports directly to the President.

a. The Federal Water Pollution Control Act

One of the major federal statutes that EPA enforces is the Federal Water Pollution Control Act (FWPCA).[26] The Act was originally passed in 1948, but attained its present form through comprehensive amendments passed in 1972 and 1977. The FWPCA as it now exists is designed to accomplish three basic objectives: (1) the regulation of discharges of pollutants from particular "point sources," such as industrial plants, municipal sewage treatment plants, and agricultural facilities; (2) regulation of oil spills and hazardous substances; and (3) financial assistance for sewage-treatment plant construction. The Act requires that persons who cause such discharges into water must adopt a certain level of control technology by dates set forth in the Act. Numerous standards and timetables have been specified in guidelines and regulations issued by the administrator of the Environmental Protection Agency. These include detailed requirements for particular industries and activities, such as the chemical industry, the oil industry, and sewage treatment facilities. The basic enforcement mechanism for the standards set forth in the Act and EPA's regulations is the "National Pollution Discharge Elimination System" permit system. EPA has various administrative and judicial remedies against violations of the conditions and standards specified in these permits issued to dischargers.

b. The Clean Air Act of 1970

The Clean Air Act (as amended in 1970 and 1977) is to air pollution control what the Federal Water Pollution Control Act is to water pollution control.[27] As with the FWPCA, the EPA has been given authority to regulate and implement the Clean Air Act. The Act is subdivided into three titles. Title I includes the general policy statement, authorizations of programs for financial and technical assistance, research authorizations, and the overall framework for the control of pollutants and emissions from stationary sources. Title II includes controls relating to emissions from moving sources, primarily automobiles, although it also pertains to buses, trucks, and airplanes. Title III includes various administrative and judicial authorizations.

The Act provides that all emission sources and other factors contributing to air pollutants that adversely affect public health and welfare and "result from numerous or diverse mobile or stationary sources" are subject to a comprehensive regulatory program developed through several steps. The steps are accomplished through a joint federal-state program, with each level of government having particular responsibilities under the general supervisory authority of the EPA administrator. The Act grants enforcement authority to the EPA administrator, including fines up to $25,000 per day and imprisonment up to one year.

---

[26] Federal Water Pollution Control Act, 33 U.S.C., section 1151 et seq.
[27] Clean Air Act, 42 U.S.C., section 1857 et seq.

c. Miscellaneous Federal Statutes

The following list of existing federal statutes illustrates the broad scope of environmental regulation as undertaken by the federal government:

Water

Coastal Zone Management Act of 1972, 16 U.S.C. Sections 1451–64 (Supp. 1973)

Federal Water Project Recreation Act, 16 U.S.C. Sections 4001–12 through 4601–21 1970)

Federal Hazardous Substances Act, 15 U.S.C. Section 1261 et seq. (1970)

Federal Water Pollution Control Act, 33 U.S.C. Section 1151 et seq.

Outer Continental Shelf Lands Act, 43 U.S.C. Section 1337(a) (1970)

Rivers and Harbors Act of 1899, 33 U.S.C. Section 407 (1970)

Wild and Scenic Rivers Act of 1968, 16 U.S.C. Sections 1271–87 (1970)

Air

Clean Air Act, 42 U.S.C. Sections 1857 et seq.

Wildlife and Wilderness

Anadromous Fish Conservation Act, 16 U.S.C. Sections 757a–f (1970)

Estuarine Areas Act, 16 U.S.C. Sections 1221–26 (1970)

Fish and Wildlife Coordination Act of March 10, 1934, 16 U.S.C. Sections 661–67e (1970)

Marine Protection, Research and Sanctuaries Act of 1972, 33 U.S.C. Sections 1401–44 (Supp. 1973)

National Wilderness Act of 1964, 16 U.S.C. Sections 1131–36 (1970)

Organic Act of the National Parks Service of 1960, 16 U.S.C. Section 1 et seq. (1970)

Other

Antiquities Act of 1906, 16 U.S.C. Sections 431–33 (1970)

Federal Environmental Pesticide Control Act of 1972, 7 U.S.C. Section 136 et seq. (Supp. 1973)

Federal Food, Drug and Cosmetic Act, 21 U.S.C. Sections 346, 346a, 348 (1970)

Federal Insecticide, Fungicide and Rodenticide Act, 7 U.S.C. Section 135 et seq. (1970)

Federal Land Policy and Management Act of 1976, 43 U.S.C. Sections 661 et seq., 931 et seq., 1701 et seq.

Historic Sites Act of 1935, 16 U.S.C. Sections 461–67 (1970)

National Environmental Policy Act, 42 U.S.C. Sections 4321, 4331–35, 4341–47

National Historic Preservation Act of 1966, 16 U.S.C. Sections 470–470m (1970)

Noise Control Act of 1972, 42 U.S.C. Section 4901 et seq. (Supp. 1973)

Occupational, Safety and Health Act, 29 U.S.C. Section 651 et seq. (1970)

Poison Prevention Packaging Act, 15 U.S.C. Sections 1471–73 (1970)

Resource Conservation and Recovery Act of 1976, 42 U.S.C. Section 6901 et seq. (1970)

Surface Mining Control and Reclamation Act of 1977, 30 U.S.C. Sections 1201–1328 (Supp. 1978)

Technology Assessment Act of 1972, 2 U.S.C. Section 471 et seq. (Supp. 1973), 42 U.S.C. Section 862 (Supp. 1973)

This list is not exhaustive and of course does not include any *state* environmental legislation. It is easy to see, however, that the federal government, through its many agencies, regulates many aspects of our lives in terms of environmental controls.

QUESTIONS

1. Is the basic concept of separation of power in danger of being destroyed by Congress's delegation of power to administrative agencies?

2. If the U.S. Department of Transportation promulgated a rule stating that all persons must wear their automobile seat belts whenever they are driving, who could challenge such a rule? How would someone challenge the rule? What, if any, court would have jurisdiction to review the agency's action?

3. President Carter has been attempting to persuade Congress to establish a federal consumer-protection agency. What arguments can be made in favor of and against the formation of such an agency?

4. Which of the following actions would require the preparation of an environmental impact statement under Section 102(2)(C) of the National Environmental Policy Act? Explain why or why not: (a) permission by the New York Port Authority for the Concorde SST to land at JFK Airport; (b) construction of a dam in California by the Army Corps of Engineers; (c) building of the Alaska oil pipeline; (d) construction of an office building in downtown Chicago; (e) issuance of a lease to an oil company by the state of Michigan allowing drilling for oil in Lake Superior.

11

Criminal Law

A. Substantive Criminal Law

1. Definition

A crime is an act or omission prohibited by a statute enacted for the public's protection, the violation of which is prosecuted by the state in a judicial proceeding in its own name, and for which a fine or imprisonment may be imposed.[1] A crime is a wrong committed against the public, as distinguished from a civil wrong, which is committed against an individual. In a criminal action a representative of the state or the people, namely the prosecuting or district attorney (or city attorney if a violation of a municipal ordinance is involved) seeks to have a fine imposed upon the defendant, or seeks his or her imprisonment, or possibly both. A few jurisdictions have instituted programs of state-provided compensation to the victims of crimes.[2] However, in the vast majority of cases there is no pecuniary compensation in any respect to the complaining or injured party in a criminal action. The victim must normally resort to a civil action in order to recover damages.

As stated in the definition, one necessary element for an act or omission to be a crime is that it be prohibited by *statute*. This was not always true. There was a time when a person could be convicted of a crime, jailed, and fined, even though the crime he or she was charged with was not codified. In other words there were crimes whose elements were established by case law rather than legislation. Even now a few states have not abolished common law crimes.[3] Except for these states, unless

---

[1] See 21 *AmJur* 2d, "Criminal Law," section 1.

[2] See, e.g., Revised Code of Washington Annotated 7.68010–7.68910 (1976). There are even some states that have begun programs in which the defendant works for the injured party in order to pay for the damage caused by his or her criminal conduct. These states are North Carolina, Florida, and Pennsylvania.

[3] "While the court has no right to invent new crimes, it has the right to ascertain and declare what were crimes at common law." 21 *AmJur* 2d, Criminal Law, section 10, citing State v. Schleifer, 99 Conn. 432, 121 A. 805 (1923). However, there are no federal common law crimes. United States v. Rosa, 404 F.Supp. 602 (W.D. Penn. 1975).

the act is prohibited by statute at the time it is committed, it does not constitute an offense punishable by the state or the federal government; no crime exists, regardless of the actor's criminal intent or state of mind.[4]

Because the great majority of modern criminal statutes in all jurisdictions have developed out of the common law definitions of crimes, we will refer frequently to common law elements throughout this chapter. We will compare the original common law crimes with the present-day criminal statutes, in order to explain the basis for certain elements in the latter, to show the logic behind these requirements, and to place them in their proper perspective. In the majority of jurisdictions, where the crimes are codified, the statutory law is still construed in light of the common law as defined early in English history, because most of the terms in the statutes have well-known and identifiable meanings relating back to that time.[5]

Before examining selected crimes, this chapter will first present some principles and concepts that are common to all crimes.

2. Classification of Crimes

Most jurisdictions classify crimes as felonies, misdemeanors, or petty offenses, depending upon the grievousness of the offense and the severity of the punishment for it.[6] In a transposed definition, the punishment for a particular crime usually determines whether it is a felony, misdemeanor, or petty offense under modern statutes. This inverse manner of categorizing crimes is not as illogical as it may seem at first glance, because it is simply assumed that no one will be imprisoned in a penitentiary for any crime that is not historically regarded as a serious crime, that is, a felony. With this in mind, most jurisdictions state that a felony is a crime that is punishable by imprisonment in the state penitentiary. There are several classes of felonies. A misdemeanor or a petty offense is usually a crime for which the punishment is other than imprisonment in the penitentiary; there are several classes of misdemeanors and petty offenses.[7]

Crimes are also classified according to their nature or the degree of moral turpitude involved. There are two broad categories: *malum in se* and *malum prohibitum*. The former includes most felonies and misdemeanors and generally encompasses all crimes that are morally reprehensible in and of themselves.[8] The term defined

---

[4] United States v. Nill, 518 F.2d 793 (5th Cir. 1975); Hotch v. United States, 212 F.2d 280 (9th Cir. 1954).

[5] State v. Pyles, 86 W. Va. 636, 104 S.E. 100 (1920). See also State v. Woodworth, 234 N.W.2d 243 (N.D. 1975), where the court stated that the common law definition applies unless redefined by state law.

[6] State v. Lewis, 142 N.C. 626, 55 S.E. 600 (1906). However, if the legislation designates an offense as a misdemeanor or felony, such designation is conclusive even if the punishment provided would indicate otherwise. People v. Harvey, 307 N.Y. 588, 123 N.E.2d 81 (1954).

[7] Merritt v. Jones, 533 S.W.2d 497 (Ark. 1976); Commonwealth v. Sheeran, 345 N.E.2d 362 (Mass. 1976); People v. Collins, 345 N.E.2d 730 (Ill. App. 1976). See also 21 *AmJur* 2d, "Criminal Law," sections 19 and 21.

[8] J. Miller, *Handbook of Criminal Law* (St. Paul: West Publishing Co., 1934), p. 23. See also *Black's Law Dictionary,* 4th ed. (St. Paul: West Publishing Co., 1968), p. 1112.

literally means "bad in itself." Thus these crimes are inherently wrong and threaten a breach of public order, or injury to person or property. The *malum prohibitum* crimes are offenses that are bad only because they are prohibited by a statute.[9] These are largely regulatory offenses with relatively minor penalties, such as traffic offenses, illegal sales of liquor, or unintentional sales of impure or mislabeled food and drugs. They are not otherwise wrongful or immoral.

3. Basic Elements of a Crime and Proof of Guilt

Just as the establishment of a *prima facie* case is necessary for recovery in a civil action, criminal law requires a similar showing of the necessary basic elements in order for the prosecution to establish that a particular crime has been committed. Every crime is made up of two components: the *actus reus* (the act) and the *mens rea* (the mental state).[10] The *actus reus* is the particular culpable act of the specific crime involved. It may consist of a voluntary physical act specifically forbidden by law, or it may be an omission or failure to perform an act that the law requires a person to perform.[11] Mere thoughts are insufficient to constitute the *actus reus;* there must be some overt act.[12] In some circumstances, however, speech may constitute the *actus reus.*[13] In no situation does the law punish a person for mere criminal thoughts or unexecuted intent to commit a crime. If no act has been done to further the wrongful intent, there is no social harm sufficient to justify any criminal sanctions.

The second element of every crime—the *mens rea*—is a subjective one, that is, the presence of a culpable state of mind, which must accompany the *actus reus.* It could be described as the necessary criminal intent, except that there are crimes whose elements are satisfied by criminal negligence. Therefore the term *intent* is not sufficiently inclusive.

There are varying degrees or levels of *mens rea;* a state of mind that may be sufficiently culpable for one crime will not necessarily satisfy the *mens rea* requirement for another crime. There are three levels of *mens rea*:

a. General intent: This is the intent to perform a prohibited act. General intent is sufficient for crimes for which a voluntary performance of the prohibited act constitutes an offense, regardless of whether the person intended to violate the law. Examples would be most traffic offenses (sometimes called civil offenses) or the delivery of liquor to a person under the age of twenty-one years, whether or not the defendant was aware that the recipient was below the minimum legal

---

[9] See *Black's Law Dictionary,* p. 1112, citing People v. Pavlic, 227 Mich. 562, 199 N.W. 373 (1924).

[10] People v. Gray, 344 N.E.2d 683 (Ill. App. 1976).

[11] State v. Laemoa, 533 P.2d 370 (Ore. App. 1975).

[12] An overt act or a specific omission to act must occur in order to establish the existence of a criminal offense. People v. Shaughnessy, 319 N.Y.S.2d 626, 66 Misc.2d 19 (1971).

[13] See R. Perkins, *Criminal Law,* 2d ed. (Mineola, N.Y.: The Foundation Press, 1969), pp. 549, 616, 635.

age. In these cases the law presumes the general intent, as evidenced by the commission of the act.[14]

b. Specific intent: This state of mind is required for many crimes. The accused must be shown to have had a specific state of mind in addition to the intent to perform the act. Such specific-intent crimes require by definition an element such as malice, knowledge, willfulness, or fraud.

c. Criminal negligence: This is the lowest of the three levels of *mens rea* required for criminal liability and is usually sufficient only when a grievous harm to the victim is involved. This level of culpability is a conscious disregard of a substantial risk of which a reasonable person would have been aware. The standard required to establish criminal negligence is higher than the standard required for civil negligence, that is, a greater probability of harm or a greater degree of unreasonableness is necessary.[15]

If the prosecution fails to establish the presence of the type of intent required for a particular crime, it may nevertheless succeed in convicting for a lesser, included offense. For example, if the prosecution is unable to prove the specific intent required for murder, it may still be possible to convict the defendant for a lesser degree of homicide, such as involuntary manslaughter, which requires only a general intent. The intent is determined by looking at the circumstances surrounding the offense, such as the suspect's acts and statements during the perpetration of the offense and any statement or confession that was made before or after it. Many jurisdictions have statutes specifically stating that a minor of a certain age cannot be held guilty for a crime, on the theory that a child is not capable of possessing or forming a criminal state of mind. Instead the child is subject to various children's codes that do not require the *mens rea* concept in order to discipline juveniles.[16]

All material elements or requirements of the crime as set forth in the statute must be proven "beyond a reasonable doubt," whereas there must be a preponderance of the evidence in civil cases. Preponderance of the evidence requires only that the "scales be tipped" in favor of one party or the other, in the opinion of the fact finder.[17] Proof beyond a reasonable doubt requires a greater degree of certainty on the part of the fact finder. "[P]roof beyond a reasonable doubt is such proof as precludes every reasonable hypothesis except that which it tends to support and is consistent with the defendant's guilt and inconsistent with any other rational conclu-

---

[14] State v. Jamison, 110 Ariz. 245, 517 P.2d 1241 (1974); State v. Lassley, 545 P.2d 379 (Kan. 1976).

[15] Commonwealth v. Olivo, 337 N.E.2d 904 (Mass. 1975) (higher degree of negligence must be shown than for liability in a civil action; conduct must be wanton or flagrant); Commonwealth v. Tackett, 299 Ky. 731, 187 S.W.2d 297 (1945); State v. Cope, 204 N.C. 28, 167 S.E. 456 (1932); People v. Angelo, 246 N.Y. 451, 159 N.E. 394 (1927).

[16] See, e.g., Georgia Code Annotated, section 26-701 (1972) (must be 13 years old at time of alleged crime); Illinois Annotated Statutes 38, section 6-1 (1961) (must be 13 years of age). The constitutionality of such statutes was upheld in People v. Boclaire, 337 N.E.2d 728 (Ill. App. 1975). The concept of the lack of capacity of minors was also recognized at common law. Porter v. State, 327 So.2d 820 (Fla. App. 1976).

[17] Stuebgen v. State, 548 P.2d 870 (Wyo. 1976).

sion."[18] The majority of jurisdictions allow such a determination to be arrived at by circumstantial evidence, rather than requiring that there be an eyewitness or other direct identification or proof.[19] Earlier cases, particularly under the common law, required that there be absolute proof in order to establish that the result of the defendant's act was criminally caused. A few jurisdictions still require that direct evidence of murder be presented. Usually this means eyewitness testimony or unusually strong circumstantial evidence.[20]

4. Causation

Just as proximate cause is an essential element of the *prima facie* case of negligence, there must be a causal relationship between the act of the accused and the harm or loss suffered, in order for the defendant to be convicted of any crime. The act must be both *actually* and *legally* the cause of the harm. Basically the rules for causation in criminal law are the same as in the law of torts, except that the range of foreseeability expands in criminal law to encompass more remote victims. Thus, where the act is unlawful, the defendant may be held liable even for consequences that would be deemed unforeseen and unintended under tort principles.[21]

Most jurisdictions use the "but for" test in order to establish actual causation. That is, the question is whether the harm would have occurred but for the act of the accused. If the combination of two acts is responsible for the harm, each actor will be guilty.[22] For example, defendants X and Y both inflict wounds on the victim, who would have recovered from either wound by itself; however, the combination of the two causes the victim's death. In this case both defendants may be found guilty of murder.

In other jurisdictions the "substantial factor" test is used. Under this test the question is whether the defendant's act was a substantial factor in bringing about the harm.[23] For example, the defendant threatened the victim with a gun, as a result of which the victim became frightened and suffered a fatal heart attack. The fact that the victim had a preexisting heart condition is not material to this analysis, because the defendant's act caused the fright that was the substantial factor in bringing about the fatal heart attack. In another example, the defendant stabbed and killed the victim, shortly after he or she had been *mortally* wounded by another person.

[18] State v. Hall, 165 Conn. 599, 345 A.2d 17 (1973). However, the jury is not required to find that all possible explanations constitute a "reasonable doubt." People v. Johnson, 32 Ill. App.3d 36, 335 N.E.2d 144 (1975).

[19] State v. Steward, 219 Kan. 256, 547 P.2d 773 (1976); State v. Jackson, 28 N.C. App. 136, 220 S.E.2d 186 (1975); Williams v. State, 535 S.W.2d 637 (Tex. Crim. App. 1976).

[20] See, e.g., State v. Collington, 259 S.C. 466, 192 S.E.2d 856 (1972) (direct evidence must be used if obtainable); State v. Durham, 195 S.E.2d 144 (W. Va. 1973) (direct evidence of the death of the victim is required, but circumstantial evidence is permissible and sufficient to prove causation of the death).

[21] 21 *AmJur* 2d, "Criminal Law," section 83.

[22] Payne v. Commonwealth, 255 Ky. 533, 75 S.W.2d 14 (1935); Hall v. State, 199 Ind. 592, 159 N.E. 420 (1927).

[23] See W. Clark & W. Marshall, *Law of Crimes* (Chicago: Callaghan & Co., 1958), section 4.01.

In this case the defendant as well as the other person would be guilty of homicide. The fact that the victim would have died without the action of the defendant is not material, since that action was in fact a substantial factor in bringing about the death that occurred.

The substantial factor test is sometimes regarded as a test to determine only legal rather than factual or actual causation. The but for test in some jurisdictions is limited to determining the actual causation.[24] In addition, legal causation concerns the question of whether any unforeseeable independent intervening factors are relevant to the causation analysis. Unlike civil law, contributory negligence on the part of the victim is not relevant and has no bearing on the defendant's guilt. However, that negligence may constitute such a substantial factor as to supersede the requirement of causation by the defendant, in which case the necessary causation element would be absent from the *prima facie* case, thereby relieving the defendant of any guilt.

5. Parties to the Crime

Culpability for a criminal act is often not limited only to the person who actually committed the act. Since common law days it has been recognized that culpability extends also to persons who significantly aided in causing the crime. Such persons are held liable in different degrees as parties to the criminal act. At common law these parties to a felony were divided into two classes: principals and accessories. The actual perpetrator of the felony was called the principal in the first degree. Such a perpetrator needed not commit the crime by his or her own hand but might do so through an inanimate agency, such as using the mail system to defraud the victim, or by an innocent human agent, such as causing a person to administer poison to the victim.[25]

An abettor at common law, that is, one who was either present at the scene of the felony or was aiding in a direct manner, was considered a principal in the second degree. An abettor is one who incites, counsels, demands, aids, or abets the commission of the felony.[26] An example of a principal in the second degree would be one who is stationed outside the place of the commission of the felony as a lookout while the felony is being committed.

At common law one who was not present at the scene of the crime, but aided or incited its commission, was considered an accessory before the fact. There had to be some active furtherance or encouragement of the crime in order for one to be an accessory before the fact. Mere knowledge that the offense was to be committed was not sufficient.[27] The question of what constitutes incitement or abetting has been the

---

[24] See Clark & Marshall, section 4.01.

[25] State v. Scott, 80 Conn. 317, 68 A. 258 (1907); Hazel v. United States, 353 A.2d 280 (D.C. Ct. App. 1976); People v. Nunnley, 344 Ill. App.3d 4, 339 N.E.2d 537 (1975); State v. Minton, 234 N.C. 716, 68 S.E.2d 844 (1952).

[26] State v. Thibodeau, 353 A.2d 595 (Me. 1976); McBryde v. State, 352 A.2d 324 (Md. App. 1976) (the person's presence need not be actual; it may be constructive).

[27] Ray v. State, 330 So.2d 580 (Miss. 1976); State v. Branch, 288 N.C. 514, 220 S.E.2d 495 (1975).

subject of numerous cases and considerable controversy. *Incitement* generally includes any encouragement to the perpetrator to commit the crime, either by words, gestures, or other conduct. *Abetting* has come to mean assisting the commission of the crime in any manner.[28]

The final category of parties to the crime under the common law was that of accessory after the fact. An accessory after the fact was one who received, comforted, or assisted another person—knowing that the latter had committed a felony—for the specific purpose of hindering that person's arrest. In order to be guilty of being an accessory after the fact, the defendant must have had actual knowledge that the perpetrator committed the felony, and the perpetrator must have actually committed it. The comfort or assistance required to establish guilt must have been given to the perpetrator personally, such as in the form of shelter, disposing of incriminating evidence, using force to protect the perpetrator or help him or her escape, or by giving false information to the governmental officials investigating the crime.[29]

In misdemeanors under the common law, all parties except accessories after the fact were treated as principals. Accessories after the fact were not considered to be parties to the misdemeanor at all, and there was no penalty for comforting or aiding its perpetrator.

These various classes of parties to criminal acts were recognized under common law principles, prior to the time that the criminal laws were codified in state statutes and in federal criminal law. These common law classifications of parties have now been largely limited or abolished. The majority of jurisdictions now tend to treat all persons who are concerned in the commission of a crime as principals, whether or not they are actual perpetrators or merely aiding or abetting in the crime, and whether or not they were present at the scene of the crime. Modern law has merged the common law classifications of principal in the first degree, principal in the second degree, and accessory before the fact. However, the common law classification of accessory *after* the fact has largely been kept intact. Thus, even under modern statutes, a person who gives aid or comfort to the perpetrator of a felony with the intent of aiding his or her escape is an accessory after the fact, provided that the

---

[28] Gurrieri v. Gunn, 404 F.Supp. 21 (C.D. Cal. 1975) ("test is whether the accused in any way, directly or indirectly, aided the perpetrator by acts or encouraged him by words or gestures"); United States v. Rosa, 404 F.Supp. 602 (W.D. Pa. 1975) (mere presence is not enough). See also State v. Dowd, 28 N.C. App. 32, 220 S.E.2d 393 (1975). United States v. Goodwyn, 410 F.Supp. 52 (E.D. Pa. 1976) states that the defendant must have had criminal intent and knowledge of the substantive offense in order to be convicted of aiding and abetting.

[29] Roberts v. State, 318 So.2d 166 (Fla. App. 1975); Collison v. State, 333 N.E.2d 787 (Ind. App. 1975). Examples of conduct constituting an accessory after the fact include harboring or concealing a criminal; providing a weapon, transportation, disguise, or other means of escape; concealing or destroying evidence of the crime; warning a criminal of impending discovery or apprehension; or volunteering false information to a law enforcement officer. Commonwealth v. Wright, 344 A.2d 512 (Pa. Super. 1975); see 18 Pennsylvania Criminal Statutes Annotated, section 5105.

accessory knows that the perpetrator has committed the felony, and provided that the felony was actually committed.[30]

B. Ancillary Crimes

The crimes of conspiracy, solicitation, and attempt are called ancillary because one or more of them generally precedes and is only incidental or ancillary to the commission of some other, substantive crime. They are nevertheless independent and complete crimes in themselves. All three consist of preliminary conduct that, although constituting a crime in itself, is aimed toward the commission of a later substantive crime that need not necessarily take place in order for the defendant to be convicted of the ancillary crime. Society regards these ancillary crimes as conduct that is sufficiently outside acceptable boundaries to justify independent criminal sanctions.

1. Conspiracy

A majority of state statutes provide criminal sanctions for "an agreement or understanding between two or more persons to commit a crime together with an overt act in pursuance of such commission." [31] Most jurisdictions require that there be a "real agreement, combination, or confederation with a common design" in order to satisfy the element of "agreement or understanding." However, there need be no express words or written agreement; a tacit understanding satisfies this element. On the other hand, a mere passive awareness or cognizance of the planning of the crime is insufficient. A further aspect of "agreement or understanding" is that a party may be a conspirator even though he or she does not know the identity of his or her coconspirator. An example of this would be the defendant obtaining narcotics through an intermediary from an unidentified source for the purpose of selling those narcotics. In this case the unidentified source and the defendant would be coconspirators, even though the defendant was unaware of the identity of the other person.[32]

---

[30] United States v. Blanton, 531 F.2d 442 (10th Cir. 1975); Dozier v. State, 343 N.E.2d 783 (Ind. 1976); State v. Dirgo, 196 Neb. 36, 241 N.W.2d 351 (1976).

[31] United States v. King, 521 F.2d 61 (10th Cir. 1975); State v. Bindyke, 288 N.C. 608, 220 S.E.2d 521 (1975).

[32] United States v. Van Hee, 531 F.2d 352 (6th Cir. 1976); United States v. Crocker, 510 F.2d 1129 (10th Cir. 1975) (agreement need not take any particular form but must be a meeting of the minds in the common design, purpose, or objects of the conspiracy). This element is further explained in the following cases: United States v. Bastone, 526 F.2d 971 (7th Cir. 1975) (common goal); United States v. Peterson, 524 F.2d 167 (4th Cir. 1975) (distinguished from aiding and abetting); Commonwealth v. Minnich, 344 A.2d 525 (Pa. Super. 1975) (common-understanding element needs no formal agreement); United States v. James, 528 F.2d 999 (5th Cir. 1976); United States v. Edwards, 488 F.2d 1154 (5th Cir. 1974); United States v. Purin, 486 F.2d 1363 (2d Cir. 1973); United States v. Gentile, 530 F.2d 461 (2d Cir. 1976) (need not know identity of coconspirators nor the scope of their activities); United States v. Braverman, 522 F.2d 218 (7th Cir. 1975) (need not know identity nor the number of coconspirators).

The second element is that the agreement or understanding must be "between two or more persons." Analysis of this requirement illustrates the fundamental purpose and theory behind the law of conspiracy. Why has the law taken a situation in which a substantive crime may not have actually been committed and made it into a separate crime? As we will see later, if *one* person were to take an overt act in planning to commit a crime alone, having decided to commit the crime, that individual would not be subject to arrest for the commission of any crime. However, if the same intent and overt act in planning the crime is coupled with an agreement or understanding with another person, then both individuals are subject to arrest for the crime of conspiracy, even though their actions and states of mind are no different than those of the single individual planning such a crime. The law, then, singles out this particular situation and makes it a separate offense because the coupling of one person's criminal intent with another person's criminal intent is regarded as a much more dangerous situation, and one which justifies otherwise premature criminal sanctions in order to protect society and to prevent the dangerous situation from proceeding further. The gist of the crime of conspiracy is that it takes at least one more person than is required to commit the substantive crime itself.[33] For example, if it takes two persons to commit the substantive crime, then it will take *more than* two to be guilty of conspiring to commit that crime. In crimes in which consent is an element, such as adultery, incest, bigamy, and bribery, there can be no prosecution for conspiracy if there are only two participants to be involved in the substantive criminal act. In such cases it would take the two consenting parties plus one additional party in order for anyone participating to be convicted for the crime of conspiracy. If there are only two persons involved, the theory that a dangerous situation has been created (because one more person than is required to commit the crime has participated in its planning) does not apply, because that one additional person is not present.

The third element in the definition of conspiracy is that the agreement or understanding between the two or more persons must be "to commit a crime." [34] It is not sufficient that the parties agree to an act or to accomplish a purpose that is unlawful. The prosecution must also show that all parties *knew* the act or purpose to be unlawful. A reasonable mistake or a reasonable lack of knowledge of the law may be a valid defense to a charge of conspiracy.[35] If a person conspires to commit a number of different crimes, he or she will nevertheless be guilty of only one conspiracy, provided such multiple crimes are part of a "single criminal episode." [36]

The last requirement is that of an "overt act." Under modern statutes no person may be convicted of a conspiracy to commit a crime unless at least one of the conspirators performs an overt act to carry out such a conspiracy. At common law it

---

[33] This is known as Wharton's rule. See United States v. Finazzo, 407 F. Supp. 1127 (E.D. Mich. 1975).

[34] State v. Karsten, 194 Nebr. 227, 231 N.W.2d 335 (1975).

[35] United States v. Bridgeman, 523 F.2d 1099 (D.C. Cir. 1975).

[36] United States v. Bastone, 526 F.2d 971 (7th Cir. 1975); United States v. Campanale, 518 F.2d 352 (9th Cir. 1975); State v. Georgi, 339 A.2d 268 (R.I. 1975).

was unlawful merely to have the combination or agreement; no further overt act was necessary, on the rationale that conspiracy was so evil in itself that it should be punished regardless of any further evil that it sought to accomplish. The modern statutes' requirement of an overt act coincides with the generally accepted principle in our society, and the First Amendment principle, that persons should not be punished for mere thoughts or ideas. However, the overt act required in furtherance of the conspiracy does not have to be a very substantial one. It need not be an attempt to perpetrate the crime.[37] In addition, an overt act committed by any one of the conspirators renders all the conspirators guilty as having satisfied all the elements of the crime.[38]

PEOPLE v. HINTZ

69 Mich. App. 207, 244 N.W.2d 414 (1976)

Court of Appeals of Michigan

T. M. BURNS, Presiding Judge.

The defendants were charged in separate counts with conspiring to aid and abet in the placing of an explosive with intent to destroy and conspiracy to murder one Myron J. Whipple. After a nonjury trial, the court found defendants guilty of the second count, conspiracy to murder. The defendants were sentenced to 15 to 25 years in prison.

In his opinion, the trial court set out the following statement of facts:

"On April 25, 1974, during the evening hours, an explosion occurred outside of the front portion of the residence of Robert Schlosser, a Midland Police Officer, located at 408 Cottonwood Street, in the City of Midland. Fragments of pipe, residue of powder and a piece of burnt dynamite fuse were discovered at the scene of the explosion as the result of an investigation made at the scene.

"Portions of the front of the house were damaged, as well as the porch on the residence. The explosion apparently occurred in front of a picture window in the front of the home.

"The explosion was under investigation by the law enforcement authorities until the arrest of the Defendants on June 20, 1974.

"On or about April 26, 1974, one Edward Shannon was talking with the Defendant, Lawrence Hintz, at the home of Shannon on St. Charles Street in the City of Midland. During the course of this conversation, the Defendant, Lawrence Hintz, stated to Shannon substantially as follows: Did you read about the big bang? That he had thrown a bomb at Schlosser's house; that it didn't do the damage that they intended; that the bomb bounced away from the house.

"A short time later, on or about the 1st of May, another conversation occurred with the Defendant, Lawrence Hintz, at the home of Mr. and Mrs. Wayne Gardner, located at 4512 W. Wackerly Road. The Gardners and the Shannons were friends and were visiting and

---

[37] United States v. Eucker, 532 F.2d 249 (2d Cir. 1976) (must be a planned act; if intended to facilitate the conspiracy, it is sufficient as an overt act); People v. Ambrose, 28 Ill. App.3d 627, 329 N.E.2d 11 (1975) (act of planning is sufficient overt act; defendant had "cased the joint" in preparation for a future armed robbery—held sufficient as an overt act).

[38] United States v. James, 528 F.2d 999 (5th Cir. 1976) ("The fact that a conspirator is not present at, or does not participate in, the commission of any of the overt acts does not, by itself, exonerate him.").

eating a meal and Lawrence Hintz was present at this time. Mrs. Shannon and Mrs. Gardner were talking together regarding the explosion at the Schlosser home on April 25th which had been mentioned in the newspaper. The newspaper article did not give the name of the officer, nor had either Mrs. Gardner nor Mrs. Shannon referred to the Schlosser home. Defendant, Lawrence Hintz, overhearing the conversation, said—"You mean Schlosser's home. Next time there will be a bigger bang." The fact that the Defendant, Hintz, referred to the location of the explosion as being the Schlosser home drew the attention of Mrs. Shannon and Mrs. Gardner because of the fact as stated above that the name had not been previously mentioned and they had, apparently, no knowledge whose home it was.

"A short time later, the Defendant, Lawrence Hintz, came to the farm of Edward Shannon and stated that he wished to obtain some more dynamite fuses and that he wanted Shannon to make some bombs for him. It appears that approximately two weeks prior to this conversation that Shannon had given the Defendant, Lawrence Hintz, some dynamite fuses at his request, the Defendant stating at that time that he wanted to blow a stream (apparently the stunning of fish). The Defendant stated at this time that his brother, Gregory, had hidden the fuses previously given to him and that he, therefore, needed some more. He further stated that he and Thomas Hintz, his cousin, desired to make seven bombs in all; that three of these bombs were to be used in Midland—one against Myron Whipple, a detective in the Sheriff's Department; one against William Maxwell, a Midland County Sheriff's Officer; and one against Robert Schlosser, a Midland City Police Officer, being the same police officer referred to hereinbefore.

"Edward Shannon lives in the City of Midland, at 425 St. Charles Street. He was employed at the time of the occurrences as a custodian for the Midland Public Schools. He also operated a farm which he owned in Homer Township, Midland County. Shannon was acquainted with both Defendants, but had known Lawrence Hintz for a number of years and was quite friendly with him.

"On or about the 2nd or 3rd of May, the Defendant, Lawrence Hintz, came to the Shannons' home on St. Charles Street and stayed for the evening meal. During this visit Shannon asked the Defendant if he still intended to go through with the making of bombs. The Defendant answered that he did. Shannon then informed the Defendant that if he desired him to make bombs that he (Lawrence) would have to furnish the pipe, the caps for the pipe and the powder. Lawrence also stated at this time that he and his cousin, Thomas, wanted the bombs.

"Shortly after this conversation Lawrence Hintz delivered to Edward Shannon some pipe, caps and four pounds of powder, making the delivery at Shannon's farm in Homer Township. The powder was Hercules smokeless powder of a type readily purchased at a sporting goods store.

"Shannon discussed these events with his wife and they both became concerned about the information that had been conveyed to them and it was decided that Shannon would contact Detective Whipple, which he did on or about May 1, 1974, advising him of the conversations that he had had with Lawrence Hintz, as well as the other facts in connection therewith. At this time Detective Whipple took a statement and arranged to have Shannon work with him and the Michigan State Police. Shannon's kitchen at his farm was wired by the State Police with a tape recording device and arrangements were made to place a body transmitter with Shannon to be used by him whenever the opportunity arose and arrangements could be made to have State Police officers listening in the immediate vicinity.

"On or about May 8, 1974, the Defendant, Lawrence Hintz, again came to the farm home to talk with Shannon about the building of bombs and they, at this time, discussed the matter including the size of the bombs that should be used, the length of the fuses that should be used. At this time Defendant, Lawrence, stated that Thomas was supposed to come to this meeting but that he had to work and couldn't make it. Lawrence stated that Thomas wanted the bombs right away. The next day Shannon met Lawrence Hintz on St. Charles Street in the City of Midland. At this time Lawrence wanted to get together with Shannon and with his cousin, Thomas. He also asked Shannon if he could make the bombs right away. . . .

"It appears that Shannon was having contact with Lawrence Hintz on almost a daily basis during the months of May and into the month of June. In the latter part of May, Lawrence informed Shannon that Thomas Hintz wished to obtain an electric bomb to be attached to Whipple's car. A short time later Lawrence delivered to Shannon a set of spark plug wires, as well as connectors for the spark plugs and a distributor of a type commonly obtainable from an automobile supply store. These were delivered to Shannon in order to enable him to build a bomb to be placed in Whipple's car which would detonate when the ignition key was turned on. Lawrence stated that Thomas had asked for the electric bomb.

"On or about the 25th of May, a conversation occurred between Shannon and Thomas Hintz at which time Thomas stated that there were several bombings that he wanted to accomplish stating that he wanted to blow up Myron Whipple, John Lapp (a Sheriff's Department Officer), and Schlosser. He also stated that he was intending to bomb another State Police Officer in Lansing and another one in Grand Rapids.

". . . Shannon discussed with Thomas Hintz the fact that he would place a pipe bomb which he had made in his pick-up truck and that his truck would be parked at Central Junior High where Shannon worked on the evening of June 20.

"On this particular evening, Detective Whipple was at a point where he could observe the pick-up truck of Edward Shannon, parked by the school. At 10:20 P.M. Thomas Hintz came to the truck, removed an article and placed it in his car. Thomas Hintz was driving a Buick Skylark. At 10:30 P.M. that evening the State Police stopped Defendant, Thomas Hintz's car

and removed the pipe bomb from the car. . . .

"There was a great deal of testimony in the case from expert witnesses. This expert testimony established the fact that the powder furnished by Defendant, Lawrence Hintz, to Shannon was of the same type, to-wit: Hercules smokeless, as that used in the bomb which had been exploded at the Schlosser home on the 25th of April 1974. It was also shown that a fragment from the bomb exploded at the Schlosser residence was of the same type of pipe that had been furnished by the Defendant, Lawrence Hintz, to Shannon. . . ."

The trial court found that there was a conspiracy between defendants Hintz to use explosive devices in order to injure or kill Schlosser. He found that both defendants made statements and took action in furtherance of the conspiracy to make another attempt on the life of Schlosser and that the conspiracy broadened to include other police officers, including Whipple. The court found that both defendants knew of the plan and intended to inflict great bodily harm upon Whipple calculated to cause his death.

Both defendants appeal their convictions and sentences.

The principal arguments of the defendants on appeal are that the evidence was legally insufficient to support a verdict of guilty of conspiracy and that the evidence was insufficient to prove guilt beyond a reasonable doubt.

Criminal conspiracy is a mutual understanding or agreement between two or more persons, express or implied, to do or accomplish some criminal or unlawful act. To prove conspiracy in the instant case, it must be established that the defendants intended to murder Whipple, and to establish that intent, there must be evidence of *knowledge* of the unlawful purpose of murder. Furthermore, it must be proven that that intent, including that knowledge, was possessed by both Thomas and Lawrence Hintz. Cf. People v. Atley, 392 Mich. at 310, 220 N.W.2d 465.

"The gist of the offense of conspiracy lies in the unlawful agreement between two or more persons. [Citations omitted.] Direct proof of agreement is not required, nor is it necessary that a formal agreement be proven. It is sufficient if the circumstances, acts, and conduct of the parties establish an agreement in fact. [Citations omitted.]

"Furthermore, conspiracy may be established, and frequently is established by circumstantial evidence, [Citations omitted] and may be based on inference." People v. Atley at 311, 220 N.W.2d at 471.

Most of the evidence against the defendants came from the testimony of Edward Shannon, pertinent parts of which are as follows:

"*A*. He [Lawrence Hintz] said that him [Lawrence Hintz] and Tom wanted some bombs. They wanted seven. And I asked him what he wanted them for. And he said that they wanted to use three right here in Midland. And I asked what for. And he told me one for Myron Whipple, one for a fellow in the Sheriff's Department by the name of Maxwell, and one for Mr. Schlosser. . . .

"*A*. I told him [Lawrence Hintz] that if he wanted the bombs made he had to furnish the materials to do it. I would furnish the wick. . . .

"*A*. He [Lawrence Hintz] brought some pipe caps and chunks of pipe; he brought powder, he brought—well, it was a four pound can pretty near full of powder. . . .

"*Q*. Where were these items delivered to you at?

"*A*. At my home in town.

"*Q*. Why were they delivered to you?

"*A*. I was asked to make an electrical bomb to blow Myron Whipple's car up. . . ."

Defendants make a forceful argument concerning the sufficiency of the evidence, but after a painstaking review of the transcripts and exhibits, we find that the argument must fail. While the record before us indicates that a less than perfect case of criminal conspiracy was made out by the prosecutor, there was sufficient evidence to find the defendants guilty beyond a reasonable doubt of criminal conspiracy to murder Officer Whipple.

There was no proof that Thomas, Lawrence and Shannon met together at any one time and planned or agreed to kill Whipple with an explosive device. Such ideal evidence of a conspiracy is rarely found. The prosecutor must, perforce, rely upon circumstantial evidence and reasonable inferences drawn from proven facts to make his case. . . .

Does the record support a finding that Lawrence Hintz withdrew from the conspiracy before it came to fruition?

The following trial testimony of Shannon raises an issue of Lawrence's withdrawal from the conspiracy:

"*Q*. When was the last time you had any contact with Larry Hintz prior to their arrests?

"*A*. It was around the last part of May.

"*Q*. And where was this at?

"*A*. At my home.

"*Q*. Why was Larry at your home?

"*A*. Larry had stopped over to—after work. He was real upset. He said that Tom had been pestering him at work and what we were doing was getting too big for him. He was getting out of it. And he wanted me to get out of it. . . .

"*Q*. Is that the last time you saw Larry Hintz?

"*A*. It was the last time that I saw him. Yes. . . .

"*Q*. Did he indicate any way to you whether or not he didn't want to be involved with the Whipple situation?

"*A*. All Larry said was he didn't want anything more to do with the whole deal.

"*Q*. Were those his exact words?

"*A*. Those were his exact words."

It is generally recognized that once formed, the conspiracy continues to exist until consummated, abandoned or otherwise terminated by some affirmative act.

"Where an agreement to commit a crime constitutes a completed conspiracy without any overt act, it is held that an alleged withdrawal by one of the conspirators before anything is done in furtherance of the agreement is no atonement and will not justify reversal of a verdict of guilty of conspiracy."

In Michigan, allegation and proof of an overt

act in furtherance of the illegal agreement is not required to prove criminal conspiracy.

In the instant case, Lawrence's "withdrawal" from the conspiracy was ineffectual; it was too little, too late. The expressed intention of "getting out of it" came after he had actively participated in the planning of the murders and manufacture of the bomb. There is no indication that Lawrence took any steps to prevent further criminal activity in furtherance of the conspiracy. . . .

We find no reversible error.

Affirmed.

---

2. Solicitation

Except as to bona fide acts of persons authorized by law to investigate and detect the commission of offenses by others, a person is guilty of criminal solicitation if he or she commands, induces, entreats, or otherwise attempts to persuade another person to commit a felony, whether as principal or accomplice, with the intent to promote or facilitate the commission of that crime, and under circumstances strongly corroborative of that intent.[39]

It is important that the crime of solicitation be carefully distinguished not only from the two other ancillary crimes but from the relationship of the principal and accessory as well. Solicitation is the inducing or counseling of another to commit the crime, and it is immaterial whether the person counseled actually committed the crime, whether he or she took the counseling seriously or not, or whether he or she was even capable of committing the crime. Generally both common law and modern statutes require no additional act beyond inducing the commission of the crime.[40] However, it is possible that if the person solicited did proceed to commit the crime, then the party who would otherwise be guilty of solicitation may now be guilty as an accessory before the fact to the completed offense. However, even if the person solicited did commit the crime, the solicitor cannot be convicted of *both* the solicitation *and* the substantive crime as an accessory before the fact. As distinguished from conspiracy, one cannot be convicted of both the substantive crime and the solicitation. In addition, conspiracy requires an agreement or understanding, but the crime of solicitation does not.

3. Attempt

Attempt is the intent to commit a crime, accompanied by an act toward the commission of the crime, but failing in such commission.[41] An analysis of this crime

---

[39] People v. Gordon, 120 Cal. Rptr. 840 (Cal. App. 1975). Most modern statutes limit the crime of solicitation to situations where specified crimes are solicited. See, e.g., West's Annotated California Penal Code, Section 653f (1970).

[40] The crime itself need not ever be committed. Greenblatt v. Munro, 161 Cal. App.2d 596, 326 P.2d 929 (1958); State v. Ciocca, 125 Vt. 64, 209 A.2d 507 (1965). The commission of the crime may even be impossible. Benson v. Superior Court of L.A. County, 57 Cal.2d 240, 368 P.2d 116 (1962). The crime is complete even if the person solicited could not have acquiesced in the scheme. State v. Keen, 25 N.C. App. 567, 214 S.E.2d 242 (1975).

[41] See R. Perkins, *Criminal Law* (Mineola, N.Y.: The Foundation Press, 2nd ed., 1969) pp. 552–77.

calls for examination of only two requirements: intent and overt act. First there must be an intent to do a particular act that if completed would be a particular substantive crime.[42] If the act intended would not be a crime if completed, then the defendant cannot be guilty of an attempt, although the defendant may believe that he or she would have been committing a crime by performing such an act. For example, if the defendant intends to pass currency which he or she believes to be counterfeit, and the currency is in fact genuine, the defendant could not be convicted of any crime. The crime of attempt must be connected with a specific and particular crime. That is, there is no crime just called "attempt." It must be attempted murder, attempted robbery, attempted burglary, etc. Thus this crime always involves prosecution for attempt of a substantive crime.

The crime of attempt requires an overt act closer to the commission of the substantive crime than the crime of conspiracy. Mere planning and preparation may be sufficient for the overt act requirement in conspiracy, whereas in order for a defendant to be guilty of attempt, a further step toward accomplishing the intended crime must be made.

The interpretation of the requirement of the overt act under the crime of attempt is a classic example of the problem of rendering useful and practical a broad legal doctrine. Somewhere between the formation of the criminal intent to commit a substantive crime and the actual commission of that crime, an overt act is performed that goes far enough to offend the public and to constitute criminal attempt. At what point does mere preparation end and attempt begin? In order to answer this question, most courts apply tests or various key phrases such as "substantial step" or "dangerously near." [43] The fact finder in the trial considers whether the defendant came dangerously near the commission of the crime or even commenced the consummation of that crime. The answer to these questions will ultimately be a subjective determination. However, useful guidelines make the analysis easier and give these legal principles greater uniformity. No legal principle can absolutely answer the question of what constitutes the dangerously near act. However, most people in society will agree within a certain range as to what is dangerous and what is not.

In the case of Lynnette ("Squeaky") Fromme's attempt to assassinate former President Ford in 1976, she actually pointed the gun at the president and attempted to pull the trigger. This was surely dangerously near the commission of the crime of murder and thus constituted attempted murder. But what if the defendant had merely purchased the gun? This would seem to be mere preparation, not commencement of the consummation of murder. However, what if the gun had been purchased, loaded, and placed on the table to be taken in five minutes by Fromme to

---

[42] State v. Vitale, 23 Ariz. App. 37, 530 P.2d 394 (1975); State v. Curry, 43 Ohio St.2d 66, 330 N.E.2d 720 (1975). Such intent may be implied, rather than expressed. People v. Cheatem, 35 Ill. App.3d 414, 342 N.E.2d 410 (1976).

[43] Hutchinson v. State, 315 So.2d 546 (Fla. App. 1975) ("approximate accomplishment" of the crime); People v. Anderson, 22 Ill. App.3d 679, 318 N.E.2d 238 (1974) ("substantial step"); State v. Stewart, 537 S.W.2d 579 (Mo. App. 1976) (beyond mere preparation, but need not be ultimate step toward last act of the crime); People v. Distefano, 382 N.Y.S.2d 5, 345 N.E.2d 548, 38 N.Y.2d 640 (1976) ("very near" accomplishing the crime).

the place of the attempted murder? What if she had purchased and loaded the gun, left it in her car five blocks away from the park where the President was to speak, and went to the park and watched him in order to further plan her course of action that afternoon? This illustrates that gray areas may often arise in the analyses of what constitutes dangerously near. Other factors in analyzing a sufficient overt act are time, distance, and the number of acts that remain to be completed before the crime can be committed.[44]

In the final analysis the question is one of how rigidly or strictly the fact finder believes that the crime of attempt should be enforced. That is, what is the proper balance between an individual's right to possess evil thoughts and perform harmless acts to further them, and the right of society to protect itself against the perpetration and consummation of those thoughts?

The requirement of *intent* must be carefully distinguished from the requirement of an overt act. In the preceding examples, it is assumed that the intent requirement is satisfied—that the defendant *does* possess the requisite intent. As stated in the definition, intent alone does not constitute the crime of attempt; it must be accompanied by a sufficient overt act.

Attempt also requires that the defendant has the *apparent* ability to commit the crime, and that the commission must be legally possible. In order to be punishable the act committed by the defendant must have had an apparent chance of success.[45] If the defendant's act objectively appears to be inadequate to accomplish the crime, there can be no crime of attempt. However, if the act objectively appears to be adequate to cause the injury intended, the defendant will be guilty of attempt even though it was *actually* impossible for him or her to commit the crime. For example, when the defendant points a gun at someone and pulls the trigger, he or she is guilty of attempted murder even though the gun was not loaded, provided it appeared to be loaded and the defendant believed it was loaded. In addition, the crime intended must be *legally* possible of commission by the defendant.[46] This requirement is relevant in those jurisdictions where minors under a certain age cannot legally commit a particular crime, as provided in state statutes, or where a husband cannot be guilty of attempt to rape his own wife, as provided in the definitions of rape in most jurisdictions.

Finally, the crime of attempt is always a "lesser included offense." Thus a person cannot be convicted of both the attempted crime and the substantive crime itself. This same principle applies under the law of solicitation, but both solicitation and attempt are different from the law of conspiracy, under which the defendant can be convicted of both conspiracy and the substantive crime. By definition in most juris-

---

[44] See People v. Hernandez, 378 N.Y.S.2d 879 (N.Y. Super. 1975); State v. Martinez, 220 N.W.2d 530 (S.D. 1974); State v. Stewart, 537 S.W.2d 579 (Mo. App. 1976).

[45] State v. Stewart, in preceding note; State v. Miles, 510 S.W.2d 787 (Mo. App. 1974); Commonwealth v. Kelly, 162 Pa. Super. 526, 58 A.2d 375 (1948).

[46] In re Appeal No. 568, (Sept. Term, 1974 from the Circuit Court of Baltimore City sitting as a Juvenile Court), 25 Md. App. 218, 333 A.2d 649 (1975) (*legal* impossibility may excuse attempt, but *factual* impossibility will never serve as a valid defense). See also United States v. Berrigan, 482 F.2d 171 (3d Cir. 1973).

dictions, the crime of attempt requires that the substantive crime not be completed, not fully committed. But can a defendant be charged and convicted for the attempt alone if the crime *was* in fact completed? That is, is the attempt completely merged into the crime if it was successfully completed, thereby precluding the charge of attempt and requiring the prosecution to prove commission and guilt for the substantive crime only? A minority of jurisdictions regard the failure to consummate the crime as an essential element of criminal attempt, thus holding that there can be no conviction for attempt if the crime was completed.[47] However, the trend of authority is to the contrary, stating that the accused may be charged and convicted for the attempt *only,* even though the substantive crime was consummated.[48] This should not be confused with a situation in which the prosecution attempts to convict the defendant for *both* the attempt and the substantive crime if the latter was completed. The attempt is clearly part of the completed offense, and once successful, attempt cannot possibly support two convictions, that is, one for the attempt, and one for the completed offense.

C. Homicide

Homicide is the killing of one human being by another human being, although not every killing justifies criminal sanctions. There are three types of homicide, and every killing of one human by another falls into one of these three classifications. The first is *justifiable* homicide, which is a killing commanded or authorized by law, and in which the slayer is therefore deemed to be faultless in his or her actions. These include killings as a result of court order, and necessary killings by private persons or peace officers in suppression of riot or revolt or under other circumstances.[49] The second type of homicide is *excusable* homicide, which is a killing in which the slayer is not necessarily faultless, but in which the degree of fault does not justify imposing criminal sanctions. These include killings resulting from accident or misfortune during the course of performing a lawful act, when there is no intent to hurt the victim and no negligence. Excusable homicide also includes killings resulting from a reasonable mistake of fact, and killings by persons who are legally incapable of committing a crime, such as infants or insane persons. These latter examples are excusable because of legal principles that state that such persons cannot possess a criminal state of mind. Finally, excusable homicide includes uintentional killings in the course of a reasonable defense of oneself.[50]

The third type of homicide is *criminal* homicide, killings that are neither justifiable nor excusable. This is the type of homicide we are concerned with here. Crimi-

---

[47] Commonwealth v. McCloskey, 341 A.2d 500 (Pa. Super. 1975).

[48] See, e.g., People v. Delk, 345 N.E.2d 197 (Ill. App. 1976); State v. Gallegos, 193 Nebr. 651, 228 N.W.2d 615 (1976) (success or failure of the attempt is immaterial).

[49] Justifiable homicide implies intentional act of killing, which is nevertheless justified by exigent circumstances enumerated by statutes. State v. Kerr, 14 Wash. App. 584, 544 P.2d 38 (1975); Adami v. State, 535 S.W.2d 643 (Tex. Cir. App. 1976) (committed for purpose of preventing certain criminal offenses enumerated by statute).

[50] See Collier v. State, 328 So.2d 626 (Ala. Cr. App. 1975).

nal homicide may result from either an affirmative act or a negative act (an omission) by another human being, provided such act or omission is proven to be the proximate cause of the death of the victim. The act does not have to involve the actual touching of the victim, provided the element of proximate cause is present. For example, if the defendant threatens the victim with death, which causes such fear or shock that the victim succumbs to a heart attack, or if the victim, in attempting to escape, accidentally causes his or her own death, the defendant may still be convicted of criminal homicide.

In analyzing criminal homicide, the difficult problem is not usually to ascertain whether a criminal act was committed; rather it is to ascertain the *mens rea,* the criminal intent. The *mens rea* is extremely important because its level or degree generally determines both the severity of the crime and the resulting penalty.

1. Murder

Murder is defined as the unlawful killing of a human being by another human being with malice aforethought.[51] The term *unlawful* requires that the killing be without justification or excuse, thus placing it in the category of criminal homicide. The other major requirement is *malice aforethought.* This phrase has a particular meaning apart from any other definition of malice. One normally thinks of the term *malice* as meaning ill will or hatred toward another person. However, in the context of criminal law the term refers to several specific types of intent, each of which could be described as a "man-endangering state of mind." The phrase malice aforethought includes not only the intent to kill but also the intent to inflict great bodily injury; the intent to commit a dangerous felony; the intent to resist lawful arrest or force; or the intent to do any act under circumstances indicating that there is an obvious risk of death or great bodily injury.[52] The result of this definition of malice aforethought is that many different types of criminal homicide are categorized under murder, even though the defendant did not necessarily have a specific intent to kill a specific person.

For example, many jurisdictions define murder in the first degree as follows: "With the premeditated intent to cause the death of a person other than oneself, the defendant causes the death of that person or of another person." [53] But they also

---

[51] See, e.g., State v. Robinson, 139 N.J. Super. 475, 354 A.2d 374 (1976); Lopez v. State, 535 S.W.2d 643 (Tex. Crim. App. 1976).

[52] Malice may be expressed or implied; malice is not necessarily confined to an intent to kill, but includes intent to do any unlawful act which may probably result in depriving the victim of life. Humphreys v. State, 531 S.W.2d 127 (Tenn. Crim. App. 1975); People v. Matta, 129 Cal. Rptr. 205, 57 Cal. App.3d 472 (1976). Malice aforethought does not necessarily require a showing of ill will toward the victim. Commonwealth v. Festa, 341 N.E.2d 276 (Mass. 1976). See also State v. Robinson, 139 N.J. Super. 475, 354 A.2d 374 (1976), where the court pointed out the trend toward using the term *malice* and dropping *aforethought* and further discussed meaning of malice.

[53] See, e.g., State v. Hammonds, 224 S.E.2d 595 (N.C. 1976); General Statutes of North Carolina, Section 14-17 (1969); *Purdon's Consolidated Pennsylvania Statutes Annotated,* section 18-2502(a)(1973).

categorize as murder in the first degree "the intentional engaging in conduct which creates a grave risk of death to other people, and thereby causes the death of another." [54] In this situation the defendant has manifested an extreme indifference to the value of human life, but did not have the specific intent to kill someone.

Many jurisdictions define murder in the second degree as the causing of a person's death intentionally without premeditation, or the causing of a person's death with the intent to do serious bodily injury.[55] Thus both in first- and second-degree murder there must be malice aforethought present, yet the specific intent to cause the person's death need not be present. Nevertheless, all such deaths could fall under murder.

COMMONWEALTH v. CARROLL

412 Pa. 525, 194 A.2d 911 (1963)

Supreme Court of Pennsylvania

BELL, Chief Justice.

The defendant, Carroll, pleaded guilty generally to an indictment charging him with the murder of his wife, and was tried by a Judge without a jury in the Court of Oyer and Terminer of Allegheny County. That Court found him guilty of first degree murder and sentenced him to life imprisonment. Following argument and denial of motions in arrest of judgment and for a new trial, defendant took this appeal. The only questions involved are thus stated by the appellant:

(1) "Does not the evidence sustain a conviction no higher than murder in the second degree?

(2) "Does not the evidence of defendant's good character, together with the testimony of medical experts, including the psychiatrist for the Behavior Clinic of Allegheny County, that the homicide was not premeditated or intentional, *require* the Court below to fix the degree of guilt of defendant no higher than murder in the second degree?"

The defendant married the deceased in 1955, when he was serving in the Army in California. Subsequently he was stationed in Alabama, and later in Greenland. During the latter tour of duty, defendant's wife and two children lived with his parents in New Jersey. Because this arrangement proved incompatible, defendant returned to the United States on emergency leave in order to move his family to their own quarters. On his wife's insistence, defendant was forced first to secure a "compassionate transfer" back to the States, and subsequently to resign from the Army in July of 1960, by which time he had attained the rank of Chief Warrant Officer. Defendant was a hard worker, earned a substantial salary and bore a very good reputation among his neighbors.

In 1958, decedent-wife suffered a fractured skull while attempting to leave defendant's car in the course of an argument. Allegedly this contributed to her mental disorder which was later diagnosed as a schizoid personality type. In 1959 she underwent psychiatric treatment at

---

[54] State v. Bush, 289 N.C. 159, 221, S.E.2d 333 (1976) (first-degree murder includes commission of a felony which creates any substantial foreseeable risk that actually results in loss of human life).

[55] State v. Arney, 218 Kan. 369, 544 P.2d 334 (1975); State v. Cousins, 223 S.E.2d 338 (N.C. 1976).

the Mental Hygiene Clinic in Aberdeen, Maryland. She complained of nervousness and told the examining doctor "I feel like hurting my children." This sentiment sometimes took the form of sadistic "discipline" toward their very young children. Nevertheless, upon her discharge from the Clinic, the doctors considered her much improved. With this background we come to the immediate events of the crime.

In January, 1962, defendant was selected to attend an electronics school in Winston-Salem, North Carolina, for nine days. His wife greeted this news with violent argument. Immediately prior to his departure for Winston-Salem, at the suggestion and request of his wife, he put a *loaded* .22 calibre pistol on the window sill at the head of their common bed, so that she would feel safe. On the evening of January 16, 1962, defendant returned home and told his wife that he had been temporarily assigned to teach at a school in Chambersburg, which would necessitate his absence from home four nights out of seven for a ten week period. A violent and protracted argument ensued at the dinner table and continued until four o'clock in the morning.

Defendant's own statement after his arrest details the final moments before the crime: "We went into the bedroom a little before 3 o'clock on Wednesday morning where we continued to argue in short bursts. Generally she laid with her back to me facing the wall in bed and would just talk over her shoulder to me. I became angry and more angry especially what she was saying about my kids and myself, and sometime between 3 and 4 o'clock in the morning I remembered the gun on the window sill over my head. I think she had dozed off. *I reached up and grabbed the pistol and brought it down and shot her twice in the back of the head.*"

Defendant's testimony at the trial elaborated this theme. He started to think about the children, "seeing my older son's feet what happened to them. I could see the bruises on him and Michael's chin was split open, four stitches. I didn't know what to do. I wanted to help my boys. Sometime in there she said something in

there, she called me some kind of name. I kept thinking of this. *During this time I either thought or felt—I thought of the gun, just thought of the gun.* I am not sure whether I felt my hand move toward the gun—I saw my hand move, the next thing—the only thing I can recollect after this is right after the shots or right during the shots I saw the gun in my hand just pointed at my wife's head. She was still lying on her back—I mean her side. I could smell the gunpowder and I could hear something—it sounded like running water. I didn't know what it was at first, didn't realize what I'd done at first. Then I smelled it. I smelled blood before...."

"*Q*. At the time you shot her, Donald, were you fully aware and intend to do what you did?
"*A*. I don't know positively. All I remember hearing was two shots and feeling myself go cold all of a sudden."

Shortly thereafter defendant wrapped his wife's body in a blanket, spread and sheets, tied them on with a piece of plastic clothesline and took her down to the cellar. He tried to clean up as well as he could. That night he took his wife's body, wrapped in a blanket with a rug over it to a desolate place near a trash dump. He then took the children to his parents' home in Magnolia, New Jersey. He was arrested the next Monday in Chambersburg where he had gone to his teaching assignment.

Although defendant's brief is voluminous, the narrow and only questions which he raises on this appeal are as hereinbefore quoted. Both are embodied in his contention that the crime amounted only to second degree murder and that his conviction should therefore be reduced to second degree or that a new trial should be granted. . . .

". . . 'Murder in Pennsylvania was authoritatively defined in the famous case of Commonwealth v. Drum, 58 Pa. 9, 15. *"Murder"*, . . . *"is defined as an unlawful killing of another with malice aforethought, express or implied."* The legislature divided murder into two classifications, murder in the first degree and murder in the second degree; and provided that (1) all murder perpetrated by poison or lying in wait; or by any other kind of wilful, deliberate [and] premeditated killing, or any murder which shall be committed in the perpetration of or attempt to perpetrate certain specified felonies [arson, rape, robbery, burglary, or kidnapping], is murder in the first degree and (2) every other kind of murder is murder in the second degree. . . .

" 'Malice express or implied is [the hallmark] the criterion and absolutely essential ingredient of murder. Malice in its legal sense exists not only where there is a particular ill will, but also whenever there is a wickedness of disposition, hardness of heart, wanton conduct, cruelty, recklessness of consequences and a mind regardless of social duty. Legal malice may be inferred and found from the attending circumstances. . . .

" 'The test of the sufficiency of the evidence —irrespective of whether it is direct or circumstantial—is whether accepting as true all the evidence upon which, if believed, the jury could properly have based its verdict, it is sufficient in law to prove beyond a reasonable doubt that the defendant is guilty of the crime charged. . . .

" '. . . It has become customary for a defendant in his argument before an Appellate Court to base his claims and contentions upon his own testimony or that of his witnesses even after a jury has found him guilty. This, of course, is basic error. After a plea or verdict of guilty, we accept as true all of the Commonwealth's evidence upon which, if believed, the jury could have properly based its verdict.

" '. . . Proof by eye witnesses or direct evidence of the corpus delicti or of identity or of the commission by the defendant of the crime charged is not necessary. . . . It is clearly settled that a man may be convicted on circumstantial evidence alone, and a criminal intent may be inferred by the jury from facts and circumstances which are of such a nature as to prove defendant's guilt beyond a reasonable doubt.'

"The essential difference in a non-felony murder-killing between murder in the first degree and murder in the second degree is that murder in the first degree requires a specific intent to take the life of another human being. . . ."

The specific intent to kill which is necessary to constitute in a nonfelony murder, murder in the first degree, may be found from a defendant's words or conduct or from the attendant circumstances together with all reasonable inferences therefrom, and may be inferred from the intentional use of a deadly weapon on a vital part of the body of another human being. . . .

If we consider only the evidence which is favorable to the Commonwealth, it is without the slightest doubt sufficient in law to prove first degree. However, even if we believe all of defendant's statements and testimony, there is no doubt that this killing constituted murder in the first degree. Defendant first urges that there was insufficient time for premeditation in the light of his good reputation. This is based on an isolated and oft repeated statement in Commonwealth v. Drum, 58 Pa. 9, 16, that " 'no time is too short for a wicked man to frame in his mind the scheme of murder.' " Defendant argues that, conversely, a long time is necessary to find premeditation in a "good man." We find no merit in defendant's analogy or contention. . . .

Defendant further contends that the time and place of the crime, the enormous difficulty of removing and concealing the body, and the obvious lack of an escape plan, militate against and make a finding of premeditation legally impossible. This is a "jury argument"; it is clear as crystal that such circumstances do not negate premeditation. This contention of defendant is likewise clearly devoid of merit. . . .

Since this is a case of murder, we have carefully reviewed the record. It is crystal clear, from the record, that defendant was justifiably convicted of murder in the first degree.

Judgment and sentence affirmed.

Murder does not require that the person at whom the action is directed be the victim of the defendant's conduct. That is, the defendant's intent may be transferred to a person other than the intended victim.[56] This is an application of the doctrine of transferred intent, which is identical to the concepts discussed under intentional torts in Chapter 9. Thus if it appears that the defendant has malice aforethought as to his or her intended victim, but through the occurrence of events not anticipated by the defendant another person is killed, the defendant will nevertheless be deemed to have malice aforethought as to the person actually killed.

The definition of malice aforethought stated earlier includes an "intent to commit a dangerous felony." This state of mind forms the basis for what is known in most jurisdictions as the felony murder rule. This doctrine requires that if a death occurs during the course of a specific felony named in the felony murder statute, then it is considered to be murder in the first degree, even if the death was accidental.[57] Thus premeditation and deliberation need not be proven. The specific felonies named in the felony murder statutes of most jurisdictions are dangerous crimes such as robbery, rape, assault, or kidnapping. The obvious purpose of the felony murder rule is to discourage the perpetration of such felonies, a possible prosecution for murder being an added deterrent.

The rule applies where the defendant has perpetrated or attempted to perpetrate some other crime that is completely distinct and apart from the homicide but that occurs in connection with such a perpetration or attempt. As stated in the definition, the other crime must be a felony under the state statute under which the defendant is prosecuted. For example, a defendant assisted his or her partner in breaking and entering a victim's home at night, with intent to steal valuables; during the course of the burglary the victim surprised the defendant and the partner, and in the ensuing struggle the victim was accidentally killed *by the partner*. The rule applies in this situation even though the defendant did not intend to kill the victim and did not directly cause his or her death. A death occurred "during the course of a specific felony," namely burglary. Thus the would-be burglar may have become a murderer in the first degree by application of the felony murder rule.

---

[56] Henderson v. State, 343 N.E.2d 776 (Ind. 1976) (doctrine of transferred intent applied in first-degree murder case in which the accused shot one of two occupants of an automobile after arguing with the other).

[57] Colorado Revised Statutes Annotated, section 18-3-102(1)(b), provides that it is first-degree murder if defendant causes the death of another while committing or attempting arson, robbery, burglary, kidnapping, rape, or any other sexual offense.

RICHMOND v. STATE

554 P.2d 1217 (1976)

Supreme Court of Wyoming

RAPER, Justice.

In this appeal from a judgment and sentence following a jury verdict finding the defendant-appellant guilty of first-degree murder in killing a human being during an attempt to perpetrate a robbery in violation of §6-54, W.S. 1957, as amended,[a] the defendant raises the following questions: . . .

3. Did the court err in refusing to instruct the jury on lesser included offenses, to-wit: manslaughter and assault and battery pursuant to defendant's written requests to charge? . . .

We will hold there was no error and affirm.

Briefly, the murder facts are that William Johnson, the operator of an automobile service station, was found shot to death by two different guns, causing three wounds, the one in his chest resulting in demise. Upon investigation, the defendant and another, Nathan Jones, were arrested on the date of the crime. The defendant was arrested at 4:00 P.M., and at about 5:00 P.M., he made a tape-recorded statement to the Carbon County undersheriff, in which he related the details of how he and Nathan Jones planned to and did rob the deceased, the defendant trying to tie him up with a T-shirt and an electric cord and Jones shooting the service station operator with both a .22 automatic and a .38 revolver. . . .

In the case now before us, the defendant was charged with first degree felony-murder and the felony alleged was attempted robbery. The trial judge meticulously instructed the jury that one of the essential elements of an attempt to commit robbery is a specific intent to forcibly take

from the person or possession of another any property of value. Section 6-54, W.S. 1957, as amended, the statute creating the crime of felony-murder, which is set out in footnote a, is in several alternatives, of which our concern is only one: "Whoever . . . in the perpetration of, or attempt to perpetrate any . . . robbery . . . kills any human being, is guilty of murder in the first degree." Put in other terms: if someone gets killed by one in the course of attempting a robbery, the robber is guilty of first degree murder.

As we understand the notion of the defendant's defense, his intoxication or being under the influence of drugs created a reasonable doubt that he was capable of formulating the specific intent to commit robbery and therefore he could not properly be found guilty of first degree murder. The trial judge instructed the jury in these aspects and informed them that intoxication or being under the influence of drugs is to be considered in determining whether or not the defendant acted with a specific intent. The defendant then asserts that since he was entitled to have the jury consider his theory of defense that since he was incapable of intending to rob the now dead victim, he was also entitled to have jury consideration of what he claims to be the lesser included offenses of manslaughter and assault and battery, in each of which specific intent is not a necessary element. . . .

In Keeble v. United States, 1973, 412 U.S. 205, 208, it was held, in interpreting Rule 31(c), F.R.Cr.P.: "[I]t is now beyond dispute that the defendant is entitled to an instruction on a lesser included offense if the evidence would permit a jury rationally to find him guilty of the lesser offense and acquit him of the greater." Oldham v. State, Wyo. 1975, 534 P.2d 107, cites and recognizes the *Keeble* doctrine but also declares:

---

a Section 6-54, W.S. 1957 . . . is as follows:
"(a) Whoever purposely and with premeditated malice, or in the perpetration of, or attempt to perpetrate any rape, arson, robbery, or burglary, or by administering poison or causing the same to be done, kills any human being, is guilty of murder in the first degree."

". . . The rule in this state is clear that the trial court should only give such instructions as arise from the evidence and that when the evidence shows that the defendant is either guilty or not guilty of the higher grade of the offense, the court is not required to instruct on the lesser offense. . . ."

Is the situation such in the case before us that there is just evidence that would sustain only a guilty or not guilty verdict for felony-murder?

This court has not previously dealt with this particular offense in the light of the appropriateness of instructing on any lesser included offenses. Felony-murder is an unusual offense in that the death arising out of the robbery is purely an incident of the basic offense. It makes no difference whether or not there was an intent to kill. The statutory law implies all of the malevolence found and necessary in the crime of first-degree murder alone. Perhaps we can convey a better understanding of that concept if we explain the purpose of the prohibition against felony-murder and the reason it is automatically first-degree murder with its accompanying heavy penalty, usually the greatest society can impose upon a violator, though in Wyoming only life imprisonment is mandatory. We find an excellent summary of the function in society of the felony-murder crime in a reference the defendant has cited, "The Diminished Capacity Defense to Felony-Murder," 23 Stan. L. Rev. 799:

"The purpose of the felony-murder rule, according to the California supreme court, is 'to deter felons from killing negligently or accidentally by holding them strictly responsible for killings they commit.' The rule relates the initial intent to commit a felony to the resultant homicide, based on the following rationale: All persons are presumed sane and competent and are presumed to know and intend the natural consequences of their acts; such persons, contemplating the commission of one of the enumerated felonies, are also presumed to recognize and reflect upon the high degree of risk of causing death involved in that act. Therefore, the requisite malice for murder is implied from the commission or attempted commission of the enumerated felony, and premeditation and deliberation are established by the presumed consideration of the risks involved. A killing committed in a felon's perpetration of one of the enumerated felonies is thus considered first degree murder."

Since the necessary elements of first degree murder—premeditation, deliberation and malice aforethought are imputed by a conclusive presumption, there can be no lesser degrees of homicide recognized. Murder committed in the perpetration of a robbery is not divisible into lesser degrees of homicide. There is no room for the exercise of a power to find the defendant guilty of a lesser degree of felonious homicide depending upon the existence or non-existence of intent. In our search we find that to be the general rule. . . . We therefore hold that manslaughter is not an offense necessarily included in robbery and therefore not included in the crime of felony-murder here charged.

The subject must be discussed a bit further because of defendant's assertion that assault and battery is an included offense upon which the jury should have been instructed. Keep in mind that the evidence here was that the fatal shots were fired by Nathan Jones and not the defendant but the robbery was the act of both. As an aider and abettor, the defendant was chargeable as a principal. The jury was appropriately instructed in that regard and defendant raises no question that the defendant was not an accomplice of Nathan Jones. There is no doubt whatsoever that death of the victim ensued during the course of the robbery. It would be a travesty on justice to allow a jury to even consider a minor offense of assault and battery. The homicide cannot be disassociated from the attempted robbery. If the defendant was incapable of entertaining an intent to commit the robbery, then he should have been acquitted. That is the only area in which intent is an issue. Intent is not an element in the homicide that was connected to the robbery. We can see no reason for submitting the issue of any lesser offense when the evidence conclusively shows the defendant guilty of the highest degree of homicide. While the jury might, if that question were submitted to them, return some verdict of a lesser crime, this does not require the court to invite them to do so by submitting to them a theory of the case not rationally supported by the evidence.

The evidence is such that the jury could not have acquitted the defendant of murder unless it found him to be incapable of forming an intent to rob or insane at the time of the offense, both of which questions were submitted to the jury. . . .

There was no error.

Affirmed.

McCLINTOCK, J., filed a separate concurring opinion in which ROSE, J., joined.

The question has arisen as to whether the rule should apply in a circumstance in which two or more felons were participating in a crime, and during it one of the felons was killed. Should the other participant be subject to the felony murder rule for the death of his or her partner? Although not specifically stated in most jurisdictions, the statute has been interpreted to require that the death be of a person *other than* a participant of the crime, although the person killed need not be the victim of the offense.[58]

Another important question in analyzing this doctrine is whether the felony murder rule may be applied to an attempted *justifiable* homicide, such as by a police officer. Most jurisdictions hold that if a police officer attempts a justifiable homicide, that is, attempts to stop the perpetration of the crime or the flight of the participants, and the officer kills an innocent bystander, then that attempted justifiable homicide cannot constitute the basis for applying the felony murder rule to the prosecution of the criminal participants.[59] Thus situations involving the death of a participant in the crime are excluded from the rule, as well as the death of a person by conduct that, if successful, would have been justified homicide.

On the other hand, some jurisdictions apply the rule strictly and maintain that the felon must be held responsible for *any* killing that proximately results from his or her crime, primarily on the theory that the acts of the policeman or other persons in the examples just given are deemed to be the normal or anticipated responses to the acts of the perpetrator.[60] Such results are not so extraordinary that they are sufficiently substantial factors to constitute superseding causes of the defendant's acts; they do not remove the element of proximate cause from the analysis of the defendant's criminal culpability.

---

[58] See, e.g., People v. Morris, 1 Ill. App.3d 566, 274 N.E.2d 898 (1971). However, in People v. Warren, 44 Mich. App. 567, 205 N.W.2d 599 (1973), the court held the felony-murder rule applicable if victim was a cofelon, as long as the killing was done by the defendant.

[59] See, e.g., People v. Antick, 123 Cal. Rptr. 475, 539 P.2d 43 (1975).

[60] See Commonwealth v. Almeida, 362 Pa. 596, 68 A.2d 595 (1949), overruled in Commonwealth ex rel. Smith v. Meyers, 438 Pa. 218, 261 A.2d 550 (1970). The modern rule is that felony murder applies only when the killing is by the felon or an accomplice. People v. Washington, 62 Cal.2d 777, 402 P.2d 130 (1965). See also *McKinney's Consolidated Laws of New York,* Penal Code, section 125.25(3) (1969); Oregon Statutes, section 163.115 (1972).

2. Manslaughter

Manslaughter is the unlawful killing of one human being by another without malice aforethought.[61] As in the case of murder, the unlawfulness element means that the killing was unjustified and unexcused. The primary distinction between murder and manslaughter is that malice aforethought is not present in the case of manslaughter, whereas it is required for a conviction of murder.

Most jurisdictions divide manslaughter into two categories—voluntary manslaughter and involuntary manslaughter. However, many jurisdictions have categorized voluntary manslaughter as the only type of manslaughter, and placed involuntary manslaughter into a category entitled "criminally negligent homicide."

a. Voluntary

Regardless of the terminology used, voluntary manslaughter includes killing with the intent to cause a person's death under circumstances in which the act causing the death was performed without premeditation, in a sudden heat of passion caused by a serious, highly provoking act. It is an express requirement that such a highly provoking act would have excited an irresistible passion in a reasonable person. Voluntary manslaughter also includes "recklessly" causing the death of another person, and in some jurisdictions it includes intentionally causing or aiding another person to commit suicide.[62]

The most common definition of voluntary manslaughter is the first, namely causing death in a sudden heat of passion. The "highly provoking act" must be so provoking that even a reasonable person would have had an "irresistible passion" excited in him or her. The standard used is that a reasonable person would have been excited, but would not have attempted to *kill* another person. The point is that if the defendant is able to show that the act was so provoking in a reasonable person as to excite an irresistible passion, then the defendant may be able to reduce the severity of the crime from murder in the first or second degree to this lesser type of criminal homicide, namely voluntary manslaughter.

Voluntary manslaughter prosecutions often arise out of situations in which the defendant was involved in some altercation. Another common situation involving manslaughter is one in which a man discovers his wife in the act of adultery. In most jurisdictions this constitutes a legally sufficient provocation to reduce the husband's killing of the wife's lover from murder to manslaughter. Similarly, the defendant's enraged killing of another who has raped or seduced his wife or his daughter is generally held to be sufficient provocation to reduce the crime to voluntary manslaughter.[63] On the other hand, insulting words or gestures alone are never adequate

---

[61] J. Miller, *Handbook of Criminal Law* (St. Paul: West Publishing Co., 1934), p. 278.

[62] State v. Ulin, 13 Ariz. 141, 548 P.2d 19 (1976); Commonwealth v. Zukoski, 345 N.E.2d 690 (Mass. 1976); State v. Ginsberg, 15 Wash. App. 244, 548 P.2d 329 (1976) (recklessly causing death of another person).

[63] Henderson v. State, 136 Ga. App. 496, 221 S.E.2d 633 (1975).

provocation to reduce a homicide to manslaughter, despite the degree of insult contained in such words or gestures.[64]

The causing of the death must occur during a "sudden heat of passion." The defendant cannot have acted out of reason; the action must have been directed by passion, and there must have been no opportunity to cool off between the time of the provocation and the time of the killing.

b. Involuntary

Involuntary manslaughter is an unintentional killing, committed without excuse or justification, and not under circumstances constituting malice aforethought. This usually covers unintentional killings during the course of unlawful acts that are inherently dangerous, and those that are the result of such a great degree of negligence as to constitute criminal negligence. For example, if a person intentionally causes the death of a person in the good faith but *unreasonable* belief that grounds for justification exist, then he or she may be convicted of involuntary manslaughter. In addition, if a person fails to perceive a substantial justifiable risk, and that risk is of such a nature and degree that the failure to perceive it constitutes a gross deviation from the standard of due care in society, and if he or she causes the death of another person during such activity, it may constitute involuntary manslaughter.[65] For example, a doctor who treats a patient with a known and serious illness in a totally unapproved or unreasonable manner may be guilty of involuntary manslaughter for the patient's death. That is, the doctor's failure to use known or approved methods that would have saved the patient's life evidences such an indifference to the consequences as to constitute criminal negligence. This situation is different from one in which the doctor simply makes a good faith mistake in his or her diagnosis or improperly performs an operation as a result of which the patient dies. The doctor would not be guilty of manslaughter or murder, but probably would be liable in a civil action.

D. Assault and Battery

Although the terms *assault* and *battery* are frequently used together, they actually represent two distinct crimes. The former is an attempted or threatened battery, while the latter is an unlawful, intentional touching of another person. Thus, although every battery includes an assault, the reverse is not true. These crimes are similar in many respects to the torts of assault and battery.

---

[64] People v. Robles, 30 Ill. App.3d 335, 332 N.E.2d 460 (1975); Commonwealth v. Bermudez, 348 N.E.2d 802 (Mass. 1976).

[65] State v. Bonano, 59 N.J. 515, 284 A.2d 345 (1971) (recklessness); De Lee v. Knight, 221 S.E.2d 844 (S.C. 1975) (mere negligence is not enough; state must prove heedlessness or willfulness).

1. Battery

A criminal battery consists of an unlawful, unconsented-to touching of another, even where the touching is extremely slight.[66] The *actus reus* consists of the actual touching of the victim, which may be accomplished either by the defendant or by any force or substance that he or she puts in motion. A minority of courts require a specific intent, that is, that the *actus reus* be performed in an angry, revengeful, or rude state of mind. However, the majority of courts require that there be a general *mens rea,* that is, a showing that the *actus reus* was done intentionally, without regard to any malice or anger that may have been in the defendant's mind.[67]

2. Assault

The defendant may be found guilty of assault where the prosecution shows either: (1) that the defendant attempted to commit a battery upon his or her victim, regardless of whether the defendant succeeded or failed in such attempt; or (2) that the defendant "menaced his or her victim," that is, succeeded in placing the victim in apprehension of an immediate battery.[68] The trend in most jurisdictions is to recognize only the first type of assault. The second situation, namely placing the victim in apprehension of a battery, is not a criminal act in those jurisdictions.

In order to prove, based on the first type of assault, that the defendant assaulted the victim, it must be shown that: (1) the defendant intended to commit a battery; and (2) the defendant had undertaken a direct act toward its commission. When this type of assault is involved, only a general *mens rea* is required, because battery itself requires such a *mens rea* in the majority of jurisdictions.[69] Thus it is sufficient to show that the defendant intended to willfully commit an act whose direct and probable consequence would be to injure another person. However, the prosecution need not prove that the defendant intended to harm or to inflict any serious or particular injury upon the victim.

Unlike the *tort* of assault, the criminal defendant must have had the actual (as opposed to the apparent) present ability to commit the battery.[70] Some statutes

---

[66] People v. McEvoy, 33 Ill. App.3d 409, 337 N.E.2d 437 (1975); State v. Thompson, 27 N.C. App. 576, 219 S.E.2d 566 (1975).

[67] State v. Berger, 235 N.W.2d 254 (N.D. 1975); State v. Kotowski, 183 N.E.2d 262 (Ohio Com. Pl. 1962). See also People v. Barrington, 15 Ill. App.3d 445, 304 N.E.2d 525 (1973) (recklessness is not enough, doesn't satisfy intent requirement); State v. Comeaux, 249 La. 914, 192 So.2d 122 (1966) (specific intent is not required). 6 *AmJur* 2d, "Assault and Battery," section 14, notes that recklessness *is* sufficient *mens rea* in some jurisdictions.

[68] United States v. Bell, 505 F.2d 539 (7th Cir. 1974). See also State v. Seeley, 350 A.2d 569 (Me. 1976) (type 1); People v. Sanford, 237 N.W.2d 201 (Mich. App. 1975) (type 2).

[69] State v. Neal, 26 Ariz. App. 423, 549 P.2d 203 (1976) (intent required); State v. Westphal, 399 A.2d 168 (Me. 1975) (need not be specific intent); Battles v. State, 288 So.2d 573 (Fla. App. 1974) (overt act required); United States v. Bell, 505 F.2d 539 (7th Cir. 1974) (apprehension on part of victim not required).

[70] People v. Puckett, 188 Cal. Rptr. 884 (Cal. App. 1975); People v. Cardwell, 181 Colo. 421, 510 P.2d 317 (1973); Allison v. State, 299 N.E.2d 618 (Ind. App. 1973). But see State v. Little, 343 A.2d 180 (Me. 1975) (need only show "objective potential" for harm).

specifically require the actual present ability, while courts in other jurisdictions have imposed this requirement through interpretation of the statute. In effect, therefore, the defense of factual impossibility is made available to the defendant in a criminal case involving the first type of assault, while that defense would not be available in a civil case of assault.

Where the charge of assault is based upon placing the victim in apprehension of immediate battery, it must be shown that: (1) the defendant had the specific intent to commit a battery upon his or her victim, or place the victim in apprehension of an immediate battery; and (2) that the defendant succeeded in creating such apprehension in his or her victim by some affirmative act or gesture.[71] As with the civil law of assault, one must examine the state of mind of both the victim and the defendant. There can be no apprehension in the victim unless he or she is aware of the potential menace. Further, such awareness must be present at the time of the defendant's acts. In the second type of criminal assault the defendant's conduct must have created an apprehension of an *immediate* battery. If the words are conditional in any respect, or tend to negate any immediate threat, such as "I'd punch you in the nose, if I wasn't in such a hurry," then the menacing gestures do not constitute an assault.[72]

Unlike the requirement in the first type of assault, it is sufficient that the defendant *appear* to have the ability to inflict the battery, even if the defendant does not actually have the present ability to do so, because only an apprehension of harm need be created in this second type of assault.[73]

E. Robbery

At common law robbery was defined as the taking and carrying away of the personal property of another, from his or her person or immediate presence, accomplished by force or by putting that person in fear, with the intent to steal.[74] Even the slightest degree of violence or force satisfies this element of the crime of robbery. Thus even shoving or mishandling the victim is sufficient; the breaking of any chain or guard by which the property is secured to the owner's person is also sufficient force.[75]

However, it is not robbery if the force is used in taking property that either actu-

---

[71] See, e.g., State v. Wilson, 276 So.2d 45 (Fla. 1973); but see Woods v. State, 14 Md. App. 627, 288 A.2d 215 (1972) (apprehension, awareness is *not* required for the crime); 6 *AmJur* 2d, "Assault and Battery," section 4, states that some authorities refer to apprehension as part of the definition of assault, but that it has been held that such apprehension is not an essential element, citing, *inter alia,* State v. Godfrey, 17 Ore. 300, 20 P. 625 (1889) (one may be victim of assault although in complete ignorance of the fact).

[72] See 6 *AmJur* 2d, "Assault and Battery," section 30, and cases cited therein.

[73] State v. Wilson, 276 So.2d 45 (Fla. 1973); Hudson v. State, 135 Ga. App. 739, 218 S.E.2d 905 (1975); Casey v. State, 491 S.W.2d 90 (Tenn. Crim. App. 1972).

[74] See, e.g., Dozier v. State, 4 Div. 429, 337 So.2d 148 (Ala. App. 1976).

[75] People v. Morales, 49 Cal. App.2d 134, 122 Cal. Rptr. 157 (1975); Merritt v. State, 139 Ga. App. 171, 228 S.E.2d 149 (1976).

ally belongs to the defendant or that he or she believes is actually his or her property. In such a case the defendant lacks the specific intent to steal, because the force or intimidation is being used to recover property that the defendant in good faith believes to be his or hers. The defendant does not possess the adequate *mens rea*. There is, however, nothing to prevent the defendant from being charged with a separate crime for the use of such force, such as battery.

As the case of *Moses* v. *State* indicates, the taking may be accompanied by fear or force, so that the property owner expects some injury to his or her person or property. In either case the fear or force used to perpetrate the robbery must precede or accompany the taking.[76] If the property is taken without force and the defendant subsequently uses force to prevent the retaking of the property by the victim, the crime would be theft or larceny, not robbery.

MOSES v. STATE

352 N.E.2d 851 (1976)

Court of Appeals of Indiana, First District

LYBROOK, Judge.

The defendants-appellants, Gene Moses and Kim Moody, jointly appeal the following issues for review: . . . (2) Whether there is sufficient evidence to support the jury's verdict.

I.

The evidence most favorable to the State reveals that at approximately 10:00 P.M. on the 4th of July, 1975, Kevin Oxendine, age 13, was riding a bicycle home, and was stopped by three individuals, Gene Moses, Kimberly Moody and Frank Williams, in front of a tavern in Terre Haute. Oxendine testified that as he was riding past the tavern Moses grabbed his arm and led him down the street. Williams and Moody walked along with the boy on the bike and Moses. Oxendine stated that at the time he was acquainted with Moses and Moody. Moody asked Oxendine if he had any money and if so could Moody borrow it. Oxendine stated that he did have money but that he

needed it to pay his paper bill. At trial Oxendine testified that he was a newspaper boy. Williams threatened to hit the boy in the eye if he refused to give the money to Moody and Moses grabbed at the boy's wallet, while flipping cigarette ashes on his arms. Moody promised to pay the boy back at the bank in the morning if the boy would lend him the money. Oxendine testified at trial that he did not believe at the time he surrendered the money that he would be repaid in the morning as Moody represented; however, fearing that he would be hit by Williams, he took his money, counted it, and handed it ($27.00) to Moody. Moody grabbed the money and walked into the tavern with Moses and Williams. A witness testified that he saw Moody dispensing the money to Williams and Moses inside the tavern.

On July 9, 1975, Moody and Moses were charged with robbery and assault and battery with intent to commit a felony. The defendants pleaded "not guilty" and requested a trial by

---

[76] Commonwealth v. Farmer, 361 A.2d 701 (Pa. Super. 1976) ("immediate fear"); Hicks v. State, 232 Ga. 393, 207 S.E.2d 30 (1974) (dismissed because victim was alseep at time and thus not in fear).

jury. At the close of the State's evidence, the trial court directed a verdict of acquittal for both defendants on the charge of assault and battery with intent to commit a felony. On September 11, 1975, the jury returned a verdict of guilty against both defendants on the charge of robbery and they were sentenced to the Indiana Department of Corrections for ten years. From this conviction defendants appeal. . . .

II.

The defendants contend that there was insufficient evidence of probative value adduced to support the jury's verdict. The defendants specifically argue that the evidence fails to show that: (1) they had the necessary criminal intent to commit the crime of robbery; and (2) they used violence or placed the victim in fear. We disagree.

The essential elements which the State must prove beyond a reasonable doubt to sustain a conviction of robbery are: (1) an unlawful taking (2) from the person of another of (3) an article of value (4) by violence or putting in fear. Criminal intent is, also, an essential element of the crime of robbery.

It must be remembered that when reviewing an appeal on sufficiency of the evidence, this Court will not weigh the evidence nor determine the credibility of witnesses. We will consider only that evidence most favorable to the State, together with all logical and reasonable inferences to be drawn therefrom. The conviction will be affirmed if, from that viewpoint, there exists substantial evidence of probative value from which the trier of facts could reasonably infer that the defendants were guilty beyond a reasonable doubt.

The defendants urge that the evidence fails to show any criminal intent on their part to commit this crime. They assert that this money transaction was a loan which was to be repaid the next day. Defendants point out that the record shows that the prosecuting witness had loaned money to them on prior occasions.

The State argues that the evidence is sufficient to show the necessary criminal intent in that the victim did not willingly part with his money nor did he expect to be repaid.

It is well established in Indiana that criminal intent is a question of fact to be determined by the trier of fact from all the evidence. Furthermore, the criminal intent to commit the crime of robbery may be inferred from the surrounding circumstantial evidence. If two reasonable inferences arise from the evidence, this court will not determine which inference controls, that being within the province of the jury.

We conclude that the jury could have reasonably inferred from the evidence presented that the defendants had the necessary criminal intent to commit the crime.

The defendants further argue that the evidence fails to show that they took the money by using violence or placing the victim in fear.

The prosecuting witness testified that he had no reason to fear the defendants Moody and Moses. He also stated that neither Moses nor Moody threatened him in any way. However, he did testify that he was afraid of being hit by the third individual, Frank Williams, if he did not turn over the money.

While defendants argue that they did not use violence or place the victim in fear, the direct testimony of the victim demonstrates that he was placed in fear by the defendants' confederate. Thus, the defendants' contention must fail because it ignores a fundamental principle of our criminal law [that] . . .

"Every person who shall aid or abet in the commission of a felony, or who shall counsel, encourage, hire, command, or otherwise procure a felony to be committed, may be charged by indictment, or information, tried and convicted in the same manner as if he were a principal, either before or after the principal offender is charged, indicted or convicted; and, upon such conviction he shall suffer the same punishment and penalties as are prescribed by law for the punishment of the principal."

As stated in Cline v. State (1969), 253 Ind. 264, 267, 252 N.E.2d 793, 795:

"A defendant is responsible for the acts of his confederates as well as his own. It is not essential that participation of any one defendant in each element of robbery be established. Here the appellants acted in unison. Any act of one is attributable to them all."

In the case at bar, the defendants acted in unison with Frank Williams in committing this robbery. Therefore, Williams' actions which placed the victim in fear may be attributed to the defendants, Moses and Moody, making the evidence sufficient to support the jury's verdict.

No reversible error having been shown, the judgment of the trial court is affirmed.

Affirmed.

In its codified form robbery has been divided into several degrees in most jurisdictions, or else it is defined in terms of simple robbery and aggravated robbery. The severity of the degree of robbery and the punishment for it depends upon the severity of the violence used or threatened. For example, aggravated robbery in many jurisdictions includes robbery if the defendant is armed with a deadly weapon with intent to injure the person, or if the defendant wounds or strikes the person, or by the use of force, threats, or intimidation puts the person robbed in reasonable fear of death or bodily injury.[77]

F. Burglary

The common law offense of burglary consisted of the breaking and entering of the dwelling place of another at night with the intent to commit a felony therein.[78] In England each of the elements in this definition developed very special and overly refined connotations. As will be seen in the following discussion, the interpretation of these terms brought about illogical results that have now been eliminated by the modern and reasonable statutory definitions of the crime of burglary.

The first element of burglary is that the defendant's entrance must have been committed by physical force or by fraudulent means, and against the will of the occupant.[79] This is the "breaking" element. It includes the most minute moving of any part of the house. Thus, if a door or a window is already open, and the defendant merely steps inside, there is no breaking and no burglary. However, if the defendant merely pushes the door open a little wider than it already was, or the window a little higher, that is sufficient force to constitute the breaking. The breaking may also be a "constructive breaking," such as entry gained by fraud, duress, threats, or trick. Because the breaking must be against the will of the occupant, the issue of authority to enter may become a critical one, particularly where the defendant is an employee or friend of the occupant and normally has the right to be on the premises or may even have a key to enter. However, if the defendant had no

---

[77] Commonwealth v. Farmer, 361 A.2d 701 (Pa. Super 1976); Johnson v. State, 541 S.W.2d 185 (Tex. Crim. App. 1976).

[78] State v. Bell, 153 Conn. 540, 219 A.2d 218 (1966). See also 13 *AmJur* 2d, "Burglary," section 1.

[79] Brooks v. State, 277 Md. 155, 353 A.2d 217 (1976); State v. Keys, 419 P.2d 943 (Ore. 1966).

authority to be on the premises at the very time of the breaking and in the particular place where he or she gained entry, it would be a sufficient breaking.[80]

The second requirement for the common law crime of burglary was an "entering." The slightest entry of a person is sufficient to satisfy this element. Even if only the fingertips of the defendant enter the building, this element is satisfied.[81] Similarly, if only a tool or instrument being manipulated by the defendant entered the dwelling place, and the defendant intended to commit the felony by use of that tool or instrument, this is a sufficient entering. However, if the tool or instrument was used merely to enable the defendant to enter personally, then the entry of such tool or instrument is merely part of the breaking.

The "dwelling place" of another was defined as a place where a person regularly sleeps, regardless of whether it is a house, barn, warehouse, or any other structure.[82] The requirement that the dwelling house belong to "another" is fairly self-explanatory. However, the ownership of the dwelling place is not the issue; the occupancy is what determines this element. Thus a landlord may be convicted of burglarizing premises that he owns, but which he has leased to a tenant.[83] Taking this concept even further, one tenant in an apartment may be guilty of burglarizing another tenant within the same apartment, because the former had no right to the possession of the latter's room.

The requirement that the offense be committed "at night" was defined literally under common law, requiring that the offense take place between sunset and sunrise. The guilt of defendants in early common law cases in England sometimes rested upon the simple question of whether the sun had set prior to the time of the breaking and entering.

The "intent to commit a felony" in the dwelling place had to prompt both the breaking and the entering. Thus if the defendant broke and entered with the intent merely to commit a misdemeanor, and once inside the dwelling changed his or her mind and decided to commit a felony, there would not be sufficient intent to support a charge of burglary at common law.[84] On the other hand, the crime is complete once the breaking and entering with the requisite intent takes place. Thus if the defendant entered with the requisite intent and thereafter abandoned his or her intent to commit a felony, the defendant would still be guilty of burglary.[85]

Many jurisdictions have enacted statutes that define the crime of burglary more reasonably than under common law. Under such statutes a person commits burglary

[80] People v. Norris, 33 Ill. App.3d 600, 338 N.E.2d 129 (1975) (general authority to enter building open to public extends only to those who enter for purposes consistent with the reasons for which the building is public); People v. Castille, 34 Ill. App.3d 220, 339 N.E.2d 366 (1975) (assistant manager had no authority to consent to an entry for purposes of theft —access does not necessarily mean authority).

[81] People v. Lamica, 274 Cal. App.2d 640, 79 Cal. Rptr. 491 (1969); People v. Failla, 51 Cal. Rptr. 103, 414 P.2d 39 (1966).

[82] Herbert v. State, 31 Md. App. 48, 354 A.2d 449 (1976).

[83] 13 *AmJur* 2d, "Burglary," section 37.

[84] People v. Polansky, 6 Ill. App.3d 773, 287 N.E.2d 747 (1972); People v. Evans, 85 Misc.2d 1088, 379 N.Y.S.2d 912 (1975).

[85] Richardson v. State, 351 N.E.2d 904 (Ind. App. 1976).

when he or she unlawfully enters or remains in or upon premises with intent to commit a crime there. The requirement that the defendant "unlawfully" enter does not change the common law requirement that the breaking be by physical force or fraudulent means, because "unlawfully" includes entrance by trick or fraud. However, the requirement of entering a "dwelling place" has been changed to any "premises," and the requirement that the intent relate to a felony has been broadened to include any crime. In addition, the unreasonable restriction that the unlawful entry take place at night has been eliminated. Also a person may enter lawfully, but cannot "remain in or upon the premises." Thus a person who enters lawfully and without any criminal intent, but who remains there in violation of a lawful order to leave, is guilty of the crime of burglary in most jurisdictions. As with robbery, most statutes divide burglary into degrees, distinguishing, for example, burglary of an inhabited dwelling house (first degree) from breaking into a vault, safe, cash register, coin-vending machine, or other equipment (second or third degree).[86]

G. Larceny and Theft

There are four related common law crimes, one or more of which may be involved in the taking by one person of property that belongs to another: larceny, larceny by bailee, embezzlement, and obtaining property by false pretenses. Although many modern theft statutes incorporate the crimes of larceny, larceny by bailee, embezzlement, and false pretenses, embezzlement and false pretenses have been the subject of separate criminal statutes for many years. In an effort to eliminate the legal technicalities and illogical requirement of these crimes, many jurisdictions have merged all four of them into the statutory crime of theft.[87] In the definition of the common law crime of burglary, each word possesses a special and highly technical meaning. This is also true in the case of these four crimes. Examining the requirements of each one leads to understanding the concepts contained in the modern theft statutes.

1. Larceny

At common law, larceny was the taking and carrying away of the personal property of another without the consent of that person and with the specific intent to steal that property.[88] The "taking" element of the crime of larceny required that the defendant have complete physical control of the property at some time.[89] At common law the taking element was called the caption. It did not require that the defendant have the property actually within his or her hands. The defendant may, instead effect such a caption through an innocent human agent or mechanical de-

[86] *McKinney's Consolidated Laws of New York,* Penal Law, section 140.00 (1975).
[87] See 47 *Cal.Jur.* 2d, Theft, section 2 (1959). See also *Vernon's Texas Code Annotated,* Penal Code, section 31.02 (1974).
[88] See 50 *AmJur* 2d, "Larceny," section 2.
[89] State v. Knabe, 538 S.W.2d 589 (Mo. App. 1976).

vice. For example, if the defendant pointed to a bicycle on the sidewalk in front of the defendant's house and said to the prospective buyer, "I'll sell you this bicycle for $50," and the buyer accepted and paid the money and rode the bicycle away, and the bicycle actually belonged to a third party not present at the time, then the defendant was guilty of larceny at common law. The caption was effected by an innocent human agent.

The element of "carrying away" (called asportation at common law) of the personal property was satisfied by the slightest removal of the property. Thus, if an automobile or any other personal property was moved only a few feet from its original location by the defendant, and the other elements of the crime were present, then the defendant may have been guilty of larceny. It was more than an attempted larceny because the "taking and carrying away" elements were satisfied, and there was nothing in the definition to suggest that the defendant must have actually succeeded in keeping the personal property for any particular length of time.

The common law definition required that the caption and asportation concern the "personal property of another without the consent of that person." The subject of the larceny could not be realty or services, and the property must have belonged to one who had a legally protected possession.

The final element, and the one most difficult to prove in any larceny charge, was that the property must have been taken "with the specific intent to steal." The intent or *mens rea* element of any crime is always difficult to prove because no one can read the defendant's mind. The criminal intent must be ascertained through the defendant's outward manifestations and by objective analysis of conduct that tends to suggest what the defendant's state of mind actually was. The requirement that the defendant have the specific intent to steal meant that he or she must have had the intent to permanently deprive the owner of his or her property, as opposed to taking it with the intent to return it at some future time. Thus, if a person took an automobile for a "joy-ride" intending to return it after a few hours, he or she could not be convicted of larceny at common law, the intent to permanently deprive the owner being absent.[90] However, if the defendant took the property and abandoned it in such a way as to make it unlikely that anyone would be able to locate it within a reasonable time, such abandonment was tantamount to a permanent deprivation. Although the defendant may not have intended to permanently *keep* the personal property, the fact that the action permanently *deprived the owner* of its possession satisfied the *mens rea* requirement.[91]

2. Larceny by Bailee

The primary distinction between larceny by bailee and the larceny described in Section G-1 was that in the case of larceny by bailee the victim either voluntarily

---

[90] State v. Thibodeau, 353 A.2d 595 (Me. 1976); People v. Goodchild, 242 N.W.2d 465 (Mich. App. 1976); Simmons v. State, 549 P.2d 111 (Okla. Crim. App. 1976); People v. Rivera, 524 P.2d 1082 (Colo. 1974); People v. Woods, 17 Ill. App.3d 835, 308 N.E.2d 856 (1974).
[91] State v. Watts, 25 N.C. App. 194, 212 S.E.2d 557 (1975).

delivered possession of the property to the defendant, or the victim lost property which was subsequently found by the defendant. In larceny, on the other hand, the defendant does not obtain possession with the victim's consent.

One type of bailment arises where one delivers personal property in trust for a particular purpose and upon a contract, either express or implied. A bailment may also arise where the person holds possession under such circumstances that the law imposes an obligation to deliver the personal property to the rightful owner. The first type of bailment is quite common, such as where a person delivers a watch to a jeweler for its repair—a bailment takes place by delivery. In this case the criminal conversion takes place when the bailee, the jeweler, begins to treat the property as his or her own and either retains it, denying ever having received it in the first place, or sells it to an innocent third party. An example of the other type of bailment just described is where property is lost. Larceny by bailee arises when a person keeps a lost article that provides a clue as to its ownership and therefore might have been restored to its owner if the person had attempted to locate the owner as the law requires. Such "clues to possession" may be provided by the nature of the item lost or by the place where it was found.[92]

3. Embezzlement

Embezzlement at common law was the fraudulent appropriation of the personal property of another by one to whom it was entrusted, either by or for its owner.[93] This crime was similar to larceny by bailee because in both crimes possession of the personal property was obtained lawfully by the defendant, and the conversion with intent to steal occurred later. However, the distinction was that in larceny by bailee the lawful possession was obtained by virtue of a contract between the bailor and the bailee, such as delivering a watch to a jeweler for its repair. In embezzlement, however, the defendant's initial rightful possession arose as a result of some particular office or employment held by the defendant, such as a bank teller who has initially gained rightful possession of the bank's funds.

4. False Pretenses

A person commits the crime of false pretenses when he or she knowingly obtains the title to another's property by means of untrue representations of facts, with the specific intent to defraud.[94] At common law it was a crime to obtain another's property through the use of false tokens, weights, or measures (known as

---

[92] State v. Campbell, 536 P.2d 105 (Alas. 1975) (circumstances surrounding the finding must afford some reasonable clues for determining the identity of the rightful owner); Commonwealth v. Metcalfe, 212 S.W. 434 (Ky. App. 1919) ("clues to ownership" test).

[93] State v. Gomez, 27 Ariz. App. 248, 553 P.2d 1233 (1976); Uriciolo v. State, 272 Md. 607, 325 A.2d 876 (1974).

[94] Andresen v. Maryland, 427 U.S. 463 (1976); People v. Gordon, 64 Ill.2d 166, 355 N.E.2d 3 (1976).

cheats), yet it was not a crime to obtain property by false statements. Therefore statutes were enacted to fill this gap. The common law crime of larceny did not cover this situation, because by definition larceny was a crime against possession and did not necessarily include instances in which the rightful owner intentionally passed title to the defendant. Thus the distinguishing factor between false pretenses and larceny was the victim's intent. If the victim *intended* to surrender his or her entire legal interest at the time the defendant gained possession of the property, the crime is false pretenses. If the victim did not intend to give up his or her interest, it is larceny.

In order for the necessary elements to be proven, the victim must have believed an untrue representation of fact, and must have significantly relied upon it in surrender of the property; however, such representation need not have been the sole factor of reliance.[95] It does not matter how reasonable the victim's reliance was. The defendant must have had the specific *mens rea* to deprive the owner permanently of the property, and the defendant must have made the representation with knowledge of its falsity.[96]

5. Theft

As stated before, many jurisdictions have combined the preceding crimes into the one statutory crime of theft. The new statutes do not necessarily repeal those covering larceny, embezzlement, or false pretenses, or related crimes such as stealing, the confidence game, or shoplifting. Instead the statutes state that whenever any of these other related crimes are mentioned, they are to be interpreted as if the word *theft* were substituted for them. The obvious purpose of establishing the one crime of theft is to remove distinctions and technicalities previously required in both the pleading and the proof of such similar crimes. Therefore, under the crime of theft in these jurisdictions it is no longer necessary for the prosecutor to specify whether, for example, the defendant formed an intent to steal the victim's goods prior to the time they were received (larceny), or subsequent to the time that the victim entrusted the defendant with such goods (embezzlement). It is now sufficient if an indictment or information merely alleges theft of a specific thing of value from another named person.

The elements of the offense of theft in many of these jurisdictions are met if the prosecutor can prove the defendant knowingly obtained or exercised control over anything of value of another without authorization, or gained control by the use of threat or deception, or exercised control while knowing that thing of value to have been stolen.[97] The fact that the defendant obtained or exercised control without

95 People v. Gross, 51.A.D.2d 191, 379 N.Y.S.2d 885 (1976). But see State v. Lemken, 136 N.J. Super. 310, 346 A.2d 92 (1974) (reliance need not be great or excessive); State v. McDonald, 534 S.W.2d 650 (Tenn. 1976) (reliance by victim not essential element under Tennessee statute, T.C.A. 39-1901).
96 People v. Faubus, 48 Cal. App.3d 1, 121 Cal. Rptr. 167 (1975).
97 Illinois Statutes Annotated, Ch. 38, section 16-1 (1970); Pocket Part (1977); *West's Annotated California Code,* Penal Code, section 484 (1970).

authorization covers what has been described before as larceny, larceny by bailee, embezzlement, and false pretenses.

As with the crimes of burglary and robbery, the statutory crime of theft is generally divided into two or more classes, usually distinguished by the value of the items stolen. In returning a verdict of guilty of theft under such a statute, the jury is required to determine the value of the property that the defendant took, based upon the evidence presented during the trial, in order to determine which class of theft is applicable.

H. Rape

At common law rape was defined as "carnal knowledge by a male of a woman not his wife by force and against her will." [98] The "carnal knowledge" element required actual sexual intercourse, with the slightest penetration sufficient to constitute the crime. Although no limitation concerning the defendant's age was expressly stated in the definition, at common law a male under fourteen years of age was presumed to be incapable of rape. However, he could still be guilty of attempted rape. The requirement that the woman not be the defendant's wife simply meant that a man could not rape his own wife at common law. However, he could be an accomplice or conspirator in her rape by another man, and he could be guilty of assault arising from or in connection with involuntary intercourse with his wife.

The requirement that the carnal knowledge be obtained "by force and against her will" encompassed situations in which the victim's resistance was overcome by physical force or threats of immediate bodily harm and in which the woman reasonably believed that the man had the capacity to carry out such threats. It also involved situations in which the victim was incapacitated, such as being unconscious or intoxicated. A third situation fulfilling this requirement was one in which the victim was deceived concerning the identity of the male, or concerning the nature of the act, such as where she was told that it was necessary for medical treatment.

The chastity or reputation of a woman was not a defense to the crime of rape; a prostitute could be raped.[99] However, evidence of the victim's lack of chastity or poor reputation was admissible on the issue of whether she gave consent to the defendant.[100]

Most jurisdictions have enacted statutes which have expanded the common law crime of rape in one significant respect, namely that regardless of whether a female consents or not, if she is under an age specifically designated in the statute, then carnal knowledge constitutes rape; the law will not recognize actual consent given by a woman under a certain age.

---

[98] See J. Miller, *Handbook of Criminal Law* (St. Paul, Minn.: West Publishing Co., 1934), pp. 293–301.

[99] In the matter of J.W.Y., 363 A.2d 674 (D.C. App. 1976); Commonwealth v. Pilosky, 362 A.2d 253 (Pa. Super. 1976); State ex rel Pope v. Superior Court, 545 P.2d 946 (Ariz. 1976).

[100] State v. Hill, 244 N.W.2d 728 (Minn. 1976).

As the case of *People* v. *Hernandez* illustrates, in some jurisdictions it is an affirmative defense to statutory rape that the defendant "reasonably believed" the female to be over the age specified in the statute, while in other jurisdictions it is immaterial that the defendant was reasonably mistaken as to her age.[101] However, in these latter jurisdictions, efforts to remedy certain shortcomings in the administration of justice in rape cases are reflected in the allowance of evidence of consent, or the good faith belief in the female's age, for the court to consider in determining the defendant's punishment.

PEOPLE v. HERNANDEZ

39 Cal. Rptr. 361, 393 P.2d 673 (1964)

Supreme Court of California

PEEK, Justice.

By information defendant was charged with statutory rape. Following his plea of not guilty he was convicted as charged by the court sitting without a jury and the offense determined to be a misdemeanor.

Section 261 of the Penal Code provides in part as follows: "Rape is an act of sexual intercourse, accomplished with a female not the wife of the perpetrator, under . . . the following circumstances: 1. Where the female is under the age of 18 years. . . ."

The sole contention raised on appeal is that the trial court erred in refusing to permit defendant to present evidence going to his guilt for the purpose of showing that he had in good faith a reasonable belief that the prosecutrix was 18 years or more of age.

The undisputed facts show that the defendant and the prosecuting witness were not married and had been companions for several months prior to January 3, 1961—the date of the commission of the alleged offense. Upon that date the prosecutrix was 17 years and 9 months of age and voluntarily engaged in an act of sexual intercourse with defendant.

In support of his contention defendant relies upon Penal Code, §20, which provides that "there must exist a union, or joint operation of act and intent, or criminal negligence" to constitute the commission of a crime. He further relies upon section 26 of that code which provides that one is not capable of committing a crime who commits an act under an ignorance or mistake of fact which disapproves any criminal intent.

Thus the sole issue relates to the question of intent and knowledge entertained by the defendant at the time of the commission of the crime charged.

Consent of the female is often an unrealistic and unfortunate standard for branding sexual intercourse a crime as serious as forcible rape. Yet the consent standard has been deemed to be required by important policy goals. We are dealing here, of course, with statutory rape where, in one sense, the lack of consent of the female is not an element of the offense. In a broader sense, however, the lack of consent is deemed to remain an element but the law makes a conclusive presumption of the lack thereof because she is presumed too innocent and naive to understand the implications and nature of her act. The law's concern with her capacity or lack thereof to so understand is explained in part by a popular conception of

---

[101] People v. Plewka, 27 Ill. App.3d 553, 327 N.E.2d 457 (1975) (is a defense); People v. Gengels, 218 Mich. 632, 188 N.W. 398 (1922) (is not a defense).

the social, moral and personal values which are preserved by the abstinence from sexual indulgence on the part of a young woman. An unwise disposition of her sexual favor is deemed to do harm both to herself and the social mores by which the community's conduct patterns are established. Hence the law of statutory rape intervenes in an effort to avoid such a disposition. This goal, moreover, is not accomplished by penalizing the naive female but by imposing criminal sanctions against the male, who is conclusively presumed to be responsible for the occurrence.

The assumption that age alone will bring an understanding of the sexual act to a young woman is of doubtful validity. Both learning from the cultural group to which she is a member and her actual sexual experiences will determine her level of comprehension. The sexually experienced 15-year old may be far more acutely aware of the implications of sexual intercourse than her sheltered cousin who is beyond the age of consent. A girl who belongs to a group whose members indulge in sexual intercourse at an early age is likely to rapidly acquire an insight into the rewards and penalties of sexual indulgence. Nevertheless, even in circumstances where a girl's actual comprehension contradicts the law's presumption, the male is deemed criminally responsible for the act, although himself young and naive and responding to advances which may have been made to him.

The law as presently constituted does not concern itself with the relative culpability of the male and female participants in the prohibited sexual act. Even where the young woman is knowledgeable it does not impose sanctions upon her. The knowledgeable young man, on the other hand, is penalized and there are none who would claim that under any construction of the law this should be otherwise. However, the issue raised by the rejected offer of proof in the instant case goes to the culpability of the young man who acts *without* knowledge that an essential factual element exists and has, on the other hand, a positive reasonable belief that it does not exist.

The primordial concept of *mens rea,* the guilty mind, expresses the principle that it is not conduct alone but conduct accompanied by certain specific mental states which concerns, or should concern the law. In a broad sense the concept may be said to relate to such important doctrines as justification, excuse, mistake, necessity and mental capacity, but in the final analysis it means simply that there must be a "joint operation of act and intent," as expressed in section 20 of the Penal Code, to constitute the commission of a criminal offense. The statutory law, however, furnishes no assistance to the courts beyond that, and the casebooks are filled to overflowing with the courts' struggles to determine just what state of mind should be considered relevant in particular contexts. In numerous instances culpability has been completely eliminated as a necessary element of criminal conduct in spite of the admonition of section 20 to the contrary. . . . More recently, however, this court has moved away from the imposition of criminal sanctions in the absence of culpability where the governing statute, by implication or otherwise, expresses no legislative intent or policy to be served by imposing strict liability.

Statutory rape has long furnished a fertile background upon which to argue that the lack of knowledgeable conduct is a proper defense. The law in this state now rests, as it did in 1896, with this court's decision in People v. Ratz, 115 Cal. 132, 46 P.915. . . .

The rationale of the Ratz decision, rather than purporting to eliminate intent as an element of the crime, holds that the wrongdoer must assume the risk; that, subjectively, when the act is committed, he consciously intends to proceed regardless of the age of the female and the consequences of his act, and that the circumstances involving the female, whether she be a day or a decade less than the statutory age, are irrelevant. There can be no dispute that a criminal intent exists when the perpetrator proceeds with utter disregard of, or in the lack of grounds for, a belief that the female has reached the age of consent. But if he participates in a mutual act of sexual intercourse, believing his partner to be beyond the age of consent, with reasonable grounds for such belief, where is his criminal intent? In such circumstances he has not consciously taken any risk. Instead he has subjectively eliminated the risk by satisfying himself on reasonable evidence that the crime cannot be committed. If it occurs that he has been misled, we cannot realistically conclude that for such reason alone the intent with which he undertook the act suddenly becomes more heinous. . . .

We are persuaded that the reluctance to accord to a charge of statutory rape the defense of a lack of criminal intent has no greater justification than in the case of other statutory crimes, where the Legislature has made identical provision with respect to intent. " 'At common law an honest and reasonable belief in the existence of circumstances, which, if true, would make the act for which the person is indicted an innocent act, has always been held to be a good defense. . . . So far as I am aware it has never been suggested that these exceptions do not equally apply to the case of statutory offenses unless they are excluded expressly or by necessary implication.' " Our departure from the views expressed in Ratz is in no manner indicative of a withdrawal from the sound policy that it is in the public interest to protect the sexually naive female from exploitation. No responsible person would hesitate to condemn as untenable a claimed good faith belief in the age of consent of an "infant" female whose obviously tender years preclude the existence of reasonable grounds for that belief. However, the prosecutrix in the instant case was but three months short of 18 years of age and there is nothing in the record to indicate that the purposes of the law as stated in Ratz can be better served by foreclosing the defense of a lack of intent. This is not to say that the granting of consent by even a sexually sophisticated girl known to be less than the statutory age is a defense. We hold only that in the absence of a legislative direction otherwise, a charge of statutory rape is defensible wherein a criminal intent is lacking.

For the foregoing reasons People v. Ratz, 115 Cal. 132, 46 P. 915, and People v. Griffin, 117 Cal. 583, 49 P. 717 are overruled, and People v. Sheffield, 9 Cal. App. 130, 98 P. 67 is disproved to the extent that such decisions are inconsistent with the views expressed herein. . . .

The judgment is reversed.

In addition to statutory provisions regarding the age of consent, some statutes also specify that consent will not be recognized as a defense if the female is in the defendant's custody or detained in a hospital or other institution where the defendant has supervisory or disciplinary authority over her.[102] In other respects the statutory crime of rape and its necessary elements remain the same as those discussed in connection with common law rape.[103]

I. Defenses

There are five categories of defenses to crimes: alibi, entrapment, duress, insanity, and defenses relating to justification. Criminal defenses embody the same concept as defenses to torts, namely that even though all the basic and necessary elements of the offense may have been proven, the possibility remains that the defendant was

---

[102] See, e.g., Colorado Revised Statutes Annotated 18-3-401 (1973); Michigan Comp. Laws Annotated 750–20b (Supp. 1974).

[103] See, e.g., Harris v. State, 6 Div. 133, 333 So.2d 871 (Ala. App. 1976); Arnold v. United States, 358 A.2d 335 (D.C. App. 1976); Dewey v. State, 345 N.E.2d 842 (Ind. 1976).

justified in his or her actions or did not possess the necessary state of mind. However, there is one significant difference between criminal defenses and the defenses to negligence and intentional torts, namely that the victim's negligence in criminal proceedings is not relevant to the defendant's guilt.

The only defense in which the defendant attempts to prove that he or she *did not intend* to commit the particular act alleged to be criminal is that of duress. In raising the defenses of entrapment, insanity, and defenses relating to justification, the defendant does not deny that he or she actually *acted with intent* to commit the act. However, such defenses introduce other considerations negating the criminal aspect from that element necessary in the prosecution's case. The defense of alibi raises a concept different than the four other defenses, because the intent element is not dispositive or even relevant to successfully raising this defense.

1. Alibi

As a result of common misuse, the term *alibi* has acquired a connotation almost opposite to its actual legal meaning. In the context of defenses to crimes, an alibi is a *provable* account of the defendant's whereabouts at the time of the commission of the crime, making it impossible for the defendant to have been at the scene of the crime. That is, an alibi negates the physical possibility that the defendant could have committed the crime. However, the term has acquired a negative implication that an alibi is an *untruth,* fabricated by the defendant in an effort to avoid guilt.

Some statutes specify procedures to be followed when the defendant intends to invoke this defense.[104] For example, the defendant may have to give notice to the prosecution that he or she was at a place other than the location specified by the prosecution. In this situation neither the prosecuting attorney nor the defendant is permitted to introduce evidence at the time of the trial inconsistent with their respective specifications. The prosecution and defendant may also be required to transmit other information related to their respective contentions, such as a list of witnesses who may be called to refute the defendant's defense of alibi.

2. Entrapment

The defense of entrapment may be successfully invoked by the defendant if it can be proved that his or her acts, which would have otherwise constituted a crime, were not criminal because the defendant engaged in them as a result of being induced to do so by a law enforcement official (or other person acting under such an official's direction), seeking to obtain evidence for the purpose of prosecution. The defendant must further prove that the methods used to obtain that evidence were such as to create a substantial risk that the acts would be committed by the

---

[104] See, e.g., *McKinney's Consolidated Laws of New York,* Penal Laws, section 250.20 (1976 Supp.).

defendant, who, but for the inducement, would not have conceived of or engaged in that conduct. The theory behind this defense is that "but for" the actions of the law officer, there would not have been a crime. The defense is difficult to prove because there must be strong evidence of the seduction of an innocent mind, and police officers must have been the creative force in instigating the offense.[105] The defense must be clearly distinguished from a situation in which the police or other law enforcement officials merely offer an opportunity to commit a crime to one who is already predisposed to commit the crime. In this situation there is no entrapment, although the officials made representations or inducements in an effort to overcome the defendant's fear of detection. If the commission of the offense was already in the mind of the defendant, there was no entrapment.

The defense is usually invoked in connection with "victimless crimes" such as narcotics offenses and prostitution. A typical example is where a policeman disguises himself as a drug addict and asks the defendant drug dealer to sell him some drugs. In this case the criminal intent of the defendant was already present, and the fact that the opportunity was furnished by the policeman does not constitute the defense of entrapment. Evidence that the jury can objectively scrutinize, such as that the defendant responded readily to the inducement, is generally sufficient to negate any claim of entrapment and to prove that the defendant was already predisposed to commit the offense. However, a few courts have found entrapment if there was reprehensible police conduct, regardless of the defendant's predisposition. The rationale behind such decisions is that the primary purpose of the entrapment defense is to control police conduct.[106]

3. Duress

With the exception of capital offenses, a criminal act may be excused by a showing that the defendant did not act of his or her own free will. If the defendant can prove that he or she acted under compulsion or coercion by another person or acted in the reasonable belief that a greater harm would otherwise occur, such as a danger to other persons, this defense may successfully be raised.[107] Generally it must be shown that some third person threatened the defendant, or some member of the defendant's immediate family, with death or serious bodily injury. The fact that there was the threat of damage to the defendant's reputation, business, or property is insufficient to raise the defense of duress.[108]

---

[105] Hampton v. United States, 423 U.S. 837 (1976); United States v. Jackson, 539 F.2d 1087 (6th Cir. 1976); Commonwealth v. Jones, 363 A.2d 1281 (Pa. Super. 1976).

[106] See cases cited in note 105.

[107] United States v. Gordon, 526 F.2d 406 (9th Cir. 1975) (for defendant to successfully urge duress as a defense it must be shown that the threat and the fear which the threat caused were immediate and involved death or serious bodily injury; he or she must also show that the fear was well grounded and that there was no reasonable opportunity to escape). See also Wentworth v. State, 29 Md. App. 110, 349 A.2d 421 (1975) (capital offense exception).

[108] People v. Patton, 25 Ill. App.3d 840, 322 N.E.2d 592 (1975); State v. Gann, 244 N.W.2d 746 (N.D. 1976). But see, 25 *AmJur* 2d, "Duress and Undue Influence," section 6.

This defense was an integral part of the highly publicized 1976 trial of Patty Hearst. It appears that duress by the Symbionese Liberation Army was relied upon heavily as a defense by Patty Hearst's attorney, F. Lee Bailey. This raises two other aspects of the defense of duress that were probably critical to the jury's final determination of guilt in the Hearst case. First, it must be shown that the defendant was not at fault in intentionally or recklessly placing himself or herself in a situation in which it was foreseeable that he or she would be subject to the illegal force of threats.[109] In the Patty Hearst trial the prosecution attempted to show that the defense of duress was not available to the defendant because she recklessly exposed herself to the compulsion by remaining with her accomplices, knowing that they planned to commit crimes. A second question during that trial was whether the defendant's submission to participation in the robbery of the Hibernia Bank was reasonable under the circumstances, that is, whether there appeared to be any way available to avoid the harm that was allegedly threatened to her if she did not participate in the robbery.[110] Could she have fled at any time or called the police?

Although the main purpose for the parade of expert psychiatry and psychology witnesses for the defense was apparently to establish duress, the defense seemingly intended to integrate duress with the idea that the defendant was psychologically forced ("brainwashed") into possessing the requisite *mens rea* for the crime of robbery. Throughout the course of the trial the term *brainwashing* was used extensively, and the defense relied heavily upon witnesses who were experts in brainwashing during war and other situations of severe mental stress. However, it is unclear what the purpose of the brainwashing approach was, because if a person is brainwashed, then that person actually changes his or her fundamental beliefs. Therefore, if the defense in the Patty Hearst trial was that she was brainwashed, her attorneys were maintaining that she did indeed possess the requisite *mens rea,* but that this *mens rea* was forcefully and unfairly imposed upon her way of thinking. On the other hand, if the defense was duress, her attorneys were not saying that she had any criminal intent, but that she was completely forced into all of her criminal conduct—the opposite of the brainwashing theory. Because no defense called "brainwashing" exists, it is difficult to ascertain the reason for the brainwashing approach. If it had been successfully proved that the brainwashing changed the defendant's concept of right and wrong in American society, such proof would have gone directly against the real defense of duress, which requires physical submission without any accompanying criminal state of mind.

4. Insanity

A person is not criminally accountable for his or her acts if: (a) he or she is so diseased or defective in mind at the time of the commission of the act (i) as to

---

[109] See, e.g., Model Penal Code, Proposed Official Draft (1962), Section 2.09(2).
[110] See, e.g., Model Penal Code, Proposed Official Draft (1962), Section 2.09(1); State v. St. Clair, 262 S.W.2d 25 (Mo. 1953).

be incapable of understanding the nature of the act, or (ii) even if able to understand the nature of the act, so diseased as to be incapable of distinguishing right from wrong with respect to the act; or (b) being able to so distinguish, has suffered such an impairment of mind by disease or defect as to destroy the will power and render him or her incapable of choosing the right and refraining from doing the wrong. The result of the insanity defense is to find the defendant's acts nonvolitional, and to hold the defendant incapable of forming criminal intent. The insanity defense is comparable to duress "from *within* the person."

The effect of pleading insanity in some jurisdictions is to create a separate triable issue in which a jury is empaneled to determine the defendant's insanity prior to the trial for the substantive crime charged. If the first jury finds the defendant sane, a separate and second jury then tries the substantive crime. In determining criminal culpability, the court is concerned only with the defendant's sanity at the time of the commission of the offense.[111] Although the defendant's lack of sanity at the time of arraignment or trial may raise procedural problems requiring continuance of the proceedings until the defendant is able to comprehend their nature, his or her present mental condition does not affect ultimate criminal liability if it is determined that the defendant was actually sane at the time of the alleged crime.

The definition of insanity just stated incorporates two well-established principles of this defense. The defendant's inability to understand the nature of his or her act or to distinguish whether the act was "right or wrong"—(a)(i) and (ii) above—is also known as the McNaghten Rule, which is followed by the majority of jurisdictions today. Such courts hold that a person is excused from a criminal act if by reason of the diseased condition of his or her mind he or she was unable to understand the nature of the act or unable to distinguish whether that act was right or wrong.[112] In this context the terms *right* and *wrong* are used in the moral rather than the legal sense.

The other part of the definition, concerning the lack of will power—(b) above—is called the irresistible impulse test; it is implemented in a substantial minority of jurisdictions. Such states do not necessarily use the one test of insanity and exclude the other, but may use both the McNaghten Rule and the irresistible impulse test. The latter test finds sufficient insanity if the defendant was unable to control himself or herself on the occasion in question. The test requires a sudden loss of self-control, rather than a prolonged breakdown of will power, and focuses on the defendant's ability to control himself or herself rather than the ability to distinguish right from wrong.[113]

---

111 United States v. Walker, 537 F.2d 1192 (4th Cir. 1976) (distinction between question of present ability to understand nature of charges and different question of whether defendant had capacity to understand and control his or her conduct at the time of the criminal act).

112 State v. Brosie, 113 Ariz. 329, 553 P.2d 1203 (1976); State v. Bott, 246 N.W.2d 48 (Minn. 1976); State v. Harris, 228 S.E.2d 424 (N.C. 1976).

113 Commonwealth v. Walzack, 360 A.2d 914 (Pa. 1976) ("Under the irresistible impulse test a person may avoid criminal responsibility even though he is capable of distinguishing between right and wrong, and is fully aware of the nature and quality of his act provided he establishes that he is unable to refrain from action").

A few jurisdictions have adopted the Durham Rule, which impliedly rejects the theory that the other tests can adequately determine insanity. The Durham (or New Hampshire) Rule simply presents a factual question to the jury of whether or not the accused was insane, and whether his or her insanity was the cause of the criminal act.[114]

The majority of courts do not recognize partial insanity or insane delusions and require that the defendant had a *complete* loss of capacity at the time of the offense.[115] However, a minority recognize that a person may be insane as to certain objects or certain subjects only, and perfectly sane with respect to everything else at the time of the criminal act. For example, a man may possess an irrational belief only with respect to his wife's relationship with another man.[116]

Even where a defendant has not raised the defense of insanity, evidence of mental condition may nevertheless be admissible on the issue of whether the defendant possessed the requisite specific *mens rea*.[117] This is a minority position and is called the doctrine of diminished capacity. Proof of diminished capacity may reduce the degree or nature of an offense so that, for example, the jury may find a defendant incapable of the premeditation required for first-degree murder. This approach is distinguished from the McNaghten and irresistible impulse tests, which seek an acquittal on the ground that the defendant was incapable of forming the *general* intent to commit the crime, rather than the specific *mens rea* sought to be disproved by the defense of diminished capacity.

5. Defenses Relating to Justification

a. *Defense of Self or Others*

As a general rule, a person is justified in using physical force upon another person in order to defend himself or herself, or a third person, from what the defendant reasonably believes to be the use or imminent use of unlawful physical force by that other person.[118] The defendant may use the degree of force that he or she reasonably believes necessary for that purpose. However, deadly physical force may be used only if a person reasonably believes that a lesser degree of force will be inadequate, and provided that the defendant has reasonable grounds to believe, and does believe, that he or she (or another person) is in imminent danger of being

---

[114] Based on Durham v. United States, 214 F.2d 862 (D.C. Cir. 1954). It is further explained in Carter v. United States, 252 F.2d 608 (D.C. Cir. 1957).

[115] See 21 *AmJur* 2d, "Criminal Law," sections 40–41. Compare Biddy v. State, 138 Ga. App. 4, 225 S.E.2d 448 (1976) ("delusional insanity" applies only if actual delusion was a causative factor and the delusion, if true, would justify the act).

[116] Ford v. State, 73 Miss. 734, 19 So. 665 (1896). And the delusion must arise from mental disease, not from mere religious belief or intellectual error. 21 *AmJur* 2d, "Criminal Law," section 41.

[117] People v. Nance, 25 Cal. App.3d 925, 102 Cal. Rptr. 266 (1972); Commonwealth v. Walzack, 360 A.2d 914 (Pa. 1976).

[118] Commonwealth v. Martin, 341 N.E.2d 885 (Mass. 1976); People v. Miller, 384 N.Y.S.2d 741, 349 N.E.2d 841 (1976).

killed or of receiving great bodily injury.[119] Also deadly physical force may be used where a lesser degree of force is inadequate and the victim is using, or reasonably appears to use, physical force against an occupant of a dwelling or business establishment while committing or attempting to commit burglary or another felony.[120]

A person is not justified in using physical force if he or she provoked the use of the victim's unlawful physical force, and at the same time had the intent to cause physical injury or death to another person. Also the defendant is not justified in using physical force if he or she was the initial aggressor.[121]

b. Defense of Property

The majority rule concerning the use of physical force in defense of premises is that the person in possession or control of any building or other premises, or a person who is privileged to be on those premises, is justified in using reasonable and appropriate physical force upon another person to the extent reasonably necessary to prevent the commission of an unlawful trespass by that other person.[122] However, the defendant may not use deadly force unless it is in defense of himself or herself (or another person, as described), or where the defendant reasonably believes it necessary to prevent destruction of the building or premises.[123]

   (i) the person against whom the force is used is attempting to dispossess him of his dwelling otherwise than under a claim of right to its possession; or
   (ii) the person against whom the force is used is attempting to commit or consummate arson, burglary, robber, or other felonious theft or property destruction and either
      (1) has employed or threatened deadly force against or in the presence of the actor; or
      (2) the use of force other than deadly force to prevent the commission or the consummation of the crime would expose the actor or another in his presence to substantial danger of serious bodily harm.

The general rule concerning use of physical force in defense of property, real or personal, is that a person is justified in using the reasonable and appropriate physical force to the extent the person reasonably believes necessary to prevent a theft or other criminal tampering involving that property.[124] The rule concerning the use of deadly force in connection with property in general is the same as that concerning the use of deadly force in defense of premises.

---

[119] People v. Fink, 552 P.2d 529 (Colo. App. 1976); People v. Williams, 56 Ill. App.2d 159, 205 N.E.2d 749 (1965).
[120] Collier v. State, 328 So.2d 626 (Ala. Crim. App. 1976); State v. Edwards, 220 S.E.2d 158 (N.C. App. 1975). See also People v. Sizemore, 69 Mich. App. 672, 245 N.W.2d 159 (1976) (unlawful entering of home does not necessarily give right to shoot the intruder).
[121] Tate v. State, 337 So.2d 13 (Ala. Crim. App. 1976); People v. Echoles, 36 Ill. App.3d 845, 344 N.E.2d 620 (1976); People v. Lenzi, 41 Ill. App.3d 825, 355 N.E.2d 153 (1976); State v. Adkins, 537 S.W.2d 246 (Mo. App. 1976).
[122] State v. Edwards, 28 N.C. App. 196, 220 S.E.2d 158 (1975). See also *McKinney's Consolidated Laws of New York*, Penal Law, section 35.20 (1975).
[123] People v. Jones, 12 Cal. Rptr. 777 (1961). See also Model Penal Code, Proposed Official Draft 1962, Section 306.(3): Deadly force to protect property is not justifiable unless the actor believes that:
[124] People v. Ceballos, 12 Cal.3d 470, 526 P.2d 241 (1974).

c. Law Enforcement Privileges

The majority view on the privileges of arrest and crime prevention is that a police officer is justified in using deadly force to apprehend or prevent the escape of a felon if the felony committed involved violence or surprise. This view also maintains that deadly force is not justified in capturing or preventing the escape of a person who committed a misdemeanor only.[125]

As may be inferred from the discussion of premises and property, a defendant in a law-enforcement case is privileged to use deadly force in preventing any felony attempted by violence that threatens to cause serious injury to the defendant or another person, or threatens to cause serious damage to the premises or property that the defendant was trying to protect.

6. Intoxication and Mistake

a. Intoxication

Intoxication, mistake of fact, and mistake of law are sometimes used as defenses to crimes. Similar to entrapment, insanity, and defenses relating to justification, these defenses also have the effect of eliminating the requisite element of criminal intent. Thus, where the crime requires proof of intent or knowledge, the defendant may seek to prove that he or she acted without such intent or knowledge because he or she was drugged or forced to consume alcohol involuntarily. Where the intoxication is voluntary, the traditional common law and statutory rule is that no defense is available.[126] However, where the crime charged requires proof of a *specific mens rea,* proof of the defendant's intoxication, voluntary or involuntary, is admissible to determine whether the defendant was able to formulate the requisite *mens rea.*[127]

---

[125] Jones v. Marshall, 528 F.2d 132 (2d Cir. 1975); State v. Kerr, 14 Wash. App. 584, 544 P.2d 38 (1975). A leading case is Durham v. State, 199 Ind. 567, 159 N.E. 145 (1927). There is some authority that only more violent felonies justify deadly force. See, e.g., Henderson v. State, 221 S.E.2d 663 (Ga. App. 1975); New York Penal Code 35.30 (1975); Model Penal Code, Proposed Official Draft 1962, Section 3.07.

[126] Lucas v. City of Long Beach, 131 Cal. Rptr. 470 (Cal. App. 1976); State v. Pickering, 245 N.W.2d 634 (S.D. 1976).

[127] State v. Clemons, 168 Conn. 395, 363 A.2d 33 (1975); People v. Fleming, 42 Ill. App.3d 1, 355 N.E. 2d 345 (1976); People v. Lerma, 66 Mich. App. 566, 239 N.W.2d 424 (1976).

PEOPLE v. HOOD

82 Cal. Rptr. 618, 462 P.2d 370 (1969)

Supreme Court of California

TRAYNOR, Chief Justice.

An indictment charged defendant in Count I with assault with a deadly weapon upon a peace officer, Alfred Elia, in Count II with battery upon a peace officer, Donald Kemper, and in Count III with assault with intent to murder Officer Elia. A jury found him guilty on Counts I and III and not guilty on Count II. . . . Defendant appeals.

On September 11, 1967, at about 2:00 A.M., defendant, his brother Donald, and a friend, Leo Chilton, all of whom had been drinking for several hours, knocked on the door of the house of Susan Bueno, defendant's former girlfriend, and asked if they could use the bathroom. Susan said no, but defendant forced his way in and started to hit her. He knocked her to the floor and kicked her. Donald Hood then took Susan aside, and defendant, Chilton, and Gene Saunders, a friend of Susan's who was staying at the house, went to the kitchen and sat down.

Gilbert A. Nielsen, Susan's next-door neighbor, was awakened by the sound of Susan's screams and called the police. Officers Elia and Kemper responded to his call. After talking to Nielsen, they went to Susan's house, knocked on the door, which was opened by Stella Gonzales, Susan's cousin, and asked if "Susie" was there. Miss Gonzales said, "Yes, just a minute," and in a few seconds Susan came running to the door crying. Officer Elia asked Susan if she had been beaten and who did it. She pointed to the kitchen and said, "They're in there right now." The two officers walked through the living room, where Susan, Susan's seven-year-old son, Ronnie, and Stella remained, and went into the kitchen. There they observed defendant on the right-hand side of the room leaning against a door. On the left side of the kitchen, the three other men were seated at a table. Officer Elia walked to the middle of the room and questioned the men at the table. Defendant interrupted the questioning and asked Officer Elia if he had a search warrant. Officer Elia replied that he did not need one since the person who rented the house had given him permission to enter. Defendant then directed a stream of obscenities at Officer Elia, who turned and, according to his testimony, started to place defendant under arrest for a violation of Penal Code section 415 (using vulgar, profane, or indecent language within the presence or hearing of women or children). He got no further than to say, "Okay fella, you are . . .," when defendant swung at him with his fist. When Officer Kemper attempted to go to Officer Elia's assistance, Donald Hood jumped on him from behind. During the ensuing struggle, Officer Elia fell with defendant on top of him in a corner of a pantry adjoining the kitchen at the rear. While struggling on the floor, Officer Elia felt a tug at his gun belt and then heard two shots fired.

A third officer, Laurence Crocker, who had arrived at the house shortly after the other two officers, came into the kitchen as the scuffle between Officer Elia and defendant was beginning. After he had control of Donald Hood, he looked across the kitchen and saw defendant with a gun in his right hand. He testified that defendant pointed the gun towards Officer Elia's mid-section and pulled the trigger twice.

Both Officers Crocker and Kemper testified that after the shots, defendant's arm came up over his head with the revolver in his hand. The struggle continued into the bathroom. Defendant was finally subdued when Officer Elia regained possession of the gun and held it against the side of defendant's neck. Officer Elia then noticed that defendant had shot him once in each leg.

The foregoing evidence is clearly sufficient to support the verdicts.

Defendant contends that the court . . . erred in instructing on the effect of intoxication with respect to the offenses charged in both Counts I and III. . . .

. . . [T]he court gave hopelessly conflicting instructions on the effect of intoxication. . . .

To guide the trial court on retrial, we consider the question of the effect of intoxication on the crime of assault with a deadly weapon.

Many cases have held that neither assault with a deadly weapon nor simple assault is a specific intent crime. A number of these cases held that an assault with a deadly weapon could be predicated on reckless, as well as intentional, conduct. . . .

The distinction between specific and general intent crimes evolved as a judicial response to the problem of the intoxicated offender. That problem is to reconcile two competing theories of what is just in the treatment of those who commit crimes while intoxicated. On the one hand, the moral culpability of a drunken criminal is frequently less than that of a sober person effecting a like injury. On the other hand, it is commonly felt that a person who voluntarily gets drunk and while in that state commits a crime should not escape the consequences.

Before the nineteenth century, the common law refused to give any effect to the fact that an accused committed a crime while intoxicated. The judges were apparently troubled by this rigid traditional rule, however, for there were a number of attempts during the early part of the nineteenth century to arrive at a more humane, yet workable, doctrine. The theory that these judges explored was that evidence of intoxication could be considered to negate intent, whenever intent was an element of the crime charged. . . . To limit the operation of the doctrine and achieve a compromise between the conflicting feelings of sympathy and reprobation for the intoxicated offender, later courts both in England and this country drew a distinction between so-called specific intent and general intent crimes.

Specific and general intent have been notoriously difficult terms to define and apply, and a number of textwriters recommend that they be abandoned altogether. . . . Too often the characterization of a particular crime as one of specific or general intent is determined solely by the presence or absence of words describing psychological phenomena—"intent" or "malice," for example—in the statutory language of defining the crime. When the definition of a crime consists of only the description of a particular act, without reference to intent to do a further act or achieve a future consequence, we ask whether the defendant intended to do the proscribed act. This intention is deemed to be a general criminal intent. When the definition refers to defendant's intent to do some further act or achieve some additional consequence, the crime is deemed to be one of specific intent. There is no real difference, however, only a linguistic one, between an intent to do an act already performed and an intent to do that same act in the future.

The language of Penal Code section 22, drafted in 1872 when "specific" and "general" intent were not yet terms of art, is somewhat broader than those terms: "No act committed by a person while in a state of voluntary intoxication is less criminal by reason of his having been in such condition. But whenever the actual existence of any particular purpose, motive, or intent is a necessary element to constitute any particular species or degree of crime, the jury may take into consideration the fact that the accused was intoxicated at the time, in determining the purpose, motive, or intent with which he committed the act." Even this statement of the relevant policy is no easier to apply to particular crimes. We are still confronted with the difficulty of characterizing the mental element of a given crime as a particular purpose, motive, or intent necessary to constitute the offense, or as something less than that to which evidence of intoxication is not pertinent. . . . Accordingly, on retrial the court should not instruct the jury to consider evidence of defendant's intoxication in determining whether he committed assault with a deadly weapon on a peace officer or any of the lesser assaults included therein. . . .

The judgment is reversed.

Recently crimes involving drug addiction and intoxication as defenses have raised issues similar to those involved in the insanity defense discussed earlier. For example, the Supreme Court has held that it is unconstitutional to punish a person for being a narcotic addict.[128] Similarly, chronic alcoholism has been determined to be a "status" or "condition" and thus cannot be made a crime by itself. Extremely difficult legal questions arise in connection with these defenses, and that of insanity, as to whether these conditions should be recognized as defenses. Is a drug addict or an alcoholic any more responsible for the crimes to which he or she is driven by addiction than an insane person who is driven by an irresistible impulse?

b. Mistake

Ignorance or mistake of fact and ignorance or mistake of law are also relied on as defenses to crimes. A bona fide and reasonable belief in the existence of facts that would justify or excuse the defendant's act if such facts existed is a valid defense to any crime.[129] The defendant must prove that such a belief was based on reasonable grounds. However, like the intoxication defense, even an unreasonable mistake may be a complete defense to a crime that requires a specific *mens rea* rather than a general *mens rea*.[130] In *malum prohibitum* crimes, sometimes referred to as civil offenses or public welfare offenses, if actual criminal intent is not a requirement, mistake of fact is not a defense.[131]

Because a general criminal intent only requires proof that the defendant intended to commit the prohibited act, ignorance or mistake of the *law* is not a valid defense, regardless of the degree of *mens rea* required in the particular crime.[132] Contrary to the defense of mistake of fact, the reasonableness of the defendant's mistake of law is not material. Thus, even where the defendant acts in good faith and reasonable reliance upon the advice of counsel, no defense is available. There are even cases holding that reliance upon the decision of a lower court or administrative tribunal is not a defense, thus allowing conviction if such a decision or ruling is later reversed.[133] In these jurisdictions the defendant may rely only upon the highest court

---

[128] Robinson v. California, 370 U.S. 660 (1962), held that a statute making it a misdemeanor "to be addicted to the use of narcotics" (making the status of addiction a criminal offense) was cruel and unusual punishment in violation of the Eighth and Fourteenth Amendments.

[129] People v. Wong, 35 Cal. App.3d 812, 111 Cal. Rptr. 314 (1974); Aarco American, Inc. v. Baylor, 18 Ill. App.3d 14, 309 N.E.2d 380 (1974); State v. Henderson, 296 So.2d 805 (La. 1974).

[130] Requirement that mistake must be such as does not arise from a want of proper care on part of person acting does not apply to acts that require a fraudulent or felonious intent in order to be criminal. Green v. State, 221 S.W.2d 612 (Tex. Crim. App. 1949).

[131] People v. Famalett, 346 N.Y.S.2d 957 (D.C. 1973).

[132] United States v. Manning, 509 F.2d 1230 (9th Cir. 1974); United States v. Toomey, 404 F. Supp. 1377 (S.D.N.Y. 1975). But see United States v. Ehrlichman, 376 F. Supp. 29 (D.C. 1974) (may be a defense to *malum prohibitum* crimes requiring specific intent, such as federal tax laws); United States v. Jonas Bros., Inc., 368 F. Supp. 783 (D. Alas. 1974) (may be a defense if statute establishes knowledge of the law as an element of the offense).

[133] State v. VFW Post #3722, 527 P.2d 1020 (Kan. 1974) (reliance on courts); Giant of Maryland, Inc. v. State's Attorney, 274 Md. 158, 334 A.2d 107 (1975) (advice of attorney); State v. Smith, 12 Wash. App. 514, 530 P.2d 354 (1974) (reliance on administrative decision).

in the jurisdiction, or the United States Supreme Court in the case of a federal issue. The sounder view and majority position is that a person may rely on the decisions of a lower court or administrative tribunal.[134]

QUESTIONS

actus facie – The act
Mens Rhea – Mental state

1. Describe the two basic elements of every crime.

2. Brown and Green planned to break into the corner grocery store down the street from their apartment and burglarize the cash register. About eight hours prior to the time of the scheduled break-in, they were arrested by a police officer who had been tipped off by an anonymous third party. → *no*
   Can Brown and Green be convicted of any crime? Would it make any difference if they were in the process of purchasing burglary tools at the time of the arrest? *yes*
   What if they were loading their own tools into a tool box at the time of the arrest? Explain. *yes*

3. While White waited in the getaway car outside, Johnson and Jones entered the First National Bank with intent to commit a robbery. When confronted with Johnson's revolver, the bank guard drew his own gun. Johnson and Jones thereupon immediately ran toward the door and the waiting getaway car. However, just seconds before, White had left the scene when he had spotted a patrol car that was coincidentally proceeding down the street in the direction of White and the bank. White sped away, and five blocks from his house (in a busy intersection about one mile from the bank) White accidentally hit and killed a pedestrian. White, Johnson, and Jones were apprehended within hours after these events occurred.
   Explain any possible basis for charging any or all of the suspects with first-degree murder. What, if any, other crimes could they be convicted of? *Manslaughter – involv. accomplice*

4. Give an example of a situation in which the defendant should seek to prove that he or she caused the death of a person because of a highly provoking act by that person. *Heat of passion*

5. Which of the two types of criminal assault most closely resembles the tort of assault? Explain.

6. Give an example of a burglary, under the modern statutory definition, in which the defendant "unlawfully remains upon premises." *Hi Tech – work –*

7. By establishing the crime of statutory rape, did the legislature intend to eliminate the defense that the defendant reasonably believed the consenting female was

---

[134] See, e.g., *United States v. Marcen Laboratories, Inc.*, 416 F. Supp. 453 (S.D.N.Y. 1976); *United States v. Ehrlichman*, in note 132; *Commonwealth v. Duncan*, 363 A.2d 803 (Pa. Super. 1976); *State v. Davis*, 63 Wis.2d 75, 216 N.W.2d 31 (1974).

beyond the age of consent? Does the *mens rea* consist solely of the intent to do the physical act? *no — Mental attitude at the time*

8. Is there any basis for establishing a completely new defense called brainwashing, under which the defendant would have to prove that he or she developed certain moral and social principles as a direct result of a particular external force, for example, a person or group of persons who influenced him or her, television indoctrination, or reading material? *? How could they themselves prove it if they really were Brainwashed.*

12

Criminal Procedure

A. Scope of Subject

Criminal procedure is much broader in scope than civil procedure. Rules of criminal procedure govern formal proceedings leading up to and including criminal trials, just as with civil procedure. But the law of criminal procedure goes considerably beyond that of civil procedure. It also governs the permissible scope of police detection of criminal activity, the manner in which police gather evidence against a suspect, and, if the defendant is found guilty, the manner in which punishment is imposed.

All laws pertaining to criminal procedure must be in accord with the United States Constitution. Over the past decade more and more principles of criminal procedure have been tested against the Constitution and are now based upon constitutional provisions, primarily the Fourth, Fifth, Sixth, and Eighth Amendments in the case of federal criminal proceedings, and the Fourteenth Amendment due process and equal protection clauses in the case of state proceedings. The other sources of the law of criminal procedure are the various state constitutions, state and federal criminal statutes (including the rules of criminal procedure), and procedural rules and regulations promulgated by the judicial branch as part of its authority to promote the administration of criminal justice (all of which must be in accord with the United States Constitution). Criminal procedure of the states and federal government differ in several material respects. The basic steps of criminal procedure can be summarized as follows:

STATE CRIMINAL PROCEDURE

1. Arrest, search, and seizure—the gathering of evidence. — *The crime*
2. Defendant booked at the police station. — *Logging in at jail*
3. Defendant charged with specific crime (charges may be based on warrant obtained prior to arrest). *Before or after crime*

4. Proceedings before judge (to advise defendant of rights and to set bond).
5. Preliminary hearing (defendant entitled to preliminary hearing when charged with felony; no hearing required when defendant has been indicted by grand jury).
6. Filing of indictment or information.
7. Arraignment.
8. Motions and plea.
9. Discovery. ——→ *getting to look a defenses files.*
10. ~~Extraordinary writs.~~
11. Trial. —— *all the rights are protected.*
12. Sentencing. → *pre sentence investigation*
13. Motions after trial.
14. Appeal.

FEDERAL CRIMINAL PROCEDURE

1. Arrest, search, and seizure—the gathering of evidence.
2. Appearance before judge.
3. Preliminary hearing (only permitted when grand jury has not yet returned indictment).
4. Grand jury indictment.
5. Filing of indictment by government.
6. Arraignment.
7. Motions and plea.
8. Discovery.
9. Extraordinary writs.
10. Trial.
11. Sentencing.
12. Motions after trial.
13. Appeal.

These steps, to be discussed in this chapter, indicate the chronological progression of all criminal proceedings. The importance of each step in any particular proceeding will differ depending upon the facts of the individual case.

B. Arrest, Search, and Seizure

Police conduct plays a very significant role in arrest, search, and seizure, as well as in confessions and identifications (Parts D. and E.). Indeed it is primarily police activities that have prompted the establishment of elaborate guidelines in these areas of criminal procedure. An agent of the state (the public) prosecutes the defendant in a criminal case.[1] The police too are agents of the executive branch of government acting on behalf of the public, according to the direction of the criminal statutes

---

[1] See Chapter 5, pp. 83–85.

that the executive must "execute and enforce the criminal laws." Here lies an important distinction between the initial stages of a criminal matter and the initial stages of civil litigation. In civil litigation there is no "agent" acting on behalf of the plaintiff to detect the tort or breach of contract or prevent it from occurring. In civil litigation, once the tort or breach has occurred, there is no governmental agent attempting to obtain evidence in support of the allegations in the complaint.

The fact that police conduct has prompted the establishment of elaborate guidelines for their activities does not suggest that they should not utilize the available methods to obtain evidence or to detect or prevent crimes. However, the need for the guidelines points out the competing values involved in the criminal process, particularly in the areas of arrest, search and seizure, confessions and identifications. Although the police must utilize all methods available to them, such as observation, surveillance, searches, seizures, interrogations, and third-party witnesses, it is inevitable that without statutory and constitutional safeguards police activities will tend to endanger the individual rights and freedoms that are fundamental to this society. The goal of criminal procedure is to obtain the efficient and expeditious investigation of crimes while maintaining the citizen's constitutional freedoms.

1. The Exclusionary Rule

The exclusionary rule provides that when any aspect of Fourth Amendment requirements regarding search and seizure has been violated, evidence illegally obtained as the result of that violation may be suppressed or excluded in the criminal prosecution. The practical result is that the prosecution must attempt to prove the essential elements of its case without the help of the important evidence illegally obtained. One major purpose of the principle is to reduce the amount of police abuse of the citizens' constitutional rights.

The exclusionary rule is founded upon the Fourth Amendment of the United States Constitution, which provides in part that "the right of the people to be secure in their persons, houses, papers, and effects, against unreasonable searches and seizures, shall not be violated." This does not prevent the government from conducting searches and seizures that are offensive or objectionable; it only protects against "unreasonable" searches and seizures. Of course, whether a particular search is unreasonable will depend on the facts surrounding each situation. The Supreme Court has established Fourth Amendment guidelines against which such searches are measured.

The exclusionary rule was first enunciated in the case of *Weeks* v. *United States,* in which the Supreme Court limited the application of the Fourth Amendment protection to prosecutions for federal crimes.[2] Thereafter, in *Mapp* v. *Ohio*[3] and several subsequent cases,[4] the principle was extended to prosecutions by state govern-

---

[2] Weeks v. United States, 232 U.S. 383 (1914).
[3] Mapp v. Ohio, 367 U.S. 643 (1961).
[4] See, e.g., One 1958 Plymouth Sedan v. Pennsylvania, 380 U.S. 693 (1965); Aguilar v. Texas, 378 U.S. 108 (1964).

ments by incorporating the Fourth Amendment prohibitions into the Fourteenth Amendment, which states that: "No *state* shall make or enforce any law which shall abridge the privileges or immunities of citizens of the United States; nor shall any *state* deprive any person of life, liberty, or property without due process of the law; nor deny person within its jurisdiction equal protection of the laws." In the case of searches and seizures, the United States Supreme Court has taken the words of the Fourteenth Amendment regarding (a) privileges and immunities, (b) due process, and (c) equal protection, and has firmly established the concept that these three phrases incorporate certain prohibitions that are *expressly* stated in the First, Fourth, Fifth, Sixth, and Eighth Amendments (even though those prohibitions appear to refer only to actions by the Congress rather than actions by states). Therefore, even though there is no prohibition against unreasonable search and seizure in the Fourteenth Amendment regarding state action, the provisions of the Fourth Amendment are said to be incorporated by the Fourteenth and applied to the states.

MAPP v. OHIO

367 U.S. 643 (1961)

Supreme Court of the United States

Mr. Justice CLARK delivered the opinion of the Court.

Appellant stands convicted of knowingly having had in her possession and under her control certain lewd and lascivious books, pictures, and photographs in violation of §2905.34 of Ohio's Revised Code. As officially stated in the syllabus to its opinion, the Supreme Court of Ohio found that her conviction was valid though "based primarily upon the introduction in evidence of lewd and lascivious books and pictures unlawfully seized during an unlawful search of defendant's home. . . ."

On May 23, 1957, three Cleveland police officers arrived at appellant's residence in that city pursuant to information that "a person [was] hiding out in the home, who was wanted for questioning in connection with a recent bombing, and that there was a large amount of policy paraphernalia being hidden in the home." Miss Mapp and her daughter by a former marriage lived on the top floor of the two-family dwelling. Upon their arrival at that house, the officers knocked on the door and demanded entrance but appellant, after telephoning her attorney, refused to admit them without a search warrant. They advised their headquarters of the situation and undertook a surveillance of the house.

The officers again sought entrance some three hours later when four or more additional officers arrived on the scene. When Miss Mapp did not come to the door immediately, at least one of the several doors to the house was forcibly opened and the policemen gained admittance. Meanwhile Miss Mapp's attorney arrived, but the officers, having secured their own entry, and continuing in their defiance of the law, would permit him neither to see Miss Mapp nor to enter the house. It appears that Miss Mapp was halfway down the stairs from the upper floor to the front door when the officers, in this highhanded manner, broke into the hall. She demanded to see the search warrant. A paper, claimed to be a warrant, was held up by one of the officers. She grabbed the "warrant" and placed it in her bosom. A struggle ensued in which the officers recovered the piece of paper and as a result of which they handcuffed appellant because she had been "belligerent" in resisting their official rescue of the "warrant" from her person. Running roughshod over appellant, a policeman "grabbed" her, "twisted [her] hand," and she "yelled [and] pleaded with him" because it "was hurting." Appellant, in handcuffs, was then forcibly taken upstairs to her bedroom where the officers searched a dresser, a chest of drawers, a closet and some suitcases. They also looked into a photo album and through personal papers belonging to the appellant. The search spread to the rest of the second floor including the child's bedroom, the living room, the kitchen and a dinette. The basement of the building and a trunk found therein were also searched. The obscene materials for possession of which she was ultimately convicted were discovered in the course of that widespread search.

At the trial no search warrant was produced by the prosecution, nor was the failure to produce one explained or accounted for. At best, "There is, in the record, considerable doubt as to whether there ever was any warrant for the search of defendant's home." The Ohio Supreme Court believed a "reasonable argument" could be made that the conviction should be reversed "because the 'methods' employed to obtain the [evidence] . . . were such as to 'offend "a sense of justice" ' " but the court found determinative the fact that the evidence had not been taken "from defendant's person by the use of brutal or offensive physical force against defendant."

The State says that even if the search were made without authority, or otherwise unreasonably, it is not prevented from using the unconstitutionally seized evidence at trial, citing Wolf v. Colorado, 338 U.S. 25 (1949), in which this Court did indeed hold "that in a prosecution in a State court for a State crime the Fourteenth Amendment does not forbid the admission of evidence obtained by an unreasonable search and seizure." At p. 33. On this appeal, of which we have noted probable jurisdiction, 364 U.S. 868, it is urged once again that we review that holding.

I.

Seventy-five years ago, in Boyd v. United States, 116 U.S. 616, 630 (1886), considering the Fourth and Fifth Amendments as running "almost into each other" on the facts before it,

this Court held that the doctrines of those Amendments "apply to all invasions on the part of the government and its employees of the sanctity of a man's home and the privacies of life. It is not the breaking of his doors, and the rummaging of his drawers, that constitutes the essence of the offence; but it is the invasion of his indefeasible right of personal security, personal liberty and private property. . . . Breaking into a house and opening boxes and drawers are circumstances of aggravation; but any forcible and compulsory extortion of a man's own testimony or of his private papers to be used as evidence to convict him of crime or to forfeit his goods, is within the condemnation . . . [of those Amendments]."

The Court noted that "constitutional provisions for the security of person and property should be liberally construed. . . . It is the duty of courts to be watchful for the constitutional rights of the citizen, and against any stealthy encroachments thereon." At p. 635.

In this jealous regard for maintaining the integrity of individual rights, the Court gave life to Madison's prediction that "independent tribunals of justice . . . will be naturally led to resist every encroachment upon rights expressly stipulated for in the Constitution by the declaration of rights." I Annals of Cong. 439 (1789). Concluding, the Court specifically referred to the use of the evidence there seized as "unconstitutional." At p. 638.

Less than 30 years after *Boyd,* this Court, in Weeks v. United States, 232 U.S. 383 (1914), stated that "the Fourth Amendment . . . put the courts of the United States and Federal officials, in the exercise of their power and authority, under limitations and restraints [and] . . . forever secure[d] the people, their persons, houses, papers and effects against all unreasonable searches and seizures under the guise of law . . . and the duty of giving to it force and effect is obligatory upon all entrusted under our Federal system with the enforcement of the laws." At pp. 391, 392.

Specifically dealing with the use of the evidence unconstitutionally seized, the Court concluded:

"If letters and private documents can thus be

seized and held and used in evidence against a citizen accused of an offense, the protection of the Fourth Amendment declaring his right to be secure against such searches and seizures is of no value, and, so far as those thus placed are concerned, might as well be stricken from the Constitution. The efforts of the courts and their officials to bring the guilty to punishment, praiseworthy as they are, are not to be aided by the sacrifice of those great principles established by years of endeavor and suffering which have resulted in their embodiment in the fundamental law of the land." At p. 393.

Finally, the Court in that case clearly stated that use of the seized evidence involved "a denial of the constitutional rights of the accused." At p. 398. Thus, in the year 1914, in the *Weeks* case, this Court "for the first time" held that "in a federal prosecution the Fourth Amendment barred the use of evidence secured through an illegal search and seizure." Wolf v. Colorado, 338 U.S. at 28. This Court has ever since required of federal law officers a strict adherence to that command which this Court has held to be a clear, specific, and constitutionally required—even if judicially implied—deterrent safeguard without insistence upon which the Fourth Amendment would have been reduced to "a form of words.". . .

II.

In 1949, 35 years after *Weeks* was announced, this Court, in Wolf v. Colorado, again for the first time discussed the effect of the Fourth Amendment upon the States through the operation of the Due Process Clause of the Fourteenth Amendment. It said:

"[W]e have no hesitation in saying that were a State affirmatively to sanction such police incursion into privacy it would run counter to the guaranty of the Fourteenth Amendment." At p. 28.

Nevertheless, after declaring that the "security of one's privacy against arbitrary intrusion by the police" is "implicit in 'the concept of ordered liberty' and as such enforceable against the States through the Due Process Clause," cf. Palko v. Connecticut, 302 U.S. 319 (1937),

and announcing that it "stoutly adhere[d]" to the *Weeks* decision, the Court decided that the *Weeks* exclusionary rule would not then be imposed upon the States as "an essential ingredient of the right." 338 U.S. at 27–29. The Court's reason for not considering essential to the right to privacy, as a curb imposed upon the States by the Due Process Clause, that which decades before had been posited as part and parcel of the Fourth Amendment's limitation upon federal encroachment of individual privacy, were bottomed on factual considerations. . . .

[T]he factual considerations supporting the failure of the Wolf Court to include the *Weeks* exclusionary rule when it recognized the enforceability of the right to privacy against the States in 1949, while not basically relevant to the constitutional consideration, could not, in any analysis, now be deemed controlling. . . .

III.

. . . Today we once again examine *Wolf*'s constitutional documentation of the right to privacy free from unreasonable state intrusion, and, after its dozen years on our books, are led by it to close the only courtroom door remaining open to evidence secured by official lawlessness in flagrant abuse of that basic right, reserved to all persons as a specific guarantee against that very same unlawful conduct. We hold that all evidence obtained by searches and seizures in violation of the Constitution is, by that same authority, inadmissible in a state court.

IV.

Since the Fourth Amendment's right of privacy has been declared enforceable against the States through the Due Process Clause of the Fourteenth, it is enforceable against them by the same sanction of exclusion as is used against the Federal Government. Were it otherwise, then just as without the *Weeks* rule the assurance against unreasonable federal searches and seizures would be "a form of words," valueless and undeserving of mention in a perpetual charter of inestimable human liberties, so too, without that rule the freedom from state invasions of privacy would be so ephemeral and so neatly severed from its conceptual nexus with the freedom from all brutish means of coercing evidence as not to merit this Court's high regard as a freedom "implicit in the concept of ordered liberty.". . .

. . . The right to privacy, no less important than any other right carefully and particularly reserved to the people, would stand in marked contrast to all other rights declared as "basic to a free society." Wolf v. Colorado, 338 U.S. at 27. This Court has not hesitated to enforce as strictly against the States as it does against the Federal Government the rights of free speech and of a free press, the rights to notice and to a fair, public trial, including, as it does, the right not to be convicted by use of a coerced confession, however logically relevant it be, and without regard to its reliability. Rogers v. Richmond, 365 U.S. 534 (1961). And nothing could be more certain than that when a coerced confession is involved, "the relevant rules of evidence" are overridden without regard to "the incidence of such conduct by the police," slight or frequent. Why should not the same rule apply to what is tantamount to coerced testimony by way of unconstitutional seizure of goods, papers, effects, documents, etc.? We find that, as to the Federal Government, the Fourth and Fifth Amendments and, as to the States, the freedom from unconscionable invasions of privacy and the freedom from convictions based upon coerced confessions do enjoy an "intimate relation" in their perpetuation of "principles of humanity and civil liberty [secured] . . . only after years of struggle," Bram v. United States, 168 U.S. 532, 543, 544 (1897). They express "supplementing phases of the same constitutional purpose—to maintain inviolate large areas of personal privacy." Feldman v. United States, 322 U.S. 487, 489, 490 (1944). The philosophy of each Amendment and of each freedom is complementary to, although not dependent upon, that of the other in its sphere of influence—the very least that together they assure in either sphere is that no man is to be convicted on unconstitutional evidence. Cf. Rochin v. California, 342 U.S. 165, 173 (1952).

V.

Moreover, our holding that the exclusionary rule is an essential part of both the Fourth and Fourteenth Amendments is not only the logical dictate of prior cases, but it also makes very good sense. There is no war between the Constitution and common sense. Presently, a federal prosecutor may make no use of evidence illegally seized, but a State's attorney across the street may, although he supposedly is operating under the enforceable prohibitions of the same Amendment. Thus the State, by admitting evidence unlawfully seized, serves to encourage disobedience to the Federal Constitution which it is bound to uphold. . . .

The ignoble shortcut to conviction left open to the State tends to destroy the entire system of constitutional restraints on which the liberties of the people rest. Having once recognized that the right to privacy embodied in the Fourth Amendment is enforceable against the States, and that the right to be secure against rude invasions of privacy by state officers is, therefore, constitutional in origin, we can no longer permit that right to remain an empty promise. Because it is enforceable in the same manner and to like effect as other basic rights secured by the Due Process Clause, we can no longer permit it to be revocable at the whim of any police officer who, in the name of law enforcement itself, chooses to suspend its enjoyment. Our decision, founded on reason and truth, gives to the individual no more than that which the Constitution guarantees him, to the police officer no less than that to which honest law enforcement is entitled, and, to the courts, that judicial integrity so necessary in the true administration of justice.

The judgment of the Supreme Court of Ohio is reversed and the cause remanded for further proceedings not inconsistent with this opinion.

Reversed and remanded.

In order to complain of the violation of one's constitutional rights and invoke the exclusionary rule, a person must be "aggrieved" by an unlawful search. It isn't necessary that the government has illegally invaded the defendant's property. In many situations the police violate the constitutional rights of A, yet on A's property they discover drugs or other evidence belonging to B. Nonetheless, B may still complain of such a violation, provided B has some interest in the property seized or has some reasonable expectation of being free of such governmental intrusion.[5]

If the trial court mistakenly admitted the introduction of evidence that should have been suppressed, appellate courts do not automatically reverse convictions obtained in such trials. It must appear from the record that the error was likely to have resulted in prejudice to the accused. That is, it must appear that a different result might have been reached if the trial court had not made the error. If the error appears to have been harmless, the conviction will not be overturned.[6] However, even though most situations are subject to this "harmless error rule," there are some situations, such as where a coerced confession has been obtained or a defendant has been denied the right to counsel, which result in automatic reversal despite additional evidence that may remain to support the conviction.[7]

The scope of the exclusionary rule extends beyond evidence that has been *directly* acquired by illegal means and encompasses all evidence that has also been *indirectly* acquired through the use of evidence illegally seized. This is known as the "fruit of the poisonous tree" doctrine. It may even extend to confessions when, for example, the defendant is not informed that his or her confession, illegally secured, cannot be used against him or her, and the police then obtain stolen property from the defendant. In this case the stolen property had a direct causal relationship to the confession and would not have been obtained without the confession.[8] The case of *Wong Sun* v. *United States* applied the "fruit of the poisonous tree" doctrine to a situation in which a confession and the names of witnesses are excluded if obtained as a result of an unlawful arrest.[9] Prior to the *Wong Sun* case the doctrine was limited to the exclusion of *goods* illegally seized and testimony related to such goods. Also, prior to *Wong Sun* it was not automatically assumed, in the case of an illegal arrest or search, that the confession did not result from an independent act of free will. Now, in an effort to deter the police from such illegal conduct in the future, these "fruits" are automatically excluded.

Yet the Supreme Court has modified this principle somewhat, because if the prosecution is able to overcome that assumption and prove that the confession was the product of free will, it and its fruits will not be excluded; the question of whether

---

[5] Jones v. United States, 362 U.S. 257 (1960); Alderman v. United States, 394 U.S. 165 (1969); Mancusi v. DeForte, 392 U.S. 364 (1968); Simmons v. United States, 390 U.S. 377 (1968).

[6] Fahy v. Connecticut, 375 U.S. 85 (1963); Chapman v. California, 386 U.S. 18 (1967).

[7] Haynes v. Washington, 373 U.S. 503 (1963); Gideon v. Wainwright, 372 U.S. 335 (1963).

[8] People v. Martin, 240 Cal. App.2d 653, 49 Cal. Rptr. 888 (1966); United States v. Bayer, 331 U.S. 532 (1947); Killough v. United States, 315 F.2d 241 (D.C. App. 1962); also see Smith and Bowden v. United States, 324 F.2d 879 (D.C. Cir. 1963), in which the court held that the chain of events (the causation) was broken.

[9] Wong Sun v. United States, 371 U.S. 471 (1963).

the incriminating statement was voluntary depends upon factors more recently outlined in the case of *Brown* v. *Illinois,* namely the time elapsing between the illegality and the statement, the presence of intervening circumstances, and the flagrancy of the illegality.

confession type case

BROWN v. ILLINOIS

422 U.S. 590 (1975)

Supreme Court of the United States

Mr. Justice BLACKMUN delivered the opinion of the Court.

This case lies at the crossroads of the Fourth and Fifth Amendments. Petitioner was arrested without probable cause and without a warrant. He was given, in full, the warnings prescribed by Miranda v. Arizona, 384 U.S. 436 (1966). Thereafter, while in custody, he made two inculpatory statements. The issue is whether evidence of those statements was properly admitted, or should have been excluded, in petitioner's subsequent trial for murder in state court. Expressed another way, the issue is whether the statements were to be excluded as the fruit of the illegal arrest, or were admissible because the giving of the *Miranda* warnings sufficiently attenuated the taint of the arrest. See Wong Sun v. United States, 371 U.S. 471 (1963). The Fourth Amendment, of course, has been held to be applicable to the States through the Fourteenth Amendment. Mapp v. Ohio, 367 U.S. 643 (1961).

I.

As petitioner Richard Brown was climbing the last of the stairs leading to the rear entrance of his Chicago apartment in the early evening of May 13, 1968, he happened to glance at the window near the door. He saw, pointed at him through the window, a revolver held by a stranger who was inside the apartment. The man said: "Don't move, you are under arrest." Another man, also with a gun, came up behind Brown and repeated the statement that he was under arrest. It was about 7:45 P.M. The two men turned out to be Detectives William Nolan

and William Lenz of the Chicago police force. It is not clear from the record exactly when they advised Brown of their identity, but it is not disputed that they broke into his apartment, searched it, and then arrested Brown, all without probable cause and without any warrant, when he arrived. They later testified that they made the arrest for the purpose of questioning Brown as part of their investigation of the murder of a man named Roger Corpus.

Corpus was murdered one week earlier, on May 6, with a .38-caliber revolver in his Chicago West Side second-floor apartment. Shortly thereafter, Detective Lenz obtained petitioner's name, among others, from Corpus' brother. Petitioner and the others were identified as acquaintances of the victim, not as suspects.

On the day of petitioner's arrest, Detectives Lenz and Nolan, armed with a photograph of Brown, and another officer arrived at petitioner's apartment about 5 P.M. . . . While the third officer covered the front entrance downstairs, the two detectives broke into Brown's apartment and searched it. Lenz then positioned himself near the rear door and watched through the adjacent window which opened onto the back porch. Nolan sat near the front door. He described the situation at the later suppression hearing: "After we were there for a while, Detective Lenz told me that somebody was coming up the back stairs. I walked out the front door through the hall and around the corner, and I stayed there behind a door leading on to the back porch. At this time I heard Detective Lenz say, 'Don't move, you are under arrest.' I looked out. I saw Mr. Brown backing away from the window. I walked up behind him, I told him he is under arrest, come back inside the apartment with us." As both officers held him at gunpoint, the three entered the apartment. Brown was ordered to stand against the wall and was searched. No weapon was found. . . . He was asked his name. When he denied being Richard Brown, Detective Lenz showed him the photograph, informed him that he was under arrest for the murder of Roger Corpus, handcuffed him, and escorted him to the squad car.

The two detectives took petitioner to the Maxwell Street police station. During the 20-minute drive Nolan again asked Brown, who then was sitting with him in the back seat of the car, whether his name was Richard Brown and whether he owned a 1966 Oldsmobile. Brown alternately evaded these questions or answered them falsely. Upon arrival at the stationhouse Brown was placed in the second-floor central interrogation room. The room was bare, except for a table and four chairs. He was left alone, apparently without handcuffs, for some minutes while the officers obtained the file on the Corpus homicide. They returned with the file, sat down at the table, one across from Brown and the other to his left, and spread the file on the table in front of him. . . .

The officers warned Brown of his rights under *Miranda.* They then informed him that they knew of an incident that had occurred in a poolroom on May 5, when Brown, angry at having been cheated at dice, fired a shot from a revolver into the ceiling. Brown answered: "Oh, you know about that." Lenz informed him that a bullet had been obtained from the ceiling of the poolroom and had been taken to the crime laboratory to be compared with bullets taken from Corpus' body. Brown responded: "Oh, you know that, too." At this point—it was about 8:45 P.M.—Lenz asked Brown whether he wanted to talk about the Corpus homicide. Petitioner answered that he did. For the next 20 to 25 minutes Brown answered questions put to him by Nolan, as Lenz typed.

This questioning produced a two-page state-ment in which Brown acknowledged that he and a man named Jimmy Claggett visited Corpus on the evening of May 5; that the three for some time sat drinking and smoking mari-huana; that Claggett ordered him at gunpoint to bind Corpus' hands and feet with cord from the headphone of a stereo set; and that Clagget, using a .38-caliber revolver sold to him by Brown, shot Corpus three times through a pillow. The statement was signed by Brown.

About 9:30 P.M. the two detectives and Brown left the stationhouse to look for Claggett in an area of Chicago Brown knew him to frequent. They made a tour of that area but did not locate their quarry. They then went to police headquarters where they endeavored, without success, to obtain a photograph of Clagget. They resumed their search—it was now about 11 P.M.—and they finally observed Claggett crossing at an intersection. Lenz and Nolan arrested him. All four, the two detectives and the two arrested men, returned to the Maxwell Street station about 12:15 A.M.

Brown was again placed in the interrogation room. He was given coffee and was left alone, for the most part, until 2 A.M. when Assistant State's Attorney Crilly arrived.

Crilly, too, informed Brown of his *Miranda* rights. After a half hour's conversation, a court reporter appeared. Once again the *Miranda* warnings were given: "I read him the card." Crilly told him that he "was sure he would be charged with murder." Brown gave a second statement, providing a factual account of the murder substantially in accord with his first statement, but containing factual inaccuracies with respect to his personal background. When the statement was completed, at about 3 A.M., Brown refused to sign it. An hour later he made a phone call to his mother. At 9:30 that morning, about 14 hours after his arrest, he was taken before a magistrate.

On June 20 Brown and Claggett were jointly indicted by a Cook County grand jury for Corpus' murder. Prior to trial, petitioner moved to suppress the two statements he had made. He alleged that his arrest and detention had been

[handwritten annotation in top margin]

illegal and that the statements were taken from him in violation of his constitutional rights. After a hearing, the motion was denied.

The case proceeded to trial. The State introduced evidence of both statements. Detective Nolan testified as to the contents of the first, but the writing itself was not placed in evidence. The second statement was introduced and was read to the jury in full. Brown was 23 at the time of the trial.

The jury found petitioner guilty of murder. He was sentenced to imprisonment for not less than 15 years nor more than 30 years.

On appeal, the Supreme Court of Illinois affirmed the judgment of conviction. The court refused to accept the State's argument that Brown's arrest was lawful. "Upon review of the record, we conclude that the testimony fails to show that at the time of his apprehension there was probable cause for defendant's arrest, [and] that his arrest was, therefore, unlawful." But it went on to hold in two significant and unembellished sentences: "[W]e conclude that the giving of the *Miranda* warnings, in the first instance by the police officer and in the second by the assistant State's Attorney, served to break the causal connection between the illegal arrest and the giving of the statements, and that defendant's act in making the statements was 'sufficiently an act of free will to purge the primary taint of the unlawful invasion.' (Wong Sun v. United States, 371 U.S. 471, at 486). We hold, therefore, that the circuit court did not err in admitting the statements into evidence." Aside from its reliance upon the presence of the *Miranda* warnings, no specific aspect of the record or of the circumstances was cited by the court in support of its conclusion. The court, in other words, appears to have held that the *Miranda* warnings in and of themselves broke the causal chain so that any subsequent statement, even one induced by the continuing effects of unconstitutional custody, was admissible so long as, in the traditional sense, it was voluntary and not coerced in violation of the Fifth and Fourteenth Amendments.

Because of our concern about the implication of our holding in Wong Sun v. United States, 371 U.S. 471 (1963), to the facts of Brown's case, we granted certiorari. 419 U.S. 894 (1974).

II.

In *Wong Sun,* the Court pronounced the principles to be applied where the issue is whether statements and other evidence obtained after an illegal arrest or search should be excluded. In that case, federal agents elicited an oral statement from defendant Toy after forcing entry at 6 A.M. into his laundry, at the back of which he had his living quarters. . . .

The exclusionary rule was applied in *Wong Sun primarily* to protect Fourth Amendment rights. Protection of the Fifth Amendment right against self-incrimination was not the Court's paramount concern there. To the extent that the question whether Toy's statement was voluntary was considered, it was only to judge whether it "was *sufficiently* an act of free will to purge the primary taint of the unlawful invasion." Id., at 486 (emphasis added).

The Court in *Wong Sun,* as is customary, emphasized that application of the exclusionary rule on Toy's behalf protected Fourth Amendment guarantees in two respects: "in terms of deterring lawless conduct by federal officers," and by "closing the doors of the federal courts to any use of evidence unconstitutionally obtained." These considerations of deterrence and of judicial integrity, by now, have become rather commonplace in the Court's cases. "The rule is calculated to prevent, not to repair. Its purpose is to deter—to compel respect for the constitutional guaranty in the only effectively available way—by removing the incentive to disregard it." Elkins v. United States, 364 U.S. 206 (1960). But "[d]espite its broad deterrent purpose, the exclusionary rule has never been interpreted to proscribe the use of illegally seized evidence in all proceedings or against all persons." United States v. Calandra, 414 U.S. at 348.

III.

The Illinois courts refrained from resolving the question, as apt here as it was in *Wong Sun,* whether Brown's statements were obtained by exploitation of the illegality of his arrest. They assumed that the *Miranda* warnings, by themselves, assured that the statements (verbal acts, as contrasted with physical evidence) were of sufficient free will as to purge the primary taint of the unlawful arrest. *Wong Sun,* of course, preceded *Miranda.*

. . . The function of the warnings relates to the Fifth Amendment's guarantee against coerced self-incrimination, and the exclusion of a statement made in the absence of the warnings, it is said, serves to deter the taking of an incriminating statement without first informing the individual of his Fifth Amendment rights.

Although, almost 90 years ago, the Court observed that the Fifth Amendment is in "intimate relation" with the Fourth, Boyd v. United States, 116 U.S. 616, 633 (1886), the *Miranda* warnings thus far have not been regarded as a means either of remedying or deterring violations of Fourth Amendment rights. Frequently, as here, rights under the two Amendments may appear to coalesce since "the 'unreasonable searches and seizures' condemned in the Fourth Amendment are almost always made for the purpose of compelling a man to give evidence against himself, which in criminal cases is condemned in the Fifth Amendment." The exclusionary rule, however, when utilized to effectuate the Fourth Amendment, serves interests and policies that are distinct from those it serves under the Fifth. It is directed at all unlawful searches and seizures, and not merely those that happen to produce incriminating material or testimony as fruits. In short, exclusion of a confession made without *Miranda* warnings might be regarded as necessary to effectuate the Fifth Amendment, but it would not be sufficient fully to protect the Fourth. *Miranda* warnings, and the exclusion of a confession made without them, do not alone sufficiently deter a Fourth Amendment violation.

Thus, even if the statements in this case were found to be voluntary under the Fifth Amendment, the Fourth Amendment issue remains. In order for the causal chain, between the illegal arrest and the statements made subsequent thereto, to be broken, *Wong Sun* requires not merely that the statement meet the Fifth Amendment standard of voluntariness but that it be "sufficiently an act of free will to purge the primary taint." 371 U.S. at 486. *Wong Sun* thus mandates consideration of a statement's admissibility in light of the distinct policies and interests of the Fourth Amendment.

If *Miranda* warnings, by themselves, were held to attenuate the taint of an unconstitutional arrest, regardless of how wanton and purposeful the Fourth Amendment violation, the effect of the exclusionary rule would be substantially diluted. Arrests made without warrant or without probable cause, for questioning or "investigation," would be encouraged by the knowledge that evidence derived therefrom could well be made admissible at trial by the simple expedient of giving *Miranda* warnings. Any incentive to avoid Fourth Amendment violations would be eviscerated by making the warnings, in effect, a "cure-all," and the constitutional guarantee against unlawful searches and seizures could be said to be reduced to "a form of words." See Mapp v. Ohio, 367 U.S. at 648. . . .

Brown's first statement was separated from his illegal arrest by less than two hours, and there was no intervening event of significance whatsoever. In its essentials, his situation is remarkably like that of James Wah Toy in *Wong Sun*. We could hold Brown's first statement admissible only if we overrule *Wong Sun*. We decline to do so. And the second statement was clearly the result and the fruit of the first.

The judgment of the Supreme Court of Illinois is reversed and the case is remanded for further proceedings not inconsistent with this opinion.

It is so ordered.

The case of *Katz* v. *United States* extended the concept of protection from unreasonable searches and seizures beyond actual physical trespass on the defendant's tangible property.[10] In *Katz* the FBI monitored a number of the defendant's telephone conversations by attaching a listening device to the outside of a public telephone booth. The information gathered was subsequently used as evidence in the trial against him. The United States Supreme Court reversed the conviction on the rationale that areas or places are not necessarily protected, but people are, no matter where they may be located. Wherever a person may reasonably expect to have privacy, that person is protected from invasion. However, as will be discussed later, what made the gathering of this information unreasonable was that the FBI did not first obtain a search warrant. The *Katz* case holds that no electronic surveillance may be undertaken without a search warrant.

2. Probable Cause

a. Constitutional Basis

The question of whether a warrant should be obtained prior to engaging in a search or seizure is part of the question of whether a search is unreasonable. The requirements for obtaining a warrant are stated in the Fourth Amendment: "[N]o Warrants shall issue, but upon probable cause, supported by Oath or Affirmation, and particularly describing the place to be searched, and the persons or things to be seized." Most state constitutions have provisions similar to the Fourth Amendment, both as to unreasonable searches and seizures and the warrant requirement. The rationale for this requirement is that the police should not have the sole discretion in determining whether a search and seizure should take place. Under the probable cause requirement, this decision is shared between the police and a judge, who must determine on a legal basis whether such "probable cause" exists. Thus the police must state to the judge sufficient facts, either from direct knowledge or from a reliable source. With these facts the judge will determine whether to issue a warrant for the search or arrest of the defendant. Probable cause to *arrest* a defendant consists of reasonable grounds to believe that a crime has been committed. Probable cause to *search* the defendant consists of reasonable grounds to believe that the items sought are connected with criminal activity, and that they will be found in the place to be searched.

b. Arrest Warrants

Numerous Supreme Court cases have refined the concept of probable cause as applied to arrest warrants. It is now held that an affidavit supporting and requesting the issuance of such a warrant must set forth: (1) the basis for the assertion by the police that the informant (from whom the police obtained their informa-

---

[10] Katz v. United States, 389 U.S. 347 (1967).

tion) was reliable; and (2) the underlying circumstances on which the informant based the conclusion that the suspect was engaging in criminal activities.[11]

In *Spinelli* v. *United States* the Court stated, however, that the affidavits supporting the warrant are not necessarily deficient (in which case the arrest would be invalid) if *other facts* had been attested to (by the affiant at the probable cause hearing) that were sufficient to establish probable cause.[12] Thus if the affiant could swear to additional personal observations sufficient to establish probable cause, or if the affiant had independent observations that could establish the reliability both of the informant and of the informant's information, then probable cause could be established. The "other facts" mentioned in Spinelli were further clarified in the case of *United States* v. *Harris*.[13] In this case the Court upheld a search warrant issued on a police officer's affidavit based on hearsay from an unidentified informant who had not previously supplied information to the police. The Court stated that warrants cannot be issued on uncorroborated hearsay, but that probable cause existed because of: (a) the informant's "personal and recent observations of the defendant's criminal activity," indicating that the information had been gained in a reliable manner; (b) the informant's statement against his own interest; and (c) the affiant-officer's knowledge of the defendant's background, which was consistent with the illegal activity alleged by the unidentified informant.

c. Search Warrants

Rule 41 of the Federal Rules of Criminal Procedure sets forth the conditions that must be met before a federal search warrant can be issued. The various state rules of criminal procedure also mandate most of these requirements. (Unless otherwise indicated, the following discussion of search warrants pertains to federal criminal procedure.) Any federal judge in the federal district where the property sought is located may issue a search warrant for that property. The case of *Coolidge* v. *New Hampshire* interpreted this requirement to mean that such a judge must be "neutral and detached." [14] Thus a search warrant cannot be issued by a person who is likely to be biased against the potential defendants, as was true in the *Coolidge* case, in which the issuing magistrate also happened to be the state's chief investigator and prosecutor. As explained earlier, the warrant is issued if the judge is satisfied that there is probable cause to believe that grounds for the warrant exist. There must be probable cause to believe that the items desired to be seized are connected with criminal activity, and that they will be found in the place named in the warrant. The warrant must state the grounds for its issuance and the names of those persons who gave affidavits in support of its issuance.

The federal government and several states have enacted statutes requiring an

---

[11] Spinelli v. United States, 394 U.S. 410 (1969); Aquilar v. Texas, in note 4.
[12] Spinelli v. United States, in preceding note.
[13] United States v. Harris, 403 U.S. 443 (1971).
[14] Coolidge v. New Hampshire, 403 U.S. 443 (1971).

officer to announce his or her purpose and authority prior to breaking into a dwelling after obtaining a validly issued search or arrest warrant.[15] This allows for the possible consent or voluntary compliance with the announced request, thereby avoiding violence. Failure to make such a required announcement results in an unlawful entry and search, thereby invoking the exclusionary rule regarding any evidence obtained as a result of that illegal entry. However, there are statutory exceptions to this requirement, as in the case of an emergency. Many states have also enacted statutes which expressly authorize judges to issue "no knock" search warrants.[16]

As stated previously, the general rule is that a search warrant must first be obtained in order to render lawful any search or arrest, and evidence obtained by it. However, there are a number of situations in which, for various policy and practical considerations, a search warrant is not required:

i. SEARCH INCIDENT TO AN ARREST

Search incident to an arrest is the most important exception to the general search warrant requirement. If a lawful arrest has been made pursuant to a valid arrest warrant, a search without a search warrant may be made incident to such an arrest. However, where the arrest to which the search is incident has been made without an arrest warrant, the arrest must have been made with probable cause in order for the search to have been valid. Therefore, any evidence obtained during an invalid arrest is not admissible in a subsequent trial. This requirement has been further limited by the case of *Gerstein* v. *Pugh,* in which the Supreme Court held that a prosecutor's assessment of probable cause by itself does not satisfy the Fourth Amendment requirement of probable cause for arrest.[17] That amendment requires a fair and reliable determination of probable cause as a condition of any significant pretrial restraint on liberty, which determination must be made by a judicial officer either before or promptly after the arrest. Further, a warrantless search incident to an arrest must be reasonable under all the circumstances and cannot be based upon the impracticability of procuring a search warrant.[18]

The rationale for the exception allowing a search without a warrant if it is incident to an arrest is that the suspect may have a concealed weapon or a concealed means of escaping, or may attempt to destroy evidence. Using this rationale, the Supreme Court in the case of *Chimel* v. *California* explained that reasonableness

---

[15] See, e.g., 18 U.S.C. section 3109: "The officer may break open any outer or inner door or window of a house, or any part of a house, or anything therein, to execute a search warrant, if, *after notice of his authority and purpose,* he is refused admittance or [it becomes] necessary to liberate himself or a person aiding him in the execution of the warrant" (emphasis added). For a discussion of common law history and state statutes, see Miller v. United States, 357 U.S. 301 (1957).

[16] See, e.g., 18 U.S.C. section 3109. Case law exceptions are listed in 68 *AmJur* 2d, "Searches and Seizures," section 91. A typical no-knock warrant statute is *McKinney's Consolidated Laws of New York,* Criminal Procedure Law 690.45 (1971).

[17] Gerstein v. Pugh, 420 U.S. 103 (1975).

[18] United States v. Rabinowitz, 339 U.S. 56 (1950); Chimel v. California, 395 U.S. 752 (1969).

under these circumstances limits the search to a search of the person and the area within that person's immediate control.[19] Any broader right under this exception would be contrary to the rationale just stated, because the arresting officer should only be concerned with the area from within which the suspect may grab a weapon or destructible evidence. Any area beyond the person's reach must be searched after obtaining a warrant to do so.

CHIMEL v. CALIFORNIA

395 U.S. 752 (1969)

Supreme Court of the United States

Mr. Justice STEWART delivered the opinion of the Court.

This case raises basic questions concerning the permissible scope under the Fourth Amendment of a search incident to a lawful arrest.

The relevant facts are essentially undisputed. Late in the afternoon of September 13, 1965, three police officers arrived at the Santa Ana, California, home of the petitioner with a warrant authorizing his arrest for the burglary of a coin shop. The officers knocked on the door, identified themselves to the petitioner's wife, and asked if they might come inside. She ushered them into the house, where they waited 10 or 15 minutes until the petitioner returned home from work. When the petitioner entered the house, one of the officers handed him the arrest warrant and asked for permission to "look around." The petitioner objected, but was advised that "on the basis of the lawful arrest," the officers would nonetheless conduct a search. No search warrant had been issued.

Accompanied by the petitioner's wife, the officers then looked through the entire three-bedroom house, including the attic, the garage, and a small workshop. In some rooms the search was relatively cursory. In the master bedroom and sewing room, however, the officers directed the petitioner's wife to open drawers and "to physically move contents of the drawers from side to side so that [they] might view any items that would have come from [the] burglary." After completing the search, they seized numerous items—primarily coins, but also several medals, tokens, and a few other objects. The entire search took between 45 minutes and an hour.

At the petitioner's subsequent state trial on two charges of burglary, the items taken from his house were admitted into evidence against him, over his objection that they had been unconstitutionally seized. He was convicted, and the judgments of conviction were affirmed by both the California Court of Appeal, and the California Supreme Court. Both courts accepted the petitioner's contention that the arrest warrant was invalid because the supporting affidavit was set out in conclusory terms, but held that since the arresting officers had procured the warrant "in good faith," and since in any event they had had sufficient information to constitute probable cause for the petitioner's arrest, that arrest had been lawful. From this conclusion the appellate courts went on to hold that the search of the petitioner's home had been justified, despite the absence of a search warrant, on the ground that it had been incident to a valid arrest. We granted certiorari in order to consider the petitioner's substantial constitutional claims.

Without deciding the question, we proceed on the hypothesis that the California courts

---

[19] Chimel v. California, 395 U.S. 752 (1969).

*Consent to
search has to
Be against the
person itself.*

were correct in holding that the arrest of the petitioner was valid under the Constitution. This brings us directly to the question whether the warrantless search of the petitioner's entire house can be constitutionally justified as incident to that arrest. The decisions of this Court bearing upon that question have been far from consistent, as even the most cursory review makes evident.

Approval of a warrantless search incident to a lawful arrest seems first to have been articulated by the Court in 1914 as dictum in Weeks v. United States, 232 U.S. 383. . . .

Eleven years later the case of Carroll v. United States, 267 U.S. 132, brought the following embellishment of the *Weeks* statement: "When a man is legally arrested for an offense, whatever is found upon his person *or in his control* which it is unlawful for him to have and which may be used to prove the offense may be seized and held as evidence in the prosecution." (Emphasis added.) Still, that assertion too was far from a claim that the "place" where one is arrested may be searched so long as the arrest is valid. . . .

. . . [The Fourth] Amendment's proscription of "unreasonable searches and seizures" must be read in light of "the history that gave rise to the words"—a history of "abuses so deeply felt by the Colonies as to be one of the potent causes of the Revolution. . . ." 339 U.S. at 69. The Amendment was in large part a reaction to the general warrants and warrantless searches that had so alienated the colonists and had helped the movement for independence. In the scheme of the Amendment, therefore, the requirement that "no Warrants shall issue, but upon probable cause," plays a crucial part. As the Court put it in McDonald v. United States, 335 U.S. 451:

"We are not dealing with formalities. The presence of a search warrant serves a high function. Absent some grave emergency, the Fourth Amendment has interposed a magistrate between the citizen and the police. This was done not to shield criminals nor to make the home a safe haven for illegal activities. It was done so that an objective mind might weigh the

need to invade that privacy in order to enforce the law. The right of privacy was deemed too precious to entrust to the discretion of those whose job is the detection of crime and the arrest of criminals. . . . And so the Constitution requires a magistrate to pass on the desires of the police before they violate the privacy of the home. We cannot be true to that constitutional requirement and excuse the absence of a search warrant without a showing by those who seek exemption from the constitutional mandate that the exigencies of the situation made that course imperative." Id., at 455–456. . . .

Only last Term in Terry v. Ohio, 392 U.S. 1, we emphasized that "the police must, whenever practicable, obtain advance judicial approval of searches and seizures through the warrant procedure," id., at 20, and that "[t]he scope of [a] search must be 'strictly tied to and justified by' the circumstances which rendered its initiation permissible." Id., at 19. The search undertaken by the officer in that "stop and frisk" case was sustained under that test, because it was no more than a "protective . . . search for weapons." Id., at 29. But in a companion case, Sibron v. New York, 392 U.S. 40, we applied the same standard to another set of facts and reached a contrary result, holding that a policeman's action in thrusting his hand into a suspect's pocket had been neither motivated by nor limited to the objective of protection. Rather, the search had been made in order to find narcotics, which were in fact found.

A similar analysis underlies the "search incident to arrest" principle, and marks its proper extent. When an arrest is made, it is reasonable for the arresting officer to search the person arrested in order to remove any weapons that the latter might seek to use in order to resist arrest or effect his escape. Otherwise, the officer's safety might well be endangered, and the arrest itself frustrated. In addition, it is entirely reasonable for the arresting officer to search for and seize any evidence on the arrestee's person in order to prevent its concealment or destruction. And the area into which an arrestee might reach in order to grab a weapon or evidentiary items must, of course, be governed by a like rule. A gun on a table or in a drawer in front of one who is arrested can be as dangerous to the arresting officer as one concealed in the clothing of the person arrested. There is ample justification, therefore, for a search of the arrestee's person and the area "within his immediate control"—construing that phrase to mean the area from within which he might gain possession of a weapon or destructible evidence.

There is no comparable justification, however, for routinely searching any room other than that in which an arrest occurs—or, for that matter, for searching through all the desk drawers or other closed or concealed areas in that room itself. Such searches, in the absence of well-recognized exceptions, may be made only under the authority of a search warrant.

The "adherence to judicial processes" mandated by the Fourth Amendment requires no less. . . .

Application of sound Fourth Amendment principles to the facts of this case produces a clear result. The search here went far beyond the petitioner's person and the area from within which he might have obtained either a weapon or something that could have been used as evidence against him. There was no constitutional justification, in the absence of a search warrant, for extending the search beyond that area. The scope of the search was, therefore, "unreasonable" under the Fourth and Fourteenth Amendments, and the petitioner's conviction cannot stand.

Reversed.

The time lapse between the arrest and the search incident to it is also important in determining the reasonableness of the search. In the case of *Preston* v. *United States* the defendants were convicted on the basis of evidence found in their car, which had been towed to a garage where it was then searched.[20] The Supreme Court reversed the conviction and held that the search was "too remote in time or place to have been made as incidental to the arrest." [21] However, in *Cooper* v. *California* the Court upheld a conviction based upon evidence obtained from an automobile that was searched a week after the defendant's arrest.[22] The Court held that although the search was not actually incident to the arrest, it was not an unreasonable search. The *Preston* case was not overruled but was distinguished on the basis that because the defendant in *Preston* was arrested for vagrancy, the retention of the car had nothing to do with the search that occurred; in *Cooper* the car was seized specifically because of the crime for which the defendant was arrested, namely narcotics charges.

If a search of the person, rather than the vehicle, is involved incident to an arrest, the Court has not made the *Preston-Cooper* distinction regarding the reason for the arrest. Under some circumstances a person stopped for a traffic violation may be properly subjected to a full-scale search. In *United States* v. *Robinson*[23] the defendant had been stopped by a police officer who, based on prior investigation, had reason to believe the defendant was driving without a valid driver's license. The defendant was pulled over and lawfully arrested for that offense. In a subsequent search of the defendant's person, the officer discovered a cigarette package that con-

---

[20] Preston v. United States, 376 U.S. 364 (1964).
[21] Preston, at 368.
[22] Cooper v. California, 386 U.S. 58 (1967).
[23] United States v. Robinson, 414 U.S. 218 (1973).

tained fourteen capsules of heroin. The defendant was later convicted for possession of heroin. On appeal of the conviction, the Court held that a full search incident to a lawful arrest is reasonable and thus not barred by the Fourth Amendment. This is true even though, as in *Robinson,* the search does not and is not intended to uncover weapons or evidence of the crime for which the arrest was made. The rationale is that an arrest based on probable cause is reasonable under the Fourth Amendment, and because that intrusion is justified, the search incident to that arrest requires no additional justification. Thus once a person is *lawfully* arrested, even for a traffic violation, that person is subject to a full search, and the Fourth Amendment does not require exclusion of any evidence discovered in such a search.[24]

ii. Emergency situations

If it reasonably appears that contraband or otherwise illegal or dangerous objects may be destroyed before they can be obtained by a warrant, or where life is in danger, a search may be made without a warrant. The Supreme Court has even upheld emergency situations in which a blood test was administered to the defendant, who was arrested for drunken driving, on the theory that delay in testing would threaten the loss of evidence because alcohol disappears from the blood rapidly.[25]

iii. Hot pursuit

When the police are on the immediate trail (in "hot pursuit") of a suspect, they may follow him or her inside the dwelling place and conduct a search. Although the precise scope of such a search is somewhat uncertain, it must be a reasonable one, such as for the purpose of locating the suspect or others who may pose a threat to the safety of the police or the public, or to locate weapons or other contraband, illegal, or dangerous items.[26]

iv. Vehicle searches

Where a police officer has probable cause to believe that a vehicle contains contraband or other items that would normally be subject to seizure with a warrant, the officer may search the vehicle without a warrant. In the case of *Chambers* v. *Maroney,* the Supreme Court established the principle that, where

---

[24] See also Gustafson v. Florida, 414 U.S. 260 (1973), a companion case to *Robinson.* The major distinction between *Robinson* and *Gustafson* was that in the latter the police officer had had no previous encounters with the defendant that would give rise to the probable cause held by the officer in *Robinson.* The Court dismissed this argument, holding the case indistinguishable from *Robinson.* The lack of department regulations requiring that the arrestee be taken into custody (present in *Robinson*) was also deemed irrelevant.

[25] Schmerber v. California, 386 U.S. 757 (1966). See also Chambers v. Maroney, 399 U.S. 42 (1970); Harris v. United States, 390 U.S. 234 (1968); Cady v. Dombrowski, 413 U.S. 1074 (1973).

[26] Warden v. Hayden, 387 U.S. 294 (1967).

probable cause existed on the highway for a warrantless search, the police may take the car to the police station and validly search it there without a warrant.[27]

v. OBJECT IN PLAIN VIEW

In the course of a warrantless search during an emergency or during hot pursuit, it was seen that the police may validly obtain contraband or dangerous objects. In addition, items that are not contraband or dangerous and that come or fall into the plain view of a police officer during a valid but warrantless search may be admissible evidence.

The "plain view" principle is somewhat unclear as a result of the split decision in the case of *Coolidge* v. *New Hampshire*.[28] Four justices held that the plain view exception to the necessity for search warrants applies only when a valid search is taking place, and the discovery of evidence in plain view is totally inadvertent on the part of the officer. The other four justices felt that any item in plain view of officers who are lawfully present may be seized without a warrant, if there is probable cause, regardless of whether its discovery is inadvertent or not.

vi. CONSENT TO SEARCHES

Of course, if the defendant consents or gives permission for the search, no warrant is required. If incriminating evidence is obtained by such a search, and the defendant later claims that entrance was coerced by the police, the question of proof may become a problem for the prosecution. Therefore police generally obtain a written waiver whenever possible. The question of voluntariness is determined from all the surrounding circumstances. The defendant's knowledge of the right to refuse consent may be a factor in determining whether the consent was voluntary.[29] However, the defendant does not *have* to know that he or she has a right to refuse consent in order for voluntariness to be found in the situation.

If the defendant has given the consent, there is little question that evidence obtained by it is admissible. However, problems arise in cases in which persons other than the defendant grant such consent, as in *Stoner* v. *California,* in which the police received consent from the hotel clerk for a search of the defendant's hotel room.[30] The Court held that the search violated the defendant's constitutional rights. In *United States* v. *Matlock* the Court stated that effective consent to a warrantless search may be given either by the accused or by any third party who possesses common authority or any other sufficient relationship regarding the premises sought to be inspected.[31] This case followed the earlier decision of *Frazier v. Cupp,* in which

---

[27] Chambers v. Maroney, 399 U.S. 42 (1970). See also Cardwell v. Lewis, 417 U.S. 583 (1974).

[28] Coolidge v. New Hampshire, 403 U.S. 443 (1971). See also Harris v. United States, 390 U.S. 234 (1968).

[29] Schneckloth v. Bustamonte, 412 U.S. 218 (1973).

[30] Stoner v. California, 376 U.S. 483 (1964). See also Chapman v. United States, 365 U.S. 610 (1961).

[31] United States v. Matlock, 415 U.S. 164 (1974).

the Court upheld a search that was conducted after consent was given by one occupant of an apartment and resulted in the conviction of the other occupant, who was absent at the time of the search.[32] Thus family members or other persons who share a house or apartment have sufficient joint access and control over the premises so that the consent of any such occupant is effective against the absent, nonconsenting person with whom the premises are shared.

The concept of consent has been liberally construed under the case of *United States* v. *White,* in which the Court held that eavesdropping upon one party to a conversation, if the consent of the other party has been given, is not an unreasonable search.[33] The Court's rationale is that a person making incriminating statements "assumes the risk" that the person in the conversation may testify against him or her. The Court's reasoning in this case does not follow logically, particularly when one considers that a person cannot "consent" to facts of which that person is unaware, namely that the person in the conversation is an informer, and that there is a third party listening to the conversation.

There have been suggestions that the *Miranda* requirements (to be discussed later in this chapter) should be expanded to require a warning that the suspect has a right to refuse consent to search, that if such consent is refused the officer must obtain a warrant, and that such refusal cannot later be used against the defendant. In the case of *Gentile* v. *United States,* consent to search the defendant's home was obtained from him during the actual custodial interrogation subsequent to the giving of the *Miranda* warnings, but without any warning regarding his right to refuse consent to search his home without a warrant.[34] Although the Supreme Court has had the opportunity to address this question of expanding the *Miranda* warnings, it has not done so. In view of recent *Miranda*-related decisions, it is unlikely that any such expansion will occur in the foreseeable future.[35]

3. Stop and Frisk

One further aspect of arrest, search, and seizure is the authority of the police to actually stop persons for the purpose of "frisking," questioning, or detaining them. The important distinction between the right to stop and frisk and the right to arrest is that the police have the authority to conduct such a stop and frisk even though they may not possess sufficient information to constitute probable cause for arrest. Even in the absence of probable cause, the Supreme Court recognizes a basis for such police conduct short of actual arrest. The definitive decision regarding the law of stop and frisk continues to be the 1968 case of *Terry* v. *Ohio.*[36] In *Terry* the

---

[32] Frazier v. Cupp, 394 U.S. 731 (1969).
[33] United States v. White, 401 U.S. 745 (1971).
[34] Gentile v. United States, 419 U.S. 979 (1974).
[35] See, e.g., Collins v. Brierly, 492 F.2d 735 (3d Cir. 1974); United States v. Vasquez, 476 F.2d 730 (5th Cir. 1973); Massimo v. United States, 463 F.2d 1171 (2d Cir. 1972); United States v. Springer, 460 F.2d 1344 (7th Cir. 1972); United States v. Gallagher, 430 F.2d 1222 (7th Cir. 1970).
[36] Terry v. Ohio, 392 U.S. 1 (1968).

Supreme Court stated that there is no question that a "pat-down" (that is, a frisk) constitutes a search under the Fourth Amendment. The question then becomes whether such a "search" is reasonable and thus constitutionally permissible. The Court employed a two-part test to determine reasonableness: (1) whether the officer's action in stopping the defendant was justified at its inception; and (2) whether the officer's conduct in frisking the suspect was reasonably related in scope to the circumstances that justified the stop in the first place.

Thus there need be no warrant or probable cause for arrest to justify a stop and frisk. The whole idea is that, as a practical matter, the police must be able to take prompt action based on their on-the-spot observations. On the other hand, the officer must be able to point to "specific and articulable" facts that, taken with rational inferences from those facts, reasonably warrant intrusion. That is, would a person of reasonable caution have believed that the action was necessary? [37] For example, was it reasonable to believe that the detainee was armed?

However, the exigency which leads to the conclusion that pat-downs are permissible also gives rise to a limit on the scope of the pat-down. It is limited "to that which is necessary for the discovery of weapons which might be used to harm the officer or others nearby." [38]

Although the frisk question is the primary thrust of the *Terry* decision, that case also noted the power of a police officer to *stop* an individual, to *question* that individual, and to *detain* that individual. Apparently the considerations applicable to the frisk question also apply to these matters. For example, according to *Terry,* detention for questioning, to be lawful, requires (1) reasonable suspicion that the detainee has committed a crime or is about to commit a crime, (2) that the purpose of detention must be reasonable, and (3) that the nature of the detention must be reasonable in light of its purpose.[39]

C. Wiretapping and Electronic Eavesdropping

Prior to the mid-1960s, the United States Supreme Court had held that the Fourth Amendment of the United States Constitution did not prohibit wiretapping because the Amendment is intended to protect only against the search and seizure of tangible, material items. This conclusion was based primarily on the actual wording of the Fourth Amendment, which only mentions protection of "persons, papers, houses, and effects." For many years wiretaps were upheld on the basis that the evidence was secured without actually entering the suspect's house. In recent years, however, the Fourth Amendment has acquired a new meaning under Supreme Court decisions. Current decisions adhere to the concept that the Fourth Amendment is intended to protect a person's right of privacy, not just the right to possession of

---

[37] Just what facts justify such a belief are unclear, but see Adams v. Williams, 407 U.S. 143 (1972), in which the only information the officer had was a tip by an informant whom he knew to be reliable. The officer's seizure of defendant's weapon was upheld.

[38] Terry v. Ohio, 392 U.S. 1 (1968).

[39] Terry v. Ohio, 392 U.S. 1 (1968).

certain tangible items. Thus, if there has been an intrusion into an area which the defendant would normally expect to retain the right of privacy, there has been an illegal search under the Fourth Amendment.[40]

Because information obtained through wiretapping and electronic surveillance is now considered to fall under the Fourth Amendment, without a proper search warrant such communications are beyond the reach of the police. The Supreme Court has held unconstitutional state statutes that improperly allow the issuance of search warrants for such confidential communications. The Court has stated that such statutes must require the warrants to contain sufficient particularity as to the crime that has been or was being committed, the place to be searched, or the persons or things (including conversations) to be seized.

BERGER v. NEW YORK

388 U.S. 41 (1967)

Supreme Court of the United States

Mr. Justice CLARK delivered the opinion of the Court.

This writ tests the validity of New York's permissive eavesdrop statute, under the Fourth, Fifth, Ninth, and Fourteenth Amendments. The claim is that the statute sets up a system of surveillance which involves trespassory intrusions into private, constitutionally protected premises, authorizes "general searches" for "mere evidence," and is an invasion of the privilege against self-incrimination.... We have concluded that the language of New York's statute is too broad in its sweep resulting in a trespassory intrusion into a constitutionally protected area and is, therefore, violative of the Fourth and Fourteenth Amendments. This disposition obviates the necessity for any discussion of the other points raised.

I.

Berger, the petitioner, was convicted on two counts of conspiracy to bribe the Chairman of the New York State Liquor Authority. The case arose out of the complaint of one Ralph Pansini to the District Attorney's office that agents of the State Liquor Authority had en-

tered his bar and grill and without cause seized his books and records. Pansini asserted that the raid was in reprisal for his failure to pay a bribe for a liquor license. Numerous complaints had been filed with the District Attorney's office charging the payment of bribes by applicants for liquor licenses. On the direction of that office, Pansini, while equipped with a "minifon" recording device, interviewed an employee of the Authority. The employee advised Pansini that the price for a license was $10,000 and suggested that he contact attorney Harry Neyer. Neyer subsequently told Pansini that he worked with the Authority employee before and that the latter was aware of the going rate on liquor licenses downtown.

On the basis of this evidence an eavesdrop order was obtained from a Justice of the State Supreme Court, as provided by §813-a. The order permitted the installation, for a period of 60 days, of a recording device in Neyer's office. On the basis of leads obtained from this eavesdrop a second order permitting the installation, for a like period, of a recording device in the office of one Harry Steinman was obtained. After some two weeks of eavesdropping a con-

[40] Katz v. United States, 389 U.S. 347 (1967).

spiracy was uncovered involving the issuance of liquor licenses for the Playboy and Tenement Clubs, both of New York City. Petitioner was indicted as "a go-between" for the principal conspirators, who though not named in the indictment were disclosed in a bill of particulars. Relevant portions of the recordings were received in evidence at the trial and were played to the jury, all over the objection of the petitioner. The parties have stipulated that the District Attorney "had no information upon which to proceed to present a case to the Grand Jury, or on the basis of which to prosecute" the petitioner except by the use of the eavesdrop evidence.

II.

Eavesdropping is an ancient practice which at common law was condemned as a nuisance. At one time the eavesdropper listened by naked ear under the eaves of houses or their windows, or beyond their walls seeking out private discourse. The awkwardness and undignified manner of this method as well as its susceptibility to abuse was immediately recognized. Electricity, however, provided a better vehicle and with the advent of the telegraph surreptitious interception of messages began. As early as 1862 California found it necessary to prohibit the practice by statute. . . .

The telephone brought on a new and more modern eavesdropper known as the "wiretapper." Interception was made by a connection with a telephone line. This activity has been with us for three-quarters of a century. Like its cousins, wiretapping proved to be a commercial as well as a police technique. Illinois outlawed it in 1895 and in 1905 California extended its telegraph interception prohibition to the telephone. Some 50 years ago a New York legislative committee found that police, in cooperation with the telephone company, had been tapping telephone lines in New York despite an Act passed in 1895 prohibiting it. During prohibition days wiretaps were the principal source of information relied upon by the police as the basis for prosecutions. In 1934 the Congress outlawed the interception without authoriza-

tion, and the divulging or publishing of the contents of wiretaps by passing §605 of the Communications Act of 1934. New York, in 1938, declared by constitutional amendment that "[t]he right of the people to be secure against unreasonable interception of telephone and telegraph communications shall not be violated," but permitted by ex parte order of the Supreme Court of the State the interception of communications on a showing of "reasonable ground to believe that evidence of crime" might be obtained. . . .

Sophisticated electronic devices have now been developed (commonly known as "bugs") which are capable of eavesdropping on anyone in almost any given situation. They are to be distinguished from "wiretaps" which are confined to the interception of telegraphic and telephonic communications. Miniature in size (⅜″ x ⅜″ x ⅛″)—no larger than a postage stamp—these gadgets pick up whispers within a room and broadcast them half a block away to a receiver. It is said that certain types of electronic rays beamed at walls or glass windows are capable of catching voice vibrations as they are bounced off the surfaces. Since 1940 eavesdropping has become a big business. Manufacturing concerns offer complete detection systems which automatically record voices under most any conditions by remote control. A microphone concealed in a book, a lamp, or other unsuspected place in a room, or made into a fountain pen, tie clasp, lapel button, or cuff link increases the range of these powerful wireless transmitters to a half mile. Receivers pick up the transmission with interference-free reception on a special wave frequency. And, of late, a combination mirror transmitter has been developed which permits not only sight but voice transmission up to 300 feet. Likewise, parabolic microphones, which can overhear conversations without being placed within the premises monitored, have been developed.

As science developed these detection techniques, lawmakers, sensing the resulting invasion of individual privacy, have provided some statutory protection for the public. Seven states, California, Illinois, Maryland, Massachusetts, Nevada, New York, and Oregon, prohibit surreptitious eavesdropping by mechanical or electronic device. However, all save Illinois permit official court-ordered eavesdropping. Some 36 states prohibit wiretapping. But of these, 27 permit "authorized" interception of some type. Federal law, as we have seen, prohibits interception and divulging or publishing of the content of wiretaps without exception. In sum, it is fair to say that wiretapping on the whole is outlawed, except for permissive use by law enforcement officials in some states; while electronic eavesdropping is—save for seven states—permitted both officially and privately. And, in six of the seven states electronic eavesdropping ("bugging") is permissible on court order.

III.

The law, though jealous of individual privacy, has not kept pace with these advances in scientific knowledge. This is not to say that individual privacy has been relegated to a second-class position for it has been held since Lord Camden's day that intrusions into it are "subversive of all the comforts of society." And the Founders so decided a quarter of a century later when they declared in the Fourth Amendment that the people had a right "to be secure in their persons, houses, papers, and effects, against unreasonable searches and seizures. . . ."

IV.

The Court was faced with its first wiretap case in 1928, Olmstead v. United States, 277 U.S. 438. There the interception of Olmstead's telephone line was accomplished without entry upon his premises and was, therefore, found not to be proscribed by the Fourth Amendment. The basis of the decision was that the Constitution did not forbid the obtaining of evidence by wiretapping unless it involved actual unlawful entry into the house. Statements in the opinion that a conversation passing over a telephone wire cannot be said to come within the Fourth Amendment's enumeration of "persons, houses, papers, and effects" have been negated by our subsequent cases as hereinafter

noted. They found "conversation" was within the Fourth Amendment's protections, and that the use of electronic devices to capture it was a "search" within the meaning of the Amendment, and we so hold. In any event, Congress soon thereafter, and some say in answer to Olmstead, specifically prohibited the interception without authorization and the divulging or publishing of the contents of telephonic communications. And the Nardone cases, 302 U.S. 379 (1937) and 308 U.S. 338 (1939), extended the exclusionary rule to wiretap evidence offered in federal prosecutions.

The first "bugging" case reached the Court in 1942 in Goldman v. United States, 316 U.S. 129. There the Court found that the use of a dictaphone placed against an office wall in order to hear private conversations in the office next door did not violate the Fourth Amendment because there was no physical trespass in connection with the relevant interception. And in On Lee v. United States, 343 U.S. 747 (1952), we found that since "no trespass was committed" a conversation between Lee and a federal agent, occurring in the former's laundry and electronically recorded, was not condemned by the Fourth Amendment. Thereafter in Silverman v. United States, 365 U.S. 505 (1961), the Court found "that the eavesdropping was accomplished by means of an unauthorized physical penetration into the premises occupied by the petitioners." At 509. A spike a foot long with a microphone attached to it was inserted under a baseboard into a party wall until it made contact with the heating duct that ran through the entire house occupied by Silverman, making a perfect sounding board through which the conversations in question were overheard. Significantly, the Court held that its decision did "not turn upon the technicality of a trespass upon a party wall as a matter of local law. It is based upon the reality of an actual intrusion into a constitutionally protected area." At 512.

In Wong Sun v. United States, 371 U.S. 471 (1963), the Court for the first time specifically held that verbal evidence may be the fruit of official illegality under the Fourth Amendment along with the more common tangible fruits of unwarranted intrusion. . . .

And in Lopez v. United States, 373 U.S. 427 (1963), the Court confirmed that it had "in the past sustained instances of 'electronic eavesdropping' against constitutional challenge, when devices have been used to enable government agents to overhear conversations which would have been beyond the reach of the human ear. . . . It has been insisted only that the electronic device not be planted by an unlawful physical invasion of a constitutionally protected area." At 438–439.

In this case a recording of a conversation between a federal agent and the petitioner in which the latter offered the agent a bribe was admitted in evidence. Rather than constituting "eavesdropping" the Court found that the recording "was used only to obtain the most reliable evidence possible of a conversation in which the Government's own agent was a participant and which that agent was fully entitled to disclose." At 439.

V.

It is now well settled that "the Fourth Amendment's right of privacy has been declared enforceable against the states through the Due Process Clause of the Fourteenth" Amendment. Mapp v. Ohio, 367 U.S. 643, 655 (1961). "The security of one's privacy against arbitrary intrusion by the police—which is at the core of the Fourth Amendment—is basic to a free society." Wolf v. Colorado, 338 U.S. 25, 27 (1949). And its "fundamental protections . . . are guaranteed . . . against invasion by the states." Stanford v. Texas, 379 U.S. 476, 481 (1965). . . .

We, therefore, turn to New York's statute to determine the basis of the search and seizure authorized by it upon the order of a state supreme court justice, a county judge or general sessions judge of New York County. Section 813-a authorizes the issuance of an "ex parte order for eavesdropping" upon "oath or affirmation of a district attorney, or of the attorney-general or of an officer above the rank of sergeant of any police department of the state

or of any political subdivision thereof. . . ." The oath must state "that there is reasonable ground to believe that evidence of crime may be thus obtained, and particularly describing the person or persons whose communications, conversations or discussions are to be overheard or recorded and the purpose thereof, and . . . identifying the particular telephone number or telegraph line involved." The judge "may examine on oath the applicant and any other witness he may produce and shall satisfy himself of the existence of reasonable grounds for the granting of such application." The order must specify the duration of the eavesdrop—not exceeding two months unless extended—and "[a]ny such order together with the papers upon which the application was based, shall be delivered to and retained by the applicant as authority for the eavesdropping authorized therein."

While New York's statute satisfies the Fourth Amendment's requirement that a neutral and detached authority be interposed between the police and the public, Johnson v. United States 333 U.S. 10, 14 (1948), the broad sweep of the statute is immediately observable. It permits the issuance of the order, or warrant for eavesdropping, upon the oath of the attorney general, the district attorney or any police officer above the rank of sergeant stating that "there is reasonable ground to believe that evidence of crime may be thus obtained . . . ." Such a requirement raises a serious probable-cause question under the Fourth Amendment. Under it warrants may only issue "but upon probable cause, supported by Oath or affirmation, and particularly describing the place to be searched, and the persons or things to be seized." Probable cause under the Fourth Amendment exists where the facts and circumstances within the affiant's knowledge, and of which he has reasonably trustworthy information, are sufficient unto themselves to warrant a man of reasonable caution to believe that an offense has been or is being committed. . . .

The Fourth Amendment commands that a warrant issue not only upon probable cause supported by oath or affirmation, but also "particularly describing the place to be searched, and the persons or things to be seized." New York's statute lacks this particularization. It merely says that a warrant may issue on reasonable ground to believe that evidence of crime may be obtained by the eavesdrop. It lays down no requirement for particularity in the warrant as to what specific crime has been or is being committed, nor "the place to be searched," or "the persons or things to be seized" as specifically required by the Fourth Amendment. The need for particularity and evidence of reliability in the showing required when judicial authorization of a search is sought is especially great in the case of eavesdropping. By its very nature eavesdropping involves an intrusion on privacy that is broad in scope. As was said in Osborn v. United States, 385 U.S. 323 (1966), the "indiscriminate use of such devices in law enforcement raises grave constitutional questions under the Fourth and Fifth Amendments," and imposes "a heavier responsibility on this Court in its supervision of the fairness of procedures. . . ." At 329, note 7. There, two judges acting jointly authorized the installation of a device on the person of a prospective witness to record conversations between him and an attorney for a defendant then on trial in the United States District Court. The judicial authorization was based on an affidavit of the witness setting out in detail previous conversations between the witness and the attorney concerning the bribery of jurors in the case. The recording device was, as the Court said, authorized "under the most precise and discriminate circumstances, circumstances which fully met the 'requirement of particularity' " of the Fourth Amendment. . . .

By contrast, New York's statute lays down no such "precise and discriminate" requirements. Indeed, it authorizes the "indiscriminate use" of electronic devices as specifically condemned in *Osborn.* "The proceeding by search warrant is a drastic one," Sgro v. United States, 287 U.S. 206, 210 (1932), and must be carefully circumscribed so as to prevent unauthorized invasions of "the sanctity of a man's home and the privacies of life." Boyd v. United States, 116 U.S. 616, at 630. New York's broadside

authorization rather than being "carefully circumscribed" so as to prevent unauthorized invasions of privacy actually permits general searches by electronic devices, the truly offensive character of which was first condemned in Entick v. Carrington, 19 How. St. Tr. 1029, and which were then known as "general warrants." The use of the latter was a motivating factor behind the Declaration of Independence. In view of the many cases commenting on the practice it is sufficient here to point out that under these "general warrants" customs officials were given blanket authority to conduct general searches for goods imported to the Colonies in violation of the tax laws of the Crown. The Fourth Amendment's requirement that a warrant "particularly describ[e] the place to be searched, and the persons or things to be seized," repudiated these general warrants and "makes general searches . . . impossible and prevents the seizure of one thing under a warrant describing another. As to what is to be taken, nothing is left to the discretion of the officer executing the warrant." Marron v. United States, 275 U.S. 192, 196 (1927).

We believe the statute here is equally offensive. First, as we have mentioned, eavesdropping is authorized without requiring belief that any particular offense has been or is being committed; nor that the "property" sought, the conversations, be particularly described. The purpose of the probable-cause requirements of the Fourth Amendment, to keep the state out of constitutionally protected areas until it has reason to believe that a specific crime has been or is being committed, is thereby wholly aborted. Likewise the statute's failure to describe with particularity the conversations sought gives the officer a roving commission to "seize" any and all conversations. It is true that the statute requires the naming of "the person or persons whose communications, conversations or discussions are to be overheard or recorded. . . ." But this does no more than identify the person whose constitutionally protected area is to be invaded rather than "particularly describing" the communications, conversations, or discussions to be seized. As with general warrants this leaves too much to the discretion of the officer executing the order. Secondly, authorization of eavesdropping for a two-month period is the equivalent of a series of intrusions, searches, and seizures pursuant to a single showing of probable cause. Prompt execution is also avoided. During such a long and continuous (24 hours a day) period the conversations of any and all persons coming into the area covered by the device will be seized indiscriminately and without regard with their connection to the crime under investigation. Moreover, the statute permits, and there were authorized here, extensions of the original two-month period—presumably for two months each—one a mere showing that such extension is "in the public interest." Apparently the original grounds on which the eavesdrop order was initially issued also form the basis of the renewal. This we believe insufficient without a showing of present probable cause for the continuance of the eavesdrop. Third, the statute places no termination date on the eavesdrop once the conversation sought is seized. This is left entirely in the discretion of the officer. Finally, the statute's procedure, necessarily because its success depends on secrecy, has no requirement for notice as do conventional warrants, nor does it overcome this defect by requiring some showing of special facts. On the contrary, it permits unconsented entry without any showing of exigent circumstances. Such a showing of exigency, in order to avoid notice, would appear more important in eavesdropping, with its inherent dangers, than that required when conventional procedures of search and seizure are utilized. Nor does the statute provide for a return on the warrant thereby leaving full discretion in the officer as to the use of seized conversations of innocent as well as guilty parties. In short, the statute's blanket grant of permission to eavesdrop is without adequate judicial supervision or protective procedures.

VI.

It is said with fervor that electronic eavesdropping is a most important technique of law enforcement and that outlawing it will severely cripple crime detection. The monumental report of the President's Commission on Law Enforcement and Administration of Justice entitled "The Challenge of Crime in a Free Society" informs us that the majority of law enforcement officials say that this is especially true in the detection of organized crime. As the Commission reports, there can be no question about the serious proportions of professional criminal activity in this country. However, we have found no empirical statistics on the use of electronic devices (bugging) in the fight against organized crime. Indeed, there are even figures available in the wiretap category which indicate to the contrary. As the Commission points out," [w]iretapping was the mainstay of the New York attack against organized crime until Federal court decisions intervened. Recently chief reliance in some offices has been placed on bugging, where the information is to be used in court. Law enforcement officials believe that the successes achieved in some parts of the State are attributable primarily to a combination of dedicated and competent personnel and adequate legal tools; and that the failure to do more in New York has resulted primarily from the failure to commit additional resources of time and men," rather than electronic devices. At 201–202. Moreover, Brooklyn's District Attorney Silver's poll of the State of New York indicates that during the 12-year period (1942–1954) duly authorized wiretaps in bribery and corruption cases constituted only a small percentage of the whole. It indicates that this category involved only 10% of the total wiretaps. The overwhelming majority were in the categories of larceny, extortion, coercion, and blackmail, accounting for almost 50%. Organized gambling was about 11%. Statistics are not available on subsequent years.

An often repeated statement of District Attorney Hogan of New York County was made at a hearing before the Senate Judiciary Committee at which he advocated the amendment of the Communications Act of 1934, so as to permit "telephonic interception" of conversations. As he testified, "Federal statutory law [the 1934 Act] has been interpreted in such a way as to bar us from divulging wiretap evidence, even in the courtroom in the course of criminal prosecution." Mr. Hogan then said that "[w]ithout it [wiretaps] my own office could not have convicted" "top figures in the underworld." He then named nine persons his office had convicted and one on whom he had furnished "leads" secured from wiretaps to the authorities of New Jersey. Evidence secured from wiretaps, as Mr. Hogan said, was not admissible in "criminal prosecutions." He was advocating that the Congress adopt a measure that would make it admissible. The President's Commission also emphasizes in its report the need for wiretapping in the investigation of organized crime because of the telephone's "relatively free use" by those engaged in the business and the difficulty of infiltrating their organizations. The Congress, though long importuned, has not amended the 1934 Act to permit it.

We are also advised by the Solicitor General of the United States that the Federal Government has abandoned the use of electronic eavesdropping for "prosecutorial purposes." Despite these actions of the Federal Government there has been no failure of law enforcement in that field. . . .

In any event we cannot forgive the requirements of the Fourth Amendment in the name of law enforcement. This is no formality that we require today but a fundamental rule that has long been recognized as basic to the privacy of every home in America. . . .

Our concern with the statute here is whether its language permits a trespassory invasion of the home or office, by general warrant, contrary to the command of the Fourth Amendment. As it is written, we believe that it does.

Reversed.

D. Confessions

The subject of police interrogation and confessions raises questions about the basis of the criminal system in the United States. Ours is an accusatorial system, in which society carries the burden of proving its charge against the defendant. The prosecution must establish its case by evidence independently secured through investigation, not by interrogation or inquisition of the accused as in other countries that employ the "inquisitorial" system of criminal law. But many cases simply cannot be solved by investigation of physical evidence; often it is not available, and so interrogation becomes essential to investigation and prosecution.

Recognizing the need for interrogation, the Supreme Court has never prevented questioning by the police. However, it has protected the suspect from the type of interrogation that may elicit involuntary or false confessions. Because the Supreme Court cannot address the issue of voluntariness on a case-by-case basis, it has sought to implement specific guidelines for determining this question. The constitutional basis for the establishment of these guidelines is the Fifth Amendment protection against self-incrimination, the Sixth Amendment right to counsel, and the Fourteenth Amendment due process guarantee.

The Fifth Amendment protection against self-incrimination is embodied in the famous case of *Miranda* v. *Arizona,* decided by the Supreme Court in 1966.[41] Miranda was arrested and questioned at the police station without being advised of the right to remain silent and to have an attorney. Based on these facts the Supreme Court held the defendant's subsequent confession inadmissible under the

---

[41] Miranda v. Arizona, 384 U.S. 436 (1966).

exclusionary rule, as evidence obtained in violation of the defendant's constitutional rights. The primary principle established in this case by the Court was that the prosecution cannot use statements which arise out of "custodial interrogation" of the defendant, unless the prosecution shows that certain procedural safeguards were applied to protect the defendant against self-incrimination. The key to this concept is the meaning of custodial interrogation. The Court stated that custodial interrogation begins after a person has been taken into custody or is otherwise significantly deprived of freedom of action. The interrogation itself must have been initiated by the police in order for the defendant to be entitled to the advice that he or she may remain silent and obtain an attorney. Of course defendants may waive the privileges established under *Miranda,* but such waivers cannot be presumed from the mere silence of defendants after being warned of their rights. They must expressly state such a waiver, and even after doing so they may later withdraw it. The burden is on the prosecution to prove that defendants were informed that (1) they have the right to remain silent; (2) anything they say may be used against them in a subsequent criminal proceeding; (3) they have the right to an attorney; and (4) if they can't afford an attorney, the court will appoint one. The prosecution must also prove that defendants knowingly and intelligently waived these rights.

The problem with the *Miranda* guidelines, as with any general rules, is that the result in many specific instances is undesirable and contrary to their original intent. Under *Miranda,* the requirement that the defendant be given the warnings and advice concerning the right to remain silent or to have an attorney has superseded the original intent to prevent involuntary confessions. Thus even if a confession was actually voluntary, failure to provide the *Miranda* warnings automatically renders such a voluntary confession inadmissible. As a result the *Miranda* concept has been criticized for going beyond the point necessary to protect citizens' rights against self-incrimination. Surely the criminal system should protect innocent people and the privacy of all persons, but the courts should be careful not to prevent the system from obtaining convictions when a person has provided the information and basis on which to do so. Recent Supreme Court decisions evidence a trend toward a stricter application of the *Miranda* principle, including a more limited interpretation of custodial interrogation.[42]

For many years the Fifth and Sixth Amendment protections for the defendant were restricted to federal prosecutions; the states remained free to use police interrogation in any manner they desired. However, continuing abusive behavior by the police during arrest and interrogation prompted the Supreme Court to apply the concepts embodied in the Fifth and Sixth Amendments to state investigations and prosecutions. The Court first did this by applying the Fourteenth Amendment due process concept to such state activities, as it did with Fourth Amendment search and seizure requirements.[43] Today any indication of coercion or police interrogation

---

[42] See cases cited in note 35.
[43] Brown v. Mississippi, 297 U.S. 278 (1936).

without counsel and before giving the *Miranda* warnings automatically renders any confession involuntary, because it violates the defendant's Fifth Amendment privilege against self-incrimination and due process rights.[44]

E. Identifications

Once a suspect has been taken into custody, the police use a variety of procedures in trying to verify that the suspect was actually the perpetrator of the crime. One of these procedures is identification. Its purpose is not only to solve the crime but also to provide evidence during the subsequent trial. The evidence will be obtained through the testimony of a person who is able to identify the defendant. Past identification procedures have indicated certain infringements on the suspect's rights. These complaints have been founded upon violations of the person's Fifth Amendment due process guarantee and privilege against self-incrimination.

Due process embodies basic, common sense concepts of the rights and treatment to which a citizen is entitled under all circumstances, including criminal proceedings. In determining what is unfair or "undue," the courts consider all of the circumstances surrounding the identification, including the necessity for prompt identification, which is essential in avoiding the witness's or victim's inability to remember what the suspect looked or sounded like. Another factor the court considers is whether the method used by the police for such an identification was a reliable one. For example, does it violate the defendant's right against self-incrimination to bring him or her in front of the victim for identification? In the case of *Stovall* v. *Denno* the Supreme Court held that when the New York police took the defendant to the hospital room of his victim, where she identified him by sight and voice, the defendant's right to due process was not violated.[45] The need for quick identification outweighed other factors in the Court's opinion, even though the defendant was the only black person in the room at the time of the identification. This is an extreme situation and may not be the law today.

Fairness in connection with photographic identifications has also been addressed by the Supreme Court in many cases. In *Simmons* v. *United States* the witnesses of a robbery were shown photographs immediately after the incident, including photographs of the defendant.[46] The defendant was identified in the course of this procedure and was later identified by the witnesses in court. The Supreme Court upheld this procedure on the basis that identification by photograph should not be set aside unless the procedure was "so impermissibly suggestive as to give rise to a very substantial likelihood of irreparable misidentification." [47]

---

[44] *Miranda;* Escobedo v. Illinois, 378 U.S. 478 (1964); Massiah v. United States, 377 U.S. 201 (1964); Malloy v. Hogan, 378 U.S. 1 (1964); Haynes v. Washington, 373 U.S. 503 (1963).
[45] Stovall v. Denno, 388 U.S. 293 (1967).
[46] Simmons v. United States, 390 U.S. 377 (1968).
[47] Simmons, at 384.

F. Grand Jury

Formal criminal proceedings begin with either a grand jury indictment or an "information," which is comparable to a complaint in a civil action. An *indictment* is the product of a grand jury proceeding against the accused. A grand jury indictment is required in federal criminal cases by the Fifth Amendment of the United States Constitution "for a capital, or otherwise infamous crime." This is now interpreted to mean all crimes punishable by at least a one-year imprisonment. Although the Fifth Amendment requires an indictment in federal cases, the Supreme Court has held that it is not a denial of due process for states to proceed by information rather than indictment in felony cases.[48] This is an example of a federal constitutional requirement that has *not* been interpreted through the Fourteenth Amendment as applying to the states. The Court reasoned that a proceeding by *information,* which includes examination by a judge or magistrate together with the right to counsel and the right to cross-examine witnesses, is as fair to the defendant as a grand jury indictment. Approximately half the states require a grand jury indictment for all or most felonies, while the other half provide for prosecution by either information or indictment, leaving the option to the prosecutor.

The grand jury proceeding should not be confused with the ordinary type of jury (the "petit" jury), which decides questions of fact during an actual trial. The grand jury is an arm of the prosecution, an agent of the executive branch of government, while the petit jury is part of court proceedings and the judicial branch. Other than the fact that both types of juries have roles at different stages of a criminal proceeding, they are entirely different and unrelated to each other. The grand jury usually consists of sixteen to twenty-three members, with a vote of twelve required for indictment of the defendant. After the selection of the grand jury from members of the community, the prosecuting attorney submits to it a "bill of indictment," which consists of a written accusation of the crime. The grand jury then holds secret hearings, during which the prosecutor presents evidence to substantiate the accusations, and witnesses are examined. The reason for the secrecy is that because the charges are not yet proven, it would not be fair to the defendant to publicize them. During these proceedings the prosecutor acts as legal advisor to the grand jury and exercises a significant influence, though not absolute control, over it. Although the grand jury is theoretically intended to protect innocent defendants from overly zealous prosecutors, in practice many grand juries are merely a stamp of approval for the prosecutor.

The evidentiary rules followed in grand jury proceedings are less stringent than in the actual trial. Because the grand jury is primarily an investigatory body, it should not be hampered by technical rules of procedure or evidence. Thus there are no constitutional limitations on the types of evidence that may be introduced in a grand jury investigation, and indictments have been held valid by the Supreme Court based entirely on hearsay evidence or illegally obtained evidence.[49]

---

[48] Hurtado v. California, 110 U.S. 516 (1884).
[49] Costello v. United States, 350 U.S. 359 (1956); United States v. Arcuri, 282 F.Supp. 347 (E.D.N.Y. 1968); United States v. Blue, 384 U.S. 251 (1966).

Recent critics of grand jury proceedings have suggested that many investigations are simply "fishing" expeditions: potential defendants are subpoenaed as witnesses, and the prosecutor's intent is to examine such witnesses about offenses with which they were allegedly familiar and then indict them on the basis of that testimony. This method of proceeding is particularly dangerous to prospective defendants, because the *Miranda* warnings are not required in grand jury proceedings; the hearing is an inquisitorial proceeding that does not determine innocence or guilt, and the Fifth Amendment is usually not applicable. The possibility that a witness may subsequently become a defendant in a criminal case often does not protect against the real motives of the prosecutor or the consequences of not being informed of the right to refuse to answer self-incriminating questions.

The "information" is used in many jurisdictions as an alternative to the grand jury indictment. In an effort to prevent abuse in criminal accusations, most states provide that prosecution by information can begin only after a preliminary hearing by a judge has taken place. The finding of probable cause, elsewhere made by the grand jury, is furnished by the reviewing judge in the case of a proceeding by information. The information must reasonably apprise the accused of the charges so that he or she may have an opportunity to prepare and present a defense.

G. Additional Formal Proceedings

1. Preliminary Hearing

In jurisdictions that permit prosecutions by information as an alternative to grand jury indictments, a preliminary hearing (also called preliminary examination) is usually required before a prosecutor is allowed to file the information. In federal courts, where an indictment is required for felonies, the accused is entitled to a preliminary hearing if arrested prior to the time of indictment by the grand jury. The main purpose of the preliminary hearing is to examine the prosecution's case to determine whether probable cause exists concerning the commission of the offense, and whether the person arrested is responsible for that offense. The preliminary hearing also provides a means of discovery of facts through the defendant's cross-examination of the prosecution's witnesses at the hearing. In addition, the defendant may present evidence on his or her behalf, and the testimony taken at the hearing may be used to impeach later testimony at trial. The hearing may also assist in subsequent plea bargaining and the determination of bail and pretrial release. Thus, although the defendant may waive the preliminary hearing, in many situations the defendant may desire the hearing. Even if a grand jury investigation has already begun, the defendant has a right to a prompt preliminary hearing.[50] The President's Commission on Law Enforcement has recommended a maximum delay of seventy-two hours between arrest and preliminary hearing if the defendant is in jail, and a maximum of seven days if the defendant is not in custody. Federal

---

[50] United States, ex rel. Wheeler v. Flood, 269 F.Supp. 194 (S.D.N.Y. 1967).

statutes provide that defendants shall be released if not given a preliminary hearing within ten days if in jail, or within twenty days if not in jail.[51]

The question in preliminary hearings in *federal* court is whether there is sufficient evidence to require the defendant to post bail in order to obtain release from custody. This step in the formal proceedings should not be confused with the determination of whether the defendant shall stand trial, because the grand jury takes up that question irrespective of the outcome of the preliminary hearing. On the other hand, in most *state* preliminary hearings the prosecution must prove that there is competent evidence of each element of the crime for which the accused is being held. Also in state preliminary hearings the defendant must be given the opportunity to present any defense desired. As part of deciding whether competent evidence exists, probable cause must be found. This consists of showing that "a man of ordinary prudence would be led to entertain a strong suspicion of the guilt of the accused."[52] Inferences may be drawn in favor of the defendant, and as long as there is some evidence to support the information, the court will not question the sufficiency of such evidence. If probable cause is found, the defendant is required to answer the information and is then bound over for trial or for a grand jury hearing. If no probable cause is found, the defendant is released. However, this discharge is not tantamount to an adjudication of innocence. The prosecution may file charges in the future if it obtains additional evidence. Also, because there has been no actual acquittal as a result of trial, the doctrine of double jeopardy does not apply.[53]

2. Arraignment

Once the prosecution's indictment or information is filed, the defendant is called into court to be informed of the charges and to be given an opportunity to plead in response to the charges. This hearing is called the arraignment. At this time the defendant is informed of his or her constitutional rights, and the indictment or information is read. The judge then requests the defendant to plead to the indictment or information, although some states allow a reasonable time in which to plead. Also the defendant may be asked whether he or she wishes to be tried by a jury or by the court without a jury.

3. Pleading to the Charge

Approximately 80 percent of all criminal prosecutions terminate in a guilty plea. Most of these guilty pleas are entered after considerable "plea bargaining" between the prosecution and the defendant. In such bargaining the defendant agrees to plead guilty to an offense less serious than the one originally charged, or agrees to plead guilty to one or more, but less than all, of the crimes originally charged.

---

[51] 18 U.S.C., section 3060.
[52] Rideout v. Superior Court, 67 Cal.2d 471, 62 Cal. Rptr. 581, 432 P.2d 197 (1967).
[53] See Part J of this chapter.

The prosecution agrees to dismiss certain charges. Thus plea bargaining avoids a time-consuming and costly trial. This is an essential aspect of the criminal process; without this result the courts simply could not administer the number of trials that would be necessary. Even at present, many cases that should be dealt with in more detail are disposed of through plea bargaining—an outgrowth of the enormous number of criminal cases in the system. The plea of guilty has the effect of a waiver by the defendant of the right to trial and of any chance of appeal.

Criminal law authorities differ as to whether the plea of guilty should be taken into consideration by the judge in sentencing the defendant. Some feel that the defendant should receive more lenient treatment if a guilty plea is offered.[54] They regard such a plea as the first step toward the defendant's rehabilitation and as an aid to the administration of justice in the criminal system. Most authorities believe that the plea should not result in lighter punishment.[55] As a practical matter, the courts do give lighter sentences to defendants who plead guilty. Because plea bargaining is so widely practiced and is an accepted part of the criminal system, there are efforts now under the Federal Rules of Criminal Procedure to protect the rights of those who do plead guilty.[56] In addition, standards published by the American Bar Association recognize several factors as justifications for the judge's consideration of the guilty plea in the disposition of the defendant's sentence. For example, the guilty plea is necessary to reduce the case load of the court system; the defendant recognizes and assumes responsibility for guilt by such a plea; the plea obviates the need for a public trial, thus eliminating the cost and the emotional trauma often associated with criminal trials; and the defendant frequently cooperates with the prosecution by giving information that leads to the arrest and conviction of other criminals.

In *Boykin* v. *Alabama* the court stated that criminal defendants who plead guilty waive their Fifth Amendment privilege against self-incrimination and their Sixth Amendment rights to trial by jury and confrontation and cross-examination of witnesses.[57] However, the defendants' waiver of these rights must indicate on the face of the record that there was "an affirmative showing that the waiver was intelligent and voluntary." [58] In the case of *Shelton* v. *United States* the defendant attacked his own guilty plea as being involuntary, after he had made it in reliance on the prosecutor's promise that he would be sentenced to only a year in prison and that a federal charge against him would be dismissed.[59] He based his claim of involuntariness on the theory that he was induced to make such plea because of the promises made to him. The Supreme Court found that the plea was voluntary, and that guilty

[54] See, e.g., A.B.A. Standards—Pleas of Guilty (1968 Draft, American Bar Association), section 1.8(a).
[55] See, e.g., Comment, "The Influence of the Defendant's Plea on Judicial Determination of Sentence," 66 *Yale Law Journal* 204 (1956).
[56] Rule 11, Federal Rules of Criminal Procedure.
[57] Boykin v. Alabama, 395 U.S. 238 (1969).
[58] Boykin, at 242.
[59] Shelton v. United States, 242 F.2d 101 (5th Cir. 1957).

pleas can be attacked as involuntary in only two situations: (1) if the plea was induced by improper physical or mental pressures, or by the threats of such pressures; and (2) if the defendant was not fully aware of all the consequences of the plea.

4. Discovery and Disclosure

Defendants in a criminal case have no *constitutional* right to inspect the prosecution's physical evidence against them, to obtain names of persons who will testify as witnesses or copies of their statements, or to obtain any discovery as to the prosecution's case. This provides a balance between the adversaries in criminal proceedings, because defendants do not have to disclose any of their evidence or theories regarding their defense. The rationale for the denial of this right further rests upon the fear that the defendant may attempt to falsify evidence, make up false alibis, or coerce or intimidate witnesses. Recently there have been indications of a trend to expand the defendant's right of discovery. For example, the American Bar Association Standards recommend disclosure to the defendant of the prosecution's witnesses, statements made by the defendant, results of examinations, statements of experts, and relevant grand jury testimony. Also, as discussed in Chapter 11, when the defendant raises the defense of alibi, a reciprocal right of discovery is recognized.[60]

Despite the lack of any constitutional right to discovery, Rule 16 of the Federal Rules of Criminal Procedure provides a broad right of discovery for defendants in criminal proceedings. Under the Rule they may inspect their own pretrial statements, confessions, and grand jury testimony. In addition, they may obtain the results of medical and scientific tests, such as autopsy reports, psychiatric reports, and ballistics tests. They are allowed to obtain any information that is "material to the preparation of [their] defense" except pretrial statements of third-party witnesses. However, once a government witness has testified at trial, the defendant is entitled to inspect any *pretrial* statements made by the witness in order to aid the defendant during cross-examination. These principles under Rule 16 are commonly known as the Jencks Rule.[61] The Jencks Rule does not extend to grand jury testimony.[62] Rule 16 also provides that if the court grants discovery to the defendant, it may, upon motion of the government, condition its order by requiring the defendant to allow the government to inspect and copy material that the defense intends to produce at trial and that is in its possession, custody, or control, such as medical reports, books, papers, documents, or tangible objects. In order to inspect these items, the government must show that they are material to the preparation of its case and that the request is reasonable.

The statutes, rules, and decisions on discovery in state courts vary significantly. Some jurisdictions deny discovery by the defendant of confessions, signed written

---

[60] See Chapter 11, p. 329. See also Wardius v. Oregon, 412 U.S. 470 (1973).
[61] Named after Jencks v. United States, 353 U.S. 657 (1957).
[62] Pittsburgh Plate Glass v. United States, 360 U.S. 395 (1959).

statements, and names of persons who purportedly know relevant facts.[63] Other jurisdictions allow the inspection of such information, believing that the defendant should have the right to determine the completeness of the confessions, and that when the police have unilaterally examined the defendant, he or she should have the opportunity to determine the accuracy of the prosecutor's report of the facts in the course of the confession.[64] In state proceedings, whenever the defendant is allowed pretrial discovery in a criminal case, an equivalent right is generally recognized in favor of the prosecution. However, whenever this principle conflicts with the attorney-client privilege or the privilege against self-incrimination, it is outweighed by those privileges.

H. Trial by Jury

1. The Jury

The Sixth Amendment of the United States Constitution states: "In all criminal prosecutions, the accused shall enjoy the right to speedy and public trial, by an impartial jury of the State and District wherein the crime shall have been committed." This has been interpreted by the Supreme Court to entitle the defendant to a trial by jury in all cases involving a serious offense.[65] Trial by jury in a petty offense is not guaranteed by the Sixth Amendment. The factors determining whether the crime is serious or petty are the nature of the offense and the maximum potential sentence. Any offense which carries a *potential* sentence of more than six months is a serious offense, despite the actual sentence imposed.

Although not constitutionally required, the number of jurors required by statutes in federal criminal trials is twelve. A unanimous verdict is required in *federal* criminal trials, although this is not expressly required by the Constitution either. In fact, in the case of *Williams* v. *Florida* the Supreme Court implied the possibility of permitting less than a unanimous verdict.[66]

The Supreme Court has expressly held that a conviction by less than a unanimous jury in a state trial does not violate the Sixth Amendment or the due process clause of the Fourteenth Amendment, provided the jury is an adequate cross-section of the community.[67]

A defendant may waive the right to a trial by jury, even without the advice of

---

[63] See Leland v. Oregon, 343 U.S. 790 (1952); Cicenia v. LaGay, 357 U.S. 504 (1978). Compare Clewis v. Texas, 386 U.S. 707, 712 n.8 (1967).

[64] E.g., State v. Johnson, 68 N.J. 349, 346 A.2d 66 (1975). Compare State v. Tune, 13 N.J. 203, 98 A.2d 881 (1953).

[65] Duncan v. Louisiana, 391 U.S. 145 (1968); Baldwin v. New York, 399 U.S. 66 (1970); Dyke v. Taylor Implement Manufacturing Co., 391 U.S. 216 (1968); Patton v. United States, 281 U.S. 276 (1930).

[66] Williams v. Florida, 399 U.S. 78 (1970). See discussion concerning jury in Chapter 6, pp. 106–08.

[67] Apodaca v. Oregon, 406 U.S. 404 (1972); Johnson v. Louisiana, 406 U.S. 356 (1972).

counsel, provided such a waiver is expressly and intelligently made.[68] A defendant cannot be coerced into making such a waiver. The Supreme Court has held that a statute providing that the death penalty could only be imposed by a jury verdict is unconstitutional, because it operated to coerce defendants into waiving their right to a jury trial for fear of exposing themselves to the death penalty if they lost.[69] If the defendant waives the jury trial, this does not affect the prosecution's right to demand a jury. There is nothing in the Constitution that allows the defendant to *avoid* a trial by jury.[70]

The Sixth Amendment requires an "impartial jury." The Supreme Court has held that this means that jurors must be chosen from representative cross-sections of the community, consistent with reasonable minimum character and literacy requirements. Numerous Supreme Court cases have invalidated discriminatory state statutes and other methods of systematic discrimination, both racial and sexual, in the selection of jurors.[71] The jury panel, both in civil and criminal cases, is usually selected through the use of voter registration rolls, telephone directories, or other sources that list a general cross-section of the community.

As part of the process of determining which of the jury candidates will comprise the final twelve members, questions may be directed to all the prospective jurors (usually a large group of candidates) to determine whether there are grounds for challenging their qualifications to serve on the jury. The trial judge may allow the prosecutor and attorney for the defendant to question the prospective jurors, or may have them submit questions to be asked of the jurors. This is called *voir dire* (pronounced vwár dēr). Although it varies from state to state, during *voir dire* the prosecution and defense counsel are entitled to a certain number of challenges, allowing the attorneys to dismiss any prospective jurors. Challenges are made either for cause, when a juror is dismissed for actual bias, implied bias, or general cause (incompetence or conviction of a felony), or on the basis of a peremptory challenge —one entirely within the discretion of the prosecutor or defense attorney.

An interesting question in connection with the jury selection process arises when the defendant has been charged with a capital offense. The prosecution will use its peremptory challenges to excuse jurors who indicate any opposition to the death penalty, and the defense will use its peremptory challenges on those who favor the death penalty. Should jurors be excused for *cause* (bias) because they favor or oppose the death penalty? The Supreme Court has ruled that it cannot be assumed that a juror favoring the death penalty is more likely to find a defendant guilty than a juror who opposes it.[72] However, in the same case the Court stated that a jury

---

[68] Adams v. United States ex rel. McCann, 317 U.S. 269 (1942).
[69] United States v. Jackson, 390 U.S. 570 (1968).
[70] Singer v. United States, 380 U.S. 24 (1965).
[71] Ballard v. United States, 329 U.S. 187 (1946); Strauder v. West Virginia, 100 U.S. 303 (1880); Whitus v. Georgia, 385 U.S. 545 (1967); Avery v. Georgia, 345 U.S. 559 (1953); Norris v. Alabama, 294 U.S. 587 (1935); Alexander v. Louisiana, 405 U.S. 625 (1972); Peters v. Kiff, 407 U.S. 493 (1972).
[72] Witherspoon v. Illinois, 391 U.S. 510 (1968).

composed only of jurors favoring the death penalty, and which finds a defendant guilty, cannot also decide the penalty to be imposed upon that defendant. This would violate the due process clause of the Fourteenth Amendment, and any death sentence imposed must be set aside.

2. Trial Procedure

The actual trial proceedings will begin shortly after the jurors have been selected, impaneled, and sworn in. At the commencement of the trial the indictment or information will be read to the jury by the clerk, and the defendant's plea will also be given. The prosecuting attorney will then make an opening statement, followed by an opening statement by the defense counsel; either or both attorneys may waive the right to make such opening statement if they so desire. Because the burden is on the government to prove the allegations contained in the indictment or information, the government must proceed first with the evidence in support of the charge. Afterwards the defense offers its evidence in an attempt to disprove the facts introduced by the prosecution, and in support of any defense theories it may raise. The process of presenting evidence may take a very short time, a matter of hours in some cases, or even weeks, depending upon the complexity of the facts and charges. At the conclusion of the evidence each side may then present its final arguments to the jury, with the government proceeding first.

At the end of the trial the judge instructs the jury on all principles of law relevant to the issues raised by the evidence. Although it varies from jurisdiction to jurisdiction, the judge may also be allowed to make comments on the evidence. Many of the judge's instructions are made to the jury according to requests made by the prosecution or defense, although the judge maintains the right to give, refuse, or modify the requested instructions.

3. Judgment and Sentencing

The directed verdict was discussed in Chapter 6 in connection with civil cases.[73] In criminal cases the trial judge may not direct a verdict of guilty. However, the judge may take the case from the jury on his or her own motion, or in response to the defendant's motion for lack of sufficient evidence to support a conviction (also called motion for acquittal). The standard applied to the motion for a directed verdict in criminal cases is that the defendant is entitled to acquittal if reasonable persons could not conclude on the evidence taken in the light most favorable to the prosecution that guilt has been proven beyond a reasonable doubt.

If a motion for a directed verdict is not granted, the jury will be instructed to deliberate and arrive at a verdict based upon the evidence presented to them. A jury verdict of guilty results in the defendant's conviction. However, the actual judgment will not be entered into the official records until the sentence has been imposed.

---

[73] See Chapter 6, pp. 117–18.

A separate hearing, which introduces additional arguments and evidence, may be held solely to determine the proper sentence. Pending this determination, the court may order the defendant committed to custody or continued on bail. However, Rule 32 of the Federal Rules of Criminal Procedure provides that the sentence shall be imposed "without unreasonable delay." The sentencing may consist of incarceration, death, a fine, forfeiture of property, or probation.

After sentencing, in federal courts and in many state courts, the judge must notify the defendant of the right to an appeal. There is no federal constitutional right to appeal a conviction, although the right is recognized by state constitutions and federal and state statutes. The appeal must be made within the time limit provided in such statutes, usually ten days following entry of judgment in the case of an appeal by the defendant, or thirty days in the case of an appeal by the government. Although the state does have the right to appeal an acquittal, the states' right of appeal is limited by the doctrine of double jeopardy, as discussed in Part J of this chapter. The state may only appeal orders that were made before the "jeopardy" commenced, such as orders that set aside the indictment or information or orders suppressing evidence.

I. Right to Counsel

The Supreme Court has established a general principle that the constitutional right to counsel arises only when the accused has been formally charged with the commission of a crime so that an adversary criminal prosecution is pending.[74] Thus, before actual charges have been filed against the defendant, such as at a police lineup, there is no right to counsel. However, as pointed out earlier, under *Miranda* and the Fifth Amendment privilege against self-incrimination, an accused is entitled to the assistance of counsel in any custodial interrogation. Once charges have been filed, the defendant is entitled to counsel at all critical stages of the proceedings.

The courts have continually moved toward broadening the scope of situations requiring the assistance of counsel. The guiding principle behind this trend is that defendants may not be discriminated against as a result of their poverty.[75] However, there are practical problems inherent in this concept. For example, should indigent persons be entitled to appointed lawyers in any situation in which a wealthy person could have one? If indigent defendants were given the aids that they would normally be entitled to if they could afford it, such as counsel and transcripts, then a much larger number of trials and appeals would result, thereby administratively crippling the criminal system. The line must be drawn somewhere short of unlimited right to counsel for indigents, while still protecting the defendant's constitutional rights to a fair trial and against police overreaches. Thus the right has been limited to those situations in which discrimination based on wealth may result in an inequality so significant as to amount to fundamental unfairness under the due process clause of

---

[74] Kirby v. Illinois, 406 U.S. 682 (1972).
[75] Griffin v. Illinois, 351 U.S. 12 (1956); Douglas v. California, 372 U.S. 353 (1963).

the Fifth and Fourteenth Amendments. The requirement to provide counsel is not absolute, but is balanced against certain practical considerations. The Supreme Court has imposed a duty on the government to allow the assistance of counsel so as to conduct the criminal justice system without regard to a person's financial status.

The following discussion outlines the situations in which a defendant may or may not be entitled to assistance by counsel.

1. Lineups

In the case of *United States* v. *Wade* the Supreme Court held that the Sixth Amendment right to counsel extends to postindictment, pretrial lineups, on the theory that this is a critical stage of the criminal proceedings.[76] The *Wade* principle recognizes the need to protect the defendant's basic right to a fair trial as affected by the right to meaningfully cross-examine witnesses at trial in view of any unfairness at the lineup. The case of *Kirby* v. *Illinois* expressly limited the *Wade* principle to those situations commencing after a formal accusation, such as the indictment, information, preliminary hearing, or arraignment.[77]

In the case of *Gilbert* v. *California,* the Supreme Court made the *Wade* rule applicable to the states through the Fourteenth Amendment.[78] That is, the right to counsel in postindictment lineups was held to be a fundamental right guaranteed by the due process clause. However, the *Gilbert* decision also found that the Fifth and Sixth Amendments, guaranteeing the privilege against self-incrimination and the right to counsel, allow the obtaining of a defendant's handwriting sample in the absence of counsel and without any advice that it may be used against him or her.

GILBERT v. CALIFORNIA

388 U.S. 263 (1967)

Supreme Court of the United States

Mr. Justice BRENNAN delivered the opinion of the Court.

This case was argued with United States v. Wade, 388 U.S. 218, and presents the same alleged constitutional error in the admission in evidence of in-court identifications there considered. In addition, petitioner alleges constitutional errors in the admission in evidence of testimony of some of the witnesses that they also identified him at the lineup, in the admission of handwriting exemplars taken from him after his arrest, and in the admission of out-of-court statements by King, a co-defendant, mentioning petitioner's part in the crimes, which statements, on the co-defendant's appeal decided with petitioner's, were held to have been improperly admitted against the co-defendant. Finally, he alleges that his Fourth Amendment

---

[76] United States v. Wade, 388 U.S. 218 (1967).
[77] Kirby v. Illinois, in note 74.
[78] Gilbert v. California, 388 U.S. 263 (1967).

rights were violated by a police seizure of photographs of him from his locked apartment after entry without a search warrant, and the admission of testimony of witnesses that they identified him from those photographs within hours after the crime.

Petitioner was convicted in the Superior Court of California of the armed robbery of the Mutual Savings and Loan Association of Alhambra and the murder of a police officer who entered during the course of the robbery. There were separate guilt and penalty stages of the trial before the same jury, which rendered a guilty verdict and imposed the death penalty. The California Supreme Court affirmed. We granted certiorari, and set the case for argument with *Wade* and with Stovall v. Denno, 388 U.S. 293. If our holding today in *Wade* is applied to this case, the issue whether admission of the in-court and lineup identifications is constitutional error which requires a new trial could be resolved on this record only after further proceedings in the California courts. We must therefore first determine whether petitioner's other contentions warrant any greater relief.

I. THE HANDWRITING EXEMPLARS

Petitioner was arrested in Philadelphia by an FBI agent and refused to answer questions about the Alhambra robbery without the advice of counsel. He later did answer questions of another agent about some Philadelphia robberies in which the robber used a handwritten note demanding that money be handed over to him, and during that interrogation gave the agent the handwriting exemplars. They were admitted in evidence at trial over objection that they were obtained in violation of petitioner's Fifth and Sixth Amendment rights. The California Supreme Court upheld admission of the exemplars on the sole ground that petitioner had waived any rights that he might have had not to furnish them. "[The agent] did not tell Gilbert that the exemplars would not be used in any other investigation. Thus, even if Gilbert believed that his exemplars would not be used in California, it does not appear that the

authorities improperly induced such belief." The court did not, therefore, decide petitioner's constitutional claims.

We pass the question of waiver since we conclude that the taking of the exemplars violated none of petitioner's constitutional rights.

First. The taking of the exemplars did not violate petitioner's Fifth Amendment privilege against self-incrimination. The privilege reaches only compulsion of "an accused's communications, whatever form they might take, and the compulsion of responses which are also communications, for example, compliance with a subpoena to produce one's papers," and not "compulsion which makes a suspect or accused the source of 'real or physical evidence.' . . ." Schmerber v. California, 384 U.S. 757, 763–764. One's voice and handwriting are, of course, means of communication. It by no means follows, however, that every compulsion of an accused to use his voice or write compels a communication within the cover of the privilege. A mere handwriting exemplar, in contrast to the content of what is written, like the voice or body itself, is an identifying physical characteristic outside its protection. United States v. Wade, at 222–223. No claim is made that the content of the exemplars was testimonial or communicative matter.

Second. The taking of the exemplars was not a "critical" stage of the criminal proceedings entitling petitioner to the assistance of counsel. Putting aside the fact that the exemplars were taken before the indictment and appointment of counsel, there is minimal risk that the absence of counsel might derogate from his right to a fair trial. Cf. United States v. Wade, 388 U.S. 218. If, for some reason, an unrepresentative exemplar is taken, this can be brought out and corrected through the adversary process at trial since the accused can make an unlimited number of additional exemplars for analysis and comparison by government and defense handwriting experts. Thus, "the accused has the opportunity for a meaningful confrontation of the [State's] case at trial through the ordinary processes of cross-examination of the [State's] expert [handwriting] witnesses and the presentation of the evidence of his own [handwriting] experts." United States v. Wade, at 227–228. . . .

IV. THE IN-COURT AND LINEUP IDENTIFICATIONS

Since none of the petitioner's other contentions warrants relief, the issue becomes what relief is required by application to this case of the principles today announced in United States v. Wade, 388 U.S. 218.

Three eyewitnesses to the Alhambra crimes who identified Gilbert at the guilt stage of the trial had observed him at a lineup conducted without notice to his counsel in a Los Angeles auditorium 16 days after his indictment and after appointment of counsel. The manager of the apartment house in which incriminating evidence was found, and in which Gilbert allegedly resided, identified Gilbert in the courtroom and also testified, in substance, to her prior lineup identification on examination by the State. Eight witnesses who identified him in the courtroom at the penalty stage were not eyewitnesses to the Alhambra crimes but to other robberies allegedly committed by him. In addition to their in-court identifications, these witnesses also testified that they identified Gilbert at the same lineup.

The lineup was on a stage behind bright lights which prevented those in the line from seeing the audience. Upwards of 100 persons were in the audience, each an eyewitness to one of the several robberies charged to Gilbert. The record is otherwise virtually silent as to what occurred at the lineup.

At the guilt stage, after the first witness, a cashier of the savings and loan association, identified Gilbert in the courtroom, defense counsel moved, out of the presence of the jury, to strike her testimony on the ground that she identified Gilbert at the pretrial lineup conducted in the absence of counsel in violation of the Sixth Amendment made applicable to the States by the Fourteenth Amendment. Gideon v. Wainwright, 372 U.S. 335. He requested a hearing outside the presence of the jury to present evidence supporting his claim that her

in-court identification was, and others to be elicited by the State from other eyewitnesses would be, "predicated at least in large part upon their identification or purported identification of Mr. Gilbert at the showup. . . ." The trial judge denied the motion as premature. Defense counsel then elicited the fact of the cashier's lineup identification on cross-examination and again moved to strike her identification testimony. Without passing on the merits of the Sixth Amendment claim, the trial judge denied the motion on the ground that, assuming a violation, it would not in any event entitle Gilbert to suppression of the in-court identification. Defense counsel thereafter elicited the fact of lineup identifications from two other eyewitnesses who on direct examination identified Gilbert in the courtroom. Defense counsel unsuccessfully objected at the penalty stage, to the testimony of the eight witnesses to the other robberies that they identified Gilbert at the lineup.

The admission of the in-court identifications without first determining that they were not tainted by the illegal lineup but were of independent origin was constitutional error. United States v. Wade, 388 U.S. 218. We there held that a postindictment pretrial lineup at which the accused is exhibited to identifying witnesses is a critical stage of the criminal prosecution; that police conduct of such a lineup without notice to and in the absence of his counsel denies the accused his Sixth Amendment right to counsel and calls in question the admissibility at trial of the in-court identifications of the accused by witnesses who attended the lineup. However, as in Wade, the record does not permit an informed judgment whether the in-court identifications at the two stages of the trial had an independent source. Gilbert is therefore entitled only to a vacation of his conviction pending the holding of such proceedings as the California Supreme Court may deem appropriate to afford the State the opportunity to establish that the in-court identifications had an independent source, or that their introduction in evidence was in any event harmless error.

Quite different considerations are involved as to the admission of the testimony of the manager of the apartment house at the guilt phase and of the eight witnesses at the penalty stage that they identified Gilbert at the lineup. That testimony is the direct result of the illegal lineup "come at by exploitation of [the primary] illegality." Wong Sun v. United States, 371 U.S. 471, 488. The State is therefore not entitled to an opportunity to show that that testimony had an independent source. Only a per se exclusionary rule as to such testimony can be an effective sanction to assure that law enforcement authorities will respect the accused's constitutional right to the presence of his counsel at the critical lineup. In the absence of legislative regulations adequate to avoid the hazards to a fair trial which inhere in lineups as presently conducted, the desirability of deterring the constitutionally objectionable practice must prevail over the undesirability of excluding relevant evidence. That conclusion is buttressed by the consideration that the witness' testimony of his lineup identification will enhance the impact of his in-court identification on the jury and seriously aggravate whatever derogation exists of the accused's right to a fair trial. Therefore, unless the California Supreme Court is "able to declare a belief that it was harmless beyond a reasonable doubt," Chapman v. California, 386 U.S. 18, Gilbert will be entitled on remand to a new trial or, if no prejudicial error is found on the guilt stage but only in the penalty stage, to whatever relief California law affords where the penalty stage must be set aside.

The judgment of the California Supreme Court and the conviction are vacated, and the case is remanded to that court for further proceedings not inconsistent with this opinion.

It is so ordered.

2. Grand Jury Proceedings

If a person has not yet been indicted or formally charged with any crime and is testifying as a witness in a grand jury proceeding, he or she is not entitled to have counsel present during such a proceeding. The reason for this is to preserve grand jury secrecy. Witnesses may, however, leave the room during the course of the hearing to confer with their attorney and obtain advice concerning their legal rights. The witness is entitled to advice concerning testimonial privileges, such as the attorney-client privilege or the doctor-patient privilege, the privilege against self-incrimination, or the obtaining of immunity.[79]

The rationale behind excluding attorneys during the hearing has been much criticized. It certainly does not appear that an attorney in the hearing room will hamper any grand jury investigations. Some jurisdictions permit attorneys to be present, and the trend seems to be in that direction.

3. Preliminary Hearing

The Supreme Court, in the case of *Coleman* v. *Alabama,* held that assistance of counsel must be provided at preliminary hearings to determine the existence of probable cause against the defendant.[80] This is clearly a critical stage in the pro-

---

[79] People v. Inaniello, 21 N.Y.2d 418, 288 N.Y.S.2d 462, 235 N.E.2d 439 (1968).
[80] Coleman v. Alabama, 399 U.S. 1 (1970).

ceeding and always occurs after the defendant has been formally charged with the commission of a crime.

4. Plea Bargaining

The defendant cannot be denied assistance of counsel during the plea bargaining process prior to the trial. In order to fully protect his or her interests, the defendant should have counsel during this stage of the proceedings, particularly since any statement made by the defendant during the plea bargaining process may be admissible evidence against him or her at trial.

If the plea bargaining agreement between the prosecutor and the defendant's attorney turns out to be undesirable for the defendant after the guilty plea, the defendant is nevertheless bound by the law, having accepted his or her lawyer's judgment at the time of the plea. The only time a defendant may withdraw a guilty plea is when he or she is able to show "serious dereliction on the part of counsel sufficient to show that his plea was not . . . a knowing and intelligent act." [81]

ANDERSON v. NORTH CAROLINA

221 F. Supp. 930 (1963)

United States District Court,
Western District North Carolina

CRAVEN, Chief Judge.

This is a civil action begun by application for a writ of habeas corpus. . . .

From competent evidence to which no objection was taken, the court finds the facts to be as follows:

1. That about 2:30 P.M. on the 23rd of October, 1961, petitioner Horace Anderson was arrested upon a warrant for assault on an eight year old minor female child, and was subsequently released about 6:00 P.M. of the same day upon a $1,000.00 bond.

2. That about 8:30 P.M. on October 30, 1961, petitioner Horace Anderson was again arrested, put in jail, and on the following morning, October 31, warrants charging him with incest and rape were served on him. All warrants (October 23 and 31) arise out of the

same occurrence alleged to have happened on October 21.

3. About the first of November, the Honorable Grover C. Mooneyham was contacted by Horace Anderson's father, and they discussed employment to represent Horace Anderson; Mooneyham interviewed Anderson in jail "the first part of November"; because of lack of money, Mooneyham was not employed, but was subsequently appointed by the Superior Court of the State of North Carolina to represent the defendant—the said appointment being made on November 21, 1961.

4. That Horace Anderson was indicted for the capital crime of rape on or about November 21, 1961.

5. That Grover C. Mooneyham discussed the case with Horace Anderson fifteen or twenty

---

[81] McMann v. Richardson, 397 U.S. 759 (1970). See also Tollet v. Henderson, 411 U.S. 258 (1973).

times; that he inquired for witnesses who might be favorable to Horace Anderson, and sought and received permission of the State to confer and talk with the prosecuting witness, Patricia Anderson, and her mother, wife of the defendant, and talked with them; that after his appointment as counsel for the defendant, Mr. Mooneyham moved the court for a continuance, which continuance was granted for the purpose of giving Mooneyham sufficient time to study the case and to understand it and competently advise his client; that as a result of Mooneyham's motion for a continuance, the case was continued from the November 20 term until the December term, pursuant to N.C.G.S. §15–4.1.

6. On the 14th day of December, 1961, Horace Anderson was brought to the superior courtroom of Buncombe County, and on the *morning* of that day entered a plea of not guilty; the trial was again postponed until January 8, 1962.

7. At 4:30 P.M. on the same day, Anderson pleaded guilty to a lesser offense.

8. At the time of entry of the guilty plea, December 14, 1961, the record shows that the Solicitor stated to the court that "[t]he defendant, through his counsel, in open court, tenders to the state a plea of guilty of assault upon a female with intent to commit rape, which plea the state accepts." (Tran. p. 1) Immediately thereafter, and sufficiently important to be set out verbatim, occurred the following:

"*The Court:* Is that correct? That is the plea you enter?"
"*The Defendant:* Yes." (Ibid)
"*The Court:* You do it freely and voluntarily, knowing the probability is you will get an extended prison term, is that right?"
"*The Defendant:* Yes sir." (Id. at p. 2)

9. Thereafter, the court proceeded to hear evidence going to the question of guilt for the purpose of determining proper punishment.

10. After the evidence had been heard, Mr. Mooneyham addressed the court asking for leniency, and in the course of his remarks, advised the court that the defendant was submit-

ting to this lesser offense (as compared with the capital felony) because of his prior record, *and that he still asserted his innocence*. (Tran. p. 10) Whereupon it appears the court said in response: "I thought this man was pleading guilty. I am not finding him guilty. I don't want any misunderstanding about that because he has plead guilty now, and if there is any misunderstanding, I want him to withdraw it and continue the matter."

"*Mr. Mooneyham:* No, sir, he knows he has plead guilty."
"*The Court:* I don't want him to go out and say he was sentenced for something he didn't do." (Tran. pp. 10 and 11)

11. Thereafter, the court afforded the defendant the right of allocution. Nothing was said by the defendant with respect to his plea or with respect to whether he was truly guilty or innocent.

12. After the defendant had spoken at some length, the court again addressed him in words as follows:

"Well, you understand you have plead guilty to this thing. That is what you wanted to do, wasn't it?"
"*The Defendant:* Yes." (Tran. p. 13)

13. Thereupon, the court sentenced the defendant to a term of not less than 12 nor more than 15 years, and the defendant was immediately taken back to jail.

14. The defendant is alert and his demeanor is such as to convey the impression that he grasps and understands the nature of the present habeas corpus proceedings. During cross-examination and questioning by the court, his responses to questions indicated complete understanding of the matters being inquired into. He has a sixth grade education and is not lacking in intelligence. According to Dr. Sargent, prison physician, he is "not quite right." But, also according to Dr. Sargent, he appreciates and understands the nature of the proceedings and is not "insane." He knows and understands the difference between right and wrong. At the time of sentencing he understood the signif-

icance of the relevant facts and the nature of the proceeding.

15. No evidence is forthcoming from the petitioner to seriously put in issue the question of his mental competence at the time of his trial; his own medical witness negates the contention.

16. Anderson pleaded not guilty to the capital offense at 11:30 A.M. on the 14th of December and pleaded guilty to the lesser felony at 4:30 P.M. the same day. The evidence does not make entirely clear why he changed his mind. But, immediately before his plea of guilty on the afternoon of December 14, 1961, the Solicitor and members of his staff talked with the prisoner in jail *in the absence of his counsel* but apparently with counsel's consent. Although no specific words of threat or promise were used, it is fair to say that the following impression was conveyed to the petitioner Anderson and was intended to be conveyed:

That he was charged with a capital offense and that the Solicitor would put him on trial for his life with the probability of a sentence of death unless Anderson agreed to plead guilty to the lesser offense of assault with intent to commit rape, and that if he so pleaded he could not be imprisoned under the law for longer than fifteen years and, in all probability, the presiding judge would give him as little as two to three or three to five years in prison. Anderson was further assured that the Solicitor "would talk to the judge." It does not appear that the Solicitor ever did so.

17. Anderson exhausted all state court remedies and never received a state court hearing to review the constitutionality of his sentence and judgment of imprisonment.

Only one of Anderson's several allegations of constitutionality of his imprisonment has sufficient merit to require discussion—his contention that he was effectively denied his right to counsel. At the time of trial, Gideon v. Wainwright, 372 U.S. 335 (1963), had not been decided. But, even then, since he had been indicted for a capital crime, he was constitutionally entitled to counsel at every stage of the proceeding terminating in his guilty plea to the non-capital felony. Powell v. Alabama, 287 U.S. 45 (1932).

There is thus a causal relationship between the imprisonment for the non-capital felony and the alleged denial of counsel in the capital case—as will more clearly appear hereinafter.

The right to counsel is not merely a matter of form. It can be waived by the defendant—but not by his counsel. It is, therefore, irrelevant that counsel may have consented for the Solicitor to conduct—in counsel's absence—what amounted to a pre-trial conference with the prisoner in jail. Unquestionably, the most important part of the proceedings against Anderson occurred in jail—when his counsel was not present to advise him. It was at that time and place that the decision was made to plead guilty to the lesser felony. Otherwise, he would not have been returned to the courtroom—for the jury had long since gone, and his trial had been set for the next term. What happened in the courtroom was to merely make a formal record of a decision arrived at upstairs in jail in a conference between the Solicitor and the defendant. Counsel's presence at the sentencing (he was sent for by the Solicitor) does not give it validity. The most he could have done was to ratify a decision previously made. More than this is implicit in the right to counsel: petitioner was entitled to have counsel aid and help him *in making the decision*.

Compromise pleas in criminal cases occur very frequently in the administration of the criminal law. Seldom are such instances reflected in the law books for the simple reason that both sides are by hypothesis usually satisfied, i.e., the defendant has escaped a greater penalty, and the state has avoided a protracted and expensive trial.

The constitutional validity of the time-honored compromise plea is assumed for purposes of this opinion. But, a compromise necessarily involves negotiation, and here Anderson was without the assistance of his lawyer in negotiating the compromise with the Solicitor. Not infrequently counsel succeed in getting the Solicitor to affirmatively recommend to the court a specific sentence in return for a guilty plea.

It is not unheard of for the trial judge to be informed of the negotiations and to indicate whether or not he will likely follow the Solicitor's recommendation. Sometimes Solicitor and counsel relate the facts to the judge, and he will then indicate the probable sentence in the event of a plea of guilty. If the sentence comes out as indicated, everyone is satisfied. If the judge changes his mind after learning more of the case, he need only permit the withdrawal of the guilty plea. The trial may then proceed as if the negotiations had never occurred— preferably before another judge and at another time.

Unquestionably petitioner Anderson could not bargain on equal terms with the Solicitor. The conference in the jail was inherently unfair, and the agreement made there infects all subsequent proceedings.

It is idle to speculate whether petitioner's counsel could have, if present, worked out a better deal with the Solicitor. The point is Anderson was entitled to have him *try*. For lack of effective counsel at a "critical" stage of the proceedings against him, those proceedings are constitutionally defective. White v. Maryland, 373 U.S. 59 (1963); Hamilton v. Alabama, 368 U.S. 52 (1961).

Petitioner Anderson is unlawfully confined and is entitled to be released unless the State of North Carolina elects to re-try him for either the capital offense or the lesser felony within a reasonable period of time. Unless the Attorney General of North Carolina shall file with this court within thirty days a certificate of the State's election to proceed with re-trial, an appropriate order will be entered commanding Anderson's release from imprisonment.

5. Trial

In 1972, in the case of *Argersinger* v. *Hamlin,* the United States Supreme Court held that under the Sixth and Fourteenth Amendments, no person may be imprisoned for any offense, no matter what the classification—petty, misdemeanor, or felony—unless afforded access to counsel at trial.[82] This decision was the culmination of a long line of previous cases which gradually expanded the defendant's right to counsel. It was first held, in *Betts* v. *Brady,* that because the Fourteenth Amendment due process clause does not incorporate the Sixth Amendment right to counsel (except in "special circumstances"), the states were not compelled to provide counsel for defendants in state court proceedings.[83] Later it was held that the states must provide counsel during all critical stages of capital cases only.[84] The most famous case expanding the right to counsel at trial in felony cases was *Gideon* v. *Wainwright,* in which the defendant was charged by the state of Florida for a particular felony.[85] After his request for counsel was denied, he appealed. The Supreme Court held that the Sixth Amendment's guarantee of counsel is such a fundamental right in felony cases that it is protected and incorporated by the due process clause of the Fourteenth Amendment, thereby making it applicable to all state criminal proceedings.

---

[82] Argersinger v. Hamlin, 407 U.S. 25 (1972).
[83] Betts v. Brady, 316 U.S. 455 (1942).
[84] Bute v. Illinois, 333 U.S. 640 (1948); Hamilton v. Alabama, 368 U.S. 52 (1961).
[85] Gideon v. Wainwright, 372 U.S. 335 (1963). This case was the subject of the book *Gideon's Trumpet,* by Anthony Lewis (New York: Random House, Inc., 1964).

Of course the defendant has the right to waive counsel, provided certain constitutional requirements are satisfied. The waiver must be an express waiver, and the defendant must be mentally competent, both as to understanding his or her action and acting as his or her own counsel, before the judge can accept the waiver.[86]

6. Appeal

In the case of *Douglas* v. *California* the Supreme Court held that it was an unconstitutional discrimination against the indigent defendant to deny counsel for an *initial* appeal.[87] In the more recent case of *Ross* v. *Moffitt,* the Court held that states are not required to provide counsel to indigent defendants for appeals to the state supreme court granted at its discretion or for a petition for *certiorari* to the United States Supreme Court.[88] This did not contradict the earlier decision in *Douglas,* because the *Ross* decision did not reverse the position that counsel must be provided for an *initial* appeal in the state court system. In *Ross* the Supreme Court held that neither the equal protection nor due process concepts of the Fourteenth Amendment were offended by not requiring counsel after an initial appeal. The Court distinguished between the need for counsel during the trial and counsel on appeal, because an appeal is used to upset a prior determination of guilt, and constitutionally a state does not have to provide any appeal at all. A violation of due process occurs only where indigents are singled out and denied meaningful access to the appellate process as a result of their indigency.

J. Double Jeopardy

The Fifth Amendment of the United States Constitution contains the requirement that "No person . . . shall be subject for the same offense to be twice put in jeopardy of life or limb." The first problem in interpreting this phrase is determining at what point the defendant has been "put in jeopardy." It is now well settled that the first jeopardy begins when the jury has been impaneled and sworn in. If the defendant is being tried by the judge alone, without a jury, the first jeopardy does not begin until the introduction of evidence has commenced. Thereafter the defendant may not be tried again "for the same offense." However, if the defendant successfully appeals the conviction, the state or federal government may retry him on the theory that the double jeopardy defense was waived by asking for a new trial.[89] As a practical matter, when convictions have been overturned on appeal, the prosecu-

---

[86] Faretta v. California, 422 U.S. 806 (1975); Adams v. United States, ex rel. McCann, 317 U.S. 269 (1942); Johnson v. Zerbst, 304 U.S. 458 (1938); Westbrook v. Arizona, 384 U.S. 150 (1966).
[87] Douglas v. California, 372 U.S. 353 (1963).
[88] Ross v. Moffitt, 417 U.S. 600 (1974).
[89] United States v. Tateo, 377 U.S. 463 (1964); Forman v. United States, 361 U.S. 416 (1960); United States v. Ball, 163 U.S. 662 (1896).

tion often drops the case at that point, rather than incurring the additional time and expense of a second trial.

The government may appeal, provided it does not raise the possibility of a second trial. For example, in the case of *United States* v. *Wilson,* the Supreme Court held that a government appeal of a posttrial court ruling does not constitute double jeopardy.[90] The defendant made a motion at trial to dismiss the government prosecution on grounds that delay had denied the defendant an opportunity for a fair trial; he had lost a witness who he had previously anticipated would testify. The defendant's motion was denied. Subsequently the jury found the defendant guilty. But the trial judge reversed the conviction by changing his mind on the previous motion regarding delay. The Supreme Court found that the government's subsequent appeal did not pose a danger of subjecting the defendant to a second trial for the same offense, because if the government were to win on the appeal of the motion, the jury's verdict of guilty would be reinstated. If the government were to lose, the judge's granting of the defendant's motion to dismiss would remain valid.

If a defendant is acquitted in federal court and is subsequently indicted, tried, and found guilty by the state, there is no double jeopardy violation.[91] This is based on the rationale that federal and state governments are separate sovereigns. Even though the facts recited in the state proceeding are nearly identical to those contained in the prior federal charge, and the federal government turns over all of its evidence to the state, it cannot be assumed that the second prosecution is conducted at the direction or as a tool of the federal government authorities.

QUESTIONS

1. Is there any validity to the contention that Supreme Court decisions in *Mapp* v. *Ohio* and *Miranda* have significantly reduced law enforcement effectiveness?

2. What percentage of police time and effort should be devoted to narcotics-related crimes?

3. What is the rationale behind the exclusionary rule?

4. Discuss the principle established in the *Katz* case. Does the Fourth Amendment protect a person regardless of where the person may be located?

5. Discuss each of the six exceptions to the search warrant requirement, and the soundness of the reasoning upon which each is based.

6. What should the defendant in a federal criminal case take into consideration in deciding whether to request or waive a preliminary hearing?

7. What constitutional arguments can be made in support of requiring a unanimous verdict by a twelve-person jury in all state and federal criminal prosecutions?

---

[90] United States v. Wilson, 420 U.S. 332 (1975).
[91] Bartkus v. Illinois, 35 U.S. 121 (1959).

8. Describe all the differences between civil trial procedures (including jury selection), as discussed in Chapter 6, and criminal trial procedure, as described in this chapter.

9. Should the defendant's right to counsel also include an assurance of "competent" counsel? Why or why not? If so, how can the legal system provide such an assurance?

Epilogue

It is hoped that this book has eliminated some of the mystery and confusion shrouding the American legal system. It should also have explained why many legal principles can be interpreted in various ways, as well as provided an understanding of the complexity and minute detail of the hundreds of legal principles discussed in the chapters on substantive law.

However, it is not the purpose of this book or any legal treatise to require memorization of those many legal principles. Continued contact with any area of the law will provide increasingly detailed knowledge of that area, including an understanding of the nuances of its principles. More importantly, initial contact with the legal system should bring an understanding of broad principles and of how the system develops those principles through the courts and, as Llewellyn suggests, a perception of the "interplay of causation between law and the world outside." [1]

In fact, a law school graduate could not possibly rely on the knowledge in law school to furnish a client with a legal opinion of any significant detail. He would have to conduct research, as explained in the discussion of the *Pope* v. *Drake* case in Chapter 6. That is why legal training places so much emphasis on the development of legal principles and the importance of being able not only to locate those principles through research tools and techniques but also to interpret the principles and place them in their proper context. "If rules were results, there would be little need of lawyers." [2]

It is not possible to gain a comprehensive knowledge of all areas of the law. The important thing is to learn how to approach and analyze the facts of a situation and how to ascertain and research the legal issues presented by such facts, as described in Chapter 3. The inadequacy of any single source of law or set of principles is evidenced in the practice of law, as in medicine, by a growing tendency toward and demand for specialization. A lawyer beginning as a general practitioner soon finds

---

[1] K. Llewellyn, *The Bramble Bush* (New York: Oceana Publications, 1951), p. 107.
[2] *Ibid.*, p. 18.

himself gravitating toward one narrow area of the law. He either discovers a stronger interest in that narrow area, seeks that type of work, and slowly develops an expertise in it, or he has no choice in the matter and is given a substantial amount of work in the area by a senior partner in his firm, for example, and thus becomes the firm's "expert" in the area. More often than not, the area of specialty is one with which the lawyer dealt only superficially in law school. For example, in New York City alone, literally tens of thousands of lawyers hold themselves out as specializing in the field of securities law,[3] and in the western United States, thousands of lawyers specialize in oil and gas law or mining law.[4]

Studying law and the legal system is sometimes a tedious endeavor. It takes significant concentration, dedication, and a positive attitude, and still questions remain and arguments persist among the brightest of judges, lawyers, and legal scholars. However, the openness to interpretation of our legal system's principles does not need apology or rationalization. The primary function of the law is to prevent or, if necessary, resolve disputes, and in a society that is continuously dealing with and producing many disputes, the law must allow for differing interpretations: if a matter is disputed, if there is doubt, rules of law do not *determine* the decisions; they provide a method by which people may resolve the dispute. Chapter 3 made this point in the discussion of the need for both stability and flexibility in the legal system.

Law students can do little to eliminate the initial feelings of confusion or competition they experience in their first year. Yet, there are many ways of reducing their confusion, increasing their knowledge of the legal system, and preparing for law school. This overview of the system was intended to contribute to that understanding. Also, the discussion of the substantive areas of the law in Chapters 7 through 12 should have made it clear that studying the law is not a process of learning by rote. The law student should bear in mind that the system is largely a reflection of society's values and needs and that, although knowledge of substantive principles is essential, such knowledge isolated from its social context is useless. Remembering these points will also help to keep law school study in perspective.

Thus, one begins to appreciate a blend of the substantive principles, the procedural framework for using those principles, the system of precedents and legal reasoning, the practical considerations with which a lawyer must deal—that is, the personalities of the clients, lawyers, and judges involved—and the overall relationship of the legal system to society's values and needs.

At some point in time—perhaps late in law school or after a few years of practice—the role of the law in our society begins to become clear and one is able to view the legal system as an element of the entire American political and economic system, rather than as an isolated discipline. Many lawyers come to view a legal education in law as a stepping stone to other careers such as politics, corporate management, or lobbying. Thus, for some people an understanding of the relation-

---

[3] See Chapter 8, pp. 170–76.
[4] See Chapter 8, p. 202.

ship between the system and the society as a whole may be more valuable than knowledge of any particular legal principles. Yet, no matter what direction one chooses after law school, he or she has been provided a comprehensive and firm basis on which to build.

In his introductory law book *The Bramble Bush*,[5] the famous legal scholar Karl Llewellyn attempted to soften the harsh impact of the reader's first year of law school by describing the philosophy of the American legal system and of the law schools, and by suggesting methods of studying, taking notes, and otherwise preparing for that difficult time. He also discussed the goals one should seek both as a law student and as a lawyer. The book begins with a short poem intended to serve as an analogy illustrating the transformation during law school from the somewhat lost feeling that so many first-year law students experience to the "enlightenment" supposedly achieved at the conclusion of law school and during the practice of law. The poem reads:

> There was a man in our town
>   And he was wondrous wise:
> He jumped into a BRAMBLE BUSH
>   And scratched out both his eyes—
> And when he saw that he was blind,
>   With all his might and main
> He jumped into another one
>   And scratched them in again.

Llewellyn believed that this broadening of the student's vision is gained not only through a greater understanding of the legal system but to an even greater degree through his knowledge of the interaction between the law and society. This introduction to the legal system has actually gone substantially beyond what is normally considered an introduction to the law, and the author hopes that the book has been able to "scratch in" the eyes of the reader and provide an understanding of the role the law plays in this complex society.

---

[5] Llewellyn (epigraph).

APPENDIX A

The Constitution of the United States

We the People of the United States, in Order to form a more perfect Union, establish Justice, insure domestic Tranquility, provide for the common defence, promote the general Welfare, and secure the Blessings of Liberty to ourselves and our Posterity, do ordain and establish this Constitution for the United States of America.

ARTICLE I

Section 1. All legislative Powers herein granted shall be vested in a Congress of the United States, which shall consist of a Senate and House of Representatives.

Section 2. The House of Representatives shall be composed of Members chosen every second Year by the People of the several States, and the Electors in each State shall have the Qualifications requisite for Electors of the most numerous Branch of the State Legislature.

No Person shall be a Representative who shall not have attained to the Age of twenty-five Years, and been seven Years a Citizen of the United States, and who shall not, when elected, be an Inhabitant of that State in which he shall be chosen.

Representatives and direct Taxes shall be apportioned among the several States which may be included within this Union, according to their respective Numbers, which shall be determined by adding to the whole Number of free Persons, including those bound to Service for a Term of Years, and excluding Indians not taxed, three fifths of all other Persons. The actual Enumeration shall be made within three Years after the first Meeting of the Congress of the United States, and within every subsequent Term of ten Years, in such Manner as they shall by Law direct. The Number of Representatives shall not exceed one for every thirty Thousand, but each State shall have at Least one Representative; and until such enumeration shall be made, the State of New Hampshire shall be entitled to chuse three, Massachusetts eight, Rhode-Island and Providence Plantations one, Connecticut five, New-York six, New Jersey four, Pennsylvania eight, Delaware one, Maryland six, Virginia ten, North Carolina five, South Carolina five, and Georgia three.

When vacancies happen in the Representation from any State, the Executive Authority thereof shall issue Writs of Election to fill such Vacancies.

The House of Representatives shall chuse their Speaker and other Officers; and shall have the sole Power of Impeachment.

Section 3. The Senate of the United States shall be composed of two Senators from each State, chosen by the Legislature thereof, for six Years; and each Senator shall have one Vote.

Immediately after they shall be assembled in Consequence of the first Election, they shall be divided as equally as may be into three Classes. The Seats of the Senators of the first Class shall be vacated at the Expiration of the second Year, of the second Class at the Expiration of the fourth Year, and of the third Class at the Expiration of the sixth Year, so that one third may be chosen every second Year; and if Vacancies happen by Resignation, or otherwise, during the Recess of the Legislature of any State, the Executive thereof may make temporary Appointments until the next Meeting of the Legislature, which shall then fill such Vacancies.

No Person shall be a Senator who shall not have attained to the Age of thirty Years, and been nine Years a Citizen of the United States, and who shall not, when elected, be an Inhabitant of that State for which he shall be chosen.

The Vice President of the United States shall be President of the Senate, but shall have no Vote, unless they be equally divided.

The Senate shall chuse their other Officers, and also a President pro tempore, in the absence of the Vice President, or when he shall exercise the Office of President of the United States.

The Senate shall have the sole Power to try all Impeachments. When sitting for that Purpose, they shall be on Oath or Affirmation. When the President of the United States is tried, the Chief Justice shall preside: And no Person shall be convicted without the Concurrence of two thirds of the Members present.

Judgment in Cases of Impeachment shall not extend further than to removal from Office, and disqualification to hold and enjoy any Office of honor, Trust, or Profit under the United States: but the Party convicted shall nevertheless be liable and subject to Indictment, Trial, Judgment, and Punishment, according to Law.

Section 4.   The Times, Places and Manner of holding Elections for Senators and Representatives, shall be prescribed in each State by the Legislature thereof; but the Congress may at any time by Law make or alter such Regulations, except as to the Places of chusing Senators.

The Congress shall assemble at least once in every Year, and such Meeting shall be on the first Monday in December unless they shall by Law appoint a different Day.

Section 5.   Each House shall be the Judge of the Elections, Returns, and Qualifications of its own Members, and a Majority of each shall constitute a Quorum to do Business; but a smaller Number may adjourn from day to day, and may be authorized to compel the Attendance of absent Members, in such Manner, and under such Penalties as each House may provide.

Each House may determine the Rules of its Proceedings, punish its Members for disorderly Behavior, and, with the Concurrence of two thirds, expel a Member.

Each House shall keep a journal of its Proceedings, and from time to time publish the same, excepting such Parts as may in their Judgment require Secrecy; and the Yeas and Nays of the Members of either House on any question shall, at the Desire of one fifth of those Present, be entered on the Journal.

Neither House, during the Session of Congress, shall, without the Consent of the other, adjourn for more than three days, nor to any other Place than that in which the two Houses shall be sitting.

Section 6.   The Senators and Representatives shall receive a Compensation for their Services, to be ascertained by Law, and paid out of the Treasury of the United States. They shall in all Cases, except Treason, Felony and Breach of the Peace, be privileged from Arrest during their Attendance at the Session of their respective Houses, and in going to and returning from the same; and for any Speech or Debate in either House, they shall not be questioned in any other Place.

No Senator or Representative shall, during the Time for which he was elected, be appointed to any civil Office under the Authority of the United States, which shall have been created, or the Emoluments whereof shall have been encreased during such time; and no Person holding any Office under the United States, shall be a Member of either House during his Continuance in Office.

Section 7.   All Bills for raising Revenue shall originate in the House of Representatives; but the Senate may propose to concur with Amendments as on other Bills.

Every Bill which shall have passed the House of Representatives and the Senate, shall, before it become a Law, be presented to the President of the United States; if he approve he shall sign it, but if not he shall return it, with his Objections to that House in which it shall have originated, who shall enter the Objections at large on their Journal, and proceed to reconsider it. If after such Reconsideration two thirds of that House shall agree to pass the Bill, it shall be sent, together with the Objections, to the other House, by which it shall likewise be reconsidered, and if approved by two thirds of that House, it shall become a Law. But in all such Cases the Votes of both Houses shall be determined by Yeas and Nays, and the Names of the Persons voting for and against the Bill shall be entered on the Journal of each House respectively. If any Bill shall not be returned by the President within ten Days (Sundays excepted) after it shall have been presented to him, the Same shall be a Law, in like Manner as if he had signed it, unless the Congress by their Adjournment prevent its Return, in which Case it shall not be a Law.

Every Order, Resolution, or Vote to which the Concurrence of the Senate and House of Representatives may be necessary (except on a question of Adjournment) shall be presented to the President of the United States; and before the Same shall take Effect, shall be approved by him, or being disapproved by him, shall be repassed by two thirds of the Senate and House of Representatives, according to the Rules and Limitations prescribed in the Case of a Bill.

Section 8.   The Congress shall have Power To lay and collect Taxes, Duties, Imposts and Excises, to pay the Debts and provide for the common Defence and general Welfare of the United States; but all Duties, Imposts and Excises shall be uniform throughout the United States;

To borrow money on the credit of the United States;

To regulate Commerce with foreign Nations, and among the several States, and with the Indian Tribes;

To establish an uniform Rule of Naturalization, and uniform Laws on the subject of Bankruptcy throughout the United States;

To coin Money, regulate the Value thereof, and of foreign Coin, and fix the Standard of Weights and Measures;

To provide for the Punishment of counterfeiting the Securities and current Coin of the United States;

To Establish Post Offices and post Roads;

To promote the Progress of Science and useful Arts, by securing for limited Times to Authors and Inventors the exclusive Right to their respective Writings and Discoveries;

To constitute Tribunals inferior to the supreme Court;

To define and punish Piracies and Felonies committed on the high Seas, and Offenses against the Law of Nations;

To declare War, grant Letters of Marque and Reprisal, and make Rules concerning Captures on Land and Water;

To raise and support Armies, but no Appropriation of Money to that Use shall be for a longer Term than two Years;

To provide and maintain a Navy;

To make Rules for the Government and Regulation of the land and naval Forces;

To provide for calling forth the Militia to execute the Laws of the Union, suppress Insurrections and repel Invasions;

To provide for organizing, arming, and disciplining the Militia, and for governing such Part of them as may be employed in the Service of the United States, reserving to the States respectively, the Appointment of the Officers, and the Authority of training the Militia according to the discipline prescribed by Congress;

To exercise exclusive Legislation in all Cases whatsoever, over such District (not exceeding ten Miles square) as may, by Cession of particular States, and the acceptance of Congress, become the Seat of the Government of the United States, and to exercise like Authority over all Places purchased by the Consent of the Legislature of the State in which the Same shall be, for the Erection of Forts, Magazines, Arsenals, dock-Yards, and other needful Buildings;—And

To make all Laws which shall be necessary and proper for carrying into Execution the foregoing Powers, and all other Powers vested by this Constitution in the Government of the United States, or in any Department or Officer thereof.

Section 9.   The Migration or Importation of Such Persons as any of the States now existing shall think proper to admit, shall not be prohibited by the Congress prior to the Year one thousand eight hundred and eight, but a tax or duty may be imposed on such Importation, not exceeding ten dollars for each Person.

The privilege of the Writ of Habeas Corpus shall not be suspended, unless when in Cases of Rebellion or Invasion the public Safety may require it.

No Bill of Attainder or ex post facto Law shall be passed.

No capitation, or other direct, Tax shall be laid, unless in Proportion to the Census or Enumeration herein before directed to be taken.

No Tax or Duty shall be laid on Articles exported from any State.

No preference shall be given by any Regulation of Commerce or Revenue to the Ports of one State over those of another: nor shall Vessels bound to, or from, one State be obliged to enter, clear, or pay Duties in another.

No money shall be drawn from the Treasury, but in Consequence of Appropriations made by Law; and a regular Statement and Account of the Receipts and Expenditures of all public Money shall be published from time to time.

No Title of Nobility shall be granted by the United States: And no Person holding any Office of Profit or Trust under them, shall, without the Consent of the Congress, accept of any present, Emolument, Office, or Title, of any kind whatever, from any King, Prince, or foreign State.

Section 10.   No State shall enter into any Treaty, Alliance, or Confederation; grant Letters of Marque and Reprisal; coin Money; emit Bills of Credit; make any Thing but gold and silver Coin a Tender in Payment of Debts; pass any Bill of Attainder, ex post facto Law, or Law impairing the Obligation of Contracts, or grant any Title of Nobility.

No State shall, without the Consent of the Congress, lay any Imposts or Duties on Imports or Exports, except what may be absolutely necessary for executing its inspection Laws: and the net Produce of all Duties and Imposts, laid by any State on Imports or Exports, shall be for the Use of the Treasury of the United States; and all such Laws shall be subject to the Revision and Control of the Congress.

No State shall, without the Consent of Congress, lay any duty of Tonnage, keep Troops, or Ships of War in time of Peace, enter into any Agreement or Compact with another State. or with a foreign Power, or engage in War, unless actually invaded, or in such imminent Danger as will not admit of delay.

ARTICLE II

Section 1. The executive Power shall be vested in a President of the United States of America. He shall hold his Office during the Term of four Years, and, together with the Vice-President, chosen for the same Term, be elected, as follows:

Each State shall appoint, in such Manner as the Legislature thereof may direct, a Number of Electors, equal to the whole Number of Senators and Representatives to which the State may be entitled in the Congress: but no Senator or Representative, or Person holding an Office of Trust or Profit under the United States, shall be appointed an Elector.

The Electors shall meet in their respective States, and vote by Ballot for two persons, of whom one at least shall not be an Inhabitant of the same State with themselves. And they shall make a List of all the Persons voted for, and of the Number of Votes for each; which List they shall sign and certify, and transmit sealed to the Seat of the Government of the United States, directed to the President of the Senate. The President of the Senate shall, in the Presence of the Senate and House of Representatives, open all the Certificates, and the Votes shall then be counted. The Person having the greatest Number of Votes shall be the President, if such Number be a Majority of the whole Number of Electors appointed; and if there be more than one who have such Majority, and have an equal Number of Votes, then the House of Representatives shall immediately chuse by Ballot one of them for President; and if no Person have a Majority, then from the five highest on the List the said House shall in like Manner chuse the President. But in chusing the President, the Votes shall be taken by States, the Representation from each State having one Vote: A quorum for this Purpose shall consist of a Member or Members from two thirds of the States, and a Majority of all the States shall be necessary to a Choice. In every Case, after the Choice of the President, the Person having the greatest Number of Votes of the Electors shall be the Vice President. But if there should remain two or more who have equal Votes, the Senate shall chuse from them by Ballot the Vice President.

The Congress may determine the Time of chusing the Electors, and the Day on which they shall give their Votes; which Day shall be the same throughout the United States.

No person except a natural born Citizen, or a Citizen of the United States, at the time of the Adoption of this Constitution, shall be eligible to the Office of President; neither shall any Person be eligible to that Office who shall not have attained to the Age of thirty-five Years, and been fourteen Years a Resident within the United States.

In case of the removal of the President from Office, or of his Death, Resignation, or Inability to discharge the Powers and Duties of the said Office, the same shall devolve on the Vice President, and the Congress may by Law provide for the Case of Removal, Death, Resignation or Inability, both of the President and Vice President, declaring what

Officer shall then act as President, and such Officer shall act accordingly, until the Disability be removed, or a President shall be elected.

The President shall, at stated Times, receive for his Services, a Compensation, which shall neither be encreased nor diminished during the Period for which he shall have been elected, and he shall not receive within that Period any other Emolument from the United States, or any of them.

Before he enter on the Execution of his Office, he shall take the following Oath or Affirmation:—"I do solemnly swear (or affirm) that I will faithfully execute the Office of President of the United States, and will to the best of my Ability, preserve, protect and defend the Constitution of the United States."

Section 2. The President shall be Commander in Chief of the Army and Navy of the United States, and of the Militia of the several States, when called into the actual Service of the United States; he may require the Opinion, in writing, of the principal Officer in each of the executive Departments, upon any subject relating to the Duties of their respective Offices, and he shall have Power to grant Reprieves and Pardons for Offenses against the United States, except in Cases of Impeachment.

He shall have Power, by and with the Advice and Consent of the Senate, to make Treaties, provided two thirds of the Senators present concur; and he shall nominate, and by and with the Advice and Consent of the Senate, shall appoint Ambassadors, other public Ministers and Consuls, Judges of the supreme Court, and all other Officers of the United States, whose Appointments are not herein otherwise provided for, and which shall be established by Law; but the Congress may by Law vest the Appointment of such inferior Officers, as they think proper, in the President alone, in the Courts of Law, or in the Heads of Departments.

The President shall have the Power to fill up all Vacancies that may happen during the Recess of the Senate, by granting Commissions which shall expire at the End of their next Session.

Section 3. He shall from time to time give to the Congress Information of the State of the Union, and recommend to their Consideration such Measures as he shall judge necessary and expedient; he may, on extraordinary Occasions, convene both Houses, or either of them, and in Case of Disagreement between them, with Respect to the Time of Adjournment, he may adjourn them to such Time as he shall think proper; he shall receive Ambassadors and other public Ministers; he shall take Care that the Laws be faithfully executed, and shall Commission all the Officers of the United States.

Section 4. The President; Vice President and all civil Officers of the United States, shall be removed from Office on Impeachment for, and Conviction of, Treason, Bribery, or other high Crimes and Misdemeanors.

ARTICLE III

Section 1. The judicial Power of the United States, shall be vested in one supreme Court, and in such inferior Courts as the Congress may from time to time ordain and establish. The Judges, both of the supreme and inferior Courts, shall hold their Offices during good Behaviour, and shall, at stated Times, receive for their Services a Compensation which shall not be diminished during their Continuance in Office.

Section 2. The judicial Power shall extend to all Cases, in Law and Equity, arising under this Constitution, the Laws of the United States, and Treaties made, or which shall be made, under their Authority;—to all Cases affecting Ambassadors, other public Ministers and Consuls;—to all Cases of admiralty and maritime Jurisdiction;—to Controversies to which the United States shall be a Party;—to Controversies between two or more States;—between a State and Citizens of another State;—between Citizens of different States;—between Citizens of the same State claiming Lands under Grants of different States, and between a State, or the Citizens thereof, and foreign States, Citizens or Subjects.

In all Cases affecting Ambassadors, other public Ministers and Consuls, and those in which a State shall be Party, the supreme Court shall have original Jurisdiction. In all the other Cases before mentioned, the supreme Court shall have appellate Jurisdiction, both as to Law and Fact, with such Exceptions, and under such Regulations as the Congress shall make.

The trial of all Crimes, except in Cases of Impeachment, shall be by Jury; and such Trial shall be held in the State where the said Crimes shall have been committed; but when not committed within any State, the Trial shall be at such Place or Places as the Congress may by Law have directed.

Section 3.   Treason against the United States, shall consist only in levying War against them, or, in adhering to their Enemies, giving them Aid and Comfort. No Person shall be convicted of Treason unless on the Testimony of two Witnesses to the same overt Act, or on Confession in open Court.

The Congress shall have power to declare the Punishment of Treason, but no Attainder of Treason shall work Corruption of Blood, or Forfeiture except during the Life of the Person attainted.

ARTICLE IV

Section 1.   Full Faith and Credit shall be given in each State to the public Acts, Records, and judicial Proceedings of every other State. And the Congress may by general Laws prescribe the Manner in which such Acts, Records and Proceedings shall be proved, and the Effect thereof.

Section 2.   The Citizens of each State shall be entitled to all Privileges and Immunities of Citizens in the several States.

A Person charged in any State with Treason, Felony, or other Crime, who shall flee from Justice, and be found in another State, shall on demand of the executive Authority of the State from which he fled, be delivered up, to be removed to the State having Jurisdiction of the Crime.

No Person held to Service or Labour in one State, under the Laws thereof, escaping into another, shall, in Consequence of any Law or Regulation therein, be discharged from such Service or Labour, but shall be delivered up on Claim of the Party to whom such Service or Labour may be due.

Section 3.   New States may be admitted by the Congress into this Union; but no new State shall be formed or erected within the Jurisdiction of any other State; nor any State be formed by the Junction of two or more States, or parts of States, without the Consent of the Legislatures of the States concerned as well as of the Congress.

The Congress shall have Power to dispose of and make all needful Rules and Regulations respecting the Territory or other Property belonging to the United States; and nothing in this Constitution shall be so construed as to Prejudice any Claims of the United States, or of any particular State.

Section 4.   The United States shall guarantee to every State in this Union a Republican   Form of Government, and shall protect each of them against Invasion; and on Application of the Legislature, or of the Executive (when the Legislature cannot be convened) against domestic Violence.

ARTICLE V

The Congress, whenever two thirds of both Houses shall deem it necessary, shall propose Amendments to this Constitution, or, on the Application of the Legislatures of two thirds of the several States, shall call a Convention for proposing Amendments, which, in either Case, shall be valid to all Intents and Purposes, as part of this Constitution, when ratified by the Legislatures of three fourths of the several States, or by Conventions in three fourths thereof, as the one or the other Mode of Ratification may be proposed by the Congress; Provided that no Amendment which may be made prior to the Year One thousand eight hundred and eight shall in any Manner affect the first and fourth Clauses in the Ninth Section of the first Article; and that no State, without its Consent, shall be deprived of its equal Suffrage in the Senate.

ARTICLE VI

All Debts contracted and Engagements entered into, before the Adoption of this Constitution shall be as valid against the United States under this Constitution, as under the Confederation.

This Constitution, and the Laws of the United States which shall be made in Pursuance thereof; and all Treaties made, or which shall be made, under the Authority of the United States, shall be the supreme Law of the Land; and the Judges in every State shall be bound thereby, any Thing in the Constitution or Laws of any State to the Contrary notwithstanding.

The Senators and Representatives before mentioned, and the Members of the several State Legislatures, and all executive and judicial Officers, both of the United States and of the several States, shall be bound by Oath or Affirmation, to support this Constitution; but no religious Test shall ever be required as a Qualification to any Office or public Trust under the United States.

ARTICLE VII

The Ratification of the Conventions of nine States shall be sufficient for the Establishment of this Constitution between the States so ratifying the Same.

ARTICLES IN ADDITION TO, AND AMENDMENT OF, THE CONSTITUTION OF THE UNITED STATES OF AMERICA, PROPOSED BY CONGRESS AND RATIFIED BY THE SEVERAL STATES, PURSUANT TO THE FIFTH ARTICLE OF THE ORIGINAL CONSTITUTION

AMENDMENT I

Congress shall make no law respecting an establishment of religion, or prohibiting the free exercise thereof; or abridging the freedom of speech, or of the press; or the right of the people peaceably to assemble, and to petition the Government for a redress of grievances.

AMENDMENT II

A well regulated Militia, being necessary to the security of a free State, the right of the people to keep and bear Arms, shall not be infringed.

AMENDMENT III

No Soldier shall, in time of peace be quartered in any house, without the consent of the Owner, nor in time of war, but in a manner to be prescribed by law.

AMENDMENT IV

The right of the people to be secure in their persons, houses, papers, and effects, against unreasonable searches and seizures, shall not be violated, and no Warrants shall issue, but upon probable cause, supported by Oath or affirmation, and particularly describing the place to be searched, and the persons or things to be seized.

AMENDMENT V

No person shall be held to answer for a capital, or otherwise infamous crime, unless on a presentment or indictment of a Grand Jury, except in cases arising in the land or naval forces, or in the Militia, when in actual service in time of War or public danger; nor shall any person be subject for the same offence to be twice put in jeopardy of life or limb; nor shall be compelled in any criminal case to be a witness against himself, nor be deprived of life, liberty, or property, without due process of law; nor shall private property be taken for public use, without just compensation.

AMENDMENT VI

In all criminal prosecutions, the accused shall enjoy the right to a speedy and public trial, by an impartial jury of the State and district wherein the crime shall have been committed, which district shall have been previously ascertained by law, and to be informed of the nature and cause of the accusation; to be confronted with the witnesses against him; to have compulsory process for obtaining witnesses in his favor, and to have the Assistance of Counsel for his defence.

AMENDMENT VII

In suits at common law, where the value in controversy shall exceed twenty dollars, the right of trial by jury shall be preserved, and no fact tried by jury, shall be otherwise re-examined in any Court of the United States, than according to the rules of the common law.

AMENDMENT VIII

Excessive bail shall not be required, nor excessive fines imposed, nor cruel and unusual punishments inflicted.

AMENDMENT IX

The enumeration in the Constitution, of certain rights, shall not be construed to deny or disparage others retained by the people.

AMENDMENT X

The powers not delegated to the United States by the Constitution, nor prohibited by it to the States, are reserved to the States respectively, or to the people.

AMENDMENT XI [1798]

The Judicial power of the United States shall not be construed to extend to any suit in law or equity, commenced or prosecuted against one of the United States by Citizens of another State, or by Citizens or Subjects of any Foreign State.

AMENDMENT XII [1804]

The electors shall meet in their respective states and vote by ballot for President and Vice-President, one of whom, at least, shall not be an inhabitant of the same state with themselves; they shall name in their ballots the person voted for as President, and in distinct ballots the person voted for as Vice-President, and they shall make distinct lists of all persons voted for as President, and of all persons voted for as Vice-President, and of the number of votes for each, which lists they shall sign and certify, and transmit sealed to the seat of the government of the United States, directed to the President of the Senate;—The President of the Senate shall, in presence of the Senate and House of Representatives, open all the certificates and the votes shall then be counted;—The person having the greatest number of votes for President, shall be the President, if such number be a majority of the whole number of Electors appointed; and if no person have such majority, then from the persons having the highest numbers not exceeding three on the list of those voted for as President, the House of Representatives shall choose immediately, by ballot, the President. But in choosing the President, the votes shall be taken by states, the representation from each state having one vote; a quorum for this purpose shall consist of a member or members from two-thirds of the states, and a majority of all the states shall be necessary to a choice. And if the House of Representatives shall not choose a President whenever the right of choice shall devolve upon them, before the fourth day of March next following, then the Vice-President shall act as President, as in the case of the death or other constitutional disability of the President.—The person having the greatest number of votes as Vice-President, shall be the Vice-President, if such number be a majority of the whole number of Electors appointed, and if no person have a majority, then from the two highest numbers on the list, the Senate shall choose the Vice-President; a quorum for the purpose shall consist of two-thirds of the whole number of Senators, and a majority of the whole number shall be necessary to a choice. But no person constitutionally ineligible to the office of President shall be eligible to that of Vice-President of the United States.

AMENDMENT XIII [1865]

Section 1. Neither slavery nor involuntary servitude, except as a punishment for crime whereof the party shall have been duly convicted, shall exist within the United States, or any place subject to their jurisdiction.

Section 2. Congress shall have power to enforce this article by appropriate legislation.

AMENDMENT XIV [1868]

Section 1. All persons born or naturalized in the United States, and subject to the jurisdiction thereof, are citizens of the United States and of the State wherein they reside. No State shall make or enforce any law which shall abridge the privileges or immunities of citizens of the United States; nor shall any State deprive any person of life, liberty, or property, without due process of law; nor deny to any person within its jurisdiction the equal protection of the laws.

Section 2. Representatives shall be apportioned among the several States according to their respective numbers, counting the whole number of persons in each State, excluding Indians not taxed. But when the right to vote at any election for the choice of electors for President and Vice President of the United States, Representatives in Congress, the Executive and Judicial officers of a State, or the members of the Legislature thereof, is denied to any of the male inhabitants of such State, being twenty-one years of age, and citizens of the United States, or in any way abridged, except for participation in rebellion, or other crime, the basis of representation therein shall be reduced in the proportion which the number of such male citizens shall bear to the whole number of male citizens twenty-one years of age in such State.

Section 3. No person shall be a Senator or Representative in Congress, or elector of President and Vice President, or hold any office, civil or military, under the United States, or under any State, who, having previously taken an oath, as a member of Congress, or as an officer of the United States, or as a member of any State legislature, or as an executive or judicial officer of any State, to support the Constitution of the United States, shall have engaged in insurrection or rebellion against the same, or given aid or comfort to the enemies thereof. But Congress may by a vote of two-thirds of each House, remove such disability.

Section 4. The validity of the public debt of the United States, authorized by law, including debts incurred for payment of pensions and bounties for services in suppressing insurrection or rebellion, shall not be questioned. But neither the United States nor any State shall assume or pay any debt or obligation incurred in aid of insurrection or rebellion against the United States, or any claim for the loss or emancipation of any slave; but all such debts, obligations and claims shall be held illegal and void.

Section 5. The Congress shall have power to enforce, by appropriate legislation, the provisions of this article.

AMENDMENT XV [1870]

Section 1. The right of citizens of the United States to vote shall not be denied or abridged by the United States or by any State on account of race, color, or previous condition of servitude.

Section 2. The Congress shall have power to enforce this article by appropriate legislation.

AMENDMENT XVI [1913]

The Congress shall have power to lay and collect taxes on incomes, from whatever source derived, without apportionment among the several States, and without regard to any census or enumeration.

AMENDMENT XVII [1913]

The Senate of the United States shall be composed of two Senators from each State, elected by the people thereof, for six years; and each Senator shall have one vote. The electors in each State shall have the qualifications requisite for electors of the most numerous branch of the State legislatures.

When vacancies happen in the representation of any State in the Senate, the executive authority of such State shall issue writs of election to fill such vacancies: *Provided,* That the legislature of any State may empower the executive thereof to make temporary appointments until the people fill the vacancies by election as the legislature may direct.

This amendment shall not be construed as to affect the election or term of any Senator chosen before it becomes valid as part of the Constitution.

AMENDMENT XVIII [1919]

Section 1. After one year from the ratification of this article the manufacture, sale, or transportation of intoxicating liquors within, the importation thereof into, or the exportation thereof from the United States and all territory subject to the jurisdiction thereof for beverage purposes is hereby prohibited.

Section 2. The Congress and the several States shall have concurrent power to enforce this article by appropriate legislation.

Section 3. This article shall be inoperative unless it shall have been ratified as an amendment to the Constitution by the legislatures of the several States, as provided in the Constitution, within seven years from the date of the submission hereof to the States by the Congress.

AMENDMENT XIX [1920]

The right of citizens of the United States to vote shall not be denied or abridged by the United States or by any State on account of sex.

Congress shall have power to enforce this article by appropriate legislation.

AMENDMENT XX [1933]

Section 1. The terms of the President and Vice President shall end at noon on the 20th day of January, and the terms of Senators and Representatives at noon on the 3d day of January, of the years in which such terms would have ended if this article had not been ratified; and the terms of their successors shall then begin.

Section 2. The Congress shall assemble at least once in every year, and such meeting shall begin at noon on the 3d day of January, unless they shall by law appoint a different day.

Section 3. If, at the time fixed for the beginning of the term of the President, the President elect shall have died, the Vice President elect shall become President. If a President shall not have been chosen before the time fixed for the beginning of his term, or if the President elect shall have failed to qualify, then the Vice President elect shall act as President until a President shall have qualified; and the Congress may by law provide for the case wherein neither a President elect nor a Vice President elect shall have qualified, declaring who shall then act as President, or the manner in which one who is to act shall be selected, and such person shall act accordingly until a President or Vice President shall have qualified.

Section 4. The Congress may by law provide for the case of the death of any of the persons from whom the House of Representatives may choose a President whenever the right of choice shall have devolved upon them, and for the case of the death of any of the persons from whom the Senate may choose a Vice President whenever the right of choice shall have devolved upon them.

Section 5. Sections 1 and 2 shall take effect on the 15th day of October following the ratification of this article.

Section 6. This article shall be inoperative unless it shall have been ratified as an amendment to the Constitution by the legislatures of three-fourths of the several States within seven years from the date of its submission.

AMENDMENT XXI [1933]

Section 1. The eighteenth article of amendment to the Constitution of the United States is hereby repealed.

Section 2. The transportation or importation into any State, Territory, or possession of the United States for delivery or use therein of intoxicating liquors, in violation of the laws thereof, is hereby prohibited.

Section 3. This article shall be inoperative unless it shall have been ratified as an amendment to the Constitution by conventions in the several States, as provided in the Constitution, within seven years from the date of the submission hereof to the States by the Congress.

AMENDMENT XXII [1951]

Section 1. No person shall be elected to the office of the President more than twice, and no person who has held the office of President, or acted as President, for more than two years of a term to which some other person was elected President shall be elected to the office of the President more than once. But this Article shall not apply to any person holding the office of President when this Article was proposed by the Congress, and shall not prevent any person who may be holding the office of President, or acting as President, during the term within which this Article becomes operative from holding the office of President or acting as President during the remainder of such term.

Section 2.   This article shall be inoperative unless it shall have been ratified as an amendment to the Constitution by the legislatures of three-fourths of the several States within seven years from the date of its submission to the States by the Congress.

AMENDMENT XXIII [1961]

Section 1.   The District constituting the seat of Government of the United States shall appoint in such manner as the Congress may direct:

A number of electors of President and Vice President equal to the whole number of Senators and Representatives in Congress to which the District would be entitled if it were a State, but in no event more than the least populous State; they shall be in addition to those appointed by the States, but they shall be considered, for the purposes of the election of President and Vice President, to be electors appointed by a State; and they shall meet in the District and perform such duties as provided by the twelfth article of amendment.

Section 2.   The Congress shall have power to enforce this article by appropriate legislation.

AMENDMENT XXIV [1964]

Section 1.   The right of citizens of the United States to vote in any primary or other election for President or Vice President, for electors for President or Vice President, or for Senator or Representative in Congress, shall not be abridged by the United States or any State by reason of failure to pay any poll tax or other tax.

Section 2.   The Congress shall have power to enforce this article by appropriate legislation.

AMENDMENT XXV [1967]

Section 1.   In case of the removal of the President from office or of his death or resignation, the Vice President shall become President.

Section 2.   Whenever there is a vacancy in the office of the Vice President, the President shall nominate a Vice President who shall take office upon confirmation by a majority vote of both Houses of Congress.

Section 3.   Whenever the President transmits to the President pro tempore of the Senate and the Speaker of the House of Representatives his written declaration that he is unable to discharge the powers and duties of his office, and until he transmits to them a written declaration to the contrary, such powers and duties shall be discharged by the Vice President as Acting President.

Section 4.   Whenever the Vice President and a majority of either the principal officers of the executive departments or of such other body as Congress may by law provide, transmit to the President pro tempore of the Senate and the Speaker of the House of Representatives their written declaration that the President is unable to discharge the powers and duties of his office, the Vice President shall immediately assume the powers and duties of the office as Acting President.

Thereafter, when the President transmits to the President pro tempore of the Senate and the Speaker of the House of Representatives his written declaration that no inability exists, he shall resume the powers and duties of his office unless the Vice President and a majority of either the principal officers of the executive department or of such other body as Congress may by law provide, transmit within four days to the President pro tempore of the Senate and the Speaker of the House of Representatives their written declaration that the President is unable to discharge the powers and duties of his office. Thereupon Congress shall decide the issue, assembling within forty-eight hours for that purpose if not in session. If the Congress, within twenty-one days after receipt of the latter written declaration, or, if Congress is not in session, within twenty-one days after Congress is required to assemble, determines by two-thirds vote of both Houses that the President is unable to discharge the powers and duties of his office, the Vice President shall continue to discharge the same as Acting President; otherwise, the President shall resume the powers and duties of his office.

AMENDMENT XXVI [1971]

Section 1.   The right of citizens of the United States, who are eighteen years of age or older, to vote shall not be denied or abridged by the United States or by any State on account of age.

Section 2.   The Congress shall have power to enforce this article by appropriate legislation.

APPENDIX B

IN THE SUPERIOR COURT
OF THE STATE OF CALIFORNIA
IN AND FOR THE CITY AND COUNTY
OF SAN FRANCISCO

JOHN POPE, Plaintiff v. RICHARD DRAKE, Defendant	Number 459 371 COMPLAINT

COMES NOW the Plaintiff, by and through his undersigned attorney, and hereby complains against Defendant as follows:

1. On January 1, 1977, at approximately 4:00 A.M., Plaintiff was proceeding eastbound on California Street in his vehicle approaching the intersection of California Street and Powell Street. At the same time, Defendant was proceeding westbound on California Street and approaching the same intersection.
2. Upon reaching the center of the intersection, at which time Plaintiff remained approximately one hundred (100) feet away from said intersection, Defendant slowed down and turned his car so as to indicate that he would make a left-hand turn after permitting Plaintiff to pass through the intersection. However, Defendant thereupon proceeded further into Plaintiff's lane immediately prior to the time that Plaintiff entered the intersection, thereby forcing Plaintiff to swerve to the left in order to avoid colliding with Defendant's vehicle.
3. Defendant's blocking of Plaintiff's lane proximately caused Plaintiff to collide with a lamppost on the northeast corner of said intersection, thereby directly and proximately causing severe, painful, and permanent injuries to Plaintiff.
4. Defendant's conduct described above was negligent and reckless and was the sole cause of Plaintiff's injuries.

WHEREFORE, Plaintiff requests the Court to order Defendant to pay damages to Plaintiff in the amount of $250,000, plus costs, including attorney's fees, and such other relief as the Court deems appropriate under the circumstances.

Respectfully submitted,

James Wilson
Suite 1500
236 Montgomery Street
San Francisco, California 94104

ATTORNEY FOR PLAINTIFF

APPENDIX C

IN THE SUPERIOR COURT
OF THE STATE OF CALIFORNIA
IN AND FOR THE CITY AND COUNTY
OF SAN FRANCISCO

JOHN POPE, Plaintiff v. RICHARD DRAKE, Defendant	Number 459 371 ANSWER

COMES NOW the Defendant, by and through his undersigned attorney, and in response to Plaintiff's Complaint states as follows:

1. Defendant admits that at some time on January 1, 1977, he was proceeding westbound on California Street, San Francisco near the intersection of California Street and Powell Street. With respect to all other allegations contained in paragraph 1 of Plaintiff's Complaint, Defendant is without sufficient knowledge to respond and therefore denies same.
2. Defendant denies the allegations contained in paragraphs 2, 3, and 4 of Plaintiff's Complaint.

AFFIRMATIVE DEFENSES

3. Plaintiff has failed to allege any contact between Plaintiff's and Defendant's vehicles, and, therefore, Plaintiff has failed to state a claim upon which relief can be granted.
4. Plaintiff was the sole and proximate cause of any injuries he may have suffered.
5. Upon reaching the intersection described in paragraph 1 of Plaintiff's Complaint, Plaintiff thereupon came to a complete stop and yielded the right-of-way to Defendant who had entered said intersection prior to Plaintiff.

WHEREFORE, Defendant requests that Plaintiff's Complaint be dismissed, that no relief be granted plaintiff, and that Defendant be granted costs, including attorney's fees and such other relief as the Court deems appropriate under the circumstances.

Respectfully submitted,

Harold R. Braden
Suite 900
210 Sutter Street
San Francisco, California 94104

ATTORNEY FOR DEFENDANT

APPENDIX D

IN THE SUPERIOR COURT
OF THE STATE OF CALIFORNIA
IN AND FOR THE CITY AND COUNTY
OF SAN FRANCISCO

JOHN POPE, Plaintiff v. RICHARD DRAKE, Defendant	Number 459 371 DEFENDANT'S MOTION TO DISMISS

COMES NOW the Defendant, by and through his undersigned attorney, and moves the Court as follows:

For a dismissal of Plaintiff's Complaint and this action upon the ground that the Complaint fails to state a claim against Defendant upon which relief can be granted.

Respectfully submitted,

_____

Harold R. Braden
Suite 900
210 Sutter Street
San Francisco, California 94104

ATTORNEY FOR DEFENDANT

APPENDIX E

IN THE SUPERIOR COURT
OF THE STATE OF CALIFORNIA
IN AND FOR THE CITY AND COUNTY
OF SAN FRANCISCO

JOHN POPE,
              Plaintiff
v.
RICHARD DRAKE,
              Defendant
	Number 459 371
	
	PLAINTIFF'S FIRST SET
	OF INTERROGATORIES
	TO DEFENDANT

COMES NOW the Plaintiff, by and through his undersigned attorney, and pursuant to Rule 33 of California Rules of Civil Procedure hereby requests Defendant to provide answers to the following interrogatories:

1. Describe in detail your whereabouts and all events that occurred at approximately 4:00 A.M. on January 1, 1977, in particular the events which occurred at the point in time when you were approaching the intersection of California and Powell Streets at said time.

2. State in detail your estimates of the following with respect to events described in the Complaint:
   a. The distances from the center of said intersection to Plaintiff's vehicle and your vehicle at the point in time when you first saw Plaintiff's vehicle.
   b. Plaintiff's speed at a point two hundred feet from the center of said intersection and his speed at fifty-foot intervals thereafter.

3. Describe whether the traffic light at said intersection was red, yellow, or green with respect to each of the following circumstances:

   a. At the point in time when you entered the intersection.
   b. At the time you began to make your turn.
   c. At the time Plaintiff was (1) two hundred, (2) one hundred, (3) fifty, and (4) ten feet, from the center of the intersection.
   d. At the time Plaintiff entered the intersection.

4. Describe the physical and operating condition of your vehicle at the time described in Interrogatory No. 1, including:

   a. Whether either of your headlights was not working at such time.
   b. Whether and at what time you had knowledge of the malfunction of your headlight or of any other defect concerning your vehicle.

5. Describe in detail all statements that you made to the police officers investigating the accident, to Plaintiff and to all other persons, immediately after the incident described in the Complaint.
6. Describe your activities during the period from 8. P.M., December 31, 1976, to 4 A.M., January 1, 1977, including, but not limited to, whether, in what quantity and at what locations, you consumed any alcoholic beverages or other intoxicants during said period.
7. Do you wear corrective lenses, and, if so, were they required as a condition of your driver's license at the time of the accident?
8. Were you wearing corrective lenses at the time of the accident?
9. Describe your physical condition at the time of the accident, including your eyesight and hearing abilities.

Respectfully submitted,

James Wilson
Suite 1500
236 Montgomery Street
San Francisco, California 94104

ATTORNEY FOR PLAINTIFF

APPENDIX F

UNIFORM PARTNERSHIP ACT

(Adopted in 43 jurisdictions: Alaska, Arizona, Arkansas, California, Colorado, Connecticut, Delaware, District of Columbia, Guam, Idaho, Illinois, Indiana, Kentucky, Maryland, Massachusetts, Michigan, Minnesota, Missouri, Montana, Nebraska, Nevada, New Jersey, New Mexico, New York, North Carolina, North Dakota, Ohio, Oklahoma, Oregon, Pennsylvania, Rhode Island, South Carolina, South Dakota, Tennessee, Texas, Utah, Vermont, Viriginia, Virgin Islands, Washington, West Virginia, Wisconsin, and Wyoming.)

Part and Section Analysis

An Act to Make Uniform the Law of Partnerships
Be it enacted, etc., as follows:

PART I.   PRELIMINARY PROVISIONS

§1. Name of Act

This act may be cited as Uniform Partnership Act.

§2. Definition of Terms

In this act, "Court" includes every court and judge having jurisdiction in the case.

"Business" includes every trade, occupation, or profession.

"Person" includes individuals, partnerships, corporations, and other associations.

"Bankrupt" includes bankrupt under the Federal Bankruptcy Act or insolvent under any state insolvent act.

"Conveyance" includes every assignment, lease, mortgage, or encumbrance.

"Real property" includes land and any interest or estate in land.

§3. Interpretation of Knowledge and Notice

(1) A person has "knowledge" of a fact within the meaning of this act not only when he has actual knowledge thereof, but also when he has knowledge of such other facts as in the circumstances shows bad faith.

(2) A person has "notice" of a fact within the meaning of this act when the person who claims the benefit of the notice

(a) States the fact to such person, or
(b) Delivers through the mail, or by other means of communication, a written statement of the fact to such person or to a proper person at his place of business or residence.

§4. Rules of Construction

(1) The rule that statutes in derogation of the common law are to be strictly construed shall have no application to this act.

(2) The law of estoppel shall apply under this act.

(3) The law of agency shall apply under this act.

(4) This act shall be so interpreted and construed as to effect its general purpose to make uniform the law of those states which enact it.

(5) This act shall not be construed so as to impair the obligations of any contract existing when the act goes into effect, nor to affect any action or proceedings begun or right accrued before this act takes effect.

§5. Rules for Cases Not Provided for in this Act

In any case not provided for in this act the rules of law and equity, including the law merchant, shall govern.

PART II. NATURE OF PARTNERSHIP

§6. Partnership Defined

(1) A partnership is an association of two or more persons to carry on as co-owners a business for profit.

(2) But any association formed under any other statute of this state, or any statute adopted by authority, other than the authority of this state, is not a partnership under this act, unless such association would have been a partnership in this state prior to the adoption of this act; but this act shall apply to limited partnerships except in so far as the statutes relating to such partnerships are inconsistent herewith.

§7. Rules for Determining the Existence of a Partnership

In determining whether a partnership exists, these rules shall apply:

(1) Except as provided by Section 16 persons who are not partners as to each other are not partners as to third persons.

(2) Joint tenancy, tenancy in common, tenancy by the entireties, joint property, common property, or part ownership does not of itself establish a partnership, whether such co-owners do or do not share any profits made by the use of the property.

(3) The sharing of gross returns does not of itself establish a partnership, whether or not the persons sharing them have a joint or common right or interest in any property from which the returns are derived.

(4) The receipt by a person of a share of the profits of a business is prima facie evidence that he is a partner in the business, but no such inference shall be drawn if such profits were received in payment:

(a) As a debt by installments or otherwise,
(b) As wages of an employee or rent to a landlord,
(c) As an annuity to a widow or representative of a deceased partner,
(d) As interest on a loan, though the amount of payment vary with the profits of the business,

(e) As the consideration for the sale of a good-will of a business or other property by installments or otherwise.

§8. Partnership Property

(1) All property originally brought into the partnership stock or subsequently acquired by purchase or otherwise, on account of the partnership, is partnership property.

(2) Unless the contrary intention appears, property acquired with partnership funds is partnership property.

(3) Any estate in real property may be acquired in the partnership name. Title so acquired can be conveyed only in the partnership name.

(4) A conveyance to a partnership in the partnership name, though without words of inheritance, passes the entire estate of the grantor unless a contrary intent appears.

PART III. RELATIONS OF PARTNERS TO PERSONS DEALING WITH THE PARTNERSHIP

§9. Partner Agent of Partnership as to Partnership Business

(1) Every partner is an agent of the partnership for the purpose of its business, and the act of every partner, including the execution in the partnership name of any instrument, for apparently carrying on in the usual way the business of the partnership of which he is a member binds the partnership, unless the partner so acting has in fact no authority to act for the partnership in the particular matter, and the person with whom he is dealing has knowledge of the fact that he has no such authority.

(2) An act of a partner which is not apparently for the carrying on of the business of the partnership in the usual way does not bind the partnership unless authorized by the other partners.

(3) Unless authorized by the other partners or unless they have abandoned the business, one or more but less than all the partners have no authority to:

(a) Assign the partnership property in trust for creditors or on the assignee's promise to pay the debts of the partnership,

(b) Dispose of the good-will of the business,

(c) Do any other act which would make it impossible to carry on the ordinary business of a partnership,

(d) Confess a judgment,

(e) Submit a partnership claim or liability to arbitration or reference.

(4) No act of a partner in contravention of a restriction on authority shall bind the partnership to persons having knowledge of the restriction.

§10. Conveyance of Real Property of the Partnership

(1) Where title to real property is in the partnership name, any partner may convey title to such property by a conveyance executed in the partnership name; but the partnership may recover such property unless the partner's act binds the partnership under the provisions of paragraph (1) of section 9 or unless such property has been conveyed by the grantee or a person claiming through such grantee to a holder for value without knowledge that the partner, in making the conveyance, has exceeded his authority.

(2) Where title to real property is in the name of the partnership, a conveyance executed by a partner, in his own name, passes the equitable interest of the partnership, provided the act is one within the authority of the partner under the provisions of paragraph (1) of section 9.

(3) Where title to real property is in the name of one or more but not all the partners, and the record does not disclose the right of the partnership, the partners in whose name the title stands may convey title to such property, but the partnership may recover such property if the partners' act does not bind the partnership under the provisions of paragraph

(1) of section 9, unless the purchaser or his assignee, is a holder for value, without knowledge.

(4) Where the title to real property is in the name of one or more or all the partners, or in a third person in trust for the partnership, a conveyance executed by a partner in the partnership name, or in his own name, passes the equitable interest of the partnership, provided the act is one within the authority of the partner under the provisions of paragraph (1) of section 9.

(5) Where the title to real property is in the names of all the partners a conveyance executed by all the partners passes all their rights in such property.

§11. Partnership Bound by Admission of Partner

An admission or representation made by any partner concerning partnership affairs within the scope of his authority as conferred by this act is evidence against the partnership.

§12. Partnership Charged with Knowledge of or Notice to Partner

Notice to any partner of any matter relating to partnership affairs, and the knowledge of the partner acting in the particular matter, acquired while a partner or then present to his mind, and the knowledge of any other partner who reasonably could and should have communicated it to the acting partner, operate as notice to or knowledge of the partnership, except in the case of a fraud on the partnership committed by or with the consent of that partner.

§13. Partnership Bound by Partner's Wrongful Act

Where, by any wrongful act or omission of any partner acting in the ordinary course of the business of the partnership or with the authority of his co-partners, loss or injury is caused to any person, not being a partner in the partnership, or any penalty is incurred, the partnership is liable therefor to the same extent as the partner so acting or omitting to act.

§14. Partnership Bound by Partner's Breach of Trust

The partnership is bound to make good the loss:

(a) Where one partner acting within the scope of his apparent authority receives money or property of a third person and misapplies it; and

(b) Where the partnership in the course of its business receives money or property of a third person and the money or property so received is misapplied by any partner while it is in the custody of the partnership.

§15. Nature of Partner's Liability

All partners are liable

(a) Jointly and severally for everything chargeable to the partnership under sections 13 and 14.

(b) Jointly for all other debts and obligations of the partnership; but any partner may enter into a separate obligation to perform a partnership contract.

§16. Partner by Estoppel

(1) When a person, by words spoken or written or by conduct, represents himself, or consents to another representing him to any one, as a partner in an existing partnership or with one or more persons not actual partners, he is liable to any such person to whom such representation has been made, who has, on the faith of such representation, given credit to the actual or apparent partnership, and if he has made such representation or consented to its being made in a public manner he is liable to such person, whether the representation has or has not been made or communicated to such person so giving credit by or with the knowledge of the apparent partner making the representation or consenting to its being made.

(a) When a partnership liability results, he is liable as though he were an actual member of the partnership.

(b) When no partnership liability results, he is liable jointly with the other persons, if any, consenting to the contract or representation as to incur liability, otherwise separately.

(2) When a person has been thus represented to be a partner in an existing partnership, or with one or more persons not actual partners, he is an agent of the persons consenting to such representation to bind them to the same extent and in the same manner as though he were a partner in fact, with respect to persons who rely upon the representation. Where all the members of the existing partnership consent to the representation, a partnership act or obligation results; but in all other cases it is the joint act or obligation of the person acting and the persons consenting to the representation.

§17. Liability of Incoming Partner

A person admitted as a partner into an existing partnership is liable for all the obligations of the partnership arising before his admission as though he had been a partner when such obligations were incurred, except that this liability shall be satisfied only out of partnership property.

PART IV. RELATIONS OF PARTNERS TO ONE ANOTHER

§18. Rules Determining Rights and Duties of Partners

The rights and duties of the partners in relation to the partnership shall be determined, subject to any agreement between them, by the following rules:

(a) Each partner shall be repaid his contributions, whether by way of capital or advances to the partnership property and share equally in the profits and surplus remaining after all liabilities, including those to partners, are satisfied; and must contribute towards the losses, whether of capital or otherwise, sustained by the partnership according to his share in the profits.

(b) The partnership must indemnify every partner in respect of payments made and personal liabilities reasonably incurred by him in the ordinary and proper conduct of its business, or for the preservation of its business or property.

(c) A partner, who in aid of the partnership makes any payment or advance beyond the amount of capital which he agreed to contribute, shall be paid interest from the date of the payment or advance.

(d) A partner shall receive interest on the capital contributed by him only from the date when repayment should be made.

(e) All partners have equal rights in the management and conduct of the partnership business.

(f) No partner is entitled to remuneration for acting in the partnership business, except that a surviving partner is entitled to reasonable compensation for his services in winding up the partnership affairs.

(g) No person can become a member of a partnership without the consent of all the partners.

(h) Any difference arising as to ordinary matters connected with the partnership business may be decided by a majority of the partners; but no act in contravention of any agreement between the partners may be done rightfully without the consent of all the partners.

§19. Partnership Books

The partnership books shall be kept, subject to any agreement between the partners, at the principal place of business of the partnership, and every partner shall at all times have access to and may inspect and copy any of them.

§20. Duty of Partners to Render Information

Partners shall render on demand true and full information of all things affecting the partnership to any partner or the legal representative of any deceased partner or partner under legal disability.

§21. Partner Accountable as a Fiduciary

(1) Every partner must account to the partnership for any benefit, and hold as trustee for it any profits derived by him without the consent of the other partners from any transaction connected with the formation, conduct, or liquidation of the partnership or from any use by him of its property.

(2) This section applies also to the representatives of a deceased partner engaged in the liquidation of the affairs of the partnership as the personal representatives of the last surviving partner.

§22. Right to an Account

Any partner shall have the right to a formal account as to partnership affairs:

(a) If he is wrongfully excluded from the partnership business or possession of its property by his co-partners,

(b) If the right exists under the terms of any agreement,

(c) As provided by section 21,

(d) Whenever other circumstances render it just and reasonable.

§23. Continuation of Partnership Beyond Fixed Term

(1) When a partnership for a fixed term or particular undertaking is continued after the termination of such term or particular undertaking without any express agreement, the rights and duties of the partners remain the same as they were at such termination, so far as is consistent with a partnership at will.

(2) A continuation of the business by the partners or such of them as habitually acted therein during the term, without any settlement or liquidation of the partnership affairs, is prima facie evidence of a continuation of the partnership.

Part V. PROPERTY RIGHTS OF A PARTNER

§24. Extent of Property Rights of a Partner

The property rights of a partner are (1) his rights in specific partnership property, (2) his interest in the partnership, and (3) his right to participate in the management.

§25. Nature of a Partner's Right in Specific Partnership Property

(1) A partner is co-owner with his partners of specific partnership property holding as a tenant in partnership.

(2) The incidents of this tenancy are such that:

(a) A partner, subject to the provisions of this act and to any agreement between the partners, has an equal right with his partners to possess specific partnership property for partnership purposes; but he has no right to possess such property for any other purpose without the consent of his partners.

(b) A partner's right in specific partnership property is not assignable except in connection with the assignment of rights of all the partners in the same property.

(c) A partner's right in specific partnership property is not subject to attachment or execution, except on a claim against the partnership. When partnership property is attached for a partnership debt the partners, or any of them, or the representatives of a deceased partner, cannot claim any right under the homestead or exemption laws.

(d) On the death of a partner his right in specific partnership property vests in the surviving partner or partners, except where the deceased was the last surviving partner, when his right in such property vests in his legal representative. Such surviving partner or partners, or the legal representative of the last surviving partner, has no right to possess the partnership property for any but a partnership purpose.

(e) A partner's right in specific partnership property is not subject to dower, curtesy, or allowances to widows, heirs, or next of kin.

§26. Nature of Partner's Interest in the Partnership

A partner's interest in the partnership is his share of the profits and surplus, and the same is personal property.

§27. Assignment of Partner's Interest

(1) A conveyance by a partner of his interest in the partnership does not of itself dissolve the partnership, nor, as against the other partners in the absence of agreement, entitle the assignee, during the continuance of the partnership to interfere in the management or administration of the partnership business or affairs, or to require any information or account of partnership transactions, or to inspect the partnership books; but it merely entitles the assignee to receive in accordance with his contract the profits to which the assigning partner would otherwise be entitled.

(2) In case of a dissolution of the partnership, the assignee is entitled to receive his assignor's interest and may require an account from the date only of the last account agreed to by all the partners.

§28. Partner's Interest Subject to Charging Order

(1) On due application to a competent court by any judgment creditor of a partner, the court which entered the judgment, order, or decree, or any other court, may charge the interest of the debtor partner with payment of the unsatisfied amount of such judgment debt with interest thereon; and may then or later appoint a receiver of his share of the profits, and of any other money due or to fall due to him in respect of the partnership, and make all other orders, directions, accounts and inquiries which the debtor partner might have made, or which the circumstances of the case may require.

(2) The interest charged may be redeemed at any time before foreclosure, or in case of a sale being directed by the court may be purchased without thereby causing a dissolution:

(a) With separate property, by any one or more of the partners, or

(b) With partnership property, by any one or more of the partners with the consent of all the partners whose interests are not so charged or sold.

(3) Nothing in this act shall be held to deprive a partner of his right, if any, under the exemption laws, as regards his interest in the partnership.

PART VI. DISSOLUTION AND WINDING UP

§29. Dissolution Defined

The dissolution of a partnership is the change in the relation of the partners caused by any partner ceasing to be associated in the carrying on as distinguished from the winding up of the business.

§30. Partnership Not Terminated by Dissolution

On dissolution the partnership is not terminated, but continues until the winding up of partnership affairs is completed.

§31. Causes of Dissolution

Dissolution is caused: (1) Without violation of the agreement between the partners,

(a) By the termination of the definite term or particular undertaking specified in the agreement,

(b) By the express will of any partner when no definite term or particular undertaking is specified,

(c) By the express will of all the partners who have not assigned their interests or suffered them to be charged for their separate debts, either before or after the termination of any specified term or particular undertaking,

(d) By the expulsion of any partner from the business bona fide in accordance with such a power conferred by the agreement between the partners;

(2) In contravention of the agreement between the partners, where the circumstances do not permit a dissolution under any other provision of this section, by the express will of any partner at any time;

(3) By any event which makes it unlawful for the business of the partnership to be carried on or for the members to carry it on in partnership;

(4) By the death of any partner;

(5) By the bankruptcy of any partner or the partnership;

(6) By decree of court under section 32.

§32. Dissolution by Decree of Court

(1) On application by or for a partner the court shall decree a dissolution whenever:

(a) A partner has been declared a lunatic in any judicial proceeding or is shown to be of unsound mind,

(b) A partner becomes in any other way incapable of performing his part of the partnership contract,

(c) A partner has been guilty of such conduct as tends to affect prejudicially the carrying on of the business,

(d) A partner wilfully or persistently commits a breach of the partnership agreement, or otherwise so conducts himself in matters relating to the partnership business that it is not reasonably practicable to carry on the business in partnership with him,

(e) The business of the partnership can only be carried on at a loss,

(f) Other circumstances render a dissolution equitable.

(2) On the application of the purchaser of a partner's interest under sections 27 or 28:

(a) After the termination of the specified term or particular undertaking,

(b) At any time if the partnership was a partnership at will when the interest was assigned or when the charging order was issued.

§33. General Effect of Dissolution on Authority of Partner

Except so far as may be necessary to wind up partnership affairs or to complete transactions begun but not then finished, dissolution terminates all authority of any partner to act for the partnership,

(1) With respect to the partners,

(a) When the dissolution is not by the act, bankruptcy or death of a partner; or

(b) When the dissolution is by such act, bankruptcy or death of a partner, in cases where section 34 so requires.

(2) With respect to persons not partners, as declared in section 35.

§34. Right of Partner to Contribution From Copartners After Dissolution

Where the dissolution is caused by the act, death or bankruptcy of a partner, each partner is liable to his copartners for his share of any liability created by any partner acting for the partnership as if the partnership had not been dissolved unless

(a) The dissolution being by act of any partner, the partner acting for the partnership had knowledge of the dissolution, or

(b) The dissolution being by the death or bankruptcy of a partner, the partner acting for the partnership had knowledge or notice of the death or bankruptcy.

§35. Power of Partner to Bind Partnership to Third Persons After Dissolution

(1) After dissolution a partner can bind the partnership except as provided in Paragraph (3)

(a) By any act appropriate for winding up partnership affairs or completing transactions unfinished at dissolution;

(b) By any transaction which would bind the partnership if dissolution had not taken place, provided the other party to the transaction

(I) Had extended credit to the partnership prior to dissolution and had no knowledge or notice of the dissolution; or

(II) Though he had not so extended credit, had nevertheless known of the partnership prior to dissolution, and, having no knowledge or notice of dissolution, the fact of dissolution had not been advertised in a newspaper of general circulation in the place (or in each place if more than one) at which the partnership business was regularly carried on.

(2) The liability of a partner under paragraph (1b) shall be satisfied out of partnership assets alone when such partner had been prior to dissolution

(a) Unknown as a partner to the person with whom the contract is made; and

(b) So far unknown and inactive in partnership affairs that the business reputation of the partnership could not be said to have been in any degree due to his connection with it.

(3) The partnership is in no case bound by any act of a partner after dissolution

(a) Where the partnership is dissolved because it is unlawful to carry on the business, unless the act is appropriate for winding up partnership affairs; or

(b) Where the partner has become bankrupt; or

(c) Where the partner has no authority to wind up partnership affairs; except by a transaction with one who

(I) Had extended credit to the partnership prior to dissolution and had no knowledge or notice of his want or authority; or

(II) Had not extended credit to the partnership prior to dissolution, and, having no knowledge or notice of his want of authority, the fact of his want of authority has not been advertised in the manner provided for advertising the fact of dissolution in paragraph (1bII).

(4) Nothing in this section shall affect the liability under section 16 of any person who after dissolution represents himself or consents to another representing him as a partner in a partnership engaged in carrying on business.

§36. Effect of Dissolution on Partner's Existing Liability

(1) The dissolution of the partnership does not of itself discharge the existing liability of any partner.

(2) A partner is discharged from any existing liability upon dissolution of the partnership by an agreement to that effect between himself, the partnership creditor and the person or partnership continuing the business; and such agreement may be inferred from the course of dealing between the creditor having knowledge of the dissolution and the person or partnership continuing the business.

(3) Where a person agrees to assume the existing obligations of a dissolved partnership, the partners whose obligations have been assumed shall be discharged from any liability to any creditor of the partnership who, knowing of the agreement, consents to a material alteration in the nature or time of payment of such obligations.

(4) The individual property of a deceased partner shall be liable for all obligations of the partnership incurred while he was a partner but subject to the prior payment of his separate debts.

§37. Right to Wind Up

Unless otherwise agreed the partners who have not wrongfully dissolved the partnership or the legal representative of the last surviving partner, not bankrupt, has the right to wind up the partnership affairs; provided, however, that any partner, his legal representative or his assignee, upon cause shown, may obtain winding up by the court.

§38. Rights of Partners to Application of Partnership Property

(1) When dissolution is caused in any way, except in contravention of the partnership agreement, each partner as against his co-partners and all persons claiming through them in respect of their interests in the partnership, unless otherwise agreed, may have the partnership property applied to discharge its liabilities, and the surplus applied to pay in cash the net amount owing to the respective partners. But if dissolution is caused by expulsion of a partner, bona fide under the partnership agreement and if the expelled partner is discharged from all partnership liabilities, either by payment or agreement under section 36(2), he shall receive in cash only the net amount due him from the partnership.

(2) When dissolution is caused in contravention of the partnership agreement the rights of the partners shall be as follows:

(a) Each partner who has not caused dissolution wrongfully shall have,

    (I) All the rights specified in paragraph (1) of this section, and

    (II) The right, as against each partner who has caused the dissolution wrongfully, to damages for breach of the agreement.

(b) The partners who have not caused the dissolution wrongfully, if they all desire to continue the business in the same name, either by themselves or jointly with others, may do so, during the agreed term for the partnership and for that purpose may possess the partnership property, provided they secure the payment by bond approved by the court, or pay to any partner who has caused the dissolution wrongfully, the value of his interest in the partnership at the dissolution, less any damages recoverable under clause (2aII) of the section, and in like manner indemnify him against all present or future partnership liabilities.

(c) A partner who has caused the dissolution wrongfully shall have:

    (I) If the business is not continued under the provisions of paragraph (2b) all the rights of a partner under paragraph (1), subject to clause (2aII), of this section,

    (II) If the business is continued under paragraph (2b) of this section the right as against his co-partners and all claiming through them in respect of their interests in the partnership, to have the value of his interest in the partnership, less any damages caused to his co-partners by the dissolution, ascertained and paid to him in cash, or the payment secured by bond approved by the court, and to be released from all existing liabilities of the partnership; but in ascertaining the value of the partner's interest the value of the good-will of the business shall not be considered.

§39. Rights Where Partnership is Dissolved for Fraud or Misrepresentation

Where a partnership contract is rescinded on the ground of the fraud or misrepresentation of one of the parties thereto, the party entitled to rescind is, without prejudice to any other right, entitled,

(a) To a lien on, or right of retention of, the surplus of the partnership property after satisfying the partnership liabilities to third persons for any sum of money paid by him for the purchase of an interest in the partnership and for any capital or advances contributed by him; and

(b) To stand, after all liabilities to third persons have been satisfied, in the place of the creditors of the partnership for any payments made by him in respect of the partnership liabilities; and

(c) To be indemnified by the person guilty of the fraud or making the representation against all debts and liabilities of the partnership.

§40. Rules for Distribution

In settling accounts between the partners after dissolution, the following rules shall be observed, subject to any agreement to the contrary:

(a) The assets of the partnership are:
(I) The partnership property,
(II) The contributions of the partners necessary for the payment of all the liabilities specified in clause (b) of this paragraph.
(b) The liabilities of the partnership shall rank in order of payment, as follows:
(I) Those owing to creditors other than partners,
(II) Those owing to partners other than for capital and profits,
(III) Those owing to partners in respect of capital,
(IV) Those owing to partners in respect of profits.
(c) The assets shall be applied in the order of their declaration in clause (a) of this paragraph to the satisfaction of the liabilities.
(d) The partners shall contribute, as provided by section 18(a) the amount necessary

to satisfy the liabilities; but if any, but not all, of the partners are insolvent, or, not being subject to process, refuse to contribute, the other parties shall contribute their share of the liabilities, and, in the relative proportions in which they share the profits, the additional amount necessary to pay the liabilities.
(e) An assignee for the benefit of creditors or any person appointed by the court shall have the right to enforce the contributions specified in clause (d) of this paragraph.
(f) Any partner or his legal representative shall have the right to enforce the contributions specified in clause (d) of this paragraph, to the extent of the amount which he has paid in excess of his share of the liability.
(g) The individual property of a deceased partner shall be liable for the contributions specified in clause (d) of this paragraph.
(h) When partnership property and the individual properties of the partners are in possession of a court for distribution, partnership creditors shall have priority on partnership property and separate creditors on individual property, saving the rights of lien or secured creditors as heretofore.
(i) Where a partner has become bankrupt or his estate is insolvent the claims against his separate property shall rank in the following order:
(I) Those owing to separate creditors,
(II) Those owing to partnership creditors,
(III) Those owing to partners by way of contribution.

§41. Liability of Persons Continuing the Business in Certain Cases

(1) When any new partner is admitted into an existing partnership, or when any partner retires and assigns (or the representative of the deceased partner assigns) his rights in partnership property to two or more of the partners, or to one or more of the partners and one or more third persons, if the business is continued without liquidation of the partnership affairs,

creditors of the first or dissolved partnership are also creditors of the partnership so continuing the business.

(2) When all but one partner retire and assign (or the representative of a deceased partner assigns) their rights in partnership property to the remaining partner, who continues the business without liquidation of partnership affairs, either alone or with others, creditors of the dissolved partnerships are also creditors of the person or partnership so continuing the business.

(3) When any partner retires or dies and the business of the dissolved partnership is continued as set forth in paragraphs (1) and (2) of this section, with the consent of the retired partners or the representative of the deceased partner, but without any assignment of his right in partnership property, rights of creditors of the dissolved partnership and of the creditors of the person or partnership continuing the business shall be as if such assignment had been made.

(4) When all the partners or their representatives assign their rights in partnership property to one or more third persons who promise to pay the debts and who continue the business of the dissolved partnership, creditors of the dissolved partnership are also creditors of the person or partnership continuing the business.

(5) When any partner wrongfully causes a dissolution and the remaining partners continue the business under the provisions of section 38(2b), either alone or with others, and without liquidation of the partnership affairs, creditors of the dissolved partnership are also creditors of the person or partnership continuing the business.

(6) When a partner is expelled and the remaining partners continue the business either alone or with others, without liquidation of the partnership affairs, creditors of the dissolved partnership are also creditors of the person or partnership continuing the business.

(7) The liability of a third person becoming a partner in the partnership continuing the business, under this section, to the creditors of the dissolved partnership shall be satisfied out of partnership property only.

(8) When the business of a partnership after dissolution is continued under any conditions set forth in this section the creditors of the dissolved partnership, as against the separate creditors of the retiring or deceased partner or the representative of the deceased partner, have a prior right to any claim of the retired partner or the representative of the deceased partner against the person or partnership continuing the business, on account of the retired or deceased partner's interest in the dissolved partnership or on account of any consideration promised for such interest or for his right in partnership property.

(9) Nothing in this section shall be held to modify any right of creditors to set aside any assignment on the ground of fraud.

(10) The use by the person or partnership continuing the business of the partnership name, or the name of a deceased partner as part thereof, shall not of itself make the individual property of the deceased partner liable for any debts contracted by such person or partnership.

§42. Rights of Retiring or Estate of Deceased Partner When the Business is Continued

When any partner retires or dies, and the business is continued under any of the conditions set forth in section 41(1, 2, 3, 5, 6), or section 38(2b), without any settlement of accounts as between him or his estate and the person or partnership continuing the business, unless otherwise agreed, he or his legal representative may have the value of his interest at the date of dissolution ascertained, and shall receive as an ordinary creditor an amount equal to the value of his interest in the dissolved partnership with interest, or, at his option or at the option of his legal representative, in lieu of interest, the profits attributable to the use of his right in the property of the dissolved partnership as against the separate creditors, or the representative of the retired or deceased partner, shall have priority on any claim arising under this section, as provided by section 41(8) of this act.

§43. Accrual of Actions

The right to an account of his interest shall accrue to any partner, or his legal representative, as against the winding up partners or the surviving partners or the person or partnership continuing the business, at the date of dissolution, in the absence of any agreement to the contrary.

PART VII. MISCELLANEOUS PROVISIONS

§44. When Act Takes Effect

This act shall take effect on the ——— day of ——— one thousand nine hundred and ———.

§45. Legislation Repealed

All acts or parts of acts inconsistent with this act are hereby repealed.

APPENDIX G

UNIFORM LIMITED PARTNERSHIP ACT

(Adopted in 47 jurisdictions: Alaska, Arizona, Arkansas, California, Colorado, Connecticut, District of Columbia, Florida, Georgia, Hawaii, Idaho, Illinois, Indiana, Iowa, Kansas, Maine, Maryland, Massachusetts, Michigan, Minnesota, Mississippi, Missouri, Montana, Nebraska, Nevada, New Hampshire, New Jersey, New Mexico, New York, North Carolina, North Dakota, Ohio, Oklahoma, Oregon, Pennsylvania, Rhode Island, South Carolina, South Dakota, Tennessee, Texas, Utah, Vermont, Virginia, Virgin Islands, Washington, West Virginia, Wisconsin.)

27. Name of Act
28. Rules of Construction
29. Rules for Cases Not Provided for in This Act
30. Provisions for Existing Limited Partnerships
31. Act (Acts) Repealed

An Act to Make Uniform the Law Relating to Limited Partnerships
Be it enacted, etc., as follows:

§1. Limited Partnership Defined

A limited partnership is a partnership formed by two or more persons under the provisions of Section 2, having as members one or more general partners and one or more limited partners. The limited partners as such shall not be bound by the obligations of the partnership.

§2. Formation

(1) Two or more persons desiring to form a limited partnership shall
(a) Sign and swear to a certificate, which shall state
I. The name of the partnership,
II. The character of the business,
III. The location of the principal place of business,
IV. The name and place of residence of each member; general and limited partners being respectively designated,
V. The term for which the partnership is to exist,
VI. The amount of cash and a description of and the agreed value of the other property contributed by each limited partner,
VII. The additional contributions, if any, agreed to be made by each limited partner and the times at which or events on the happening of which they shall be made,
VIII. The time, if agreed upon, when the contribution of each limited partner is to be returned,
IX. The share of the profits or the other compensation by way of income which each limited partner shall receive by reason of his contribution,
X. The right, if given, of a limited partner to substitute an assignee as contributor in his place, and the terms and conditions of the substitution,
XI. The right, if given, of the partners to admit additional limited partners,
XII. The right, if given, of one or more of the limited partners to priority over other limited partners, as to contributions or as to compensation by way of income, and the nature of such priority,
XIII. The right, if given, of the remaining general partner or partners to continue the business on the death, retirement or insanity of a general partner, and
XIV. The right, if given, of a limited partner to demand and receive property other than cash in return for his contribution.
(b) File for record the certificate in the office of [here designate the proper office].

(2) A limited partnership is formed if there has been substantial compliance in good faith with the requirements of paragraph (1).

§3. Business Which May Be Carried On

A limited partnership may carry on any business which a partnership without limited partners may carry on, except [here designate the business to be prohibited].

§4. Character of Limited Partner's Contribution

The contributions of a limited partner may be cash or other property, but not services.

§5. A Name Not to Contain Surname of Limited Partner; Exceptions

(1) The surname of a limited partner shall not appear in the partnership name, unless

(a) It is also the surname of a general partner, or
(b) Prior to the time when the limited partner became such the business had been carried on under a name in which his surname appeared.

(2) A limited partner whose name appears in a partnership name contrary to the provisions of paragraph (1) is liable as a general partner to partnership creditors who extend credit to the partnership without actual knowledge that he is not a general partner.

§6. Liability for False Statements in Certificate

If the certificate contains a false statement, one who suffers loss by reliance on such statement may hold liable any party to the certificate who knew the statement to be false.

(a) At the time he signed the certificate, or
(b) Subsequently, but within a sufficient time before the statement was relied upon to enable him to cancel or amend the certificate, or to file a petition for its cancellation or amendment as provided in Section 25(3).

§7. Limited Partner Not Liable to Creditors

A limited partner shall not become liable as a general partner unless, in addition to the exercise of his rights and powers as a limited partner, he takes part in the control of the business.

§8. Admission of Additional Limited Partners

After the formation of a limited partnership, additional limited partners may be admitted upon filing an amendment to the original certificate in accordance with the requirements of Section 25.

§9. Rights, Powers and Liabilities of a General Partner

(1) A general partner shall have all the rights and powers and be subject to all the restrictions and liabilities of a partner in a partnership without limited partners, except that without the written consent or ratification of the specific act by all the limited partners, a general partner or all of the general partners have no authority to

(a) Do any act in contravention of the certificate,
(b) Do any act which would make it impossible to carry on the ordinary business of the partnership,
(c) Confess a judgment against the partnership,
(d) Possess partnership property, or assign their rights in specific partnership property, for other than a partnership purpose,
(e) Admit a person as a general partner,
(f) Admit a person as a limited partner, unless the right so to do is given in the certificate,
(g) Continue the business with partnership property on the death, retirement or insanity of a general partner, unless the right so to do is given in the certificate.

§10. Rights of a Limited Partner

(1) A limited partner shall have the same rights as a general partner to

(a) Have the partnership books kept at the principal place of business of the partnership, and at all times to inspect and copy any of them,
(b) Have on demand true and full information of all things affecting the partnership, and a formal account of partnership affairs, whenever circumstances render it just and reasonable, and

(c) Have dissolution and winding up by decree of court.

(2) A limited partner shall have the right to receive a share of the profits or other compensation by way of income, and to the return of his contribution as provided in Sections 15 and 16.

§11. Status of Person Erroneously Believing Himself a Limited Partner

A person who has contributed to the capital of a business conducted by a person or partnership erroneously believing that he has become a limited partner in a limited partnership, is not, by reason of his exercise of the rights of a limited partner, a general partner with the person or in the partnership carrying on the business, or bound by the obligations of such person or partnership; provided that on ascertaining the mistake he promptly renounces his interest in the profits of the business, or other compensation by way of income.

§12. One Person Both General and Limited Partner

(1) A person may be a general partner and a limited partner in the same partnership at the same time.

(2) A person who is a general, and also at the same time a limited partner, shall have all the rights and powers and be subject to all the restrictions of a general partner; except that, in respect to his contribution, he shall have the rights against the other members which he would have had if he were not also a general partner.

§13. Loans and Other Business Transactions with Limited Partner

(1) A limited partner also may loan money to and transact other business with the partnership, and, unless he is also a general partner, receive on account of resulting claims against the partnership, with general creditors, a pro rata share of the assets. No limited partner shall in respect to any such claim

(a) Receive or hold as collateral security any partnership property, or
(b) Receive from a general partner or the partnership any payment, conveyance, or release from liability, if at the time the assets of the partnership are not sufficient to discharge partnership liabilities to persons not claiming as general or limited partners.

(2) The receiving of collateral security, or a payment, conveyance, or release in violation of the provisions of paragraph (1) is a fraud on the creditors of the partnership.

§14. Relation of Limited Partners Inter Se

Where there are several limited partners the members may agree that one or more of the limited partners shall have a priority over other limited partners as to the return of their contributions, as to their compensation by way of income, or as to any other matter. If such an agreement is made it shall be stated in the certificate, and in the absence of such a statement all the limited partners shall stand upon equal footing.

§15. Compensation of Limited Partner

A limited partner may receive from the partnership the share of the profits or the compensation by way of income stipulated for in the certificate; provided, that after such payment is made, whether from the property of the partnership or that of a general partner, the partnership assets are in excess of all liabilities of the partnership except liabilities to limited partners on account of their contribution and to general partners.

§16. Withdrawal or Reduction of Limited Partner's Contribuition

(1) A limited partner shall not receive from a general partner or out of partnership property any part of his contribution until

(a) All liabilities of the partnership, except liabilities to general partners and to limited partners on account of their contributions, have been paid or there remains property of the partnership sufficient to pay them,

(b) The consent of all members is had, unless the return of the contribution may be rightfully demanded under the provisions of paragraph (2), and

(c) The certificate is cancelled or so amended as to set forth the withdrawal or reduction.

(2) Subject to the provisions of paragraph (1) a limited partner may rightfully demand the return of his contribution

(a) On the dissolution of a partnership, or

(b) When the date specified in the certificate for its return has arrived, or

(c) After he has given six months' notice in writing to all other members, if no time is specified in the certificate either for the return of the contribution or for the dissolution of the partnership.

(3) In the absence of any statement in the certificate to the contrary or the consent of all members, a limited partner, irrespective of the nature of his contribution, has only the right to demand and receive cash in return for his contribution.

(4) A limited partner may have the partnership dissolved and its affairs wound up when

(a) He rightfully but unsuccessfully demands the return of his contribution, or

(b) The other liabilities of the partnership have not been paid, or the partnership property is insufficient for their payment as required by paragraph (1a) and the limited partner would otherwise be entitled to the return of his contribution.

§17. Liability of Limited Partner to Partnership

(1) A limited partner is liable to the partnership

(a) For the difference between his contribution as actually made and that stated in the certificate as having been made, and

(b) For any unpaid contribution which he agreed in the certificate to make in the future at the time and on the conditions stated in the certificate.

(2) A limited partner holds as trustee for the partnership

(a) Specific property stated in the certificate as contributed by him, but which was not contributed or which has been wrongfully returned, and

(b) Money or other property wrongfully paid or conveyed to him on account of his contribution.

(3) The liabilities of a limited partner as set forth in this section can be waived or compromised only by the consent of all members; but a waiver or compromise shall not affect the right of a creditor of a partnership, who extended credit or whose claim arose after the filing and before a cancellation or amendment of the certificate, to enforce such liabilities.

(4) When a contributor has rightfully received the return in whole or in part of the capital of his contribution, he is nevertheless liable to the partnership for any sum, not in excess of such return with interest, necessary to discharge its liabilities to all creditors who extended credit or whose claims arose before such return.

§18. Nature of Limited Partner's Interest in Partnership

A limited partner's interest in the partnership is personal property.

§19. Assignment of Limited Partner's Interest

(1) A limited partner's interest is assignable.

(2) A substituted limited partner is a person admitted to all the rights of a limited partner who has died or has assigned his interest in a partnership.

(3) An assignee, who does not become a substituted limited partner, has no right to require any information or account of the partnership transactions or to inspect the partnership books;

he is only entitled to receive the share of the profits or other compensation by way of income, or the return of his contribution, to which his assignor would otherwise be entitled.

(4) An assignee shall have the right to become a substituted limited partner if all the members (except the assignor) consent thereto or if the assignor, being thereunto empowered by the certificate, gives the assignee that right.

(5) An assignee becomes a substituted limited partner when the certificate is appropriately amended in accordance with Section 25.

(6) The substituted limited partner has all the rights and powers, and is subject to all the restrictions and liabilities of his assignor, except those liabilities of which he was ignorant at the time he became a limited partner and which could not be ascertained from the certificate.

(7) The substitution of the assignee as a limited partner does not release the assignor from liability to the partnership under Sections 6 and 17.

§20. Effect of Retirement, Death, or Insanity of a General Partner

The retirement, death or insanity of a general partner dissolves the partnership, unless the business is continued by the remaining general partners

(a) Under a right so to do stated in the certificate, or

(b) With the consent of all members.

§21. Death of Limited Partner

(1) On the death of a limited partner his executor or administrator shall have all the rights of a limited partner for the purpose of settling his estate, and such power as the deceased had to constitute his assignee a substituted limited partner.

(2) The estate of a deceased limited partner shall be liable for his liabilities as a limited partner.

§22. Rights of Creditors of Limited Partner

(1) On due application to a court of competent jurisdiction by any judgment creditor of a limited partner, the court may charge the interest of the indebted limited partner with payment of the unsatisfied amount of the judgment debt; and may appoint a receiver, and make all other orders, directions, and inquiries which the circumstances of the case may require.

[In those states where a creditor on beginning an action can attach debts due the defendant before he has obtained a judgment against the defendant it is recommended that paragraph (1) of this section read as follows:

On due application to a court of competent jurisdiction by any creditor of a limited partner, the court may charge the interest of the indebted limited partner with payment of the unsatisfied amount of such claim; and may appoint a receiver, and make all other orders, directions, and inquiries which the circumstances of the case may require.]

(2) The interest may be redeemed with the separate property of any general partner, but may not be redeemed with partnership property.

(3) The remedies conferred by paragraph (1) shall not be deemed exclusive of others which may exist.

(4) Nothing in this act shall be held to deprive a limited partner of his statutory exemption.

§23. Distribution of Assets

(1) In settling accounts after dissolution the liabilities of the partnership shall be entitled to payment in the following order:

(a) Those to creditors, in the order of priority as provided by law, except those to limited partners on account of their contributions, and to general partners,

(b) Those to limited partners in respect to their share of the profits and other compensation by way of income on their contributions,

(c) Those to limited partners in respect to the capital of their contributions,

(d) Those to general partners other than for capital and profits,

(e) Those to general partners in respect to profits,

(f) Those to general partners in respect to capital.

(2) Subject to any statement in the certificate or to subsequent agreement, limited partners share in the partnership assets in respect to their claims for capital, and in respect to their claims for profits or for compensation by way of income on their contributions respectively, in proportion to the respective amounts of such claims.

§24. When Certificate Shall be Cancelled or Amended

(1) The certificate shall be cancelled when the partnership is dissolved or all limited partners cease to be such.

(2) A certificate shall be amended when

(a) There is a change in the name of the partnership or in the amount or character of the contribution of any limited partner,

(b) A person is substituted as a limited partner,

(c) An additional limited partner is admitted,

(d) A person is admitted as a general partner,

(e) A general partner retires, dies or becomes insane, and the business is continued under section 20,

(f) There is a change in the character of the business of the partnership,

(g) There is a false or erroneous statement in the certificate,

(h) There is a change in the time as stated in the certificate for the dissolution of the partnership or for the return of a contribution,

(i) A time is fixed for the dissolution of the partnership, or the return of a contribution,

no time having been specified in the certificate, or

(j) The members desire to make a change in any other statement in the certificate in order that it shall accurately represent the agreement between them.

§25. Requirements for Amendment and for Cancellation of Certificate

(1) The writing to amend a certificate shall

(a) Conform to the requirements of Section 2(1a) as far as necessary to set forth clearly the change in the certificate which it is desired to make, and

(b) Be signed and sworn to by all members, and an amendment substituting a limited partner or adding a limited or general partner shall be signed also by the member to be substituted or added, and when a limited partner is to be substituted, the amendment shall also be signed by the assigning limited partner.

(2) The writing to cancel a certificate shall be signed by all members.

(3) A person desiring the cancellation or amendment of a certificate, if any person designated in paragraphs (1) and (2) as a person who must execute the writing refuses to do so, may petition the [here designate the proper court] to direct a cancellation or amendment thereof.

(4) If the court finds that the petitioner has a right to have the writing executed by a person who refuses to do so, it shall order the [here designate the responsible official in the office designated in Section 2] in the office where the certificate is recorded to record the cancellation or amendment of the certificate; and where the certificate is to be amended, the court shall also cause to be filed for record in said office a certified copy of its decree setting forth the amendment.

(5) A certificate is amended or cancelled when there is filed for record in the office [here designate the office designated in Section 2] where the certificate is recorded

(a) A writing in accordance with the provisions of paragraph (1), or (2) or

(b) A certified copy of the order of court in accordance with the provisions of paragraph (4).

(6) After the certificate is duly amended in accordance with this section, the amended certificate shall thereafter be for all purposes the certificate provided for by this act.

§26. Parties to Actions

A contributor, unless he is a general partner, is not a proper party to proceedings by or against a partnership, except where the object is to enforce a limited partner's right against or liability to the partnership.

§27. Name of Act

This act may be cited as The Uniform Limited Partnership Act.

§28. Rules of Construction

(1) The rule that statutes in derogation of the common law are to be strictly construed shall have no application to this act.

(2) This act shall be so interpreted and construed as to effect its general purpose to make uniform the law of those states which enact it.

(3) This act shall not be so construed as to impair the obligations of any contract existing when the act goes into effect, nor to affect any action on proceedings begun or right accrued before this act takes affect.

§29. Rules for Cases Not Provided for in this Act

In any case not provided for in this act the rules of law and equity, including the law merchant, shall govern.

§30.[1] Provisions for Existing Limited Partnerships

(1) A limited partnership formed under any statute of this state prior to the adoption of this act, may become a limited partnership under this act by complying with the provisions of Section 2; provided the certificate sets forth

(a) The amount of the original contribution of each limited partner, and the time when the contribution was made, and

(b) That the property of the partnership exceeds the amount sufficient to discharge its liabilities to persons not claiming as general or limited partners by an amount greater than the sum of the contributions of its limited partners.

(2) A limited partnership formed under any statute of this state prior to the adoption of this act, until or unless it becomes a limited partnership under this act, shall continue to be governed by the provisions of [here insert proper reference to the existing limited partnership act or acts], except that such partnership shall not be renewed unless so provided in the original agreement.

§31.[1] Act [Acts] Repealed

Except as affecting existing limited partnerships to the extent set forth in Section 30, the act (acts) of [here designate the existing limited partnership act or acts] is (are) hereby repealed.

---

1 Sections 30, 31, will be omitted in any state which has not a limited partnership act.

APPENDIX H

MODEL BUSINESS CORPORATION ACT

Prepared by the
Committee on Corporate Laws
(Section of Corporation, Banking and Business Law)
of the
American Bar Association
(1969 Official Text)

Not Indiana nor Michigan

(Adopted, in whole or in part, by 31 jurisdictions. Alabama, Alaska, Arkansas, Colorado, Connecticut, District of Columbia, Georgia, Illinois, Iowa, Louisiana, Maryland, Massachusetts, Mississippi, Montana, Nebraska, New Jersey, New Mexico, New York, North Carolina, North Dakota, Oregon, Rhode Island, South Carolina, South Dakota, Tennessee, Texas, Utah, Virginia, Washington, Wisconsin, and Wyoming.)

Table of Sections

FORMATION OF CORPORATIONS

PENALTIES

MISCELLANEOUS PROVISIONS

§1. Short Title

This Act shall be known and may be cited as the ".......* Business Corporation Act."

§2. Definitions

As used in this Act, unless the context otherwise requires, the term:

(a) "Corporation" or "domestic corporation" means a corporation for profit subject to the provisions of this Act, except a foreign corporation.

(b) "Foreign corporation" means a corporation for profit organized under laws other than the laws of this State for a purpose or purposes for which a corporation may be organized under this Act.

(c) "Articles of incorporation" means the original or restated articles of incorporation or articles of consolidation and all amendments thereto including articles of merger.

(d) "Shares" means the units into which the

---

* Supply name of state.

---

proprietary interests in a corporation are divided.

(e) "Subscriber" means one who subscribes for shares in a corporation, whether before or after incorporation.

(f) "Shareholder" means one who is a holder of a record of shares in a corporation.

(g) "Authorized shares" means the shares of all classes which the corporation is authorized to issue.

(h) "Treasury shares" means shares of a corporation which have been issued, have been subsequently acquired by and belong to the corporation, and have not, either by reason of the acquisition or thereafter, been cancelled or restored to the status of authorized but unissued shares. Treasury shares shall be deemed to be "issued" shares, but not "outstanding" shares.

(i) "Net assets" means the amount by which the total assets of a corporation exceed the total debts of the corporation.

(j) "Stated capital" means, at any particular time, the sum of (1) the par value of all shares of the corporation having a par value that have been issued, (2) the amount of the consideration received by the corporation for all shares of the corporation without par value that have been issued, except such part of the consideration therefor as may have been allocated to capital surplus in a manner permitted by law, and (3) such amounts not included in clauses (1) and (2) of this paragraph as have been transferred to stated capital of the corporation, whether upon the issue of shares as a share dividend or otherwise, minus all reductions from such sum as have been effected in a manner permitted by law. Irrespective of the manner of designation thereof by the laws under which a foreign corporation is organized, the stated capital of a foreign corporation shall be determined on the same basis and in the same manner as the stated capital of a domestic corporation, for the purpose of computing fees, franchise taxes and other charges imposed by this Act.

(k) "Surplus" means the excess of the net assets of a corporation over its stated capital.

(l) "Earner surplus" means the portion of the surplus of a corporation equal to the balance of its net profits, income, gains and losses from the date of incorporation, or from the latest date when a deficit was eliminated by an application of its capital surplus or stated capital or otherwise, after deducting subsequent distributions to shareholders and transfers to stated capital and capital surplus to the extent such distribution and transfers are made out of earned surplus. Earned surplus shall include also any portion of surplus allocated to earned surplus in mergers, consolidations or acquisitions of all or substantially all of the outstanding shares or of the property and assets of another corporation, domestic or foreign.

(m) "Capital surplus" means the entire surplus of a corporation other than its earned surplus.

(n) "Insolvent" means inability of a corporation to pay its debts as they become due in the usual course of its business.

(o) "Employee" includes officers but not directors. A director may accept duties which make him also an employee.

§3. Purposes

Corporations may be organized under this Act for any lawful purpose or purposes, except for the purpose of banking or insurance.

§4. General Powers

Each corporation shall have power:

(a) To have perpetual succession by its corporate name unless a limited period of duration is stated in its articles of incorporation.

(b) To sue and be sued, complain and defend, in its corporate name.

(c) To have a corporate seal which may be altered at pleasure, and to use the same by causing it, or a facsimile thereof, to be impressed or affixed or in any other manner reproduced.

(d) To purchase, take, receive, lease, or otherwise acquire, own, hold, improve, use and otherwise deal in and with, real or personal property, or any interest therein, wherever situated.

(e) To sell, convey, mortgage, pledge, lease, exchange, transfer and otherwise dispose of all or any part of its property and assets.

(f) To lend money and use its credit to assist its employees.

(g) To purchase, take, receive, subscribe for, or otherwise acquire, own, hold, vote, use, employ, sell, mortgage, lend, pledge, or otherwise use and deal in and with, shares or other interests in, or obligations of, other domestic or foreign corporations, associations, partnerships or individuals, or direct or indirect obligations of the United States or of any other government, state, territory, governmental district or municipality or any instrumentality thereof.

(h) To make contracts and guarantees and incur liabilities, borrow money at such rates of interest as the corporation may determine, issue its notes, bonds, and other obligations, and secure any of its obligations by mortgage or pledge of all or any of its property, franchises and income.

(i) To lend money for its corporate purposes, invest and reinvest its funds, and take and hold real and personal property as security for the payment of funds so loaned or invested.

(j) To conduct its business, carry on its operations and have offices and exercise the powers granted by this Act, within or without this State.

(k) To elect or appoint officers and agents of the corporation, and define their duties and fix their compensation.

(l) To make and alter by-laws, not inconsistent with its articles of incorporation or with the laws of this State, for the administration and regulation of the affairs of the corporation.

(m) To make donations for the public welfare or for charitable, scientific or educational purposes.

(n) To transfer any lawful business which the board of directors shall find will be in aid of governmental policy.

(o) To pay pensions and establish pension plans, pension trusts, profit sharing plans, stock bonus plans, stock option plans and other incentive plans for any or all of its directors, officers and employees.

(p) To be a promoter, partner, member, associate, or manager of any partnership, joint venture, trust or other enterprise.

(q) To have and exercise all powers necessary or convenient to effect its purposes.

§5. Indemnification of Officers, Directors, Employees and Agents

(a) A corporation shall have power to indemnify any person who was or is a party or is threatened to be made a party to any threatened, pending or completed action, suit or proceeding, whether civil, criminal, administrative or investigative (other than an action by or in the right of the corporation) by reason of the fact that he is or was a director, officer, employee or agent of the corporation, or is or was serving at the request of the corporation as a director, officer, employee or agent of another corporation, partnership, joint venture, trust or other enterprise, against expenses (including attorneys' fees),

judgments, fines and amounts paid in settlement actually and reasonably incurred by him in connection with such action, suit or proceeding if he acted in good faith and in a manner he reasonably believed to be in or not opposed to the best interests of the corporation, and, with respect to any criminal action or proceeding, had no reasonable cause to believe his conduct was unlawful. The termination of any action, suit or proceeding by judgment, order, settlement, conviction, or upon a plea of nolo contendere or its equivalent, shall not, of itself, create a presumption that the person did not act in good faith and in a manner which he reasonably believed to be in or not opposed to the best interests of the corporation, and, with respect to any criminal action or proceeding, had no reasonable cause to believe his conduct was unlawful.

(b) A corporation shall have power to indemnify any person who was or is a party or is threatened to be made a party to any threatened, pending or completed action or suit by or in the right of the corporation to procure a judgment in its favor by reason of the fact that he is or was a director, officer, employee or agent of the corporation, or is or was serving at the request of the corporation as a director, officer, employee or agent of another corporation, partnership, joint venture, trust or other enterprise against expenses (including attorneys' fees) actually and reasonably incurred by him in connection with the defense or settlement of such action or suit if he acted in good faith and in a manner he reasonably believed to be in or not opposed to the best interests of the corporation and except that no indemnification shall be made in respect of any claim, issue or matter as to which such person shall have been adjudged to be liable for negligence or misconduct in the performance of his duty to the corporation unless and only to the extent that the court in which such action or suit was brought shall determine upon application that, despite the adjudication of liability but in view of all circumstances of the case, such person is fairly and reasonably entitled to indemnity for such expenses which such court shall deem proper.

(c) To the extent that a director, officer, employee or agent of a corporation has been successful on the merits or otherwise in defense of any action, suit or proceeding referred to in subsections (a) or (b), or in defense of any claim, issue or matter therein, he shall be indemnified against expenses (including attorneys' fees) actually and reasonably incurred by him in connection therewith.

(d) Any indemnification under subsections (a) or (b) (unless ordered by a court) shall be made by the corporation only as authorized in the specific case upon a determination that indemnification of the director, officer, employee or agent is proper in the circumstances because he has met the applicable standard of conduct set forth in subsections (a) or (b). Such determination shall be made (1) by the board of directors by a majority vote of a quorum consisting of directors who were not parties to such action, suit or proceeding, or (2) if such a quorum is not obtainable, or, even if obtainable a quorum of disinterested directors so directs, by independent legal counsel in a written opinion, or (3) by the shareholders.

(e) Expenses (including attorneys' fees) incurred in defending a civil or criminal action, suit or proceeding may be paid by the corporation in advance of the final disposition of such action, suit or proceeding as authorized in the manner provided in subsection (d) upon receipt of an undertaking by or on behalf of the director, officer, employee or agent to repay such amount unless it shall ultimately be determined that he is entitled to be indemnified by the corporation as authorized in this section.

(f) The indemnification provided by this section shall not be deemed exclusive of any other rights to which those indemnified may be entitled under any by-law, agreement, vote of shareholders or disinterested directors or otherwise, both as to action in his official capacity and as to action in another capacity while holding such office, and shall continue as to a person who has ceased to be a director, officer, employee or agent and shall inure to the benefit of the heirs, executors and administrators of such a person.

(g) A corporation shall have power to purchase and maintain insurance on behalf of any person who is or was a director, officer, employee or agent of the corporation, or is or was serving at the request of the corporation as a director, officer, employee or agent of another corporation, partnership, joint venture, trust or other enterprise against any liability asserted against him and incurred by him in any such capacity or arising out of his status as such, whether or not the corporation would have the power to indemnify him against such liability under the provisions of this section.

§6. Right of Corporation to Acquire and Dispose of Its Own Shares

A corporation shall have the right to purchase, take, receive or otherwise acquire, hold, own, pledge, transfer or otherwise dispose of its own shares, but purchases of its own shares, whether direct or indirect, shall be made only to the extent of unreserved and unrestricted earned surplus available therefor, and, if the articles of incorporation so permit or with the affirmative vote of the holders of a majority of all shares entitled to vote thereon, to the extent of unreserved and unrestricted capital surplus available therefor.

To the extent that earned surplus or capital surplus is used as the measure of the corporation's right to purchase its own shares, such surplus shall be restricted so long as such shares are held as treasury shares, and upon the disposition or cancellation of any such shares the restriction shall be removed pro tanto.

Notwithstanding the foregoing limitation, a corporation may purchase or otherwise acquire its own shares for the purpose of:

(a) Eliminating fractional shares.

(b) Collecting or compromising indebtedness to the corporation.

(c) Paying dissenting shareholders entitled to

payment for their shares under the provisions of this Act.

(d) Effecting, subject to the other provisions of this Act, the retirement of its redeemable shares by redemption or by purchase at not to exceed the redemption price.

No purchase of or payment for its own shares shall be made at a time when the corporation is insolvent or when such purchase or payment would make it insolvent.

§7. Defense of Ultra Vires

No act of a corporation and no conveyance or transfer of real or personal property to or by a corporation shall be invalid by reason of the fact that the corporation was without capacity or power to do such act or to make or receive such conveyance or transfer, but such lack of capacity or power may be asserted:

(a) In a proceeding by a shareholder against the corporation to enjoin the doing of any act or the transfer of real or personal property by or to the corporation. If the unauthorized act or transfer sought to be enjoined is being, or is to be, performed or made pursuant to a contract to which the corporation is a party, the court may, if all of the parties to the contract are parties to the proceeding and if it deems the same to be equitable, set aside and enjoin the performance of such contract, and in so doing may allow to the corporation or to the other parties to the contract, as the case may be, compensation for the loss or damage sustained by either of them which may result from the action of the court in setting aside and enjoining the performance of such contract, but anticipated profits to be derived from the performance of the contract shall not be awarded by the court as a loss or damage sustained.

(b) In a proceeding by the corporation, whether acting directly or through a receiver, trustee, or other legal representative, or through shareholders in a representative suit, against the incumbent or former officers or directors of the corporation.

(c) In a proceeding by the Attorney General,

as provided in this Act, to dissolve the corporation, or in a proceeding by the Attorney General to enjoin the corporation from the transaction of unauthorized business.

§8. Corporate Name

The corporate name:

(a) Shall contain the word "corporation," "company," "incorporated" or "limited," or shall contain an abbreviation of one of such words.

(b) Shall not contain any word or phrase which indicates or implies that it is organized for any purpose other than one or more of the purposes contained in its articles of incorporation.

(c) Shall not be the same as, or deceptively similar to, the name of any domestic corporation existing under the laws of this State or any foreign corporation authorized to transact business in this State, or a name the exclusive right to which is, at the time, reserved in the manner provided in this Act, or the name of a corporation which has in effect a registration of its corporate name as provided in this Act, except that this provision shall not apply if the applicant files with the Secretary of State either of the following: (1) the written consent of such corporation or holder of a reserved or registered name to use the same or deceptively similar name and one or more words are added to make such name distinguishable from such other name, or (2) a certified copy of a final decree of a court of competent jurisdiction establishing the prior right of the applicant to the use of such name in this State.

A corporation with which another corporation, domestic or foreign, is merged, or which is formed by the reorganization or consolidation of one or more domestic or foreign corporations or upon a sale, lease or other disposition to or exchange with, a domestic corporation of all or substantially all the assets of another corporation, domestic or foreign including its name, may have the same name as that used in this State by any of such corporations if such other corporation was organized under the laws of, or is authorized to transact business in, this State.

§9. Reserved Name

The exclusive right to the use of a corporate name may be reserved by:

(a) Any person intending to organize a corporation under this Act.
(b) Any domestic corporation intending to change its name.
(c) Any foreign corporation intending to make application for a certificate of authority to transact business in this State.
(d) Any foreign corporation authorized to transact business in this State intending to change its name.
(e) Any person intending to organize a foreign corporation and intending to have such corporation make application for a certificate of authority to transact business in this State.

The reservation shall be made by filing with the Secretary of State an application to reserve a specified corporate name, executed by the applicant. If the Secretary of State finds that the name is available for corporate use, he shall reserve the same for the exclusive use of the applicant for a period of one hundred and twenty days.

The right of the exclusive use of a specified corporate name so reserved may be transferred to any other person or corporation by filing in the office of the Secretary of State a notice of such transfer, executed by the applicant for whom the name was reserved, and specifying the name and address of the transferee.

§10. Registered Name

Any corporation organized and existing under the laws of any state or territory of the United States may register its corporate name under this Act, provided its corporate name is not the same as, or deceptively similar to, the name of any domestic corporation existing under the laws of this State, or the name of any foreign corporation authorized to transact business in this State, or any corporate name reserved or registered under this Act.

Such registration shall be made by:

(a) Filing with the Secretary of State (1) an application for registration executed by the corporation by an officer thereof, setting forth the name of the corporation, the state or territory under the laws of which it is incorporated, the date of its incorporation, a statement that it is carrying on or doing business, and a brief statement of the business in which it is engaged, and (2) a certificate setting forth that such corporation is in good standing under the laws of the state or territory wherein it is organized, executed by the Secretary of State of such state or territory or by such other official as may have custody of the records pertaining to corporations, and
(b) Paying to the Secretary of State a registration fee in the amount of . . . . for each month, or fraction thereof, between the date of filing such application and December 31st of the calendar year in which such application is filed.

Such registration shall be effective until the close of the calendar year in which the application for registration is filed.

§11. Renewal of Registered Name

A corporation which has in effect a registration of its corporate name, may renew such registration from year to year by annually filing an application for renewal setting forth the facts required to be set forth in an original application for registration and a certificate of good standing as required for the original registration and by paying a fee of . . . . A renewal application may be filed between the first day of October and the thirty-first day of December in each year, and shall extend the registration for the following calendar year.

§12. Registered Office and Registered Agent

Each corporation shall have and continuously maintain in this State:

(a) A registered office which may be, but need not be, the same as its place of business.
(b) A registered agent, which agent may be either an individual resident in this State whose business office is identical with such registered office, or a domestic corporation, or a foreign corporation authorized to transact business in this State, having a business office identical with such registered office.

§13. Change of Registered Office or Registered Agent

A corporation may change its registered office or change its registered agent, or both, upon filing in the office of the Secretary of State a statement setting forth:

(a) The name of the corporation.
(b) The address of its then registered office.
(c) If the address of its registered office is to be changed, the address to which the registered office is to be changed.
(d) The name of its then registered agent.
(e) If its registered agent is to be changed, the name of its successor registered agent.
(f) That the address of its registered office and the address of the business office of its registered agent, as changed, will be identical.
(g) That such change was authorized by resolution duly adopted by its board of directors.

Such statement shall be executed by the corporation by its president, or a vice president, and verified by him, and delivered to the Secretary of State. If the Secretary of State finds that such statement conforms to the provisions of this Act, he shall file such statement in his office, and upon such filing the change of address of the registered office, or the appointment of a new registered agent, or both, as the case may be, shall become effective.

Any registered agent of a corporation may resign as such agent upon filing a written notice thereof, executed in duplicate, with the Secretary of State, who shall forthwith mail a copy thereof to the corporation at its registered office. The appointment of such agent shall terminate upon the expiration of thirty days after receipt of such notice by the Secretary of State.

If a registered agent changes his or its business address to another place within the same . . . . ,* he or it may change such address and the address of the registered office of any corporation of which he or it is registered agent by filing a statement as required above except that it need be signed only by the registered agent and need not be responsive to (e) or (g) and must recite that a copy of the statement has been mailed to the corporation.

§14. Service of Process on Corporation

The registered agent so appointed by a corporation shall be an agent of such corporation upon whom any process, notice or demand required or permitted by law to be served upon the corporation may be served.

Whenever a corporation shall fail to appoint or maintain a registered agent in this State, or whenever its registered agent cannot with reasonable diligence be found at the registered office, then the Secretary of State shall be an agent of such corporation upon whom any such process, notice, or demand may be served. Service on the Secretary of State of any such process, notice, or demand shall be made by delivering to and leaving with him, or with any clerk having charge of the corporation department of his office, duplicate copies of such process, notice or demand. In the event any such process, notice or demand is served on the Secretary of State, he shall immediately cause one of the copies thereof to be forwarded by registered mail, addressed to the corporation at its registered office. Any service so had on the Secretary of State shall be returnable in not less than thirty days.

The Secretary of State shall keep a record of all processes, notices and demands served upon him under this section, and shall record therein the time of such service and his action with reference thereto.

Nothing herein contained shall limit or affect the right to serve any process, notice or demand required or permitted by law to be

---

* Supply designation of jurisdiction, such as county, etc., in accordance with local practice.

served upon a corporation in any other manner now or hereafter permitted by law.

§15. Authorized Shares

Each corporation shall have power to create and issue the number of shares stated in its articles of incorporation. Such shares may be divided into one or more classes, any or all of which classes may consist of shares with par value or shares without par value, with such designations, preferences, limitations, and relative rights as shall be stated in the articles of incorporation. The articles of incorporation may limit or deny the voting rights of or provide special voting rights for the shares of any class to the extent not inconsistent with the provisions of this Act.

Without limiting the authority herein contained, a corporation, when so provided in its articles of incorporation, may issue shares of preferred or special classes:

(a) Subject to the right of the corporation to redeem any of such shares at the price fixed by the articles of incorporation for the redemption thereof.

(b) Entitling the holders thereof to cumulative, noncumulative or partially cumulative dividends.

(c) Having preference over any other class or classes of shares as to the payment of dividends.

(d) Having preference in the assets of the corporation over any other class or classes of shares upon the voluntary or involuntary liquidation of the corporation.

(e) Convertible into shares of any other class or into shares of any series of the same or any other class, except a class having prior or superior rights and preferences as to dividends or distribution of assets upon liquidation, but shares without par value shall not be converted into shares with par value unless that part of the stated capital of the corporation represented by such shares without par value is, at the time of conversion, at least equal to the aggregate par value of the shares into which the shares without par value are to be converted or the amount of any such deficiency is transferred from surplus to stated capital.

§16. Issuance of Shares of Preferred or Special Classes in Series

If the articles of incorporation so provide, the shares of any preferred or special class may be divided into and issued in series. If the shares of any such class are to be issued in series, then each series shall be so designated as to distinguish the shares thereof from the shares of all other series and classes. Any or all of the series of any such class and the variations in the relative rights and preferences as between different series may be fixed and determined by the articles of incorporation, but all shares of the same class shall be identical except as to the following relative rights and preferences, as to which there may be variations between different series:

(A) The rate of dividend.

(B) Whether shares may be redeemed and, if so, the redemption price and the terms and conditions of redemption.

(C) The amount payable upon shares in event of voluntary and involuntary liquidation.

(D) Sinking fund provisions, if any, for the redemption or purchase of shares.

(E) The terms and conditions, if any, on which shares may be converted.

(F) Voting rights, if any.

If the articles of incorporation shall expressly vest authority in the board of directors, then, to the extent that the articles of incorporation shall not have established series and fixed and determined the variations in the relative rights and preferences as between series, the board of directors shall have authority to divide any or all of such classes into series and, within the limitations set forth in this section and in the articles of incorporation, fix and determine the relative rights and preferences of the shares of any series so established.

In order for the board of directors to establish a series, where authority so to do is contained in the articles of incorporation, the board of directors shall adopt a resolution setting forth the designation of the series and fixing and determining the relative rights and preferences thereof, or so much thereof as shall not be fixed and determined by the articles of incorporation.

Prior to the issue of any shares of a series established by resolution adopted by the board of directors, the corporation shall file in the office of the Secretary of State a statement setting forth:

(a) The name of the corporation.
(b) A copy of the resolution establishing and designating the series, and fixing and determining the relative rights and preferences thereof.
(c) The date of adoption of such resolution.
(d) That such resolution was duly adopted by the board of directors.

Such statement shall be executed in duplicate by the corporation by its president or a vice president and by its secretary or an assistant secretary, and verified by one of the officers signing such statement, and shall be delivered to the Secretary of State. If the Secretary of State finds that such statement conforms to law, he shall, when all franchise taxes and fees have been paid as in this Act prescribed:

(1) Endorse on each of such duplicate originals the word "Filed," and the month, day, and year of the filing thereof.
(2) File one of such duplicate originals in his office.
(3) Return the other duplicate original to the corporation or its representative.

Upon the filing of such statement by the Secretary of State, the resolution establishing and designating the series and fixing and determining the relative rights and preferences thereof shall become effective and shall constitute an amendment of the articles of incorporation.

§17. Subscriptions for Shares

A subscription for shares of a corporation to be organized shall be irrevocable for a period of six months, unless otherwise provided by the terms of the subscription agreement or unless all of the subscribers consent to the revocation of such subscription.

Unless otherwise provided in the subscription agreement, subscriptions for shares, whether made before or after the organization of a corporation, shall be paid in full at such time, or in such installments and at such times, as shall be determined by the board of directors. Any call made by the board of directors for payment on subscriptions shall be uniform as to all shares of the same class or as to all shares of the same series, as the case may be. In case of default in the payment of any installment or call when such payment is due, the corporation may proceed to collect the amount due in the same manner as any debt due the corporation. The by-laws may prescribe other penalties for failure to pay installments or calls that may become due, but no penalty working a forfeiture of a subscription, or of the amounts paid thereon, shall be declared as against any subscriber unless the amount due thereon shall remain unpaid for a period of twenty days after written demand has been made therefor. If mailed, such written demand shall be deemed to be made when deposited in the United States mail in a sealed envelope addressed to the subscriber at his last post-office address known to the corporation, with postage thereon prepaid. In the event of the sale of any shares by reason of any forfeiture, the excess of proceeds realized over the amount due and unpaid on such shares shall be paid to the delinquent subscriber or to his legal representative.

§18. Consideration for Shares

Shares having a par value may be issued for such consideration expressed in dollars, not less than the par value thereof, as shall be fixed from time to time by the board of directors.

Shares without par value may be issued for such consideration expressed in dollars as may be fixed from time to time by the board of directors unless the articles of incorporation reserve to the shareholders the right to fix the consideration. In the event that such right be reserved as to any shares, the shareholders shall, prior to the issuance of such shares, fix the consideration to be received for such shares, by a vote of the holders of a majority of all shares entitled to vote thereon.

Treasury shares may be disposed of by the corporation for such consideration expressed in dollars as may be fixed from time to time by the board of directors.

That part of the surplus of a corporation which is transferred to stated capital upon the issuance of shares as a share dividend shall be deemed to be the consideration for the issuance of such shares.

In the event of the issuance of shares upon the conversion or exchange of indebtedness or shares, the consideration for the shares so issued shall be (1) the principal sum of, and accrued interest on, the indebtedness so exchanged or converted, or the stated capital then represented by the shares so exchanged or converted, and (2) that part of surplus, if any, transferred to stated capital upon the issuance of shares for the shares so exchanged or converted, and (3) any additional consideration paid to the corporation upon the issuance of shares for the indebtedness or shares so exchanged or converted.

§19. Payment for Shares

The consideration for the issuance of shares may be paid, in whole or in part, in money, in other property, tangible or intangible, or in labor or services actually performed for the corporation. When payment of the consideration for which shares are to be issued shall have been received by the corporation, such shares shall be deemed to be fully paid and non-assessable.

Neither promissory notes nor future services shall constitute payment or part payment for the issuance of shares of a corporation.

In the absence of fraud in the transaction, the judgment of the board of directors or the shareholders, as the case may be, as to the value of consideration received for shares shall be conclusive.

§20. Stock Rights and Options

Subject to any provisions in respect thereof set forth in its articles of incorporation, a corporation may create and issue, whether or not in connection with the issuance and sale of any of its shares or other securities, rights or options entitling the holders thereof to purchase from the corporation shares of any class or classes. Such rights or options shall be evidenced in such manner as the board of directors shall approve and, subject to the provisions of the articles of incorporation, shall set forth the terms upon which the time or times within which and the price or prices at which such shares may be purchased from the corporation upon the exercise of any such right or option. If such rights or options are to be issued to directors, officers or employees as such of the corporation or of any subsidiary thereof, and not to the shareholders generally, their issuance shall be approved by the affirmative vote of the holders of a majority of the shares entitled to vote there on or shall be authorized by and consistent with a plan approved or ratified by such a vote of shareholders. In the absence of fraud in the transaction, the judgment of the board of directors as to the adequacy of the consideration received for such rights or options shall be conclusive. The price or prices to be received for any shares having a par value, other than treasury shares to be issued upon the exercise of such rights or options, shall not be less than the par value thereof.

§21. Determination of Amount of Stated Capital

In case of the issuance by a corporation of shares having a par value, the consideration received therefor shall constitute stated capital to the extent of the par value of such shares, and the excess, if any, of such consideration shall constitute capital surplus.

In case of the issuance by a corporation of shares without par value, the entire consideration received therefor shall constitute stated capital unless the corporation shall determine as provided in this section that only a part thereof shall be stated capital. Within a period of sixty days after the issuance of any shares without par value, the board of directors may allocate to capital surplus any portion of the consideration received for the issuance of such shares. No such allocation shall be made of any portion of the consideration received for shares without par value having a preference in the assets of the corporation in the event of involuntary liquidation except the amount, if any, of such consideration in excess of such preference.

If shares have been or shall be issued by a corporation in merger or consolidation or in acquisition of all or substantially all of the outstanding shares or of the property and assets of another corporation, whether domestic or foreign, any amount that would otherwise constitute capital surplus under the foregoing provisions of this section may instead be allocated to earned surplus by the board of directors of the issuing corporation except that its aggregate earned surplus shall not exceed the sum of the earned surpluses as defined in this Act to the issuing corporation and of all other corporations, domestic or foreign, that were merged or consolidated or of which the shares or assets were acquired.

The stated capital of a corporation may be increased from time to time by resolution of the board of directors directing that all or a part of the surplus of the corporation be transferred to stated capital. The board of directors may direct that the amount of the surplus so transferred shall be deemed to be stated capital in respect of any designated class of shares.

§22. Expense of Organization, Reorganization and Financing

The reasonable charges and expenses of organization or reorganization of a corporation, and the reasonable expenses of and compensation for the sale or underwriting of its shares, may be paid or allowed by such corporation out of the consideration received by it in payment for its shares without thereby rendering such shares not fully paid or assessable.

§23. Certificates Representing Shares

The shares of a corporation shall be represented by certificates signed by the president or a vice president and the secretary or an assistant secretary of the corporation, and may be sealed with the seal of the corporation or a facsimile thereof. The signatures of the president or vice president and the secretary or assistant secretary upon a certificate may be facsimiles if the certificate is manually signed on behalf of a transfer agent or a registrar, other than the corporation itself or an employee of the corporation. In case any officer who has signed or whose facsimile signature had been placed upon such certificate shall have ceased to be such officer before such certificate is issued, it may be issued by the corporation with the same effect as if he were such officer at the date of its issue.

Every certificate representing shares issued by a corporation which is authorized to issue shares of more than one class shall set forth upon the face or back of the certificate, or shall state that the corporation will furnish to any shareholder upon request and without charge, a full statement of the designations, preferences, limitations, and relative rights of the shares of each class authorized to be issued, and if the corporation is authorized to issue any preferred or special class in series, the variations in the relative rights and preferences between the shares of each such series so far as the same have been fixed and determined and the authority of the board of directors to fix and determine the relative rights and preferences of subsequent series.

Each certificate representing shares shall state upon the face thereof:

(a) That the corporation is organized under the laws of this State.
(b) The name of the person to whom issued.
(c) The number and class of shares, and the

designation of the series, if any, which such certificate represents.

(d) The par value of each share represented by such certificate, or a statement that the shares are without par value.

No certificate shall be issued for any share until such share is fully paid.

§24. Fractional Shares

A corporation may (1) issue fractions of a share, (2) arrange for the disposition of fractional interests by those entitled thereto, (3) pay in cash the fair value of fractions of a share as of the time when those entitled to receive such fractions are determined, or (4) issue scrip in registered or bearer form which shall entitle the holder to receive a certificate for a full share upon the surrender of such scrip aggregating a full share. A certificate for a fractional share shall, but scrip shall not unless otherwise provided therein, entitle the holder to exercise voting rights, to receive dividends thereon, and to participate in any of the assets of the corporation in the event of liquidation. The board of directors may cause scrip to be issued subject to the condition that it shall become void if not exchanged for certificates representing full shares before a specified date, or subject to the condition that the shares for which scrip is exchangeable may be sold by the corporation and the proceeds thereof distributed to the holders of scrip, or subject to any other conditions which the board of directors may deem advisable.

§25. Liability of Subscribers and Shareholders

A holder of or subscriber to shares of a corporation shall be under no obligation to the corporation or its creditors with respect to such shares other than the obligation to pay to the corporation the full consideration for which such shares were issued or to be issued.

Any person becoming an assignee or transferee of shares or of a subscription for shares in good faith and without knowledge or notice that the full consideration therefor has not been paid shall not be personally liable to the corporation or its creditors for any unpaid portion of such consideration.

An executor, administrator, conservator, guardian, trustee, assignee for the benefit of creditors, or receiver shall not be personally liable to the corporation as a holder of or subscriber to shares of a corporation but the estate and funds in his hands shall be so liable.

No pledge or other holder of shares as collateral security shall be personally liable as a shareholder.

§26. Shareholders' Preemptive Rights

The shareholders of a corporation shall have no preemptive right to acquire unissued or treasury shares of the corporation, or securities of the corporation convertible into or carrying a right to subscribe to or acquire shares, except to the extent, if any, that such right is provided in the articles of incorporation.

§26A. Shareholders' Preemptive Rights [Alternative]

Except to the extent limited or denied by this section or by the articles of incorporation, shareholders shall have a preemptive right to acquire unissued or treasury shares or securities convertible into such shares or carrying a right to subscribe to or acquire shares.

Unless otherwise provided in the articles of incorporation,

(a) No preemptive right shall exist
  (1) to acquire any shares issued to directors, officers or employees pursuant to approval by the affirmative vote of the holders of a majority of the shares entitled to vote thereon or when authorized by and consistent with a plan theretofore approved by such a vote of shareholders; or
  (2) to acquire any shares sold otherwise than for cash.

(b) Holders of shares of any class that is preferred or limited as to dividends or assets shall not be entitled to any preemptive right.

(c) Holders of shares of common stock shall not be entitled to any preemptive right to shares of any class that is preferred or limited as to dividends or assets or to any obligations, unless convertible into shares of common stock or carrying a right to subscribe to or acquire shares of common stock.

(d) Holders of common stock without voting power shall have no preemptive right to shares of common stock with voting power.

(e) The preemptive right shall be only an opportunity to acquire shares or other securities under such terms and conditions as the board of directors may fix for the purpose of providing a fair and reasonable opportunity for the exercise of such right.

§27. By-Laws

The initial by-laws of a corporation shall be adopted by its board of directors. The power to alter, amend or repeal the by-laws or adopt new by-laws, subject to repeal or change by action of the shareholders, shall be vested in the board of directors unless reserved to the shareholders by the articles of incorporation. The by-laws may contain any provisions for the regulation and management of the affairs of the corporation not inconsistent with law or the articles of incorporation.

§27A. By-Laws and Other Powers in Emergency [Optional]

The board of directors of any corporation may adopt emergency by-laws, subject to repeal or change by action of the shareholders, which shall, notwithstanding any different provision elsewhere in this Act or in the articles of incorporation or by-laws, be operative during any emergency in the conduct of the business of the corporation resulting from an attack on the United States or any nuclear or atomic disaster. The emergency by-laws may make any provision that may be practical and necessary for the circumstances of the emergency, including provisions that:

(a) A meeting of the board of directors may be called by any officer or director in such manner and under such conditions as shall be prescribed in the emergency by-laws;

(b) The director or directors in attendance at the meeting, or any greater number fixed by the emergency by-laws, shall constitute a quorum; and

(c) The officers or other persons designated on a list approved by the board of directors before the emergency, all in such order of priority and subject to such conditions, and for such period of time (not longer than reasonably necessary after the termination of the emergency) as may be provided in the emergency by-laws or in the resolution approving the list shall, to the extent required to provide a quorum at any meeting of the board of directors, be deemed directors for such meeting.

The board of directors, either before or during any such emergency, may provide, and from time to time modify, lines of succession in the event that during such an emergency any or all officers or agents of the corporation shall for any reason be rendered incapable of discharging their duties.

The board of directors, either before or during any such emergency, may, effective in the emergency, change the head office or designate several alternative head offices or regional offices, or authorize the officers so to do.

To the extent not inconsistent with any emergency by-laws so adopted, the by-laws of the corporation shall remain in effect during any such emergency and upon its termination the emergency by-laws shall cease to be operative.

Unless otherwise provided in emergency by-laws, notice of any meeting of the board of directors during any such emergency may be given only to such of the directors as it may be feasible to reach at the time and by such means as may be feasible at the time, including publication or radio.

To the extent required to constitute a quorum at any meeting of the board of directors during any such emergency, the officers of the corporation who are present shall, unless otherwise provided in emergency by-laws, be deemed, in order of rank and within the same rank in order of seniority, directors for such meeting.

No officer, director or employee acting in accordance with any emergency by-laws shall be liable except for willful misconduct. No officer, director or employee shall be liable for any action taken by him in good faith in such an emergency in furtherance of the ordinary business affairs of the corporation even though not authorized by the by-laws then in effect.

§28. Meetings of Shareholders

Meetings of shareholders may be held at such place within or without this State as may be stated in or fixed in accordance with the by-laws. If no other place is stated or so fixed, meetings shall be held at the registered office of the corporation.

An annual meeting of the shareholders shall be held at such time as may be stated in or fixed in accordance with the by-laws. If the annual meeting is not held within any thirteen-month period the Court of . . . . may, on the application of any shareholder, summarily order a meeting to be held.

Special meetings of the shareholders may be called by the board of directors, the holders of not less than one-tenth of all the shares entitled to vote at the meeting, or such other persons as may be authorized in the articles of incorporation or the by-laws.

§29. Notice of Shareholders' Meetings

Written notice stating the place, day and hour of the meeting and, in case of a special meeting, the purpose or purposes for which the meeting is called, shall be delivered not less than ten nor more than fifty days before the date of the meeting, either personally or by mail, by or at the direction of the president, the secretary or the officer or persons calling the meeting, to each shareholder of record entitled to vote at such meeting. If mailed, such notice shall be deemed to be delivered when deposited in the United States mail addressed to the shareholder at his address as it appears on the stock transfer books of the corporation, with postage thereon prepaid.

§30. Closing of Transfer Books and Fixing Record Date

For the purpose of determining shareholders entitled to notice of or to vote at any meeting of shareholders or any adjournment thereof, or entitled to receive payment of any dividend, or in order to make a determination of shareholders for any other proper purpose, the board of directors of a corporation may provide that the stock transfer books shall be closed for a stated period but not to exceed, in any case, fifty days. If the stock transfer books shall be closed for the purpose of determining shareholders entitled to notice of or to vote at a meeting of shareholders, such books shall be closed for at least ten days immediately preceding such meeting. In lieu of closing the stock transfer books, the by-laws, or in the absence of an applicable by-law the board of directors, may fix in advance a date as the record date for any such determination of shareholders, such date in any case to be not more than fifty days and, in case of a meeting of shareholders, not less than ten days prior to the date on which the particular action, requiring such determination of shareholders, is to be taken. If the stock transfer books are not closed and no record date is fixed for the determination of shareholders entitled to notice of or to vote at a meeting of shareholders, or shareholders entitled to receive payment of a dividend, the date on which notice of the meeting is mailed or the date on which the resolution of the board of directors declaring such dividend is adopted, as the case may be, shall be the record date for such determination of shareholders. When a determination of shareholders entitled to vote at any meeting of shareholders has been made as provided in this section, such determination shall apply to any adjournment thereof.

§31. Voting Record

The officer or agent having charge of the stock transfer books for shares of a corporation shall make a complete record of the shareholders entitled to vote at such meeting or any adjournment thereof, arranged in alphabetical order, with the address of and the number of shares held by each. Such record shall be produced and kept open at the time and place of the meeting and shall be subject to the inspection of any shareholder during the whole time of the meeting for the purposes thereof.

Failure to comply with the requirements of this section shall not affect the validity of any action taken at such meeting.

An officer or agent having charge of the stock transfer books who shall fail to prepare the record of shareholders, or produce and keep it open for inspection at the meeting, as provided in this section, shall be liable to any shareholder suffering damage on account of such failure, to the extent of such damage.

§32. Quorum of Shareholders

Unless otherwise provided in the articles of incorporation, a majority of the shares entitled to vote, represented in person or by proxy, shall constitute a quorum at a meeting of shareholders, but in no event shall a quorum consist of less than one-third of the shares entitled to vote at the meeting. If a quorum is present, the affirmative vote of the majority of the shares represented at the meeting and entitled to vote on the subject matter shall be the act of the shareholders, unless the vote of a greater number of voting by classes is required by this Act or the articles of incorporation or by-laws.

§33. Voting of Shares

Each outstanding share, regardless of class, shall be entitled to one vote on each matter submitted to a vote at a meeting of shareholders, except as may be otherwise provided in the articles of incorporation. If the articles of incorporation provide for more or less than one vote for any share, on any matter, every reference in this Act to a majority or other proportion of shares shall refer to such a majority or other proportion of votes entitled to be cast.

Neither treasury shares, nor shares held by another corporation if a majority of the shares entitled to vote for the election of directors of such other corporation is held by the corporation, shall be voted at any meeting or counted in determining the total number of outstanding shares at any given time.

A shareholder may vote either in person or by proxy executed in the writing by the shareholder or by his duly authorized attorney-in-fact. No proxy shall be valid after eleven months from the date of its execution, unless otherwise provided in the proxy.

[Either of the following prefatory phrases may be inserted here: "The articles of incorporation may provide that" or "Unless the articles of incorporation otherwise provide"] . . . at each election for directors every shareholder entitled to vote at such election shall have the right to vote, in person or by proxy, the number of shares owned by him for as many persons as there are directors to be elected and for whose election he has a right to vote, or to cumulate his votes by giving one candidate as many votes as the number of such directors multiplied by the number of his shares shall equal, or by distributing such votes on the same principle among any number of such candidates.

Shares standing in the name of another corporation, domestic or foreign, may be voted by such officer, agent or proxy as the by-laws of such other corporation may prescribe, or, in the absence of such provision, as the board of directors of such other corporation may determine.

Shares held by an administrator, executor, guardian or conservator may be voted by him, either in person or by proxy, without a transfer of such shares into his name. Shares standing in the name of a trustee may be voted by him, either in person or by proxy, but no trustee shall be entitled to vote shares held by him without a transfer of such shares into his name.

Shares standing in the name of a receiver may be voted by such receiver, and shares held by or under the control of a receiver may be voted by such receiver without the transfer thereof into his name if authority so to do be contained in an appropriate order of the court by which such receiver was appointed.

A shareholder whose shares are pledged shall be entitled to vote such shares until the shares have been transferred into the name of the pledgee, and thereafter the pledgee shall be entitled to vote the shares so transferred.

On and after the date on which written notice of redemption of redeemable shares has been mailed to the holders thereof and a sum sufficient to redeem such shares has been deposited with a bank or trust company with irrevocable instruction and authority to pay the redemption price to the holders thereof upon surrender of certificates therefor, such shares shall not be entitled to vote on any matter and shall not be deemed to be outstanding shares.

§34. Voting Trusts and Agreements Among Shareholders

Any number of shareholders of a corporation may create a voting trust for the purpose of conferring upon a trustee or trustees the right to vote or otherwise represent their shares, for a period of not to exceed ten years, by entering into a written voting trust agreement specifying the terms and conditions of the voting trust, by depositing a counterpart of the agreement with the corporation at its registered office, and by transferring their shares to such trustee or trustees for the purposes of the agreement. Such trustee or trustees shall keep a record of the holders of voting trust certificates evidencing a beneficial interest in the voting trust, giving the names and addresses of all such holders and the number and class of the shares in respect of which the voting trust certificates held by each are issued, and shall deposit a copy of such record with the corporation at its registered office. The counterpart of the voting trust agreement and the copy of such record so deposited with the corporation shall be subject to the same right of examination by a shareholder of the corporation, in person or by agent or attorney, as are the books and records of the corporation, and such counterpart and such copy of such record shall be subject to examination by any holder of record of voting trust certificates, either in person or by agent or attorney, at any reasonable time for any proper purpose.

Agreements among shareholders regarding the voting of their shares shall be valid and enforceable in accordance with their terms. Such agreements shall not be subject to the provisions of this section regarding voting trusts.

§35. Board of Directors

The business and affairs of a corporation shall be managed by a board of directors except as may be otherwise provided in the articles of incorporation. If any such provision is made in the articles of incorporation, the powers and duties conferred or imposed upon the board of directors by this Act shall be exercised or performed to such extent and by such person or persons as shall be provided in the articles of incorporation. Directors need not be residents of this State or shareholders of the corporation unless the articles of incorporation or by-laws so require. The articles of incorporation or by-laws may prescribe other qualifications for directors. The board of directors shall have authority to fix the compensation of directors unless otherwise provided in the articles of incorporation.

§36. Number and Election of Directors

The board of directors of a corporation shall consist of one or more members. The number of directors shall be fixed by, or in the manner provided in, the articles of incorporation or the by-laws, except as to the number constituting the initial board of directors, which number shall be fixed by the articles of incorporation. The number of directors may be increased or decreased from time to time by amendment to, or in the manner provided in, the articles of incorporation or the by-laws, but no decrease shall have the effect of shortening the term of any incumbent director. In the absence of a by-law providing for the number of directors, the number shall be the same as that provided for in the articles of incorporation. The names and addresses of the members of the first board of directors shall be stated in the articles of incorporation. Such persons shall hold office until the first annual meeting of shareholders, and until their successors shall have been elected and qualified. At the first annual meeting of shareholders and at each annual meeting thereafter the shareholders shall elect directors to hold office until the next succeeding annual meeting, except in case of the classification of directors as permitted by this Act. Each director shall hold office for the term for which he is elected and until his successor shall have been elected and qualified.

§37. Classification of Directors

When the board of directors shall consist of nine or more members, in lieu of electing the whole number of directors annually, the articles of incorporation may provide that the directors be divided into either two or three classes, each class to be as nearly equal in number as possible, the term of office of directors of the first class to expire at the first annual meeting of shareholders after their election, that of the second class to expire at the second annual meeting after their election, and that of the third class, if any, to expire at the third annual meeting after their election. At each annual meeting after such classification the number of directors equal to the number of the class whose term expires at the time of such meeting shall be elected to hold office until the second succeeding annual meeting, if there be two classes, or until the third succeeding annual meeting, if there be three classes. No classification of directors shall be effective prior to the first annual meeting of shareholders.

§38. Vacancies

Any vacancy occurring in the board of directors may be filled by the affirmative vote of a majority of the remaining directors though less than a quorum of the board of directors. A director elected to fill a vacancy shall be elected for the unexpired term of his predecessor in office. Any directorship to be filled by reason of an increase in the number of directors may be filled by the board of directors for a term of office continuing only until the next election of directors by the shareholders.

§39. Removal of Directors

At a meeting of shareholders called expressly for that purpose, directors may be removed in the manner provided in this section. Any director or the entire board of directors may be removed, with or without cause, by a vote of the holders of a majority of the shares then entitled to vote at an election of directors.

In the case of a corporation having cumulative voting, if less than the entire board is to be removed, no one of the directors may be removed if the votes cast against his removal would be sufficient to elect him if then cumulatively voted at an election of the entire board of directors, or, if there be classes of directors, at an election of the class of directors of which he is a part.

Whenever the holders of the shares of any class are entitled to elect one or more directors by the provisions of the articles of incorporation, the provisions of this section shall apply, in respect to the removal of a director or directors so elected, to the vote of the holders of the outstanding shares of that class and not to the vote of the outstanding shares as a whole.

§40. Quorum of Directors

A majority of the number of directors fixed by or in the manner provided in the by-laws or in the absence of a by-law fixing or providing for the number of directors, then of the number stated in the articles of incorporation, shall constitute a quorum for the transaction of business unless a greater number is required by the articles of incorporation or the by-laws. The act of the majority of the directors present at a meeting at which a quorum is present shall be the act of the board of directors, unless the act of a greater number is required by the articles of incorporation or the by-laws.

§41. Director Conflicts of Interest

No contract or other transaction between a corporation and one or more of its directors or any other corporation, firm, association or entity in which one or more of its directors are directors or officers or are financially interested, shall be either void or voidable because of such relationship or interest or because such director or directors are present at the meeting of the board of directors or a committee thereof which authorizes, approves or ratifies such contract or transaction or because his or their votes are counted for such purpose, if:

(a) the fact of such relationship or interest is disclosed or known to the board of directors or committee which authorizes, approves or ratifies the contract or transaction by a vote or consent sufficient for the purpose without counting the votes or consents of such interested directors; or

(b) the fact of such relationship or interest is disclosed or known to the shareholders entitled to vote and they authorize, approve or ratify such contract or transaction by vote or written consent; or

(c) the contract or transaction is fair and reasonable to the corporation.

Common or interested directors may be counted in determining the presence of a quorum at a meeting of the board of directors or a committee thereof which authorizes, approves or ratifies such contract or transaction.

§42. Executive and Other Committees

If the articles of incorporation or the by-laws so provide, the board of directors, by resolution adopted by a majority of the full board of directors, may designate from among its members an executive committee and one or more other committees each of which, to the extent provided in such resolution or in the articles of incorporation or the by-laws of the corporation, shall have and may exercise all the authority of the board of directors, but no such committee shall have the authority of the board of directors in reference to amending the articles of in-

corporation, adopting a plan of merger or consolidation, recommending to the shareholders the sale, lease, exchange or other disposition of all or substantially all the property and assets of the corporation otherwise than in the usual and regular course of its business, recommending to the shareholders a voluntary dissolution of the corporation or a revocation thereof, or amending the by-laws of the corporation. The designation of any such committee and the delegation thereto of authority shall not operate to relieve the board of directors, or any member thereof, of any responsibility imposed by law.

§43. Place and Notice of Directors' Meetings

Meetings of the board of directors, regular or special, may be held either within or without this State.

Regular meetings of the board of directors may be held with or without notice as prescribed in the by-laws. Special meetings of the board of directors shall be held upon such notice as is prescribed in the by-laws. Attendance of a director at a meeting shall constitute a waiver of notice of such meeting, except where a director attends a meeting for the express purpose of objecting to the transaction of any business because the meeting is not lawfully called or convened. Neither the business to be transacted at, nor the purpose of, any regular or special meeting of the board of directors need be specified in the notice or waiver of notice of such meeting unless required by the by-laws.

§44. Action by Directors Without a Meeting

Unless otherwise provided by the articles of incorporation or by-laws, any action required by this Act to be taken at a meeting of the directors of a corporation, or any action which may be taken at a meeting of the directors or of a committee, may be taken without a meeting if a consent in writing, setting forth the action so taken, shall be signed by all of the directors, or all of the members of the committee, as the case may be. Such consent shall have the same effect as a unanimous vote.

§45. Dividends

The board of directors of a corporation may, from time to time, declare and the corporation may pay dividends in cash, property, or its own shares, except when the corporation is insolvent or when the payment thereof would render the corporation insolvent or when the declaration or payment thereof would be contrary to any restriction contained in the articles of incorporation, subject to the following provisions:

(a) Dividends may be declared and paid in cash or property only out of the unreserved and unrestricted earned surplus of the corporation, except as otherwise provided in this section.

[Alternative] (a) Dividends may be declared and paid in cash or property only out of the unreserved and unrestricted earned surplus of the corporation, or out of the unreserved and unrestricted net earnings of the current fiscal year and the next preceding fiscal year taken as a single period, except as otherwise provided in this section.

(b) If the articles of incorporation of a corporation engaged in the business of exploiting natural resources so provide, dividends may be declared and paid in cash out of the depletion reserves, but each such dividend shall be identified as a distribution of such reserves and the amount per share paid from such reserves shall be disclosed to the shareholders receiving the same concurrently with the distribution thereof.

(c) Dividends may be declared and paid in its own treasury shares.

(d) Dividends may be declared and paid in its own authorized but unissued shares out of any unreserved and unrestricted surplus of the corporation upon the following conditions:

(1) If a dividend is payable in its own shares having a par value, such shares shall be issued at not less than the par value thereof and there shall be transferred to stated capital at the time such dividend is paid an amount of surplus equal to the aggregate par value of the shares to be issued as a dividend.

(2) If a dividend is payable in its own shares without par value, such shares shall be issued at such stated value as shall be fixed by the board of directors by resolution adopted at the time such dividend is declared, and there shall be transferred to stated capital at the time such dividend is paid an amount of surplus equal to the aggregate stated value so fixed in respect of such shares; and the amount per share so transferred to stated capital shall be disclosed to the shareholders receiving such dividend concurrently with the payment thereof.

(e) No dividend payable in shares of any class shall be paid to the holders of shares of any other class unless the articles of incorporation so provide or such payment is authorized by the affirmative vote or the written consent of the holders of at least a majority of the outstanding shares of the class in which the payment is to be made.

A split-up or division of the issued shares of any class into a greater number of shares of the same class without increasing the stated capital of the corporation shall not be construed to be a share dividend within the meaning of this section.

§46. Distributions from Capital Surplus

The board of directors of a corporation may, from time to time, distribute to its shareholders out of capital surplus of the corporation a portion of its assets, in cash or property, subject to the following provisions:

(a) No such distribution shall be made at a time when the corporation is insolvent or when such distribution would render the corporation insolvent.

(b) No such distribution shall be made unless the articles of incorporation so provide or such distribution is authorized by the affirmative vote of the holders of a majority of the outstanding shares of each class whether or not entitled to vote thereon by the provisions of the articles of incorporation of the corporation.

(c) No such distribution shall be made to the holders of any class of shares unless all cumulative dividends accrued on all preferred or special classes of shares entitled to preferential dividends shall have been fully paid.

(d) No such distribution shall be made to the holders of any class of shares which would reduce the remaining net assets of the corporation below the aggregate preferential amount payable in event of involuntary liquidation to the holders of shares having preferential rights to the assets of the corporation in the event of liquidation.

(e) Each such distribution, when made, shall be identified as a distribution from capital surplus and the amount per share disclosed to the shareholders receiving the same concurrently with the distribution thereof.

The board of directors of a corporation may also, from time to time, distribute to the holders of its outstanding shares having a cumulative preferential right to receive dividends, in discharge of their cumulative dividend rights, dividends payable in cash out of the capital surplus of the corporation, if at the time the corporation has no earned surplus and is not insolvent and would not thereby be rendered insolvent. Each such distribution when made, shall be identified as a payment of cumulative dividends out of capital surplus.

§47. Loans to Employees and Directors

A corporation shall not lend money to or use its credit to assist its directors without authorization in the particular case by its shareholders, but may lend money to and use its credit to assist any employee of the corporation or of a subsidiary, including any such employee who is a director of the corporation, if the board of directors decides that such loan or assistance may benefit the corporation.

§48. Liability of Directors in Certain Cases

In addition to any other liabilities imposed by law upon directors of a corporation:

(a) Directors of a corporation who vote for or assent to the declaration of any dividend or other distribution of the assets of a corporation to its shareholders contrary to the provisions of this Act or contrary to any restrictions contained in the articles of incorporation, shall be jointly and severally liable to the corporation for the amount of such dividend which is paid or the value of such assets which are distributed in excess of the amount of such dividend or distribution which could have been paid or distributed without a violation of the provisions of this Act or the restrictions in the articles of incorporation.

(b) Directors of a corporation who vote for or assent to the purchase of its own shares contrary to the provisions of this Act shall be jointly and severally liable to the corporation for the amount of consideration paid for such shares which is in excess of the maximum amount which could have been paid therefor without a violation of the provisions of this Act.

(c) The directors of a corporation who vote for or assent to any distribution of assets of a corporation to its shareholders during the liquidation of the corporation without the payment and discharge of, or making adequate provision for, all known debts, obligations, and liabilities of the corporation shall be jointly and severally liable to the corporation for the value of such assets which are distributed, to the extent that such debts, obligations and liabilities of the corporation are not thereafter paid and discharged.

A director of a corporation who is present at a meeting of its board of directors at which action on any corporate matter is taken shall be presumed to have assented to the action taken unless his dissent shall be entered in the minutes of the meeting or unless he shall file his written dissent to such action with the secretary of the meeting before the adjournment thereof or shall forward such dissent by registered mail to the secretary of the corporation immediately after the adjournment of the meeting. Such right to dissent shall not apply to a director who voted in favor of such action.

A director shall not be liable under (a), (b) or (c) of this section if he relied and acted in good faith upon financial statements of the corporation represented to him to be correct by the president or the officer of such corporation having charge of its books of account, or stated in a written report by an independent public or certified public accountant or firm of such accountants fairly to reflect the financial condition of such corporation, nor shall he be so liable if in good faith in determining the amount available for any such dividend or distribution he considered the assets to be of their book value.

Any director against whom a claim shall be asserted under or pursuant to this section for the payment of a dividend or other distribution of assets of a corporation and who shall be held liable thereon, shall be entitled to contribution from the shareholders who accepted or received any such dividend or assets, knowing such dividend or distribution to have been made in violation of this Act, in proportion to the amounts received by them.

Any director against whom a claim shall be asserted under or pursuant to this section shall be entitled to contribution from the other directors who voted for or assented to the action upon which the claim is asserted.

§49. Provisions Relating to Actions by Shareholders

No action shall be brought in this State by a shareholder in the right of a domestic or foreign corporation unless the plaintiff was a holder of record of shares or of voting trust certificates therefor at the time of the transaction of which he complains, or his shares or voting trust certificates thereafter devolved upon him by operation of law from a person who was a holder of record at such time.

In any action hereafter instituted in the right of any domestic or foreign corporation by the holder or holders of record of shares of such corporation or of voting trust certificates therefor, the court having jurisdiction, upon final judgment and a finding that the action was brought without reasonable cause, may require the plaintiff or plaintiffs to pay to the parties named as defendant the reasonable expenses, including fees of attorneys, incurred by them in the defense of such action.

In any action now pending or hereafter instituted or maintained in the right of any domestic or foreign corporation by the holder or holders of record of less than five per cent of the outstanding shares of any class of such corporation or of voting trust certificates therefor, unless the shares or voting trust certificates so held have a market value in excess of twenty-five thousand dollars, the corporation in whose right such action is brought shall be entitled at any time before final judgment to require the plaintiff or plaintiffs to give security for the reasonable expenses, including fees of attorneys, that may be incurred by it in connection with such action or may be incurred by other parties named as defendant for which it may become legally liable. Market value shall be determined as of the date that the plaintiff institutes the action or, in the case of an intervenor, as of the date that he becomes a party to the action. The amount of such security may from time to time be increased or decreased, in the discretion of the court, upon showing that the security provided has or may become inadequate or is excessive. The corporation shall have recourse to such security in such amount as the court having jurisdiction shall determine upon the termination of such action, whether or not the court finds the action was brought without reasonable cause.

§50. Officers

The officers of a corporation shall consist of a president, one or more vice presidents as may be prescribed by the by-laws, a secretary, and a treasurer, each of whom shall be elected by the board of directors at such time and in such manner as may be prescribed by the by-laws. Such other officers and assistant officers and agents as may be deemed necessary may be elected or appointed by the board of directors or chosen in such other manner as may be prescribed by the by-laws. Any two or more offices may be held by the same person, except the offices of president and secretary.

All officers and agents of the corporation, as between themselves and the corporation, shall have such authority and perform such duties in the management of the corporation as may be provided in the by-laws, or as may be determined by resolution of the board of directors not inconsistent with the by-laws.

§51. Removal of Officers

Any officer or agent may be removed by the board of directors whenever in its judgment the best interests of the corporation will be served thereby, but such removal shall be without prejudice to the contract rights, if any, of the person so removed. Election or appointment of an officer or agent shall not of itself create contract rights.

§52. Books and Records

Each corporation shall keep correct and complete books and records of account and shall keep minutes of the proceedings of its shareholders and board of directors and shall keep at its registered office or principal place of business, or at the office of its transfer agent or registrar, a record of its shareholders, giving the names and addresses of all shareholders and the number and class of the shares held by each. Any books, records and minutes may be in written form or in any other form capable of being converted into written form within a reasonable time.

Any person who shall have been a holder of record of shares or of voting trust certificates therefor at least six months immediately preceding his demand or shall be the holder of record of, or the holder of record of voting trust certificates for, at least five per cent of all the outstanding shares of the corporation, upon written demand stating the purpose thereof, shall have the right to examine, in person, or by agent or attorney, at any reasonable time or times, for any proper purpose its relevant books and records of account, minutes, and record of shareholders and to make extracts therefrom.

Any officer or agent who, or a corporation which, shall refuse to allow any such shareholder or holder of voting trust certificates, or his agent or attorney, so to examine and make extracts from its books and records of account, minutes, and record of shareholders, for any proper purpose, shall be liable to such shareholder or holder of voting trust certificates in a penalty of ten per cent of the value of the shares owned by such shareholder, or in respect of which such voting trust certificates are issued, in addition to any other damages or remedy afforded him by law. It shall be a defense to any action for penalties under this section that the person suing therefor has within two years sold or offered for sale any list of shareholders or of holders of voting trust certificates for shares of such corporation or any other corporation or has aided or abetted any person in procuring any list of shareholders or of holders of voting trust certificates for any such purpose, or has improperly used any information secured through any prior examination of the books and records of account, or minutes, or record of shareholders or of holders of voting trust certificates for shares of such corporation or any other corporation, or was not acting in good faith or for a proper purpose in making his demand.

Nothing herein contained shall impair the power of any court of competent jurisdiction, upon proof by a shareholder or holder of voting trust certificates of proper purpose, irrespective of the period of time during which such shareholder or holder of voting trust certificates shall have been a shareholder of record or a holder of record of voting trust certificates, and irrespective of the number of shares held by him or represented by voting trust certificates held by him, to compel the production for examination by such shareholder or holder of voting trust certificates of the books and records of account, minutes and record of shareholders of a corporation.

Upon the written request of any shareholder or holder of voting trust certificates for shares of a corporation, the corporation shall mail to such shareholder or holder of voting trust certificates its most recent financial statements showing in reasonable detail its assets and liabilities and the results of its operations.

§53. Incorporators

One or more persons, or a domestic or foreign corporation, may act as incorporator or incorporators of a corporation by signing and delivering in duplicate to the Secretary of State articles of incorporation for such corporation.

§54. Articles of Incorporation

The articles of incorporation shall set forth:

(a) The name of the corporation.

(b) The period of duration, which may be perpetual.

(c) The purpose or purposes for which the corporation is organized which may be stated to be, or to include, the transaction of any or all lawful business for which corporations may be incorporated under this Act.

(d) The aggregate number of shares which the corporation shall have authority to issue; if such shares are to consist of one class only, the par value of each of such shares, or a statement that all of such shares are without par value; or, if such shares are to be divided into classes, the number of shares of each class, and a statement of the par value of the shares of each such class or that such shares are to be without par value.

(e) If the shares are to be divided into classes, the designation of each class and a statement of the preferences, limitations and relative rights in respect of the shares of each class.

(f) If the corporation is to issue the shares of any preferred or special class in series, then the designation of each series and a statement of the variations in the relative rights and preferences as between series insofar as the same are to be fixed in the articles of incorporation, and a statement of any authority to be vested in the board of directors to establish series and fix and determine the variations in the relative rights and preferences as between series.

(g) If any preemptive right is to be granted to shareholders, the provisions therefor.

(h) Any provision, not inconsistent with law, which the incorporators elect to set forth in the articles of incorporation for the regulation of the internal affairs of the corporation, including any provision restricting the transfer of shares and any provision which under this Act is required or permitted to be set forth in the by-laws.

(i) The address of its initial registered office, and the name of its initial registered agent at such address.

(j) The number of directors constituting the initial board of directors and the names and addresses of the persons who are to serve as directors until the first annual meeting of shareholders or until their successors be elected and qualify.

(k) The name and address of each incorporator.

It shall not be necessary to set forth in the articles of incorporation any of the corporate powers enumerated in this Act.

§55. Filing of Articles of Incorporation

Duplicate originals of the articles of incorporation shall be delivered to the Secretary of State. If the Secretary of State finds that the articles of incorporation conform to law, he shall, when all fees have been paid as in this Act prescribed:

(a) Endorse on each of such duplicate originals the word "Filed," and the month, day and year of the filing thereof.

(b) File one of such duplicate originals in his office.

(c) Issue a certificate of incorporation to which he shall affix the other duplicate original.

The certificate of incorporation, together with the duplicate original of the articles of incorporation affixed thereto by the Secretary of State, shall be returned to the incorporators or their representative.

§56. Effect of Issuance of Certificate of Incorporation

Upon the issuance of the certificate of incorporation, the corporate existence shall begin, and such certificate of incorporation shall be conclusive evidence that all conditions precedent required to be performed by the incorporators have been complied with and that the corporation has been incorporated under this Act, except as against this State in a proceeding to cancel or revoke the certificate of incorporation or for involuntary dissolution of the corporation.

§57. Organization Meeting of Directors

After the issuance of the certificate of incorporation an organization meeting of the board of directors named in the articles of incorporation shall be held, either within or without this State, at the call of a majority of the directors named in the articles of incorporation, for the purpose of adopting by-laws, electing officers and transacting such other business as may come before the meeting. The directors calling the meeting shall give at least three days' notice thereof by mail to each director so named, stating the time and place of the meeting.

§58. Right to Amend Articles of Incorporation

A corporation may amend its articles of incorporation, from time to time, in any and as many respects as may be desired, so long as its articles of incorporation as amended contain only such provisions as might be lawfully contained in original articles of incorporation at the time of making such amendment, and, if a change in shares or the rights of shareholders, or an exchange, reclassification or cancellation of shares or rights of shareholders is to be made, such provisions as may be necessary to effect such change, exchange, reclassification or cancellation.

In particular, and without limitation upon such general power of amendment, a corporation may amend its articles of incorporation, from time to time, so as:

(a) To change its corporate name.

(b) To change its period of duration.

(c) To change, enlarge or diminish its corporate purposes.

(d) To increase or decrease the aggregate number of shares, or shares of any class, which the corporation has authority to issue.

(e) To increase or decrease the par value of the authorized shares of any class having a par value, whether issued or unissued.

(f) To exchange, classify, reclassify or cancel all or any part of its shares, whether issued or unissued.

(g) To change the designation of all or any part of its shares, whether issued or unissued, and to change the preferences, limitations, and the relative rights in respect of all or any part of its shares, whether issued or unissued.

(h) To change shares having the par value, whether issued or unissued, into the same or a different number of shares without par value, and to change shares without par value, whether issued or unissued, into the same or a different number of shares having a par value.

(i) To change the shares of any class, whether issued or unissued and whether with or without par value, into a different number of shares of the same class or into the same or a different number of shares, either with or without par value, of other classes.

(j) To create new classes of shares having rights and preferences either prior and superior or subordinate and inferior to the shares of any class then authorized, whether issued or unissued.

(k) To cancel or otherwise affect the right of the holders of the shares of any class to receive dividends which have accrued but have not been declared.

(l) To divide any preferred or special class of shares, whether issued or unissued, into series and fix and determine the designations of such series and the variations in the relative rights and preferences as between the shares of such series.

(m) To authorize the board of directors to establish, out of authorized but unissued shares, series of any preferred or special class of shares and fix and determine the relative rights and preferences of the shares of any series so established.

(n) To authorize the board of directors to fix and determine the relative rights and preferences of the authorized but unissued shares of series theretofore established in respect of which either the relative rights and preferences have not been fixed and determined or the relative rights and preferences theretofore fixed and determined are to be changed.

(o) To revoke, diminish, or enlarge the authority of the board of directors to establish series out of authorized but unissued shares of any preferred or special class and fix and determine the relative rights and preferences of the shares of any series so established.

(p) To limit, deny or grant to shareholders of any class the preemptive right to acquire additional or treasury shares of the corporation, whether then or thereafter authorized.

§59. Procedure to Amend Articles of Incorportion

Amendments to the articles of incorporation shall be made in the following manner:

(a) The board of directors shall adopt a resolution setting forth the proposed amendment and, if shares have been issued, directing that it be submitted to a vote at a meeting of shareholders, which may be either the annual or a special meeting. If no shares have been issued, the amendment shall be adopted by resolution of the board of directors and the provisions for adoption by shareholders shall not apply. The resolution may incorporate the proposed amendment in restated articles of incorporation which contain a statement that except for the designated amendment the restated articles of incorporation correctly set forth without change the corresponding provisions of the articles of incorporation as theretofore amended, and that the restated articles of incorporation together with the designated amendment supersede the original articles of incorporation and all amendments thereto.

(b) Written notice setting forth the proposed amendment or a summary of the changes to be effected thereby shall be given to each shareholder of record entitled to vote thereon within the time and in the manner provided in this Act for the giving of notice of meetings of shareholders. If the meeting be an annual meeting, the proposed amendment of such summary may be included in the notice of such annual meeting.

(c) At such meeting a vote of the shareholders entitled to vote thereon shall be taken on the proposed amendment. The proposed amendment shall be adopted upon receiving the affirmative vote of the holders of a majority of the shares entitled to vote thereon, unless any class of shares is entitled to vote thereon as a class, in which event the proposed amendment shall be adopted upon receiving the affirmative vote of the holders of a majority of the shares of each class of shares entitled to vote thereon as a class and of the total shares entitled to vote thereon.

Any number of amendments may be submitted to the shareholders, and voted upon by them, at one meeting.

§60. Class Voting on Amendments

The holders of the outstanding shares of a class shall be entitled to vote as a class upon a proposed amendment, whether or not entitled to vote thereon by the provisions of the articles of incorporation, if the amendment would:

(a) Increase or decrease the aggregate number of authorized shares of such class.

(b) Increase or decrease the par value of the shares of such class.

(c) Effect an exchange, reclassification or cancellation of all or part of the shares of such class.

(d) Effect an exchange, or create a right of exchange, of all or any part of the shares of another class into the shares of such class.

(e) Change the designations, preferences, limitations or relative rights of the shares of such class.

(f) Change the shares of such class, whether with or without par value, into the same or a different number of shares, either with or without par value, of the same class or another class or classes.

(g) Create a new class of shares having rights and preferences prior and superior to the shares of such class, or increase the rights and preferences or the number of authorized shares, of any class having rights and preferences prior or superior to the shares of such class.

(h) In the case of a preferred or special class of shares, divide the shares of such class into series and fix and determine the designation of such series and the variations in the relative rights and preferences between the shares of such series, or authorize the board of directors to do so.

(i) Limit or deny any existing preemptive rights of the shares of such class.

(j) Cancel or otherwise affect dividends on the shares of such class which have accrued but have not been declared.

§61. Articles of Amendment

The articles of amendment shall be executed in duplicate by the corporation by its president or a vice president and by its secretary or an assistant secretary, and verified by one of the officers signing such articles, and shall set forth:

(a) The name of the corporation.

(b) The amendments so adopted.

(c) The date of the adoption of the amendment by the shareholders, or by the board of directors where no shares have been issued.

(d) The number of shares outstanding, and the number of shares entitled to vote thereon, and if the shares of any class are entitled to vote thereon as a class, the designation and number of outstanding shares entitled to vote thereon of each such class.

(e) The number of shares voted for and against such amendment, respectively, and, if the shares of any class are entitled to vote thereon as a class, the number of shares of each such class voted for and against such amendment, respectively, or if no shares have

been issued, a statement to that effect.

(f) If such amendment provides for an exchange, reclassification or cancellation of issued shares, and if the manner in which the same shall be effected is not set forth in the amendment, then a statement of the manner in which the same shall be effected.

(g) If such amendment effects a change in the amount of stated capital, then a statement of the manner in which the same is effected and a statement, expressed in dollars, of the amount of stated capital as changed by such amendment.

§62. Filing of Aricles of Amendment

Duplicate originals of the articles of amendment shall be delivered to the Secretary of State. If the Secretary of State finds that the articles of amendment conform to law, he shall, when all fees and franchise taxes have been paid as in this Act prescribed:

(a) Endorse on each of such duplicate originals the word "Filed," and the month, day and year of the filing thereof.

(b) File one of such duplicate originals in his office.

(c) Issue a certificate of amendment to which he shall affix the other duplicate original.

The certificate of amendment, together with the duplicate original of the articles of amendment affixed thereto by the Secretary of State, shall be returned to the corporation or its representative.

§63. Effect of Certificate of Amendment

Upon the issuance of the certificate of amendment by the Secretary of State, the amendment shall become effective and the articles of incorporation shall be deemed to be amended accordingly.

No amendment shall affect any existing cause of action in favor of or against such corporation, or any pending suit to which such corporation shall be a party, or the existing rights of persons other than shareholders; and, in the event the corporate name shall be changed by amendment, no suit brought by or against such corporation under its former name shall abate for that reason.

§64. Restated Articles of Incorporation

A domestic corporation may at any time restate its articles of incorporation as theretofore amended, by a resolution adopted by the board of directors.

Upon the adoption of such resolution, restated articles of incorporation shall be executed in duplicate by the corporation by its president or a vice president and by its secretary or assistant secretary and verified by one of the officers signing such articles and shall set forth all of the operative provisions of the articles of incorporation as theretofore amended together with a statement that the restated articles of incorporation correctly set forth without change the corresponding provisions of the articles of incorporation as theretofore amended and that the restated articles of incorporation supersede the original articles of incorporation and all amendments thereto.

Duplicate originals of the restated articles of incorporation shall be delivered to the Secretary of State. If the Secretary of State finds that such restated articles of incorporation conform to law, he shall, when all fees and franchise taxes have been paid as in this Act prescribed:

(1) Endorse on each of such duplicate originals the word "Filed," and the month, day and year of the filing thereof.
(2) File one of such duplicate originals in his office.
(3) Issue a restated certificate of incorporation, to which he shall affix the other duplicate original.

The restated certificate of incorporation, together with the duplicate original of the restated articles of incorporation affixed thereto by the Secretary of State, shall be returned to the corporation or its representative.

Upon the issuance of the restated certificate of incorporation by the Secretary of State, the restated articles of incorporation shall become effective and shall supersede the original articles of incorporation and all amendments thereto.

§65. Amendment of Articles of Incorporation in Reorganization Proceedings

Whenever a plan of reorganization of a corporation has been confirmed by decree or order of a court of competent jurisdiction in proceedings for the reorganization of such corporation, pursuant to the provisions of any applicable statute of the United States relating to reorganizations of corporations, the articles of incorporation of the corporation may be amended, in the manner provided in this section, in as many respects as may be necessary to carry out the plan and put it into effect, so long as the articles of incorporation as amended contain only such provisions as might be lawfully contained in original articles of incorporation at the time of making such amendment.

In particular and without limitation upon such general power of amendment, the articles of incorporation may be amended for such purpose so as to:

(A) Change the corporate name, period of duration or corporate purposes of the corporation;
(B) Repeal, alter or amend the by-laws of the corporation;
(C) Change the aggregate number of shares or shares of any class, which the corporation has authority to issue;
(D) Change the preferences, limitations and relative rights in respect of all or any part of the shares of the corporation, and classify, reclassify or cancel all or any part thereof, whether issued or unissued;
(E) Authorize the issuance of bonds, debentures or other obligations of the corporation, whether or not convertible into shares of any class or bearing warrants or other evidences of optional rights to purchase or subscribe for shares of any class, and fix the terms and conditions thereof; and
(F) Constitute or reconstitute and classify or reclassify the board of directors of the cor-

poration, and appoint directors and officers in place of or in addition to all or any of the directors or officers then in office.

Amendments to the articles of incorporation pursuant to this section shall be made in the following manner:

(a) Articles of amendment approved by decree or order of such court shall be executed and verified in duplicate by such person or persons as the court shall designate or appoint for the purpose, and shall set forth the name of the corporation, the amendments of the articles of incorporation approved by the court, the date of the decree or order approving the articles of amendment, the title of the proceedings in which the decree or order was entered, and a statement that such decree or order was entered by a court having jurisdiction of the proceedings for the reorganization of the corporation pursuant to the provisions of an applicable statute of the United States.

(b) Duplicate originals of the articles of amendment shall be delivered to the Secretary of State. If the Secretary of State finds that the articles of amendment conform to law, he shall, when all fees and franchise taxes have been paid as in this Act prescribed:

(1) Endorse on each of such duplicate originals the word "Filed," and the month, day and year of the filing thereof.

(2) File one of such duplicate originals in his office.

(3) Issue a certificate of amendment to which he shall affix the other duplicate original.

The certificate of amendment, together with the duplicate original of the articles of amendment affixed thereto by the Secretary of State, shall be returned to the corporation or its representative.

Upon the issuance of the certificate of amendment by the Secretary of State, the amendment shall become effective and the articles of incorporation shall be deemed to be amended accordingly, without any action

thereon by the directors or shareholders of the corporation and with the same effect as if the amendment had been adopted by unanimous action of the directors and shareholders of the corporation.

§66. Restriction on Redemption or Purchase of Redeemable Shares

No redemption or purchase of redeemable shares shall be made by a corporation when it is insolvent or when such redemption or purchase would render it insolvent, or which would reduce the net assets below the aggregate amount payable to the holders of shares having prior or equal rights to the assets of the corporation upon involuntary dissolution.

§67. Cancellation of Redeemable Shares by Redemption or Purchase

When redeemable shares of a corporation are redeemed or purchased by the corporation, the redemption or purchase shall effect a cancellation of such shares, and a statement of cancellation shall be filed as provided in this section. Thereupon such shares shall be restored to the status of authorized but unissued shares, unless the articles of incorporation provide that such shares when redeemed or purchased shall not be reissued, in which case the filing of the statement of cancellation shall constitute an amendment to the articles of incorporation and shall reduce the number of shares of the class so cancelled which the corporation is authorized to issue by the number of shares so cancelled.

The statement of cancellation shall be executed in duplicate by the corporation by its president or a vice president and by its secretary or an assistant secretary, and verified by one of the officers signing such statement, and shall set forth:

(a) The name of the corporation.

(b) The number of redeemable shares cancelled through redemption or purchase, itemized by classes and series.

(c) The aggregate number of issued shares,

itemized by classes and series, after giving effect to such cancellation.

(d) The amount, expressed in dollars, of the stated capital of the corporation after giving effect to such cancellation.

(e) If the articles of incorporation provide that the cancelled shares shall not be reissued, the number of shares which the corporation will have authority to issue itemized by classes and series, after giving effect to such cancellation.

Duplicate originals of such statement shall be delivered to the Secretary of State. If the Secretary of State finds that such statement conforms to law, he shall, when all fees and franchise taxes have been paid as in this Act prescribed:

(1) Endorse on each of such duplicate originals the word "Filed," and the month, day and year of the filing thereof.

(2) File one of such duplicate originals in his office.

(3) Return the other duplicate original to the corporation or its representative.

Upon the filing of such statement of cancellation, the stated capital of the corporation shall be deemed to be reduced by that part of the stated capital which was, at the time of such cancellation, represented by the shares so cancelled.

Nothing contained in this section shall be construed to forbid a cancellation of shares or a reduction of stated capital in any other manner permitted by this Act.

§68. Cancellation of Other Reacquired Shares

A corporation may at any time, by resolution of its board of directors, cancel all or any part of the shares of the corporation of any class reacquired by it, other than redeemable shares redeemed or purchased, and in such event a statement of cancellation shall be filed as provided in this section.

The statement of cancellation shall be executed in duplicate by the corporation by its president or a vice president and by its secretary or an assistant secretary, and verified by one of the officers signing such statement, and shall set forth:

(a) The name of the corporation.

(b) The number of reacquired shares cancelled by resolution duly adopted by the board of directors, itemized by classes and series, and the date of its adoption.

(c) The aggregate number of issued shares, itemized by classes and series, after giving effect to such cancellation.

(d) The amount, expressed in dollars, of the stated capital of the corporation after giving effect to such cancellation.

Duplicate originals of such statement shall be delivered to the Secretary of State. If the Secretary of State finds that such statement conforms to law, he shall, when all fees and franchise taxes have been paid as in this Act prescribed:

(1) Endorse on each of such duplicate originals the word "Filed," and the month, day and year of the filing thereof.

(2) File one of such duplicate originals in his office.

(3) Return the other duplicate original to the corporation or its representative.

Upon the filing of such statement of cancellation, the stated capital of the corporation shall be deemed to be reduced by that part of the stated capital which was, at the time of such cancellation, represented by the shares so cancelled, and the shares so cancelled shall be restored to the status of authorized but unissued shares.

Nothing contained in this section shall be construed to forbid a cancellation of shares or a reduction of stated capital in any other manner permitted by this Act.

§69. Reduction of Stated Capital in Certain Cases

A reduction of the stated capital of a corporation, where such reduction is not accompanied by any action requiring an amendment of the articles of incorporation and not accompanied by a cancellation of shares, may be made in the following manner:

(A) The board of directors shall adopt a resolution setting forth the amount of the proposed reduction and the manner in which the reduction shall be effected, and directing that the question of such reduction be submitted to a vote at a meeting of shareholders, which may be either an annual or a special meeting.
(B) Written notice, stating that the purpose or one of the purposes of such meeting is to consider the question of reducing the stated capital of the corporation in the amount and manner proposed by the board of directors, shall be given to each shareholder of record entitled to vote thereon within the time and in the manner provided in this Act for the giving of notice of meetings of shareholders.
(C) At such meeting a vote of the shareholders entitled to vote thereon shall be taken on the question of approving the proposed reduction of stated capital, which shall require for its adoption the affirmative vote of the holders of a majority of the shares entitled to vote thereon.

When a reduction of the stated capital of a corporation has been approved as provided in this section, a statement shall be executed in duplicate by the corporation by its president or a vice president and by its secretary or an assistant secretary, and verified by one of the officers signing such statement, and shall set forth:

(a) The name of the corporation.
(b) A copy of the resolution of the shareholders approving such reduction, and the date of its adoption.
(c) The number of shares outstanding, and the number of shares entitled to vote thereon.
(d) The number of shares voted for and against such reduction, respectively.
(e) A statement of the manner in which such reduction is effected, and a statement, expressed in dollars, of the amount of stated capital of the corporation after giving effect to such reduction.

Duplicate originals of such statement shall be delivered to the Secretary of State. If the Secretary of State finds that such statement conforms to law, he shall, when all fees and franchise taxes have been paid as in this Act prescribed:

(1) Endorse on each of such duplicate originals the word "Filed," and the month, day and year of the filing thereof.
(2) File one of such duplicate originals in his office.
(3) Return the other duplicate original to the corporation or its representative.

Upon the filing of such statement, the stated capital of the corporation shall be reduced as therein set forth.

No reduction of stated capital shall be made under the provisions of this section which would reduce the amount of the aggregate stated capital of the corporation to an amount equal to or less than the aggregate preferential amounts payable upon all issued shares having a preferential right in the assets of the corporation in the event of involuntary liquidation, plus the aggregate par value of all issued shares having a par value but no preferential right in the assets of the corporation in the event of involuntary liquidation.

§70. Special Provisions Relating to Surplus and Reserves

The surplus, if any, created by or arising out of a reduction of the stated capital of a corporation shall be capital surplus.

The capital surplus of a corporation may be increased from time to time by resolution of the board of directors directing that all or a part of the earned surplus of the corporation be transferred to capital surplus.

A corporation may, by resolution of its board of directors, apply any part or all of its capital surplus to the reduction or elimination of any deficit arising from losses, however incurred, but only after first eliminating the earned surplus, if any, of the corporation by applying such losses against earned surplus and only to the extent that such losses exceed the earned surplus, if any. Each such application of capital surplus shall, to the extent thereof, effect a reduction of capital surplus.

A corporation may, by resolution of its board of directors, create a reserve or reserves out of its earned surplus for any proper purpose or purposes, and may abolish any such reserve in the same manner. Earned surplus of the corporation to the extent so reserved shall not be available for the payment of dividends or other distributions by the corporation except as expressly permitted by this Act.

§71. Procedure for Merger

Any two or more domestic corporations may merge into one of such corporations pursuant to a plan of merger approved in the manner provided in this Act.

The board of directors of each corporation shall, by resolution adopted by each such board, approve a plan of merger setting forth:

(a) The names of the corporations proposing to merge, and the name of the corporation into which they propose to merge, which is hereinafter designated as the surviving corporation.
(b) The terms and conditions of the proposed merger.
(c) The manner and basis of converting the shares of each corporation into shares, obligations or other securities of the surviving corporation or of any other corporation or, in whole or in part, into cash or other property.
(d) A statement of any changes in the articles of incorporation of the surviving corporation to be effected by such merger.
(e) Such other provisions with respect to the proposed merger as are deemed necessary or desirable.

§72. Procedure for Consolidation

Any two or more domestic corporations may consolidate into a new corporation pursuant to a plan of consolidation approved in the manner provided in this Act.

The board of directors of each corporation shall, by a resolution adopted by each such board, approve a plan of consolidation setting forth:

(a) The names of the corporations proposing to consolidate, and the name of the new corporation into which they propose to consolidate, which is hereinafter designated as the new corporation.
(b) The terms and conditions of the proposed consolidation.
(c) The manner and basis of converting the shares of each corporation into shares, obligations or other securities of the new corporation or of any other corporation or, in whole or in part, into cash or other property.
(d) With respect to the new corporation, all of the statements required to be set forth in articles of incorporation for corporations organized under this Act.
(e) Such other provisions with respect to the proposed consolidation as are deemed necessary or desirable.

§73. Approval by Shareholders

The board of directors of each corporation, upon approving such plan of merger or plan of consolidation, shall, by resolution, direct that the plan be submitted to a vote at a meeting of shareholders, which may be either an annual or a special meeting. Written notice shall be given to each shareholder of record, whether or not entitled to vote at such meeting, not less than twenty days before such meeting, in the manner provided in this Act for the giving of notice of meetings of shareholders, and, whether the meeting be an annual or a special meeting, shall state that the purpose or one of the purposes is to consider the proposed plan of merger or consolidation. A copy or a summary of the plan of merger or plan of consolidation, as the case may be,.shall be included in or enclosed with such notice.

At each such meeting, a vote of the shareholders shall be taken on the proposed plan of merger or consolidation. The plan of merger or consolidation shall be approved upon receiving the affirmative vote of the holders of a majority of the shares entitled to vote thereon of each such corporation, unless any class of shares of any such corporation is entitled to vote thereon as a class, in which event, as to such corporation, the plan of merger, or consolidation shall be approved upon receiving the affirmative vote of the holders of a majority of the shares of each class of shares entitled to vote thereon as a class and of the total shares entitled to vote thereon. Any class of shares of any such corporation shall be entitled to vote as a class if the plan of merger or consolidation, as the case may be, contains any provision which, if contained in a proposed amendment to articles of incorporation, would entitle such class of shares to vote as a class.

After such approval by a vote of the shareholders of each corporation, and at any time prior to the filing of the articles of merger or consolidation, the merger or consolidation may be abandoned pursuant to provisions therefor, if any, set forth in the plan of merger or consolidation.

§74. Articles of Merger or Consolidation

Upon such approval, articles of merger or articles of consolidation shall be executed in duplicate by each corporation by its president or a vice president and by its secretary or an assistant secretary, and verified by one of the officers of each corporation signing such articles, and shall set forth:

(a) The plan of merger or the plan of consolidation.
(b) As to each corporation, the number of shares outstanding, and, if the shares of any class are entitled to vote as a class, the designation and number of outstanding shares of each such class.
(c) As to each corporation, the number of shares voted for and against such plan, respectively, and, if the shares of any class are entitled to vote as a class, the number of shares of each such class voted for and against such plan, respectively.

Duplicate originals of the articles of merger or articles of consolidation shall be delivered to the Secretary of State. If the Secretary of State finds that such articles conform to law, he shall, when all fees and franchise taxes have been paid as in this Act prescribed:

(1) Endorse on each of such duplicate originals the word "Filed," and the month, day and year of the filing thereof.
(2) File one of such duplicate originals in his office.
(3) Issue a certificate of merger or a certificate of consolidation to which he shall affix the other duplicate original.

The certificate of merger or certificate of consolidation, together with the duplicate original of the articles of merger or articles of consolidation affixed thereto by the Secretary of State, shall be returned to the surviving or new corporation, as the case may be, or its representative.

§75. Merger of Subsidiary Corporation

Any corporation owning at least ninety percent of the outstanding shares of each class of another corporation may merge such other corporation into itself without approval by a vote of the shareholders of either corporation. Its board of directors shall, by resolution, approve a plan of merger setting forth:

(A) The name of the subsidiary corporation and the name of the corporation owning at least ninety percent of its shares, which is hereinafter designated as the surviving corporation.
(B) The manner and basis of converting the shares of the subsidiary corporation into shares, obligations or other securities of the surviving corporation or of any other corporation or, in whole or in part, into cash or other property.

A copy of such plan of merger shall be mailed to each shareholder of record of the subsidiary corporation.

Articles of merger shall be executed in duplicate by the surviving corporation by its president or a vice president and by its secretary or an assistant secretary, and verified by one of its officers signing such articles, and shall set forth:

(a) The plan of merger;

(b) The number of outstanding shares of each class of the subsidiary corporation and the number of such shares of each class owned by the surviving corporation; and

(c) The date of the mailing to shareholders of the subsidiary corporation of a copy of the plan of merger.

On and after the thirtieth day after the mailing of a copy of the plan of merger to shareholders of the subsidiary corporation or upon the waiver thereof by the holders of all outstanding shares duplicate originals of the articles of merger shall be delivered to the Secretary of State. If the Secretary of State finds that such articles conform to law, he shall, when all fees and franchise taxes have been paid as in this Act prescribed:

(1) Endorse on each of such duplicate originals the word "Filed," and the month, day and year of the filing thereof,

(2) File one of such duplicate originals in his office, and

(3) Issue a certificate of merger to which he shall affix the other duplicate original.

The certificate of merger, together with the duplicate original of the articles of merger affixed thereto by the Secretary of State, shall be returned to the surviving corporation or its representative.

§76. Effect of Merger or Consolidation

Upon the issuance of the certificate of merger or the certificate of consolidation by the Secretary of State, the merger or consolidation shall be effected.

When such merger or consolidation has been effected:

(a) The several corporations parties to the plan of merger or consolidation shall be a single corporation, which, in the case of a merger, shall be that corporation designated in the plan of merger as the surviving corporation, and, in the case of a consolidation, shall be the new corporation provided for in the plan of consolidation.

(b) The separate existence of all corporations parties to the plan of merger or consolidation, except the surviving or new cortion, shall cease.

(c) Such surviving or new corporation shall have all the rights, privileges, immunities and powers and shall be subject to all the duties and liabilities of a corporation organized under this Act.

(d) Such surviving or new corporation shall thereupon and thereafter possess all the rights, privileges, immunities, and franchises, of a public as well as of a private nature, of each of the merging or consolidating corporations; and all property, real, personal and mixed, and all debts due on whatever account, including subscriptions to shares, and all other choses in action, and all and every other interest of or belonging to or due to each of the corporations so merged or consolidated, shall be taken and deemed to be transferred to and vested in such single corporation without further act or deed; and the title to any real estate, or any interest therein, vested in any of such corporations shall not revert or be in any way impaired by reason of such merger or consolidation.

(e) Such surviving or new corporation shall thenceforth be responsible and liable for all the liabilities and obligations of each of the corporations so merged or consolidated; and any claim existing or action or proceeding pending by or against any of such corporations may be prosecuted as if such merger or consolidation had not taken place, or such surviving or new corporation may be substituted in its place. Neither the rights of creditors nor any liens upon the property of any such corporation shall be impaired by such merger or consolidation.

(f) In the case of a merger, the articles of

incorporation of the surviving corporation shall be deemed to be amended to the extent, if any, that changes in its articles of incorporation are stated in the plan of merger; and, in the case of a consolidation, the statements set forth in the articles of consolidation and which are required or permitted to be set forth in the articles of incorporation of corporations organized under this Act shall be deemed to be the original articles of incorporation of the new corporation.

§77. Merger or Consolidation of Domestic and Foreign Corporations

One or more foreign corporations and one or more domestic corporations may be merged or consolidated in the following manner, if such merger or consolidation is permitted by the laws of the state under which each such foreign corporation is organized.

(a) Each domestic corporation shall comply with the provisions of this Act with respect to the merger or consolidation, as the case may be, of domestic corporations and each foreign corporation shall comply with the applicable provisions of the laws of the state under which it is organized.

(b) If the surviving or new corporation, as the case may be, is to be governed by the laws of any state other than this State, it shall comply with the provisions of this Act with respect to foreign corporations if it is to transact business in this State, and in every case it shall file with the Secretary of State of this State:

(1) An agreement that it may be served with process in this State in any proceeding for the enforcement of any obligation of any domestic corporation which is a party to such merger or consolidation and in any proceeding for the enforcement of the rights of a dissenting shareholder of any such domestic corporation against the surviving or new corporation;

(2) An irrevocable appointment of the Secretary of State of this State as its agent to accept service of process in any such proceeding; and

(3) An agreement that it will promptly pay to the dissenting shareholders of any such domestic corporation the amount, if any, to which they shall be entitled under the provisions of this Act with respect to the rights of dissenting shareholders.

The effect of such merger or consolidation shall be the same as in the case of the merger or consolidation of domestic corporations, if the surviving or new corporation is to be governed by the laws of this State. If the surviving or new corporation is to be governed by the laws of any state other than this State, the effect of such merger or consolidation shall be the same as in the case of the merger or consolidation of domestic corporations except insofar as the laws of such other state provide otherwise.

At any time prior to the filing of the articles of merger or consolidation, the merger or consolidation may be abandoned pursuant to provisions therefor, if any, set forth in the plan of merger or consolidation.

§78. Sale of Assets in Regular Course of Business and Mortgage or Pledge of Assets

The sale, lease, exchange, or other disposition of all, or substantially all, the property and assets of a corporation in the usual and regular course of its business and the mortgage or pledge of any or all property and assets of a corporation whether or not in the usual and regular course of business may be made upon such terms and conditions and for such consideration, which may consist in whole or in part of cash or other property, including shares, obligations or other securities of any other corporation, domestic or foreign, as shall be authorized by its board of directors; and in any such case no authorization or consent of the shareholders shall be required.

§79. Sale of Assets Other Than in Regular Course of Business

A sale, lease, exchange, or other disposition of all, or substantially all, the property and assets, with or without the good will, of a corporation, if not in the usual and regular course of its business, may be made upon such terms and conditions and for such consideration, which may consist in whole or in part of cash or other property, including shares, obligations or other securities of any other corporation, domestic or foreign, as may be authorized in the following manner:

(a) The board of directors shall adopt a resolution recommending such sale, lease, exchange, or other disposition and directing the submission thereof to a vote at a meeting of shareholders, which may be either an annual or a special meeting.

(b) Written notice shall be given to each shareholder of record, whether or not entitled to vote at such meeting, not less than twenty days before such meeting, in the manner provided in this Act for the giving of notice of meetings of shareholders, and, whether the meeting be an annual or a special meeting, shall state that the purpose, or one of the purposes is to consider the proposed sale, lease, exchange, or other disposition.

(c) At such meeting the shareholders may authorize such sale, lease, exchange, or other disposition and may fix, or may authorize the board of directors to fix, any or all of the terms and conditions thereof and the consideration to be received by the corporation therefor. Such authorization shall require the affirmative vote of the holders of a majority of the shares of the corporation entitled to vote thereon, unless any class of shares is entitled to vote thereon as a class, in which event such authorization shall require the affirmative vote of the holders of a majority of the shares of each class of shares entitled to vote as a class thereon and of the total shares entitled to vote thereon.

(d) After such authorization by a vote of shareholders, the board of directors never-theless, in its discretion, may abandon such sale, lease, exchange, or other disposition of assets, subject to the rights of third parties under any contracts relating thereto, without further action or approval by shareholders.

§80. Right of Shareholders to Dissent

Any shareholder of a corporation shall have the right to dissent from any of the following corporate actions:

(a) Any plan of merger or consolidation to which the corporation is a party; or

(b) Any sale or exchange of all or substantially all of the property and assets of the corporation not made in the usual and regular course of its business, including a sale in dissolution, but not including a sale pursuant to an order of a court having jurisdiction in the premises or a sale for cash on terms requiring that all or substantially all of the net proceeds of sale be distributed to the shareholders in accordance with their respective interests within one year after the date of sale.

A shareholder may dissent as to less than all of the shares registered in his name. In that event, his rights shall be determined as if the shares as to which he has dissented and his other shares were registered in the names of different shareholders.

This section shall not apply to the shareholders of the surviving corporation in a merger if a vote of the shareholders of such corporation is not necessary to authorize such merger. Nor shall it apply to the holders of shares of any class or series if the shares of such class or series were registered on a national securities exchange on the date fixed to determine the shareholders entitled to vote at the meeting of shareholders at which a plan of merger or consolidation or a proposed sale or exchange of property and assets is to be acted upon unless the articles of incorporation of the corporation shall otherwise provide.

§81. Rights of Dissenting Shareholders

Any shareholder electing to exercise such right of dissent shall file with the corporation, prior to or at the meeting of shareholders at which such proposed corporate action is submitted to a vote, a written objection to such proposed corporate action. If such proposed corporate action be approved by the required vote and such shareholder shall not have voted in favor thereof, such shareholder may, within ten days after the date on which the vote was taken or if a corporation is to be merged without a vote of its shareholders into another corporation, any of its shareholders may, within fifteen days after the plan of such merger shall have been mailed to such shareholders, make written demand on the corporation, or, in the case of a merger or consolidation, on the surviving or new corporation, domestic or foreign, for payment of the fair value of such shareholder's shares, and, if such proposed corporate action is effected, such corporation shall pay to such shareholder, upon surrender of the certificate or certificates representing such shares, the fair value thereof as of the day prior to the date on which the vote was taken approving the proposed corporate action, excluding any appreciation or depreciation in anticipation of such corporate action. Any shareholder failing to make demand within the applicable ten-day or fifteen-day period shall be bound by the terms of the proposed corporate action. Any shareholder making such demand shall thereafter be entitled only to payment as in this section provided and shall not be entitled to vote or to exercise any other rights of a shareholder.

No such demand may be withdrawn unless the corporation shall consent thereto. If, however, such demand shall be withdrawn upon consent, or if the proposed corporate action shall be abandoned or rescinded or the shareholders shall revoke the authority to effect such action, or if, in the case of a merger, on the date of the filing of the articles of merger the surviving corporation is the owner of all the outstanding shares of the other corporations, domestic and foreign, that are parties to the merger, or if no demand or petition for the determination of fair value by a court shall have been made or filed within the time provided in this section, or if a court of competent jurisdiction shall determine that such shareholder is not entitled to the relief provided by this section, then the right of such shareholder to be paid the fair value of his shares shall cease and his status as a shareholder shall be restored, without prejudice to any corporate proceedings which may have been taken during the interim.

Within ten days after such corporate action is effected, the corporation, or, in the case of a merger or consolidation, the surviving or new corporation, domestic or foreign, shall give written notice thereof to each dissenting shareholder who has made demand as herein provided, and shall make a written offer to each such shareholder to pay for such shares at a specified price deemed by such corporation to be the fair value thereof. Such notice and offer shall be accompanied by a balance sheet of the corporation the shares of which the dissenting shareholder holds, as of the latest available date and not more than twelve months prior to the making of such offer, and a profit and loss statement of such corporation for the twelve months' period ended on the date of such balance sheet.

If within thirty days after the date on which such corporate action was effected the fair value of such shares is agreed upon between any such dissenting shareholder and the corporation, payment therefor shall be made within ninety days after the date on which such corporate action was effected, upon surrender of the certificate or certificates representing such shares. Upon payment of the agreed value the dissenting shareholder shall cease to have any interest in such shares.

If within such period of thirty days a dissenting shareholder and the corporation do not so agree, then the corporation, within thirty days after receipt of written demand from any dissenting shareholder given within sixty days after the date on which such corporate action was effected, shall, or at its election at any time within such period of sixty days may, file a petition in any court of competent jurisdiction in the county in this State where the registered office of the corporation is located requesting that the fair value of such shares be found and determined. If, in the case of a merger or consolidation, the surviving or new corporation is a foreign corporation without a registered office in this State, such petition shall be filed in the county where the registered office of the domestic corporation was last located. If the corporation shall fail to institute the proceeding as herein provided, any dissenting shareholder may do so in the name of the corporation. All dissenting shareholders, wherever residing, shall be made parties to the proceeding as an action against their shares quasi in rem. A copy of the petition shall be served on each dissenting shareholder who is a resident of this State and shall be served by registered or certified mail on each dissenting shareholder who is a nonresident. Service on nonresidents shall also be made by publication as provided by law. The jurisdiction of the court shall be plenary and exclusive. All shareholders who are parties to the proceeding shall be entitled to judgment against the corporation for the amount of the fair value of their shares. The court may, if it so elects, appoint one or more persons as appraisers to receive evidence and recommend a decision on the question of fair value. The appraisers shall have such power and authority as shall be specified in the order of their appointment or an amendment thereof. The judgment shall be payable only upon and concurrently with the surrender to the corporation of the certificate or certificates representing such shares. Upon payment of the judgment, the dissenting shareholder shall cease to have any interest in such shares.

The judgment shall include an allowance for interest at such rate as the court may find to be fair and equitable in all the circumstances, from the date on which the vote was taken on the proposed corporate action to the date of payment.

The costs and expenses of any such proceed-ing shall be determined by the court and shall be assessed against the corporation, but all or any part of such costs and expenses may be apportioned and assessed as the court may deem equitable against any or all of the dissenting shareholders who are parties to the proceeding to whom the corporation shall have made an offer to pay for the shares if the court shall find that the action of such shareholders in failing to accept such offer was arbitrary or vexatious or not in good faith. Such expenses shall include reasonable compensation for and reasonable expenses of the appraisers, but shall exclude the fees and expenses of counsel for and experts employed by any party; but if the fair value of the shares as determined materially exceeds the amount which the corporation offered to pay therefor, or if no offer was made, the court in its discretion may award to any shareholder who is a party to the proceeding such sum as the court may determine to be reasonable compensation to any expert or experts employed by the shareholder in the proceeding.

Within twenty days after demanding payment for his shares, each shareholder demanding payment shall submit the certificate or certificates representing his shares to the corporation for notation thereon that such demand has been made. His failure to do so shall, at the option of the corporation, terminate his rights under this section unless a court of competent jurisdiction, for good and sufficient cause shown, shall otherwise direct. If shares represented by a certificate on which notation has been so made shall be transferred, each new certificate issued therefor shall bear similar notation, together with the name of the original dissenting holder of such shares, and a transferee of such shares shall acquire by such transfer no rights in the corporation other than those which the original dissenting shareholder had after making demand for payment of the fair value thereof.

Shares acquired by a corporation pursuant to payment of the agreed value therefor or to payment of the judgment entered therefor, as in this section provided, may be held and disposed of by such corporation as in the case of other treasury shares, except that, in the case of a merger or consolidation, they may be held and disposed of as the plan of merger or consolidation may otherwise provide.

§82. Voluntary Dissolution by Incorporators

A corporation which has not commenced business and which has not issued any shares, may be voluntarily dissolved by its incorporators at any time in the following manner:

(a) Articles of dissolution shall be executed in duplicate by a majority of the incorporators, and verified by them, and shall set forth:
    (1) The name of the corporation.
    (2) The date of issuance of its certificate of incorporation.
    (3) That none of its shares has been issued.
    (4) That the corporation has not commenced business.
    (5) That the amount, if any, actually paid in on subscriptions for its shares, less any part thereof disbursed for necessary expenses, has been returned to those entitled thereto.
    (6) That no debts of the corporation remain unpaid.
    (7) That a majority of the incorporators elect that the corporation be dissolved.
(b) Duplicate originals of the articles of dissolution shall be delivered to the Secretary of State. If the Secretary of State finds that the articles of dissolution conform to law, he shall, when all fees and franchise taxes have been paid as in this Act prescribed:
    (1) Endorse on each of such duplicate originals the word "Filed," and the month, day and year of the filing thereof.
    (2) File one of such duplicate originals in his office.
    (3) Issue a certificate of dissolution to which he shall affix the other duplicate original.

The certificate of dissolution, together with the duplicate original of the articles of dissolution affixed thereto by the Secretary of State,

shall be returned to the incorporators or their representative. Upon the issuance of such certificate of dissolution by the Secretary of State, the existence of the corporation shall cease.

§83. Voluntary Dissolution by Consent of Shareholders

A corporation may be voluntarily dissolved by the written consent of all of its shareholders.

Upon the execution of such written consent, a statement of intent to dissolve shall be executed in duplicate by the corporation by its president or a vice president and by its secretary or an assistant secretary, and verified by one of the officers signing such statement, which statement shall set forth:

(a) The name of the corporation.
(b) The names and respective addresses of its officers.
(c) The names and respective addresses of its directors.
(d) A copy of the written consent signed by all shareholders of the corporation.
(e) A statement that such written consent has been signed by all shareholders of the corporation or signed in their names by their attorneys thereunto duly authorized.

§84. Voluntary Dissolution by Act of Corporation

A corporation may be dissolved by the act of the corporation, when authorized in the following manner:

(a) The board of directors shall adopt a resolution recommending that the corporation be dissolved, and directing that the question of such dissolution be submitted to a vote at a meeting of shareholders, which may be either an annual or a special meeting.
(b) Written notice shall be given to each shareholder of record entitled to vote at such meeting within the time and in the manner provided in this Act for the giving of notice of meetings of shareholders, and, whether the meeting be an annual or special meeting,

shall state that the purpose, or one of the purposes, of such meeting is to consider the advisability of dissolving the corporation.

(c) At such meeting a vote of shareholders entitled to vote thereat shall be taken on a resolution to dissolve the corporation. Such resolution shall be adopted upon receiving the affirmative vote of the holders of a majority of the shares of the corporation entitled to vote thereon, unless any class of shares is entitled to vote thereon as a class, in which event the resolution shall be adopted upon receiving the affirmative vote of the holders of a majority of the shares of each class of shares entitled to vote thereon as a class and of the total shares entitled to vote thereon.

(d) Upon the adoption of such resolution, a statement of intent to dissolve shall be executed in duplicate by the corporation by its president or a vice president and by its secretary or an assistant secretary, and verified by one of the officers signing such statement, which statement shall set forth:

(1) The name of the corporation.

(2) The names and respective addresses of its officers.

(3) The names and respective addresses of its directors.

(4) A copy of the resolution adopted by the shareholders authorizing the dissolution of the corporation.

(5) The number of shares outstanding, and, if the shares of any class entitled to vote as a class, the designation and number of outstanding shares of each such class.

(6) The number of shares voted for and against the resolution, respectively, and, if the shares of any class are entitled to vote as a class, the number of shares of each such class voted for and against the resolution, respectively.

§85. Filing of Statement of Intent to Dissolve

Duplicate originals of the statement of intent to dissolve, whether by consent of shareholders or by act of the corporation, shall be delivered to the Secretary of State. If the Secretary of State finds that such statement conforms to law, he shall, when all fees and franchise taxes have been paid as in this Act prescribed:

(a) Endorse on each of such duplicate originals the word "Filed," and the month, day and year of the filing thereof.

(b) File one of such duplicate originals in his office.

(c) Return the other duplicate original to the corporation or its representative.

§86. Effect of Statement of Intent to Dissolve

Upon the filing by the Secretary of State of a statement of intent to dissolve, whether by consent of shareholders or by act of the corporation, the corporation shall cease to carry on its business, except insofar as may be necessary for the winding up thereof, but its corporate existence shall continue until a certificate of dissolution has been issued by the Secretary of State or until a decree dissolving the corporation has been entered by a court of competent jurisdiction as in this Act provided.

§87. Procedure after Filing of Statement of Intent to Dissolve

After the filing by the Secretary of State of a statement of intent to dissolve:

(a) The corporation shall immediately cause notice thereof to be mailed to each known creditor of the corporation.

(b) The corporation shall proceed to collect its assets, convey and dispose of such of its properties as are not to be distributed in kind to its shareholders, pay, satisfy and discharge its liabilities and obligations and do all other acts required to liquidate its business and affairs, and, after paying or adequately providing for the payment of all its obligations, distribute the remainder of its assets, either in cash or in kind, among its shareholders according to their respective rights and interests.

(c) The corporation, at any time during the liquidation of its business and affairs, may make application to a court of competent jurisdiction within the state and judicial subdivision in which the registered office or principal place of business of the corporation is situated, to have the liquidation continued under the supervision of the court as provided in this Act.

§88. Revocation of Voluntary Dissolution Proceedings by Consent of Shareholders

By the written consent of all of its shareholders, a corporation may, at any time prior to the issuance of a certificate of dissolution by the Secretary of State, revoke voluntary dissolution proceedings theretofore taken, in the following manner:

Upon the execution of such written consent, a statement of revocation of voluntary dissolution proceedings shall be executed in duplicate by the corporation by its president or a vice president and by its secretary or an assistant secretary, and verified by one of the officers signing such statement, which statement shall set forth:

(a) The name of the corporation.

(b) The names and respective addresses of its officers.

(c) The names and respective addresses of its directors.

(d) A copy of the written consent signed by all shareholders of the corporation revoking such voluntary dissolution proceedings.

(e) That such written consent has been signed by all shareholders of the corporation or signed in their names by their attorneys thereunto duly authorized.

§89. Revocation of Voluntary Dissolution Proceedings by Act of Corporation

By the act of the corporation, a corporation may, at any time prior to the issuance of a certificate of dissolution by the Secretary of State, revoke voluntary dissolution proceedings theretofore taken, in the following manner:

(a) The board of directors shall adopt a resolution recommending that the voluntary dissolution proceedings be revoked, and directing that the question of such revocation be submitted to a vote at a special meeting of shareholders.

(b) Written notice, stating that the purpose or one of the purposes of such meeting is to consider the advisability of revoking the voluntary dissolution proceedings, shall be given to each shareholder of record entitled to vote at such meeting within the time and in the manner provided in this Act for the giving of notice of special meetings of shareholders.

(c) At such meeting a vote of the shareholders entitled to vote thereat shall be taken on a resolution to revoke the voluntary dissolution proceedings, which shall require for its adoption the affirmative vote of the holders of a majority of the shares entitled to vote thereon.

(d) Upon the adoption of such resolution, a statement of revocation of voluntary dissolution proceedings shall be executed in duplicate by the corporation by its president or a vice president and by its secretary or an assistant secretary, and verified by one of the officers signing such statement, which statement shall set forth:

(1) The name of the corporation.

(2) The names and respective addresses of its officers.

(3) The names and respective addresses of its directors.

(4) A copy of the resolution adopted by the shareholders revoking the voluntary dissolution proceedings.

(5) The number of shares outstanding.

(6) The number of shares voted for and against the resolution, respectively.

§90. Filing of Statement of Revocation of Voluntary Dissolution Proceedings

Duplicate originals of the statement of revocation of voluntary dissolution proceedings, whether by consent of shareholders or by act of the corporation, shall be delivered to the Secretary of State. If the Secretary of State finds that such statement conforms to law, he shall, when all fees and franchise taxes have been paid as in this Act prescribed:

(a) Endorse on each of such duplicate originals the word "Filed," and the month, day and year of the filing thereof.

(b) File one of such duplicate originals in his office.

(c) Return the other duplicate original to the corporation or its representative.

§91. Effect of Statement of Revocation of Voluntary Dissolution Proceedings

Upon the filing by the Secretary of State of a statement of revocation of voluntary dissolution proceedings, whether by consent of shareholders or by act of the corporation, the revocation of the voluntary dissolution proceedings shall become effective and the corporation may again carry on its business.

§92. Articles of Dissolution

If voluntary dissolution proceedings have not been revoked, then when all debts, liabilities and obligations of the corporation have been paid and discharged, or adequate provision has been made therefor, and all of the remaining property and assets of the corporation have been distributed to its shareholders, articles of dissolution shall be executed in duplicate by the corporation by its president or a vice president and by its secretary or an assistant secretary, and verified by one of the officers signing such statement, which statement shall set forth:

(a) The name of the corporation.

(b) That the Secretary of State has theretofore filed a statement of intent to dissolve the corporation, and the date on which such statement was filed.

(c) That all debts, obligations and liabilities of the corporation have been paid and discharged or that adequate provision has been made therefor.

(d) That all the remaining property and assets of the corporation have been distributed among its shareholders in accordance with their respective rights and interests.

(e) That there are no suits pending against the corporation in any court, or that adequate provision has been made for the satisfaction of any judgment, order or decree which may be entered against it in any pending suit.

§93. Filing of Articles of Dissolution

Duplicate originals of such articles of dissolution shall be delivered to the Secretary of State. If the Secretary of State finds that such articles of dissolution conform to law, he shall, when all fees and franchise taxes have been paid as in this Act prescribed:

(a) Endorse on each of such duplicate originals the word "Filed," and the month, day and year of the filing thereof.

(b) File one of such duplicate originals in his office.

(c) Issue a certificate of dissolution to which he shall affix the other duplicate original.

The certificate of dissolution, together with the duplicate original of the articles of dissolution affixed thereto by the Secretary of State, shall be returned to the representative of the dissolved corporation. Upon the issuance of such certificate of dissolution the existence of the corporation shall cease, except for the purpose of suits, other proceedings and appropriate corporate action by shareholders, directors and officers as provided in this Act.

§94. Involuntary Dissolution

A corporation may be dissolved involuntarily by a decree of the . . . . court in an action filed by the Attorney General when it is established that:

(a) The corporation has failed to file its annual report within the time required by this Act, or has failed to pay its franchise tax on or before the first day of August of the year in which such franchise tax becomes due and payable; or

(b) The corporation procured its articles of incorporation through fraud; or

(c) The corporation has continued to exceed or abuse the authority conferred upon it by law; or

(d) The corporation has failed for thirty days to appoint and maintain a registered agent in this State; or

(e) The corporation has failed for thirty days after change of its registered office or registered agent to file in the office of the Secretary of State a statement of such change.

§95. Notification to Attorney General

The Secretary of State, on or before the last day of December of each year, shall certify to the Attorney General the names of all corporations which have failed to file their annual reports or to pay franchise taxes in accordance with the provisions of this Act, together with the facts pertinent thereto. He shall also certify, from time to time, the names of all corporations which have given other cause for dissolution as provided in this Act, together with the facts pertinent thereto. Whenever the Secretary of State shall certify the name of a corporation to the Attorney General as having given any cause for dissolution, the Secretary of State shall concurrently mail to the corporation at its registered office a notice that such certification has been made. Upon the receipt of such certification, the Attorney General shall file an action in the name of the State against such corporation for its dissolution. Every such certificate from the Secretary of State to the Attorney General pertaining to the failure of a corporation to file an annual report or pay a franchise tax shall be taken and received in all courts as prima facie evidence of the facts therein stated. If, before action is filed, the corporation shall file its annual report or pay its franchise tax, together with all penalties thereon, or shall appoint or maintain a registered agent as provided in this Act, or shall file with the Secretary of State the required statement of change of registered office or registered agent, such fact shall be forthwith certified by the Secretary of State to the Attorney General and he shall not file an action against such corporation for such cause. If, after action is filed, the corporation shall file its annual report or pay its franchise tax, together with all penalties

thereon, or shall appoint or maintain a registered agent as provided in this Act, or shall file with the Secretary of State the required statement of change of registered office or registered agent, and shall pay the costs of such action, the action for such cause shall abate.

§96. Venue and Process

Every action for the involuntary dissolution of a corporation shall be commenced by the Attorney General either in the . . . . court of the county in which the registered office of the corporation is situated, or in the . . . . court of . . . . county. Summons shall issue and be served as in other civil actions. If process is returned not found, the Attorney General shall cause publication to be made as in other civil cases in some newspaper published in the county where the registered office of the corporation is situated, containing a notice of the pendency of such action, the title of the court, the title of the action, and the date on or after which default may be entered. The Attorney General may include in one notice the names of any number of corporations against which actions are then pending in the same court. The Attorney General shall cause a copy of such notice to be mailed to the corporation at its registered office within ten days after the first publication thereof. The certificate of the Attorney General of the mailing of such notice shall be prima facie evidence thereof. Such notice shall be published at least once each week for two successive weeks, and the first publication thereof may begin at any time after the summons has been returned. Unless a corporation shall have been served with summons, no default shall be taken against it earlier than thirty days after the first publication of such notice.

§97. Jurisdiction of Court to Liquidate Assets and Business of Corporation

The . . . . . . courts shall have full power to liquidate the assets and business of a corporation:

(a) In an action by a shareholder when it is established:

> (1) That the directors are deadlocked in the management of the corporate affairs and the shareholders are unable to break the deadlock, and that irreparable injury to the corporation is being suffered or is threatened by reason thereof; or
>
> (2) That the acts of the directors or those in control of the corporation are illegal, oppressive or fraudulent; or
>
> (3) That the shareholders are deadlocked in voting power, and have failed, for a period which includes at least two consecutive annual meeting dates, to elect successors to directors whose terms have expired or would have expired upon the election of their successors; or
>
> (4) That the corporate assets are being misapplied or wasted.

(b) In an action by a creditor:

> (1) When the claim of the creditor has been reduced to judgment and an execution thereon returned unsatisfied and it is established that the corporation is insolvent; or
>
> (2) When the corporation has admitted in writing that the claim of the creditor is due and owing and it is established that the corporation is insolvent.

(c) Upon application by a corporation which has filed a statement of intent to dissolve, as provided in this Act, to have its liquidation continued under the supervision of the court.

(d) When an action has been filed by the Attorney General to dissolve a corporation and it is established that liquidation of its business and affairs should precede the entry of a decree of dissolution.

Proceedings under clause (a), (b) or (c) of this section shall be brought in the county in which the registered office of the principal office of the corporation is situated.

It shall not be necessary to make shareholders parties to any such action or proceeding unless relief is sought against them personally.

§98. Procedure in Liquidation of Corporation by Court

In proceedings to liquidate the assets and business of a corporation the court shall have power to issue injunctions, to appoint a receiver or receivers pendente lite, with such powers and duties as the court, from time to time, may direct, and to take such other proceedings as may be requisite to preserve the corporate assets wherever situated, and carry on the business of the corporation until a full hearing can be had.

After a hearing had upon such notice as the court may direct to be given to all parties to the proceedings and to any other parties in interest designated by the court, the court may appoint a liquidating receiver or receivers with authority to collect the assets of the corporation, including all amounts owing to the corporation by subscribers on account of any unpaid portion of the consideration for the issuance of shares. Such liquidating receiver or receivers shall have authority, subject to the order of the court, to sell, convey and dispose of all or any part of the assets of the corporation wherever situated, either at public or private sale. The assets of the corporation or the proceeds resulting from a sale, conveyance or other disposition thereof shall be applied to the expenses of such liquidation and to the payment of the liabilities and obligations of the corporation, and any remaining assets or proceeds shall be distributed among its shareholders according to their respective rights and interests. The order appointing such liquidating receiver or receivers shall state their powers and duties. Such powers and duties may be increased or diminished at any time during the proceedings.

The court shall have power to allow from time to time as expenses of the liquidation compensation to the receiver or receivers and to attorneys in the proceeding, and to direct the payment thereof out of the assets of the corporation or the proceeds of any sale or disposition of such assets.

A receiver of a corporation appointed under the provisions of this section shall have authority to sue and defend in all courts in his own name as receiver of such corporation. The court appointing such receiver shall have exclusive jurisdiction of the corporation and its property, wherever situated.

§99. Qualifications of Receivers

A receiver shall in all cases be a natural person or a corporation authorized to act as receiver, which corporation may be a domestic corporation or a foreign corporation authorized to transact business in this State, and shall in all cases give such bond as the court may direct with such sureties as the court may require.

§100. Filing of Claims in Liquidation Proceedings

In proceedings to liquidate the assets and business of a corporation the court may require all creditors of the corporation to file with the clerk of the court or with the receiver, in such form as the court may prescribe, proofs under oath of their respective claims. If the court requires the filing of claims it shall fix a date, which shall be not less than four months from the date of the order, as the last day for the filing of claims, and shall prescribe the notice that shall be given to creditors and claimants of the date so fixed. Prior to the date so fixed, the court may extend the time for the filing of claims. Creditors and claimants failing to file proofs of claim on or before the date so fixed may be barred, by order of court, from participating in the distribution of the assets of the corporation.

§101. Discontinuance of Liquidation Proceedings

The liquidation of the assets and business of a corporation may be discontinued at any time during the liquidation proceedings when it is established that cause for liquidation no longer exists. In such event the court shall dismiss the proceedings and direct the receiver to redeliver to the corporation all its remaining property and assets.

§102. Decree of Involuntary Dissolution

In proceedings to liquidate the assets and business of a corporation, when the costs and expenses of such proceedings and all debts, obligations and liabilities of the corporation shall have been paid and discharged and all of its remaining property and assets distributed to its shareholders, or in case its property and assets are not sufficient to satisfy and discharge such costs, expenses, debts and obligations, all the property and assets have been applied so far as they will go to their payment, the court shall enter a decree dissolving the corporation, whereupon the existence of the corporation shall cease.

§103. Filing of Decree of Dissolution

In case the court shall enter a decree dissolving a corporation, it shall be the duty of the clerk of such court to cause a certified copy of the decree to be filed with the Secretary of State. No fee shall be charged by the Secretary of State for the filing thereof.

§104. Deposit with State Treasurer of Amount Due Certain Shareholders

Upon the voluntary or involuntary dissolution of a corporation, the portion of the assets distributable to a creditor or shareholder who is unknown or cannot be found, or who is under disability and there is no person legally competent to receive such distributive portion, shall be reduced to cash and deposited with the State Treasurer and shall be paid over to such creditor or shareholder or to his legal representative upon proof satisfactory to the State Treasurer of his right thereto.

§105. Survival of Remedy after Dissolution

The dissolution of a corporation either (1) by the issuance of a certificate of dissolution by the Secretary of State, or (2) by a decree of court when the court has not liquidated the assets and business of the corporation as provided in this Act, or (3) by expiration of its period of duration, shall not take away or impair any remedy available to or against such corporation, its directors, officers, or shareholders, for any right or claim existing, or any liability incurred, prior to such dissolution if action or other proceeding thereon is commenced within two years after the date of such dissolution. Any such action or proceeding by or against the corporation may be prosecuted or defended by the corporation in its corporate name. The shareholders, directors and officers shall have power to take such corporate or other action as shall be appropriate to protect such remedy, right or claim. If such corporation was dissolved by the expiration of its period of duration, such corporation may amend its articles of incorporation at any time during such period of two years so as to extend its period of duration.

§106. Admission of Foreign Corporation

No foreign corporation shall have the right to transact business in this State until it shall have procured a certificate of authority so to do from the Secretary of State. No foreign corporation shall be entitled to procure a certificate of authority under this Act to transact in this State any business which a corporation organized under this Act is not permitted to transact. A foreign corporation shall not be denied a certificate of authority by reason of the fact that the laws of the state or country under which such corporation is organized governing its organization and internal affairs differ from the laws of this State, and nothing in this Act contained shall be construed to authorize this State to regulate the organization or the internal affairs of such corporation.

Without excluding other activities which may not constitute transacting business in this State, a foreign corporation shall not be considered to be transacting business in this State, for the purposes of this Act, by reason of carrying on in this State any one or more of the following activities:

(a) Maintaining or defending any action or suit or any administrative or arbitration proceeding, or effecting the settlement thereof or the settlement of claims or disputes.

(b) Holding meetings of its directors or shareholders or carrying on other activities concerning its internal affairs.

(c) Maintaining bank accounts.

(d) Maintaining offices or agencies for the transfer, exchange and registration of its securities, or appointing and maintaining trustees or depositaries with relation to its securities.

(e) Effecting sales through independent contractors.

(f) Soliciting or procuring orders, whether by mail or through employees or agents or otherwise, where such orders require acceptance without this State before becoming binding contracts.

(g) Creating evidences of debt, mortgages or liens on real or personal property.

(h) Securing or collecting debts or enforcing any rights in property securing the same.

(i) Transacting any business in interstate commerce.

(j) Conducting an isolated transaction completed within a period of thirty days and not in the course of a number of repeated transactions of like nature.

§107. Powers of Foreign Corporation

A foreign corporation which shall have received a certificate of authority under this Act shall, until a certificate of revocation or of withdrawal shall have been issued as provided in this Act, enjoy the same, but no greater, rights and privileges as a domestic corporation organized for the purposes set forth in the application pursuant to which such certificate of authority is issued; and, except as in this Act otherwise provided, shall be subject to the same duties, restrictions, penalties and liabilities now or hereafter imposed upon a domestic corporation of like character.

§108. Corporate Name of Foreign Corporation

No certificate of authority shall be issued to a foreign corporation unless the corporate name of such corporation:

(a) Shall contain the word "corporation," "company," "incorporated," or "limited," or shall contain an abbreviation of one of such words, or such corporation shall, for use in this State, add at the end of its name one of such words or an abbreviation thereof.

(b) Shall not contain any word or phrase which indicates or implies that it is organized for any purpose other than one or more of the purposes contained in its articles of incorporation or that it is authorized or empowered to conduct the business of banking or insurance.

(c) Shall not be the same as, or deceptively similar to, the name of any domestic corporation existing under the laws of this State or any foreign corporation authorized to transact business in this State, or a name the exclusive right to which is, at the time, reserved in the manner provided in this Act, or the name of a corporation which has in effect a registration of its name as provided in this Act, except that this provision shall not apply if the foreign corporation applying for a certificate of authority files with the Secretary of State any one of the following:

(1) a resolution of its board of directors adopting a fictitious name for use in transacting business in this State which fictitious name is not deceptively similar to the name of any domestic corporation or of any foreign corporation authorized to transact business in this State or to any name reserved or registered as provided in this Act, or

(2) the written consent of such other corporation or holder of a reserved or registered name to use the same or deceptively similar name and one or more words are added to make such name distinguishable from such other name, or

(3) a certified copy of a final decree of a court of competent jurisdiction establishing the prior right of such foreign corporation to the use of such name in this State.

§109. Change of Name by Foreign Corporation

Whenever a foreign corporation which is authorized to transact business in this State shall change its name to one under which a certificate of authority would not be granted to it on application therefor, the certificate of authority of such corporation shall be suspended and it shall not thereafter transact any business in this State until it has changed its name to a name which is available to it under the laws of this State or has otherwise complied with the provisions of this Act.

§110. Application for Certificate of Authority

A foreign corporation, in order to procure a certificate of authority to transact business in this State, shall make application therefor to the Secretary of State, which application shall set forth:

(a) The name of the corporation and the state or country under the laws of which it is incorporated.

(b) If the name of the corporation does not contain the word "corporation," "company," "incorporated," or "limited," or does not contain an abbreviation of one of such words, then the name of the corporation with the word or abbreviation which it elects to add thereto for use in this State.

(c) The date of incorporation and the period of duration of the corporation.

(d) The address of the principal office of the corporation in the state or country under the laws of which it is incorporated.

(e) The address of the proposed registered office of the corporation in this State, and the name of its proposed registered agent in this State at such address.

(f) The purpose or purposes of the corporation which it proposes to pursue in the transaction of business in this State.

(g) The names and respective addresses of the directors and officers of the corporation.

(h) A statement of the aggregate number of shares which the corporation has authority to issue, itemized by classes, par value of shares, shares without par value, and series, if any, within a class.

(i) A statement of the aggregate number of issued shares itemized by classes, par value of shares, shares without par value, and series, if any, within a class.

(j) A statement, expressed in dollars, of the amount of stated capital of the corporation, as defined in this Act.

(k) An estimate, expressed in dollars, of the value of all property to be owned by the corporation for the following year, wherever located, and an estimate of the value of the property of the corporation to be located within this State during such year, and an estimate, expressed in dollars, of the gross amount of business which will be transacted by the corporation during such year, and an estimate of the gross amount thereof which will be transacted by the corporation at or from places of business in this State during such year.

(l) Such additional information as may be necessary or appropriate in order to enable the Secretary of State to determine whether such corporation is entitled to a certificate of authority to transact business in this State and to determine and assess the fees and franchise taxes payable as in this Act prescribed.

Such application shall be made on forms prescribed and furnished by the Secretary of State and shall be executed in duplicate by the corporation by its president or a vice president and by its secretary or an assistant secretary, and verified by one of the officers signing such application.

§111. Filing of Application for Certificate of Authority

Duplicate originals of the application of the corporation for a certificate of authority shall be delivered to the Secretary of State, together with a copy of its articles of incorporation and all amendments thereto, duly authenticated by the proper officer of the state or country under the laws of which it is incorporated.

If the Secretary of State finds that such application conforms to law, he shall, when all fees and franchise taxes have been paid as in this Act prescribed:

(a) Endorse on each of such documents the word "Filed," and the month, day and year of the filing thereof.

(b) File in his office one of such duplicate originals of the application and the copy of the articles of incorporation and amendments thereto.

(c) Issue a certificate of authority to transact business in this State to which he shall affix the other duplicate original application.

The certificate of authority, together with the duplicate original of the application affixed thereto by the Secretary of State, shall be returned to the corporation or its representative.

§112. Effect of Certificate of Authority

Upon the issuance of a certificate of authority by the Secretary of State, the corporation shall be authorized to transact business in this State for those purposes set forth in its application, subject, however, to the right of this State to suspend or to revoke such authority as provided in this Act.

§113. Registered Office and Registered Agent of Foreign Corporation

Each foreign corporation authorized to transact business in this State shall have and continuously maintain in this State:

(a) A registered office which may be, but need not be, the same as its place of business in this State.

(b) A registered agent, which agent may be either an individual resident in this State whose business office is identical with such registered office, or a domestic corporation, or a foreign corporation authorized to transact business in this State, having a business office identical with such registered office.

§114. Change of Registered Office or Registered Agent of Foreign Corporation

A foreign corporation authorized to transact business in this State may change its registered office or change its registered agent, or both, upon filing in the office of the Secretary of State a statement setting forth:

(a) The name of the corporation.

(b) The address of its then registered office.

(c) If the address of its registered office be changed, the address to which the registered office is to be changed.

(d) The name of its then registered agent.

(e) If its registered agent be changed, the name of its successor registered agent.

(f) That the address of its registered office and the address of the business office of its registered agent, as changed, will be identical.

(g) That such change was authorized by resolution duly adopted by its board of directors.

Such statement shall be executed by the corporation by its president or a vice president, and verified by him, and delivered to the Secretary of State. If the Secretary of State finds that such statement conforms to the provisions of this Act, he shall file such statement in his office, and upon such filing the change of address of the registered office, or the appointment of a new registered agent, or both, as the case may be, shall become effective.

Any registered agent of a foreign corporation may resign as such agent upon filing a written notice thereof, executed in duplicate, with the Secretary of State, who shall forthwith mail a copy thereof to the corporation at its principal office in the state or country under the laws of which it is incorporated. The appointment of such agent shall terminate upon the expiration of thirty days after receipt of such notice by the Secretary of State.

If a registered agent changes his or its business address to another place within the same ....,* he or it may change such address and the address of the registered office of any corporation of which he or it is registered agent by filing a statement as required above except that it need be signed only by the registered agent and need not be re-

sponsive to (e) or (g) and must recite that a copy of the statement has been mailed to the corporation.

§115. Service of Process on Foreign Corporation

The registered agent so appointed by a foreign corporation authorized to transact business in this State shall be an agent of such corporation upon whom any process, notice or demand required or permitted by law to be served upon the corporation may be served.

Whenever a foreign corporation authorized to transact business in this State shall fail to appoint or maintain a registered agent in this State, or whenever any such registered agent cannot with reasonable diligence be found at the registered office, or whenever the certificate of authority of a foreign corporation shall be suspended or revoked, then the Secretary of State shall be an agent of such corporation upon whom any such process, notice, or demand may be served. Service on the Secretary of State of any such process, notice or demand shall be made by delivering to and leaving with him, or with any clerk having charge of the corporation department of his office, duplicate copies of such process, notice or demand. In the event any such process, notice or demand is served on the Secretary of State, he shall immediately cause one of such copies thereof to be forwarded by registered mail, addressed to the corporation at its principal office in the state or country under the laws of which it is incorporated. Any service so had on the Secretary of State shall be returnable in not less than thirty days.

The Secretary of State shall keep a record of all processes, notices and demands served upon him under this section, and shall record therein the time of such service and his action with reference thereto.

Nothing herein contained shall limit or affect the right to serve any process, notice or demand, required or permitted by law to be served upon a foreign corporation in any other manner now or hereafter permitted by law.

---

* Supply designation of jurisdiction, such as county, etc., in accordance with local practice.

§116. Amendment to Articles of Incorporation of Foreign Corporation

Whenever the articles of incorporation of a foreign corporation authorized to transact business in this State are amended, such foreign corporation shall, within thirty days after such amendment becomes effective, file in the office of the Secretary of State a copy of such amendment duly authenticated by the proper officer of the state or country under the laws of which it is incorporated; but the filing thereof shall not of itself enlarge or alter the purpose or purposes which such corporation is authorized to pursue in the transaction of business in this State, nor authorize such corporation to transact business in this State under any other name than the name set forth in its certificate of authority.

§117. Merger of Foreign Corporation Authorized to Transact Business in This State

Whenever a foreign corporation authorized to transact business in this State shall be a party to a statutory merger permitted by the laws of the state or country under the laws of which it is incorporated, and such corporation shall be the surviving corporation, it shall, within thirty days after such merger becomes effective, file with the Secretary of State a copy of the articles of merger duly authenticated by the proper officer of the state or country under the laws of which such statutory merger was effected; and it shall not be necessary for such corporation to procure either a new or amended certificate of authority to transact business in this State unless the name of such corporation be changed thereby or unless the corporation desires to pursue in this State other or additional purposes than those which it is then authorized to transact in this State.

§118. Amended Certificate of Authority

A foreign corporation authorized to transact business in this State shall procure an amended certificate of authority in the event it changes its corporate name, or desires to pursue in this State other or additional purposes than those set forth in its prior application for a certificate of authority, by making application therefor to the Secretary of State.

The requirements in respect to the form and contents of such application, the manner of its execution, the filing of duplicate originals thereof with the Secretary of State, the issuance of an amended certificate of authority and the effect thereof, shall be the same as in the case of an original application for a certificate of authority.

§119. Withdrawal of Foreign Corporation

A foreign corporation authorized to transact business in this State may withdraw from this State upon procuring from the Secretary of State a certificate of withdrawal. In order to procure such certificate of withdrawal, such foreign corporation shall deliver to the Secretary of State an application for withdrawal, which shall set forth:

(a) The name of the corporation and the state or country under the laws of which it is incorporated.

(b) That the corporation is not transacting business in this State.

(c) That the corporation surrenders its authority to transact business in this State.

(d) That the corporation revokes the authority of its registered agent in this State to accept service of process and consents that service of process in any action, suit or proceeding based upon any cause of action arising in this State during the time the corporation was authorized to transact business in this State may thereafter be made on such corporation by service thereof on the Secretary of State.

(e) A post-office address to which the Secretary of State may mail a copy of any process against the corporation that may be served on him.

(f) A statement of the aggregate number of shares which the corporation has authority to issue, itemized by classes, par value of shares,

shares without par value, and series, if any, within a class, as of the date of such application.

(g) A statement of the aggregate number of issued shares, itemized by classes, par value of shares, shares without par value, and series, if any, within a class, as of the date of such application.

(h) A statement, expressed in dollars, of the amount of stated capital of the corporation, as of the date of such application.

(i) Such additional information as may be necessary or appropriate in order to enable the Secretary of State to determine and assess any unpaid fees or franchise taxes payable by such foreign corporation as in this Act prescribed.

The application for withdrawal shall be made on forms prescribed and furnished by the Secretary of State and shall be executed by the corporation by its president or a vice president and by its secretary or an assistant secretary, and verified by one of the officers signing the application, or, if the corporation is in the hands of a receiver or trustee, shall be executed on behalf of the corporation by such receiver or trustee and verified by him.

§120. Filing of Application for Withdrawal

Duplicate originals of such application for withdrawal shall be delivered to the Secretary of State. If the Secretary of State finds that such application conforms to the provisions of this Act, he shall, when all fees and franchise taxes have been paid as in this Act prescribed:

(a) Endorse on each of such duplicate originals the word "Filed," and the month, day and year of the filing thereof.

(b) File one of such duplicate originals in his office.

(c) Issue a certificate of withdrawal to which he shall affix the other duplicate original.

The certificate of withdrawal, together with the duplicate original of the application for withdrawal affixed thereto by the Secretary of State, shall be returned to the corporation or its representative. Upon the issuance of such certificate of withdrawal, the authority of the corporation to transact business in this State shall cease.

§121. Revocation of Certificate of Authority

The certificate of authority of a foreign corporation to transact business in this State may be revoked by the Secretary of State upon the conditions prescribed in this section when:

(a) The corporation has failed to file its annual report within the time required by this Act, or has failed to pay any fees, franchise taxes or penalties prescribed by this Act when they have become due and payable; or

(b) The corporation has failed to appoint and maintain a registered agent in this State as required by this Act; or

(c) The corporation has failed, after change of its registered office or registered agent, to file in the office of the Secretary of State a statement of such change as required by this Act; or

(d) The corporation has failed to file in the office of the Secretary of State any amendment to its articles of incorporation or any articles of merger within the time prescribed by this Act; or

(e) A misrepresentation has been made of any material matter in any application, report, affidavit, or other document submitted by such corporation pursuant to this Act.

No certificate of authority of a foreign corporation shall be revoked by the Secretary of State unless (1) he shall have given the corporation not less than sixty days' notice thereof by mail addressed to its registered office in this State, and (2) the corporation shall fail prior to revocation to file such annual report, or pay such fees, franchise taxes or penalties, or file the required statement of change of registered agent or registered office, or file such articles of amendment or articles of merger, or correct such misrepresentation.

§122. Issuance of Certificate of Revocation

Upon revoking any such certificate of authority, the Secretary of State shall:

(a) Issue a certificate of revocation in duplicate.

(b) File one of such certificates in his office.

(c) Mail to such corporation at its registered office in this State a notice of such revocation accompanied by one of such certificates.

Upon the issuance of such certificate of revocation, the authority of the corporation to transact business in this State shall cease.

§123. Application to Corporations Heretofore Authorized to Transact Business in this State

Foreign corporations which are duly authorized to transact business in this State at the time this Act takes effect, for a purpose or purposes for which a corporation might secure such authority under this Act, shall, subject to the limitations set forth in their respective certificates of authority, be entitled to all the rights and privileges applicable to foreign corporations procuring certificates of authority to transact business in this State under this Act, and from the time this Act takes effect such corporations shall be subject to all the limitations, restrictions, liabilities, and duties prescribed herein for foreign corporations procuring certificates of authority to transact business in this State under this Act.

§124. Transacting Business Without Certificate of Authority

No foreign corporation transacting business in this State without a certificate of authority shall be permitted to maintain any action, suit or proceeding in any court of this State, until such corporation shall have obtained a certificate of authority. Nor shall any action, suit or proceeding be maintained in any court of this State by any successor or assignee of such corporation on any right, claim or demand arising out of the transaction of business by such corporation in this State, until a certificate of authority shall have been obtained by such corporation or by a corporation which has acquired all or substantially all of its assets.

The failure of a foreign corporation to obtain a certificate of authority to transact business in this State shall not impair the validity of any contract or act of such corporation, and shall not prevent such corporation from defending any action, suit or proceeding in any court of this State.

A foreign corporation which transacts business in this State without a certificate of authority shall be liable to this State, for the years or parts thereof during which it transacted business in this State without a certificate of authority, in an amount equal to all fees and franchise taxes which would have been imposed by this Act upon such corporation had it duly applied for and received a certificate of authority to transact business in this State as required by this Act and thereafter filed all reports required by this Act, plus all penalties imposed by this Act for failure to pay such fees and franchise taxes. The Attorney General shall bring proceedings to recover all amounts due this State under the provisions of this Section.

§125. Annual Report of Domestic and Foreign Corporations

Each domestic corporation, and each foreign corporation authorized to transact business in this State, shall file, within the time prescribed by this Act, an annual report setting forth:

(a) The name of the corporation and the state or country under the laws of which it is incorporated.

(b) The address of the registered office of the corporation in this State, and the name of its registered agent in this State at such address, and, in case of a foreign corporation, the address of its principal office in the state or country under the laws of which it is incorporated.

(c) A brief statement of the character of the

business in which the corporation is actually engaged in this State.

(d) The names and respective addresses of the directors and officers of the corporation.

(e) A statement of the aggregate number of shares which the corporation has authority to issue, itemized by classes, par value of shares, shares without par value, and series, if any, within a class.

(f) A statement of the aggregate number of issued shares, itemized by classes, par value of shares, shares without par value, and series, if any, within a class.

(g) A statement, expressed in dollars, of the amount of stated capital of the corporation, as defined in this Act.

(h) A statement, expressed in dollars, of the value of all the property owned by the corporation, wherever located, and the value of the property of the corporation located within this State, and a statement, expressed in dollars, of the gross amount of business transacted by the corporation for the twelve months ended on the thirty-first day of December preceding the date herein provided for the filing of such report and the gross amount thereof transacted by the corporation at or from places of business in this State. If, on the thirty-first day of December preceding the time herein provided for the filing of such report, the corporation had not been in existence for a period of twelve months, or in the case of a foreign corporation had not been authorized to transact business in this State for a period of twelve months, the statement with respect to business transacted shall be furnished for the period between the date of incorporation or the date of its authorization to transact business in this State, as the case may be, and such thirty-first day of December. If all the property of the corporation is located in this State and all of its business is transacted at or from places of business in this State, or if the corporation elects to pay the annual franchise tax on the basis of its entire stated capital, then the information required by this subparagraph need not be set forth in such report.

(i) Such additional information as may be necessary or appropriate in order to enable the Secretary of State to determine and assess the proper amount of franchise taxes payable by such corporation.

Such annual report shall be made on forms prescribed and furnished by the Secretary of State, and the information therein contained shall be given as of the date of the execution of the report, except as to the information required by subparagraphs (g), (h) and (i) which shall be given as of the close of business on the thirty-first day of December next preceding the date herein provided for the filing of such report. It shall be executed by the corporation by its president, a vice president, secretary, an assistant secretary, or treasurer, and verified by the officer executing the report, or, if the corporation is in the hands of a receiver or trustee, it shall be executed on behalf of the corporation and verified by such receiver or trustee.

§126. Filing of Annual Report of Domestic and Foreign Corporations

Such annual report of a domestic or foreign corporation shall be delivered to the Secretary of State between the first day of January and the first day of March of each year, except that the first annual report of a domestic or foreign corporation shall be filed between the first day of January and the first day of March of the year next succeeding the calendar year in which its certificate of incorporation or its certificate of authority, as the case may be, was issued by the Secretary of State. Proof to the satisfaction of the Secretary of State that prior to the first day of March such report was deposited in the United States mail in a sealed envelope, properly addressed, with postage prepaid, shall be deemed a compliance with this requirement. If the Secretary of State finds that such report conforms to the requirements of this Act, he shall file the same. If he finds that it does not so conform, he shall promptly return the same to the corporation for any necessary corrections, in which event the penalties hereinafter prescribed for failure to file such report within the time hereinabove provided shall not apply, if such report is corrected to conform to the requirements of this Act and returned to the Secretary of State within thirty days from the date on which it was mailed to the corporation by the Secretary of State.

§127. Fees, Franchise Taxes and Charges to be Collected by Secretary of State

[Text omitted.]

§128. Fees for Filing Documents and Issuing Certificates

[Text omitted.]

§129. Miscellaneous Charges

[Text omitted.]

§130. License Fees Payable by Domestic Corporations

[Text omitted.]

§131. License Fees Payable by Foreign Corporations

[Text omitted.]

§132. Franchise Taxes Payable by Domestic Corporations

[Text omitted.]

§133. Franchise Taxes Payable by Foreign Corporations

[Text omitted.]

§134. Assessment and Collection of Annual Franchise Taxes

[Text omitted.]

§135. Penalties Imposed upon Corporations

Each corporation, domestic or foreign, that fails or refuses to file its annual report for any year within the time prescribed by this Act shall be subject to a penalty of ten per cent of the amount of the franchise tax assessed against it for the period beginning July 1 of the year in which such report should have been filed. Such penalty shall be assessed by the Secretary of State at the time of the assessment of the franchise tax. If the amount of the franchise tax as originally assessed against such corporation be thereafter adjusted in accordance with the provisions of this Act, the amount of the penalty shall be likewise adjusted to ten per cent of the amount of the adjusted franchise tax. The amount of the franchise tax and the amount of the penalty shall be separately stated in any notice to the corporation with respect thereto.

If the franchise tax assessed in accordance with the provisions of this Act shall not be paid on or before the thirty-first day of July, it shall be deemed to be delinquent, and there shall be added a penalty of one per cent for each month or part of month that the same is delinquent, commencing with the month of August.

Each corporation, domestic or foreign, that fails or refuses to answer truthfully and fully within the time prescribed by this Act interrogatories propounded by the Secretary of State in accordance with the provisions of this Act, shall be deemed to be guilty of a misdemeanor and upon conviction thereof may be fined in any amount not exceeding five hundred dollars.

§136. Penalties Imposed upon Officers and Directors

Each officer and director of a corporation, domestic or foreign, who fails or refuses within the time prescribed by this Act to answer truthfully and fully interrogatories propounded to him by the Secretary of State in accordance with the provisions of this Act, or who signs any articles, statement, report, application or other document filed with the Secretary of State which is known to such officer or director to be false in any material respect, shall be deemed to be guilty of a misdemeanor, and upon conviction thereof may be fined in any amount not exceeding . . . . dollars.

§137. Interrogatories by Secretary of State

The Secretary of State may propound to any corporation, domestic or foreign, subject to the provisions of this Act, and to any officer or director thereof, such interrogatories as may be reasonably necessary and proper to enable him to ascertain whether such corporation has complied with all the provisions of this Act applicable to such corporation. Such interrogatories shall be answered within thirty days after the mailing thereof, or within such additional time as shall be fixed by the Secretary of State, and the answers thereto shall be full and complete and shall be made in writing and under oath. If such interrogatories be directed to an individual they shall be answered by him, and if directed to a corporation they shall be answered by the president, vice president, secretary or assistant secretary thereof. The Secretary of State need not file any document to which such interrogatories relate until such interrogatories be answered as herein provided, and not then if the answers thereto disclose that such document is not in conformity with the provisions of this Act. The Secretary of State shall certify to the Attorney General, for such action as the Attorney General may deem appropriate, all interrogatories and answers thereto which disclose a violation of any of the provisions of this Act.

§138. Information Disclosed by Interrogatories

Interrogatories propounded by the Secretary of State and the answers thereto shall not be open to public inspection nor shall the Secretary of State disclose any facts or information obtained therefrom except insofar as his official duty may require the same to be made public or in the event such interrogatories or the answers thereto are required for evidence in any criminal proceedings or in any other action by this State.

§139. Powers of Secretary of State

The Secretary of State shall have the power and authority reasonably necessary to enable him to administer this Act efficiently and to perform the duties therein imposed upon him.

§140. Appeal from Secretary of State

[Text omitted.]

§141. Certificates and Certified Copies to be Received in Evidence

[Text omitted.]

§142. Forms to be Furnished by Secretary of State

[Text omitted.]

§143. Greater Voting Requirements

Whenever, with respect to any action to be taken by the shareholders of a corporation, the articles of incorporation require the vote or concurrence of the holders of a greater proportion of the shares, or of any class or series thereof, than required by this Act with respect to such action, the provisions of the articles of incorporation shall control.

§144. Waiver of Notice

Whenever any notice is required to be given to any shareholder or director of a corporation under the provisions of this Act or under the provisions of the articles of incorporation or by-laws of the corporation, a waiver thereof in writing signed by the person or persons entitled to such notice, whether before or after the time stated therein, shall be equivalent to the giving of such notice.

145. Action by Shareholders Without a Meeting

Any action required by this Act to be taken at a meeting of the shareholders of a corporation, or any action which may be taken at a meeting of the shareholders, may be taken without a meeting if a consent in writing, setting forth the action so taken, shall be signed by all of the shareholders entitled to vote with respect to the subject matter thereof.

Such consent shall have the same effect as a

unanimous vote of shareholders, and may be stated as such in any articles or document filed with the Secretary of State under this Act.

§146. Unauthorized Assumption of Corporate Powers

All persons who assume to act as a corporation without authority so to do shall be jointly and severally liable for all debts and liabilities incurred or arising as a result thereof.

§147. Application to Existing Corporations

[Text omitted.]

§148. Application to Foreign and Interstate Commerce

[Text omitted.]

§149. Reservation of Power

The . . . .* shall at all times have power

---

* Insert name of legislative body.

to prescribe such regulations, provisions and limitations as it may deem advisable, which regulations, provisions and limitations shall be binding upon any and all corporations subject to the provisions of this Act, and the . . . .* shall have power to amend, repeal or modify this Act at pleasure.

§150. Effect of Repeal of Prior Acts

[Text omitted.]

§151. Effect of Invalidity of Part of this Act

[Text omitted.]

§152. Repeal of Prior Acts

(Insert appropriate provisions) . . . .

APPENDIX I

UNIFORM COMMERCIAL CODE
(1972 Official Text)

TITLE

AN ACT

To be known as the Uniform Commercial Code, Relating to Certain Commercial Transactions in or regarding Personal Property and Contracts and other Documents concerning them, including Sales, Commercial Paper, Bank Deposits and Collections, Letters of Credit, Bulk Transfers, Warehouse Receipts, Bills of Lading, other Documents of Title, Investment Securities, and Secured Transactions, including certain Sales of Accounts, Chattel Paper, and Contract Rights; Providing for Public Notice to Third Parties in Certain Circumstances; Regulating Procedure, Evidence and Damages in Certain Court Actions Involving such Transactions, Contracts or Documents; to Make Uniform the Law with Respect Thereto; and Repealing Inconsistent Legislation.

(Adopted in District of Columbia, Virgin Islands, and 49 States)

The Code consists of 10 Articles as follows:

Article

1. General Provisions
2. Sales
3. Commercial Paper
4. Bank Deposits and Collections
5. Letters of Credit
6. Bulk Transfers
7. Warehouse Receipts, Bills of Lading and Other Documents of Title
8. Investment Securities
9. Secured Transactions: Sales of Accounts, Contract Rights and Chattel Paper
10. Effective Date and Repealer

(Articles 1, 2, and 3 are set forth below.)

Article 1. GENERAL PROVISIONS

Article 2. SALES

Article 3.   COMMERCIAL PAPER

Part 1.   SHORT TITLE, FORM AND INTERPRETATION

ARTICLE 1. GENERAL PROVISIONS

PART 1. SHORT TITLE, CONSTRUCTION, APPLICATION AND SUBJECT MATTER OF THE ACT

§1–101. Short Title

This Act shall be known and may be cited as Uniform Commercial Code.

§1–102. Purposes; Rules of Construction; Variation by Agreement

(1) This Act shall be liberally construed and applied to promote its underlying purposes and policies.

(2) Underlying purposes and policies of this Act are

(a) to simplify, clarify and modernize the law governing commercial transactions;

(b) to permit the continued expansion of commercial practices through custom, usage and agreement of the parties;

(c) to make uniform the law among the various jurisdictions.

(3) The effect of provisions of this Act may be varied by agreement, except as otherwise provided in this Act and except that the obligations of good faith, diligence, reasonableness and care prescribed by this Act may not be disclaimed by agreement but the parties may by agreement determine the standards by which the performance of such obligations is to be

measured if such standards are not manifestly unreasonable.

(4) The presence in certain provisions of this Act of the words "unless otherwise agreed" or words of similar import does not imply that the effect of other provisions may not be varied by agreement under subsection (3).

(5) In this Act unless the context otherwise requires

(a) words in the singular number include the plural, and in the plural include the singular;
(b) words of the masculine gender include the feminine and the neuter, and when the sense so indicates words of the neuter gender may refer to any gender.

§1–103. Supplementary General Principles of Law Applicable

Unless displaced by the particular provisions of this Act, the principles of law and equity, including the law merchant and the law relative to capacity to contract, principal and agent, estoppel, fraud, misrepresentation, duress, coercion, mistake, bankruptcy, or other validating or invalidating cause shall supplement its provisions.

§1–104. Construction Against Implicit Repeal

This Act being a general act intended as a unified coverage of its subject matter, no part of it shall be deemed to be impliedly repealed by subsequent legislation if such construction can reasonably be avoided.

§1–105. Territorial Application of the Act; Parties' Power to Choose Applicable Law

(1) Except as provided hereafter in this section, when a transaction bears a reasonable relation to this state and also to another state or nation the parties may agree that the law either of this state or of such other state or nation shall govern their rights and duties. Failing such agreement this Act applies to transactions bearing an appropriate relation to this state.

(2) Where one of the following provisions of this Act specifies the applicable law, that provision governs and a contrary agreement is effective only to the extent permitted by the law (including the conflict of laws rules) so specified:

Rights of creditors against sold goods. Section 2–402.
Applicability of the Article on Bank Deposits and Collections. Section 4–102.
Bulk transfers subject to the Article on Bulk Transfers. Section 6–102.
Applicability of the Article on Investment Securities. Section 8–106.
Policy and scope of the Article on Secured Transactions. Sections 9–102 and 9–103.
Perfection provisions of the Article on Secured Transactions. Section 9–103.

§1–106. Remedies to Be Liberally Administered

(1) The remedies provided by this Act shall be liberally administered to the end that the aggrieved party may be put in as good a position as if the other party had fully performed but neither consequential or special nor penal damages may be had except as specifically provided in this Act or by other rule of law.

(2) Any right or obligation declared by this Act is enforceable by action unless the provision declaring it specifies a different and limited effect.

§1–107. Waiver or Renunciation of Claim or Right After Breach

Any claim or right arising out of an alleged breach can be discharged in whole or in part without consideration by a written waiver or renunciation signed and delivered by the aggrieved party.

§1–108. Severability

If any provision or clause of this Act or application thereof to any person or circumstances is held invalid, such invalidity shall not affect other provisions or applications of the Act which can be given effect without the invalid provision or application, and to this end the provisions of this Act are declared to be severable.

§1–109. Section Captions

Section captions are parts of this Act.

PART 2.   GENERAL DEFINITIONS AND PRINCIPLES OF INTERPRETATION

§1–201. General Definitions

Subject to additional definitions contained in the subsequent Article of this Act which are applicable to specific Articles or Parts thereof, and unless the context otherwise requires, in this Act:

(1) "Action" in the sense of a judicial proceeding includes recoupment, counterclaim, setoff, suit in equity and any other proceedings in which rights are determined.

(2) "Aggrieved party" means a party entitled to resort to a remedy.

(3) "Agreement" means the bargain of the parties in fact as found in their language or by implication from other circumstances including course of dealing or usage of trade or course of performance as provided in this Act (Sections 1–205 and 2–208). Whether an agreement has legal consequences is determined by the provisions of this Act, if applicable; otherwise by the law of contracts (Section 1–103). (Compare "Contract.")

(4) "Bank" means any person engaged in the business of banking.

(5) "Bearer" means the person in possession of an instrument, document of title, or security payable to bearer or indorsed in blank.

(6) "Bill of lading" means a document evidencing the receipt of goods for shipment issued by a person engaged in the business of transporting or forwarding goods, and includes an airbill. "Airbill" means a document serving for air transportation as a bill of lading does for marine or rail transportation, and includes an air consignment note or air waybill.

(7) "Branch" includes a separately incorporated foreign branch of a bank.

(8) "Burden of establishing" a fact means the burden of persuading the triers of fact that the existence of the fact is more probable than its non-existence.

(9) "Buyer in ordinary course of business" means a person who in good faith and without knowledge that the sale to him is in violation of the ownership rights or security interest of a third party in the goods buys in ordinary course from a person in the business of selling goods of that kind but does not include a pawnbroker. All persons who sell minerals or the like (including oil and gas) at wellhead or minehead shall be deemed to be persons in the business of selling goods of that kind. "Buying" may be for cash or by exchange of other property or on secured or unsecured credit and includes receiving goods or documents of title under a pre-existing contract for sale but does not include a transfer in bulk or as security for or in total or partial satisfaction of a money debt.

(10) "Conspicuous": A term or clause is conspicuous when it is so written that a reasonable person against whom it is to operate ought to have noticed it. A printed heading in capitals (as: NON-NEGOTIABLE BILL OF LADING) is conspicuous. Language in the body of a form is "conspicuous" if it is in larger or other contrasting type or color. But in a telegram any stated term is "conspicuous." Whether a term or clause is "conspicuous" or not is for decision by the court.

(11) "Contract" means the total legal obligation which results from the parties' agreement as affected by this Act and any other applicable rules of law. (Compare "Agreement.")

(12) "Creditor" includes a general creditor, a secured creditor, a lien creditor and any representative of creditors, including an assignee for the benefit of creditors, a trustee in bankruptcy, a receiver in equity and an executor or administrator of an insolvent debtor's or assignor's estate.

(13) "Defendant" includes a person in the position of defendant in a cross-action or counterclaim.

(14) "Delivery" with respect to instruments, documents of title, chattel paper or securities means voluntary transfer of possession.

(15) "Document of title" includes bill of lading, dock warrant, dock receipt, warehouse receipt or order for the delivery of goods, and also any other document which in the regular course of business or financing is treated as adequately evidencing that the person in possession of it is entitled to receive, hold and dispose of the document and the goods it covers. To be a document of title a document must purport to be issued by or addressed to a bailee and purport to cover goods in the bailee's possession which are either identified or are fungible portions of an identified mass.

(16) "Fault" means wrongful act, omission or breach.

(17) "Fungible" with respect to goods or securities means goods or securities of which any unit is, by nature or usage of trade, the equivalent of any other like unit. Goods which are not fungible shall be deemed fungible for the purposes of this Act to the extent that under a particular agreement or document unlike units are treated as equivalents.

(18) "Genuine" means free of forgery or counterfeiting.

(19) "Good faith" means honesty in fact in the conduct or transaction concerned.

(20) "Holder" means a person who is in possession of a document of title or an instrument or an investment security drawn, issued or indorsed to him or to his order or to bearer or in blank.

(21) To "honor" is to pay or to accept and pay, or where a credit so engages to purchase or discount a draft complying with the terms of the credit.

(22) "Insolvency proceedings" includes any assignment for the benefit of creditors or other proceedings intended to liquidate or rehabilitate the estate of the person involved.

(23) A person is "insolvent" who either has ceased to pay his debts in the ordinary course of business or cannot pay his debts as they become due or is insolvent within the meaning of the federal bankruptcy law.

(24) "Money" means a medium of exchange authorized or adopted by a domestic or foreign government as a part of its currency.

(25) A person has "notice" of a fact when

(a) he has actual knowledge of it; or

(b) he has received a notice or notification of it; or

(c) from all the facts and circumstances known to him at the time in question he has reason to know that it exists.

A person "knows" or has "knowledge" of a fact when he has actual knowledge of it. "Discover" or "learn" or a word or phrase of similar import refers to knowledge rather than to reason to know. The time and circumstances under which a notice or notification may cease to be effective are not determined by this Act.

(26) A person "notifies" or "gives" a notice or notification to another by taking such steps as may be reasonably required to inform the other in ordinary course whether or not such other actually comes to know of it. A person "receives" a notice or notification when

(a) it comes to his attention; or

(b) it is duly delivered at the place of business through which the contract was made or at any other place held out by him as the place for receipt of such communications.

(27) Notice, knowledge or a notice or notification received by an organization is effective for a particular transaction from the time when it is brought to the attention of the individual conducting that transaction, and in any event from the time when it would have been brought to his attention if the organization had exercised due diligence. An organization exercises due diligence if it maintains reasonable routines for communicating significant information to the person conducting the transaction and there is rea-

sonable compliance with the routines. Due diligence does not require an individual acting for the organization to communicate information unless such communication is part of his regular duties or unless he has reason to know of the transaction and that the transaction would be materially affected by the information.

(28) "Organization" includes a corporation, government or governmental subdivision or agency, business trust, estate, trust, partnership or association, two or more persons having a joint or common interest, or any other legal or commercial entity.

(29) "Party," as distinct from "third party," means a person who has engaged in a transaction or made an agreement within this Act.

(30) "Person" includes an individual or an organization (see Section 1–102).

(31) "Presumption" or "presumed" means that the trier of fact must find the existence of the fact presumed unless and until evidence is introduced which would support a finding of its nonexistence.

(32) "Purchase" includes taking by sale, discount, negotiation, mortgage, pledge, lien, issue or re-issue, gift or any other voluntary transaction creating an interest in property.

(33) "Purchaser" means a person who takes by purchase.

(34) "Remedy" means any remedial right to which an aggrieved party is entitled with or without resort to a tribunal.

(35) "Representative" includes an agent, an officer of a corporation or association, and a trustee, executor or administrator of an estate, or any other person empowered to act for another.

(36) "Rights" includes remedies.

(37) "Security interest" means an interest in personal property or fixtures which secures payment or performance of an obligation. The retention or reservation of title by a seller of goods notwithstanding shipment or delivery to the buyer (Section 2–401) is limited in effect to a reservation of a "security interest." The term also includes any interest of a buyer of accounts, chattel paper, or contract rights which is subject to Article 9. The special property interest of a buyer of goods on identification of such goods to a contract for sale under Section 2–401 is not a "security interest," but a buyer may also acquire a "security interest" by complying with Article 9. Unless a lease or consignment is intended as security, reservation of title thereunder is not a "security interest" but a consignment is in any event subject to the provisions on consignment sales (Section 2–326). Whether a lease is intended as security is to be determined by the facts of each case; however, (a) the inclusion of an option to purchase does not of itself make the lease one intended for security, and (b) an agreement that upon compliance with the terms of the lease the lessee shall become or has the option to become the owner of the property for no additional consideration or for a nominal consideration does make the lease one intended for security.

(38) "Send" in connection with any writing or notice means to deposit in the mail or deliver for transmission by any other usual means of communication with postage or cost of transmission provided for and properly addressed and in the case of an instrument to an address specified thereon or otherwise agreed, or if there be none to any address reasonable under the circumstances. The receipt of any writing or notice within the time at which it would have arrived if properly sent has the effect of a proper sending.

(39) "Signed" includes any symbol executed or adopted by a party with present intention to authenticate a writing.

(40) "Surety" includes guarantor.

(41) "Telegram" includes a message transmitted by radio, teletype, cable, any mechanical method of transmission, or the like.

(42) "Term" means that portion of an agreement which relates to a particular matter.

(43) "Unauthorized" signature or indorsement means one made without actual, implied or apparent authority and includes a forgery.

(44) "Value." Except as otherwise provided with respect to negotiable instruments and bank collections (Sections 3–303, 4–208 and 4–209) a person gives "value" for rights if he acquires them

> (a) in return for a binding commitment to extend credit or for the extension of immediately available credit whether or not drawn upon and whether or not a charge-back is provided for in the event of difficulties in collection; or
> (b) as security for or in total or partial satisfaction of a pre-existing claim; or
> (c) by accepting delivery pursuant to a pre-existing contract for purchase; or
> (d) generally, in return for any consideration sufficient to support a simple contract.

(45) "Warehouse receipt" means a receipt issued by a person engaged in the business of storing goods for hire.

(46) "Written" or "writing" includes printing, typewriting or any other intentional reduction to tangible form.

§1–202. Prima Facie Evidence by Third Party Documents

A document in due form purporting to be a bill of lading, policy or certificate of insurance, official weigher's or inspector's certificate, consular invoice, or any other document authorized or required by the contract to be issued by a third party shall be prima facie evidence of its own authenticity and genuineness and of the facts stated in the document by the third party.

§1–203. Obligation of Good Faith

Every contract or duty within this Act imposes an obligation of good faith in its performance or enforcement.

§1–204. Time; Reasonable Time; "Seasonably"

(1) Whenever this Act requires any action to be taken within a reasonable time, any time which is not manifestly unreasonable may be fixed by agreement.

(2) What is a reasonable time for taking any action depends on the nature, purpose and circumstances of such action.

(3) An action is taken "seasonably" when it is taken at or within the time agreed or if no time is agreed at or within a reasonable time.

§1–205. Course of Dealing and Usage of Trade

(1) A course of dealing is a sequence of previous conduct between the parties to a particular transaction which is fairly to be regarded as establishing a common basis of understanding for interpreting their expressions and other conduct.

(2) A usage of trade is any practice or method of dealing having such regularity of observance in a place, vocation or trade as to justify an expectation that it will be observed with respect to the transaction in question. The existence and scope of such a usage are to be proved as facts. If it is established that such a usage is embodied in a written trade code or similar writing the interpretation of the writing is for the court.

(3) A course of dealing between parties and any usage of trade in the vocation or trade in which they are engaged or of which they are or should be aware give particular meaning to and supplement or qualify terms of an agreement.

(4) The express terms of an agreement and an applicable course of dealing or usage of trade shall be construed wherever reasonable as consistent with each other; but when such construction is unreasonable express terms control both course of dealing and usage of trade and course of dealing controls usage of trade.

(5) An applicable usage of trade in the place where any part of performance is to occur shall be used in interpreting the agreement as to that part of the performance.

(6) Evidence of a relevant usage of trade offered by one party is not admissible unless and until he has given the other party such

notice as the court finds sufficient to prevent unfair surprise to the latter.

§1-206. Statute of Frauds for Kinds of Personal Property Not Otherwise Covered

(1) Except in the cases described in subsection (2) of this section a contract for the sale of personal property is not enforceable by way of action or defense beyond five thousand dollars in amount or value of remedy unless there is some writing which indicates that a contract for sale has been made between the parties at a defined or stated price, reasonably identifies the subject matter, and is signed by the party against whom enforcement is sought or by his authorized agent.

(2) Subsection (1) of this section does not apply to contracts for the sale of goods (Section 2-201) nor of securities (Section 8-319) nor to security agreements (Section 9-203).

§1-207. Performance or Acceptance Under Reservation of Rights

A party who with explicit reservation of rights performs or promises performance or assents to performance in a manner demanded or offered by the other party does not thereby prejudice the rights reserved. Such words as "without prejudice," "under protest" or the like are sufficient.

§1-208. Option to Accelerate at Will

A term providing that one party or his successor in interest may accelerate payment or performance or require collateral or additional collateral "at will" or "when he deems himself insecure" or in words of similar import shall be construed to mean that he shall have power to do so only if he in good faith believes that the prospect of payment or performance is impaired. The burden of establishing lack of good faith is on the party against whom the power has been exercised.

§1-209. Subordinated Obligations

An obligation may be issued as subordinated to payment of another obligation of the person obligated, or a creditor may subordinate his right to payment of an obligation by agreement with either the person obligated or another creditor of the person obligated. Such a subordination does not create a security interest as against either the common debtor or a subordinated creditor. This section shall be construed as declaring the law as it existed prior to the enactment of this section and not as modifying it.

ARTICLE 2.   SALES

PART 1.   SHORT TITLE, CONSTRUCTION AND SUBJECT MATTER

§2-101. Short Title

This Article shall be known and may be cited as Uniform Commercial Code—Sales.

§2-102. Scope; Certain Security and Other Transactions Excluded From This Article

Unless the context otherwise requires, this Article applies to transactions in goods; it does not apply to any transaction which although in the form of an unconditional contract to sell or present sale is intended to operate only as a security transaction nor does this Article impair or repeal any statute regulating sales to consumers, farmers or other specified classes of buyers.

§2-103. Definitions and Index of Definitions

(1) In this Article unless the context otherwise requires

(a) "Buyer" means a person who buys or contracts to buy goods.

(b) "Good faith" in the case of a merchant means honesty in fact and the observance of reasonable commercial standards of fair dealing in the trade.

(c) "Receipt" of goods means taking physical possession of them.

(d) "Seller" means a person who sells or contracts to sell goods.

(2) Other definitions applying to this Article or to specified Parts thereof, and the sections in which they appear are:

"Acceptance." Section 2–606.
"Banker's credit." Section 2–325.
"Between merchants." Section 2–104.
"Cancellation." Section 2–106(4).
"Commercial unit." Section 2–105.
"Confirmed credit." Section 2–325.
"Conforming to contract." Section 2–106.
"Contract for sale." Section 2–106.
"Cover." Section 2–712.
"Entrusting." Section 2–403.
"Financing agency." Section 2–104.
"Future goods." Section 2–105.
"Goods." Section 2–105.
"Identification." Section 2–501.
"Installment contract." Section 2–612.
"Letter of Credit." Section 2–325.
"Lot." Section 2–105.
"Merchant." Section 2–104.
"Overseas." Section 2–323.
"Person in position of seller." Section 2–707.
"Present sale." Section 2–106.
"Sale." Section 2–106.
"Sale on approval." Section 2–326.
"Sale or return." Section 2–326.
"Termination." Section 2–106.

(3) The following definitions in other Articles apply to this Article:

"Check." Section 3–104.
"Consignee." Section 7–102.
"Consignor." Section 7–102.
"Consumer goods." Section 9–109.
"Dishonor." Section 3–507.
"Draft." Section 3–104.

(4) In addition Article 1 contains general definitions and principles of construction and interpretation applicable throughout this Article.

§2–104. Definitions: "Merchant"; "Between Merchants"; "Financing Agency"

(1) "Merchant" means a person who deals in goods of the kind or otherwise by his occupation holds himself out as having knowledge or skill peculiar to the practices or goods involved in the transaction or to whom such knowledge or skill may be attributed by his employment of an agent or broker or other intermediary who by his occupation holds himself out as having such knowledge or skill.

(2) "Financing agency" means a bank, finance company or other person who in the ordinary course of business makes advances against goods or documents of title or who by arrangement with either the seller or the buyer intervenes in ordinary course to make or collect payment due or claimed under the contract for sale, as by purchasing or paying the seller's draft or making advances against it or by merely taking it for collection whether or not documents of title accompany the draft. "Financing agency" includes also a bank or other person who similarly intervenes between persons who are in the position of seller and buyer in respect to the goods (Section 2–707).

(3) "Between merchants" means in any transaction with respect to which both parties are chargeable with the knowledge or skill of merchants.

§2–105. Definitions: Transferability; "Goods"; "Future" Goods; "Lot"; "Commercial Unit"

(1) "Goods" means all things (including specially manufactured goods) which are movable at the time of identification to the contract for sale other than the money in which the price is to be paid, investment securities (Article 8) and things in action. "Goods" also includes the unborn young of animals and growing crops and other identified things attached to realty

as described in the section on goods to be severed from realty (Section 2–107).

(2) Goods must be both existing and identified before any interest in them can pass. Goods which are not both existing and identified are "future" goods. A purported present sale of future goods or of any interest therein operates as a contract to sell.

(3) There may be a sale of a part interest in existing identified goods.

(4) An undivided share in an identified bulk of fungible goods is sufficiently identified to be sold although the quantity of the bulk is not determined. Any agreed proportion of such a bulk or any quantity thereof agreed upon by number, weight or other measure may to the extent of the seller's interest in the bulk be sold to the buyer who then becomes an owner in common.

(5) "Lot" means a parcel or a single article which is the subject matter of a separate sale or delivery, whether or not it is sufficient to perform the contract.

(6) "Commercial unit" means such a unit of goods as by commercial usage is a single whole for purposes of sale and division of which materially impairs its character or value on the market or in use. A commercial unit may be a single article (as a machine) or a set of articles (as a suite of furniture or an assortment of sizes) or a quantity (as a bale, gross, or carload) or any other unit treated in use or in the relevant market as a single whole.

§2–106. Definitions: "Contract"; "Agreement"; "Contract for Sale"; "Sale"; "Present Sale"; "Conforming" to Contract; "Termination"; "Cancellation"

(1) In this Article unless the context otherwise requires "contract" and "agreement" are limited to those relating to the present or future sale of goods. "Contract for sale" includes both a present sale of goods and a contract to sell goods at a future time. A "sale" consists in the passing of title from the seller to the buyer for a price (Section 2–401). A "present sale" means

a sale which is accomplished by the making of the contract.

(2) Goods or conduct including any part of a performance are "conforming" or conform to the contract when they are in accordance with the obligations under the contract.

(3) "Termination" occurs when either party pursuant to a power created by agreement or law puts an end to the contract otherwise than for its breach. On "termination" all obligations which are still executory on both sides are discharged but any right based on prior breach or performance survives.

(4) "Cancellation" occurs when either party puts an end to the contract for breach by the other and its effect is the same as that of "termination" except that the cancelling party also retains any remedy for breach of the whole contract or any unperformed balance.

§2–107. Goods to Be Severed From Realty: Recording

(1) A contract for the sale of minerals or the like (including oil and gas) or a structure or its materials to be removed from realty is a contract for the sale of goods within this Article if they are to be severed by the seller but until severance a purported present sale thereof which is not effective as a transfer of an interest in land is effective only as a contract to sell.

(2) A contract for the sale apart from the land of growing crops or other things attached to realty and capable of severance without material harm thereto but not described in subsection (1) or of timber to be cut is a contract for the sale of goods within this Article whether the subject matter is to be severed by the buyer or by the seller even though it forms part of the realty at the time of contracting, and the parties can by identification effect a present sale before severance.

(3) The provisions of this section are subject to any third party rights provided by the law relating to realty records, and the contract for sale may be executed and recorded as a docu-

ment transferring an interest in land and shall then constitute notice to third parties of the buyer's rights under the contract for sale.

PART 2. FORM, FORMATION AND READJUSTMENT OF CONTRACT

§2–201. Formal Requirements; Statute of Frauds

(1) Except as otherwise provided in this section a contract for the sale of goods for the price of $500 or more is not enforceable by way of action or defense unless there is some writing sufficient to indicate that a contract for sale has been made between the parties and signed by the party against whom enforcement is sought or by his authorized agent or broker. A writing is not insufficient because it omits or incorrectly states a term agreed upon but the contract is not enforceable under this paragraph beyond the quantity of goods shown in such writing.

(2) Between merchants if within a reasonable time a writing in confirmation of the contract and sufficient against the sender is received and the party receiving it has reason to know its contents, it satisfies the requirements of subsection (1) against such party unless written notice of objection to its contents is given within ten days after it is received.

(3) A contract which does not satisfy the requirements of subsection (1) but which is valid in other respects is enforceable

(a) if the goods are to be specially manufactured for the buyer and are not suitable for sale to others in the ordinary course of the seller's business and the seller, before notice of repudiation is received and under circumstances which reasonably indicate that the goods are for the buyer, has made either a substantial beginning of their manufacture or commitments for their procurement; or
(b) if the party against whom enforcement is sought admits in his pleading, testimony

or otherwise in court that a contract for sale was made, but the contract is not enforceable under this provision beyond the quantity of goods admitted; or
(c) with respect to goods for which payment has been made and accepted or which have been received and accepted (Section 2–606).

§2–202. Final Written Expression; Parol or Extrinsic Evidence

Terms with respect to which the confirmatory memoranda of the parties agree or which are otherwise set forth in a writing intended by the parties as a final expression of their agreement with respect to such terms as are included therein may not be contradicted by evidence of any prior agreement or of a contemporaneous oral agreement but may be explained or supplemented

(a) by course of dealing or usage of trade (Section 1–205) or by course of performance (Section 2–208); and
(b) by evidence of consistent additional terms unless the court finds the writing to have been intended also as a complete and exclusive statement of the terms of the agreement.

§2–203. Seals Inoperative

The affixing of a seal to a writing evidencing a contract for sale or an offer to buy or sell goods does not constitute the writing a sealed instrument and the law with respect to sealed instruments does not apply to such a contract or offer.

§2–204. Formation in General

(1) A contract for sale of goods may be made in any manner sufficient to show agreement, including conduct by both parties which recognizes the existence of such a contract.

(2) An agreement sufficient to constitute a contract for sale may be found even though the moment of its making is undetermined.

(3) Even though one or more terms are left

open a contract for sale does not fail for indefiniteness if the parties have intended to make a contract and there is a reasonably certain basis for giving an appropriate remedy.

§2–205. Firm Offers

An offer by a merchant to buy or sell goods in a signed writing which by its terms gives assurance that it will be held open is not revocable, for lack of consideration, during the time stated or if no time is stated for a reasonable time, but in no event may such period of irrevocability exceed three months; but any such term of assurance on a form supplied by the offeree must be separately signed by the offeror.

§2–206. Offer and Acceptance in Formation of Contract

(1) Unless otherwise unambiguously indicated by the language or circumstances

(a) an offer to make a contract shall be construed as inviting acceptance in any manner and by any medium reasonable in the circumstances;

(b) an order or other offer to buy goods for prompt or current shipment shall be construed as inviting acceptance either by a prompt promise to ship or by the prompt or current shipment of conforming or nonconforming goods, but such a shipment of non-conforming goods does not constitute an acceptance if the seller seasonably notifies the buyer that the shipment is offered only as an accommodation to the buyer.

(2) Where the beginning of a requested performance is a reasonable mode of acceptance an offeror who is not notified of acceptance within a reasonable time may treat the offer as having lapsed before acceptance.

§2–207. Additional Terms in Acceptance or Confirmation

(1) A definite and seasonable expression of acceptance or a written confirmation which is sent within a reasonable time operates as an acceptance even though it states terms additional to or different from those offered or agreed upon, unless acceptance is expressly made conditional on assent to the additional or different terms.

(2) The additional terms are to be construed as proposals for addition to the contract. Between merchants such terms become part of the contract unless:

(a) the offer expressly limits acceptance to the terms of the offer;

(b) they materially alter it; or

(c) notification of objection to them has already been given or is given within a reasonable time after notice of them is received.

(3) Conduct by both parties which recognizes the existence of a contract is sufficient to establish a contract for sale although the writings of the parties do not otherwise establish a contract. In such case the terms of the particular contract consist of those terms on which the writings of the parties agree, together with any supplementary terms incorporated under any other provisions of this Act.

§2–208. Course of Performance or Practical Construction

(1) Where the contract for sale involves repeated occasions for performance by either party with knowledge of the nature of the performance and opportunity for objection to it by the other, any course of performance accepted or acquiesced in without objection shall be relevant to determine the meaning of the agreement.

(2) The express terms of the agreement and any such course of performance, as well as any course of dealing and usage of trade, shall be construed whenever reasonable as consistent with each other; but when such construction is unreasonable, express terms shall control course of performance and course of performance shall control both course of dealing and usage of trade (Section 1–205).

(3) Subject to the provisions of the next section on modification and waiver, such course

of performance shall be relevant to show a waiver or modification of any term inconsistent with such course of performance.

§2–209. Modification, Rescission and Waiver

(1) An agreement modifying a contract within this Article needs no consideration to be binding.

(2) A signed agreement which excludes modification or rescission except by a signed writing cannot be otherwise modified or rescinded, but except as between merchants such a requirement on a form supplied by the merchant must be separately signed by the other party.

(3) The requirements of the statute of frauds section of this Article (Section 2–201) must be satisfied if the contract as modified is within its provisions.

(4) Although an attempt at modification or rescission does not satisfy the requirements of subsection (2) or (3) it can operate as a waiver.

(5) A party who has made a waiver affecting an executory portion of the contract may retract the waiver by reasonable notification received by the other party that strict performance will be required of any term waived, unless the retraction would be unjust in view of a material change of position in reliance on the waiver.

§2–210. Delegation of Performance; Assignment of Rights

(1) A party may perform his duty through a delegate unless otherwise agreed or unless the other party has a substantial interest in having his original promisor perform or control the acts required by the contract. No delegation of performance relieves the party delegating of any duty to perform or any liability for breach.

(2) Unless otherwise agreed all rights of either seller or buyer can be assigned except where the assignment would materially change the duty of the other party, or increase materially the burden or risk imposed on him by his contract, or impair materially his chance of obtaining return performance. A right to damages for breach of the whole contract or a

right arising out of the assignor's due performance of his entire obligation can be assigned despite agreement otherwise.

(3) Unless the circumstances indicate the contrary a prohibition of assignment of "the contract" is to be construed as barring only the delegation to the assignee of the assignor's performance.

(4) An assignment of "the contract" or of "all my rights under the contract" or an assignment in similar general terms is an assignment of rights and unless the language or the circumstances (as in an assignment for security) indicate the contrary, it is a delegation of performance of the duties of the assignor and its acceptance by the assignee constitutes a promise by him to perform those duties. This promise is enforceable by either the assignor or the other party to the original contract.

(5) The other party may treat any assignment which delegates performance as creating reasonable grounds for insecurity and may without prejudice to his rights against the assignor demand assurances from the assignee (Section 2–609).

PART 3. GENERAL OBLIGATION AND CONSTRUCTION OF CONTRACT

§2–301. General Obligations of Parties

The obligation of the seller is to transfer and deliver and that of the buyer is to accept and pay in accordance with the contract.

§2–302. Unconscionable Contract or Clause

(1) If the court as a matter of law finds the contract or any clause of the contract to have been unconscionable at the time it was made the court may refuse to enforce the contract, or it may enforce the remainder of the contract without the unconscionable clause, or it may so limit the application of any unconscionable clause as to avoid any unconscionable result.

(2) When it is claimed or appears to the court that the contract or any clause thereof

may be unconscionable the parties shall be afforded a reasonable opportunity to present evidence as to its commercial setting, purpose and effect to aid the court in making the determination.

§2–303. Allocation or Division of Risks

Where this Article allocates a risk or a burden as between the parties "unless otherwise agreed," the agreement may not only shift the allocation but may also divide the risk or burden.

§2–304. Price Payable in Money, Goods, Realty, or Otherwise

(1) The price can be made payable in money or otherwise. If it is payable in whole or in part in goods each party is a seller of the goods which he is to transfer.

(2) Even though all or part of the price is payable in an interest in realty the transfer of the goods and the seller's obligations with reference to them are subject to this Article, but not the transfer of the interest in realty or the transferor's obligations in connection therewith.

§2–305. Open Price Term

(1) The parties if they so intend can conclude a contract for sale even though the price is not settled. In such a case the price is a reasonable price at the time for delivery if

(a) nothing is said as to price; or
(b) the price is left to be agreed by the parties and they fail to agree; or
(c) the price is to be fixed in terms of some agreed market or other standard as set or recorded by a third person or agency and it is not so set or recorded.

(2) A price to be fixed by the seller or by the buyer means a price for him to fix in good faith.

(3) When a price left to be fixed otherwise than by agreement of the parties fails to be fixed through fault of one party the other may at his option treat the contract as cancelled or himself fix a reasonable price.

(4) Where, however, the parties intend not to be bound unless the price be fixed or agreed and it is not fixed or agreed there is no contract. In such a case the buyer must return any goods already received or if unable so to do must pay their reasonable value at the time of delivery and the seller must return any portion of the price paid on account.

§2–306. Output, Requirements and Exclusive Dealings

(1) A term which measures the quantity by the output of the seller or the requirements of the buyer means such actual output or requirements as may occur in good faith, except that no quantity unreasonably disproportionate to any stated estimate or in the absence of a stated estimate to any normal or otherwise comparable prior output or requirements may be tendered or demanded.

(2) A lawful agreement by either the seller or the buyer for exclusive dealing in the kind of goods concerned imposes unless otherwise agreed an obligation by the seller to use best efforts to supply the goods and by the buyer to use best efforts to promote their sale.

§2–307. Delivery in Single Lot or Several Lots

Unless otherwise agreed all goods called for by a contract for sale must be tendered in a single delivery and payment is due only on such tender but where the circumstances give either party the right to make or demand delivery in lots the price if it can be apportioned may be demanded for each lot.

§2–308. Absence of Specified Place for Delivery

Unless otherwise agreed

(a) the place for delivery of goods is the seller's place of business or if he has none his residence; but
(b) in a contract for sale of identified goods which to the knowledge of the parties at the time of contracting are in some other place,

that place is the place for their delivery; and (c) documents of title may be delivered through customary banking channels.

§2–309. Absence of Specific Time Provisions; Notice of Termination

(1) The time for shipment or delivery or any other action under a contract if not provided in this Article or agreed upon shall be a reasonable time.

(2) Where the contract provides for successive performances but is indefinite in duration it is valid for a reasonable time but unless otherwise agreed may be terminated at any time by either party.

(3) Termination of a contract by one party except on the happening of an agreed event requires that reasonable notification be received by the other party and an agreement dispensing with notification is invalid if its operation would be unconscionable.

§2–310. Open Time for Payment or Running of Credit; Authority to Ship Under Reservation

Unless otherwise agreed

(a) payment is due at the time and place at which the buyer is to receive the goods even though the place of shipment is the place of delivery; and

(b) if the seller is authorized to send the goods he may ship them under reservation, and may tender the documents of title, but the buyer may inspect the goods after their arrival before payment is due unless such inspection is inconsistent with the terms of the contract (Section 2–513); and

(c) if delivery is authorized and made by way of documents of title otherwise than by subsection (b) then payment is due at the time and place at which the buyer is to receive the documents regardless of where the goods are to be received; and

(d) where the seller is required or authorized to ship the goods on credit the credit period runs from the time of shipment but post-

dating the invoice or delaying its dispatch will correspondingly delay the starting of the credit period.

§2–311. Options and Cooperation Respecting Performance

(1) An agreement for sale which is otherwise sufficiently definite (subsection (3) of Section 2–204) to be a contract is not made invalid by the fact that it leaves particulars of performance to be specified by one of the parties. Any such specification must be made in good faith and within limits set by commercial reasonableness.

(2) Unless otherwise agreed specifications relating to assortment of the goods are at the buyer's option and except as otherwise provided in subsections (1) (c) and (3) of Section 2–319 specifications or arrangements relating to shipment are at the seller's option.

(3) Where such specification would materially affect the other party's performance but is not seasonably made or where one party's cooperation is necessary to the agreed performance of the other but is not seasonably forthcoming, the other party in addition to all other remedies

(a) is excused for any resulting delay in his own performance; and

(b) may also either proceed to perform in any reasonable manner or after the time for a material part of his own performance treat the failure to specify or to cooperate as a breach by failure to deliver or accept the goods.

§2–312. Warranty of Title and Against Infringement; Buyer's Obligation Against Infringement

(1) Subject to subsection (2) there is in a contract for sale a warranty by the seller that

(a) the title conveyed shall be good, and its transfer rightful; and

(b) the goods shall be delivered free from any security interest or other lien or encumbrance of which the buyer at the time of contracting has no knowledge.

(2) A warranty under subsection (1) will be excluded or modified only by specific language or by circumstances which give the buyer reason to know that the person selling does not claim title in himself or that he is purporting to sell only such right or title as he or a third person may have.

(3) Unless otherwise agreed a seller who is a merchant regularly dealing in goods of the kind warrants that the goods shall be delivered free of the rightful claim of any third person by way of infringement or the like but a buyer who furnishes specifications to the seller must hold the seller harmless against any such claim which arises out of compliance with the specifications.

§2–313. Express Warranties by Affirmation, Promise, Description, Sample

(1) Express warranties by the seller are created as follows:

(a) Any affirmation of fact or promise made by the seller to the buyer which relates to the goods and becomes part of the basis of the bargain creates an express warranty that the goods shall conform to the affirmation or promise.

(b) Any description of the goods which is made part of the basis of the bargain creates an express warranty that the goods shall conform to the description.

(c) Any sample or model which is made part of the basis of the bargain creates an express warranty that the whole of the goods shall conform to the sample or model.

(2) It is not necessary to the creation of an express warranty that the seller use formal words such as "warrant" or "guarantee" or that he have a specific intention to make a warranty, but an affirmation merely of the value of the goods or a statement purporting to be merely the seller's opinion or commendation of the goods does not create a warranty.

§2–314. Implied Warranty: Merchantability; Usage of Trade

(1) Unless excluded or modified (Section 2–316), a warranty that the goods shall be merchantable is implied in a contract for their sale if the seller is a merchant with respect to goods of that kind. Under this section the serving for value of food or drink to be consumed either on the premises or elsewhere is a sale.

(2) Goods to be merchantable must be at least such as

(a) pass without objection in the trade under the contract description; and

(b) in the case of fungible goods, are of fair average quality within the description; and

(c) are fit for the ordinary purposes for which such goods are used; and

(d) run, within the variations permitted by the agreement, of even kind, quality and quantity within each unit and among all units involved; and

(e) are adequately contained, packaged, and labeled as the agreement may require; and

(f) conform to the promises or affirmations of fact made on the container or label if any.

(3) Unless excluded or modified (Section 2–316) other implied warranties may arise from course of dealing or usage of trade.

§2–315. Implied Warranty: Fitness for Particular Purpose

Where the seller at the time of contracting has reason to know any particular purpose for which the goods are required and that the buyer is relying on the seller's skill or judgment to select or furnish suitable goods, there is unless excluded or modified under the next section an implied warranty that the goods shall be fit for such purpose.

§2–316. Exclusion or Modification of Warranties

(1) Words or conduct relevant to the creation of an express warranty and words or conduct tending to negate or limit warranty shall

be construed wherever reasonable as consistent with each other; but subject to the provisions of this Article on parol or extrinsic evidence (Section 2–202) negation or limitation is inoperative to the extent that such construction is unreasonable.

(2) Subject to subsection (3), to exclude or modify the implied warranty of merchantability or any part of it the language must mention merchantability and in case of a writing must be conspicuous, and to exclude or modify any implied warranty of fitness the exclusion must be by a writing and conspicuous. Language to exclude all implied warranties of fitness is sufficient if it states, for example, that "There are no warranties which extend beyond the description on the face hereof."

(3) Notwithstanding subsection (2)

(a) unless the circumstances indicate otherwise, all implied warranties are excluded by expressions like "as is," "with all faults" or other language which in common understanding calls the buyer's attention to the exclusion of warranties and makes plain that there is no implied warranty; and
(b) when the buyer before entering into the contract has examined the goods or the sample or model as fully as he desired or has refused to examine the goods there is no implied warranty with regard to defects which an examination ought in the circumstances to have revealed to him; and
(c) an implied warranty can also be excluded or modified by course of dealing or course of performance or usage of trade.

(4) Remedies for breach of warranty can be limited in accordance with the provisions of this Article on liquidation or limitation of damages and on contractual modification of remedy (Sections 2–718 and 2–719).

§2–317. Cumulation and Conflict of Warranties Express or Implied

Warranties whether express or implied shall be construed as consistent with each other and as cumulative, but if such construction is unrea-

sonable the intention of the parties shall determine which warranty is dominant. In ascertaining that intention the following rules apply:

(a) Exact or technical specifications displace an inconsistent sample or model or general language of description.
(b) A sample from an existing bulk displaces inconsistent general language of description.
(c) Express warranties displace inconsistent implied warranties other than an implied warranty of fitness for a particular purpose.

§2–318. Third Party Beneficiaries of Warranties Express or Implied

A seller's warranty whether express or implied extends to any natural person who is in the family or household of his buyer or who is a guest in his home if it is reasonable to expect that such person may use, consume or be affected by the goods and who is injured in person by breach of the warranty. A seller may not exclude or limit the operation of this section.

§2–319. F.O.B. and F.A.S. Terms

(1) Unless otherwise agreed the term F.O.B. (which means "free on board") at a named place, even though used only in connection with the stated price, is a delivery term under which

(a) when the term is F.O.B. the place of shipment, the seller must at that place ship the goods in the manner provided in this Article (Section 2–504) and bear the expense and risk of putting them into the possession of the carrier; or
(b) when the term is F.O.B. the place of destination, the seller must at his own expense and risk transport the goods to that place and there tender delivery of them in the manner provided in this Article (Section 2–503);
(c) when under either (a) or (b) the term is also F.O.B. vessel, car or other vehicle, the seller must in addition at his own expense and risk load the goods on board. If the term is F.O.B. vessel the buyer must name the ves-

sel and in an appropriate case the seller must comply with the provisions of this Article on the form of bill of lading (Section 2–323).

(2) Unless otherwise agreed the term F.A.S. vessel (which means "free alongside") at a named port, even though used only in connection with the stated price, is a delivery term under which the seller must

(a) at his own expense and risk deliver the goods alongside the vessel in the manner usual in that port or on a dock designated and provided by the buyer; and
(b) obtain and tender a receipt for the goods in exchange for which the carrier is under a duty to issue a bill of lading.

(3) Unless otherwise agreed in any case falling within subsection (1) (a) or (c) or subsection (2) the buyer must seasonably give any needed instructions for making delivery, including when the term is F.A.S. or F.O.B. the loading berth of the vessel and in an appropriate case its name and sailing date. The seller may treat the failure of needed instructions as a failure of cooperation under this Article (Section 2–311). He may also at his option move the goods in any reasonable manner preparatory to delivery or shipment.

(4) Under the term F.O.B. vessel or F.A.S. unless otherwise agreed the buyer must make payment against tender or the required documents and the seller may not tender nor the buyer demand delivery of the goods in substitution for the documents.

§2–320. C.I.F. and C. & F. Terms

(1) The term C.I.F. means that the price includes in a lump sum the cost of the goods and the insurance and freight to the named destination. The term C. & F. or C.F. means that the price so includes cost and freight to the named destination.

(2) Unless otherwise agreed and even though used only in connection with the stated price and destination, the term C.I.F. destination or its equivalent requires the seller at his own expense and risk to

(a) put the goods into the possession of a carrier at the port for shipment and obtain a negotiable bill or bills of lading covering the entire transportation to the named destination; and
(b) load the goods and obtain a receipt from the carrier (which may be contained in the bill of lading) showing that the freight has been paid or provided for; and
(c) obtain a policy or certificate of insurance, including any war risk insurance, of a kind and on terms then current at the port of shipment in the usual amount, in the currency of the contract, shown to cover the same goods covered by the bill of lading and providing for payment of loss to the order of the buyer or for the account of whom it may concern; but the seller may add to the price the amount of the premium for any such war risk insurance; and
(d) prepare an invoice of the goods and procure any other documents required to effect shipment or to comply with the contract; and
(e) forward and tender with commercial promptness all the documents in due form and with any indorsement necessary to perfect the buyer's rights.

(3) Unless otherwise agreed the term C. & F. or its equivalent has the same effect and imposes upon the seller the same obligations and risks as a C.I.F. term except the obligation as to insurance.

(4) Under the term C.I.F. or C. & F. unless otherwise agreed the buyer must make payment against tender of the required documents and the seller may not tender nor the buyer demand delivery of the goods in substitution for the documents.

§2–321. C.I.F. or C. & F.: "Net Landed Weights"; "Payment on Arrival"; Warranty of Condition on Arrival

Under a contract containing a term C.I.F. or C. & F.

(1) Where the price is based on or is to be adjusted according to "net landed weights," "delivered weights," "out turn" quantity or

quality or the like, unless otherwise agreed the seller must reasonably estimate the price. The payment due on tender of the documents called for by the contract is the amount so estimated, but after final adjustment of the price a settlement must be made with commercial promptness.

(2) An agreement described in subsection (1) or any warranty of quality or condition of the goods on arrival places upon the seller the risk of ordinary deterioration, shrinkage and the like in transportation but has no effect on the place or time of identification to the contract for sale or delivery or on the passing of the risk of loss.

(3) Unless otherwise agreed where the contract provides for payment on or after arrival of the goods the seller must before payment allow such preliminary inspection as is feasible; but if the goods are lost delivery of the documents and payment are due when the goods should have arrived.

§2–322. Delivery "Ex-Ship"

(1) Unless otherwise agreed a term for delivery of goods "ex-ship" (which means from the carrying vessel) or in equivalent language is not restricted to a particular ship and requires delivery from a ship which has reached a place at the named port of destination where goods of the kind are usually discharged.

(2) Under such a term unless otherwise agreed

(a) the seller must discharge all liens arising out of the carriage and furnish the buyer with a direction which puts the carrier under a duty to deliver the goods; and
(b) the risk of loss does not pass to the buyer until the goods leave the ship's tackle. or are otherwise properly unloaded.

§2–323. Form of Bill of Lading Required in Overseas Shipment; "Overseas"

(1) Where the contract contemplates overseas shipment and contains a term C.I.F. or

C. & F. or F.O.B. vessel, the seller unless otherwise agreed must obtain a negotiable bill of lading stating that the goods have been loaded on board or, in the case of a term C.I.F. or C. & F., received for shipment.

(2) Where in a case within subsection (1) a bill of lading has been issued in a set of parts, unless otherwise agreed if the documents are not to be sent from abroad the buyer may demand tender of the full set; otherwise only one part of the bill of lading need be tendered. Even if the agreement expressly requires a full set

(a) due tender of a single part is acceptable within the provisions of this Article on cure of improper delivery (subsection (1) of Section 2–508); and
(b) even though the full set is demanded, if the documents are sent from abroad the person tendering an incomplete set may nevertheless require payment upon furnishing an indemnity which the buyer in good faith deems adequate.

(3) A shipment by water or by air or a contract contemplating such shipment is "overseas" insofar as by usage of trade or agreement it is subject to the commercial, financing or shipping practices characteristic of international deep water commerce.

§2–324. "No Arrival, No Sale" Term

Under a term "no arrival, no sale" or terms of like meaning, unless otherwise agreed,

(a) the seller must properly ship conforming goods and if they arrive by any means he must tender them on arrival but he assumes no obligation that the goods will arrive unless he has caused the non-arrival; and
(b) where without fault of the seller the goods are in part lost or have so deteriorated as no longer to conform to the contract or arrive after the contract time, the buyer may proceed as if there had been casualty to identified goods (Section 2–613).

§2–325. "Letter of Credit" Term; "Confirmed Credit"

(1) Failure of the buyer seasonably to furnish an agreed letter of credit is a breach of the contract for sale.

(2) The delivery to seller of a proper letter of credit suspends the buyer's obligation to pay. If the letter of credit is dishonored, the seller may on seasonable notification to the buyer require payment directly from him.

(3) Unless otherwise agreed the term "letter of credit" or "banker's credit" in a contract for sale means an irrevocable credit issued by a financing agency of good repute and, where the shipment is overseas, of good international repute. The term "confirmed credit" means that the credit must also carry the direct obligation of such an agency which does business in the seller's financial market.

§2–326. Sale on Approval and Sale or Return; Consignment Sales and Rights of Creditors

(1) Unless otherwise agreed, if delivered goods may be returned by the buyer even though they conform to the contract, the transaction is

(a) a "sale on approval" if the goods are delivered primarily for use, and
(b) a "sale or return" if the goods are delivered primarily for resale.

(2) Except as provided in subsection (3), goods held on approval are not subject to the claims of the buyer's creditor until acceptance; goods held on sale or return are subject to such claims while in the buyer's possession.

(3) Where goods are delivered to a person for sale and such person maintains a place of business at which he deals in goods of the kind involved, under a name other than the name of the person making delivery, then with respect to claims of creditors of the person conducting the business the goods are deemed to be on sale or return. The provisions of this subsection are applicable even though an agreement purports to reserve title to the person making delivery

until payment or resale or uses such words as "on consignment" or "on memorandum." However, this subsection is not applicable if the person making delivery

(a) complies with an applicable law providing for a consignor's interest or the like to be evidenced by a sign, or
(b) establishes that the person conducting the business is generally known by his creditors to be substantially engaged in selling the goods of others, or
(c) complies with the filing provisions of the Article on Secured Transactions (Article 9).

(4) Any "or return" term of a contract for sale is to be treated as a separate contract for sale within the statute of frauds section of this Article (Section 2–201) and as contradicting the sale aspect of the contract within the provisions of this Article on parol or extrinsic evidence (Section 2–202).

§2–327. Special Incidents of Sale on Approval and Sale or Return

(1) Under a sale on approval unless otherwise agreed

(a) although the goods are identified to the contract the risk of loss and the title do not pass to the buyer until acceptance; and
(b) use of the goods consistent with the purpose of trial is not acceptance but failure seasonably to notify the seller of election to return the goods is acceptance, and if the goods conform to the contract acceptance of any part is acceptance of the whole; and
(c) after due notification of election to return, is at the seller's risk and expense but a merchant buyer must follow any reasonable instructions.

(2) Under a sale or return unless otherwise agreed

(a) the option to return extends to the whole or any commercial unit of the goods while in substantially their original condition, but must be exercised seasonably; and

(b) the return is at the buyer's risk and expense.

§2–328. Sale by Auction

(1) In a sale by auction if goods are put up in lots each lot is the subject of a separate sale.

(2) A sale by auction is complete when the auctioneer so announces by the fall of the hammer or in other customary manner. Where a bid is made while the hammer is falling in acceptance of a prior bid the auctioneer may in his discretion reopen the bidding or declare the goods sold under the bid on which the hammer was falling.

(3) Such a sale is with reserve unless the goods are in explicit terms put up without reserve. In an auction with reserve the auctioneer may withdraw the goods at any time until he announces completion of the sale. In an auction without reserve, after the auctioneer calls for bids on an article or lot, that article or lot cannot be withdrawn unless no bid is made within a reasonable time. In either case a bidder may retract his bid until the auctioneer's announcement of completion of the sale, but a bidder's retraction does not revive any previous bid.

(4) If the auctioneer knowingly receives a bid on the seller's behalf or the seller makes or procures such a bid, and notice has not been given that liberty for such bidding is reserved, the buyer may at his option avoid the sale or take the goods at the price of the last good faith bid prior to the completion of the sale. This subsection shall not apply to any bid at a forced sale.

PART 4. TITLE, CREDITORS AND GOOD FAITH PURCHASERS

§2–401. Passing of Title; Reservation for Security; Limited Application of This Section

Each provision of this article with regard to the rights, obligations and remedies of the seller, the buyer, purchasers or other third parties applies irrespective of title to the goods except where the provision refers to such title. Insofar as situations are not covered by the other provisions of this Article and matters concerning title became material the following rules apply:

(1) Title to goods cannot pass under a contract for sale prior to their identification to the contract (Section 2–501), and unless otherwise explicitly agreed the buyer acquires by their identification a special property as limited by this Act. Any retention or reservation by the seller of the title (property) in goods shipped or delivered to the buyer is limited in effect to a reservation of a security interest. Subject to these provisions and to the provisions of the Article on Secured Transactions (Article 9), title to goods passes from the seller to the buyer in any manner and on any conditions explicitly agreed on by the parties.

(2) Unless otherwise explicitly agreed title passes to the buyer at the time and place at which the seller completes his performance with reference to the physical delivery of the goods, despite any reservation of a security interest and even though a document of title is to be delivered at a different time or place; and in particular and despite any reservation of a security interest by the bill of lading

(a) if the contract requires or authorizes the seller to send the goods to the buyer but does not require him to deliver them at destination, title passes to the buyer at the time and place of shipment; but

(b) if the contract requires delivery at destination, title passes on tender there.

(3) Unless otherwise explicitly agreed where delivery is to be made without moving the goods,

(a) if the seller is to deliver a document of title, title passes at the time when and the place where he delivers such documents; or

(b) if the goods are at the time of contracting already identified and no documents are to be delivered, title passes at the time and place of contracting.

(4) A rejection or other refusal by the buyer to receive or retain the goods, whether or not justified, or a justified revocation of acceptance revests title to the goods in the seller. Such revesting occurs by operation of law and is not a "sale."

§2–402. Rights of Seller's Creditors Against Sold Goods

(1) Except as provided in subsections (2) and (3), rights of unsecured creditors of the seller with respect to goods which have been identified to a contract for sale are subject to the buyer's rights to recover the goods under this Article (Sections 2–502 and 2–716).

(2) A creditor of the seller may treat a sale or an identification of goods to a contract for sale as void if as against him a retention of possession by the seller is fraudulent under any rule of law of the state where the goods are situated, except that retention of possession in good faith and current course of trade by a merchant-seller for a commercially reasonable time after a sale or identification is not fraudulent.

(3) Nothing in this Article shall be deemed to impair the rights of creditors of the seller

(a) under the provisions of the Article on Secured Transactions (Article 9); or
(b) where identification to the contract or delivery is made not in current course of trade but in satisfaction of or as security for a pre-existing claim for money, security or the like and is made under circumstances which under any rule of law of the state where the goods are situated would apart from this Article constitute the transaction a fraudulent transfer or voidable preference.

§2–403. Power to Transfer; Good Faith Purchase of Goods; "Entrusting"

(1) A purchaser of goods acquires all title which his transferor had or had power to transfer except that a purchaser of a limited interest acquires rights only to the extent of the interest purchased. A person with voidable title has power to transfer a good title to a good faith purchaser for value. When goods have been delivered under a transaction of purchase the purchaser has such power even though

(a) the transferor was deceived as to the identity of the purchaser, or
(b) the delivery was in exchange for a check which is later dishonored, or
(c) it was agreed that the transaction was to be a "cash sale," or
(d) the delivery was procured through fraud punishable as larcenous under the criminal law.

(2) Any entrusting of possession of goods to a merchant who deals in goods of that kind gives him power to transfer all rights of the entruster to a buyer in ordinary course of business.

(3) "Entrusting" includes any delivery and any acquiescence in retention of possession regardless of any condition expressed between the parties to the delivery or acquiescence and regardless of whether the procurement of the entrusting or the possessor's disposition of the goods have been such as to be larcenous under the criminal law.

(4) The rights of other purchasers of goods and of lien creditors are governed by the Articles on Secured Transactions (Article 9), Bulk Transfers (Article 6) and Documents of Title (Article 7).

PART 5.   PERFORMANCE

§2–501. Insurable Interest in Goods, Manner of Identification of Goods

(1) The buyer obtains a special property and an insurable interest in goods by identification of existing goods as goods to which the contract refers even though the goods so identified are non-conforming and he has an option to return or reject them. Such identification can be made at any time and in any manner explicitly agreed to by the parties. In the absence of explicit agreement identification occurs

(a) when the contract is made if it is for the sale of goods already existing and identified;
(b) if the contract is for the sale of future goods other than those described in paragraph (c), when goods are shipped, marked or otherwise designated by the seller as goods to which the contract refers;
(c) when the crops are planted or otherwise become growing crops or the young are conceived if the contract is for the sale of unborn young to be born within twelve months after contracting or for the sale of crops to be harvested within twelve months or the next normal harvest season after contracting whichever is longer.

(2) The seller retains an insurable interest in goods so long as title to or any security interest in the goods remains in him and where the identification is by the seller alone he may until default or insolvency or notification to the buyer that the identification is final substitute other goods for those identified.

(3) Nothing in this section impairs any insurable interest recognized under any other statute or rule of law.

§2–502. Buyer's Right to Goods on Seller's Insolvency

(1) Subject to subsection (2) and even though the goods have not been shipped a buyer who has paid a part or all of the price of goods in which he has a special property under the provisions of the immediately preceding section may on making and keeping good a tender of any unpaid portion of their price recover them from the seller if the seller becomes insolvent within ten days after receipt of the first installment on their price.

(2) If the identification creating his special property has been made by the buyer he acquires the right to recover the goods only if they conform to the contract for sale.

§2–503. Manner of Seller's Tender of Delivery

(1) Tender of delivery requires that the seller put and hold conforming goods at the buyer's disposition and give the buyer any notification reasonably necessary to enable him to take delivery. The manner, time and place for tender are determined by the agreement and this Article, and in particular

(a) tender must be at a reasonable hour, and if it is of goods they must be kept available for the period reasonably necessary to enable the buyer to take possession; but
(b) unless otherwise agreed the buyer must furnish facilities reasonably suited to the receipt of the goods.

(2) Where the case is within the next section respecting shipment tender requires that the seller comply with its provisions.

(3) Where the seller is required to deliver at a particular destination tender requires that he comply with subsection (1) and also in any appropriate case tender documents as described in subsections (4) and (5) of this section.

(4) Where goods are in the possession of a bailee and are to be delivered without being moved

(a) tender requires that the seller either tender a negotiable document of title covering such goods or procure acknowledgment by the bailee of the buyer's right to possession of the goods; but
(b) tender to the buyer of a non-negotiable document of title or of a written direction to the bailee to deliver is sufficient tender unless the buyer seasonably objects, and receipt by the bailee of notification of the buyer's rights fixes those rights as against the bailee and all third persons; but risk of loss of the goods and of any failure by the bailee to honor the nonnegotiable document of title or to obey the direction remains on the seller until the buyer has had a reasonable time to present the document or direction, and a refusal by the bailee to honor the document or to obey the direction defeats the tender.

(5) Where the contract requires the seller to deliver documents

(a) he must tender all such documents in correct form, except as provided in this Article with respect to bills of lading in a set (subsection (2) of Section 2–323); and

(b) tender through customary banking channels is sufficient and dishonor of a draft accompanying the documents constitutes non-acceptance or rejection.

§2–504. Shipment by Seller

Where the seller is required or authorized to send the goods to the buyer and the contract does not require him to deliver them at a particular destination, then unless otherwise agreed he must

(a) put the goods in the possession of such a carrier and make such a contract for their transportation as may be reasonable having regard to the nature of the goods and other circumstances of the case; and

(b) obtain and promptly deliver or tender in due form any document necessary to enable the buyer to obtain possession of the goods or otherwise required by the agreement or by usage of trade; and

(c) promptly notify the buyer of the shipment.

Failure to notify the buyer under paragraph (c) or to make a proper contract under paragraph (a) is a ground for rejection only if material delay or loss ensues.

§2–505. Seller's Shipment Under Reservation

(1) Where the seller has identified goods to the contract by or before shipment:

(a) his procurement of a negotiable bill of lading to his own order or otherwise reserves in him a security interest in the goods. His procurement of the bill to the order of a financing agency or of the buyer indicates in addition only the seller's expectation of transferring that interest to the person named.

(b) a non-negotiable bill of lading to himself or his nominee reserves possession of the goods as security but except in a case of conditional delivery (subsection (2) of Section 2–507) a non-negotiable bill of lading naming the buyer as consignee reserves no security interest even though the seller retains possession of the bill of lading.

(2) When shipment by the seller with reservation of a security interest is in violation of the contract for sale it constitutes an improper contract for transportation within the preceding section but impairs neither the rights given to the buyer by shipment and identification of the goods to the contract nor the seller's powers as a holder of a negotiable document.

§2–506. Rights of Financing Agency

(1) A financing agency by paying or purchasing for value a draft which relates to a shipment of goods acquires to the extent of the payment or purchase and in addition to its own rights under the draft and any document of title securing it any rights of the shipper in the goods including the right to stop delivery and the shipper's right to have the draft honored by the buyer.

(2) The right to reimbursement of a financing agency which has in good faith honored or purchased the draft under commitment to or authority from the buyer is not impaired by subsequent discovery of defects with reference to any relevant document which was apparently regular on its face.

§2–507. Effect of Seller's Tender; Delivery on Condition

(1) Tender of delivery is a condition to the buyer's duty to accept the goods and, unless otherwise agreed, to his duty to pay for them. Tender entitles the seller to acceptance of the goods and to payment according to the contract.

(2) Where payment is due and demanded on the delivery to the buyer of goods or documents of title, his right as against the seller to retain or dispose of them is conditional upon his making the payment due.

§2–508. Cure by Seller of Improper Tender or Delivery; Replacement

(1) Where any tender or delivery by the seller is rejected because non-conforming and the time for performance has not yet expired, the seller may seasonably notify the buyer of his intention to cure and may then within the contract time make a conforming delivery.

(2) Where the buyer rejects a non-conforming tender which the seller had reasonable grounds to believe would be acceptable with or without money allowance the seller may if he seasonably notifies the buyer have a further reasonable time to substitute a conforming tender.

§2–509. Risk of Loss in the Absence of Breach

(1) Where the contract requires or authorizes the seller to ship the goods by carrier

(a) if it does not require him to deliver them at a particular destination, the risk of loss passes to the buyer when the goods are duly delivered to the carrier even though the shipment is under reservation (Section 2–505); but

(b) if it does require him to deliver them at a particular destination and the goods are there duly tendered while in the possession of the carrier, the risk of loss passes to the buyer when the goods are there duly so tendered as to enable the buyer to take delivery.

(2) Where the goods are held by a bailee to be delivered without being moved, the risk of loss passes to the buyer

(a) on his receipt of a negotiable document of title covering the goods; or

(b) on acknowledgment by the bailee of the buyer's right to possession of the goods; or

(c) after his receipt of a non-negotiable document of title or other written direction to deliver, as provided in subsection (4) (b) of Section 2–503.

(3) In any case not within subsection (1) or (2), the risk of loss passes to the buyer on his receipt of the goods if the seller is a merchant; otherwise the risk passes to the buyer on tender of delivery.

(4) The provisions of this section are subject to contrary agreement of the parties and to the provisions of this Article on sale on approval (Section 2–327) and on effect of breach on risk of loss (Section 2–510).

§2–510. Effect of Breach on Risk of Loss

(1) Where a tender or delivery of goods so fails to conform to the contract as to give a right of rejection the risk of their loss remains on the seller until cure or acceptance.

(2) Where the buyer rightfully revokes acceptance he may to the extent of any deficiency in his effective insurance coverage treat the risk of loss as having rested on the seller from the beginning.

(3) Where the buyer as to conforming goods already identified to the contract for sale repudiates or is otherwise in breach before risk of their loss has passed to him, the seller may to the extent of any deficiency in his effective insurance coverage treat the risk of loss as resting on the buyer for a commercially reasonable time.

§2–511. Tender of Payment by Buyer; Payment by Check

(1) Unless otherwise agreed tender of payment is a condition to the seller's duty to tender and complete any delivery.

(2) Tender of payment is sufficient when made by any means or in any manner current in the ordinary course of business unless the seller demands payment in legal tender and gives any extension of time reasonably necessary to procure it.

(3) Subject to the provisions of this Act on the effect of an instrument on an obligation (Section 3–802), payment by check is conditional and is defeated as between the parties by dishonor of the check on due presentment.

§2–512. Payment by Buyer Before Inspection

(1) Where the contract requires payment before inspection non-conformity of the goods does not excuse the buyer from so making payment unless

(a) the non-conformity appears without inspection; or

(b) despite tender of the required documents the circumstances would justify injunction against honor under the provisions of this Act (Section 5–114).

(2) Payment pursuant to subsection (1) does not constitute an acceptance of goods or impair the buyer's right to inspect or any of his remedies.

§2–513. Buyer's Right to Inspection of Goods

(1) Unless otherwise agreed and subject to subsection (3), where goods are tendered or delivered or identified to the contract for sale, the buyer has a right before payment or acceptance to inspect them at any reasonable place and time and in any reasonable manner. When the seller is required or authorized to send the goods to the buyer, the inspection may be after their arrival.

(2) Expenses of inspection must be borne by the buyer but may be recovered from the seller if the goods do not conform and are rejected.

(3) Unless otherwise agreed and subject to the provisions of this Article on C.I.F. contracts (subsection (3) of Section 2–321), the buyer is not entitled to inspect the goods before payment of the price when the contract provides

(a) for delivery "C.O.D." or on other like terms; or

(b) for payment against documents of title, except where such payment is due only after the goods are to become available for inspection.

(4) A place or method of inspection fixed by the parties is presumed to be exclusive but unless otherwise expressly agreed it does not postpone identification or shift the place for delivery or for passing the risk of loss. If compliance becomes impossible, inspection shall be as provided in this section unless the place or method fixed was clearly intended as an indispensable condition failure of which avoids the contract.

§2–514. When Documents Deliverable on Acceptance; When on Payment

Unless otherwise agreed documents against which a draft is drawn are to be delivered to the drawee on acceptance of the draft if it is payable more than three days after presentment; otherwise, only on payment.

§2–515. Preserving Evidence of Goods in Dispute

In furtherance of the adjustment of any claim or dispute

(a) either party on reasonable notification to the other and for the purpose of ascertaining the facts and preserving evidence has the right to inspect, test and sample the goods including such of them as may be in the possession or control of the other; and

(b) the parties may agree to a third-party inspection or survey to determine the conformity or condition of the goods and may agree that the findings shall be binding upon them in any subsequent litigation or adjustment.

PART 6.   BREACH, REPUDIATION AND EXCUSE

§2–601. Buyer's Rights on Improper Delivery

Subject to the provisions of this Article on breach in installment contracts (Section 2–612)) and unless otherwise agreed under the sections on contractual limitations of remedy (Sections 2–718 and 2–719), if the goods or the tender of delivery fail in any respect to conform to the contract, the buyer may

(a) reject the whole; or

(b) accept the whole; or

(c) accept any commercial unit or units and reject the rest.

§2–602. Manner and Effect of Rightful Rejection

(1) Rejection of goods must be within a reasonable time after their delivery or tender. It is ineffective unless the buyer seasonably notifies the seller.

(2) Subject to the provisions of the two following sections on rejected goods (Sections 2–603 and 2–604),

(a) after rejection any exercise of ownership by the buyer with respect to any commercial unit is wrongful as against the seller; and

(b) if the buyer has before rejection taken physical possession of goods in which he does not have a security interest under the provisions of this Article (subsection (3) of Section 2–711), he is under a duty after rejection to hold them with reasonable care at the seller's disposition for a time sufficient to permit the seller to remove them; but

(c) the buyer has no further obligation with regard to goods rightfully rejected.

(3) The seller's rights with respect to goods wrongfully rejected are governed by the provisions of this Article on Seller's remedies in general (Section 2–703).

§2–603. Merchant Buyer's Duties as to Rightfully Rejected Goods

(1) Subject to any security interest in the buyer (subsection (3) of Section 2–711), when the seller has no agent or place of business at the market of rejection a merchant buyer is under a duty after rejection of goods in his possession or control to follow any reasonable instructions received from the seller with respect to the goods and in the absence of such instructions to make reasonable efforts to sell them for the seller's account if they are perishable or threaten to decline in value speedily.

Instructions are not reasonable if on demand indemnity for expenses is not forthcoming.

(2) When the buyer sells goods under subsection (1), he is entitled to reimbursement from the seller or out of the proceeds for reasonable expenses of caring for and selling them, and if the expenses include no selling commission then to such commission as is usual in the trade or if there is none to a reasonable sum not exceeding ten percent on the gross proceeds.

(3) In complying with this section the buyer is held only to good faith and good faith conduct hereunder is neither acceptance nor conversion nor the basis of an action for damages.

§2–604. Buyer's Options as to Salvage of Rightfully Rejected Goods

Subject to the provisions of the immediately preceding section on perishables if the seller gives no instructions within a reasonable time after notification of rejection the buyer may store the rejected goods for the seller's account or reship them to him or resell them for the seller's account with reimbursement as provided in the preceding section. Such action is not acceptance or conversion.

§2–605. Waiver of Buyer's Objections by Failure to Particularize

(1) The buyer's failure to state in connection with rejection a particular defect which is ascertainable by reasonable inspection precludes him from relying on the unstated defect to justify rejection or to establish breach to justify rejection or to establish breach

(a) where the seller could have cured it if stated seasonably; or

(b) between merchants when the seller has after rejection made a request in writing for a full and final written statement of all defects on which the buyer proposes to rely.

(2) Payment against documents made without reservation of rights precludes recovery of the payment for defects apparent on the face of the documents.

§2-606. What Constitutes Acceptance of Goods

(1) Acceptance of goods occurs when the buyer

(a) after a reasonable opportunity to inspect the goods signifies to the seller that the goods are conforming or that he will take or retain them in spite of their nonconformity; or
(b) fails to make an effective rejection (subsection (1) of Section 2-602), but such acceptance does not occur until the buyer has had a reasonable opportunity to inspect them; or
(c) does any act inconsistent with the seller's ownership; but if such act is wrongful as against the seller it is an acceptance only if ratified by him.

(2) Acceptance of a part of any commercial unit is acceptance of that entire unit.

§2-607. Effect of Acceptance; Notice of Breach; Burden of Establishing Breach After Acceptance; Notice of Claim or Litigation to Person Answerable Over

(1) The buyer must pay at the contract rate for any goods accepted.

(2) Acceptance of goods by the buyer precludes rejection of the goods accepted and if made with knowledge of a non-conformity cannot be revoked because of it unless the acceptance was on the reasonable assumption that the non-conformity would be seasonably cured but acceptance does not of itself impair any other remedy provided by this Article for nonconformity.

(3) Where a tender has been accepted

(a) the buyer must within a reasonable time after he discovers or should have discovered any breach notify the seller of breach or be barred from any remedy; and
(b) if the claim is one for infringement or the like (subsection (3) of Section 2-312) and the buyer is sued as a result of such a breach he must so notify the seller within a reasonable time after he receives notice of the litigation or be barred from any remedy over for liability established by the litigation.

(4) The burden is on the buyer to establish any breach with respect to the goods accepted.

(5) Where the buyer is sued for breach of a warranty or other obligation for which his seller is answerable over

(a) he may give his seller written notice of the litigation. If the notice states that seller may come in and defend and that if the seller does not do so he will be bound in any action against him by his buyer by any determination of fact common to the two litigations, then unless the seller after seasonable receipt of the notice does come in and defend he is so bound.
(b) if the claim is one for infringement or the like (subsection (3) of Section 2-312) the original seller may demand in writing that his buyer turn over to him control of the litigation including settlement or else be barred from any remedy over and if he also agrees to bear all expense and to satisfy any adverse judgment, then unless the buyer after seasonable receipt of the demand does turn over control the buyer is so barred.

(6) The provisions of subsections (3), (4) and (5) apply to any obligation of a buyer to hold the seller harmless against infringement or the like (subsection (3) of Section 2-312).

§2-608. Revocation of Acceptance in Whole or in Part

(1) The buyer may revoke his acceptance of a lot or commercial unit whose non-conformity substantially impairs its value to him if he has accepted it

(a) on the reasonable assumption that its non-conformity would be cured and it has not been seasonable cured; or
(b) without discovery of such non-conformity if his acceptance was reasonably induced either by the difficulty of discovery before acceptance or by the seller's assurances.

(2) Revocation of acceptance must occur within a reasonable time after the buyer discovers or should have discovered the ground

for it and before any substantial change in condition of the goods which is not caused by their own defects. It is not effective until the buyer notifies the seller of it.

(3) A buyer who so revokes has the same rights and duties with regard to the goods involved as if he had rejected them.

§2–609. Right to Adequate Assurance of Performance

(1) A contract for sale imposes an obligation on each party that the other's expectation of receiving due performance will not be impaired. When reasonable grounds for insecurity arise with respect to the performance of either party the other may in writing demand adequate assurance of due performance and until he receives such assurance may if commercially reasonable suspend any performance for which he has not already received the agreed return.

(2) Between merchants the reasonableness of grounds for insecurity and the adequacy of any assurance offered shall be determined according to commercial standards.

(3) Acceptance of any improper delivery or payment does not prejudice the aggrieved party's right to demand adequate assurance of future performance.

(4) After receipt of a justified demand failure to provide within a reasonable time not exceeding thirty days such assurance of due performance as is adequate under the circumstances of the particular case is a repudiation of the contract.

§2–610. Anticipatory Repudiation

When either party repudiates the contract with respect to a performance not yet due the loss of which will substantially impair the value of the contract to the other, the aggrieved party may

(a) for a commercially reasonable time await performance by the repudiating party; or
(b) resort to any remedy for breach (Section 2–703 or Section 2–711), even though he has notified the repudiating party that he

would await the latter's performance and has urged retraction; and
(c) in either case suspend his own performance or proceed in accordance with the provisions of this Article on the seller's right to identify goods to the contract notwithstanding breach or to salvage unfinished goods (Section 2–704).

§2–611. Retraction of Anticipatory Repudiation

(1) Until the repudiating party's next performance is due he can retract his repudiation unless the aggrieved party has since the repudiation cancelled or materially changed his position or otherwise indicated that he considers the repudiation final.

(2) Retraction may be by any method which clearly indicates to the aggrieved party that the repudiating party intends to perform, but must include any assurance justifiably demanded under the provisions of this Article (Section 2–609).

(3) Retraction reinstates the repudiating party's rights under the contract with due excuse and allowance to the aggrieved party for any delay occasioned by the repudiation.

§2–612. "Installment Contract"; Breach

(1) An "installment contract" is one which requires or authorizes the delivery of goods in separate lots to be separately accepted, even though the contract contains a clause "each delivery is a separate contract" or its equivalent.

(2) The buyer may reject any installment which is non-conforming if the non-conformity substantially impairs the value of that installment and cannot be cured or if the non-conformity is a defect in the required documents; but if the non-conformity does not fall within subsection (3) and the seller gives adequate assurance of its cure the buyer must accept that installment.

(3) Whenever non-conformity or default with respect to one or more installments substantially impairs the value of the whole contract there is a breach of the whole. But the aggrieved

party reinstates the contract if he accepts a non-conforming installment without seasonably notifying of cancellation or if he brings an action with respect only to past installments or demands performance as to future installments.

§2–613. Casualty to Identified Goods

Where the contract requires for its performance goods identified when the contract is made, and the goods suffer casualty without fault of either party before the risk of loss passes to the buyer, or in a proper case under a "no arrival, no sale" term (Section 2–324) then

(a) if the loss is total the contract is avoided; and

(b) if the loss is partial or the goods have so deteriorated as no longer to conform to the contract the buyer may nevertheless demand inspection and at his option either treat the contract as avoided or accept the goods with due allowance from the contract price for the deterioration or the deficiency in quantity but without further right against the seller.

§2–614. Substituted Performance

(1) Where without fault of either party the agreed berthing, loading, or unloading facilities fail or an agreed type of carrier becomes unavailable or the agreed manner of delivery otherwise becomes commercially impracticable but a commercially reasonable substitute is available, such substitute performance must be tendered and accepted.

(2) If the agreed means or manner of payment fails because of domestic or foreign governmental regulation, the seller may withhold or stop delivery unless the buyer provides a means or manner of payment which is commercially a substantial equivalent. If delivery has already been taken, payment by the means or in the manner provided by the regulation discharges the buyer's obligation unless the regulation is discriminatory, oppressive or predatory.

§2–615. Excuse by Failure of Presupposed Conditions

Except so far as a seller may have assumed a greater obligation and subject to the preceding section on substituted performance:

(a) Delay in delivery or non-delivery in whole or in part by a seller who complies with paragraphs (b) and (c) is not a breach of his duty under a contract for sale if performance as agreed has been made impracticable by the occurrence of a contingency the non-occurrence of which was a basic assumption on which the contract was made or by compliance in good faith with any applicable foreign or domestic governmental regulation or order whether or not it later proves to be invalid.

(b) Where the causes mentioned in paragraph (a) affect only a part of the seller's capacity to perform, he must allocate production and deliveries among his customers but may at his option include regular customers not then under contract as well as his own requirements for further manufacture. He may so allocate in any manner which is fair and reasonable.

(c) The seller must notify the buyer seasonably that there will be delay or non-delivery and, when allocation is required under paragraph (b), of the estimated quota thus made available for the buyer.

§2–616. Procedure on Notice Claiming Excuse

(1) When the buyer receives notification of a material or indefinite delay or an allocation justified under the preceding section he may by written notification to the seller as to any delivery concerned, and where the prospective deficiency substantially impairs the value of the whole contract under the provisions of this Article relating to breach of installment contracts (Section 2–612), then also as to the whole,

(a) terminate and thereby discharge any unexecuted portion of the contract; or

(b) modify the contract by agreeing to take his available quota in substitution.

(2) If after receipt of such notification from the seller the buyer fails so to modify the contract within a reasonable time not exceeding thirty days the contract lapses with respect to any deliveries affected.

(3) The provisions of this section may not be negated by agreement except in so far as the seller has assumed a greater obligation under the preceding section.

PART 7. REMEDIES

§2–701. Remedies for Breach of Collateral Contracts Not Impaired

Remedies for breach of any obligation or promise collateral or ancillary to a contract for sale are not impaired by the provisions of this Article.

§2–702. Seller's Remedies on Discovery of Buyer's Insolvency

(1) Where the seller discovers the buyer to be insolvent he may refuse delivery except for cash including payment for all goods theretofore delivered under the contract, and stop delivery under this Article (Section 2–705).

(2) Where the seller discovers that the buyer has received goods on credit while insolvent he may reclaim the goods upon demand made within ten days after the receipt, but if misrepresentation of solvency has been made to the particular seller in writing within three months before delivery the ten day limitation does not apply. Except as provided in this subsection the seller may not base a right to reclaim goods on the buyer's fraudulent or innocent misrepresentation of solvency or of intent to pay.

(3) The seller's right to reclaim under subsection (2) is subject to the rights of a buyer in ordinary course or other good faith purchaser under this Article (Section 2–403). Suc-

cessful reclamation of goods excludes all other remedies with respect to them.

§2–703. Seller's Remedies in General

Where the buyer wrongfully rejects or revokes acceptance of goods or fails to make a payment due on or before delivery or repudiates with respect to a part or the whole, then with respect to any goods directly affected and, if the breach is of the whole contract (Section 2–612), then also with respect to the whole undelivered balance, the aggrieved seller may

(a) withhold delivery of such goods;
(b) stop delivery by any bailee as hereafter provided (Section 2–705);
(c) proceed under the next section respecting goods still unidentified to the contract;
(d) resell and recover damages as hereafter provided (Section 2–706);
(e) recover damages for non-acceptance (Section 2–708) or in a proper case the price (Section 2–709);
(f) cancel.

§2–704. Seller's Right to Identify Goods to the Contract Notwithstanding Breach or to Salvage Unfinished Goods

(1) An aggrieved seller under the preceding section may

(a) identify to the contract conforming goods not already identified if at the time he learned of the breach they are in his possession or control;
(b) treat as the subject of resale goods which have demonstrably been intended for the particular contract even though those goods are unfinished.

(2) Where the goods are unfinished an aggrieved seller may in the exercise of reasonable commercial judgment for the purposes of avoiding loss and of effective realization either complete the manufacture and wholly identify the goods to the contract or cease manufacture and resell for scrap or salvage value or proceed in any other reasonable manner.

§2–705. Seller's Stoppage of Delivery in Transit or Otherwise

(1) The seller may stop delivery of goods in the possession of a carrier or other bailee when he discovers the buyer to be insolvent (Section 2–702) and may stop delivery of carload, truckload, planeload or larger shipments of express or freight when the buyer repudiates or fails to make a payment due before delivery or if for any other reason the seller has a right to withhold or reclaim the goods.

(2) As against such buyer the seller may stop delivery until

(a) receipt of the goods by the buyer; or

(b) acknowledgment to the buyer by any bailee of the goods except a carrier that the bailee holds the goods for the buyer; or

(c) such acknowledgment to the buyer by a carrier by reshipment or as warehouseman; or

(d) negotiation to the buyer of any negotiable document of title covering the goods.

(3) (a) To stop delivery the seller must so notify as to enable the bailee by reasonable diligence to prevent delivery of the goods.

(b) After such notification the bailee must hold and deliver the goods according to the directions of the seller but the seller is liable to the bailee for any ensuing charges or damages.

(c) If a negotiable document of title has been issued for goods the bailee is not obliged to obey a notification to stop until surrender of the document.

(d) A carrier who has issued a non-negotiable bill of lading is not obliged to obey a notification to stop received from a person other than the consignor.

§2–706. Seller's Resale Including Contract for Resale

(1) Under the conditions stated in Section 2–703 on seller's remedies, the seller may resell the goods concerned or the undelivered balance thereof. Where the resale is made in good faith and in a commercially reasonable manner the seller may recover the difference between the resale price and the contract price together with any incidental damages allowed under the provisions of this Article (Section 2–710), but less expenses saved in consequence of the buyer's breach.

(2) Except as otherwise provided in subsection (3) or unless otherwise agreed resale may be at public or private sale including sale by way of one or more contracts to sell or of identification to an existing contract of the seller. Sale may be as a unit or in parcels and at any time and place and on any terms but every aspect of the sale including the method, manner, time, place and terms must be commercially reasonable. The resale must be reasonably identified as referring to the broken contract, but it is not necessary that the goods be in existence or that any or all of them have been identified to the contract before the breach.

(3) Where the resale is at private sale the seller must give the buyer reasonable notification of his intention to resell.

(4) Where the resale is at public sale

(a) only identified goods can be sold except where there is a recognized market for a public sale of futures in goods of the kind; and

(b) it must be made at a usual place or market for public sale if one is reasonably available and except in the case of goods which are perishable or threaten to decline in value speedily the seller must give the buyer reasonable notice of the time and place of the resale; and

(c) if the goods are not to be within the view of those attending the sale the notification of sale must state the place where the goods are located and provide for their reasonable inspection by prospective bidders; and

(d) the seller may buy.

(5) A purchaser who buys in good faith at a resale takes the goods free of any rights of the original buyer even though the seller fails

to comply with one or more of the requirements of this section.

(6) The seller is not accountable to the buyer for any profit made on any resale. A person in the position of a seller (Section 2–707) or a buyer who has rightfully rejected or justifiably revoked acceptance must account for any excess over the amount of his security interest, as hereinafter defined (subsection (3) of Section 2–711).

§2–707. "Person in the Position of a Seller"

(1) A "person in the position of a seller" includes as against a principal an agent who has paid or become responsible for the price of goods on behalf of his principal or anyone who otherwise holds a security interest or other right in goods similar to that of a seller.

(2) A person in the position of a seller may as provided in this Article withhold or stop delivery (Section 2–705) and resell (Section 2–706) and recover incidental damages (Section 2–710).

§2–708. Seller's Damages for Non-acceptance or Repudiation

(1) Subject to subsection (2) and to the provisions of this Article with respect to proof of market price (Section 2–723), the measure of damages for non-acceptance or repudiation by the buyer is the difference between the market price at the time and place for tender and the unpaid contract price together with any incidental damages provided in this Article (Section 2–710), but less expenses saved in consequence of the buyer's breach.

(2) If the measure of damages provided in subsection (1) is inadequate to put the seller in as good a position as performance would have done then the measure of damages is the profit (including reasonable overhead) which the seller would have made from full performance by the buyer, together with any incidental damages provided in this Article (Section

2–710), due allowance for costs reasonably incurred and due credit for payments or proceeds of resale.

§2–709. Action for the Price

(1) When the buyer fails to pay the price as it becomes due the seller may recover, together with any incidental damages under the next section, the price

(a) of goods accepted or of conforming goods lost or damaged within a commercially reasonable time after risk of their loss has passed to the buyer; and

(b) of goods identified to the contract if the seller is unable after reasonable effort to resell them at a reasonable price or the circumstances reasonably indicate that such effort will be unavailing.

(2) Where the seller sues for the price he must hold for the buyer any goods which have been identified to the contract and are still in his control except that if resale becomes possible he may resell them at any time prior to the collection of the judgment. The net proceeds of any such resale must be credited to the buyer and payment of the judgment entitles him to any goods not resold.

(3) After the buyer has wrongfully rejected or revoked acceptance of the goods or has failed to make payment due or has repudiated (Section 2–610), a seller who is held not entitled to the price under this section shall nevertheless be awarded damages for non-acceptance under the preceding section.

§2–710. Seller's Incidental Damages

Incidental damages to an aggrieved seller include any commercially reasonable charges, expenses or commissions incurred in stopping delivery, in the transportation, care and custody of goods after the buyer's breach, in connection with return or resale of the goods or otherwise resulting from the breach.

§2–711. Buyer's Remedies in General; Buyer's Security Interest in Rejected Goods

(1) Where the seller fails to make delivery or repudiates or the buyer rightfully rejects or justifiably revokes acceptance then with respect to any goods involved, and with respect to the whole if the breach goes to the whole contract (Section 2–612), the buyer may cancel and whether or not he has done so may in addition to recovering so much of the price as has been paid

    (a) "cover" and have damages under the next section as to all the goods affected whether or not they have been identified to the contract; or
    (b) recover damages for non-delivery as provided in this Article (Section 2–713).

(2) Where the seller fails to deliver or repudiates the buyer may also

    (a) if the goods have been identified recover them as provided in this Article (Section 2–502); or
    (b) in a proper case obtain specific performance or replevy the goods as provided in this Article (Section 2–716).

(3) On rightful rejection or justifiable revocation of acceptance a buyer has a security interest in goods in his possession or control for any payments made on their price and any expenses reasonably incurred in their inspection, receipt, transportation, care and custody and may hold such goods and resell them in like manner as an aggrieved seller (Section 2–706).

§2–712. "Cover"; Buyer's Procurement of Substitute Goods

(1) After a breach within the preceding section the buyer may "cover" by making in good faith and without unreasonable delay any reasonable purchase of or contract to purchase goods in substitution for those due from the seller.

(2) The buyer may recover from the seller as damages the difference between the cost of cover and the contract price together with any incidental or consequential damages as hereinafter defined (Section 2–715), but less expenses saved in consequence of the seller's breach.

(3) Failure of the buyer to effect cover within this section does not bar him from any other remedy.

§2–713. Buyer's Damages for Non-Delivery or Repudiation

(1) Subject to the provisions of this Article with respect to proof of market price (Section 2–723), the measure of damages for non-delivery or repudiation by the seller is the difference between the market price at the time when the buyer learned of the breach and the contract price together with any incidental and consequential damages provided in this Article (Section 2–715), but less expenses saved in consequence of the seller's breach.

(2) Market price is to be determined as of the place for tender or, in cases of rejection after arrival or revocation of acceptance, as of the place of arrival.

§2–714. Buyer's Damages for Breach in Regard to Accepted Goods

(1) Where the buyer has accepted goods and given notification (subsection (3) of Section 2–607) he may recover as damages for any non-conformity of tender the loss resulting in the ordinary course of events from the seller's breach as determined in any manner which is reasonable.

(2) The measure of damages for breach of warranty is the difference at the time and place of acceptance between the value of the goods accepted and the value they would have had if they had been as warranted, unless special circumstances show proximate damages of a different amount.

(3) In a proper case any incidental and consequential damages under the next section may also be recovered.

§2-715. Buyer's Incidental and Consequential Damages

(1) Incidental damages resulting from the seller's breach include expenses reasonably incurred in inspection, receipt, transportation and care and custody of goods rightfully rejected, any commercially reasonable charges, expenses or commissions in connection with effecting cover and any other reasonable expense incident to the delay or other breach.

(2) Consequential damages resulting from the seller's breach include

(a) any loss resulting from general or particular requirements and needs of which the seller at the time of contracting had reason to know and which could not reasonably be prevented by cover or otherwise; and

(b) injury to person or property proximately resulting from any breach of warranty.

§2-716. Buyer's Right to Specific Performance or Replevin

(1) Specific performance may be decreed where the goods are unique or in other proper circumstances.

(2) The decree for specific performance may include such terms and conditions as to payment of the price, damages, or other relief as the court may deem just.

(3) The buyer has a right of replevin for goods identified to the contract if after reasonable effort he is unable to effect cover for such goods or the circumstances reasonably indicate that such effort will be unavailing or if the goods have been shipped under reservation and satisfaction of the security interest in them has been made or tendered.

§2-717. Deduction of Damages From the Price

The buyer on notifying the seller of his intention to do so may deduct all or any part of the damages resulting from any breach of the contract from any part of the price still due under the same contract.

§2-718. Liquidation or Limitation of Damages; Deposits

(1) Damages for breach by either party may be liquidated in the agreement but only at an amount which is reasonable in the light of the anticipated or actual harm caused by the breach, the difficulties of proof of loss, and the inconvenience or nonfeasibility of otherwise obtaining an adequate remedy. A term fixing unreasonably large liquidated damages is void as a penalty.

(2) Where the seller justifiably withholds delivery of goods because of the buyer's breach, the buyer is entitled to restitution of any amount by which the sum of his payments exceeds

(a) the amount to which the seller is entitled by virtue of terms liquidating the seller's damages in accordance with subsection (1), or

(b) in the absence of such terms, twenty per cent of the value of the total performance for which the buyer is obligated under the contract or $500, whichever is smaller.

(3) The buyer's right to restitution under subsection (2) is subject to offset to the extent that the seller establishes

(a) a right to recover damages under the provisions of this Article other than subsection (1), and

(b) the amount or value of any benefits received by the buyer directly or indirectly by reason of the contract.

(4) Where a seller has received payment in goods their reasonable value or the proceeds of their resale shall be treated as payments for the purposes of subsection (2); but if the seller has notice of the buyer's breach before reselling goods received in part performance, his resale

is subject to the conditions laid down in this Article on resale by an aggrieved seller (Section 2–706).

§2–719. Contractual Modification or Limitation of Remedy

(1) Subject to the provisions of subsections (2) and (3) of this section and of the preceding section on liquidation and limitation of damages,

(a) the agreement may provide for remedies in addition to or in substitution for those provided in this Article and may limit or alter the measure of damages recoverable under this Article, as by limiting the buyer's remedies to return of the goods and repayment of the price or to repair and replacement of non-conforming goods or parts; and

(b) resort to a remedy as provided is optional unless the remedy is expressly agreed to be exclusive, in which case it is the sole remedy.

(2) Where circumstances cause an exclusive or limited remedy to fail of its essential purpose, remedy may be had as provided in this Act.

(3) Consequential damages may be limited or excluded unless the limitation or exclusion is unconscionable. Limitation of consequential damages for injury to the person in the case of consumer goods is prima facie unconscionable but limitation of damages where the loss is commercial is not.

§2–720. Effect of "Cancellation" or "Recission" on Claims for Antecedent Breach

Unless the contrary intention clearly appears, expressions of "cancellation" or "rescission" of the contract or the like shall not be construed as a renunciation or discharge of any claim in damages for an antecedent breach.

§2–721. Remedies for Fraud

Remedies for material misrepresentation or fraud include all remedies available under this Article for non-fraudulent breach. Neither rescission or a claim for rescission of the contract for sale nor rejection or return of the goods shall bar or be deemed inconsistent with a claim for damages or other remedy.

§2–722. Who Can Sue Third Parties for Injury to Goods

Where a third party so deals with goods which have been identified to a contract for sale as to cause actionable injury to a party to that contract

(a) a right of action against the third party is in either party to the contract for sale who has title to or a security interest or a special property or an insurable interest in the goods; and if the goods have been destroyed or converted a right of action is also in the party who either bore the risk of loss under the contract for sale or has since the injury assumed that risk as against the other;

(b) if at the time of the injury the party plaintiff did not bear the risk of loss as against the other party to the contract for sale and there is no arrangement between them for disposition of the recovery, his suit or settlement is, subject to his own interest, as a fiduciary for the other party to the contract;

(c) either party may with the consent of the other sue for the benefit of whom it may concern.

§2–723. Proof of Market Price: Time and Place

(1) If an action based on anticipatory repudiation comes to trial before the time for performance with respect to some or all of the goods, any damages based on market price (Section 2–708 or Section 2–713) shall be determined according to the price of such goods prevailing at the time when the aggrieved party learned of the repudiation.

(2) If evidence of a price prevailing at the times or places described in this Article is not readily available the price prevailing within any reasonable time before or after the time described or at any other place which in com-

mercial judgment or under usage of trade would serve as a reasonable substitute for the one described may be used, making any proper allowance for the cost of transporting the goods to or from such other place.

(3) Evidence of a relevant price prevailing at a time or place other than the one described in this Article offered by one party is not admissible unless and until he has given the other party such notice as the court finds sufficient to prevent unfair surprise.

§2–724. Admissibility of Market Quotations

Whenever the prevailing price or value of any goods regularly bought and sold in any established commodity market is in issue, reports in official publications or trade journals or in newspapers or periodicals of general circulation published as the reports of such market shall be admissible in evidence. The circumstances of the preparation of such a report may be shown to affect its weight but not its admissibility.

§2–725. Statute of Limitations in Contracts for Sale

(1) An action for breach of any contract for sale must be commenced within four years after the cause of action has accrued. By the original agreement the parties may reduce the period of limitation to not less than one year but may extend it.

(2) A cause of action accrues when the breach occurs, regardless of the aggrieved party's lack of knowledge of the breach. A breach of warranty occurs when tender of delivery is made, except that where a warranty explicitly extends to future performance of the goods and discovery of the breach must await the time of such performance the cause of action accrues when the breach is or should have been discovered.

(3) Where an action commenced within the time limited by subsection (1) is so terminated as to leave available a remedy by another action for the same breach such other action may be commenced after the expiration of the time limited and within six months after the termination resulted from voluntary discontinuance or from dismissal for failure or neglect to prosecute.

(4) This section does not alter the law on tolling of the statute of limitations nor does it apply to causes of action which have accrued before this Act becomes effective.

ARTICLE 3. COMMERCIAL PAPER

PART 1. SHORT TITLE, FORM AND INTERPRETATION

§3–101. Short Title

This Article shall be known and may be cited as Uniform Commercial Code—Commercial Paper.

§3–102. Definitions and Index of Definitions

(1) In this Article unless the context otherwise requires

(a) "Issue" means the first delivery of an instrument to a holder or a remitter.

(b) An "order" is a direction to pay and must be more than an authorization or request. It must identify the person to pay with reasonable certainty. It may be addressed to one or more such persons jointly or in the alternative but not in succession.

(c) A "promise" is an undertaking to pay and must be more than an acknowledgment of an obligation.

(d) "Secondary party" means a drawer or endorser.

(e) "Instrument" means a negotiable instrument.

(2) Other definitions applying to this Article and the sections in which they appear are:

"Acceptance." Section 3–410.
"Accommodation party." Section 3–415.
"Alteration." Section 3–407.
"Certificate of deposit." Section 3–104.
"Certification." Section 3–411.
"Check." Section 3–104.
"Definite time." Section 3–109.
"Dishonor." Section 3–507.
"Draft." Section 3–104.
"Holder in due course." Section 3–302.
"Negotiation." Section 3–202.
"Note." Section 3–104.
"Notice of dishonor." Section 3–508.
"On demand." Section 3–108.
"Presentment." Section 3–504.
"Protest." Section 3–509.
"Restrictive Indorsement." Section 3–205.
"Signature." Section 3–401.

(3) The following definitions in other Articles apply to this Article:

"Account." Section 4–104.
"Banking Day." Section 4–104.
"Clearing house." Section 4–104.
"Collecting bank." Section 4–105.
"Customer." Section 4–104.
"Depositary Bank." Section 4–105.
"Documentary Draft." Section 4–104.
"Intermediary Bank." Section 4–105.
"Item." Section 4–104.
"Midnight deadline." Section 4–104.
"Payor bank." Section 4–105.

(4) In addition Article 1 contains general definitions and principles of construction and interpretation applicable throughout this Article.

§3–103. Limitations on Scope of Article

(1) This Article does not apply to money, documents of title or investment securities.

(2) The provisions of this Article are subject to the provisions of the Article on Bank Deposits and Collections (Article 4) and Secured Transactions (Article 9).

§3–104. Form of Negotiable Instruments; "Draft"; "Check"; "Certificate of Deposit"; "Note"

(1) Any writing to be a negotiable instrument within this Article must

(a) be signed by the maker or drawer; and
(b) contain an unconditional promise or order to pay a sum certain in money and no other promise, order, obligation or power given by the maker or drawer except as authorized by this Article; and
(c) be payable on demand or at a definite time; and
(d) be payable to order or to bearer.

(2) A writing which complies with the requirements of this section is

(a) a "draft" ("bill of exchange") if it is an order;
(b) a "check" if it is a draft drawn on a bank and payable on demand;
(c) a "certificate of deposit" if it is an acknowledgment by a bank of receipt of money with an engagement to repay it;
(d) a "note" if it is a promise other than a certificate of deposit.

(3) As used in other Articles of this Act, and as the context may require, the terms "draft," "check," "certificate of deposit" and "note" may refer to instruments which are not negotiable within this Article as well as to instruments which are so negotiable.

§3–105. When Promise or Order Unconditional

(1) A promise or order otherwise unconditional is not made conditional by the fact that the instrument

(a) is subject to implied or constructive conditions; or
(b) states its consideration, whether performed or promised, or the transaction which gave rise to the instrument, or that the promise or order is made or the instrument ma-

tures in accordance with or "as per" such transaction; or

(c) refers to or states that it arises out of a separate agreement or refers to a separate agreement for rights as to prepayment or acceleration; or

(d) states that it is drawn under a letter of credit; or

(e) states that it is secured, whether by mortgage, reservation of title or otherwise; or

(f) indicates a particular account to be debited or any other fund or source from which reimbursement is expected; or

(g) is limited to payment out of a particular fund or the proceeds of a particular source, if the instrument is issued by a government or governmental agency or unit; or

(h) is limited to payment out of the entire assets of a partnership, unincorporated association, trust or estate by or on behalf of which the instrument is issued.

(2) A promise or order is not unconditional if the instrument

(a) states that it is subject to or governed by any other agreement; or

(b) states that it is to be paid only out of a particular fund or source except as provided in this section.

§3–106. Sum Certain

(1) The sum payable is a sum certain even though it is to be paid

(a) with stated interest or by stated installments; or

(b) with stated different rates of interest before and after default or a specified date; or

(c) with a stated discount or addition if paid before or after the date fixed for payment; or

(d) with exchange or less exchange, whether at a fixed rate or at the current rate; or

(e) with costs of collection or an attorney's fee or both upon default.

(2) Nothing in this section shall validate any term which is otherwise illegal.

§3–107. Money

(1) An instrument is payable in money if the medium of exchange in which it is payable is money at the time the instrument is made. An instrument payable in "currency" or "current funds" is payable in money.

(2) A promise or order to pay a sum stated in a foreign currency is for a sum certain in money and, unless a different medium of payment is specified in the instrument, may be satisfied by payment of that number of dollars which the stated foreign currency will purchase at the buying sight rate for that currency on the day on which the instrument is payable or, if payable on demand, on the day of demand. If such an instrument specifies a foreign currency as the medium of payment the instrument is payable in that currency.

§3–108. Payable on Demand

Instruments payable on demand include those payable at sight or on presentation and those in which no time for payment is stated.

§3–109. Definite Time

(1) An instrument is payable at a definite time if by its terms it is payable

(a) on or before a stated date or at a fixed period after a stated date; or

(b) at a fixed period after sight; or

(c) at a definite time subject to any acceleration; or

(d) at a definite time subject to extension at the option of the holder, or to extension to a further definite time at the option of the maker or acceptor or automatically upon or after a specified act or event.

(2) An instrument which by its terms is otherwise payable only upon an act or event uncertain as to time of occurrence is not payable at a definite time even though the act or event has occurred.

§3–110. Payable to Order

(1) An instrument is payable to order when by its terms it is payable to the order or assigns of any person therein specified with reasonable certainty, or to him or his order, or when it is conspicuously designated on its face as "exchange" or the like and names a payee. It may be payable to the order of

(a) the maker or drawer; or

(b) the drawee; or

(c) a payee who is not maker, drawer or drawee; or

(d) two or more payees together or in the alternative; or

(e) an estate, trust or fund, in which case it is payable to the order of the representative of such estate, trust or fund or his successors; or

(f) an office, or an officer by his title is such in which case it is payable to the principal but the incumbent of the office or his successors may act as if he or they were the holder; or

(g) a partnership or unincorporated association, in which case it is payable to the partnership or association and may be indorsed or transferred by any person thereto authorized.

(2) An instrument not payable to order is not made so payable by such words as "payable upon return of this instrument properly indorsed."

(3) An instrument made payable both to order and to bearer is payable to order unless the bearer words are handwritten or typewritten.

§3–111. Payable to Bearer

An instrument is payable to bearer when by its terms it is payable to

(a) bearer or the order of bearer; or

(b) a specified person or bearer; or

(c) "cash" or the order of "cash," or any other indication which does not purport to designate a specific payee.

§3–112. Terms and Omissions Not Affecting Negotiability

(1) The negotiability of an instrument is not affected by

(a) the omission of a statement of any consideration or of the place where the instrument is drawn or payable; or

(b) a statement that collateral has been given to secure obligations either on the instrument or otherwise of an obligor on the instrument or that in case of default on those obligations the holder may realize on or dispose of the collateral; or

(c) a promise or power to maintain or protect collateral or to give additional collateral; or

(d) a term authorizing a confession of judgment on the instrument if it is not paid when due; or

(e) a term purporting to waive the benefit of any law intended for the advantage or protection of any obligor; or

(f) a term in a draft providing that the payee by indorsing or cashing it acknowledges full satisfaction of an obligation of the drawer; or

(g) a statement in a draft drawn in a set of parts (Section 3–801) to the effect that the order is effective only if no other part has been honored.

(2) Nothing in this section shall validate any term which is otherwise illegal.

§3–113. Seal

An instrument otherwise negotiable is within this Article even though it is under a seal.

§3–114. Date, Antedating, Postdating

(1) The negotiability of an instrument is not affected by the fact that it is undated, antedated or postdated.

(2) Where an instrument is antedated or postdated the time when it is payable is determined by the stated date if the instrument is payable on demand or at fixed period after date.

(3) Where the instrument or any signature thereon is dated, the date is presumed to be correct.

§3–115. Incomplete Instruments

(1) When a paper whose contents at the time of signing show that it is intended to become an instrument is signed while still incomplete in any necessary respect it cannot be enforced until completed, but when it is completed in accordance with authority given it is effective as completed.

(2) If the completion is unauthorized the rules as to material alteration apply (Section 3–407), even though the paper was not delivered by the maker or drawer; but the burden of establishing that any completion is unauthorized is on the party so asserting.

§3–116. Instruments Payable to Two or More Persons

An instrument payable to the order of two or more persons

(a) if in the alternative is payable to any one of them and may be negotiated, discharged or enforced by any of them who has possession of it;

(b) if not in the alternative is payable to all of them and may be negotiated, discharged or enforced only by all of them.

§3–117. Instruments Payable With Words of Description

An instrument made payable to a named person with the addition of words describing him

(a) as agent or officer of a specified person is payable to his principal but the agent or officer may act as if he were the holder;

(b) as any other fiduciary for a specified person or purpose is payable to the payee and may be negotiated, discharged or enforced by him;

(c) in any other manner is payable to the payee unconditionally and the additional words are without effect on subsequent parties.

§3–118. Ambiguous Terms and Rules of Construction

The following rules apply to every instrument:

(a) Where there is doubt whether the instrument is a draft or a note the holder may treat it as either. A draft drawn on the drawer is effective as a note.

(b) Handwritten terms control typewritten and printed terms, and typewritten control printed.

(c) Words control figures except that if the words are ambiguous figures control.

(d) Unless otherwise specified a provision for interest means interest at the judgment rate at the place of payment from the date of the instrument, or if it is undated from the date of issue.

(e) Unless the instrument otherwise specifies two or more persons who sign as maker, acceptor or drawer or indorser and as a part of the same transaction are jointly and severally liable even though the instrument contains such words as "I promise to pay."

(f) Unless otherwise specified consent to extension authorizes a single extension for not longer than the original period. A consent to extension, expressed in the instrument, is binding on secondary parties and accommodation makers. A holder may not exercise his option to extend an instrument over the objection of a maker or acceptor or other party who in accordance with Section 3–604 tenders full payment when the instrument is due.

§3–119. Other Writings Affecting Instrument

(1) As between the obligor and his immediate obligee or any transferee the terms of an instrument may be modified or affected by any other written agreement executed as a part of

the same transaction, except that a holder in due course is not affected by any limitation of his rights arising out of the separate written agreement if he had no notice of the limitation when he took the instrument.

(2) A separate agreement does not affect the negotiability of an instrument.

§3–120. Instruments "Payable Through" Bank

An instrument which states that it is "payable through" a bank or the like designates that bank as a collecting bank to make presentment but does not of itself authorize the bank to pay the instrument.

§3-121. Instruments Payable at Bank

NOTE: *If this Act is introduced in the Congress of the United States this section should be omitted.*
(States to select either alternative)

Alternative A

A note or acceptance which states that it is payable at a bank is the equivalent of a draft drawn on the bank payable when it falls due out of any funds of the maker or acceptor in current account or otherwise available for such payment.

Alternative B

A note or acceptance which states that it is payable at a bank is not of itself an order or authorization to the bank to pay it.

§3-122. Accrual of Cause of Action

(1) A cause of action against a maker or an acceptor accrues

(a) in the case of a time instrument on the day after maturity;
(b) in the case of a demand instrument upon its date or, if no date is stated, on the date of issue.

(2) A cause of action against the obligor of a demand or time certificate of deposit accrues upon demand, but demand on a time certificate may not be made until on or after the date of maturity.

(3) A cause of action against a drawer of a draft or an indorser of any instrument accrues upon demand following dishonor of the instrument. Notice of dishonor is a demand.

(4) Unless an instrument provides otherwise, interest runs at the rate provided by law for a judgment

(a) in the case of a maker, acceptor or other primary obligor of a demand instrument, from the date of demand;
(b) in all other cases from the date of accrual of the cause of action.

PART 2.   TRANSFER AND NEGOTIATION

§3–201. Transfer: Right to Indorsement

(1) Transfer of an instrument vests in the transferee such rights as the transferor has therein, except that a transferee who has himself been a party to any fraud or illegality affecting the instrument or who as a prior holder had notice of a defense or claim against it cannot improve his position by taking from a later holder in due course.

(2) A transfer of a security interest in an instrument vests the foregoing rights in the transferee to the extent of the interest transferred.

(3) Unless otherwise agreed any transfer for value of an instrument not then payable to bearer gives the transferee the specifically enforceable right to have the unqualified indorsement of the transferor. Negotiation takes effect only when the indorsement is made and until that time there is no presumption that the transferee is the owner.

§3–202. Negotiation

(1) Negotiation is the transfer of an instrument in such form that the transferee becomes

a holder. If the instrument is payable to order it is negotiated by delivery with any necessary indorsement; if payable to bearer it is negotiated by delivery.

(2) An indorsement must be written by or on behalf of the holder and on the instrument or on a paper so firmly affixed thereto as to become a part thereof.

(3) An indorsement is effective for negotiation only when it conveys the entire instrument or any unpaid residue. If it purports to be of less it operates only as a partial assignment.

(4) Words of assignment, condition, waiver, guaranty, limitation or disclaimer of liability and the like accompanying an indorsement do not affect its character as an indorsement.

§3–203. Wrong or Misspelled Name

Where an instrument is made payable to a person under a misspelled name or one other than his own he may indorse in that name or his own or both; but signature in both names may be required by a person paying or giving value for the instrument.

§3–204. Special Indorsement; Blank Indorsement

(1) A special indorsement specifies the person to whom or to whose order it makes the instrument payable. Any instrument specially indorsed becomes payable to the order of the special indorsee and may be further negotiated only by his indorsement.

(2) An indorsement in blank specifies no particular indorsee and may consist of a mere signature. An instrument payable to order and indorsed in blank becomes payable to bearer and may be negotiated by delivery alone until specially indorsed.

(3) The holder may convert a blank indorsement into a special indorsement by writing over the signature of the indorser in blank any contract consistent with the character of the indorsement.

§3–205. Restrictive Indorsements

An indorsement is restrictive which either

(a) is conditional; or
(b) purports to prohibit further transfer of the instrument; or
(c) includes the words "for collection," "for deposit," "pay any bank," or like terms signifying a purpose of deposit or collection; or
(d) otherwise states that it is for the benefit or use of the indorser or of another person.

§3–206. Effect of Restrictive Indorsement

(1) No restrictive indorsement prevents further transfer or negotiation of the instrument.

(2) An intermediary bank, or a payor bank which is not the depository bank, is neither given notice nor otherwise affected by a restrictive indorsement of any person except the bank's immediate transferor or the person presenting for payment.

(3) Except for an intermediary bank, any transferee under an indorsement which is conditional or includes the words "for collection," "for deposit," "pay any bank," or like terms (subparagraphs (a) and (c) of Section 3–205) must pay or apply any value given by him for or on the security of the instrument consistently with the indorsement and to the extent that he does so he becomes a holder for value. In addition such transferee is a holder in due course if he otherwise complies with the requirements of Section 3–302 on what constitutes a holder in due course.

(4) The first taker under an indorsement for the benefit of the indorser or another person (subparagraph (d) of Section 3–205) must pay or apply any value given by him for or on the security of the instrument consistently with the indorsement and to the extent that he does so he becomes a holder for value. In addition such taker is a holder in due course if he otherwise complies with the requirements of Section 3–302 on what constitutes a holder in due course. A later holder for value is neither given notice nor otherwise affected by such restrictive indorsement unless he has knowledge that a

fiduciary or other person has negotiated the instrument in any transaction for his own benefit or otherwise in breach of duty (subsection (2) of Section 3–304).

§3–207. Negotiation Effective Although It May Be Rescinded

(1) Negotiation is effective to transfer the instrument although the negotiation is

(a) made by an infant, a corporation exceeding its powers, or any other person without capacity; or
(b) obtained by fraud, duress or mistake of any kind; or
(c) part of an illegal transaction; or
(d) made in breach of duty.

(2) Except as against a subsequent holder in due course such negotiation is in an appropriate case subject to rescission, the declaration of a constructive trust or any other remedy permitted by law.

§3–208. Reacquisition

Where an instrument is returned to or reacquired by a prior party he may cancel any indorsement which is not necessary to his title and reissue or further negotiate the instrument, but any intervening party is discharged as against the reacquiring party and subsequent holders not in due course and if his indorsement has been cancelled is discharged as against subsequent holders in due course as well.

Part 3.   RIGHTS OF A HOLDER

§3–301. Rights of a Holder

The holder of an instrument whether or not he is the owner may transfer or negotiate it and, except as otherwise provided in Section 3–603 on payment or satisfaction, discharge it or enforce payment in his own name.

§3–302. Holder in Due Course

(1) A holder in due course is a holder who takes the instrument

(a) for value; and
(b) in good faith; and
(c) without notice that it is overdue or has been dishonored or of any defense against or claim to it on the part of any person.

(2) A payee may be a holder in due course.
(3) A holder does not become a holder in due course of an instrument:

(a) by purchase of it at judicial sale or by taking it under legal process; or
(b) by acquiring it in taking over an estate; or
(c) by purchasing it as part of a bulk transaction not in regular course of business of the transferor.

(4) A purchaser of a limited interest can be a holder in due course only to the extent of the interest purchased.

§3–303. Taking for Value

A holder takes the instrument for value

(a) to the extent that the agreed consideration has been performed or that he acquires a security interest in or a lien on the instrument otherwise than by legal process; or
(b) when he takes the instrument in payment of or as security for an antecedent claim against any person whether or not the claim is due; or
(c) when he gives a negotiable instrument for it or makes an irrevocable commitment to a third person.

§3–304. Notice to Purchaser

(1) The purchaser has notice of a claim or defense if

(a) the instrument is so incomplete, bears such visible evidence of forgery or alteration, or is otherwise so irregular as to call into question its validity, terms or ownership or to create an ambiguity as to the party to pay; or

(b) the purchaser has notice that the obligation of any party is voidable in whole or in part, or that all parties have been discharged.

(2) The purchaser has notice of a claim against the instrument when he has knowledge that a fiduciary has negotiated the instrument in payment of or as security for his own debt or in any transaction for his own benefit or otherwise in breach of duty.

(3) The purchaser has notice that an instrument is overdue if he has reason to know

(a) that any part of the principal amount is overdue or that there is an uncured default in payment of another instrument of the same series; or

(b) that acceleration of the instrument has been made; or

(c) that he is taking a demand instrument after demand has been made or more than a reasonable length of time after its issue. A reasonable time for a check drawn and payable within the states and territories of the United States and the District of Columbia is presumed to be thirty days.

(4) Knowledge of the following facts does not of itself give the purchaser notice of a defense or claim

(a) that the instrument is antedated or postdated;

(b) that it was issued or negotiated in return for an executory promise or accompanied by a separate agreement, unless the purchaser has notice that a defense or claim has arisen from the terms thereof;

(c) that any party has signed for accommodation;

(d) that an incomplete instrument has been completed, unless the purchaser has notice of any improper completion;

(e) that any person negotiating the instrument is or was a fiduciary;

(f) that there has been default in payment of interest on the instrument or in payment of any other instrument, except one of the same series.

(5) The filing or recording of a document does not of itself constitute notice within the provisions of this Article to a person who would otherwise be a holder in due course.

(6) To be effective notice must be received at such time and in such manner as to give a reasonable opportunity to act on it.

§3–305. Rights of a Holder in Due Course

To the extent that a holder is a holder in due course he takes the instrument free from

(1) all claims to it on the part of any person; and

(2) all defenses of any party to the instrument with whom the holder has not dealt except

(a) infancy, to the extent that it is a defense to a simple contract; and

(b) such other incapacity, or duress, or illegality of the transaction, as renders the obligation of the party a nullity; and

(c) such misrepresentation as has induced the party to sign the instrument with neither knowledge nor reasonable opportunity to obtain knowledge of its character or its essential terms; and

(d) discharge in insolvency proceedings; and

(e) any other discharge of which the holder has notice when he takes the instrument.

§3–306. Rights of One Not Holder in Due Course

Unless he has the rights of a holder in due course any person takes the instrument subject to

(a) all valid claims to it on the part of any person; and

(b) all defenses of any party which would be available in an action on a simple contract; and

(c) the defenses of want or failure of consideration, nonperformance of any condition precedent, non-delivery, or delivery for a special purpose (Section 3–408); and

(d) the defense that he or a person through whom he holds the instrument acquired it by theft, or that payment or satisfaction to such holder would be inconsistent with the terms of a restrictive indorsement. The claim of any third person to the instrument is not otherwise available as a defense to any party liable thereon unless the third person himself defends the action for such party.

§3–307. Burden of Establishing Signatures, Defenses and Due Course

(1) Unless specifically denied in the pleadings each signature on an instrument is admitted. When the effectiveness of a signature is put in issue

(a) the burden of establishing it is on the party claiming under the signature; but
(b) the signature is presumed to be genuine or authorized except where the action is to enforce the obligation of a purported signer who has died or become incompetent before proof is required.

(2) When signatures are admitted or established, production of the instrument entitles a holder to recover on it unless the defendant establishes a defense.

(3) After it is shown that a defense exists a person claiming the rights of a holder in due course has the burden of establishing that he or some person under whom he claims is in all respects a holder in due course.

Part 4.   LIABILITY OF PARTIES

§3–401. Signature

(1) No person is liable on an instrument unless his signature appears thereon.

(2) A signature is made by use of any name, including any trade or assumed name, upon an instrument, or by any word or mark used in lieu of a written signature.

§3–402. Signature in Ambiguous Capacity

Unless the instrument clearly indicates that a signature is made in some other capacity it is an indorsement.

§3–403. Signature by Authorized Representative

(1) A signature may be made by an agent or other representative, and his authority to make it may be established as in other cases of representation. No particular form of appointment is necessary to establish such authority.

(2) An authorized representative who gives his own name to an instrument

(a) is personally obligated if the instrument neither names the person represented nor shows that the representative signed in a representative capacity;
(b) except as otherwise established between the immediate parties, is personally obligated if the instrument names the person represented but does not show that the representative signed in a representative capacity, or if the instrument does not name the person represented but does show that the representative signed in a representative capacity.

(3) Except as otherwise established the name of an organization preceded or followed by the name and office of an authorized individual is a signature made in a representative capacity.

§3–404. Unauthorized Signatures

(1) Any unauthorized signature is wholly inoperative as that of the person whose name is signed unless he ratifies it or is precluded from denying it; but it operates as the signature of the unauthorized signer in favor of any person who in good faith pays the instrument or takes it for value.

(2) Any unauthorized signature may be ratified for all purposes of this Article. Such ratification does not of itself affect any rights of the person ratifying against the actual signer.

§3–405. Impostors; Signature in Name of Payee

(1) An indorsement by any person in the name of a named payee is effective if

(a) an impostor by use of the mails or otherwise has induced the maker or drawer to issue the instrument to him or his confederate in the name of the payee; or

(b) a person signing as or on behalf of a maker or drawer intends the payee to have no interest in the instrument; or

(c) an agent or employee of the maker or drawer has supplied him with the name of the payee intending the latter to have no such interest.

(2) Nothing in this section shall affect the criminal or civil liability of the person so indorsing.

§3–406. Negligence Contributing to Alteration or Unauthorized Signature

Any person who by his negligence substantially contributes to a material alteration of the instrument or to the making of an unauthorized signature is precluded from asserting the alteration or lack of authority against a holder in due course or against a drawee or other payor who pays the instrument in good faith and in accordance with the reasonable commercial standards of the drawee's or payor's business.

§3–407. Alteration

(1) Any alteration of an instrument is material which changes the contract of any party thereto in any respect, including any such change in

(a) the number of relations of the parties; or

(b) an incomplete instrument, by completing it otherwise than as authorized; or

(c) the writing as signed, by adding to it or by removing any part of it.

(2) As against any person other than a subsequent holder in due course

(a) alteration by the holder which is both fraudulent and material discharges any party whose contract is thereby changed unless that party assents or is precluded from asserting the defense;

(b) no other alteration discharges any party and the instrument may be enforced according to its original tenor, or as to incomplete instruments according to the authority given.

(3) A subsequent holder in due course may in all cases enforce the instrument according to its original tenor, and when an incomplete instrument has been completed, he may enforce it as completed.

§3–408. Consideration

Want or failure of consideration is a defense as against any person not having the rights of a holder in due course (Section 3–305), except that no consideration is necessary for an instrument or obligation thereon given in payment of or as security for an antecedent obligation of any kind. Nothing in this section shall be taken to displace any statute outside this Act under which a promise is enforceable notwithstanding lack or failure of consideration. Partial failure of consideration is a defense pro tanto whether or not the failure is in an ascertained or liquidated amount.

§3–409. Draft Not an Assignment

(1) A check or other draft does not of itself operate as an assignment of any funds in the hands of the drawee available for its payment, and the drawee is not liable on the instrument until he accepts it.

(2) Nothing in this section shall affect any liability in contract, tort or otherwise arising from any letter of credit or other obligation or representation which is not an acceptance.

§3–410. Definition and Operation of Acceptance

(1) Acceptance is the drawee's signed engagement to honor the draft as presented. It must be written on the draft, and may consist of his signature alone. It becomes operative when completed by delivery or notification.

(2) A draft may be accepted although it has not been signed by the drawer or is otherwise incomplete or is overdue or has been dishonored.

(3) Where the draft is payable at a fixed period after sight and the acceptor fails to date his acceptance the holder may complete it by supplying a date in good faith.

§3-411. Certification of a Check

(1) Certification of a check is acceptance. Where a holder procures certification the drawer and all prior indorsers are discharged.

(2) Unless otherwise agreed a bank has no obligation to certify a check.

(3) A bank may certify a check before returning it for lack of proper indorsement. If it does so the drawer is discharged.

§3-412. Acceptance Varying Draft

(1) Where the drawee's proffered acceptance in any manner varies the draft as presented the holder may refuse the acceptance and treat the draft as dishonored in which case the drawee is entitled to have his acceptance cancelled.

(2) The terms of the draft are not varied by an acceptance to pay at any particular bank or place in the United States, unless the acceptance states that the draft is to be paid only at such bank or place.

(3) Where the holder assents to an acceptance varying the terms of the draft each drawer and indorser who does not affirmatively assent is discharged.

§3-413. Contract of Maker, Drawer and Acceptor

(1) The maker or acceptor engages that he will pay the instrument according to its tenor at the time of his engagement or as completed pursuant to Section 3-115 on incomplete instruments.

(2) The drawer engages that upon dishonor of the draft and any necessary notice of dishonor or protest he will pay the amount of the draft to the holder or to any indorser who takes it up. The drawer may disclaim this liability by drawing without recourse.

(3) By making, drawing or accepting the party admits as against all subsequent parties including the drawee the existence of the payee and his then capacity to indorse.

§3-414. Contract of Indorser; Order of Liability

(1) Unless the indorsement otherwise specifies (as by such words as "without recourse") every indorser engages that upon dishonor and any necessary notice of dishonor and protest he will pay the instrument according to its tenor at the time of his indorsement to the holder or to any subsequent indorser who takes it up, even though the indorser who takes it up was not obligated to do so.

(2) Unless they otherwise agree indorsers are liable to one another in the order in which they indorse, which is presumed to be the order in which their signatures appear on the instrument.

§3-415. Contract of Accommodation Party

(1) An accommodation party is one who signs the instrument in any capacity for the purpose of lending his name to another party to it.

(2) When the instrument has been taken for value before it is due the accommodation party is liable in the capacity in which he has signed even though the taker knows of the accommodation.

(3) As against a holder in due course and without notice of the accommodation oral proof of the accommodation is not admissible to give the accommodation party the benefit of discharges dependent on his character as such. In other cases the accommodation character may be shown by oral proof.

(4) An indorsement which shows that it is not in the chain of title is notice of its accommodation character.

(5) An accommodation party is not liable to the party accommodated, and if he pays the instrument has a right of recourse on the instrument against such party.

§3–416. Contract of Guarantor

(1) "Payment guaranteed" or equivalent words added to a signature mean that the signer engages that if the instrument is not paid when due he will pay it according to its tenor without resort by the holder to any other party.

(2) "Collection guaranteed" or equivalent words added to a signature mean that the signer engages that if the instrument is not paid when due he will pay it according to its tenor, but only after the holder has reduced his claim against the maker or acceptor to judgment and execution has been returned unsatisfied, or after the maker or acceptor has become insolvent or it is otherwise apparent that it is useless to proceed against him.

(3) Words of guaranty which do not otherwise specify guarantee payment.

(4) No words of guaranty added to the signature of a sole maker or acceptor affect his liability on the instrument. Such words added to the signature of one of two or more makers or acceptors create a presumption that the signature is for the accommodation of the others.

(5) When words of guaranty are used presentment, notice of dishonor and protest are not necessary to charge the user.

(6) Any guaranty written on the instrument is enforcible notwithstanding any statute of frauds.

§3–417. Warranties on Presentment and Transfer

(1) Any person who obtains payment or acceptance and any prior transferor warrants to a person who in good faith pays or accepts that

(a) he has a good title to the instrument or is authorized to obtain payment or acceptance on behalf of one who has a good title; and

(b) he has no knowledge that the signature of the maker or drawer is unauthorized, except that this warranty is not given by a holder in due course acting in good faith

    (i) to a maker with respect to the maker's own signature; or

    (ii) to a drawer with respect to the drawer's own signature, whether or not the drawer is also the drawee; or

    (iii) to an acceptor of a draft if the holder in due course took the draft after the acceptance or obtained the acceptance without knowledge that the drawer's signature was unauthorized; and

(c) the instrument has not been materially altered, except that this warranty is not given by a holder in due course acting in good faith

    (i) to the maker of a note; or

    (ii) to the drawer of a draft whether or not the drawer is also the drawee; or

    (iii) to the acceptor of a draft with respect to an alteration made prior to the acceptance if the holder in due course took the draft after the acceptance, even though the acceptance provided "payable as originally drawn" or equivalent terms; or

    (iv) to the acceptor of a draft with respect to an alteration made after the acceptance.

(2) Any person who transfers an instrument and receives consideration warrants to his transferee and if the transfer is by indorsement to any subsequent holder who takes the instrument in good faith that

(a) he has a good title to the instrument or is authorized to obtain payment or acceptance on behalf of one who has a good title and the transfer is otherwise rightful; and

(b) all signatures are genuine or authorized; and

(c) the instrument has not been materially altered; and

(d) no defense of any party is good against him; and

(e) he has no knowledge of any insolvency proceeding instituted with respect to the maker or acceptor or the drawer of an unaccepted instrument.

(3) By transferring "without recourse" the transferor limits the obligation stated in subsection (2) (d) to a warranty that he has no knowledge of such a defense.

(4) A selling agent or broker who does not disclose the fact that he is acting only as such gives the warranties provided in this section, but if he makes such disclosure warrants only his good faith and authority.

§3–418. Finality of Payment or Acceptance

Except for recovery of bank payments as provided in the Article on Bank Deposits and Collections (Article 4) and except for liability for breach of warranty on presentment under the preceding section, payment or acceptance of any instrument is final in favor of a holder in due course, or a person who has in good faith changed his position in reliance on the payment.

§3–419. Conversion of Instrument; Innocent Representative

(1) An instrument is converted when

(a) a drawee to whom it is delivered for acceptance refuses to return it on demand; or
(b) any person to whom it is delivered for payment refuses on demand either to pay or to return it; or
(c) it is paid on a forged indorsement.

(2) In an action against a drawee under subsection (1) the measure of the drawee's liability is the face amount of the instrument. In any other action under subsection (1) the measure of liability is presumed to be the face amount of the instrument.

(3) Subject to the provisions of this Act concerning restrictive indorsements a representative, including a depositary or collecting bank, who has in good faith and in accordance with the reasonable commercial standards applicable to the business of such representative dealt with an instrument or its proceeds on behalf of one who was not the true owner is not liable in conversion or otherwise to the true owner beyond the amount of any proceeds remaining in his hands.

(4) An intermediary bank or payor bank which is not a depositary bank is not liable in conversion solely by reason of the fact that proceeds of an item indorsed restrictively (Sections 3–205 and 3–206) are not paid or applied consistently with the restrictive indorsement of an indorser other than its immediate transferor.

PART 5.   PRESENTMENT, NOTICE OF DISHONOR AND PROTEST

§3–501. When Presentment, Notice of Dishonor, and Protest Necessary or Permissible

(1) Unless excused (Section 3–511) presentment is necessary to charge secondary parties as follows:

(a) presentment for acceptance is necessary to charge the drawer and indorsers of a draft where the draft so provides, or is payable elsewhere than at the residence or place of business of the drawee, or its date of payment depends upon such presentment. The holder may at his option present for acceptance any other draft payable at a stated date;
(b) presentment for payment is necessary to charge any indorser;
(c) in the case of any drawer, the acceptor of a draft payable at a bank or the maker of a note payable at a bank, presentment for payment is necessary, but failure to make presentment discharges such drawer, acceptor or maker only as stated in Section 3–502(1) (b).

(2) Unless excused (Section 3–511)

(a) notice of any dishonor is necessary to charge any indorser;
(b) in the case of any drawer, the acceptor of a draft payable at a bank or the maker of a note payable at a bank, notice of any dishonor is necessary, but failure to give such notice discharges such drawer, acceptor or maker only as stated in Section 3–502(1) (b).

(3) Unless excused (Section 3–511) protest of any dishonor is necessary to charge the

drawer and indorsers of any draft which on its face appears to be drawn or payable outside of the states, territories, dependencies, and possessions of the United States, the District of Columbia and the Commonwealth of Puerto Rico. The holder may at his option make protest of any dishonor of any other instrument and in the case of a foreign draft may on insolvency of the acceptor before maturity make protest for better security.

(4) Notwithstanding any provision of this section, neither presentment nor notice of dishonor nor protest is necessary to charge an indorser who has indorsed an instrument after maturity.

§3–502. Unexcused Delay; Discharge

(1) Where without excuse any necessary presentment or notice of dishonor is delayed beyond the time when it is due

(a) any indorser is discharged; and
(b) any drawer or the acceptor of a draft payable at a bank or the maker of a note payable at a bank who because the drawee or payor bank becomes insolvent during the delay is deprived of funds maintained with the drawee or payor bank to cover the instrument may discharge his liability by written assignment to the holder of his rights against the drawee or payor bank in respect of such funds, but such drawer, acceptor or maker is not otherwise discharged.

(2) Where without excuse a necessary protest is delayed beyond the time when it is due any drawer or indorser is discharged.

§3–503. Time of Presentment

(1) Unless a different time is expressed in the instrument the time for any presentment is determined as follows:

(a) where an instrument is payable at or a fixed period after a stated date any presentment for acceptance must be made on or before the date it is payable;
(b) where an instrument is payable after

sight it must either be presented for acceptance or negotiated within a reasonable time after date or issue whichever is later;
(c) where an instrument shows the date on which it is payable presentment for payment is due on that date;
(d) where an instrument is accelerated presentment for payment is due within a reasonable time after the acceleration;
(e) with respect to the liability of any secondary party presentment for acceptance or payment of any other instrument is due within a reasonable time after such party becomes liable thereon.

(2) A reasonable time for presentment is determined by the nature of the instrument, any usage of banking or trade and the facts of the particular case. In the case of an uncertified check which is drawn and payable within the United States and which is not a draft drawn by a bank the following are presumed to be reasonable periods within which to present for payment or to initiate bank collection:

(a) with respect to the liability of the drawer, thirty days after date or issue whichever is later; and
(b) with respect to the liability of an indorser, seven days after his indorsement.

(3) Where any presentment is due on a day which is not a full business day for either the person making presentment or the party to pay or accept, presentment is due on the next following day which is a full business day for both parties.

(4) Presentment to be sufficient must be made at a reasonable hour, and if at a bank during its banking day.

§3–504. How Presentment Made

(1) Presentment is a demand for acceptance or payment made upon the maker, acceptor, drawee or other payor by or on behalf of the holder.

(2) Presentment may be made

(a) by mail, in which event the time of presentment is determined by the time of receipt of the mail; or

(b) through a clearing house; or

(c) at the place of acceptance or payment specified in the instrument or if there be none at the place of business or residence of the party to accept or pay. If neither the party to accept or pay nor anyone authorized to act for him is present or accessible at such place presentment is excused.

(3) It may be made

(a) to any one of two or more makers, acceptors, drawees or other payors; or

(b) to any person who has authority to make or refuse the acceptance or payment.

(4) A draft accepted or a note made payable at a bank in the United States must be presented at such bank.

(5) In the cases described in Section 4–210 presentment may be made in the manner and with the result stated in that section.

§3–505. Rights of Party to Whom Presentment Is Made

(1) The party to whom presentment is made may without dishonor require

(a) exhibition of the instrument; and

(b) reasonable identification of the person making presentment and evidence of his authority to make it if made for another; and

(c) that the instrument be produced for acceptance or payment at a place specified in it, or if there be none at any place reasonable in the circumstances; and

(d) a signed receipt on the instrument for any partial or full payment and its surrender upon full payment.

(2) Failure to comply with any such requirement invalidates the presentment but the person presenting has a reasonable time in which to comply and the time for acceptance or payment runs from the time of compliance.

§3–506. Time Allowed for Acceptance or Payment

(1) Acceptance may be deferred without dishonor until the close of the next business day following presentment. The holder may also in a good faith effort to obtain acceptance and without either dishonor of the instrument or discharge of secondary parties allow postponement of acceptance for an additional business day.

(2) Except as a longer time is allowed in the case of documentary drafts drawn under a letter of credit, and unless an earlier time is agreed to by the party to pay, payment of an instrument may be deferred without dishonor pending reasonable examination to determine whether it is properly payable, but payment must be made in any event before the close of business on the day of presentment.

§3–507. Dishonor; Holder's Right of Recourse; Term Allowing Re-Presentment

(1) An instrument is dishonored when

(a) a necessary or optional presentment is duly made and due acceptance or payment is refused or cannot be obtained within the prescribed time or in case of bank collections the instrument is seasonably returned by the midnight deadline (Section 4–301); or

(b) presentment is excused and the instrument is not duly accepted or paid.

(2) Subject to any necessary notice of dishonor and protest, the holder has upon dishonor an immediate right of recourse against the drawers and indorsers.

(3) Return of an instrument for lack of proper indorsement is not dishonor.

(4) A term in a draft or an indorsement thereof allowing a stated time for re-presentment in the event of any dishonor of the draft by nonacceptance if a time draft or by nonpayment if a sight draft gives the holder as against any secondary party bound by the term an option to waive the dishonor without affect-

ing the liability of the secondary party and he may present again up to the end of the stated time.

§3–508. Notice of Dishonor

(1) Notice of dishonor may be given to any person who may be liable on the instrument by or on behalf of the holder or any party who has himself received notice, or any other party who can be compelled to pay the instrument. In addition an agent or bank in whose hands the instrument is dishonored may give notice to his principal or customer or to another agent or bank from which the instrument was received.

(2) Any necessary notice must be given by a bank before its midnight deadline and by any other person before midnight of the third business day after dishonor or receipt of notice of dishonor.

(3) Notice may be given in any reasonable manner. It may be oral or written and in any terms which identify the instrument and state that it has been dishonored. A misdescription which does not mislead the party notified does not vitiate the notice. Sending the instrument bearing a stamp, ticket or writing stating that acceptance or payment has been refused or sending a notice of debit with respect to the instrument is sufficient.

(4) Written notice is given when sent although it is not received.

(5) Notice to one partner is notice to each although the firm has been dissolved.

(6) When any party is in insolvency proceedings instituted after the issue of the instrument notice may be given either to the party or to the representative of his estate.

(7) When any party is dead or incompetent notice may be sent to his last known address or given to his personal representative.

(8) Notice operates for the benefit of all parties who have rights on the instrument against the party notified.

§3–509. Protest; Noting for Protest

(1) A protest is a certificate of dishonor made under the hand and seal of a United States consul or vice consul or a notary public or other person authorized to certify dishonor by the law of the place where dishonor occurs. It may be made upon information satisfactory to such person.

(2) The protest must identify the instrument and certify either that due presentment has been made or the reason why it is excused and that the instrument has been dishonored by nonacceptance or nonpayment.

(3) The protest may also certify that notice of dishonor has been given to all parties or to specified parties.

(4) Subject to subsection (5) any necessary protest is due by the time that notice of dishonor is due.

(5) If, before protest is due, an instrument has been noted for protest by the officer to make protest, the protest may be made at any time thereafter as of the date of the noting.

§3–510. Evidence of Dishonor and Notice of Dishonor

The following are admissible as evidence and create a presumption of dishonor and of any notice of dishonor therein shown:

(a) a document regular in form as provided in the preceding section which purports to be a protest;

(b) the purported stamp or writing of the drawee, payor bank or presenting bank on the instrument or accompanying it stating that acceptance or payment has been refused for reasons consistent with dishonor;

(c) any book or record of the drawee, payor bank, or any collecting bank kept in the usual course of business which shows dishonor, even though there is no evidence of who made the entry.

§3–511. Waived or Excused Presentment, Protest or Notice of Dishonor or Delay Therein

(1) Delay in presentment, protest or notice of dishonor is excused when the party is without notice that it is due or when the delay is

caused by circumstances beyond his control and he exercises reasonable diligence after the cause of the delay ceases to operate.

(2) Presentment or notice of protest as the case may be is entirely excused when

(a) the party to be charged has waived it expressly or by implication either before or after it is due; or

(b) such party has himself dishonored the instrument or has countermanded payment or otherwise has no reason to expect or right to require that the instrument be accepted or paid; or

(c) by reasonable diligence the presentment or protest cannot be made or the notice given.

(3) Presentment is also entirely excused when

(a) the maker, acceptor or drawee of any instrument except a documentary draft is dead or in insolvency proceedings instituted after the issue of the instrument; or

(b) acceptance or payment is refused but not for want of proper presentment.

(4) Where a draft has been dishonored by nonacceptance a later presentment for payment and any notice of dishonor and protest for non-payment are excused unless in the meantime the instrument has been accepted.

(5) A waiver of protest is also a waiver of presentment and of notice of dishonor even though protest is not required.

(6) Where a waiver of presentment or notice or protest is embodied in the instrument itself it is binding upon all parties; but where it is written above the signature of an indorser it binds him only.

Part 6. DISCHARGE

§3-601. Discharge of Parties

(1) The extent of the discharge of any party from liability on an instrument is governed by the sections on

(a) payment or satisfaction (Section 3–603); or

(b) tender of payment(Section 3–604); or

(c) cancellation or renunciation (Section 3–605); or

(d) impairment of right of recourse or of collateral (Section 3–606); or

(e) reacquisition of the instrument by a prior party (Section 3–208); or

(f) fraudulent and material alteration (Section 3–407); or

(g) certification of a check (Section 3–411); or

(h) acceptance varying a draft (Section 3–412); or

(i) unexcused delay in presentment or notice of dishonor or protest (Section 3–502).

(2) Any party is also discharged from his liability on an instrument to another party by any other act or agreement with such party which would discharge his simple contract for the payment of money.

(3) The liability of all parties is discharged when any party who has himself no right of action or recourse on the instrument

(a) reacquires the instrument in his own right; or

(b) is discharged under any provision of this Article, except as otherwise provided with respect to discharge for impairment of recourse or of collateral (Section 3–606).

§3-602. Effect of Discharge Against Holder in Due Course

No discharge of any party provided by this Article is effective against a subsequent holder in due course unless he has notice thereof when he takes the instrument.

§3-603. Payment or Satisfaction

(1) The liability of any party is discharged to the extent of his payment or satisfaction to the holder even though it is made with knowledge of a claim of another person to the

instrument unless prior to such payment or satisfaction the person making the claim either supplies indemnity deemed adequate by the party seeking the discharge or enjoins payment or satisfaction by order of a court of competent jurisdiction in an action in which the adverse claimant and the holder are parties. This subsection does not, however, result in the discharge of the liability

(a) of a party who in bad faith pays or satisfies a holder who acquired the instrument by theft or who (unless having the rights of a holder in due course) holds through one who so acquired it; or

(b) of a party (other than an intermediary bank or a payor bank which is not a depositary bank) who pays or satisfies the holder of an instrument which has been restrictively indorsed in a manner not consistent with the terms of such restrictive indorsement.

(2) Payment or satisfaction may be made with the consent of the holder by any person including a stranger to the instrument. Surrender of the instrument to such a person gives him the rights of a transferee (Section 3–201).

§3–604. Tender of Payment

(1) Any party making tender of full payment to a holder when or after it is due is discharged to the extent of all subsequent liability for interest, costs, and attorney's fees.

(2) The holder's refusal of such tender wholly discharges any party who has a right of recourse against the party making the tender.

(3) Where the maker or acceptor of an instrument payable otherwise than on demand is able and ready to pay at every place of payment specified in the instrument when it is due, it is equivalent to tender.

§3–605. Cancellation and Renunciation

(1) The holder of an instrument may even without consideration discharge any party

(a) in any manner apparent on the face of the instrument or the indorsement, as by

intentionally cancelling the instrument or the party's signature by destruction or mutilation, or by striking out the party's signature; or

(b) by renouncing his rights by a writing signed and delivered or by surrender of the instrument to the party to be discharged.

(2) Neither cancellation nor renunciation without surrender of the instrument affects the title thereto.

§3–606. Impairment of Recourse or of Collateral

(1) The holder discharges any party to the instrument to the extent that without such party's consent the holder

(a) without express reservation of rights releases or agrees not to sue any person against whom the party has to the knowledge of the holder a right of recourse or agrees to suspend the right to enforce against such person the instrument or collateral or otherwise discharges such person, except that failure or delay in effecting any required presentment, protest or notice of dishonor with respect to any such person does not discharge any party as to whom presentment, protest or notice of dishonor is effective or unnecessary; or

(b) unjustifiably impairs any collateral for the instrument given by or on behalf of the party or any person against whom he has a right of recourse.

(2) By express reservation of rights against a party with a right of recourse the holder preserves

(a) all his rights against such party as of the time when the instrument was originally due; and

(b) the right of the party to pay the instrument as of that time; and

(c) all rights of such party to recourse against others.

PART 7. ADVICE OF INTERNATIONAL SIGHT DRAFT

§3-701. Letter of Advice of International Sight Draft

(1) A "letter of advice" is a drawer's communication to the drawee that a described draft has been drawn.

(2) Unless otherwise agreed when a bank receives from another bank a letter of advice of an international sight draft the drawee bank may immediately debit the drawer's account and stop the running of interest pro tanto. Such a debit and any resulting credit to any account covering outstanding drafts leaves in the drawer full power to stop payment or otherwise dispose of the amount and creates no trust or interest in favor of the holder.

(3) Unless otherwise agreed and except where a draft is drawn under a credit issued by the drawee, the drawee of an international sight draft owes the drawer no duty to pay an unadvised draft but if it does so and the draft is genuine, may appropriately debit the drawer's account.

PART 8. MISCELLANEOUS

§3-801. Drafts in a Set

(1) Where a draft is drawn in a set of parts, each of which is numbered and expressed to be an order only if no other part has been honored, the whole of the parts constitutes one draft but a taker of any part may become a holder in due course of the draft.

(2) Any person who negotiates, indorses or accepts a single part of a draft drawn in a set thereby becomes liable to any holder in due course of that part as if it were the whole set, but as between different holders in due course to whom different parts have been negotiated the holder whose title first accrues has all rights to the draft and its proceeds.

(3) As against the drawee the first presented part of a draft drawn in a set is the part entitled to payment, or if a time draft to acceptance

and payment. Acceptance of any subsequently presented part renders the drawee liable thereon under subsection (2). With respect both to a holder and to the drawer payment of a subsequently presented part of a draft payable at sight has the same effect as payment of a check notwithstanding an effective stop order (Section 4-407).

(4) Except as otherwise provided in this section, where any part of a draft in a set is discharged by payment or otherwise the whole draft is discharged.

§3-802. Effect of Instrument on Obligation for Which It Is Given

(1) Unless otherwise agreed where an instrument is taken for an underlying obligation

(a) the obligation is pro tanto discharged if a bank is drawer, maker or acceptor of the instrument and there is no recourse on the instrument against the underlying obligor; and

(b) in any other case the obligation is suspended pro tanto until the instrument is due or if it is payable on demand until its presentment. If the instrument is dishonored action may be maintained on either the instrument or the obligation; discharge of the underlying obligor on the instrument also discharges him on the obligation.

(2) The taking in good faith of a check which is not postdated does not of itself so extend the time on the original obligation as to discharge a surety.

§3-803. Notice to Third Party

Where a defendant is sued for breach of an obligation for which a third person is answerable over under this Article he may give the third person written notice of the litigation, and the person notified may then give similar notice to any other person who is answerable over to him under this Article. If the notice states that the person notified may come in and defend and that if the person notified does not do so he will in any action against him by the person giving the notice be bound by any determination of fact common to the two litigations, then unless after seasonable receipt of the notice the person notified does come in and defend he is so bound.

§3–804. Lost, Destroyed or Stolen Instruments

The owner of an instrument which is lost, whether by destruction, theft or otherwise, may maintain an action in his own name and recover from any party liable thereon upon due proof of his ownership, the facts which prevent his production of the instrument and its terms. The court may require security indemnifying the defendant against loss by reason of further claims on the instrument.

§3–805. Instruments Not Payable to Order or to Bearer

This Article applies to any instrument whose terms do not preclude transfer and which is otherwise negotiable within this Article but which is not payable to order or to bearer, except that there can be no holder in due course of such an instrument.

Information for Prospective Law Students

A. Case Analysis and Classwork in Law School

The vast majority of law schools in the country use what is known as the *case method* or *case system* of instruction in most of their courses, particularly in first-year courses such as civil procedure, contracts, property, torts, and criminal law. This practice is based on the theory that the best method for learning law is to study actual appellate court decisions and to derive from them an understanding of the courts' reasoning processes—as well as the general principles of law applicable to the particular fields. An important aspect of the student's reasoning process is ascertaining the facts the court regarded as crucial in making its decision, and applying the general principles to those facts.

The cases in a particular section of a casebook are related to each other in a particular way. The author has carefully selected certain opinions and reproduced either the entire opinion or part of it, as is done in Chapters 4 through 12 of this book. However, unlike this book, casebooks consist almost exclusively of such edited cases. Any section of a casebook consists of several particular cases selected to illustrate the historical development of a particular principle. For example, the first case in a section entitled "Defenses to Intentional Torts" may set forth the basic principles underlying the concept of defenses to intentional torts; the second one may contain an exception to those general principles; and the third one may show how certain statutes have affected the common law doctrines that have evolved up to the present, thereby giving the student a perspective on the entire body of law related to the subject.

Students read and "brief" the cases as described in the next section, attend class, recite cases, and take copious notes on the lectures and discussions of the cases in the casebooks. They also read additional material in textbooks and law reviews. By reading and briefing the cases and by class recitation, students are expected to learn by inductive reasoning, from the statements made by various courts in particular cases, the rules and principles most frequently applied and most likely to be applied by the courts in similar future cases.

The professor forces students, particularly through class recitation of cases, to perform the exercise of inductive reasoning without expressly telling them what important principles are embodied in the particular cases in the casebook. Through critical analysis and comparison of these cases in class students can determine their value and relate them to each other.

Law textbooks, known as "hornbooks," are also used in law schools, primarily as supplements to the classroom analysis of cases. The law textbook is a treatise on a particular field of law, usually written by an expert in the field. A textbook consists of a discussion of general principles of law similar to the discussions contained in Chapters 7 through 12 of this book, but without the edited cases.

B. Briefing a Case

1. Meanings of the Term *Brief;* Purposes of Briefing

The term *brief* may be used in two completely different senses: (1) The printed or typewritten documents that attorneys submit to appellate courts on behalf of their clients to persuade the court to rule in their favor. Such briefs consist of extensive legal arguments and citations of cases in support of such arguments (this type of brief is sometimes used in trial courts also). (2) A summary and analysis of one particular case. We will discuss here only the latter definition.

Law students are required to make briefs of almost all of the cases they read. Briefs are useful in two respects: First, they provide a handy method of refreshing the student's memory of the cases, which is especially helpful in preparing for class discussions. Briefs also aid in studying for examinations. Second, analysis of cases gives the student a better understanding of the courts' decisions and the principles contained in those decisions.

For the practicing attorney, briefing cases is a common practice, both for the purpose of determining a client's position on any particular subject and as an integral part of preparing the other type of brief to be submitted to the court on appeal.

2. Form of the Brief

A brief of a case should be organized into three separate sections:

1. *Facts:* First, the facts the court relied on in making its decision should be listed in the brief. A number of facts will not be particularly important to the final decision, and therefore need not be mentioned in the brief. The facts the court relied on are often described as the *dispositive* facts, because these particular facts were the instrumental or essential facts and thus disposed of the issue being presented to the court.

   The facts of *People* v. *Hintz,*[1] in Chapter 11, may be summarized as follows: Defendants were charged with conspiring to aid and abet in placing explosives with intent to destroy and conspiracy to murder; evidence introduced at trial indicated numerous discussions between defendants and third party in which defendants requested that said third party construct bombs to kill police officers; evidence further indicated relationship between explosions that occurred prior to arrest of defendants and powder in their possession; trial court found existence of conspiracy between defendants to use explosive devices to injure or kill and conspiracy to murder; defendants appeal their convictions.

2. *Issues:* The issues (or "questions presented,") are the legal questions the appellant submitted to the appellate court for resolution. Sometimes only one issue will be presented to the appellate court, but more often there are several questions the ap-

---

[1] People v. Hintz, 69 Mich. App. 207, 244 N.W.2d 414 (1976), appears on pages 297–301 in Chapter 11.

pellant contends the trial court ruled on incorrectly. In addition, both parties may raise questions on appeal, thereby making both parties appellants in certain respects and appellees in other respects. For example, suppose a trial court renders judgment in favor of the plaintiff, but for an amount of money much smaller than the damages the plaintiff sued for. The plaintiff may appeal on the grounds that the trial court incorrectly applied certain principles of the law of "damages" to the case, and that as a matter of law the damages are inadequate. The defendant may appeal on a different ground, such as the trial judge's failure to admit certain evidence the defendant sought to introduce.

In *Hintz* the issues were: (1) whether the evidence presented at trial was legally sufficient to support the verdict of guilty of conspiracy; (2) whether the evidence was legally sufficient to prove guilt beyond a reasonable doubt; and (3) whether defendant Lawrence Hintz withdrew from the conspiracy before criminal culpability attached.

3. *Resolution:* This portion of the brief should succinctly state the decision, or *holding,* of the court. A case is a precedent for what it holds, as opposed to its *dicta*—the observations in a court's decision that are not necessary to that decision.[2]

> [T]he thing adjudged comes to us oftentimes swathed in obscuring dicta, which must be stripped off and cast aside. Judges differ greatly in their reverence for the illustrations and comments and remarks of their predecessors, to make no mention of their own. . . . [I]t is a good deal of a mystery to me how judges, of all persons in the world, should put their faith in dicta. . . . [D]icta are not always ticketed as such, and one does not recognize them always at a glance. There is the constant need, as every law student knows, to separate the accidental and the non-essential from the essential and inherent.

The significance of each case in the precedent system is that each case presents a principle or rule, called the *ratio decidendi* of that particular case. The *ratio decidendi* can be determined by viewing the facts which were deemed important by the court, and then formulating the principle in terms of those facts. The *ratio decidendi* of a case is its rule or holding:[3]

> The implications of a decision may in the beginning be equivocal. New cases by commentary and exposition extract the essence. At last there emerges a rule or principle which becomes a datum, a point of departure, from which new lines will be run, from which new courses will be measured. Sometimes the rule or principle is found to have been formulated too narrowly or too broadly, and has to be reframed. Sometimes it is accepted as a postulate of later reasoning, its origins are forgotten, it becomes a new stock of descent, its issues unite with other strains, and persisting permeate the law. You may call the process one of analogy or of logic or of philosophy as you please. Its essence in any event is the derivation of a consequence from a rule or a principle or a precedent which, accepted as a datum, contains implicitly within itself the germ of conclusion.

Sometimes a court will expressly state what its holding is by stating, "We hold that. . . ." In such a case, the court has formulated what it conceives to be the hold-

---

[2] B. Cardozo, *The Nature of the Judicial Process* (New Haven: Yale University Press, 1970), pp. 29–30.
[3] Cardozo, pp. 48–49.

ing of that case. However, it still remains for the reader of the case to determine whether such proclamation of the court's holding coincides with the other statements made by the court in that case. Thus it is possible for a court to expressly state its holding and for a reader to objectively determine that the resolution, or *ratio decidendi,* is actually different from what the court says it is.

In the *Hintz* case, the appellate court's resolution of the three issues stated above was: (1) if the evidence indicates that intent and knowledge of unlawful purpose to murder was possessed by both defendants, who have taken overt action working together under an agreement or mutual understanding, the evidence is sufficient to sustain conviction for conspiracy to use explosive devices to injure or kill and conspiracy to commit murder; (2) evidence based on the facts in (1) was sufficient to prove guilt beyond a reasonable doubt; and (3) if the defendant's expressed intention to withdraw from the conspiracy comes after active participation in planning murders and manufacturing bombs, and defendant takes no action to prevent further criminal activity in furtherance of conspiracy, no legally recognized withdrawal has taken place.

C. Taking a Law School Examination

The typical law school examination question is a problem that contains a specific factual situation and requires the student to provide an analysis and statement of the issues and an application of legal principles to the given facts. The student is asked to resolve these issues, either as judge or as advocate on one party's side. Thus the first requirement is to recognize and clearly state the issues that are embodied within the facts. The next requirement is to state the legal principles that could possibly be applied to those issues, including the various policy considerations underlying those principles insofar as they are relevant to the stated facts. If the student is answering the question as an advocate, he or she should strongly argue the principles and policies underlying the client's position, without compromising reason, logic, or intellectual honesty. If asked to answer the question as a judge, the student should render a definite conclusion and judgment, after illustrating recognition of the range of possible solutions to the questions presented. The judge's decision should conform to what appears to be the soundest solution of the issue.

Whether the student answers a law school examination question as an advocate or as a judge, the most important thing to remember is that the professor expects an explanation of why the law requires that particular decision. This requires a proper application of legal knowledge and legal principles to solve the problem. The professor expects the student to support the conclusions with arguments based on cases, rules, and principles that have been studied throughout the course. Although a statement of particular legal principles is expected, citation of particular cases is generally not required. If the facts in a problem raise a legal question for which no precedent yet exists, the professor will expect the student to argue by analogy to cases that are closely related to such question and thereby infer a reasonable resolution of the issue.

There is no better preparation for taking a law school examination than actually writing practice answers to exams given by professors in prior years. Most law schools maintain copies of old exams in the law library. The student is then able to develop a systematic method of taking the exams, including allotting a particular amount of time and practicing outlining the answer before actually writing it out.

Bibliography

Adams, John. "A defense of the Constitution of Government of the United States of America, 1787–88." In *The Works of John Adams,* edited by Charles F. Adams. Vol. 4. Boston: Little, Brown and Co., 1851.

Administrative Office of the Illinois Courts Annotated Reports. 1974.

Administrative Office of the Maryland Courts Annotated Reports. 1973–74.

Administrative Office of the United States Courts. *Management Statistics for U.S. Courts.* Washington, D.C.: U.S. Government Printing Office, 1974.

American Bar Association. *Environmental Law: Practice and Procedure Handbook.* Chicago: American Bar Association, 1976.

American Bar Association. *Information Service Center Publications.* Chicago, 1977.

Andrews, R. *Environmental Policy and Administrative Change.* Lexington, Mass.: D. C. Heath & Co., 1976.

Annual Report. Judicial Department of the State of New Mexico. 1974.

Annual Report of the Director of the Administrative Office of the United States Courts. Washington, D.C.: U.S. Government Printing Office, 1968.

Baldwin, M., and Page, J., eds. *Law and the Environment.* New York: Walker and Co., 1970.

Barron, W.W., Holtzoff, A., and Wright, A., eds. *Federal Practice and Procedure.* St. Paul: West Publishing Co., 1960.

Beard, C. *An Economic Interpretation of the Constitution of the United States.* New York: The MacMillan Co., 1947.

Berman, H.J. and Greiner, W.R. *Nature and Functions of Law.* Mineola, N.Y.: Foundation Press, 1972.

Bickel, A. *The Supreme Court and the Idea of Progress.* New York: Harper and Row, 1970.

Billikopff, D.M. *The Exercise of Judicial Power 1789–1864.* New York: Vantage Press, 1973.

Birnbach, M. *American Political Life.* Homewood, Ill.: Dorsey Press, 1971.

Black, C. *The People and the Court: Judicial Review in a Democracy.* New York: MacMillan & Co., 1960.

Black's Law Dictionary. 4th ed. St. Paul: West Publishing Co., 1968.

Bloomstein, M. *Verdict: The Jury System.* New York: Dodd, Mead & Co., 1968.

Burby, W. *Hornbook on Real Property.* St. Paul: West Publishing Co., 1943.

Calamari, J., and Perillo, J. *The Law of Contracts.* St. Paul: West Publishing Co., 1970.

Callander, C. *American Courts: Organization and Procedure.* New York: McGraw-Hill, 1927.

Cardozo, B. *The Paradoxes of Legal Science*. New York: Columbia University Press, 1928.

————. *The Nature of the Judicial Process*. New Haven: Yale University Press, 1970.

Casner, A.J., ed. *American Law of Property*. Boston: Little, Brown and Co., 1952.

Casper, J. *American Criminal Justice: The Defendant's Perspective*. Englewood Cliffs, N.J.: Prentice-Hall, Inc., 1972.

Cataldo, B.F. *Introduction to Law and the Legal Process*. New York: John Wiley and Sons, 1973.

Cavers, D. *The Choice of Law Process*. Ann Arbor: University of Michigan Press, 1965.

Cavitch, Z. *Business Organization with Tax Planning*. New York: Matthew Bender, 1977.

Clark, W., and Marshall, W. *Law of Crimes*. Chicago: Callaghan & Co., 1958.

Colorado Annotated Statistical Report of the Colorado Judiciary. 1974.

Comment, "The Influence of the Defendant's Plea on Judicial Determination of Sentence," 66 *Yale Law Journal* 204 (1956).

Constitutions of the United States, National and State. Dobbs Ferry, N.Y.: Oceana Publishing Co., 1974.

Corley, R., and Black, R. *Legal Environment of Business*. New York: McGraw-Hill, 1973.

Cox, A. *The Role of the Supreme Court in American Government*. New York: Oxford University Press, 1976.

Curtis, G. *Constitutional History of the United States*. 2 vols. New York: Da Capo Press, 1974.

Dabin, Jean. "General Theory of Law." Translated by K. Wilk. In *The Legal Philosophies of Lask, Redbruck and Dabin*. In Morris, C. *The Great Legal Philosophers*. Philadelphia: University of Pennsylvania Press, 1971.

Dolgin, E., and Guilbert, T., eds. *Federal Environmental Law*. St. Paul: West Publishing Co., 1974.

Dominick, P., and Brody, D. "The Alaska Pipeline: Wilderness Society v. Morton and the Trans-Alaska Pipeline Authorization Act," 23 *American University Law Review* 337 (1973).

Edwards, A., and White, J. *The Lawyer as Negotiator*. St. Paul: West Publishing Co., 1977.

Eisenstein, J. *Politics and the Legal Process*. New York: Harper & Row, 1973.

Fairman, C. *History of the Supreme Court of the United States: Reconstruction and Reunion, 1864–88*. New York: MacMillan Co., 1971.

Fisher, Bruce D. *Introduction to the Legal System*. St. Paul: West Publishing Co., 1972.

Florida Judicial System Statistical Report. 1973.

Ford, S. *The American Legal System*. 20th ed. St. Paul: West Publishing Co., 1974.

Forrester, W.R. "Are We Ready for Truth in Judging?" *American Bar Association Journal* (September 1977).

Freund, P. *The Supreme Court of the United States*. New York: World Press, 1961.

Friendly, H. *Federal Jurisdiction: A General View*. New York: Columbia University Press, 1973.

Gifis, S. *Law Dictionary*. Woodbury, N.Y.: Barron's Educational Series, Inc., 1975.

Glick, H., and Vines, K. *State Court Systems*. Englewood Cliffs, N.J.: Prentice-Hall, Inc., 1973.

Goebel, J. *History of the Supreme Court of the United States: Antecedents and Beginnings to 1801*. New York: MacMillan Co., 1971.

Goldman, S., and Jahnige, T. *The Federal Courts as a Political System.* New York: Harper & Row, 1971.

Green, Leon. *The Litigation Process in Tort Law.* Indianapolis: Bobbs-Merrill Co., Inc., 1965.

Green, M. *Basic Civil Procedure.* Mineola, N.Y.: Foundation Press, 1972.

Haines, C. *The American Doctrine of Judicial Supremacy.* New York: Da Capo Press, 1973.

Haley, A. "The Law on Radio Programs." 5 *George Washington Law Review* 1157 (1937).

Hamilton, Alexander. "The Continentalist." 12 July 1781–4 July 1782. Reprinted in *The Works of Alexander Hamilton,* edited by Henry Cabot Lodge. New York: G.P. Putnam's Sons, 1904.

Harper, F., and James, F. *The Law of Torts.* Boston: Little, Brown, 1956.

Herbert A. *Uncommon Law.* London: Methuen & Co., 1935.

Hogan, W., and Warren, W. *Cases and Materials on Commercial and Consumer Transactions.* Mineola, N.Y.: Foundation Press, 1972.

Hogue, A. *Origins of the Common Law.* Bloomington: Indiana University Press, 1966.

Holdsworth, W.S. *A History of English Law.* 16 vols. London: Methuen and Co., and Boston: Little, Brown and Co. 1922–1972.

Jefferson, Thomas. *Notes on the State of Virginia.* Chapel Hill: University of North Carolina Press, 1955.

Judicial Department of Arkansas Annotated Report. 1975.

Kempin, F. "The Corporate Officer and the Law of Agency." 44 *Virginia Law Review* 1273 (1958).

Konefsky, S. *The Legacy of Holmes and Brandeis.* New York: Da Capo Press, 1974.

Laugesen, R. "Colorado Comparative Negligence." 48 *Denver Law Journal* 469 (1972).

Leflar, R. *American Conflicts of Law.* New York: Bobbs-Merrill Co., Inc., 1968.

Levi, E. *An Introduction to Legal Reasoning.* Chicago: University of Chicago Press, 1949.

Lewis, A. *Gideon's Trumpet.* New York: Random House, Inc., 1964.

Llewellyn, K. *The Bramble Bush.* New York: Oceana Publications, 1951.

Lorch, R. *Democratic Process and Administrative Law.* Detroit: Wayne State University Press, 1969.

Madison, James. "Vices of the Political System of the United States." April, 1787. Reprinted in *The Writings of James Madison,* edited by Gaillard Hunt. New York: G.P. Putnam's Sons, 1901.

Mason, A., and Leach, R. *In Quest of Freedom.* Englewood Cliffs, N.J.: Prentice-Hall, Inc., 1959.

Mayer, M. *The Lawyers.* New York: Harper and Row, 1967.

Mermin, S. *Law and the Legal System: An Introduction.* Boston: Little, Brown, and Co., 1973.

Miller, J. *Handbook of Criminal Law.* St. Paul: West Publishing Co., 1934.

Mishkin, P., and Hart, H., eds. *The Federal Courts and the Federal System.* Mineola, N.Y.: Foundation Press, 1973.

Moore, C. *The Jury.* Cincinnati: W.H. Anderson Co., 1973.

———, ed. *The Great Legal Philosophers.* Philadelphia: University of Pennsylvania Press, 1971.

Nelson, M. *A Study of Judicial Review in Virginia 1789–1928.* New York: AMS Press, 1967.

Perkins, R. *Criminal Law*. 2d ed. Mineola, N.Y.: Foundation Press, 1969.

Pfeffer, L. *This Honorable Court*. Boston: Beacon Press, 1965.

Post, C.G. *An Introduction to the Law*. Englewood Cliffs, N.J.: Prentice-Hall, Inc., 1963.

Pound, R. *The Spirit of the Common Law*. Boston: Jones Co., 1921.

————. *An Introduction to the Philosophy of Law*. New Haven: Yale University Press, 1968.

Project. "The Direct Selling Industry: An Empirical Study." 16 *U.C.L.A. Law Review* 883 (1969).

Prosser, W. *Law of Torts*. 4th ed. St. Paul: West Publishing Co., 1971.

Redford, E.S., et al. *Politics and Government in the United States*. New York: Harcourt, Brace and World, Inc., 1965.

Reitze, A. *Environmental Law*. Washington, D.C.: North American International, 1972.

Restatement of Conflict of Laws 2d. St. Paul: American Law Institute, 1971.

Restatement of the Law of Contracts 2d. St. Paul: American Law Institute, 1973.

Restatement of the Law of Torts 2d. St. Paul: American Law Institute, 1965.

Restatement of the Law of Property 2d. St. Paul: American Law Institute, 1977.

Rohan, P. *Powell on Real Property*. New York: Matthew Bender & Co., 1977.

Rostow, E., ed. *Is Law Dead?* New York: Simon and Schuster, 1971.

Rothstein, P. *Evidence in a Nutshell*. St. Paul: West Publishing Co., 1970.

Rousseau, Jean Jacques. *The Social Contract*. Translated by G.D.H. Cole. In Morris, C., *The Great Legal Philosophers*. Philadelphia: University of Pennsylvania Press, 1971.

Schwartz, B. *The Law in America*. New York: McGraw-Hill, 1974.

Simpson, L. *Law of Contracts*. St. Paul: West Publishing Co., 1965.

Smith, L.Y., and Roberson, G.G. *Business Law*. St. Paul: West Publishing Co., 1971.

Smith, M. *Jurisprudence*. New York: Columbia University Press, 1909.

Stern, R., and Gressman, E. *Supreme Court Practice*. Washington, D.C.: BNA, Inc.

Story, J. *Commentaries on the Constitution of the United States*. 3 vols. New York: Da Capo Press, 1970.

The Federalist Papers. New York: New American Library, 1961.

Tucker, E. *Administrative Law: Regulation of Enterprise and Individual Liberties*. St. Paul: West Publishing Co., 1975.

U.S. Department of Justice. *Annual Report of the Attorney General*. Washington, D.C.: U.S. Government Printing Office, 1963, 1973–75.

U.S. Department of Justice, LEAA. *National Survey of Court Organization*. Washington, D.C.: U.S. Government Printing Office, 1973.

Vold, L. "The Basis for Liability for Defamation by Radio," 19 *Minnesota Law Review* 611 (1935).

Warren, S.D., and Brandeis, L.D. "The Right to Privacy," 4 *Harvard Law Review* 193 (1890).

White, J.J., and Summers, R.S. *Uniform Commercial Code*. St. Paul: West Publishing Co., 1972.

Williams, et al. "Effective, Average and Ineffective Legal Negotiators." In *Psychology and the Law: Research Frontiers,* edited by G. Berment, et al. Lexington, Mass.: Lexington Books, 1976.

Wright, C. *Law of Federal Courts*. St. Paul: West Publishing Co., 1970.

Index of Cases

(The principal cases are in italic type. Cases cited are in roman type.)

Index